Understanding
Health
Insurance

A Guide to Billing and Reimbursement

Tenth Edition

RMA
test

248-595-2558

Understanding
Health
Insurance

A Guide to Billing and Reimbursement

Tenth Edition

Michelle A. Green, MPS, RHIA, FAHIMA, CPC

SUNY Distinguished Teaching Professor
Alfred State College, Alfred NY

JoAnn C. Rowell

Founder and Former Chairperson
Medical Assisting Department
Anne Arundel Community College, Arnold MD

DELMAR
CENGAGE Learning

Australia • Brazil • Japan • Korea • Mexico • Singapore • Spain • United Kingdom • United States

**Understanding Health Insurance,
A Guide to Billing and
Reimbursement, Tenth Edition**
Michelle A. Green, JoAnn C. Rowell

Vice President, Career and Professional
Editorial: Dave Garza

Director of Learning Solutions:
Matthew Kane

Managing Editor: Marah Bellegarde

Senior Acquisitions Editor:
Rhonda Dearborn

Product Manager:
Jadin Babin-Kavanaugh

Editorial Assistant: Chiara Astriab

Vice President, Career and Professional
Marketing: Jennifer Baker

Executive Marketing Manager:
Wendy Mapstone

Senior Marketing Manager:
Nancy Bradshaw

Marketing Coordinator: Erica Ropitzky

Technology Director: Tom Smith

Technology Product Manager:
Mary Colleen Liburdi

Technology Project Manager:
Benjamin Knapp

Technology Project Manager:
Christopher Catalina

Technology Product Manager:
Erin Zeggert

Production Director: Carolyn Miller

Senior Content Project Manager:
Andrea Majot

Senior Art Director: Jack Pendleton

For product information and technology assistance, contact us at
Cengage Learning Customer & Sales Support, 1-800-354-9706

For permission to use material from this text or product,
submit all requests online at **www.cengage.com/permissions**
Further permissions questions can be emailed to
permissionrequest@cengage.com

Library of Congress Control Number: 2009940696

ISBN-13: 978-1-111-03518-1

ISBN-10: 1-111-03518-0

Delmar
Executive Woods
5 Maxwell Drive
Clifton Park, NY 12065
USA

Cengage Learning is a leading provider of customized learning solutions with office locations around the globe, including Singapore, the United Kingdom, Australia, Mexico, Brazil, and Japan. Locate your local office at **www.cengage.com/global**

Cengage Learning products are represented in Canada by Nelson Education, Ltd.

To learn more about Delmar, visit **www.cengage.com/delmar**

Purchase any of our products at your local bookstore or at our preferred online store
www.cengagebrain.com

Printed in the United States of America
4 5 6 7 14 13 12 11

Contents

List of Tables

Some chapter material is located in tables so that content is easy to read (and learn). Tables allow additional material (e.g., history of healthcare reimbursement in Chapter 2, history of managed care in Chapter 3) to be included in the textbook. The instructor has the option of assigning the review of such content as homework instead of covering that material in class.

Preface

INTRODUCTION

Accurate processing of health insurance claims has become more exacting and rigorous as health insurance plan options have rapidly expanded. These changes, combined with modifications in state and federal regulations affecting the health insurance industry, are a constant challenge to healthcare personnel. Those responsible for processing health insurance claims require thorough instruction in all aspects of medical insurance, including plan options, payer requirements, state and federal regulations, abstracting of source documents, accurate completion of claims, and coding of diagnoses and procedures/services. *Understanding Health Insurance* provides the required information in a clear and comprehensive manner.

OBJECTIVES

The objectives of this text are to:

1. Introduce information about major insurance programs and federal healthcare legislation.

2. Provide a basic knowledge of national diagnosis and procedure coding systems.

3. Simplify the process of completing claims.

This text is designed to be used by college and vocational school programs to train medical assistants, medical insurance specialists, coding and reimbursement specialists, and health information technicians. It can also be used as an in-service training tool for new medical office personnel and independent billing services, or individually by claims processors in the healthcare field who want to develop or enhance their skills.

FEATURES OF THE TEXT

Major features of this text have been updated and expanded:

- Key terms, section headings, and learning objectives at the beginning of each chapter help to organize the material. They can be used as a self-test for checking comprehension and mastery of chapter content. Boldfaced key terms appear throughout each chapter to help learners master the technical vocabulary associated with claims processing.

- Coding exercises are located within the respective coding chapters: ICD-9-CM Coding, CPT Coding, HCPCS Level II Coding, and Coding for Medical Necessity. Answers to coding exercises are available from your instructor.

- Exercises in Chapters 11–17 help students develop claims completion skills.

- Numerous examples are provided in each chapter to illustrate the correct application of rules and guidelines.

- Notes clarify chapter content, focusing the student's attention on important concepts. Coding Tips provide practical suggestions for mastering the use of the CPT, HCPCS, and ICD-9-CM coding manuals. HIPAA Alerts draw attention to the impact of this legislation on privacy and security requirements for patient health information.

- End-of-chapter reviews reinforce learning and are in multiple-choice format. Answers to chapter reviews are available from your instructor.

- The practice CD-ROM provided with the text StudyWare™ software, as well as a free trial version of Ingenix's Encoder Pro software. SIMClaim software is located at the online companion contains case studies (also found in Appendix I and Appendix II of the textbook) that include billing data and patient histories and allow for data entry on CMS-1500 claims and immediate feedback. The complete SIMClaim *Procedure Manual* is easily accessed in the software and provides complete instructions for working with the software. StudyWare™ helps students learn key terms and concepts presented in each chapter by automating chapter exercises. This allows students to complete the exercises multiple times and receive immediate feedback about correct and incorrect answers. (Instructions for using Encoder Pro, SIMClaim and StudyWare are located at the end of this preface.)

NEW TO THIS EDITION

- Chapter 1: A new section about health insurance career opportunities was added, and the professional credentials section was renamed professionalism. New content was also added about internships, professionalism, and telephone skills.

- Chapter 2: Table 2-1 was renamed "significant events of health care reimbursement," and its content was revised to include only the most significant events. New sections covering medical documentation and the electronic health record (EHR) were added.

- Chapter 3: A table containing the "history of managed care" was relocated to the online companion. Table 3-1 was renamed "significant managed care federal legislation."

- Chapter 4: The chapter was renamed "Processing Insurance Claims." New content about electronic data interchange (EDI) was added.

- Chapter 5: New content was added, such as the Medicare Recovery Audit Contractor (RAC) Program.

- Chapter 6: New chapter sections include an overview of ICD-10-CM and ICD-10-PCS and medical necessity. ICD-9-CM coding guidelines and codes are updated. ICD-10-CM alerts were added throughout the chapter to help faculty and students become familiar with differences between ICD-9-CM and ICD-10-CM coding.

- Chapter 7: CPT coding guidelines and codes are updated.

- Chapter 8: HCPCS level II guidelines and codes are updated.

- Chapter 9: Updated content about reimbursement systems has been added.

- Chapter 11: Content about automobile, disability, and liability was relocated from chapter 2, and ICD-10-CM codes were added. (ICD-9-CM codes are also included.)

- Chapter 12: A new section about completing group health plans CMS-1500 claims has been added.

- Chapter 15: A new section about completing SCHIP claims has been added.

- Chapters 12-17: ICD-10-CM codes were added. (ICD-9-CM codes are also included.)

- Fully updated to include the latest industry guidelines and standards

- New content about the electronic health record, medical documentation, and electronic data interchange
- Additional ICD-10-CM and ICD-10-PCS coverage to anticipate the transition in 2013, including an ICD-10-CM Alert! feature that displays ICD-9-CM and ICD-10-CM codes side-by-side
- SIMClaim practice software has improved functionality in feedback mode, targeted block help with video, and the option to print completed forms to PDF for easy emailing and printing.
- StudyWare™ scenario-based coding cases have been updated and use multimedia to enhance coding practice.

ORGANIZATION OF THIS TEXTBOOK

- Chapter outlines, key terms, and end-of-chapter summaries facilitate student learning.
- A Study Checklist at the end of each chapter directs learners to various methods of review, reinforcement, and testing.
- Chapter 1, Health Insurance Specialist Career, contains an easy-to-read table that delineates training requirements for health insurance specialists.
- Chapter 2, Introduction to Health Insurance, contains content about healthcare insurance developments.
- Chapter 3, Managed Health Care, contains content about managed care plans, consumer-directed health plans, health savings accounts, and flexible spending accounts.
- Chapter 4, Processing an Insurance Claim, contains content about managing an office visit for a new or established patient, claims processing steps, and the denials/appeals process.
- Chapter 5, Legal and Regulatory Issues, emphasizes confidentiality of patient information, retention of patient information and health insurance records, the Federal False Claims Act, the Health Insurance Portability and Accountability Act of 1996, and federal laws and events that affect health care.
- Chapter 6, ICD-9-CM Coding, contains coding guidelines and coding rules with examples. The coding conventions for the Index to Diseases and the Tabular List of Diseases are located in tables within the chapter, and examples of coding manual entries are included. The chapter review includes coding exercises, which are organized according to the sections in the ICD-9-CM Tabular List of Diseases.
- Chapter 7, CPT Coding, follows the organization of CPT sections. The chapter review includes coding exercises organized by CPT section.
- Chapter 8, HCPCS Level II Coding, has been updated to reflect revised codes and descriptions.
- Chapter 9, CMS Reimbursement Methodologies, contains information about reimbursement systems implemented since 1983 (including the Medicare physician fee schedule), hospital revenue cycle management, the chargemaster, and the UB-04 (CMS-1450) claim. (A separate chapter about the UB-04 claim is not included in this textbook. The UB-04 claim is automatically generated upon entry of chargemaster data in the facility's patient accounting system.)
- Chapter 10, Coding for Medical Necessity, contains tables that allow learners to organize answers to exercises. A chapter review contains evaluation and management coding practice exercises.
- Chapter 11, Essential CMS-1500 Claim Instructions, contains updated content, and information about automobile, disability, and liability insurance.

NOTE: The ICD-9-CM chapter is sequenced before the CPT and HCPCS level II chapters in this textbook because diagnosis codes are reported for medical necessity (to justify procedures and/or services provided).

NOTE: CPT codes were updated using the AMA's downloadable CPT data files.

- Claims completion instructions in Chapters 12–17 are revised according to changes implemented by third-party and government payers. Claims completion instructions are located in an easy-to-read table format.

SUPPLEMENTS

The following supplements accompany the text:

Instructor's Manual

The Instructor's Manual contains the following sections:
- Section I – Preparing Your Course
- Section II - Answer Keys to Textbook Chapter Exercises and Reviews
- Section III - Chapter Exams and Answer Keys to Chapter Exams
- Section IV - Answer Keys to Textbook Appendix Case Studies
- Section V – Instructor's Materials
- Section VI - Answer Keys to Workbook Chapter Assignments
- Section VII - Answer Key to Mock CMRS Exam
- Section VIII - Answer Key to Mock CPC-P Exam

Student Workbook

The Workbook follows the chapter organization of the text and contains application-based assignments. Each chapter assignment includes a list of objectives, an overview of content relating to the assignment, and instructions for completing the assignment. Other components may be present depending on the assignment. Each chapter contains review questions, in multiple-choice format, to emulate credentialing exam questions. In Chapters 11 through 17, additional case studies allow more practice in completing the CMS-1500 claim. Appendix A contains a mock CMRS exam, and Appendix B contains a mock CPC-P exam.

The Workbook features billing activities using **Medical Office Simulation Software (MOSS 2.0)** that provides hands-on training of all aspects of front office practice management software, simulating online transmission of claims and insurance eligibility. Version 2.0 of MOSS features expanded insurance and billing functionality, and includes a new Claims Tracking module.

Instructor Resources CD-ROM

The Instructor Resources CD-ROM provides many aids to help the instructor plan and implement a course for health insurance specialists. Included on the CD-ROM are a computerized test bank; instructor slides contained in PowerPoint; an electronic version of the Instructor's Manual; Delmar's *Insurance, Billing and Coding Curriculum Guide;* and a grid comparing the tenth edition of *Understanding Health Insurance* with the ninth edition. To order the Instructor Resources CD-ROM, contact your sales representative. (Locate your sales representative by clicking on the Find Your Rep link at www.delmarlearning.com.)

Online Companion

Additional resources can be found online at the following Internet link: **www.delmarlearning.com/companions.** In the upper right corner, you may search by author, title, or ISBN in the search field to locate the Online Companion site for this textbook.

Items listed as Instructor Resources are password protected. For access to protected content in the Online Companion, see the username and password provided in the Instructor's Manual at the end of the Introduction (both the print version and the electronic version of the Instructor Resources CD-ROM).

Student Resources

- CMS-1500 claim (blank)
- *Ready, Set, Get a Job!*
- Revisions to the textbook and Workbook due to coding updates
- Ready, Set, Get a Job! and other career information
- Web Links
- 2010 final test for AAPC CEU approval

Instructor Resources

- Curriculum Guide
- Conversion grid mapping the 9th edition to the 10th edition to make transitioning a snap
- Revisions to the instructor's manual, computerized test bank (CTB) and WebTutor™ due to coding updates
- Grids comparing the tenth edition of *Understanding Health Insurance* with competitive titles
- Answer keys to Workbook Appendix C of MOSS billing exercises

> **NOTE:** WebTutor™ Advantage was designed to accompany *Understanding Health Insurance,* by Michelle A. Green and JoAnn C. Rowell. Its purpose is to help students organize their study of the textbook material, reinforce their learning, test their mastery of the content, and improve their performance on exams. WebTutor™ is intended to complement the textbook and course delivery. It is not intended as a substitute for either.

WebTutor™

WebTutor™ Advantage is an Internet-based course management and delivery system designed to accompany the text. Its content is available for use in either WebCT or Blackboard. Available to supplement on-campus course delivery or as the course management platform for an online course, the enhanced WebTutor contains:

- Video and audio clips
- Online quizzes for each chapter
- Discussion topics and learning links
- Additional coding exercises
- Online glossary, organized by chapter
- Answers to textbook exercises and reviews
- Instructor slides contained in PowerPoint
- Testbank
- Communication tools, including a course calendar, chat, e-mail, and threaded discussions

To learn more, visit **http://webtutor.cengage.com**.

ABOUT THE AUTHOR

Michelle A. Green, MPS, RHIA, FAHIMA, CPC, SUNY Distinguished Teaching Professor, Alfred State College, Alfred, New York, has been a full-time college professor since 1984. She taught traditional classroom-based courses until 2000, when she transitioned all of the health information technology and coding/reimbursement specialist courses to an Internet-based format. Her teaching responsibilities include health information management, insurance and reimbursement, and ICD-9-CM, ICD-10-CM, ICD-10-PCS, CPT, and HCPCS level II coding courses. Prior to 1984, she worked as a director of health information management at two acute care hospitals in the Tampa Bay, Florida, area. Both positions required her to assign ICD-9-CM codes to inpatient cases. Upon becoming employed as a college professor, she routinely spent semester breaks coding for a number of healthcare facilities so that she could further develop her inpatient and outpatient coding skills.

REVIEWERS

Special thanks are extended to the reviewers who provided recommendations and suggestions for improvement throughout the development of the tenth edition. Their experience and knowledge has been a valuable resource for the authors.

Mary M. Cantwell, RHIT, CPC, CPC-I, CPC-H, RMC
Full-time Instructor in the Health Information Management Systems
Metro Community College
Omaha, Nebraska

Julia Carlson, BS, MS, CPC, CPC-I
Associate Professor, Healthcare and Office Administration
Guilford Technical Community College
Jamestown, NC

Rashmi Gaonkar, MS
Senior Instructor
ASA Institute
Brooklyn, New York

Teena Gregory-Gooding, MS, CPC
Medical Education Consultant
Rapid City, South Dakota

Linda Hernandez
Instructor
Franklin Career College
Ontario, California

Annette Jackson, MBA, CMRS
Faculty-Subject Area Coordinator in Medical Administrative Assistant
Bryant & Stratton College
Eastlake, Ohio Campus

Shirley Jelmo, BS, CMA (AAMA), RMA, AHI
MA Program Director
PIMA Medical Institute
Colorado Springs, Colorado

Joshua Maywalt, NCICS, NCMOA
Billing Manager/Medical Billing and Coding Instructor
Medical Alternatives of America Inc./Sanford Brown Institute
Orlando, Florida

Wilsetta L. McClain
Department Chair
Baker College of Auburn Hills
Auburn Hills, Michigan

Kathleen O'Gorman, BS
Lead Instructor, Health Claims Dept.
Branford Hall Career Institute
Southington, Connecticut

Patricia L. Orr, CBCS
Program Manager
Caliber College
Phoenix, Arizona

Donna Otis, LPN
Medical Program Coordinator
Metro Business College
Rolla, Missouri

Lynne Padilla, CPC, CHI
Medical Curriculum Developer
Allied Business Schools
Laguna Hills, California

Danielle Robel, MBA, BA, Medical Assistant
Adjunct Instructor
Kaplan University
Fort Lauderdale, Florida

Linda Scarborough, MSHA, RN, CPC, CMA (AAMA)
Healthcare Management Technology Instructor
Lanier Technical College
Oakwood, Georgia

Tonia Seay-Josephina, CPC, RMC, RMM
Instructor, Medical Billing and Coding
Advanced Career Training
Morrow, Georgia

Josh VanDusen
Medical Assisting Instructor
Miller Motte Technical College
Chattanooga, Tennessee

Jan West-Boagni, BA
Program Director
American Career College
Anaheim, California

Karen Wright, MHA, RHIA
Professor/Coordinator Health Information Technology
Hocking College
Nelsonville, Ohio

TECHNICAL REVIEWERS

Deborah Farwell, BS, CCS-P, CPC, GENSG
Billing Manager, Coordinated Primary Care
Health Alliance Hospital
Fitchburg, Massachusetts

Cecile Favreau, MBA, CPC
Instructor
The Salter School
Worcester, Massachusetts

Linda Hernandez
Instructor
Franklin Career College
Ontario, California

ACKNOWLEDGMENTS

To my son, Eric, who understands and supports my passion for teaching and writing.

To my students, throughout the world, who motivate me to want to learn everything so I can teach them everything. You are my inspiration.

Special appreciation is expressed to Ingenix Publishing Group for granting permission to reprint selected tables and pages from:

- *HCPCS Level II Professional*
- *ICD-9-CM Professional for Physicians, vols. 1 & 2*
- *ICD-10-CM*
- *ICD-10-PCS*

FEEDBACK

Contact the author at **delmarauthor@yahoo.com** with questions, suggestions, or comments about the text or supplements.

How to Use This Text

Health Insurance Specialist Career

CHAPTER OUTLINE

Health Insurance Overview
Health Insurance Career Opportunities
Education and Training
Job Responsibilities
Professionalism

OBJECTIVES

Upon successful completion of this chapter, you should be able to:

1. Define key terms.
2. Discuss introductory health insurance concepts.
3. Identify career opportunities available in health insurance.
4. List the education and training requirements of a health insurance specialist.
5. Describe the job responsibilities of a health insurance specialist.
6. Explain the role of workplace professionalism in career success.

KEY TERMS

American Academy of Professional Coders (AAPC)
American Association of Medical Assistants (AAMA)
American Health Information Management Association (AHIMA)
American Medical Billing Association (AMBA)
bonding insurance
business liability insurance
Centers for Medicare and Medicaid Services (CMS)
claims examiner
coding
Current Procedural Terminology (CPT)

embezzle
errors and omissions insurance
ethics
explanation of benefits (EOB)
HCPCS level II codes
Healthcare Common Procedure Coding System (HCPCS)
healthcare provider
health information technician
health insurance claim
health insurance specialist
hold harmless clause
independent contractor
International Classification of

Diseases, 9th Revision, Clinical Modification (ICD-9-CM)
International Classification of Diseases, 10th Revision, Clinical Modification (ICD-10-CM)
International Classification of Diseases, 10th Revision, Procedural Coding System (ICD-10-PCS)
internship
liability insurance
medical assistant
Medical Association of Billers (MAB)
medical malpractice insurance
medical necessity

© Delmar, Cengage Learning 2011

Objectives and Key Terms

The **Objectives** section lists the outcomes expected of the learner after a careful study of the chapter. Review the Objectives before reading the chapter content. When you complete the chapter, read the Objectives again to see if you can say for each one, "Yes, I can do that." If you cannot, go back to the appropriate content and reread it.

Key Terms represent new vocabulary in each chapter. Each term is highlighted in color in the chapter, is used in context, and is defined on first usage. A complete definition of each term appears in the Glossary at the end of the text.

STUDY CHECKLIST

☐ Read this textbook chapter and highlight key concepts. (Use colored highlighter sparingly throughout chapter.)
☐ Create an index card for each key term. (Write the key term on one side of the index card and the concept on the other. Learn the
☐ Access chapter Internet links t
☐ Answer the chapter review que
☐ Complete WebTutor assignmen
☐ Complete Workbook chapter, w
☐ Form a study group with class

Study Checklist

The **Study Checklist** appears at the end of each chapter. This list directs you to other learning and application aids. Completing each of the items in the checklist helps you to gain confidence in your understanding of the key concepts and in your ability to apply them correctly.

NOTE: The federal Social Security Disability Insurance (SSDI) and Supplemental Security Income (SSI) disability program provide assistance to people with disabilities. Both programs are administered by the federal Social Security Administration, and only individuals who have a disability and meet medical criteria qualify for benefits und either program. Social Security Disability Insurance pays bene to you and certain members o your family if you are "insured," meaning that you worked long enough and paid Social Securi taxes. Supplemental Security Income pays benefits based or financial need.

Introduction

The **Introduction** provides a brief overview of the major topics covered in the chapter.

The Introduction and the Objectives provide a framework for your study of the content.

Notes

NOTES appear throughout the text and serve to bring important points to your attention. The notes may clarify content, refer you to reference material, provide more background for selected topics, or emphasize exceptions to rules.

INTRODUCTION

Managed health care (managed care) combines healthcare delivery with the financing of services provided. The intent was to replace conventional fee-for-service plans with more affordable quality care to healthcare consumers and providers who agreed to certain restrictions (e.g., patients would receive care only from providers who are members of a managed care organization). Managed care is currently being challenged by the growth of consumer-directed health plans (CDHPs), which define employer contributions and ask employees to be more responsible for healthcare decisions and cost-sharing. You might think of a CDHP as a sort of "401(k) plan for health care" (recalling the shift from employer defined-benefit pension plans to employer defined-contribution 401(k) plans).

HIPAA ALERT!

Traditionally, claims attachments containing medical documentation that supported procedures and services reported on claims were copied from patient records and mailed to payers. Effective 2006, providers submit electronic attachments with electronic claims or send [in response to requests for medical documentation to su] (e.g., scanned images of paper records).

CODING TIP: Make sure that diagnoses, procedures, and services listed on the encounter form are documented in the patient's medical record before reporting codes on the insurance claim.

Icons

Icons draw attention to critical areas of content or provide experience-based recommendations. For example, the **HIPAA ALERT!** identifies issues related to the security of personal health information in the medical office. The **CODING TIP** provides recommendations and hints for selecting codes and for the correct use of the coding manuals. Other icons include **MANAGED CARE ALERT, HINT, REMEMBER!,** and **CAUTION.**

INTERNET LINKS

- **Great Plains Regional Medical Center**
  Go to **www.gprmc-ok.com** and select the About Us link to learn more about Dr. Shadid and the history of the Great Plains Regional Medical Center, a managed care system started in 1929.
- **HealthEast**
  Go to **www.healtheast.org** to view information about the Health[...] grated care delivery system that provides acute care, chronic c[...] services, ambulatory/outpatient services, physician clinics, an[...]
- **The Joint Commission**
  Go to **www.jointcommission.org** to learn about The Joint Comm[...]
- **The Joint Commission Quality Check**
  Go to **www.qualitycheck.org**, and conduct a search to identify[...] Joint Commission's patient safety and quality standards.
- **Kaiser Permanente**
  Go to **www.kaiserpermanente.org** to learn about the history of[...] Permanente.
- **National Committee for Quality Assurance (NCQA)**
  Go to **www.ncqa.org** to learn about the NCQA.
- **NCQA's Health Plan Report Card**
  Go to **reportcard.ncqa.org**, and click the "create a report card"[...] a customized report card of managed care plans.

Internet Links

Internet Links are provided to encourage you to expand your knowledge at various state and federal government agency sites, commercial sites, and organization sites. Some exercises require you to obtain information from the Internet to complete the exercise.

SUMMARY

The financing of America's health care system has changed the way health care services are organized and delivered, as evidenced by a movement from traditional fee-for-service systems to managed care networks. These range from structured staff model HMOs to less structured preferred provider organizations (PPOs).

Currently, more than 60 million Americans are enrolled in some type of managed care program in response to regulatory initiatives affecting health care cost and quality.

A managed care organization (MCO) is responsible for the health of its enrollees, [...] istered by the MCO that serves as a health plan or contracts with a hospital, p[...] health system.

Most managed care financing is achieved through a method called capitation, an[...] assigned to or select a primary care provider who serves as the patient's gatek[...]

Federal legislation mandated that MCOs participate in quality assurance program[...] including utilization management, case management, requirements for secon[...] non-use of gag clauses in MCO contracts, and disclosure of any physician inc[...]

Managed care is categorized according to six models: exclusive provider organiz[...] integrated delivery systems, health maintenance organizations, point-of-servic[...] vider organizations, and triple option plans.

Consumer-directed health plans (CDHPs) provide incentives for controlling healt[...] give individuals an alternative to traditional health insurance and managed ca[...]

Accreditation organizations, such as the NCQA, evaluate MCOs according to pre[...]

Summary

The **Summary** at the end of each chapter recaps the key points of the chapter. It also serves as a review aid when preparing for tests.

EXERCISE 10-4

Coding Case Scenarios

A. List and code the procedures and diagnosis(es) for each of the following case scenarios.

B. Be sure to include all necessary CPT and/or HCPCS modifiers.

C. Underline the first-listed condition.

1. A 66-year-old Medicare patient came to the office for his annual physical. He has past history of hypertension, controlled by medication, and new complaints of dizziness and tiredness. During the course of the examination the physician found BP of 160/130. A detailed history and exam of this established patient was performed in addition to the preventive medicine encounter.

Procedures	Diagnoses
_____	_____
_____	_____
_____	_____

2. A 67-year-old woman came to the surgery center for a scheduled diagnostic arthroscopy of her right shoulder because of constant pain [...]

REVIEW

MULTIPLE CHOICE Select the most appropriate response.

1. **Which means that the patient and/or insured has authorized the payer to reimburse the provider directly?**
   a. accept assignment
   b. assignment of benefits
   c. coordination of benefits
   d. medical necessity

2. **Providers who do not accept assignment of Medicare benefits do not receive information included on the _____, which is sent to the patient.**
   a. electronic flat file
   b. encounter form
   c. ledger
   d. Medicare Summary Notice

3. **The transmission of claims data to payers or clearinghouses is called claims:**
   a. adjudication.
   b. assignment.
   c. processing.
   d. submission.

4. **Which facilitates processing of nonstandard claims data elements into standard data elements?**
   a. clearinghouse
   b. EHNAC
   c. payer
   d. provider

5. **A series of fixed-length records submitted to payers to bill for health care services is an electronic:**
   a. flat file format.
   b. funds transfer.

Reviews

The **Reviews** test student understanding about chapter content and critical thinking ability. Reviews in coding chapters require students to assign correct codes and modifiers using coding manuals. Answers are available from your instructor.

Coding Exercises appear in Chapters 6–8 and 10 to provide more practice in applying critical thinking to code selection. Answers to the coding exercises are available from your instructor.

BLUE CROSS BLUE SHIELD   413

TABLE 13-1 CMS-1500 claims completion instructions for BCBS fee-for-service plans

NOTE: Refer to Chapter 11 for clarification of claims completion (e.g., entering names, mailing addresses, ICD codes, diagnosis pointer numbers, NPI, and so on).

BLOCK	INSTRUCTIONS
1	Enter an X in the *Other* box.
1a	Enter the BCBS plan identification number as it appears on the patient's insurance card. *Do not enter hyphens or spaces in the number.*
2	Enter the patient's last name, first name, and middle initial (separated by commas).
3	Enter the patient's birth date as MM DD YYYY (with spaces). Enter an X in the appropriate box to indicate the patient's gender. If the patient's gender is unknown, leave blank.
4	Enter the policyholder's last name, first name, and middle initial (separated by commas).
5	Enter the patient's mailing address and telephone number. Enter the street address on line 1, enter the city and state on line 2, and enter the 5- or 9-digit zip code and phone number on line 3.
6	Enter an X in the appropriate box to indicate the patient's relationship to the policyholder. If the patient is an unmarried domestic partner, enter an X in the *Other* box.
7	Enter the policyholder's mailing address and telephone number. Enter the street address on line 1, enter the city and state on line 2, and enter the 5- or 9-digit zip code and phone number on line 3.
8	Enter an X in the appropriate box to [...] unmarried domestic partner, enter a[...] Enter an X in the appropriate box to [...] patient is unemployed and/or not a [...]
9, 9a-9d	Leave blank. *Blocks 9 and 9a–9d ar[...] cussed later in this chapter).*
10a-c	Enter an X in the appropriate boxes [...] ment, an automobile accident, and/[...] accident, enter the 2-character state[...]
10d	Leave blank.
11	Enter the policyholder's BCBS polic[...] or group number.
11a	Enter the policyholder's birth date a[...] Enter an X in the appropriate box to [...] unknown, leave blank.
11b	Enter the name of the policyholder'[...] provided as an employer group hea[...] a full- or part-time student). Otherw[...]
11c	Enter the name of the policyholder'[...]
11d	Enter an X in the NO box. *Block 11[...] secondary insurance coverage (disc[...]*
12	Enter SIGNATURE ON FILE. Leave [...]
13	Leave blank. *Assignment of benefits[...] authorizes BCBS to reimburse prov[...]*
14	Enter the date as MM DD YYYY (w[...] symptoms of the present illness or i[...] visits. *If the date is not documented[...] date (e.g., three weeks ago), simply [...]*

CPT copyright 2007 American Medical Association. All rights [...]

Claims Instructions

Claims instructions simplify the process of completing the CMS-1500 for various types of payers. These instructions are provided in tables in Chapters 12–17. Each table consists of step-by-step instructions for completing each block of the CMS-1500 for commercial, Blue Cross Blue Shield, Medicare, Medicaid, TRICARE, and Workers' Compensation payers.

How to Use the SIMClaim CMS-1500 Student Practice

SimClaim is an educational tool designed to familiarize you with the basics of the CMS-1500 claim form completion. Because in the real world there are many rules that can vary by payer, facility, and state, every effort was made to make the SimClaim program *generically correct* in order to provide you with a foundational understanding of the claim form.

How to Access SimClaim

To access the SimClaim student practice software program online, please refer to the information on the printed access card found in the front of this textbook. The SimClaim case studies are also available for reference in Appendix I and II of this textbook.

Main Menu

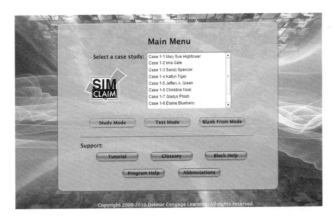

From the Main Menu, you can access the SimClaim program three different ways: Study Mode, Test Mode, and Blank Form Mode.

- Click on **Study Mode** to get feedback as you fill out claim forms for the case studies. If you need help entering information in a block of the form, you may click on Block Help for block-specific instructions while in Study Mode.
- Click on **Test Mode** to fill out claim forms for the case studies to test yourself. The completed claim is graded and can be printed and emailed to your instructor.
- Use **Blank Form Mode** if you wish to utilize the SimClaim program to fill out a blank CMS-1500 form with another case study in the textbook or student workbook.

You can access SimClaim support documentation from the Main Menu as well, including a video Tutorial, Block Help, a glossary, and list of abbreviations.

General Instructions and Hints for Completing CMS-1500 Forms in SimClaim

Please read through the following general instructions before beginning work in the SimClaim program:

- **Turn on Caps Lock**—all data entered into SimClaim must be in ALL CAPS.

- **Do not abbreviate**—spell out words like street, drive, avenue, Signature on File, Blue Cross Blue Shield, etc—no abbreviations (other than state abbreviations) will be accepted by the program.

- **Do not use "Same As" or "None" in Block 7**—if patient information is the same as insured information, enter that information again on the claim.

- **More than one Diagnosis Pointer in Block 24E**—for the SimClaim case studies, there may be more than one diagnosis pointer required in Block 24E. See the Block Help video for more information.

- **No Amount Paid Indicated**—if there is no amount paid indicated on the case study, **you must enter "0 00" in Block 29.**

- **Secondary Insurance Claims**—If a Case Study indicates that a patient's Primary Insurance carrier has paid an amount, fill out a second claim form for Secondary Insurance that reflects the amount reimbursed by primary insurance.

- **Follow NUCC form guidelines** on punctuation use in the form. The NUCC CMS-1500 Claim Form Instruction Manual may be downloaded by going to www.nucc.org.

- **For additional help, refer to the Block Help documentation within the SimClaim program.**

How to Use the StudyWare CD-ROM

STUDYWARE™

The StudyWare™ software helps you learn terms and concepts presented in this textbook. As you study each chapter, be sure to complete the activities for the corresponding content areas on the CD-ROM. Use StudyWare™ as your own private tutor to help you learn the material in your textbook. When you open the software, enter your first and last name so the software can track your quiz results. Then choose a content area from the menu to take a quiz, complete an activity, or complete a coding case.

Menus

You can access any of the menus from wherever you are in the program. The menus include Chapter Quizzes and Activities, Coding Cases, and Scores.

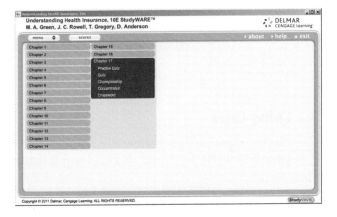

Quizzes

Quizzes include multiple choice, true/false, and fill-in-the-blank questions. You can take the quizzes in both Practice Mode and Quiz Mode.

- **Use Practice Mode to improve your mastery of the material. You have multiple tries to get the answers correct. Instant feedback tells you whether you are right or wrong and helps you learn quickly by explaining why an answer is correct or incorrect.**

- Use Quiz Mode when you are ready to test yourself and keep a record of your scores. In Quiz Mode, you have one try to get the answers right, but you can take each quiz as many times as you want.
- You can view your last scores for each quiz and print out your results to submit to your instructor.

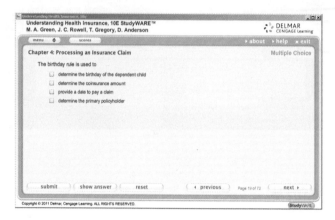

Activities

Activities include Hangman, crossword puzzles, and Concentration. Have fun while increasing your knowledge!

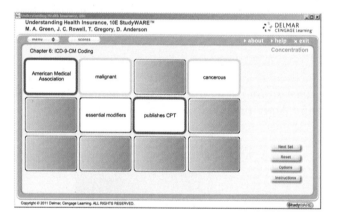

Coding Cases

Coding cases include animations, images, and video clips to challenge and test your ICD-9-CM, CPT, and HCPCS level II coding skills.

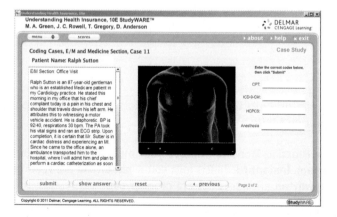

How to Use the Encoder Pro CD-ROM

INTRODUCTION TO ENCODER PRO

The Encoder Pro software included in the back cover of this textbook is a 30-day free trial of Ingenix's powerful medical coding solution that allows you to lookup ICD-9-CM, CPT, and HCPCS level II codes quickly and accurately. This software can be used to assign codes to any of the coding exercises in the *Understanding Health Insurance* textbook. (Be sure to check with your instructor before installing the Encoder Pro software because the CD-ROM bundled with your book expires 30 days after installation.)

MENUS AND TOOLBARS

Encoder Pro contains a menu that expands to allow you to easily navigate the software. Click on a menu heading to select one of its options (e.g., View, Code Book Sections).

Encoder Pro contains a toolbar with drop down menus that allow you to select the ICD-9-CM, CPT, or HCPCS level II coding system and new/revised/deleted codes (on the left) and code book sections (on the right).

- Use the coding system drop down menu on the far left to select a coding system. Then, enter a condition (e.g., diabetes) or procedure/service in the Search box. Click the Search button to view Tabular Results, which can be expanded, or click the "See index listing" to use the alphabetic index to locate a code.
- Use the drop down menu on the far right of the toolbar to quickly access New Codes, Revised Codes, Deleted Codes, and Code Book Sections. Make a selection and click the View button to access the dialog boxes.

Encoder Pro's toolbar has clickable buttons (icons) that allow you to use its unique features. Simply mouse over a button to view its complete title, and a brief description of the button will also appear in the status bar (bottom left corner of screen). Click on the button to use its function (e.g., CPT Section Notes button allows you to read notes associated with an entered CPT code).

ENCODER PRO TUTORIAL

Instructions: Use this tutorial to learn how to use Ingenix's Encoder Pro software—located inside the back cover of your textbook—as a 30-day trial.

Step 1
Retrieve the Encoder Pro disk from the cardboard sleeve inside the back cover of your textbook. You will use Encoder Pro to automate the process of locating ICD-9-CM codes for:

- Beer-drinkers' heart
- Bee sting

To install Encoder Pro . . .

- Insert the disk in the CD-ROM drive of your computer and wait for the "Install Shield Wizard" screen to display.
- Enter your name as the "User Name" and your school's name as the "Company Name." Click Next.
- Click Next when the "Welcome to Encoder Pro . . . :" screen displays.
- Click Yes to accept the terms of Ingenix's licensing agreement.
- Click Next to install the software to the predetermined destination folder.
- Click Yes to add a shortcut (Encoder Pro icon) to your computer's desktop. (This will make it easy to locate and double click on the icon.)
- Click Next after reading Ingenix's commitment to accuracy screen.
- Click Finish to complete the software installation.
- Remove the disk from your computer's CD-ROM drive and replace it in the cardboard sleeve.
- Double click on the Encoder Pro icon, which is located on your computer's desktop. Wait a moment for the opening screen to clear. Then, click OK to accept the AMA Copyright notice.
- You are now ready to begin using Ingenix's Encoder Pro software!

Step 2

Locate the toolbar that contains the "All Code Sets" drop down list, which allows you to select a coding system. (Refer to the image at right, which identifies the location of the toolbar on the Encoder Pro software screen.)

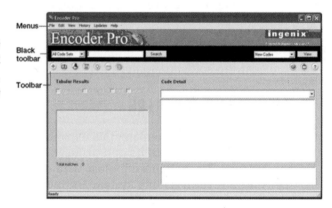

Step 3

- Click on the "All Code Sets" arrow and select "ICD-9 Vol. 1."
- Click in the empty Search box, located to the right of the "ICD-9 Vol. 1" indicator.
- Enter BEER as the condition search term. (You can enter as beer or Beer, too.)
- Click "Search."

Step 4

- A "Tabular Results" screen displays.
- Click on the "See Index listing" link.

"**Total matches: 2**" displays when the Tabular Results for ICD-9 Vol. 1 screen appears. If you click the + next to **425 Cardiomyopathy**, the second "match" (**425.5 Alcoholic cardiomyopathy**) will display. Experienced coders sometimes view "Tabular Results" directly (instead of clicking on the "See Index listing" link).

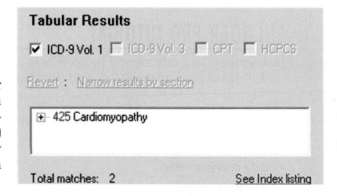

Step 5

- An "Index Listing" screen displays with the condition and its code.
- Click OK.

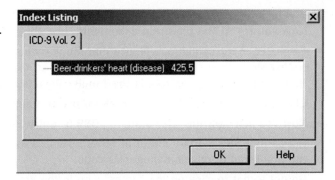

Step 6

A "Code Detail" window displays, and code **425.5** Alcoholic cardiomyopathy appears in shaded text. This means you have verified code 425.5 in the ICD-9-CM Tabular List of Diseases, and you can assign this code for "Beer-drinker's heart."

When you scroll up to category code **425** Cardiomyopathy, notice that the code number is displayed in red. This means that code 425 is incomplete, and a fourth digit is required. Notice the "Fourth Digit Code Required" instruction at the bottom of the Encoder Pro screen.

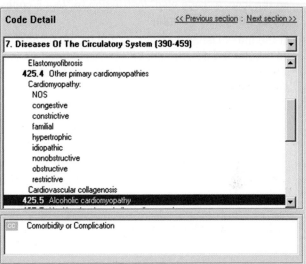

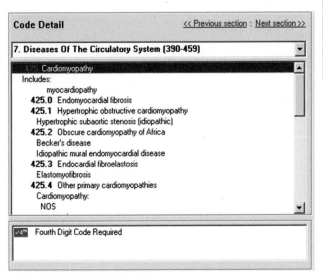

Step 7

- Click on the icons in the gray toolbar to view additional content and instructions about code 425.5.
- Notice that when you click the "Notes" icon (fourth from the left), you are directed to "Coding Clinic" references about this condition. (The American Hospital Association's *Coding Clinic for ICD-9-CM* provides additional instructions about assigning ICD-9-CM codes.)

- Be sure to click on each icon to view the additional information available to you.

Step 8

- **Now you try it!** The physician documents "bee sting" as the patient's diagnosis.
- Enter BEE in the search box. Notice that many Tabular Results display. (This condition requires more advanced coding skills than "Beer-drinker's heart." Only an experienced coder would be comfortable selecting a code from among those displayed in the Tabular Results box.)
- Click on "See Index listing," and click on the plus sign to view all index entries.
- Now you can view the "Bee sting . . . 989.5" entry. Select it by clicking OK.
- Notice that **989.5 Toxic effect of venom** displays as shaded text in the Code Detail window. Assign 989.5 as the first-listed or principal diagnosis code.
- Do not forget to click on the "notes" icon in the gray toolbar (located above the Code Detail). Once you click on the icon, a "code also" instruction to "Use E codes to identify the cause and intent of the injury or poisoning (E800-E999)" will display.
- In the Index Listing display for "Bee (sting) (venom)," click on the "Table of Drugs-Accident E905.3" Link to view its tabular list description. Select "Accidental" as the cause and assign E905.3 as the secondary code because it is not likely that the bee sting was the result of an assault, suicide attempt, or undetermined, which are your other choices.

Health Insurance Specialist Career

CHAPTER OUTLINE

Health Insurance Overview

Health Insurance Career Opportunities

Education and Training

Job Responsibilities

Professionalism

OBJECTIVES

Upon successful completion of this chapter, you should be able to:

1. Define key terms.
2. Discuss introductory health insurance concepts.
3. Identify career opportunities available in health insurance.
4. List the education and training requirements of a health insurance specialist.
5. Describe the job responsibilities of a health insurance specialist.
6. Explain the role of workplace professionalism in career success.

KEY TERMS

American Academy of Professional Coders (AAPC)

American Association of Medical Assistants (AAMA)

American Health Information Management Association (AHIMA)

American Medical Billing Association (AMBA)

bonding insurance

business liability insurance

Centers for Medicare and Medicaid Services (CMS)

claims examiner

coding

Current Procedural Terminology (CPT)

embezzle

errors and omissions insurance

ethics

explanation of benefits (EOB)

HCPCS level II codes

Healthcare Common Procedure Coding System (HCPCS)

healthcare provider

health information technician

health insurance claim

health insurance specialist

hold harmless clause

independent contractor

International Classification of

Diseases, 9th Revision, Clinical Modification (ICD-9-CM)

International Classification of Diseases, 10th Revision, Clinical Modification (ICD-10-CM)

International Classification of Diseases, 10th Revision, Procedural Coding System (ICD-10-PCS)

internship

liability insurance

medical assistant

Medical Association of Billers (MAB)

medical malpractice insurance

medical necessity

national codes
National Electronic Billers Alliance (NEBA)
preauthorization

professional liability insurance
professionalism
property insurance
reimbursement specialist

remittance advice (remit)
respondeat superior
scope of practice
workers' compensation insurance

INTRODUCTION

The career of a health insurance specialist is a challenging one, with opportunities for professional advancement. Individuals who understand claims processing and billing regulations,

> **NOTE:** Reimbursement specialist is another title for health insurance specialist.

possess accurate coding skills, can successfully appeal underpaid or denied insurance claims, and demonstrate workplace professionalism, are in demand. A review of medical office personnel help-wanted advertisements indicates the need for individuals with all of these skills.

Complete StudyWare practice quizzes and activities using the CD-ROM located inside the back cover of your textbook.

HEALTH INSURANCE OVERVIEW

Most healthcare practices in the United States accept responsibility for filing health insurance claims, and some third-party payers (e.g., Blue Cross/Blue Shield) and government programs (e.g., Medicare) require providers to file claims. A **health insurance claim** is the documentation submitted to a third-party payer or government program requesting reimbursement for healthcare services provided. In the past few years, many practices have increased the number of employees assigned to some aspect of claims processing. This increase is a result of more patients having some form of health insurance, many of whom require **preauthorization** (prior approval) for treatment by specialists and documentation of post-treatment reports. If preauthorization requirements are not met, payment of the claim is denied. If the insurance plan has a **hold harmless clause** (patient is not responsible for paying what the insurance plan denies) in the contract, the healthcare provider cannot collect the fees from the patient. In addition, patients referred to non-participating providers (e.g., a physician who does not participate in a particular healthcare plan) incur significantly higher out-of-pocket costs than anticipated. Competitive insurance companies are fine-tuning procedures to reduce administrative costs and overall expenditures. This cost-reduction campaign forces closer scrutiny of the entire claims process, which in turn increases the time and effort medical practices must devote to billing and filing claims according to the insurance policy filing requirements. Poor attention to claims requirements will result in lower reimbursement rates to the practices and increased expenses.

A number of managed care contracts are signed by healthcare providers. A **healthcare provider** is a physician or other healthcare practitioner (e.g., physician's assistant). Each new provider-managed care contract increases the practice's patient base, the number of claims requirements and reimbursement regulations, the time the office staff must devote to fulfilling contract requirements, and the complexity of referring patients for specialty care. Each insurance plan has its own authorization requirements, billing deadlines, claims requirements, and list of participating providers or networks. If a healthcare provider has signed 10 participating contracts, there are 10 different sets of requirements to follow and 10 different panels of participating healthcare providers from which referrals can be made.

Rules associated with health insurance processing (especially government programs) change frequently; to remain up-to-date, insurance specialists should be sure they are on mailing lists to receive newsletters from third-party payers. It is also important to remain current regarding news released from the

Centers for Medicare and Medicaid Services (CMS) which is the administrative agency within the federal Department of Health and Human Services (DHHS). The Secretary of the DHHS is often reported by the news media as having announced the implementation of new regulations.

The increased hiring of insurance specialists is a direct result of employers' attempts to reduce the cost of providing employee health insurance coverage. Employers renegotiate benefits with existing plans or change third-party payers altogether. The employees often receive retroactive notice of these contract changes and, in some cases, once notified may have to wait several weeks before new health benefit booklets and new insurance identification cards are issued. These changes in employer-sponsored plans have made it necessary for the healthcare provider's staff to check on patients' current eligibility and benefit status at each office visit.

HEALTH INSURANCE CAREER OPPORTUNITIES

According to the *Occupational Outlook Handbook* published by the U.S. Department of Labor—Bureau of Labor Statistics, healthcare facilities and insurance companies will hire claims examiners (health insurance specialists) to process routine medical claims at an increased rate of 9 to 17 percent through the year 2014.

Health insurance specialists (or **reimbursement specialists**) review health-related claims to determine the medical necessity for procedures or services performed before payment (reimbursement) is made to the provider. A **claims examiner** employed by a third-party payer reviews health-related claims to determine whether the charges are reasonable and for medical necessity. **Medical necessity** involves *linking every procedure or service code reported on the claim to an ICD-9-CM condition code that justifies the necessity for performing that procedure or service.*

The claims review process requires verification of the claim for completeness and accuracy and comparison with third-party payer guidelines (e.g., expected treatment practices) to (1) authorize appropriate payment or (2) refer the claim to an investigator for a more thorough review. A **medical assistant** is employed by a provider to perform administrative and clinical tasks that keep the office or clinic running smoothly. Medical assistants who specialize in administrative aspects of the profession answer telephones, greet patients, update and file patient medical records, complete insurance claims, process correspondence, schedule appointments, arrange for hospital admission and laboratory services, and manage billing and bookkeeping.

> **NOTE:** Health insurance specialists and medical assistants obtain employment in clinics, healthcare clearinghouses, healthcare facility billing departments, insurance companies, and physicians' offices, and with third-party administrators (TPAs). When employed by clearinghouses, insurance companies, or TPAs, they often have the opportunity to work at home, where they process and verify healthcare claims using an Internet-based application server provider (ASP).

EXAMPLE 1: Procedure: Knee x-ray

Diagnosis: Shoulder pain

In this example, the provider is not reimbursed because the reason for the x-ray (shoulder pain) does not match the type of x-ray performed (knee). For medical necessity, the provider would need to document a diagnosis such as "fractured patella (knee bone)."

EXAMPLE 2: Procedure: Chest x-ray

Diagnosis: Severe shortness of breath

In this example, the provider is reimbursed because medical necessity for performing the procedure is demonstrated.

Coding is the process of assigning ICD-9-CM and CPT/HCPCS codes to diagnoses, procedures, and services. Coding systems include:

- International Classification of Diseases, 9th Revision, Clinical Modification (ICD-9-CM) (coding system used to report diagnoses and reasons for encounters, such as an annual physical examination, on outpatient and physician office claims)
- Healthcare Common Procedure Coding System (HCPCS, pronounced "hick picks"), which consists of two levels:
  - Current Procedural Terminology (CPT) (coding system published by the American Medical Association that is used to report (1) procedures and services performed during outpatient and physician office encounters and (2) professional services provided to inpatients)
  - HCPCS level II codes (or national codes) (coding system published by CMS that is used to report procedures, services, and supplies not classified in CPT)

In addition to an increase in insurance specialist positions available in healthcare practices, opportunities are also increasing in other settings, and include:

- Claims benefit advisors in health, malpractice, and liability insurance companies.
- Coding or insurance specialists in state, local, and federal government agencies, legal offices, private insurance billing offices, and medical societies. Medical billing and insurance verification specialists in healthcare organizations.
- Educators in schools and companies specializing in medical office staff training.
- Writers and editors of health insurance textbooks, newsletters, and other publications.
- Self-employed consultants who provide assistance to medical practices with billing practices and claims appeal procedures.
- Consumer claims assistance professionals, who file claims and appeal low reimbursement for private individuals. In the latter case, individuals may be dissatisfied with the handling of their claims by the healthcare provider's insurance staff.
- Practices with poorly trained health insurance staff who are unwilling or unable to file a proper claims appeal.
- Private billing practices dedicated to claims filing for elderly or disabled patients.

EDUCATION AND TRAINING

Training and entry requirements vary widely for health insurance specialists, and the *Occupational Outlook Handbook* states that opportunities will be best for those with a college degree. Academic programs should include coursework (Table 1-1) in general education (e.g., anatomy and physiology, English composition, oral communications, human relations, computer applications, and so on) and health insurance specialist education (e.g., health information management, medical terminology, pharmacology, coding and reimbursement, insurance processing, and so on). The characteristics of a successful health insurance specialist include an ability to work independently, a strong sense of ethics, attention to detail, and the ability to think critically. The *American Heritage Concise Dictionary* defines ethics as the principles of right or good conduct, and rules that govern the conduct of members of a profession.

Student Internship

An internship benefits students and facilities that accept students for placement. Students receive on-the-job experience prior to graduation, and the internship assists them in obtaining permanent employment. Facilities benefit from the

TABLE 1-1 Training requirements for health insurance specialists

COURSEWORK	DESCRIPTION
Anatomy and Physiology, Medical Terminology, Pharmacology, and Pathophysiology	Knowledge of anatomic structures and physiological functioning of the body, medical terminology and essentials of pharmacology are necessary to recognizing abnormal conditions (pathophysiology). Fluency in the language of medicine and the ability to use a medical dictionary as a reference are crucial skills.
Diagnosis and Procedure/ Service Coding	Understanding the rules, conventions, and applications of coding systems ensures proper selection of diagnosis and procedure/service codes, which are reported on insurance claims for reimbursement purposes. **EXAMPLE:** Patient undergoes simple suture treatment of 3 cm facial laceration. When referring to the CPT index, there is no listing for "Suture, facial laceration." There is, however, an instructional notation below the entry for "Suture" that refers the coder to "Repair." When "Repair" is referenced in the index, the coder must then locate the subterms "Skin," "Wound," and "Simple." The code range in the index is reviewed, and the coder must refer to the tabular section of the coding manual to select the correct code.
Verbal and Written Communication	Health insurance specialists explain complex insurance concepts and regulations to patients and must effectively communicate with providers regarding documentation of procedures and services (to reduce coding and billing errors). Written communication skills are necessary when preparing effective appeals for unpaid claims.
Critical Thinking	Differentiating among technical descriptions of similar procedures requires critical thinking skills. **EXAMPLE:** Patient is diagnosed with spondylosis, which is defined as any condition of the spine. A code from category 721 of ICD would be assigned. If the specialist read the diagnosis as spondylolysis, which is a defect of the articulating portion of the vertebra, and assigned a code from ICD category 756 (if congenital) or 738 (if acquired), the coder would be in error.
Data Entry	Federal regulations require electronic submission of most government claims, which means that health insurance specialists need excellent keyboarding skills and basic finance and math skills. Because insurance information screens with different titles often contain identical information, the health insurance specialist must carefully and accurately enter data about patient care. **EXAMPLE:** Primary and secondary insurance computer screens require entry of similar information. Claims are rejected by insurance companies if data is missing or erroneous.
Internet Access	Online information sources provide access to medical references, insurance company manuals, and procedure guidelines. The federal government posts changes to reimbursement methodologies and other policies on Web sites. Internet forums allow health insurance specialists to network with other professionals.

NOTE: Chapter 1 of the *Workbook to Accompany Understanding Health Insurance* contains an assignment entitled "Ready, Set, Get a Job" that teaches students how to create a résumé and cover letter, and helps them prepare for a job interview.

opportunity to participate in and improve the formal education process. Quite often, students who complete internships obtain employment at the internship facility. The internship supervisor is the person to whom the student reports at the site. Students are often required to submit a professional résumé to the internship supervisor and schedule an interview prior to acceptance for placement. While this process can be intimidating, students gain experience with the interview process that is part of obtaining permanent employment. Students should research résumé writing and utilize interview technique services available from their school's career services office. This office typically reviews résumés and provides interview tips. (Some offices even videotape mock interviews for students.)

The internship is on-the-job training even though it is unpaid, and students should expect to provide proof of immunizations (available from a physician) and possibly undergo a pre-employment physical examination and participate in an orientation. In addition, because of the focus on privacy and security of patient information, the facility will likely require students to sign a nondisclosure agreement (to protect patient confidentiality), which is kept on file at the school college and by the internship site.

During the internship, students are expected to report to work on time. Students who cannot attend the internship on a particular day (or who arrive late) should contact their internship supervisor or program faculty, whoever is designated for that purpose. Students are also required to make up any lost time. Because the internship is a simulated job experience, students are to be well groomed and should dress professionally. Students should show interest in all aspects of the experience, develop good working relationships with coworkers, and react appropriately to criticism and direction. If any concerns arise during the internship, students should discuss them with their internship supervisor or program faculty.

JOB RESPONSIBILITIES

This section provides an overview of the major responsibilities delegated to health insurance specialists. In practices where just one or two persons work with insurance billing, each individual must be capable of performing all the listed responsibilities. In multispecialty practices that employ many health insurance specialists, each usually processes claims for a limited number of insurance companies (e.g., an insurance specialist may be assigned to processing only Medicare claims). Some practices have a clear division of labor, with specific individuals accepting responsibility for only a few assigned tasks. Typical tasks are listed in the following job description.

Health Insurance Specialist Job Description

1. Review patient record documentation to accurately code all diagnoses, procedures, and services using ICD-9-CM for diagnoses and CPT and HCPCS level II for procedures and services.

   The accurate coding of diagnoses, procedures, and services rendered to the patient allows a medical practice to

   - **Communicate diagnostic and treatment data to a patient's insurance plan to assist the patient in obtaining maximum benefits.**
   - **Facilitate analysis of the practice's patient base to improve patient care delivery and efficiency of practice operations to contain costs.**

2. Research and apply knowledge of all insurance rules and regulations for major insurance programs in the local or regional area.

3. Accurately post charges, payments, and adjustments to patient accounts and office accounts receivable records.

4. Prepare or review claims generated by the practice to ensure that all required data are accurately reported and to ensure prompt reimbursement for services provided (contributing to the practice's cash flow).

5. Review all insurance payments and remittance advice documents to ensure proper processing and payment of each claim. The patient receives an **explanation of benefits (EOB)**, which is a report detailing the results of processing a claim (e.g., payer reimburses provider $80 on a submitted charge of $100). The provider receives a **remittance advice** (or **remit)**, which is a notice sent by the insurance company that contains payment information about a claim. (EOBs and remits are further discussed in Chapter 4.)

6. Correct all data errors and resubmit all unprocessed or returned claims.

7. Research and prepare appeals for all underpaid, unjustly recoded, or denied claims.

8. Rebill all claims not paid within 30 to 45 days, depending on individual practice policy and the payers' policies.

9. Inform healthcare providers and staff of changes in fraud and abuse laws, coding changes, documentation guidelines, and third-party payer requirements that may affect the billing and claims submission procedures.

10. Assist with timely updating of the practice's internal documents, patient registration forms, and billing forms as required by changes in coding or insurance billing requirements.

11. Maintain an internal audit system to ensure that required pretreatment authorizations have been received and entered into the billing and treatment records. Audits comparing provider documentation with codes assigned should also be performed.

12. Explain insurance benefits, policy requirements, and filing rules to patients.

13. Maintain confidentiality of patient information.

Scope of Practice and Employer Liability

Regardless of the employment setting, health insurance specialists are guided by a **scope of practice** that defines the profession, delineates qualifications and responsibilities, and clarifies supervision requirements (Table 1-2). Health insurance specialists who are self-employed are considered independent contractors. The *'Lectric Law Library's Lexicon* defines an **independent contractor** as "a person who performs services for another under an express or implied agreement and who is not subject to the other's control, or right to control, of the manner and means of performing the services. The organization that hires an independent contractor is not liable for the acts or omissions of the independent contractor."

Independent contractors should purchase **professional liability insurance** (or **errors and omissions insurance)**, which provides protection from claims that contain errors and omissions resulting from professional services provided to clients as expected of a person in the contractor's profession. Professional associations often include a membership benefit that allows purchase of liability insurance coverage at reduced rates.

NOTE: One way to determine independent contractor status is to apply the common law "right to control" test, which includes five factors: (1) amount of control the hiring organization exerted over the worker's activities; (2) responsibility for costs of operation (e.g., equipment and supplies); (3) method and form of payment and benefits; (4) length of job commitment made to the worker; (5) nature of occupation and skills required. The Internal Revenue Service applies a 20-factor independent contractor test to decide whether an organization has correctly classified a worker as an independent contractor for purposes of wage withholdings. The Department of Labor uses the "economic reality" test to determine worker status for purposes of compliance with the minimum wage and overtime requirements of the Fair Labor Standards Act.

TABLE 1-2   Scope of practice for health insurance specialists

Definition of Profession:	One who interacts with patients to clarify health insurance coverage and financial responsibility, completes and processes insurance claims, and appeals denied claims.
Qualifications:	Graduate of health insurance specialist certificate or degree program or equivalent. One year of experience in health insurance or related field. Detailed working knowledge and demonstrated proficiency in at least one insurance company's billing and/or collection process. Excellent organizational skills. Ability to manage multiple tasks in a timely manner. Proficient use of computerized registration and billing systems and personal computers, including spreadsheet and word processing software applications. Certification through AAPC, AHIMA, or AMBA.
Responsibilities:	Use medical management computer software to process health insurance claims, assign codes to diagnoses and procedures/services, and manage patient records. Communicate with patients, providers, and insurance companies about coverage and reimbursement issues. Remain up-to-date regarding changes in healthcare industry laws and regulations.
Supervision Requirements:	Active and continuous supervision of a health insurance specialist is required. However, the physical presence of the supervisor at the time and place responsibilities are performed is not required.

> **EXAMPLE:** The American Health Information Management Association makes information about the purchase of a professional liability plan available to its membership. If a member is sued for malpractice, the plan covers legal fees, court costs, court judgments, and out-of-court settlements. The coverage includes up to $2 million per incident and up to $4 million in any one policy year.

A healthcare facility (or physician) that employs health insurance specialists is legally responsible for employees' actions performed within the context of their employment. This is called *respondeat superior*, Latin for "let the master answer," which means that the employer is liable for the actions and omissions of employees as performed and committed within the scope of their employment. Employers purchase many types of insurance to protect their business assets and property (Table 1-3).

> **EXAMPLE:** Linda Starling is employed by Dr. Pederson's office as a health insurance specialist. As part of her job, Linda has access to confidential patient information. While processing claims, she notices that her mother-in-law has been a patient, and she later tells her husband about the diagnosis and treatment. Her mother-in-law finds out about the breach of confidentiality and contacts her lawyer. Legally, Dr. Pederson can be sued by the mother-in-law. Although Linda could also be named in the lawsuit, it is more likely that she will be terminated.

TABLE 1-3 Types of professional insurance purchased by employers

INSURANCE	DESCRIPTION
Bonding insurance	An insurance agreement that guarantees repayment for financial losses resulting from an employee's act or failure to act. It protects the financial operations of the employer. **NOTE:** Physician offices should bond employees who have financial responsibilities. The U.S. Department of Commerce estimates $500 billion in annual losses to all types of employers due to employees who **embezzle** (steal).
Business liability insurance	Protects business assets and covers the cost of lawsuits resulting from bodily injury (e.g., customer slips on wet floor), personal injury (e.g., slander or libel), and false advertising. **Medical malpractice insurance** is a type of liability insurance, which covers physicians and other healthcare professionals for liability as to claims arising from patient treatment. **NOTE:** Liability insurance does *not* protect an employer from nonperformance of a contract, sexual harassment, race and gender discrimination lawsuits, or wrongful termination of employees. **NOTE:** An alternative to purchasing liability insurance from an insurance company is to *self-fund*, which involves setting aside money to pay damages or paying damages with current operating revenue should the employer ever be found liable. Another option is to join a *risk retention* or *risk purchasing group*, which provides lower-cost commercial liability insurance to its members. A third option is to obtain coverage in a *surplus lines market* that has been established to insure unique risks.
Property insurance	Protects business contents (e.g., buildings and equipment) against fire, theft, and other risks.
Workers' compensation insurance	Protection mandated by state law that covers employees and their dependents against injury and death occurring during the course of employment. Workers' compensation is not health insurance, and it is not intended to compensate for disability other than that caused by injury arising from employment. The purpose of workers' compensation is to provide financial and medical benefits to those with work-related injuries, and their families, regardless of fault.

PROFESSIONALISM

The *Merriam-Webster Dictionary* defines **professionalism** as the conduct or qualities that characterize a professional person. Developing workplace professionalism is the result of individual work on the following skills:

Attitude and Self-esteem

"For success, attitude is equally as important as ability."

Harry F. Banks

Attitude impacts an individual's capacity to effectively perform job functions, and an employee's attitude is perceived as positive, negative, or neutral. This subconscious transfer of feelings results in colleagues determining whether someone has a positive attitude about their work. Self-esteem impacts attitude: low self-esteem causes lack of confidence, and higher self-esteem leads to self-confidence, improved relationships, self-respect, and a successful career.

Communication

"And he goes through life, his mouth open, and his mind closed."

William Shakespeare

Successful interpersonal communication includes self-expression and active listening to develop understanding about what others are saying. To listen effectively, be sure to understand the message instead of just hearing words. This active involvement in the communication process helps avoid miscommunication.

Conflict Management

"When angry, count to ten before you speak; if very angry, a hundred."

Thomas Jefferson

Conflict occurs as a part of the decision-making process, and the way it is handled makes it positive or negative. People often have different perspectives about the same situation, and actively listening to the other's viewpoint helps neutralize what could become negative conflict.

Customer Service

"If we don't take care of our customers, someone else will."

Unknown

Health insurance specialists serve as a direct point of contact for a provider's patients, and they are responsible for ensuring that patients receive an excellent level of service or assistance with questions and concerns. It is equally important to remember that colleagues deserve the same respect and attention as patients.

Diversity Awareness

"The real death of America will come when everyone is alike."

James T. Ellison

Diversity is defined as differences among people and includes demographics of age, education, ethnicity, gender, geographic location, income, language, marital status, occupation, parental status, physical and mental ability, race, religious beliefs, sexual orientation, and veteran status. Developing tolerance, which is the opposite of bigotry and prejudice, means dealing with personal attitudes, beliefs, and experiences. Embracing the differences that represent the demographics of our society is crucial to becoming a successful health professional.

Leadership

"The difference between a boss and a leader: a boss says, 'Go!' A leader says, 'Let's go!'"

E. M. Kelly

Leadership is the ability to motivate team members to complete a common organizational goal display. Leaders have earned the trust of their team, which is the reason the entire team is able to achieve its objective and set the standard for productivity, and even revenue goals. Interestingly, the leader identified by the team might not be the organization's manager or supervisor. Leaders emerge from within the organization because they have demonstrated beliefs, ethics, and values with which team members identify. Managers who are not threatened by the natural emergence of leaders benefit from team harmony and increased productivity. They receive credit for excellent management skills, and they begin the process to leadership when they begin to acknowledge the work ethic of the team and its leader.

Managing Change

"If we don't change, we don't grow. If we don't grow, we aren't really living."
Gail Sheehy

Change is crucial to the survival of an organization because it is a necessary response to implementation of new and revised federal and state programs, regulations, and so on. While the organization that does not embrace change becomes extinct, such change disrupts the organization's workflow (and productivity) and is perceived as a threat to employees. Therefore, it is the role of the organization's leadership team to provide details about the impending change, including periodic updates as work processes undergo gradual revision. Employees also need to understand what is being changed and why, and the leadership team needs to understand employees' reluctance to change.

Productivity

"Even if you are on the right track, you'll get run over if you just sit there."
Will Rogers

Healthcare providers expect health insurance and medical coding/billing specialists to be productive regarding completion of duties and responsibilities. Pursuing professional certification and participating in continuing education helps ensure individual compliance with the latest coding rules and other updates. Increased knowledge leads to increased productivity and performance improvement on the job.

Professional Ethics

"Always do right—this will gratify some and astonish the rest."
Mark Twain

The characteristics of a successful health insurance specialist include an ability to work independently, attention to detail, ability to think critically, and a strong sense of ethics. The American Heritage Concise Dictionary defines ethics as the principles of right or good conduct, and rules that govern the conduct of members of a profession.

Team-building

"Michael, if you can't pass, you can't play."
Coach Dean Smith to Michael Jordan in his freshman year.

Colleagues who share a sense of community and purpose work well together and can accomplish organizational goals more quickly and easily because they rely on one another. This means colleagues provide help to and receive help from other members of the team. Sharing the leadership role and working together to complete difficult tasks facilitates team-building.

NOTE: Although a receptionist is the initial point of contact for the office, all healthcare team members must effectively handle or transfer telephone calls. This requires sensitivity to patient concerns about healthcare problems, and the healthcare professional must communicate a caring environment that leads to patient satisfaction.

Telephone Skills for the Healthcare Setting

The telephone can be an effective means of patient access to the healthcare system because a healthcare team member serves as an immediate contact for the patient. Participating in telephone skills training and following established protocols (policies) allow healthcare team members to respond appropriately to patients. When processes for handling all calls are developed *and* followed by healthcare team members, the result is greater office efficiency and less frustration for healthcare team members and patients. Avoid problems with telephone communication in your healthcare setting by implementing the following protocols:

Establish a telephone-availability policy that works for patients and office staff. Telephone calls that are unanswered, result in a busy signal, and/or force patients to be placed on hold for long periods frustrate callers. The outcome can be a receptionist who sounds impatient and too busy to properly resolve callers' questions and concerns. Avoid such problems by increasing telephone availability so that the calls are answered outside of the typical 9 to 5 workday (which often includes not answering the telephone during lunch). Consider having employees (who have undergone telephone skills training) answer calls on a rotating basis one hour before the office opens, during the noon hour, and one hour after the office closes. This telephone protocol will result in satisfied patients (and other callers) and office employees (who do not have to return calls to individuals who otherwise leave messages on the answering machine).

Set up an appropriate number of dedicated telephone lines (e.g., appointment scheduling, insurance and billing) based on the function and size of the healthcare setting. Publish the telephone numbers on the office's Web site and in an office brochure or local telephone directory, and instruct employees to avoid using the lines when making outgoing calls. Another option is to install an interactive telephone response system that connects callers with appropriate staff (e.g., appointment scheduling, insurance and billing, and so on) based on caller keypad or voice responses to instructions provided.

Inform callers who ask to speak with the physician (or another healthcare provider) that the physician (or provider) is with a patient. Do *not* state, "The physician is busy," which implies that the physician is too busy for the patient and could offend the caller. Ask for the caller's name, telephone number, and reason for call, and explain that the call will be returned.

Assign 15-minute time periods every 2–3 hours when creating the schedule, so physicians (and other healthcare providers) can return telephone calls. The receptionist will be able to tell callers an approximate time when calls will be returned (and patient records can be retrieved).

Physically separate front desk check-in/check-out and receptionist/patient appointment scheduling offices. It is unlikely that an employee who manages the registration of patients as they arrive at the office (and the check-out of patients at the conclusion of an appointment) has time to answer telephone calls. Office receptionists and appointment schedulers who work in private offices will comply with federal and state patient privacy laws when talking with patients. In addition, appointment scheduling, telephone management, and patient check-in (registration) and check-out procedures will be performed with greater efficiency.

Require office employees to learn professional telephone skills. Schedule professional telephone skills training as part of new employee orientation, and arrange for all employees to attend an annual workshop to improve skills. Training allows everyone to learn key aspects of successful telephone communication, which include developing an effective telephone voice that focuses on tone. During a telephone conversation, each person forms an opinion based on *how* something is said (rather than *what* is said). Therefore, speak clearly and distinctly, do not speak too fast or too slow, and vary your tone by letting your voice rise and fall naturally. The following rules apply to each telephone conversation:

- **When answering the telephone, state the name of the office and your name (e.g., "Hornell Medical Center, Shelly Dunham speaking").**

- **Do not use slang (e.g., nope, yep, uh huh) or healthcare jargon (e.g., ICU—the patient hears "eye see you").**

- Use the caller's name (e.g., Betty Smith calls the office, stating her name as soon as her call is answered, and the receptionist asks, "How may I help you today, Mrs. Smith?").
- Provide clear explanations (e.g., the doctor will return your call between 3 and 4 p.m. today.).
- Be pleasant, friendly, sincere, and helpful. (e.g., smile as you talk with the caller and your tone will be friendly) (Figure 1-1).
- Give the caller your undivided attention to show personal interest, and do not interrupt.
- Before placing the caller on hold or transferring a call, ask him or her for permission to do so (e.g., "May I place you on hold?," "May I transfer you to the appropriate office?").
- When the individual with whom the caller wants to talk is unavailable, ask if you can take a message (e.g., "Dr. Smith is with a patient right now. May I take a message and have him return your call after 3 p.m.?").
- Use a preprinted message form (or commercial message pad) when taking a message (Figure 1-2).

Professional Credentials

The health insurance specialist who becomes affiliated with one or more professional associations (Table 1-4) receives useful information available in several formats, including professional journals and newsletters, access to members-only Web sites, notification of professional development, and so on. A key feature of membership is an awareness of the importance of professional certification. Once certified, the professional is responsible for maintaining that credential by fulfilling continuing education requirements established by the sponsoring association.

Figure 1-1 Tone of voice can put callers at ease during telephone conversations. (Courtesy Delmar/Cengage Learning)

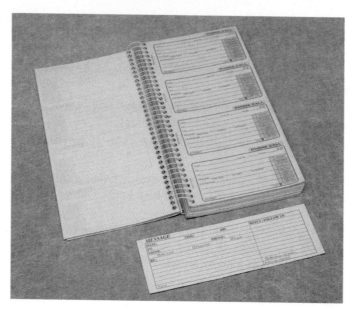

Figure 1-2 Message pads with carbonless copy (Courtesy Delmar/Cengage Learning)

TABLE 1-4   Professional associations that offer coding and reimbursement credentials

American Academy of Professional Coders (AAPC)	• Founded to elevate the standards of medical coding by providing certification, ongoing education, networking, and recognition for coders. • Publishes *Coding Edge* monthly newsmagazine, and hosts continuing education. • *Credentials:* Certified Professional Coder (CPC), Certified Professional Coder-Hospital (CPC-H), Certified Professional Coder-Payer (CPC-P), Certified Interventional Radiology Cardiovascular Coder (CIRCC), and specialty credentials in 18 different fields of expertise.
American Association of Medical Assistants (AAMA)	• Enables medical assisting professionals to enhance and demonstrate knowledge, skills, and professionalism required by employers and patients, and protects medical assistants' right to practice. • Publishes monthly *Certified Medical Assistant* journal. • *Credential:* Certified Medical Assistant, abbreviated as CMA (AAMA).
American Health Information Management Association (AHIMA)	• Founded in 1928 to improve the quality of medical records, and currently advances the health information management (HIM) profession toward an electronic and global environment, including implementation of ICD-10-CM and ICD-10-PCS. • Publishes monthly *Journal of AHIMA*. • *Credentials:* Certified Coding Assistant (CCA), Certified Coding Specialist (CCS), and Certified Coding Specialist-Physician-office (CCS-P). (Additional HIM credentials are offered by AHIMA.)
American Medical Billing Association (AMBA)	• Provides industry and regulatory education and networking opportunities for members. • *Credential:* Certified Medical Reimbursement Specialist (CMRS).
Medical Association of Billers (MAB)	• Created in 1995 to provide medical billing and coding specialists with a reliable source for diagnosis and procedure coding education and training. • Publishes *CodeTrends* bimonthly newsletter, and hosts continuing education programs. • *Credentials:* Certified Medical Billing Specialist (CMBS), Certified Medical Billing Specialist for Chiropractic Assistants (CMBS-CA), Certified Medical Billing Specialist for Hospitals (CMBS-H), and Certified Medical Billing Specialist for Instructors (CMBSI).
National Electronic Billers Alliance (NEBA)	• Created in 1996 to assist professionals entering the medical billing industry and those already working in the field. • Provides online discussion board and mentoring program. • *Credentials:* Certified Healthcare Reimbursement Specialist (CHRS) and Certified HIPAA Information Specialist (CHIS).

SUMMARY

A health insurance specialist career is challenging and requires professional training to understand claims processing and billing regulations, possess accurate coding skills, and develop the ability to successfully appeal underpaid or denied insurance claims. A health insurance claim is submitted to a third-party payer or government program to request reimbursement for healthcare services provided. Many health insurance plans require preauthorization for treatment provided by specialists.

While the requirements of health insurance specialist programs vary, successful specialists will develop skills that allow them to work independently and ethically, focus on attention to detail, and think critically. Medical practices and healthcare facilities employing health insurance specialists require them to perform various functions. Smaller practices and facilities require specialists to process claims for all types of payers, while larger practices and facilities expect specialists to process claims for a limited number of payers.

Health insurance specialists are guided by a scope of practice, which defines the profession, delineates qualification and responsibilities, and clarifies supervision requirements. Self-employed health insurance specialists are independent contractors who should purchase professional liability insurance. Healthcare providers and facilities typically purchase bonding, liability, property, and workers' compensation insurance to cover their employees. The AAMA, AAPC, AHIMA, AMBA, and MAB offer exams leading to professional credentials. Becoming credentialed demonstrates competence and knowledge in the field of health insurance processing as well as coding and reimbursement.

INTERNET LINKS

- American Academy of Professional Coders (AAPC)
  www.aapc.com
- American Association of Medical Assistants (AAMA)
  www.aama-ntl.org
- American Health Information Management Association (AHIMA)
  www.ahima.org
- American Medical Billing Association (AMBA)
  www.ambanet.net
- Centers for Medicare and Medicaid Services (CMS)
  www.cms.hhs.gov
- Medical Association of Billers (MAB)
  www.physicianwebsites.com

STUDY CHECKLIST

- ☐ Read this textbook chapter and highlight key concepts. (Use colored highlighter sparingly throughout chapter.)
- ☐ Create an index card for each key term. (Write the key term on one side of the index card and the concept on the other. Learn the definition of each key term, and match the term to the concept.)
- ☐ Access chapter Internet links to learn more about concepts.
- ☐ Answer the chapter review questions, verifying answers with your instructor.
- ☐ Complete WebTutor assignments and take online quizzes. (Refer to WebTutor content in the Preface.)
- ☐ Complete Workbook chapter, verifying answers with your instructor.
- ☐ Complete the StudyWare activities to receive immediate feedback.
- ☐ Form a study group with classmates to discuss chapter concepts in preparation for an exam.

REVIEW

MULTIPLE CHOICE Select the most appropriate response.

1. **The document submitted to the payer requesting reimbursement is called a(n)**
   a. explanation of benefits.
   b. health insurance claim.
   c. remittance advice.
   d. preauthorization form.

2. **The Centers for Medicare and Medicaid Services (CMS) is an administration within the**
   a. Administration for Children and Families.
   b. Department of Health and Human Services.
   c. Food and Drug Administration.
   d. Office of the Inspector General.

3. **A healthcare practitioner is also called a**
   a. dealer.
   b. provider.
   c. purveyor.
   d. supplier.

4. **Which is the most appropriate response to a patient who calls the office and asks to speak with the physician?**
   a. Politely state that the physician is busy and cannot be disturbed.
   b. Explain that the physician is with a patient, and ask if the patient would leave a message.
   c. Transfer the call to the exam room where the physician is located.
   d. Offer to schedule an appointment for the patient to be seen by the physician.

5. **The process of assigning diagnoses, procedures, and services using numeric and alphanumeric characters is called**
   a. coding.
   b. data processing.
   c. programming.
   d. reimbursement.

6. **If a health insurance plan's preauthorization requirements are not met by providers,**
   a. administrative costs are reduced.
   b. patients' coverage is cancelled.
   c. payment of the claim is denied.
   d. they pay a fine to the health plan.

7. **Which coding system is used to report diagnoses and conditions on claims?**
   a. CPT
   b. HCPCS
   c. ICD
   d. national codes

8. **The CPT coding system is published by the**
   a. ADA.
   b. AHIMA.
   c. AMA.
   d. CMS.

9. **National codes are associated with**

   a. CDT.

   b. CPT.

   c. HCPCS.

   d. ICD.

10. **Which report is sent to the patient by the payer to clarify the results of claims processing?**

    a. explanation of benefits

    b. health insurance claim

    c. preauthorization form

    d. remittance advice

11. **A remittance advice contains**

    a. payment information about a claim.

    b. provider qualifications and responsibilities.

    c. detected errors and omissions from claims.

    d. documentation of medical necessity.

12. **Which type of insurance guarantees repayment for financial losses resulting from an employee's act or failure to act?**

    a. bonding

    b. liability

    c. property

    d. workers' compensation

13. **Medical malpractice insurance is a type of _____ insurance.**

    a. bonding

    b. liability

    c. property

    d. workers' compensation

14. **Which mandates workers' compensation insurance to cover employees and their dependents against injury and death occurring during the course of employment?**

    a. state

    b. federal

    c. local

    d. workers' compensation coverage is optional

15. **The American Medical Billing Association offers which certification exam?**

    a. CCS

    b. CMRS

    c. CPC

    d. RHIT

Introduction to Health Insurance

CHAPTER OUTLINE

What Is Health Insurance?

Major Developments in Health Insurance

Health Insurance Coverage Statistics

Medical Documentation

Electronic Health Record (EHR)

OBJECTIVES

Upon successful completion of this chapter, you should be able to:

1. Define key terms.
2. State the difference between medical care and healthcare.
3. Discuss the significant events in healthcare reimbursement from 1860 to the present.
4. Identify and explain the impact of significant events in the history of healthcare reimbursement.
5. Interpret health insurance coverage statistics.

KEY TERMS

Ambulatory Payment Classification (APC)

American Recovery and Reinvestment Act of 2009

Balanced Budget Act of 1997 (BBA)

base period

CHAMPUS Reform Initiative (CRI)

Civilian Health and Medical Program of the Department of Veterans Affairs (CHAMPVA)

Civilian Health and Medical Program— Uniformed Services (CHAMPUS)

Clinical Laboratory Improvement Act (CLIA)

CMS-1500

coinsurance

Consolidated Omnibus Budget Reconciliation Act of 1985 (COBRA)

consumer-driven health plan

continuity of care

copayment (copay)

deductible

diagnosis-related group (DRG)

electronic health record (EHR)

electronic medical record (EMR)

Employee Retirement Income Security Act of 1974 (ERISA)

employer-based self-insurance plans

Evaluation and Management (E/M)

Federal Employees' Compensation Act (FECA)

fee schedule

Financial Services Modernization Act

Gramm-Leach-Bliley Act

group health insurance

health care

health insurance

Hill-Burton Act

individual health insurance

International Classification of Diseases (ICD)

lifetime maximum amount

major medical insurance

medical record

patient record

problem-oriented record (POR)

public health insurance

record linkage

self-insured (or self-funded) employer-sponsored group health plans

single-payer plan

19

socialized medicine
third-party administrators (TPAs)

Total practice management software
(TPMS)

universal health insurance
World Health Organization (WHO)

INTRODUCTION

According to the American Heritage Concise Dictionary, insurance is a contract that protects the insured from loss. An insurance company guarantees payment to the insured for an unforeseen event (e.g., death, accident, and illness) in return for the payment of premiums. In addition to heath insurance, types of insurance include automobile, disability, liability, malpractice, property, life (discussed in Chapter 12). (This textbook covers health insurance in detail.) This chapter includes information about terms and concepts as an introduction to health insurance processing. These terms and concepts are explained in greater detail in later chapters of this text.

StudyWARE

Complete StudyWare practice quizzes and activities using the CD-ROM located inside the back cover of your textbook.

NOTE: Some group plans can be converted to individual plans when the employee leaves the organization.

WHAT IS HEALTH INSURANCE?

Healthcare insurance or **health insurance** is a contract between a policyholder and a third-party payer or government program to reimburse the policyholder for all or a portion of the cost of medically necessary treatment or preventive care provided by healthcare professionals. Because both the government and the general public speak of "health insurance," this text uses that term exclusively. Health insurance is available to individuals who participate in group (e.g., employer sponsored), individual (or personal insurance), or prepaid health plans (e.g., managed care).

MAJOR DEVELOPMENTS IN HEALTH INSURANCE

Since the early 1900s, when solo practices prevailed, managed care and group practices have increased in number, and healthcare services (like other aspects of society in this country) have undergone tremendous changes (Table 2-1).

GLOSSARY OF HEALTH INSURANCE TERMS	
Group health insurance	Traditional healthcare coverage subsidized by employers and other organizations (e.g., labor unions, rural and consumer health cooperatives) whereby part or all of premium costs are paid for and/or discounted group rates are offered to eligible individuals.
Individual health insurance	Private health insurance policy purchased by individuals or families who do not have access to group health insurance coverage. Applicants can be denied coverage, and they can also be required to pay higher premiums due to age, gender, and/or pre-existing medical conditions.
Public health insurance	Federal and state government health programs (e.g., Medicare, Medicaid, SCHIP, TRICARE) available to eligible individuals.
Single–payer plan	Centralized healthcare system adopted by some Western nations (e.g., Canada, Great Britain) and funded by taxes. The government pays for each resident's health care, which is considered a basic social service.
Socialized medicine	A type of single-payer system in which the government owns and operates healthcare facilities and providers (e.g., physicians) receive salaries. The VA healthcare program is a form of socialized medicine.
Universal health insurance	The goal of providing every individual with access to health coverage, regardless of the system implemented to achieve that goal.

HEALTH INSURANCE COVERAGE STATISTICS

NOTE: Go to www.delmarlearning.com/companions, enter **Understanding Health Insurance** in the Companion Search box, click **Search,** and click on the most current edition of the textbook. Then, click on **Student Resources** to locate Table 2-A and view a comprehensive history of healthcare reimbursement.

U.S. Census Bureau data from 2007 estimate that almost 85 percent of people in the United States are covered by some form of health insurance; of that percentage:

- Approximately **68** percent are covered by private health insurance
- Approximately **60** percent are covered by employment-based plans
- Approximately **28** percent are covered by government plans (e.g., **Medicare, Medicaid, TRICARE**)

The reason the insurance coverage breakdown of covered persons total is greater than 85 percent is because some people are covered by more than one insurance plan (e.g., employment-based plan plus Medicare). Thus, they are counted more than once when percentages are calculated.

TABLE 2-1   Significant events in healthcare reimbursement

YEAR	EVENT	DESCRIPTION
1860	First health insurance policy	The Franklin Health Assurance Company of Massachusetts was the first commercial insurance company in the United States to provide private healthcare coverage for injuries not resulting in death.
1908	Workers' compensation	President Theodore Roosevelt signed legislation to provide workers' compensation for certain federal employees in unusually hazardous jobs. Workers' compensation is a program mandated by federal and state governments, which requires employers to cover medical expenses and loss of wages for workers who are injured on the job or who have developed job-related disorders.
1916	FECA	The **Federal Employees' Compensation Act (FECA)** replaced the 1908 workers' compensation legislation, and civilian employees of the federal government were provided medical care, survivors' benefits, and compensation for lost wages. The Office of Workers' Compensation Programs (OWCP) administers FECA as well as the Longshore and Harbor Workers' Compensation Act of 1927 and the Black Lung Benefits Reform Act of 1977.
1929	First Blue Cross policy	Justin Ford Kimball, an official at Baylor University in Dallas, introduced a plan to guarantee school teachers 21 days of hospital care for $6 a year. Other groups of employees in Dallas joined, and the idea attracted nationwide attention. This is generally considered the first Blue Cross plan.
1939	Blue Shield	The first Blue Shield plan was founded in California. The Blue Shield concept grew out of the lumber and mining camps of the Pacific Northwest at the turn of the century. Employers wanted to provide medical care for their workers, so they paid monthly fees to *medical service bureaus*, which were composed of groups of physicians.
1940s	Group health insurance	To attract wartime labor during World War II, group health insurance was offered to full-time employees. The insurance was not subject to income or Social Security taxes, making it an attractive part of an employee benefit package. *Group health insurance* is healthcare coverage available through employers and other organizations (e.g., labor unions, rural and consumer health cooperatives); employers usually pay part or all of premium costs.
1946	Hill-Burton Act	The **Hill–Burton Act** provided federal grants for modernizing hospitals that had become obsolete because of a lack of capital investment during the Great Depression and WWII (1929 to 1945). In return for federal funds, facilities were required to provide services free or at reduced rates to patients unable to pay for care.
1947	Taft-Hartley Act	The Taft-Hartley Act of 1947 amended the National Labor Relations Act of 1932, restoring a more balanced relationship between labor and management. An indirect result of Taft-Hartley was the creation of **third–party administrators (TPAs)**, which administer healthcare plans and process claims, thus serving as a system of checks and balances for labor and management.

(continues)

TABLE 2-1 (continued)

YEAR	EVENT	DESCRIPTION
1948	ICD	The World Health Organization (WHO) developed the International Classification of Diseases (ICD), a classification system used to collect data for statistical purposes.
1950	Major medical insurance is offered	Insurance companies began offering major medical insurance, which provided coverage for catastrophic or prolonged illnesses and injuries. Most of these programs incorporate large deductibles and lifetime maximum amounts. A deductible is the amount for which the patient is financially responsible before an insurance policy provides payment. A lifetime maximum amount is the maximum benefits payable to a health plan participant.
1966	Social Security Amendments of 1965 were implemented	Medicare (Title XVIII of the SSA of 1965) provides healthcare services to Americans over the age of 65. (It was originally administered by the Social Security Administration.)
		Medicaid (Title XIX of the SSA of 1965) is a cost-sharing program between the federal and state governments to provide healthcare services to low-income Americans. (It was originally administered by the Social and Rehabilitation Service [SRS].)
	Amendments to the Dependents' Medical Care Act of 1956	Amendments to the Dependents' Medical Care Act of 1956 created the Civilian Health and Medical Program—Uniformed Services (CHAMPUS), which was designed as a benefit for dependents of personnel serving in the armed forces and uniformed branches of the Public Health Service and the National Oceanic and Atmospheric Administration. The program is now called TRICARE.
	CPT is developed	*Current Procedural Terminology (CPT)* was developed by the American Medical Association in 1966. Each year an annual publication is prepared, which includes changes that correspond to significant updates in medical technology and practice.
1970	Self-insured group health plans	Self-insured (or self-funded) employer-sponsored group health plans allow large employers to assume the financial risk for providing healthcare benefits to employees. The employer does not pay a fixed premium to a health insurance payer, but establishes a trust fund (of employer and employee contributions) out of which claims are paid.
	OSHA	The Occupational Safety and Health Administration Act of 1970 (OSHA) was designed to protect all employees against injuries from occupational hazards in the workplace.
1973	CHAMPVA	The Veterans Healthcare Expansion Act of 1973 authorized Veterans Affairs (VA) to establish the Civilian Health and Medical Program of the Department of Veterans Affairs (CHAMPVA) to provide healthcare benefits for dependents of veterans rated as 100 percent permanently and totally disabled as a result of service-connected conditions, veterans who died as a result of service-connected conditions, and veterans who died on duty with less than 30 days of active service.
	HMO Act of 1973	The Health Maintenance Organization Assistance Act of 1973 authorized federal grants and loans to private organizations that wished to develop health maintenance organizations (HMOs), which are responsible for providing healthcare services to subscribers in a given geographic area for a fixed fee.

(continues)

TABLE 2-1   (continued)

YEAR	EVENT	DESCRIPTION
1974	ERISA	The **Employee Retirement Income Security Act of 1974 (ERISA)** mandated reporting and disclosure requirements for group life and health plans (including managed care plans), permitted large employers to self-insure employee healthcare benefits, and exempted large employers from taxes on health insurance premiums. A **copayment (copay)** is a provision in an insurance policy that requires the policyholder or patient to pay a specified dollar amount to a healthcare provider for each visit or medical service received. **Coinsurance** is the percentage of costs a patient shares with the health plan. For example, the plan pays 80 percent of costs and the patient pays 20 percent.
1977	HCFA	To combine healthcare financing and quality assurance programs into a single agency, the Health Care Financing Administration (HCFA) was formed within the Department of Health and Human Services (DHHS). The Medicare and Medicaid programs were also transferred to the newly created agency. (HCFA is now called the Centers for Medicare and Medicaid Services, or CMS.)
1980	DHHS	With the departure of the Office of Education, the Department of Health, Education and Welfare (HEW) became the Department of Health and Human Services (DHHS).
1981	OBRA	The **Omnibus Budget Reconciliation Act of 1981 (OBRA)** was federal legislation that expanded the Medicare and Medicaid programs.
1983	TEFRA of 1982	The **Tax Equity and Fiscal Responsibility Act of 1982 (TEFRA)** created Medicare risk programs, which allowed federally qualified HMOs and competitive medical plans that met specified Medicare requirements to provide Medicare-covered services under a risk contract. TEFRA also enacted a **prospective payment system (PPS)**, which issues a predetermined payment for inpatient services. Previously, reimbursement was generated on a *per diem* basis, which issued payment based on daily rates. The PPS implemented in 1983 is called **diagnosis–related groups (DRGs)**, which reimburses hospitals for inpatient stays.
1984	Standardization of information submitted on Medicare claims	HCFA (now called CMS) required providers to use the *HCFA-1500* (now called the **CMS-1500**) to submit Medicare claims. The HCFA Common Procedure Coding System (HCPCS) (now called Health Care Procedure Coding System) was created, which included CPT, level II (national), and level III (local) codes. (Local codes have been discontinued.) Commercial payers also adopted HCPCS coding and use of the HCFA-1500 claim.
1985	COBRA	The **Consolidated Omnibus Budget Reconciliation Act of 1985 (COBRA)** allows employees to continue healthcare coverage beyond the benefit termination date.
1988	TRICARE	The **CHAMPUS Reform Initiative (CRI)** of 1988 resulted in a new program, TRICARE, which includes options such as TRICARE Prime, TRICARE Extra, and TRICARE Standard. (Chapter 16 covers TRICARE claims processing.)
	CLIA	**Clinical Laboratory Improvement Act (CLIA)** legislation established quality standards for all laboratory testing to ensure the accuracy, reliability, and timeliness of patient test results regardless of where the test was performed.
1991	E/M codes created	The American Medical Association (AMA) and HCFA (now called CMS) implemented major revisions of CPT, creating a new section called **Evaluation and Management (E/M)**, which describes patient encounters with providers for the purpose of evaluation and management of general health status.

(continues)

TABLE 2-1   (continued)

YEAR	EVENT	DESCRIPTION
1992	RBRVS is implemented	A new fee schedule for Medicare services was implemented as part of the Omnibus Reconciliation Acts (OBRA) of 1989 and 1990, which replaced the regional "usual and reasonable" payment basis with a fixed fee schedule calculated according to the Resource–Based Relative Value Scale (RBRVS) system. The RBRVS system is a payment system that reimburses physicians' practice expenses based on relative values for three components of each physician's service: physician work, practice expense, and malpractice insurance expense. Usual and reasonable payments were based on fees typically charged by providers by specialty within a particular region of the country. A fee schedule is a list of predetermined payments for healthcare services provided to patients (e.g., a fee is assigned to each CPT code). The patient pays a copayment or coinsurance amount for services rendered, the payer reimburses the provider according to its fee schedule, and the remainder is a "write off" (or loss). **EXAMPLE:** A patient received preventive care evaluation and management services from his family practitioner. The total charges were $125, and the patient paid a $20 copayment during the office visit. The third-party payer reimbursed the physician the fee schedule amount of $75. The remaining $30 owed is recorded as a loss (write off) for his business.
1996	NCCI	The National Correct Coding Initiative (NCCI) was created to promote national correct coding methodologies and to eliminate improper coding. NCCI edits are developed based on coding conventions defined in the American Medical Association's *Current Procedural Terminology (CPT) manual*, current standards of medical and surgical coding practice, input from specialty societies, and analysis of current coding practice.
	HIPAA	The Health Insurance Portability and Accountability Act of 1996 (HIPAA) mandates regulations that govern privacy, security, and electronic transactions standards for healthcare information. The primary intent of HIPAA is to provide better access to health insurance, limit fraud and abuse, and reduce administrative costs.
1997	BBA of 1997	The Balanced Budget Act of 1997 (BBA) addresses healthcare fraud and abuse issues. The DHHS Office of the Inspector General (OIG) provides investigative and audit services in healthcare fraud cases. The State Children's Health Insurance Program (SCHIP) was also established to provide health assistance to uninsured, low-income children, either through separate programs or through expanded eligibility under state Medicaid programs.
1998	SNF PPS	The Skilled Nursing Facility Prospective Payment System (SNF PPS) is implemented (as a result of the BBA of 1997) to cover all costs (routine, ancillary, and capital) related to services furnished to Medicare Part A beneficiaries. The SNF PPS generates *per diem* payments for each admission; these payments are case-mix adjusted using a resident classification system called Resource Utilization Groups (RUGs), which is based on data collected from resident assessments (using data elements called the Minimum Data Set, or MDS) and relative weights developed from staff time data.
1999	HH PPS	The Omnibus Consolidated and Emergency Supplemental Appropriations Act (OCE-SAA) of 1999 amended the BBA of 1997 to require the development and implementation of a Home Health Prospective Payment System (HH PPS), which reimburses home health agencies at a predetermined rate for healthcare services provided to patients. The HH PPS was implemented October 1, 2000, and uses the Outcomes and Assessment Information Set (OASIS), a group of data elements that represent core items of a comprehensive assessment for an adult home care patient and form the basis for measuring patient outcomes for purposes of outcome-based quality improvement.
	Financial Services Modernization Act	Financial Services Modernization Act (or Gramm–Leach–Bliley Act) prohibits sharing of medical information among health insurers and other financial institutions for use in making credit decisions.

(continues)

TABLE 2-1 (continued)

YEAR	EVENT	DESCRIPTION
2000	OPPS	The Outpatient Prospective Payment System (OPPS), which uses Ambulatory Payment Classifications (APCs) to calculate reimbursement, is implemented for billing of hospital-based Medicare outpatient claims.
	BIPA	The Medicare, Medicaid, and SCHIP Benefits Improvement and Protection Act of 2000 (BIPA) requires implementation of a $400 billion prescription drug benefit, improved Medicare Advantage (formerly called Medicare+Choice) benefits, faster Medicare appeals decisions, and more.
	Consumer-driven health plans	Consumer-driven health plans are introduced as a way to encourage individuals to locate the best healthcare at the lowest possible price with the goal of holding down healthcare costs. These plans are organized into three categories: 1. *Employer-paid high-deductible insurance plans* with special health spending accounts to be used by employees to cover deductibles and other medical costs when covered amounts are exceeded. 2. *Defined contribution plans*, which provide a selection of insurance options; employees pay the difference between what the employer pays and the actual cost of the plan they select. 3. *After-tax savings accounts*, which combine a traditional health insurance plan for major medical expenses with a savings account that the employee uses to pay for routine care.
2001	CMS	On June 14, 2001, the Centers for Medicare and Medicaid Services (CMS) became the new name for the Health Care Financing Administration (HCFA).
2002	IRF PPS	The Inpatient Rehabilitation Facilities Prospective Payment System (IRF PPS) is implemented (as a result of the BBA of 1997), which utilizes information from a patient assessment instrument to classify patients into distinct groups based on clinical characteristics and expected resource needs. Separate payments are calculated for each group, including the application of case- and facility-level adjustments.
	QIOs	CMS announced that quality improvement organizations (QIOs) will perform utilization and quality control review of health care furnished, or to be furnished, to Medicare beneficiaries. QIOs replaced peer review organizations (PROs), which previously performed this function.
	EIN	The employer identification number (EIN), assigned by the Internal Revenue Service (IRS), is adopted by DHHS as the National Employer Identification Standard for use in healthcare transactions.
2003	MMA	The Medicare Prescription Drug, Improvement, and Modernization Act (MMA) adds new prescription drug and preventive benefits and provides extra assistance to people with low incomes. A Medicare contracting reform (MCR) initiative was also established to integrate the administration of Medicare Parts A and B fee-for-service benefits to new entities called Medicare Administrative Contractors (MACs). The goal of this reform measure is to improve and modernize the Medicare fee-for-service system and to establish a competitive bidding process to appoint MACs.
	The Medicare Contracting Reform initiative (MCR)	Established to integrate the administration of Medicare Parts A and B fee-for-service benefits with new entities called Medicare administrative contractors (MACs). MACs replaced Medicare carriers, DMERCs, and fiscal intermediaries to improve and modernize the Medicare fee-for-service system and establish a competitive bidding process for contracts.

(continues)

TABLE 2-1   (continued)

YEAR	EVENT	DESCRIPTION
2005	IPF PPS	The Inpatient Psychiatric Facility Prospective Payment System (IPF PPS) is implemented as a requirement of the Medicare, Medicaid, and SCHIP Balanced Budget Refinement Act of 1999 (BBRA). The IPF PPS includes a patient classification system that reflects differences in patient resource use and costs; the new system replaces the cost-based payment system with a per diem IPF PPS. About 1,800 inpatient psychiatric facilities, including freestanding psychiatric hospitals and certified psychiatric units in general acute care hospitals, were impacted.
	NPI	The Standard Unique Health Identifier for Health Care Providers, or National Provider Identifier (NPI), is implemented.
2009	American Recovery and Reinvestment Act of 2009	Authorized an expenditure of $1.5 billion for grants for construction, renovation, and equipment, and for the acquisition of health information technology systems.
	Health Information Technology for Economic and Clinical Health Act (HITECH Act)	Amended the Public Health Service Act to establish an Office of National Coordinator for Health Information Technology within HHS to improve healthcare quality, safety, and efficiency. The HITECH Act is included as part of the American Recovery and Reinvestment Act of 2009.
2010	PPACA	The Patient Protection and Affordable Care Act (PPACA) provides quality affordable health care for Americans, improves role of public programs, improves quality and efficiency of health care, prevents chronic disease, and improves public health. PPACA amended the time period for filing Medicare fee-for-service (FFS) claims to reduce the maximum time period for submission of all Medicare FFS claims to one calendar year after the date of service.
	HCERA	The Health Care and Education Reconciliation Act (HCERA) amended PPACA to implement a number of health-related financing (e.g., closes the Medicare Part D "donut hole" by 2011) and revenue changes (e.g., 10 percent tax on indoor tanning services effective 2010), and to modify higher education assistance provisions.

MEDICAL DOCUMENTATION

Healthcare providers are responsible for documenting and authenticating legible, complete, and timely patient records in accordance with federal regulations (e.g., Medicare *Conditions of Participation*) and accrediting agency standards (e.g., The Joint Commission). The provider is also responsible for correcting or altering errors in patient record documentation. A **patient record** (or **medical record**) documents healthcare services provided to a patient, and healthcare providers are responsible for documenting and authenticating legible, complete, and timely entries according to federal regulations and accreditation standards. The records include patient demographic (or identification) data, documentation to support diagnoses and justify treatment provided, and the results of treatment provided. The primary purpose of the record is to provide for **continuity of care**, which involves documenting patient care services so that others who treat the patient have a source of information to assist with additional care and treatment. The record also serves as a communication tool for physicians and other patient care professionals, and assists in planning individual patient care and documenting a patient's illness and treatment.

Secondary purposes of the record do not relate directly to patient care and include:

- Evaluating the quality of patient care.
- Providing data for use in clinical research, epidemiology studies, education, public policy making, facilities planning, and healthcare statistics.
- Providing information to third-party payers for reimbursement.
- Serving the medico-legal interests of the patient, facility, and providers of care.

Documentation includes dictated and transcribed, typed or handwritten, and computer-generated notes and reports recorded in the patient's records by a healthcare professional. Documentation must be dated and authenticated (with a legible signature or electronic authentication). In a teaching hospital, documentation must identify what service was furnished, how the teaching physician participated in providing the service, and whether the teaching physician was physically present when care was provided. A teaching hospital is engaged in an approved graduate medical education (GME) residency program in medicine, osteopathy, dentistry, or podiatry. A teaching physician is a physician (other than another resident physician) who supervises residents during patient care. A resident physician is an individual who participates in an approved GME program. (Physicians who are authorized to practice only in a hospital setting are called hospitalists; some facilities also call them residents.)

Documentation in the patient record serves as the basis for coding. The information in the record must support codes submitted on claims for third-party payer reimbursement processing. The patient's diagnosis must also justify diagnostic and/or therapeutic procedures or services provided. This is called *medical necessity* and requires providers to document services or supplies that are:

- Proper and needed for the diagnosis or treatment of a medical condition.
- Provided for the diagnosis, direct care, and treatment of a medical condition.
- Consistent with standards of good medical practice in the local area.
- Not mainly for the convenience of the physician or healthcare facility.

It is important to remember the familiar phrase "If it wasn't documented, it wasn't done." The patient record serves as a medico-legal document and a business record. If a provider performs a service but does not document it, the patient (or third-party payer) can refuse to pay for that service, resulting in lost revenue for the provider. In addition, because the patient record serves as an excellent defense of the quality of care administered to a patient, missing documentation can result in problems if the record has to be admitted as evidence in a court of law.

EXAMPLE:

Missing Documentation: A representative from XYZ Insurance Company reviewed 100 outpatient claims submitted by the Medical Center to ensure that all services billed were documented in the patient records. Upon reconciliation of claims with patient record documentation, the representative denied payment for 13 services (totaling $14,000) because reports of the services billed were not found in the patient records. The facility must pay back the $14,000 it received from the payer as reimbursement for the claims submitted.

Lack of Medical Necessity: The patient underwent an x-ray of his right knee, and the provider documented "severe right shoulder pain" in the record. The coder assigned a CPT code to the "right knee x-ray" and an ICD code to the "right shoulder pain." In this example, the third-party

---

payer will deny reimbursement for the submitted claim because the *reason* for the x-ray (shoulder pain) does not match the *type* of x-ray performed. For medical necessity, the provider should have documented a diagnosis such as "right knee pain."

Support of Medical Necessity: The patient underwent a chest x-ray, and the provider documented "severe shortness of breath" in the record. The coder assigned a CPT code to "chest x-ray" and an ICD code to "severe shortness of breath." In this example, the third-party payer will reimburse the provider for services rendered because medical necessity for performing the procedure has been shown.

Problem-oriented Record (POR)

The problem-oriented record (POR) is systematic method of documentation that consists of four components:

- Database
- Problem list
- Initial plan
- Progress notes

The POR database contains the following patient information collected on each patient:

- Chief complaint
- Present conditions and diagnoses
- Social data
- Past, personal, medical, and social history
- Review of systems
- Physical examination
- Baseline laboratory data

The POR problem list serves as a table of contents for the patient record because it is filed at the beginning of the record and contains a numbered list of the patient's problems, which helps to index documentation throughout the record. The POR initial plan contains the strategy for managing patient care and any actions taken to investigate the patient's condition and to treat and educate him or her. The initial plan consists of three categories:

- Diagnostic/management plans (plans to learn more about the patient's condition and the management of the conditions).
- Therapeutic plans (specific medications, goals, procedures, therapies, and treatments used to treat the patient).
- Patient education plans (plans to educate the patient about conditions for which he or she is being treated).

The POR progress notes are documented for each problem assigned to the patient, using the SOAP format:

- Subjective (S) (patient's statement about how he or she feels, including symptomatic information [e.g., "I have a headache"]).

- Objective (O) (observations about the patient, such as physical findings, or lab or x-ray results [e.g., chest x-ray negative]).
- Assessment (A) (judgment, opinion, or evaluation made by the healthcare provider [e.g., acute headache]).
- Plan (P) (diagnostic, therapeutic, and education plans to resolve the problems [e.g., patient to take Tylenol as needed for pain]).

ELECTRONIC HEALTH RECORD (EHR)

Although the terms electronic health record (EHR) and electronic medical record (EMR) are often used interchangeably, the electronic health record (EHR) is a more global concept that includes the collection of patient information documented by a number of providers at different facilities regarding one patient. The EHR uses multidisciplinary (many specialties) and multi-enterprise (many facilities) recordkeeping approaches to facilitate record linkage, which allows patient information to be created at different locations according to a unique patient identifier or identification number. The electronic health record:

- Provides access to complete and accurate patient health problems, status, and treatment data.
- Allows access to evidence-based decision support tools (e.g., drug interaction alerts) that assist providers with decision making.
- Automates and streamlines a provider's workflow, ensuring that all clinical information is communicated.
- Prevents delays in healthcare response that result in gaps in care (e.g., automated prescription renewal notices).
- Supports the collection of data for uses other than clinical care (e.g., billing, outcome reporting, public health disease surveillance/reporting, and quality management).

> **NOTE:** The personal health record (PHR) is a web-based application that allows individuals to maintain and manage their health information (and that of others for whom they are authorized, such as family members) in a private, secure, and confidential environment.

The electronic medical record (EMR) has a more narrow focus because it is the patient record created for a single medical practice using a computer, keyboard, a mouse, optical pen device, voice recognition system, scanner, and/or touch screen. The electronic medical record:

- Includes a patient's medication lists, problem lists, clinical notes, and other documentation.
- Allows providers to prescribe medications, order and view results of ancillary tests (e.g., laboratory, radiology).
- Alerts the provider about drug interactions, abnormal ancillary testing results, and when ancillary tests are needed.

Total practice management software (TPMS) (Figure 2-1) is used to generate the EMR, automating the following medical practice functions:

- Registering patients
- Scheduling appointments
- Generating insurance claims and patient statements
- Processing payments from patient and third-party payers
- Producing administrative and clinical reports

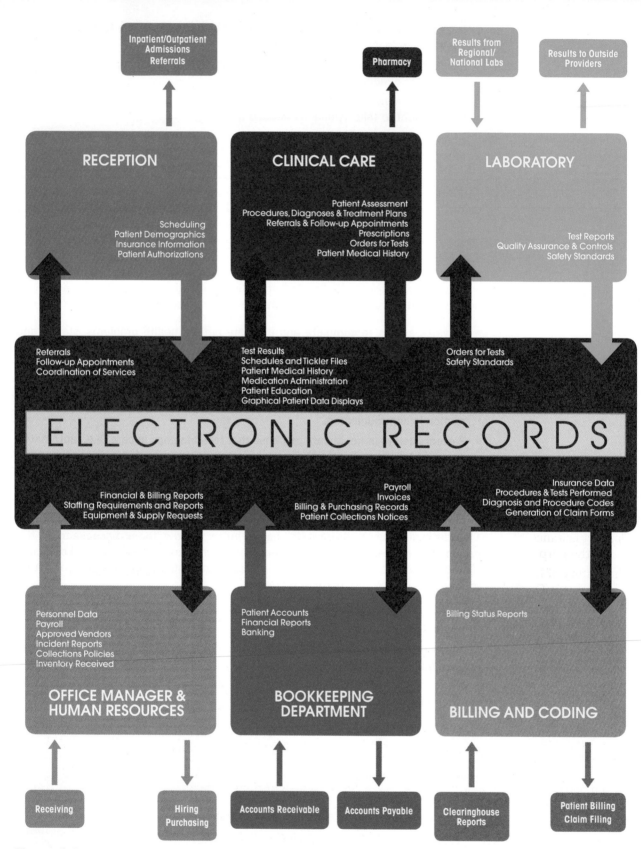

Figure 2-1 Total practice management software (TPMS) data flow (Courtesy Delmar/Cengage Learning)

MEDICAL OFFICE SIMULATION SOFTWARE (MOSS)

Delmar's Medical Office Simulation Software (MOSS) (Figure 2-2) is generic software created for educational purposes to help prepare students for using commercial software used in medical practices.

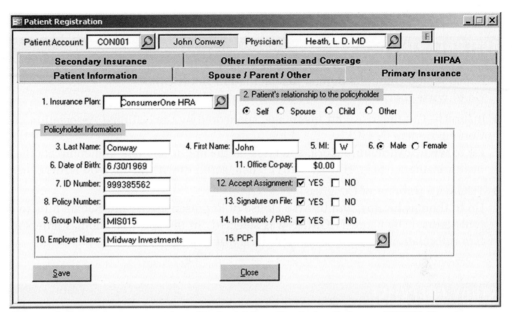

Figure 2-2 Insurance screen from Medical Office Simulation Software (MOSS) (Courtesy Delmar/Cengage Learning)

SUMMARY

Health insurance is a contract between a policyholder and a third-party payer or government program for the purpose of providing reimbursement of all or a portion of medical and heath care costs.

The history of healthcare reimbursement can be traced back to 1860, when the Franklin Health Assurance Company of Massachusetts wrote the first health insurance policy.

Subsequent years, through the present, have seen significant changes and advances in healthcare insurance and reimbursement, from the development of the first Blue Cross and Blue Shield plans to legislation that resulted in government healthcare programs (e.g., to cover individuals age 65 and older), payment systems to control healthcare costs (e.g., diagnosis-related groups), and regulations to govern privacy, security, and electronic transaction standards for healthcare information.

A *patient record* (or *medical record*) documents healthcare services provided to a patient, and healthcare providers are responsible for documenting and authenticating legible, complete, and timely entries according to federal regulations and accreditation standards. The records include patient demographic (or identification) data, documentation to support diagnoses and justify treatment provided, and the results of treatment provided. The primary purpose of the record is to provide for continuity of care, which involves documenting patient care services so that others who treat the patient have a source of information to assist with additional care and treatment. The *problem-oriented record (POR)* is a systematic method of documentation that consists of four components: database, problem list, initial plan, and progress notes (documented using the SOAP format).

The *electronic health record (EHR)* is a global concept (as compared with the EMR) that includes the collection of patient information documented by a number of providers at different facilities regarding one patient. The EHR uses multidisciplinary (many specialties) and multi-enterprise (many facilities) recordkeeping approaches to facilitate *record linkage,* which allows patient information to be created at different locations according to a unique patient identifier or identification number.

The *personal health record* (PHR) is a web-based application that allows individuals to maintain and manage their health information (and that of others for whom they are authorized, such as family members) in a private, secure, and confidential environment. The electronic medical record (EMR) has a more narrow focus (as compared with the EHR) because it is the patient record created for a single medical practice and uses total practice management software (TPMS) to generate the EMR and automate medical practice functions.

INTERNET LINKS

- Consolidated Omnibus Budget Reconciliation Act (COBRA)
  Go to **www.cobrainsurance.net** to learn more about COBRA.

- InsureU—Get Smart About Insurance, sponsored by the National Association of Insurance Commissioners (NAIC)
  Go to **www.insureuonline.org,** and click on the applicable link and complete the life stage course about health insurance (e.g., HEALTH 101). Then, scroll down and click on NAIC consumer guides links.

- THOMAS (Library of Congress)
  Go to **thomas.loc.gov,** and browse House of Representatives and Senate bills to determine their current status. (The name THOMAS was selected "in the spirit of Thomas Jefferson," to provide legislative information available from the Library of Congress.)

STUDY CHECKLIST

- ☐ Read this textbook chapter and highlight key concepts.
- ☐ Create an index card for each key term.
- ☐ Access the chapter Internet links to learn more about concepts.
- ☐ Answer the chapter review questions, verifying answers with your instructor.
- ☐ Complete WebTutor assignments and take online quizzes.
- ☐ Complete Workbook chapter, verifying answers with your instructor.
- ☐ Complete the StudyWare activities to receive immediate feedback.
- ☐ Form a study group with classmates to discuss chapter concepts in preparation for an exam.

REVIEW

MULTIPLE CHOICE Select the most appropriate response.

1. **Which was the first commercial insurance company in the United States to provide private healthcare coverage for injuries not resulting in death?**
    a. Baylor University Health Plan
    b. Blue Cross and Blue Shield Association
    c. Franklin Health Assurance Company
    d. Office of Workers' Compensation Program

2. Which replaced the 1908 workers' compensation legislation and provided civilian employees of the federal government with medical care, survivors' benefits, and compensation for lost wages?

   a. Black Lung Benefits Reform Act

   b. Federal Employees' Compensation Act

   c. Longshore and Harbor Workers' Compensation Act

   d. Office of Workers' Compensation Programs

3. The first Blue Cross policy was introduced by

   a. Baylor University in Dallas, Texas.

   b. Harvard University in Cambridge, Massachusetts.

   c. Kaiser Permanente in Los Angeles, California.

   d. American Medical Association representatives.

4. The Blue Shield concept grew out of the lumber and mining camps of the _____ region at the turn of the century.

   a. Great Plains

   b. New England

   c. Pacific Northwest

   d. Southwest

5. Healthcare coverage offered by _____ is called group health insurance.

   a. a state

   b. CMS

   c. employees

   d. employers

6. The Hill-Burton Act provided federal grants for modernizing hospitals that had become obsolete because of a lack of capital investment during the Great Depression and WWII (1929 to 1945). In return for federal funds,

   a. facilities were required to provide services free or at reduced rates to patients unable to pay for care.

   b. medical group practices were formed to allow providers to share equipment, supplies, and personnel.

   c. national coordinating agencies for physician-sponsored health insurance plans were created.

   d. universal health insurance was provided to those who could not afford private insurance.

7. Third-party administrators (TPAs) administer healthcare plans and process claims, serving as a

   a. clearinghouse for data submitted by government agencies.

   b. Medicare administrative contractor (MAC) for business owners.

   c. system of checks and balances for labor and management.

   d. third-party payer (insurance company) for employers.

8. Major medical insurance provides coverage for _____ illnesses and injuries, incorporating large deductibles and lifetime maximum amounts.

   a. acute care (short-term)

   b. catastrophic or prolonged

   c. recently diagnosed

   d. work-related

9. The government health plan that provides healthcare services to Americans over the age of 65 is called

   a. Medicare.

   b. Medicaid.

   c. CHAMPUS.

   d. TRICARE.

10. The percentage of costs a patient shares with the health plan (e.g., plan pays 80 percent of costs and patient pays 20 percent), is called

    a. coinsurance.

    b. copayment.

    c. deductible.

    d. maximum.

11. The Tax Equity and Fiscal Responsibility Act of 1982 (TEFRA) enacted the _____ prospective payment system (PPS).

    a. ambulatory payment classifications

    b. diagnosis-related groups

    c. fee-for-service reimbursement

    d. resource-based relative value scale system

12. The Clinical Laboratory Improvement Act (CLIA) established quality standards for all laboratory testing to ensure the accuracy, reliability, and timeliness of patient test results

    a. only at hospitals and other large institutions.

    b. regardless of where the test was performed.

13. The National Correct Coding Initiative (NCCI) promotes national correct coding methodologies and eliminates improper coding. NCCI edits are developed based on coding conventions defined in _____, current standards of medical and surgical coding practice, input from specialty societies, and analysis of current coding practice.

    a. CPT

    b. ICD

    c. HCPCS level II

    d. NDC

14. The primary intent of HIPAA legislation is to

    a. combine healthcare financing and quality assurance programs into a single agency.

    b. create better access to health insurance, limit fraud and abuse, and reduce administrative costs.

    c. provide health assistance to uninsured, low-income children by expanding the Medicaid program.

    d. protect all employees against injuries from occupational hazards in the workplace.

15. Utilization and quality control review of healthcare furnished, or to be furnished, to Medicare beneficiaries is currently performed by _____.

    a. consumer-driven health plans

    b. peer review organizations

    c. professional standards review organizations

    d. quality improvement organizations

16. Which is a primary purpose of the patient record?

    a. ensure continuity of care

    b. evaluate quality of care

    c. provide data for use in research

    d. submit data to third-party payers

17. The problem-oriented record (POR) includes the following four components:

    a. chief complaint, review of systems, physical examination, laboratory data

    b. database, problem list, initial plan, progress notes

    c. diagnostic plans, management plans, therapeutic plans, patient education plans

    d. subjective, objective, assessment, plan

18. The electronic health record (EHR) allows patient information to be created at different locations according to a unique patient identifier or identification number, which is called

    a. evidence-based decision support.

    b. health data management.

    c. record linkage.

    d. surveillance and reporting.

19. When a patient states, "I haven't been able to sleep for weeks," the provider who uses the SOAP format documents that statement in the _____ portion of the clinic note.

    a. assessment

    b. objective

    c. plan

    d. subjective

20. The provider who uses the SOAP format documents the physical examination in the _____ portion of the clinic note.

    a. assessment

    b. objective

    c. plan

    d. subjective

Managed Health Care

CHAPTER OUTLINE

History of Managed Health Care

Managed Care Organizations

Managed Care Models

Consumer-Directed Health Plans

Accreditation of Managed Care Organizations

Effects of Managed Care on a Physician's Practice

OBJECTIVES

Upon successful completion of this chapter, you should be able to:

1. Define key terms.
2. Discuss the history of managed care in the United States.
3. Explain the role of a managed care organization.
4. Describe six managed care models, and provide details about each.
5. List and define consumer-directed health plans.
6. Identify the organization that accredits managed care organizations.
7. Describe the effects of managed care on a physician's practice.

KEY TERMS

accreditation

Amendment to the HMO Act of 1973

adverse selection

cafeteria plan

capitation

case management

case manager

closed-panel HMO

competitive medical plan (CMP)

concurrent review

consumer-directed health plan (CDHP)

customized sub-capitation plan (CSCP)

direct contract model HMO

discharge planning

enrollees

exclusive provider organization (EPO)

external quality review organization (EQRO)

federally qualified HMO

fee-for-service

flexible benefit plan

flexible spending account (FSA)

gag clause

gatekeeper

group model HMO

group practice without walls (GPWW)

healthcare reimbursement account (HCRA)

health maintenance organization (HMO)

Health Maintenance Organization Assistance Act of 1973

Healthcare Effectiveness
    Data and Information Set
    (HEDIS)
health reimbursement
    arrangement (HRA)
health savings account (HSA)
health savings security
    account (HSSA)
independent practice
    association (IPA) HMO
individual practice
    association (IPA) HMO
integrated delivery system (IDS)
integrated provider
    organization (IPO)
legislation
managed care organization
    (MCO)
managed health care
    (managed care)
management service
    organization (MSO)
mandates
medical foundation

medical savings account
    (MSA)
Medicare+Choice
Medicare risk program
National Committee for
    Quality Assurance (NCQA)
network model HMO
network provider
Office of Managed Care
open-panel HMO
physician incentive plan
physician incentives
physician-hospital
    organization (PHO)
point-of-service plan (POS)
preadmission certification
    (PAC)
preadmission review
Preferred Provider Health
    Care Act of 1985
preferred provider
    organization (PPO)
primary care provider (PCP)

prospective review
quality assessment and
    performance improvement
    (QAPI)
quality assurance program
Quality Improvement System
    for Managed Care (QISMC)
report card
retrospective review
risk contract
risk pool
second surgical opinion (SSO)
self-referral
staff model HMO
standards
sub-capitation payment
subscribers (policyholders)
survey
triple option plan
utilization management
    (utilization review)
utilization review organization
    (URO)

INTRODUCTION

Managed health care (managed care) combines healthcare delivery with the financing of services provided. The intent was to replace conventional fee-for-service plans with more affordable quality care to healthcare consumers and providers who agreed to certain restrictions (e.g., patients would receive care only from providers who are members of a managed care organization). Managed care is currently being challenged by the growth of consumer-directed health plans (CDHPs), which define employer contributions and ask employees to be more responsible for healthcare decisions and cost-sharing. You might think of a CDHP as a sort of "401(k) plan for health care" (recalling the shift from employer defined-benefit pension plans to employer defined-contribution 401(k) plans).

StudyWARE

Complete StudyWare practice quizzes and activities using the CD-ROM located inside the back cover of your textbook.

NOTE: Go to www.delmarlearning.com/companions, enter **Understanding Health Insurance** in the Companion Search box, click **Search**, and click on the most current edition of the textbook. Then, click on **Student Resources** to locate Tables 3-A to learn about the history of managed care.

HISTORY OF MANAGED HEALTH CARE

Managed health care (or managed care) (Table 3-1) was developed as a way to provide affordable, comprehensive, prepaid healthcare services to enrollees (or subscribers or policyholders) (employees and dependents who join a managed care plan; known as *beneficiaries* in private insurance plans).

TABLE 3-1 Significant managed care federal legislation

YEAR	LEGISLATIVE TITLE	LEGISLATIVE SUMMARY
1973	Health Maintenance Organization Assistance Act of 1973	• Authorized grants and loans to develop HMOs under private sponsorship • Defined a federally qualified HMO (certified to provide healthcare services to Medicare and Medicaid enrollees) as one that has applied for and met federal standards established in the HMO Act of 1973 • Required most employers with more than 25 employees to offer HMO coverage if local plans were available
1974	Employee Retirement Income Security Act of 1974 (ERISA)	• Mandated reporting and disclosure requirements for group life and health plans (including managed care plans) • Permitted large employers to self-insure employee healthcare benefits • Exempted large employers from taxes on health insurance premiums
1981	Omnibus Budget Reconciliation Act of 1981 (OBRA)	• Provided states with flexibility to establish HMOs for Medicare and Medicaid programs • Increased managed-care enrollment resulted
1982	Tax Equity and Fiscal Responsibility Act of 1982 (TEFRA)	• Modified the HMO Act of 1973 • Created Medicare risk programs, which allowed federally qualified HMOs and competitive medical plans that met specified Medicare requirements to provide Medicare-covered services under a risk contract • Defined risk contract as an arrangement among providers to provide capitated (fixed, prepaid basis) healthcare services to Medicare beneficiaries • Defined competitive medical plan (CMP) as an HMO that meets federal eligibility requirements for a Medicare risk contract but is not licensed as a federally qualified plan
1985	Preferred Provider Health Care Act of 1985	• Eased restrictions on preferred provider organizations (PPOs) • Allowed subscribers to seek health care from providers outside of the PPO
	Consolidated Omnibus Budget Reconciliation Act of 1985 (COBRA)	• Established an employee's right to continue healthcare coverage beyond scheduled benefit termination date (including HMO coverage)
1988	Amendment to the HMO Act of 1973	• Allowed federally qualified HMOs to permit members to occasionally use non-HMO physicians and be partially reimbursed
1989	Healthcare Effectiveness Data and Information Set (HEDIS) is developed by National Committee for Quality Assurance (NCQA)	• Created standards to assess managed-care systems in terms of membership, utilization of services, quality, access, health plan management and activities, and financial indicators
1994	HCFA's Office of Managed Care is established	• Facilitated innovation and competition among Medicare HMOs
1996	Health Insurance Portability and Accountability Act of 1996 (HIPAA)	• Created federal standards for insurers, HMOs, and employer plans, including those who self-insure

(continues)

TABLE 3-1   Significant managed care federal legislation (continued)

YEAR	LEGISLATIVE TITLE	LEGISLATIVE SUMMARY
1997	Medical savings accounts pilot program created as part of IRS legislation	A **medical savings account (MSA)** allows individuals to withdraw tax-free funds for healthcare expenses that are not covered by a qualifying high-deductible health plan. Healthcare expenses that may be reimbursed from the MSA include the following: • Dental expenses, including uncovered orthodontia • Eye exams, contact lenses, and eyeglasses • Hearing care expenses • Health plan deductibles and copayments • Prescription drugs **NOTE:** 2003 legislation replaced MSAs with health savings accounts (HSAs) (Table 3-3). Existing MSAs are "grandfathered," or they can be moved to an HSA.
	Balanced Budget Act of 1997 (BBA)	• Encouraged formation of provider service networks (PSNs) and provider service organizations (PSOs) • Mandated risk-based managed care organizations to submit encounter data related to inpatient hospital stays of members • Established the Medicare+Choice program, which expanded Medicare coverage options by creating managed care plans, to include HMOs, PPOs, and MSAs (now called Medicare Advantage or Medicare Part C) • Required M+C organizations to implement a **quality assessment and performance improvement (QAPI)** program so that quality assurance activities are performed to improve the functioning of M+C organizations
	State managed care legislation	• In 1997, Texas was the first state to enact legislation allowing consumers to sue an HMO for medical malpractice. (Other states have since passed similar legislation.) • Other state-enacted legislation since 1997 includes that relating to mandated benefits, high-risk pools, method and philosophy of treatment for Alzheimer's disease, Medicaid eligibility, banning financial incentives, independent appeals measures, insuring liability, and prompt payment.
2003	Medicare Prescription Drug, Improvement, and Modernization Act (MMA) (or Medicare Modernization Act)	• Amended the Internal Revenue Code of 1986 to allow a deduction to individuals for amounts contributed to health savings security accounts and health savings accounts, and to provide for the disposition of unused health benefits in cafeteria plans and flexible spending arrangements • Title I of the Act established voluntary program for prescription drug coverage under Medicare

MANAGED CARE ORGANIZATIONS

NOTE: Some managed care organizations have discontinued capitation and have adopted fee-for-service payment plans.

A **managed care organization (MCO)** is responsible for the health of a group of enrollees and can be a health plan, hospital, physician group, or health system. Unlike traditional **fee-for-service** plans, which reimburse providers for individual healthcare services rendered, managed care is financed according to a method called **capitation**, where providers accept pre-established payments for providing healthcare services to enrollees over a period of time (usually one year). If the physician provides services that cost less than the capitation amount, there is a profit (which the physician keeps). If services provided to subscribers cost more than the capitation amount, the physician loses money.

> **EXAMPLE:** In June, Hillcrest Medical Group received a capitated payment of $15,000 for the 150 members (enrollees) of the ABC Managed Care Health Plan. The Group spent $12,500 of the capitated payment on preventive, chronic, and acute healthcare services provided to member patients. The services were provided at the Group's office and local hospital, which included inpatient, outpatient, and emergency department care. (The Group is responsible for paying the enrollees' hospital bills.) In this scenario, healthcare services provided to enrollees cost less than the capitated payment received. The Hillcrest Medical Group, therefore, made a profit of $2,500. If healthcare services had cost more than the capitated amount of $15,000, the Group would have experienced a loss.

Primary Care Providers

Managed care plan enrollees receive care from a primary care provider selected from a list of participating providers. The **primary care provider (PCP)** is responsible for supervising and coordinating healthcare services for enrollees and approves referrals to specialists and inpatient hospital admissions (except in emergencies) (Figure 3-1). The PCP serves as a **gatekeeper** by providing essential healthcare services at the lowest possible cost, avoiding nonessential care, and referring patients to specialists.

Quality Assurance

Managed care plans that are "federally qualified" and those that must comply with state quality review **mandates** (laws) are required to establish quality assurance programs. A **quality assurance program** includes activities that assess the quality of care provided in a healthcare setting. Many states have enacted **legislation** (laws) requiring an **external quality review organization (EQRO)** (e.g., QIO) to review health care provided by managed care organizations. The types of quality reviews performed include government oversight, patient satisfaction surveys, data collected from grievance procedures, and reviews conducted by independent organizations. Independent organizations that perform reviews include accreditation agencies such as the National Committee for Quality Assurance and The Joint Commission.

Medicare established the **Quality Improvement System for Managed Care (QISMC)** to ensure the accountability of managed care plans in terms of objective, measurable **standards** (requirements). Plans are required to meet minimum performance levels and to show demonstrable and measurable improvement in specified broad clinical areas (e.g., preventive services, acute ambulatory care, chronic care, and hospital care) based on performance improvement projects that each plan identifies. The Health Plan Employer Data and Information Set (HEDIS), sponsored by the National Committee for Quality Assurance, consists of performance measures used to evaluate managed care plans (e.g., rate of Pap smears performed among women of a certain age). The National Committee for Quality Assurance (NCQA) reviews managed care plans and develops report cards to allow healthcare consumers to make informed decisions when selecting a plan. The **report card** contains data regarding a managed care plan's quality, utilization, customer satisfaction, administrative effectiveness, financial stability, and cost control.

Utilization Management

Utilization management (or **utilization review**) is a method of controlling healthcare costs and quality of care by reviewing the appropriateness and necessity of care provided to patients prior to the administration of care (**prospective review**) or after

Guardian Managed Care Plan

101 Main St. ■ Anywhere, US 12345 ■ (101) 555-1234

PRIMARY CARE PROVIDER PREAUTHORIZATION REFERRAL FORM FOR CONSULTATION

Patient Name	Preauthorization Number	Name of Consulting Physician
Member Identification Number	Member Name (Last, First, MI)	Member Birthdate
Primary Care Physician Identification Number	Name of Primary Care Physician (PCP)	PCP Phone Number

This referral authorizes the services listed below. All services must be rendered by provider stated below.

Diagnosis: ICD code(s):

Medical History:

Reason for Referral:

Consultant may provide services listed below. All authorized visits must occur within 90 days of date authorized by PCP. If surgical procedure is listed below, Consultant Treatment Plan is not required. For initial consultation, specialist must submit Consultant Treatment Report of findings and treatment recommendations.

Diagnostic tests indicated: CPT code(s):

Procedure(s) to be performed: CPT code(s):

Primary Care Physician Signature	Date

Consultant billing procedures for services authorized by Primary Care Physician:
1. Enter Preauthorization Number listed above in Block 23 of the CMS-1500 claim.
2. For first submission, submit CMS-1500 claim with original PCP Preauthorization Referral Form for Consultation.
3. For subsequent submissions, no attachments are required.
4. Consultant must complete Consultant Treatment Plan to obtain authorization for any surgical procedure not specified on this form.

Improperly completed forms will be returned.

Care Management Use Only
Expiration date: _____
Referral number: _____

FIGURE 3-1 Sample primary care provider preauthorization referral for consultation (Courtesy Delmar/Cengage Learning)

care has been provided (retrospective review). Utilization management activities performed by managed care plans include:

- Preadmission certification (PAC, or preadmission review) which is a review for medical necessity of inpatient care prior to the patient's admission.
- *Preauthorization,* which is a review that grants prior approval for reimbursement of a healthcare service (e.g., elective surgery).

- **Concurrent review,** which is a review for medical necessity of tests and procedures ordered during an inpatient hospitalization.
- **Discharge planning,** which involves arranging appropriate healthcare services for the discharged patient (e.g., home health care).

Some managed care plans contract out utilization management services to a **utilization review organization (URO),** an entity that establishes a utilization management program and performs external utilization review services. Other plans contract with a *third-party administrator (TPA),* an organization that provides health benefits claims administration and other outsourced services for self-insured companies.

Case Management

Case management involves the development of patient care plans for the coordination and provision of care for complicated cases in a cost-effective manner. For example, instead of admitting a patient to the hospital, a managed care plan might authorize 24-hour home healthcare services when appropriate. The **case manager** submits written confirmation, authorizing treatment, to the provider (Figure 3-2).

Second Surgical Opinions

> **NOTE:** Managed care programs have been successful in containing costs and limiting unnecessary services, resulting in the current trend for healthcare plans to offer the SSO as a benefit, not a requirement.

Prior to scheduling elective surgery, managed care plans often require a **second surgical opinion (SSO);** that is, a second physician is asked to evaluate the necessity of surgery and recommend the most economical, appropriate facility in which to perform the surgery (e.g., outpatient clinic or doctor's office versus inpatient hospitalization).

Gag Clauses

Medicare and many states prohibit managed care contracts from containing **gag clauses,** which prevent providers from discussing all treatment options with patients, whether or not the plan would provide reimbursement for services. Medicare beneficiaries are entitled to advice from their physicians on medically necessary treatment options that may be appropriate for their condition or disease. Because a gag clause would have the practical effect of prohibiting a physician from giving a patient the full range of advice and counsel that is clinically appropriate, it would result in the managed care plan not providing all covered Medicare services to its enrollees, in violation of the managed care plan's responsibilities.

Physician Incentives

Physician incentives include payments made directly or indirectly to healthcare providers to encourage them to reduce or limit services (e.g., discharge an inpatient from the hospital more quickly) so as to save money for the managed care plan. The federal **physician incentive plan** requires managed care plans that contract with Medicare or Medicaid to disclose information about physician incentive plans to CMS or state Medicaid agencies before a new or renewed contract receives final approval.

Guardian Managed Care Plan

101 Main St. ■ Anywhere, US 12345 ■ (101) 555-1234

DATE:

RE: _____

DATE OF BIRTH: _____

IDENTIFICATION NUMBER: _____

START TREATMENT DATE: _____

NAME OF CONSULTANT: _____

MAILING ADDRESS: _____

Dear Dr. _____

_____ was referred to you by the Guardian Managed Care Plan on _____.
I am authorizing the following medically necessary treatment. This is subject to patient eligibility and contract limitations at the time treatment is performed.

Procedure	Units	From	To	Preauthorization Number
_____	_____	_____	_____	_____

When filing for reimbursement, please send the CMS-1500 claim to the Guardian Managed Care Plan at the above address. In order to expedite payment, please be certain to include in Block 23 the pre-authorization number indicated above.

Please note that any services provided beyond those listed in this letter require additional preauthorization. If you anticipate that the patient will require additional services, you must complete an outpatient treatment report two weeks prior to rendering any additional treatment. If the patient fails to keep appointments, please inform us by telephone. If treatment is discontinued, submit a written discharge summary within two weeks of termination.

Although eligibility and benefit information has been corroborated to the best of our ability, certification for medically necessary care does not guarantee financial reimbursement related to these matters. If you need further information, or if there are any significant changes in the patient's medical status, please contact me at the Guardian Managed Care Plan at (800) 555-1212, extension 1234.
Thank you for your cooperation.

Sincerely,

Case Manager
Original:
cc:

FIGURE 3-2 Sample case manager written confirmation order (Courtesy Delmar/Cengage Learning)

MANAGED CARE MODELS

NOTE: Government and private payers have implemented managed care programs to control healthcare costs. Chapters 12–17 of this textbook include details about such managed care programs (e.g., Medicare managed care plans are discussed in Chapter 14).

Managed care originally focused on cost reductions by restricting healthcare access through utilization management and availability of limited benefits. Managed care organizations (MCOs) were created to manage benefits and to develop participating provider networks. Managed care can now be categorized according to six models:

1. Exclusive provider organization (EPO).
2. Integrated delivery system (IDS).

3. Health maintenance organization (HMO).

   a. direct contract model

   b. group model

   c. individual practice association (IPA)

   d. network model

   e. staff model

4. Point-of-service plan (POS).

5. Preferred provider organization (PPO).

6. Triple option plan.

Exclusive Provider Organization (EPO)

> **NOTE:** *Exclusive provider organization (EPO)* patients must receive care from participating providers, or they pay for all costs incurred.

An **exclusive provider organization (EPO)** is a managed care plan that provides benefits to subscribers who are required to receive services from network providers. A **network provider** is a physician or healthcare facility under contract to the managed care plan. Usually, network providers sign exclusive contracts with the EPO, which means they cannot contract with other managed care plans. (Network providers are usually reimbursed on a fee-for-service basis.) Subscribers are generally required to coordinate healthcare services through their primary care physician (PCP). EPOs are regulated by state insurance departments (unlike HMOs, which are regulated by either the state commerce or department of corporations, depending on state requirements).

Integrated Delivery System (IDS)

> **NOTE:** An *integrated delivery system (IDS)* is the result of a joint venture between hospitals and members of their medical staff.

An **integrated delivery system (IDS)** is an organization of affiliated providers' sites (e.g., hospitals, ambulatory surgical centers, or physician groups) that offer joint healthcare services to subscribers. Models include physician-hospital organizations, management service organizations, group practices without walls, integrated provider organizations, and medical foundations. A **physician–hospital organization (PHO)** is owned by hospital(s) and physician groups that obtain managed care plan contracts; physicians maintain their own practices and provide healthcare services to plan members. A **management service organization (MSO)** is usually owned by physicians or a hospital and provides practice management (administrative and support) services to individual physician practices. A **group practice without walls (GPWW)** establishes a contract that allows physicians to maintain their own offices and share services (e.g., appointment scheduling and billing). An **integrated provider organization (IPO)** manages the delivery of healthcare services offered by hospitals, physicians (who are employees of the IPO), and other healthcare organizations (e.g., an ambulatory surgery clinic and a nursing facility). A **medical foundation** is a nonprofit organization that contracts with and acquires the clinical and business assets of physician practices; the foundation is assigned a provider number and manages the practice's business. An *integrated delivery system* may also be referred to by any of the following names: integrated service network (ISN), delivery system, vertically integrated plan (VIP), vertically integrated system, horizontally integrated system, health delivery network, or accountable health plan.

Health Maintenance Organization (HMO)

A **health maintenance organization (HMO)** is an alternative to traditional group health insurance coverage and provides comprehensive healthcare services to voluntarily enrolled members on a prepaid basis. In contrast, traditional health insurance coverage is usually provided on a fee-for-service basis in which reimbursement increases if the healthcare service fees increase, if multiple units of service are provided, or if more expensive services are provided instead of less expensive ones (e.g., brand-name versus generic prescription medication).

HMOs provide preventive care services to promote "wellness" or good health, thus reducing the overall cost of medical care. Annual physical examinations are encouraged for the early detection of health problems. Health risk assessment instruments (surveys) and resources are also available to subscribers. A primary care provider (PCP) assigned to each subscriber is responsible for coordinating healthcare services and referring subscribers to other healthcare providers.

HMOs often require a *copayment* (or *copay*), which is a fee paid by the patient to the provider at the time healthcare services are rendered. Copayments range from $1 to $35 per visit, and some services are exempt because coinsurance payments are required instead.

HMOs must meet the requirements of the HMO Act of 1973 as well as the rules and regulations of individual states. There are five HMO models (Table 3-2): direct contract model, group model, individual practice association, network model, and staff model.

> **EXAMPLE:** Dr. Sanders provided Nancy Jones with evaluation and management (E/M) services at the Center City HMO during an office visit. The contracted E/M service rate is $64, and Nancy is required to pay a $10 copayment. She has $100 annual deductible, which was met earlier this year. She is not required to pay a coinsurance amount.
>
> | | |
> |---|---:|
> | Provider fee (contracted E/M service rate) | $64 |
> | Patient copayment | − $10 |
> | Insurance payment | $54 |

Point-of-Service Plan (POS)

To create flexibility in managed care plans, some HMOs and preferred provider organizations have implemented a point-of-service plan (POS), under which patients have freedom to use the managed panel of providers or to self-refer to non-managed care providers. If the enrollee chooses to receive all medical care from the managed network of healthcare providers, or obtains an authorization from the POS primary care physician for specialty care outside the managed care network, he pays only the regular copayment or a small charge for the visit. Also, no deductible or coinsurance responsibility applies. If the enrollee sees a non-managed care panel specialist without a referral from the primary care physician, this is known as a self-referral. The enrollee will have greater out-of-pocket expenses, as he must pay both a large deductible (usually $200 to $250) and 20 to 25 percent coinsurance charges, similar to those paid by persons with fee-for-service plans.

Preferred Provider Organization (PPO)

A preferred provider organization (PPO) is a network of physicians and hospitals that have joined together to contract with insurance companies, employers, or other organizations to provide health care to subscribers for a discounted fee. PPOs do not routinely establish contracts for laboratory or pharmacy services, but they do offer reduced-rate contracts with specific hospitals. Most PPOs are open-ended plans allowing patients to use non-PPO providers in exchange for larger out-of-pocket expenses. Premiums, deductibles, and copayments are usually higher than those paid for HMOs, but lower than regular fee-for-service plans.

TABLE 3-2 Closed-panel and open-panel health maintenance organization models

CLOSED–PANEL HMO	Health care is provided in an HMO-owned center or satellite clinic or by physicians who belong to a specially formed medical group that serves the HMO.
CLOSED-PANEL MODELS	**DESCRIPTION**
Group Model HMO	Contracted healthcare services are delivered to subscribers by *participating physicians who are members of an independent multispecialty group practice.* The HMO reimburses the physician group, which is then responsible for reimbursing physician members and contracted healthcare facilities (e.g., hospitals). The physician group can be owned or managed by the HMO, or it can simply contract with the HMO.
Staff Model HMO	Healthcare services are provided to subscribers by *physicians employed by the HMO.* Premiums and other revenue are paid to the HMO. Usually, all ambulatory services are provided within HMO corporate buildings.
OPEN–PANEL HMO	Health care is provided by individuals who are *not* employees of the HMO or who do not belong to a specially formed medical group that serves the HMO.
OPEN-PANEL MODELS	**DESCRIPTION**
Direct Contract Model HMO	Contracted healthcare services are delivered to subscribers by *individual physicians in the community.*
Individual Practice Association (IPA) HMO	Also called **independent practice association (IPA)**, contracted health services are delivered to subscribers by *physicians who remain in their independent office settings.* The IPA is an intermediary (e.g., physician association) that negotiates the HMO contract and receives and manages the capitation payment from the HMO, so that physicians are paid on either a fee-for-service or capitation basis.
Network Model HMO	Contracted healthcare services are provided to subscribers by *two or more physician multi-specialty group practices.*

Triple Option Plan

> **NOTE:** A *triple option plan* provides patients with more choices than a traditional managed care plan.

A **triple option plan**, which is usually offered either by a single insurance plan or as a joint venture among two or more insurance payers, provides subscribers or employees with a choice of HMO, PPO, or traditional health insurance plans. It is also called a **cafeteria plan** (or **flexible benefit plan**) because of the different benefit plans and extra coverage options provided through the insurer or third-party administrator. Triple option plans are intended to prevent the problem of covering members who are sicker than the general population (called **adverse selection**). A **risk pool** is created when a number of people are grouped for insurance purposes (e.g., employees of an organization); the cost of healthcare coverage is determined by employees' health status, age, sex, and occupation.

CONSUMER-DIRECTED HEALTH PLANS

Consumer-directed health plans (CDHPs) include many choices that provide individuals with an incentive to control the costs of health benefits and health care. Individuals have greater freedom in spending healthcare dollars, up to a designated amount, and receive full coverage for in-network preventive care. In return, individuals assume significantly higher cost-sharing expenses after the designated amount has been expended. (The catastrophic limit is usually higher than those common in other plans.) CDHPs have become a popular alternative to the increased costs of traditional health insurance premiums and the limitations associated with managed care plans. They include the following tiers:

- **Tax-exempt account, which is used to pay for healthcare expenses and provides more flexibility than traditional managed care plans in terms of access to providers and services.**

- **Out-of-pocket payments for healthcare expenses, which are made after the tax-exempt account is expended and before the deductible for high-deductible insurance has been met; this tier actually represents a gap in coverage.**

- **High-deductible insurance policy, which reimburses allowable healthcare expenses after the high deductible has been paid.**

CDHPs usually provide Internet-based support so individuals can track healthcare expenses, improve their health by viewing useful information and learning about preventive services, obtain information about provider quality, and receive notification about provider group-rate pricing. Various CDHPs are available to individuals (Table 3-3), all of which are subject to modification as legislation is passed and payers alter program requirements.

ACCREDITATION OF MANAGED CARE ORGANIZATIONS

The National Committee for Quality Assurance (NCQA) evaluates managed care organizations. **Accreditation** is a voluntary process that a healthcare facility or organization (e.g., hospital or managed care plan) undergoes to demonstrate that it has met standards beyond those required by law. Accreditation organizations develop standards (requirements) that are reviewed during a **survey** (evaluation) process that is conducted both offsite (e.g., managed care plan submits an initial document for review) and onsite (at the managed care plan's facilities).

National Committee for Quality Assurance (NCQA)

The **National Committee for Quality Assurance (NCQA)** of Washington, DC, is a private, not-for-profit organization that assesses the quality of managed care plans in the United States and releases the data to the public for consideration when selecting a managed care plan. The NCQA began accrediting managed care programs in 1991 when a need for consistent, independent information about the quality of care provided to patients was originally identified.

EFFECTS OF MANAGED CARE ON A PHYSICIAN'S PRACTICE

Managed care organizations (MCOs) impact a practice's administrative procedures by requiring

- **Separate bookkeeping systems for each capitated plan to ensure financial viability of the contract.**

- **A tracking system for preauthorization of specialty care and documented requests for receipt of the specialist's treatment plan or consultation report.**

- **Preauthorization and/or precertification for all hospitalizations and continued certification if the patient's condition requires extension of the number of authorized days.**

- **Up-to-date lists for referrals to participating healthcare providers, hospitals, and diagnostic test facilities used by the practice.**

- **Up-to-date lists of special administrative procedures required by each managed care plan contract.**

NOTE: Effective January 1, 2006, The Joint Commission (formerly called the Joint Commission on Accreditation of Healthcare Organizations, or JCAHO, pronounced jāy cō) discontinued its Network Accreditation Program for Managed Care Organizations. In July 2002, The Joint Commission approved its first National Patient Safety Goals, and annual national patient safety goals were published. The Joint Commission International Collaborating Center on Patient Safety was then established in 2005 to provide patient safety solutions to healthcare organizations.

TABLE 3-3   Types of consumer-directed health plans (CDHPs)

TYPE OF CDHP	DESCRIPTION
Customized sub-capitation plan (CSCP)	• Healthcare expenses are funded by insurance coverage; the individual selects one of each type of provider to create a customized network and pays the resulting customized insurance premium • Each provider is paid a fixed amount per month to provide only the care that an individual needs from that provider (sub-capitation payment) **NOTE:** In managed care, the primary care provider usually receives a *capitation payment* and is responsible for managing *all* of an individual's health care, which includes reimbursing other caregivers (e.g., specialists).
Flexible spending account (FSA)	• Tax-exempt accounts offered by employers to any number of employees, which individuals use to pay healthcare bills • Employees contribute funds to the FSA through a salary reduction agreement and withdraw funds to pay medical bills • Funds in an FSA are exempt from both income tax and Social Security tax (employers may also contribute to FSAs) • By law, employees forfeit unspent funds remaining in the FSA at the end of the year
Health savings account (HSA); health savings security account (HSSA)	• Participants enroll in a relatively inexpensive high-deductible insurance plan, and a tax-deductible savings account is opened to cover current and future medical expenses • Money deposited (and earnings) is tax-deferred, and money withdrawn to cover qualified medical expenses is tax-free • Money can be withdrawn for purposes other than healthcare expenses after payment of income tax plus a 15 percent penalty • Unused balances "roll over" from year to year and, if an employee changes jobs, he or she can continue to use the FSA to pay for qualified healthcare expenses
Healthcare reimbursement account (HCRA)	• Tax-exempt account used to pay for healthcare expenses • Individual decides, in advance, how much money to deposit in the HCRA (unused funds are forfeited)
Health reimbursement arrangement (HRA)	• Tax-exempt accounts offered by employers with more than 50 employees, which individuals use to pay healthcare bills • United States Treasury Department and Internal Revenue Service issued a tax guidance for HRAs in 2002 • Must be used for qualified healthcare expenses, require enrollment in a high-deductible insurance policy, and accumulate unspent money for future years • If an employee changes jobs, he or she can continue to use the HRA to pay for qualified healthcare expenses

- Up-to-date lists of patient copayments and fees for each managed care plan contract.
- Special patient interviews to ensure preauthorization and to explain out-of-network requirements if the patient is self-referring.
- Additional paperwork for specialists to complete and the filing of treatment and discharge plans.
- Some case managers who are employed by the MCO to monitor services provided to enrollees and to be notified if a patient fails to keep a preauthorized appointment.
- The attachment of preauthorization documentation to health insurance claims submitted to some MCOs.

NOTE: It is important to realize that managed care is an option many payers use to reimburse healthcare, as covered in Chapters 12–17.

SUMMARY

The financing of America's healthcare system has changed the way healthcare services are organized and delivered, as evidenced by a movement from traditional fee-for-service systems to managed care networks. These range from structured staff model HMOs to less structured preferred provider organizations (PPOs).

Currently, more than 60 million Americans are enrolled in some type of managed care program in response to regulatory initiatives affecting healthcare cost and quality.

A managed care organization (MCO) is responsible for the health of its enrollees, which can be administered by the MCO that serves as a health plan or contracts with a hospital, physician group, or health system.

Most managed care financing is achieved through a method called capitation, and enrollees are assigned to or select a primary care provider who serves as the patient's gatekeeper.

Federal legislation mandated that MCOs participate in quality assurance programs and other activities, including utilization management, case management, requirements for second surgical opinions, non-use of gag clauses in MCO contracts, and disclosure of any physician incentives.

Managed care is categorized according to six models: exclusive provider organizations, integrated delivery systems, health maintenance organizations, point-of-service plans, preferred provider organizations, and triple option plans.

Consumer-directed health plans (CDHPs) provide incentives for controlling healthcare expenses and give individuals an alternative to traditional health insurance and managed care coverage.

Accreditation organizations, such as the NCQA, evaluate MCOs according to pre-established standards.

INTERNET LINKS

- Great Plains Regional Medical Center
  Go to **www.gprmc-ok.com** and select the About GPRMC link to learn more about Dr. Shadid and the history of the Great Plains Regional Medical Center, a managed care system started in 1929.

- HealthEast
  Go to **www.healtheast.org** to view information about the HealthEast Care System, which is an integrated care delivery system that provides acute care, chronic care, senior services, community-based services, ambulatory/outpatient services, physician clinics, and preventive services.

- The Joint Commission
  Go to **www.jointcommission.org** to learn about The Joint Commission.

- The Joint Commission Quality Check
  Go to **www.qualitycheck.org**, and conduct a search to identify healthcare organizations that meet The Joint Commission's patient safety and quality standards.

- Kaiser Permanente
  Go to **www.kaiserpermanente.org** to learn about the history of the country's first HMO, Kaiser Permanente.

- National Committee for Quality Assurance (NCQA)
  Go to **www.ncqa.org** to learn about the NCQA.

- NCQA's Health Plan Report Card
  Go to **reportcard.ncqa.org,** and click the Health Insurance Plans link to use an interactive tool to create a customized report card of managed care plans.

STUDY CHECKLIST

- ☑ Read this textbook chapter and highlight key concepts.
- ☐ Create an index card for each key term.
- ☐ Access the chapter Internet links to learn more about concepts.
- ☐ Answer the chapter review questions, verifying answers with your instructor.
- ☐ Complete WebTutor assignments and take online quizzes.
- ☐ Complete Workbook chapter, verifying answers with your instructor.
- ☐ Complete the StudyWare activities to receive immediate feedback.
- ☐ Form a study group with classmates to discuss chapter concepts in preparation for an exam.

REVIEW

MULTIPLE CHOICE Select the most appropriate response.

1. **The intent of managed health care was to**
   a. dramatically improve the healthcare delivery system in the United States.
   b. have employees of a managed care organization provide patient care.
   c. replace fee-for-service plans with affordable, quality care to healthcare consumers.
   d. retrospectively reimburse patients for healthcare services provided.

2. **Which term best describes those who receive managed healthcare plan services?**
   a. employees
   b. enrollees
   c. payers
   d. providers

3. **The Medical Center received a $100,000 capitation payment in January to cover the healthcare costs of 150 managed care enrollees. By the following January, $80,000 had been expended to cover services provided. The remaining $20,000 is**
   a. distributed equally among the 150 enrollees.
   b. retained by the Medical Center as profit.
   c. submitted to the managed care organization.
   d. turned over to the federal government.

4. **A nonprofit organization that contracts with and acquires the clinical and business assets of physician practices is called a**
   a. medical foundation.
   b. Medicare risk program.
   c. physician-hospital organization.
   d. triple option plan.

5. **A _____ is responsible for supervising and coordinating healthcare services for enrollees.**
   a. case manager
   b. primary care provider
   c. third-party administrator
   d. utilization review manager

6. The term that describes requirements created by accreditation organizations is
   a. laws.
   b. mandates.
   c. regulations.
   d. standards.

MATCHING: Match the term with its definition.

   a. pre-admission review
   b. preauthorization
   c. concurrent review
   d. discharge planning

_____ 7. Arranging appropriate healthcare services for discharged patients.

_____ 8. Review for medical necessity of inpatient care prior to admission.

_____ 9. Review for medical necessity of tests/procedures ordered during inpatient hospitalization.

_____ 10. Grants prior approval for reimbursement of a healthcare service.

MATCHING: Match the type of managed care model with its definition.

   a. EPO
   b. IDS
   c. HMO
   d. POS
   e. PPO

_____ 11. Contracted network of healthcare providers that provide care to subscribers for a discounted fee.

_____ 12. Organization of affiliated providers' sites that offer joint healthcare services to subscribers.

_____ 13. Provides benefits to subscribers who are required to receive services from network providers.

_____ 14. Provides comprehensive healthcare services to voluntarily enrolled members on a prepaid basis.

_____ 15. Patients are free to use the managed care panel of providers or self-refer to non-managed care providers.

Processing an Insurance Claim

CHAPTER OUTLINE

Processing an Insurance Claim

Managing New Patients

Managing Established Patients

Managing Office Insurance Finances

Insurance Claim Life Cycle

Electronic Data Interchange (EDI)

Maintaining Insurance Claim Files

Credit and Collections

OBJECTIVES

Upon successful completion of this chapter, you should be able to:

1. Define key terms.
2. Describe the processing of an insurance claim.
3. Explain how patient records and claims processing for new and established patients differ.
4. Manage the office's insurance finances.
5. Discuss the life cycle of an insurance claim.
6. Maintain a medical practice's insurance claim files.
7. Explain the role of credit and collections in processing claims.

KEY TERMS

accept assignment
accounts receivable
accounts receivable aging report
accounts receivable management
allowed charges
ANSI ASC X12 standards
appeal
assignment of benefits
bad debt
beneficiary

birthday rule
chargemaster
claims adjudication
claims attachment
claims processing
claims submission
clean claim
clearinghouse
closed claim
coinsurance

common data file
Consumer Credit Protection Act of 1968
coordination of benefits (COB)
covered entity
day sheet
deductible
delinquent account
delinquent claim
delinquent claim cycle

downcoding

electronic data interchange (EDI)

electronic flat file format

electronic funds transfer (EFT)

Electronic Funds Transfer Act

Electronic Healthcare Network Accreditation Commission (EHNAC)

electronic media claim

electronic remittance advice (ERA)

encounter form

Equal Credit Opportunity Act

Fair Credit and Charge Card Disclosure Act

Fair Credit Billing Act

Fair Credit Reporting Act

Fair Debt Collection Practices Act (FDCPA)

guarantor

litigation

manual daily accounts receivable journal

noncovered benefit

nonparticipating provider (nonPAR)

open claim

out-of-pocket payment

outsource

participating provider (PAR)

past-due account

patient account record

patient ledger

pre-existing condition

primary insurance

Provider Remittance Notice (PRN)

source document

superbill

suspense

Truth in Lending Act

two-party check

unassigned claim

unauthorized service

unbundling

value-added network (VAN)

INTRODUCTION

This chapter provides an overview of the processing of a health insurance claim in the healthcare provider's office and the major steps taken to process that claim by the insurance company.

StudyWARE

Complete StudyWare practice quizzes and activities using the CD-ROM located inside the back cover of your textbook.

NOTE: To *accept assignment* is sometimes confused with **assignment of benefits**, which means the patient and/or insured authorizes the payer to reimburse the provider directly.

NOTE: During the insurance verification and eligibility process, patient payments are determined. During the check-in process, all copayments, coinsurance, and deductibles are collected.

PROCESSING AN INSURANCE CLAIM

The processing of an insurance claim is initiated when the patient contacts a healthcare provider's office and schedules an appointment. (Procedures for obtaining information on new and established patients are discussed next in this chapter.) The insurance claim used to report professional and technical services is known as the *CMS-1500 claim* (Figure 4-1). The provider's claim for payment is generated from information located on the patient's encounter form (or super-bill), ledger/account record, and source document (e.g., patient record or chart). Information from these documents is transferred to the CMS-1500 claim. Such information includes patient and insurance policy identification, codes and charges for procedures and/or services, and codes for diagnoses treated and/or managed during the encounter. (The selection of codes for procedures, services, and diagnoses is discussed in later chapters.) The CMS-1500 claim requires responses to standard questions pertaining to whether the patient's condition is related to employment, auto accident, or any other accident; additional insurance coverage; use of an outside laboratory; and whether the provider accepts assignment. To **accept assignment** means the provider agrees to accept what the insurance company allows or approves as payment in full for the claim. The patient is responsible for paying any copayment and/or coinsurance amounts.

Accounts Receivable Management

Accounts receivable management assists providers in the collection of appropriate reimbursement for services rendered, and includes the following functions:

- **Insurance verification and eligibility (confirming patient insurance plan and eligibility information with the third-party payer to determine the patient's financial responsibility for services rendered).**

1500

HEALTH INSURANCE CLAIM FORM

APPROVED BY NATIONAL UNIFORM CLAIM COMMITTE 08/05

CARRIER

| | PICA | | | | | | | | | | PICA | |

1. MEDICARE	MEDICAID	TRICARE CHAMPUS	CHAMPVA	GROUP HEALTH PLAN	FECA BLK LUNG	OTHER	1a. INSURED'S I.D. NUMBER	(For Program in Item 1)
(Medicare #)	(Medicaid #)	(Sponsor's SSN)	(Member ID#)	(SSN or ID)	(SSN)	(ID)		

2. PATIENT'S NAME (Last Name, First Name, Middle Initial)

3. PATIENT'S BIRTH DATE MM DD YY   SEX   M   F

4. INSURED'S NAME (Last Name, First Name, Middle Initial)

5. PATIENT'S ADDRESS (No., Street)

6. PATIENT'S RELATIONSHIP TO INSURED   Self   Spouse   Child   Other

7. INSURED'S ADDRESS (No., Street)

CITY   STATE

8. PATIENT STATUS   Single   Married   Other

CITY   STATE

ZIP CODE   TELEPHONE (Include Area Code) ( )

Employed   Full-Time Student   Part-Time Student

ZIP CODE   TELEPHONE (Include Area Code) ( )

9. OTHER INSURED'S NAME (Last Name, First Name, Middle Initial)

10. IS PATIENT'S CONDITION RELATED TO:

11. INSURED'S POLICY GROUP OR FECA NUMBER

a. OTHER INSURED'S POLICY OR GROUP NUMBER

a. EMPLOYMENT? (Current or Previous)   YES   NO

a. INSURED'S DATE OF BIRTH MM DD YY   SEX   M   F

b. OTHER INSURED'S DATE OF BIRTH MM DD YY   SEX   M   F

b. AUTO ACCIDENT?   PLACE (State)   YES   NO

b. EMPLOYER'S NAME OR SCHOOL NAME

c. EMPLOYER'S NAME OR SCHOOL NAME

c. OTHER ACCIDENT?   YES   NO

c. INSURANCE PLAN NAME OR PROGRAM NAME

d. INSURANCE PLAN NAME OR PROGRAM NAME

10d. RESERVED FOR LOCAL USE

d. IS THERE ANOTHER HEALTH BENEFIT PLAN?   YES   NO   *If yes,* return to and complete item 9 a-d.

READ BACK OF FORM BEFORE COMPLETING & SIGNING THIS FORM.

12. PATIENT'S OR AUTHORIZED PERSON'S SIGNATURE I authorize the release of any medical or other information necessary to process this claim. I also request payment of government benefits either to myself or to the party who accepts assignment below.

SIGNED _____   DATE _____

13. INSURED'S OR AUTHORIZED PERSON'S SIGNATURE I authorize payment of medical benefits to the undersigned physician or supplier for services described below.

SIGNED _____

PATIENT AND INSURED INFORMATION

| 14. DATE OF CURRENT: MM DD YY   ILLNESS (First symptom) OR INJURY (Accident) OR PREGNANCY (LMP) | 15. IF PATIENT HAS HAD SAME OR SIMILAR ILLNESS, GIVE FIRST DATE MM DD YY | 16. DATES PATIENT UNABLE TO WORK IN CURRENT OCCUPATION MM DD YY   TO   MM DD YY   FROM |

17. NAME OF REFERRING PROVIDER OR OTHER SOURCE

17a.

17b. NPI

18. HOSPITALIZATION DATES RELATED TO CURRENT SERVICES MM DD YY   TO   MM DD YY   FROM

19. RESERVED FOR LOCAL USE

20. OUTSIDE LAB?   YES   NO $ CHARGES

21. DIAGNOSIS OR NATURE OF ILLNESS OR INJURY (Relate Items 1, 2, 3 or 4 to Item 24E by Line)

1. _____ . _____
2. _____ . _____
3. _____ . _____
4. _____ . _____

22. MEDICAID RESUBMISSION CODE   ORIGINAL REF. NO.

23. PRIOR AUTHORIZATION NUMBER

24. A DATE(S) OF SERVICE From To MM DD YY MM DD YY	B. PLACE OF SERVICE	C. EMG	D. PROCEDURES, SERVICES, OR SUPPLIES (Explain Unusual Circumstances) CPT/HCPCS MODIFER	E. DIAGNOSIS POINTER	F. $ CHARGES	G. DAYS OR UNITS	H. EPSDT Family Plan	I. ID. QUAL.	J. RENDERING PROVIDER ID. #
1									NPI
2									NPI
3									NPI
4									NPI
5									NPI
6									NPI

PHYSICIAN OR SUPPLIER INFORMATION

25. FEDERAL TAX I.D. NUMBER   SSN   EIN

26. PATIENT'S ACCOUNT NO.

27. ACCEPT ASSIGNMENT? (For govt. claims, see back)   YES   NO

28. TOTAL CHARGE $

29. AMOUNT PAID $

30. BALANCE DUE $

31. SIGNATURE OF PHYSICIAN OR SUPPLIER INCLUDING DEGREES OR CREDENTIALS (I certify that the statements on the reverse apply to this bill and are made a part thereof.)

SIGNED _____   DATE _____

32. SERVICE FACILITY LOCATION INFORMATION

a. NPI   b.

33. BILLING PROVIDER INFO & PH # ( )

a. NPI   b.

NUCC Instruction Manual available at: www.nucc.org

APPROVED OMB-0938-0999 FORM CMS-1500 (08/05)

FIGURE 4-1 Blank CMS-1500 claim (For instructional use only) (Courtesy of the Centers for Medicare and Medicaid Services, www.cms.hhs.gov)

- Patient and family counseling about insurance and payment issues (assessing patient financial requirements; advising patients and families about insurance benefits, co-payments, and other financial obligations; resolving patient billing questions and complaints; adjusting accounts as necessary; and establishing financial arrangements for patients as necessary).

- Patient and family assistance with obtaining community resources (assisting patients in researching financial resources, housing, transportation, and medications and pharmaceutical supplies).

- Preauthorization of services (contacting third-party payers to obtain approval before services are provided, ensuring appropriate reimbursement).

- Capturing charges and posting payments (entering charges for services and procedures in the billing system, entering adjustments to patient accounts for payments received, generating balance receipts, reconciling daily work batches, preparing an audit trail, and preparing bank deposits).

- Billing and claims submission (completing, submitting, and processing CMS-1500 claims for payment; and researching and resolving claims payment delay issues).

- Account follow-up and payment resolution (reviewing explanation of benefits and remittance advice documents, contacting payers to resolve claims denials, resubmitting CMS-1500 claims, responding to payer and patient correspondence; following up on assigned accounts, and using collection techniques to maintain current accounts, including monitoring for delinquent payments).

NOTE: Health insurance plans may include an **out-of-pocket payment** provision, which usually has limits of $1,000 or $2,000. The physician's office manager must be familiar with the out-of-pocket payments provision of a patient's health insurance plan so that when the patient has reached the limit of an out-of-pocket payment for the year, appropriate patient reimbursement to the provider is determined. For example, if the health insurance plan's annual deductible has been met, the office staff no longer collects this out-of-pocket payment from the patient. The patient may still be responsible for another out-of-pocket provision, such as 20 percent of the cost for services or procedures performed. (Not all health insurance plans include an out-of-pocket payments provision.)

Health insurance plans may also include a *pre-existing conditions clause*, which is used to determine patient eligibility for coverage. If the patient was treated for a medical condition prior to the effective date of health insurance coverage, the health insurance plan will not pay benefits for that particular illness. Usually, the clause expires one year after the health insurance plan's effective date. This means that the health care provided to the patient for a pre-existing condition is then covered by the health insurance plan.

EXAMPLE: The patient's insurance plan has a $200 deductible, and just $100.00 has been met so far this year. The insurance specialist will inform the patient that the remaining deductible amount must be met (in addition to any copayments, coinsurance, and other out-of-pocket payments).

The patient's health insurance information is verified by the insurance specialist (or office manager) by calling the health insurance company and completing an "insurance verification form."

INSURANCE VERIFICATION FORM

Patient's Last Name, First Name, Middle Initial	Patient's DOB	Patient's Mailing Address
Insurance Specialist or Office Manager's Name	Date of Call	Physician's Name
Health Insurance Plan Name	Group No.	Health Insurance Policy Number
Health Insurance Plan Effective Date	PlanID	Health Insurance Plan Termination Date

Plan Type (circle one): PPO   HMO   Regular   Group   MC   Capitated   WC

$_____ Deductible Amount $_____ Amount not Satisfied $_____ Copayment Amount

Percentage of Reimbursement: _____% Coinsurance   ☐ Yes ☐ No Pre-existing Clause

List plan exclusions: _____

Name of plan representative: _____

Completing the CMS-1500 Claim

The health insurance specialist will also complete portions of the form that identify the type of insurance, patient's sex, patient's relationship to insured, and provider's federal tax identification number. The CMS-1500 claim includes several areas that require the signature of the patient and the provider. When submitting claims, "SIGNATURE ON FILE" can be substituted for the patient's signature (as long as the patient's signature is actually on file in the office). The completed claim is proofread and double-checked for accuracy (e.g., verification that a signature statement is on file, and so on). Any supporting documentation that has to be attached to the claim is copied from the patient's chart (e.g., operative report) or developed (e.g., letter delineating unlisted service provided, referred to in the CPT coding manual as a "special report").

MANAGING NEW PATIENTS

The interview and check-in procedure for a patient who is new to the provider's practice is more extensive than for a returning patient. The purpose of the new patient interview and check-in procedure is to obtain information, schedule the patient for an appointment, and generate a patient record. Basic office policies and procedures (e.g., copayments must be paid at the time of visit) should also be explained to each new patient.

STEP 1 Preregister the new patient who calls to schedule an appointment. After determining that the patient has contacted the appropriate office, obtain the following information:

- Patient's name (last, first, and middle initial).
- Home address and telephone number.
- Name of employer and employer's address and telephone number.
- Date of birth.
- Guarantor (person responsible for paying the charges).
- Social security number.
- Spouse's name, occupation, and place of employment.
- Referring provider's name.
- Emergency contact (e.g., relative), including address and telephone number.
- Health insurance information (so the claim can be processed).
  - Name and phone number of health insurance company
  - Name of policyholder (which is the person in whose name the insurance policy is issued)
  - Health insurance identification number, which is sometimes the policyholder's social security number (SSN)
  - Health insurance group number
  - Whether healthcare treatment must be preauthorized

Be sure to explain office policies regarding appointment cancellations, billing and collections (e.g., copayments are to be paid at the time of office visit), and health insurance filing. Patients may ask whether the provider participates in their health insurance plan. A **participating provider (PAR)** contracts with a health insurance plan and accepts whatever the plan pays for procedures or services

NOTE: The Privacy Act of 1974 prohibits payers from notifying providers about payment or rejection information on claims for which the provider did not accept assignment. Therefore, *providers who do not accept assignment of Medicare benefits do not receive a copy of the Medicare Summary Notice (MSN) information* (called a provider remittance notice, or PRN) that is sent to the Medicare beneficiary (patient). Information released to providers is limited to whether the claim was received, processed, and approved or denied. To assist in an appeal of a denied claim, the patient must furnish the nonparticipating provider with a copy of the MSN, and a letter signed by the patient must accompany the request for review. If the beneficiary writes the appeal, the provider must supply supporting documentation (e.g., copy of medical record).

NOTE: To increase office efficiency, mail new patients an information form to be completed and brought to the office 15 minutes prior to the scheduled appointment.

NOTE: Steps discussed in this chapter apply both to computerized and noncomputerized practices. The ✓ icon identifies steps completed for computerized practices.

NOTE: For a minor child, obtain the name, address, and signature of the parent or guardian.

NOTE: Be sure to instruct the patient to bring his or her health insurance card (Figure 4-2) to the appointment, because the office will need to make a copy of its front and back. The card contains the subscriber's insurance and group number, as well as payer telephone numbers and provider network information.

NOTE: The patient is responsible for copayments and/or deductibles, but does not pay more than the allowed negotiated charge.

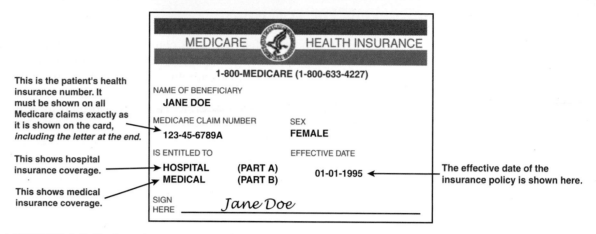

FIGURE 4-2 Medicare insurance card (Courtesy Delmar/Cengage Learning)

performed. PARs are not allowed to bill patients for the difference between the contracted rate and their normal fee.

A **nonparticipating provider (nonPAR)** (or out-of-network provider) does not contract with the insurance plan, and patients who elect to receive care from nonPARs will incur higher out-of-pocket expenses. The patient is usually expected to pay the difference between the insurance payment and the provider's fee.

In example 1, Dr. Smith collects $10 from the patient and is reimbursed a total of $40. In example 2, Dr. Jones collects $13 from the patient and is reimbursed a total of $50 (because he does not participate in the insurance plan and can collect the difference between his fee and the patient's coinsurance plus the insurance payment).

EXAMPLE 1:

Dr. Smith is a *participating provider (PAR)* for the ABC Health Insurance Plan. Kathe Bartron is treated by Dr. Smith in the office, for which a $50 fee is charged.

PAR provider fee	$50
PAR provider contracted rate (or allowable charge)	$40
Patient copayment	− $10
Insurance payment	$30
PAR provider write-off amount	$10

EXAMPLE 2:

Dr. Jones is a *nonparticipating provider (nonPAR)*. Lee Noffsker is treated by Dr. Jones in the office, for which a $50 fee is charged.

nonPAR provider fee	$50
Usual and customary rate (UCR)	$45
Patient copayment	− $8
Insurance payment	$37
nonPAR provider may bill patient	$5

MANAGED CARE ALERT!

Prior to scheduling an appointment with a specialist, a managed care patient must obtain a referral from the primary care provider (Figure 4-3) or case manager (i.e., preauthorization number is required). In addition, depending on the managed care plan, certain procedures and services must be preauthorized before the patient undergoes treatment.

Consultation Referral Form

Date of Referral:

Payer Information:

Name:

Address:

Patient Information:

Name (Last, First, MI)

Date of Birth (MM/DD/YYYY)   Phone:
(   )

Member #:

Site #:

Phone Number: (   )

Facsimile / Data #: (   )

Primary or Requesting Provider:

Name: (Last, First, MI)   Specialty:

Institution / Group Name: Provider ID #:   1   Provider ID #:   2 (If Required)

Address: (Street #, City, State, Zip)

Phone Number: (   )   Facsimile / Data Number: (   )

Consultant / Facility / Provider:

Name: (Last, First, MI)   Specialty:

Institution / Group Name: Provider ID #:   1   Provider ID #:   2 (if Required)

Address: (Street #, City, State, Zip)

Phone Number: (   )   Facsimile / Data Number: (   )

Referral Information:

Reason for Referral:

Brief History, Diagnosis and Test Results: _____

_____

Services Desired: Provide Care as indicated:

- ☐ Initial Consultation Only
- ☐ Diagnostic Test: (specify) _____
- ☐ Consultation with Specific Procedures: (specify) _____
  _____
- ☐ Specific Treatment: _____
- ☐ Global OB Care & Delivery
- ☐ Other: (explain) _____

Place of Service:

- ☐ Office
- ☐ Outpatient Medical/Surgical Center*
- ☐ Radiology   ☐ Laboratory
- ☐ Inpatient Hospital*
- ☐ Extended Care Facility*
- ☐ Other: (explain)
- *(Specific Facility Must be Named)

Number of visits: (If blank, 1 visit is assumed)	Authorization #: (If Required)	Referral is Valid Until: (Date) (See Payer Instructions)
Signature: (Individual Completing This Form)		Authorizing Signature (If Required)

Referral certification is not a guarantee of payment. Payment of benefits is subject to a member's eligibility on the date that the service is rendered and to any other contractual provisions of the plan.

White: Payer • Yellow: Primary or Requesting Provider • Pink: Consultant / Facility / Provider • Goldenrod: Patient

See Health Care Plan Manual For Specific Instructions.

FIGURE 4-3 Sample consultation referral form (Courtesy Delmar/Cengage Learning)

STEP 2 Upon arrival for the office appointment, have the patient complete a patient registration form (Figure 4-4).

NOTE: It is fraudulent for patients to withhold information about secondary health insurance coverage, and penalties may apply.

The patient registration form is used to create the patient's financial and medical records. Be sure to carefully review the completed form for identification, financial, and medical history information. Sometimes patients do not know how to answer a question or they feel that the requested information does not apply to

DOCTORS GROUP ¥ MAIN STREET ¥ ALFRED, NY 12345   **PATIENT REGISTRATION FORM**

PATIENT INFORMATION

Last Name	First Name	Middle Name

Street	City	State/Zip Code

Patient's Date of Birth	Social Security Number	Home Phone Number

Student Status
☐ Full-time   ☐ Part-time

Employment Status
☐ Full-time   ☐ Part-time   ☐ Unemployed

Marital Status
☐ Single   ☐ Married   ☐ Separated
☐ Divorced   ☐ Widowed

Sex   ☐ Male   ☐ Female

Name/Address of Employer

Occupation

Employer Phone Number	Referred by

Emergency Contact	Address	Telephone Number

Visit is related to on-the-job injury
☐ No   ☐ Yes   Date: _____

Prior treatment received for injury
☐ No   ☐ Yes   Doctor: _____   WC Number: _____

Visit is related to automobile accident   ☐ No   ☐ Yes   Date: _____   Name & Address of Insurance Company/Policy Number

GUARANTOR'S BILLING INFORMATION

Last Name	First Name	Middle Name

Street	City	State/Zip Code

Relationship to Patient	Social Security Number	Home Phone Number

Employer	Employer Address	Employer Phone Number

INSURANCE INFORMATION

PRIMARY INSURED INFORMATION   SECONDARY INSURED INFORMATION

Last Name	First Name/Middle Initial	Last Name	First Name/Middle Initial

Address	City/State/Zip Code	Address	City/State/Zip Code

Relationship to Insured   ☐ Self   ☐ Spouse   ☐ Child   ☐ Other   Relationship to Insured   ☐ Self   ☐ Spouse   ☐ Child   ☐ Other

Sex   ☐ Male ☐ Female   Sex   ☐ Male ☐ Female

Insured's Date of Birth	Home Phone Number	Insured's Date of Birth	Home Phone Number

Name and Address of Insurance Company		Name and Address of Insurance Company	

Insured Identification Number	Group Number	Effective Date	Insured Identification Number	Group Number	Effective Date

Name of Employer Sponsoring Plan	Name of Employer Sponsoring Plan

CONSENT TO PAYMENT

I have listed all health insurance plans from which I may receive benefits. I hereby authorize payment of medical benefits bill ed to my insurance to the Doctors Group. I hereby accept responsibility for payment for any service(s) provided to me that is not covered by my insurance. I also accept responsibility for fees that exceed the payment made by my insurance, if the Doctors Group does not participate with my insurance. I agree to pay all copayments, coinsurance, and deductibles at the time services are rendered. I, (Patient's Name), hereby authorize the Doctors Group to use and/or disclose my health information which specifically identifies me or which can reasonably be used to identify me to carry out my treatment, payment, and healthcare operations.

I understand that while this consent is voluntary, if I refuse to sign this consent, the Doctors Group can refuse to treat me.

I have been informed that the Doctors Group has prepared a notice ("Notice") that more fully describes the uses and disclosures that can be made of my individually identifiable health information for treatment, payment and healthcare operations. I understand that I have the right to review such Notice prior to signing this consent. I understand that I may revoke this consent at any time by notifying the Doctors Group, in writing, but if I revoke my consent, such revocation will not affect any actions that the Doctors Group took before receiving my revocation.

I understand that the Doctors Group has reserved the right to change his/her privacy practices and that I can obtain such changed notice upon request. I understand that I have the right to request that the Doctors Group restrict how my individually identifiable health information is used and/or disclosed to carry out treatment, payment or health operations. I understand that the Doctors Group does not have to agree to such restrictions, but that once such restrictions are agreed to, the Doctors Group must adhere to such restrictions.

_____   _____
Signature of Patient or Patient's Representative   Date

Printed Name of Patient: _____   Relationship of representative to patient: _____

FIGURE 4-4 Sample patient registration form (Courtesy Delmar/Cengage Learning)

their situation. If information is missing, be sure to interview the patient appropriately to complete the form.

NOTE: Generate a separate financial record and medical record for each patient to separately maintain each type of information.

STEP 3 Photocopy the front and back of the patient's insurance identification card(s), and file the copy in the patient's financial record.

STEP 4 Confirm the patient's insurance information and eligibility status by contacting the payer via telephone, Internet, or fax. (Payer contact information can be found on the insurance card.) Collect copayment from patient.

STEP 5 ✓ Enter all information using computer data entry software. Verify information with the patient or subscriber, and make appropriate changes.

NOTE: Per HIPAA privacy standards, when contacting the payer to verify insurance eligibility and benefit status, be prepared to provide the following information:

- Beneficiary last name and first initial.
- Beneficiary date of birth.
- Beneficiary health insurance claim number (HICN).
- Beneficiary gender.

When the patient has more than one policy, perform a coordination of benefits (COB) to be sure the patient has correctly determined which policy is primary, secondary, and so on. The determination of primary or secondary status for patients with two or more commercial policies is different for adults than for children.

- *Adult patient named as policyholder:* **The patient is the policyholder.**
- *Adult patient named as dependent on policy:* **The patient is a dependent on the insurance policy.**

> **EXAMPLE:** Mary Jones works for Alfred State College and is enrolled in the group health insurance's family plan. She is named as the primary policyholder on this plan. Her husband, Bill, is a full-time college student and is named as a dependent on Mary's health insurance plan. (Bill does not have other health insurance coverage.)

NOTE: Certain insurance plans are always considered primary to other plans (e.g., workers' compensation insurance is primary to an employee's group healthcare plan if the employee is injured on the job). These situations are discussed in Chapters 12 through 17.

- *Primary versus secondary insurance:* Primary insurance **is the insurance plan responsible for paying healthcare insurance claims first. Once the primary insurance is billed and pays the contracted amount (e.g., 80 percent of billed amount), the secondary plan is billed for the remainder, and so on.** *Group health insurance reimbursement cannot exceed the total cost of services rendered.*

> **EXAMPLE:** Cindy Thomas has two health insurance policies, a group insurance plan through her full-time employer and another group insurance plan through her husband's employer. Cindy's plan through her own employer is primary, and the plan through her husband's employer is secondary. When Cindy receives healthcare services at her doctor's office, the office first submits the insurance claim to Cindy's employer's health plan; once that health plan has paid, the insurance claim can be submitted to Cindy's secondary insurance (her husband's group insurance plan).
>
> **NOTE:** Total reimbursement cannot exceed the total charges for healthcare services rendered by Cindy's doctor.

- *Child of divorced parents:* **The custodial parent's plan is primary. If the parents are remarried, the custodial parent's plan is primary, the custodial stepparent's plan is secondary, and the noncustodial parent's plan is tertiary (third). An exception is made if a court order specifies that a particular parent must cover the child's medical expenses.**
- *Child living with both parents:* **If each parent subscribes to a different health insurance plan, the primary and secondary policies are determined by applying the birthday rule. Physician office staff must obtain the birth date of each policyholder because the** birthday rule **states that the policyholder whose birth month and day**

occurs earlier in the calendar year holds the primary policy for dependent children. The year of birth is not considered when applying the birthday rule determination. If the policyholders have identical birthdays, the policy in effect the longest is considered primary.

EXAMPLE 1: A child is listed as a dependent on both his father's and his mother's group policy. Which policy is primary?

    Mother—birthdate 03/06/59—works for IBM

    Father—birthdate 03/20/57—works for General Motors

Answer: Mother's policy is primary; her birthday is earlier in the calendar year.

EXAMPLE 2: A child is listed as a dependent on his father's group health insurance policy and his mother's group health insurance policy. The father was born on 01/01/1956, and the mother was born on 03/04/1945. Which policy is considered primary?

Answer: Father's policy is primary because his birthday is earlier in the calendar year.

EXAMPLE 3: A dependent child is covered by both parent group policies. The parents were born on the same day. Which policy is primary?

    Father's policy took effect 03/06/86

    Mother's policy took effect 09/06/92

Answer: Father's policy is primary because it has been in effect six years longer.

> **NOTE:** Determination of primary and secondary coverage involving one or more government-sponsored programs is discussed in detail in the respective Medicare, Medicaid, and TRICARE chapters.

- *Gender rule:* Some self-funded healthcare plans use the *gender rule*, which states that the father's plan is always primary when a child is covered by both parents. This provision can cause problems if one parent's coverage uses the *birthday rule* and the other uses the *gender rule*. Be sure to contact the health plan administrators to determine which rule to follow.

STEP 6 Create a new patient's medical record.

STEP 7 Generate the patient's encounter form (Figure 4-5).

> **NOTE:** At this point, clinical assessment and/or treatment of the patient is performed, after which the provider documents all current and pertinent diagnoses, services rendered, and special follow-up instructions on the encounter form. The medical record and encounter form are then returned to the employee responsible for checking out patients.

The **encounter form** (Figure 4-5) is the financial record source document used by healthcare providers and other personnel to record treated diagnoses and services rendered to the patient during the current encounter. In the physician's office, it is also called a **superbill**; in the hospital it is called a **chargemaster**. The minimum information entered on the form at this time is the date of service, patient's name, and balance due on the account.

Attach the encounter form to the front of the patient's medical record so that it is available for clinical staff when the patient is escorted to the treatment area.

If patient scheduling is performed on the computer, generate encounter forms for all patients scheduled on a given day by selecting the "print encounter forms" function from the computer program.

ENCOUNTER FORM

Tel: (101) 555-1111
Fax: (101) 555-2222

Kim Donaldson, M.D.
INTERNAL MEDICINE
101 Main Street, Suite A
Alfred NY 14802

EIN: 11-9876543
NPI: 1234567890

OFFICE VISITS	NEW	EST	OFFICE PROCEDURES		INJECTIONS	
☐ Level I	99201	99211	☐ EKG with interpretation	93000	☐ Influenza virus vaccine	90656
☐ Level II	99202	99212	☐ Oximetry with interpretation	94760	☐ Admin of Influenza vaccine	G0008
☐ Level III	99203	99213	**LABORATORY TESTS**		☐ Pneumococcal vaccine	90732
☐ Level IV	99204	99214	■ Blood, occult (feces)	82270	☐ Admin of pneumococcal vaccine	G0009
☐ Level V	99205	99215	☐ Skin test, Tb, intradermal (PPD)	86580	☐ Hepatitis B vaccine	90746
OFFICE CONSULTS (NEW or EST)			☐		☐ Admin of Hepatitis B vaccine	G0010
☐ Level I	99241		☐		☐ Tetanus toxoid vaccine	90703
☐ Level II	99242		☐		☐ Immunization administration	90471
☐ Level III	99243		☐		☐	
☐ Level IV	99244		☐		☐	
☐ Level V	99245		☐		☐	

DIAGNOSIS

☐ Abnormal heart sounds	785.3	☐ Chronic ischemic heart disease	414.9	☐ Hypertension	401.9
☐ Abnormal pain	789.0__	☐ Chronic obstructive lung disease	496	☐ Hormone replacement	V07.4
☐ Abnormal feces	787.7	☐ Congestive heart failure	428.0	☐ Hyperlipidemia	272.4
☐ Allergic rhinitis	477.9	☐ Cough	786.2	☐ Hyperthyroidism	242.9__
☐ Anemia, pernicious	281.0	☐ Depressive disorder	311	☐ Influenza	487.1
☐ Anxiety	300.0__	☐ Diabetes mellitus	250.____	☐ Loss of weight	783.21
☐ Asthma	493.9__	☐ Diarrhea	787.91	☐ Nausea	787.02
☐ Atrophy, cerebral	331.0	☐ Dizziness	780.4	☐ Nausea with vomiting	787.01
☐ B-12 deficiency	281.1	☐ Emphysema	492.8	☐ Pneumonia	486
☐ Back pain	724.5	☐ Fatigue and malaise	780.79	☐ Sore throat	462
☐ Bronchitis	490	☐ Fever	780.6	☐ Vaccine, hepatitis B	V05.3
☐ Cardiovascular disease	429.2	☐ Gastritis, atrophic	535.1__	☐ Vaccine, influenza	V04.81
☐ Cervicalgia	723.1	☐ Heartburn	787.1	☐ Vaccine, pneumococcus	V03.82
☐ Chest pain	786.5__	☐ Hematuria	599.70	☐ Vaccine, tetanus toxoid	V03.7
☐	____	☐	____	☐	____

PATIENT IDENTIFICATION		FINANCIAL TRANSACTION DATA	
PATIENT NAME:		INVOICE NO.	
PATIENT NUMBER:		ACCOUNT NO.	
DATE OF BIRTH:		TOTAL FOR SERVICE:	$
ENCOUNTER DATE		AMOUNT RECEIVED:	$
DATE OF SERVICE:	/ /	PAID BY:	☐ Cash ☐ Check ☐ Credit Card
RETURN VISIT DATE			
DATE OF RETURN VISIT:	/ /	CASHIER'S INITIALS:	

FIGURE 4-5 Sample encounter form (Courtesy Delmar/Cengage Learning)

MANAGING ESTABLISHED PATIENTS

STEP 1 Depending on the provider's plan of treatment, either schedule a return appointment when checking out the patient or when the patient contacts the office.

> **EXAMPLE:**
>
> In this example, a follow-up visit is scheduled only if the patient contacts the office.
>
> S: Patient states that her stomach hurts and she has been vomiting.
>
> O: Abdominal exam reveals mild tenderness. Her throat is red.
>
> A: Flu.
>
> P: Bed rest. Return to office if symptoms worsen.
>
> (SOAP notes are typically used in a provider's office to document patient visits. S = subjective, O = objective, A = assessment, and P = plan. SOAP notes are discussed in Chapter 10.)

MANAGED CARE ALERT!

Approximately one week prior to an appointment with a specialist for nonemergency services, the status of preauthorization for care must be verified. If the preauthorization has expired, the patient's nonemergency appointment may have to be postponed until the required treatment reports have been filed with the primary care provider or case manager and a new preauthorization for additional treatment has been obtained.

NOTE: Once the clinical assessment and/or treatment has been completed, the patient enters the postclinical phase of the visit. The services and diagnosis(es) are added to the encounter form, and the patient's medical record and encounter form are given to the employee responsible for checking out patients.

STEP 2 Verify the patient's registration information when the patient registers at the front desk.

As the cost of health care increases and competition for subscribers escalates among insurers, many employers who pay a portion of healthcare costs for their employees purchase health insurance contracts that cover only a three- or six-month period. Therefore, it is important to ask all returning patients if there have been any changes in their name, address, phone number, employer, or insurance plan. If the answer is yes, a new registration form should be completed and the computerized patient database should be updated.

STEP 3 Collect copayment from patient.

STEP 4 Generate an encounter form for the patient's current visit.

Attach the encounter form to the front of the patient's medical record so it is available for clinical staff when the patient is escorted to the treatment area.

MANAGING OFFICE INSURANCE FINANCES

The following procedures are the same for new and established patients.

STEP 1 Assign CPT and HCPCS level II (national) codes to procedures and services, and assign ICD-9-CM codes to diagnoses documented on the encounter form. (Coding is discussed in Chapters 6 through 8.)

> **CODING TIP:**
>
> Make sure that diagnoses, procedures, and services listed on the encounter form are documented in the patient's medical record before reporting codes on the insurance claim.

STEP 2 Enter charges for procedures and/or services performed on the encounter form (or in practice management software), and total the charges on the encounter form.

STEP 3 Post all charges to the patient's ledger/account record and the daily accounts receivable journal, either manually or using practice management software.

The **patient ledger** (Figure 4-6), known as the **patient account record** (Figure 4-7) in a computerized system, is a permanent record of all financial transactions between the patient and the practice. The charges, along with personal or third-party payments, are all posted on the patient's account.

Each procedure performed must be individually described and priced on the patient's ledger/account record.

The **manual daily accounts receivable journal**, also known as the **day sheet**, is a chronologic summary of all transactions posted to individual patient ledgers/accounts on a specific day (Figure 4-8).

BC/BS R2345678   STATEMENT   PATIENT, IMA

IMA PATIENT
900 RANDELL RD
ANYWHERE MD 20000

DATE	CODE	DESCRIPTION	CHARGE	CREDITS PAYMENTS	ADJ	CURRENT BALANCE
		BALANCE FOR WARD ⟶				30 –
5/23/YYYY		ROA per ck		30 –		0
6/25/YYYY	99213	OV copayment per check	38 –	15 –		0
6/25/YYYY		BCBS billed	23 –			23 –
8/1/YYYY		BCBS check		23 –		0 –

PLEASE PAY LAST AMOUNT IN THIS COLUMN ◆

OV — Office Visit	**HOSP** — Hospital Visit	**ROA** — Received on Account
OS — Office Surgery	**HS** — Hospital Surgery	**NC** — No Charge
TC — Telephone Consultation	**SA** — Surgical Assistant	**INS** — Insurance
FA — Failed Appointment	**SC** — Surgical Consultation	
RP — Report	**ER** — Emergency Room	

THIS IS A COPY OF YOUR ACCOUNT AS IT APPEARS ON YOUR LEDGER CARD

FIGURE 4-6 Sample patient ledger card (Courtesy Delmar/Cengage Learning)

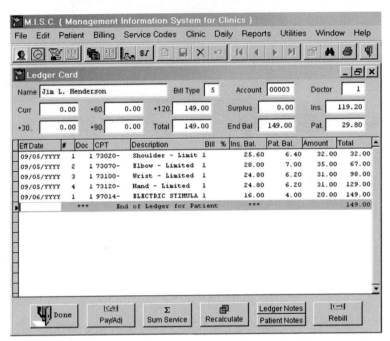

FIGURE 4-7 Sample patient account record generated from practice management software (Permission to reprint granted by DataCom Software Business Products.)

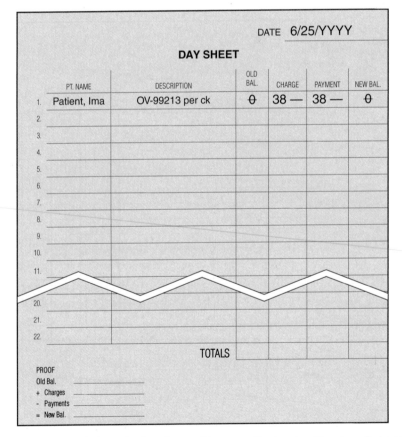

FIGURE 4-8 Sample day sheet with one patient entry (Courtesy Delmar/ Cengage Learning)

STEP 4 Bill the patient's insurance policy and then bill the patient for the coinsurance amount.

The patient's health insurance policy may stipulate a coinsurance payment (e.g., 20 percent of charges). Healthcare providers bill patients for copayment amounts after reimbursement from the third-party payer has been received and posted.

HINT:

To save the expense of mailing invoices, ask patients to pay their portion of the bill as they depart the office.

STEP 5 Post payment(s) to the patient's account.

The source of each payment should be identified, either as third-party payment (e.g., name of payer and payment type) or patient's payment (e.g., cash, check, credit card, money order, personal check). (Refer to the 5/23/YYYY entry in Figure 4-6.)

STEP 6 Complete the insurance claim.

STEP 7 Attach supporting documentation to the claim (e.g., copies of operative reports, pathology reports, and written authorization). ✓ For electronic claims, check with the payer to determine how to submit attachments (e.g., fax, postal mail, scanned image).

NOTE: In July 2000, federal electronic signature legislation was enacted. Physicians who contract with government and/or managed care plans are considered to have valid signatures on file.

STEP 8 Obtain the provider's signature on the claim, if manually processed. Special arrangements may be made with some payers to allow the provider's name to be keyboarded or a signature stamp to be used. No signature is possible on electronic claims.

STEP 9 File a copy of the claim and copies of the attachment(s) in the practice's insurance files. ✓ Electronic claims are stored in the computer.

STEP 10 Log completed claims in an insurance registry (Figure 4-9). Be sure to include the date the claim was filed with the insurance payer. ✓ For computerized claims processing, medical practice management software should generate a claims log.

STEP 11 Mail or electronically send the claims to the third-party payer.

INSURANCE CLAIMS REGISTRY

Date Filed	Patient Name	Insurance Company	Unusual Procedure Reported	Amount Due	Amount Paid
6/13/YYYY	Patient, Ima	BC/BS FEP	n/a	$ 38.00	

FIGURE 4-9 Insurance claim registry (Courtesy Delmar/Cengage Learning)

INSURANCE CLAIM LIFE CYCLE

The life cycle of a claim includes four stages (Figure 4-10):

- **Claims submission**
- **Claims processing**
- **Claims adjudication**
- **Payment**

> **NOTE:** Electronic data interchange (EDI) content is located in a separate heading within the Claims Submission section of this chapter.

For claims assigned a "pending status" by the payer, the provider can respond by correcting errors and omissions on the claim and resubmitting for reconsideration. When the claim is denied (or rejected), the provider can appeal the payer's decision and resubmit the claim for reconsideration, attaching supporting documentation to justify procedures or services provided.

Claims Submission

> **NOTE:** Providers can purchase software from a vendor, contract with a billing service or clearinghouse that will provide software or programming support, or use HIPAA-compliant free billing software that is supplied by Medicare administrative contractors.

> The American Medical Billing Association (AMBA) estimates that more than six billion insurance claims are filed each year (around 500 million claims each month) and just 40 percent are filed electronically. About 60 percent are filed manually (on a paper-based CMS-1500 claim). Medicare alone receives more than 500 million claims per year.

> **NOTE:** A healthcare clearinghouse performs centralized claims processing for providers and healthcare plans. They receive claims from providers, transmit claims to payers, receive remittance advice and payment instructions from payers, and transmit that information to providers (all in a HIPAA-compliant format). A healthcare clearinghouse also conducts eligibility and claim status queries in the format prescribed by HIPAA.

The life cycle of an insurance claim begins in the provider's office when the health insurance specialist completes CMS-1500 claims using medical management software. **Claims submission** is the electronic or manual transmission of claims data to payers or clearinghouses for processing. A **clearinghouse** is a public or private entity that processes or facilitates the processing of nonstandard data elements (e.g., paper claim) into standard data elements (e.g., electronic claim). Clearinghouses also convert standard transactions (e.g., electronic remittance advice) received from payers to nonstandard formats (e.g., remittance advice that looks like an explanation of benefits) so providers can read them. Clearinghouses use secure networks to receive and remit electronic transactions that flow among payers, providers, and employees. A **value-added network (VAN)** is a clearinghouse that involves value-added vendors, such as banks, in the processing of claims. Using a VAN is more efficient and less expensive for providers than managing their own systems to send and receive transactions directly from numerous entities.

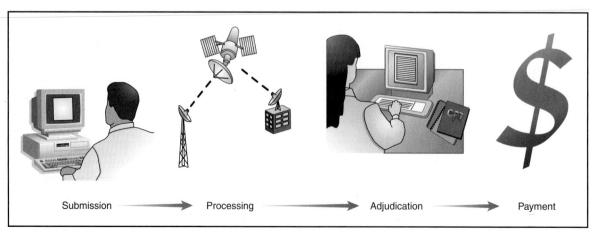

Submission   Processing   Adjudication   Payment

FIGURE 4-10 Life cycle of an insurance claim (Courtesy Delmar/Cengage Learning)

```
MSG_HDR|BCBS|ECM_Y06|SndApp|SndFac|RcApp|RcFac|YYYY01052369|56941
INS_CLM||||562697|YYYY0105|YYYY0110|ADLO5691|125.00
PRV_DT1|M_P|Smith|DKSL23659
PRV_DT1|M_H|Jones|DLEP65915
PAT_IDF|DCB5432|Green|19941205
CRD_STS|Y|Y|N
SRV_CMN|GM|YYYY0105|50.00
SRV_FEE|CP|45.00
SRV_FEE|CK|12.00
SRV_CMN|GM|YYYY0106|55.00
SRV_FEE|CO|10.00
SRV_FEE|RK|
```

FIGURE 4-11 Sample electronic flat file format (Courtesy Delmar/Cengage Learning)

When selecting a clearinghouse, it is important to determine which one processes a majority of claims for health plans billed by the provider. Although a provider might be able to contract with just one clearinghouse *if a health plan does not require submission of claims to a specific clearinghouse,* some plans have established their own clearinghouses, and providers must submit claims to them. Clearinghouses typically charge providers a start-up fee, a monthly flat fee, and/or a per-claim transaction fee based on volume. They also offer additional services, such as claims status tracking, insurance eligibility determination, and secondary billing services. (Providers may also want to determine whether a clearinghouse is accredited by the **Electronic Healthcare Network Accreditation Commission [EHNAC]**.)

Clearinghouses process claims in an electronic flat file format, which requires conversion of CMS-1500 claims data to a standard format. Providers can also use software to convert claims to an **electronic flat file format** (or **electronic media claim**) (Figure 4-11), which is a series of fixed-length records (e.g., 25 spaces for patient's name) submitted to payers as a bill for healthcare services.

ELECTRONIC DATA INTERCHANGE (EDI)

NOTE: ANSI ASC X12 is an electronic format standard that uses a variable length file format to process transactions for institutional, professional, dental, and drug claims. The ANSI organization facilitates the development of standards for health informatics and other industries (e.g., international exchange of goods and services).

Electronic data interchange (EDI) is the computer-to-computer transfer of data between providers and third-party payers (or providers and healthcare clearinghouses) in a data format agreed upon by sending and receiving parties. HIPAA's administrative simplification provisions directed the federal government to adopt national electronic standards for the automated transfer of certain healthcare data among healthcare payers (e.g., Medicare administrative contractors), payers (e.g., BCBS), and providers (e.g., hospitals, physicians). These provisions enable the entire healthcare industry to communicate electronic data using a single set of standards. Healthcare providers submit standard transactions for eligibility, authorization, referrals, claims, or attachments to any payer. This "simplifies" clinical, billing, and other financial applications and reduces costs. Three electronic formats are supported for healthcare claims transactions, including the following:

- UB-04 flat file format.
- National Standard Format (NSF).
- ANSI ASC X12 837 format (American National Standards Institute, Accredited Standards Committee, Insurance Subcommittee X12, claims validation table 837).

NOTE: Electronic claims data submission has almost entirely replaced the paper-based claims processing.

The Health Insurance Portability and Accountability Act of 1996 (HIPAA) mandated national standards for the electronic exchange of administrative and financial healthcare transactions (e.g., CMS-1500 claim) to improve the efficiency and effectiveness of the healthcare system. Standards were adopted for the following transactions:

- Eligibility for a health plan.
- Enrollment and disenrollment in a health plan.
- First report of injury.
- Healthcare payment and remittance advice.
- Health claim status.
- Health claims and equivalent encounter information.
- Health claims attachments.
- Health plan premium payments.
- Referral certification and authorization.
- Coordination of benefits (COB).

Covered entities (Figure 4-12) are required to use the standards when conducting any of the defined transactions covered under HIPAA. **Covered entities** include all private-sector health plans (excluding certain small self-administered health plans); managed care organizations; ERISA-covered health benefit plans (those covered by the Employee Retirement Income Security Act of 1974); government health plans (including Medicare, Medicaid, Military Health System for active duty and civilian personnel, Veterans Health Administration, and Indian Health Service programs); all healthcare clearinghouses; and all healthcare providers that choose to submit or receive these transactions electronically.

Implementation of the HIPAA healthcare transaction standards has caused concern among providers, especially small physician practices that are not computerized or do not currently submit electronic claims. It is important to understand that only those providers that submit electronic claims are required to

> **NOTE:** *Computer-generated paper claims are not considered electronic data interchange (EDI). Providers that generate paper-based claims submit them to healthcare clearinghouses, which convert them to a standardized electronic format for submission to payers.*

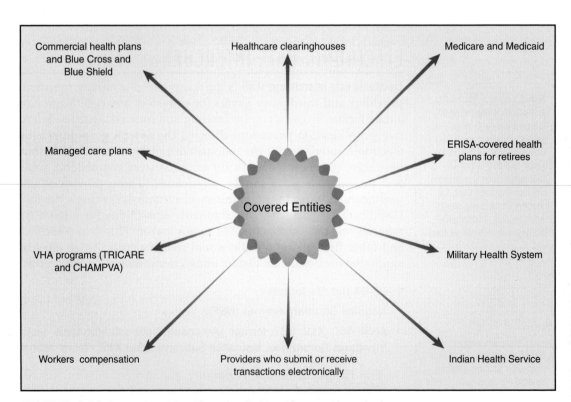

FIGURE 4-12 Covered entities (Courtesy Delmar/Cengage Learning)

comply with the transaction standards. If the provider's office uses paper CMS-1500 claims, that office can usually contracts with a healthcare clearinghouse to conduct standard electronic transactions for it. The administrative simplification provisions of HIPAA were passed with the support of the healthcare industry, which believed that standards would lower the cost and administrative burdens of health care. Industry members needed the federal government's help to establish a uniform way of processing transactions. In the past, providers had to submit transactions in whatever format the particular health plan required. Health plans could not agree on a standard without giving their competitors a (short-term) market advantage.

The American Medical Billing Association delineates the following advantages of electronic claims processing:

- **Reduction in payment turnaround time by shortening payment cycle.**
- **Reduction in claims submission error rates to 1 to 2 percent.**

Paper claims that can contain errors result in payment delays, and approximately 30 to 35 percent of all paper claims are rejected due to errors and omissions. Electronic claims are submitted directly to the payer after being checked for accuracy by billing software or a healthcare clearinghouse, and this audit/edit process reduces the normal rejection rate to 1 to 2 percent. The audit/edit process results in a **clean claim**, which contains all required data elements needed to process and pay the claim (e.g., valid diagnosis and procedure/service codes, modifiers, and so on). In addition, if an electronic claim is rejected due to an error or omission, the provider is notified more quickly than with paper claims, and the claim can be edited and resubmitted for processing.

Electronic claims are submitted using the following transmission media:

- *Dial-up* **(telephone line or digital subscriber line [DSL] is used for claims submission, and providers install software on office computers).**
- *Extranet* **(direct submission of claims to payers using Internet technology that emulates a system connection; provider can access information about collaborating parties only, such as payer and patient data elements).**
- *Internet* **(secure transmission of claims over the Internet, eliminating the need for additional software).**
- *Magnetic tape, disk, or compact disc media* **(physical movement of transmissions from one location to another using media).**

ELECTRONIC SUBMISSION OF MEDICARE CLAIMS BY PROVIDERS

The insurance claim is electronically transmitted in data "packets" (called batches) from the provider's computer modem to the Medicare administrative contractor's modem over a telephone line. Medicare administrative contractors perform a series of initial edits (called front-end edits or pre-edits), which determine whether the claims in a batch meet basic requirements of the HIPAA standard. If errors are detected at this level, the entire batch of claims is rejected and returned to the provider for correction and resubmission. Claims that pass initial edits are re-edited to compare data with implementation guide requirements in those HIPAA claim standards. If errors are detected at this level, individual claims containing errors are rejected and returned to the payer for correction and resubmission. Once the claim has passed the first two levels of edits, each claim undergoes a third editing process for compliance with Medicare coverage and payment policy requirements. Edits at this level could result in rejection of individual claims and be returned to the provider for correction. If individual claims are denied, the reason for the denial is communicated to the provider. Upon successful transmission of claims, an acknowledgement report is generated and either transmitted to the provider or placed in an electronic mailbox for downloading by the provider.

Claims Attachments

A claims attachment is a set of supporting documentation or information associated with a healthcare claim or patient encounter. Claims attachment information can be found in the remarks or notes fields of an electronic claim or paper-based claim forms. Claims attachments are used for

- Medical evaluation for payment.
- Past payment audit or review.
- Quality control to ensure access to care and quality of care.

> **NOTE:** Claims are sometimes delayed or rejected because the payer needs to obtain a copy of patient records for review prior to making a determination. In this situation, the provider is notified of the request for information and has an opportunity to submit supporting documentation from the record to justify the medical necessity of procedures or services performed. This delay in claims processing can sometimes be avoided if the practice contacts payers to request a list of CPT and HCPCS level II codes that require supporting documentation.

> **EXAMPLE:** CPT modifiers are reported on claims to provide clarification about procedures and services performed, and they are entered as two-digit numbers. Providers that submit supporting documentation when reporting the following modifiers on claims assist the payer in making payment determinations:
>
> - -22 (Unusual Procedural Services).
> - -53 (Discontinued Procedure).
> - -59 (Distinct Procedural Service).

> **EXAMPLE:** When a provider performs a procedure for which there is no CPT or HCPCS level II code and an unlisted code is reported on the claim, supporting documentation must be submitted (e.g., copy of operative report).

HIPAA ALERT!

Traditionally, claims attachments containing medical documentation that supported procedures and services reported on claims were copied from patient records and mailed to payers. Effective 2006, providers submit electronic attachments with electronic claims or send electronic attachments in response to requests for medical documentation to support claims submitted (e.g., scanned images of paper records).

How to Avoid Resubmitting Claims

In April 2002 the American Association of Health Plans (AAHP) and the National Specialty Society Insurance Coalition met with health plans and medical specialty societies to discuss claims submission concerns. A work group, which included representatives from health plans, the Healthcare Financial Management Association (HFMA), hospitals, and physician specialty organizations, was created to improve administrative processes and claims processing; among other things, the group identified ways that health plans and providers could improve claims submission processes. The result was the development of "tools & tips" documents that can assist health plans and providers to improve claims processing efficiency by decreasing duplicate, ineligible, and delayed claims.

Delayed claims contain incomplete and inaccurate information. Although hospitals and large group practices collect data about these problems and address them, smaller provider practices often do not have the tools to evaluate their claims submission processes. A major reason for delays in claims processing is incompleteness or inaccuracy of the information necessary to coordinate benefits among multiple payers. If the remittance advice from the primary payer is not attached to the claim submitted to the secondary payer, delays will also result. **Coordination of benefits (COB)** is a provision in group health insurance policies intended to keep multiple insurers from paying benefits covered by other policies; it also specifies that coverage will be provided in a specific sequence when more than one policy covers the claim. Some payers electronically transfer data to facilitate the coordination of benefits on a submitted claim. (Medicare calls this concept "crossover.") Becoming educated about how to correctly process claims for crossover patients will reduce payment delays and improve accounts receivable.

Claims Processing

Claims processing involves sorting claims upon submission to collect and verify information about the patient and provider (Figure 4-13). Clearinghouses and payers use software to automate the scanning and imaging functions associated with claims processing. Scanning technology "reads" the information reported on the claim and converts it to an image so that claims examiners can analyze, edit, and validate the data. The claims examiner views the image (or electronic data if submitted in that format) on a split computer screen (Figure 4-14) that contains the claim on the top half and information verification software on the bottom half.

Claims Adjudication

After the claim has been validated by the payer's claims examiner, it undergoes the **claims adjudication** process (Figure 4-15), in which the claim is compared to payer edits and the patient's health plan benefits to verify that the

- **Required information is available to process the claim.**
- **Claim is not a duplicate.**
- **Payer rules and procedures have been followed.**
- **Procedures performed or services provided are covered benefits.**

> **NOTE:** Edits and validation at the claims processing stage are limited to verification of insured status, patient identification number and demographic information, provider identification number, and the like. If analysis of the claim reveals incorrect or missing information that cannot be edited by the claims examination, the claim is rejected and returned to the provider. The provider can correct the errors and omissions and resubmit the claim for processing.

> **NOTE:** Patients can be billed for noncovered procedures but not for unauthorized services. Providers process denials of unauthorized services as a business loss.

The payer analyzes each claim for patient and policy identification and compares data with its computerized database. Claims are automatically rejected if the patient and subscriber names do not match exactly with names in the computerized database. Use of nicknames or typographical errors on claims will cause rejection and return, or delay in reimbursement to the provider, because the claim cannot be matched. Procedure and service codes reported on the claim are compared with the policy's master benefit list to determine if they are covered. Any procedure or service reported on the claim that is not included on the master benefit list is a **noncovered benefit**, and will result in denial (rejection) of the claim. This means that the patient's insurance plan will not reimburse the provider for having performed those procedures or services. Procedures and services provided to a patient without proper authorization from the payer, or that were not covered by a current authorization, are **unauthorized services**. This means that the payer requires the provider to obtain preauthorization before performing certain procedures and services, and because it was not obtained, the claim is denied (rejected).

MANAGED CARE ALERT!

For managed care claims, both procedures and dates of service are verified to ensure that the services performed were both preauthorized and performed within the preauthorized time frame.

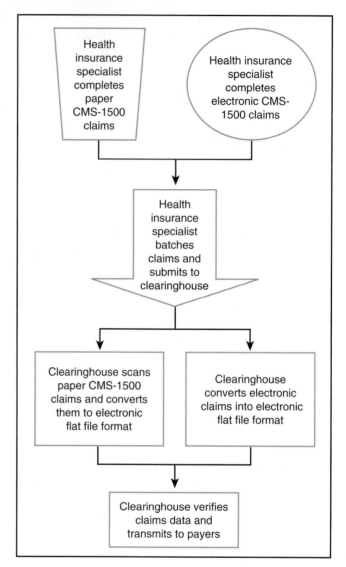

FIGURE 4-13 Claims submission and processing (Courtesy Delmar/Cengage Learning)

Insurance ID Number	First Name		Middle Initial		Last Name
123456789	Mary		S		Patient

Address					
2 Tiger Street					

City	State	Zip Code	Payer
Anywhere	NY	12345-1234	BCBS

Payer PlanID Number	Home Phone	Work Phone
987654321	(101) 111-1234	(101) 111-9876

FIGURE 4-14 Sample split screen viewed by claims examiner (Courtesy Delmar/Cengage Learning)

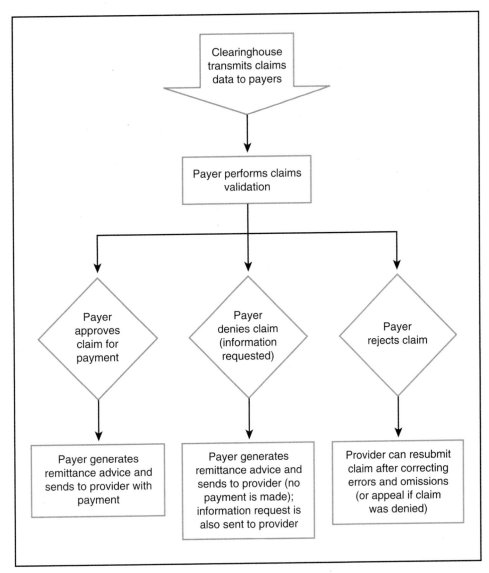

FIGURE 4-15 Claims adjudication and payment (Courtesy Delmar/Cengage Learning)

NOTE: Payers will identify a claim as a third-party liability responsibility based on review of codes. For example, submitting a claim on a patient who was injured in an automobile accident will trigger the payer to identify the automobile insurance as the primary payer on the claim.

The payer matches procedure and service codes (e.g., CPT) with diagnosis codes reported on the CMS-1500 claim to ensure the medical necessity of all procedures and services provided. Any procedure or service that is not medically necessary is denied. The claim is also checked against the **common data file**, which is an abstract of all recent claims filed on each patient. This process determines whether the patient is receiving concurrent care for the same condition by more than one provider, and it identifies services that are related to recent surgeries, hospitalizations, or liability coverage.

A determination is made as to **allowed charges**, which is the maximum amount the payer will allow for each procedure or service, according to the patient's policy. If no irregularity or inconsistency is found on the claim, the allowed charge for each covered procedure is determined. Allowed charges vary from policy to policy, and they are less than or equal to the fee charged by the provider. This means that payment is never greater than the fee submitted by the provider. A determination of the patient's annual deductible, copayment, and/or coinsurance amounts, is also made. The **deductible** is the total amount

NOTE: Physician claims are adjudicated by line item (not for total charges), which means that payers bundle and edit code numbers for individual procedures and services. Because rules and procedures vary among payers, what one payer bundles, another may not. In addition, payers routinely change the rules and procedures that affect coverage policies and reimbursement to the provider. Another concern is that payers often do not apply official coding guidelines for diagnosis and procedure/service coding. Thus, CPT and HCPCS level II codes reported on a claim are sometimes changed by the payer, affecting payment to the provider.

of covered medical expenses a policyholder must pay each year out-of-pocket before the insurance company is obligated to pay any benefits. A policyholder (or subscriber or **beneficiary**) is the person in whose name the insurance policy is issued. **Coinsurance** is the percentage the patient pays for covered services after the deductible has been met and the copayment has been paid. For example, with an 80/20 plan, the insurance company pays 80 percent and the patient pays 20 percent. A *copayment* (or *copay*) is the fixed amount the patient pays each time he or she receives healthcare services.

Once the claims adjudication process has been completed, the payer generates a remittance advice that contains information about payment, denials, and pending status of claims. If a claim is denied, the provider can appeal the decision by resubmitting the claim and attaching supporting documentation. Claims that are assigned pending status contain errors and omissions, and providers can correct those problems and resubmit the claim for processing.

> **EXAMPLE:** CPT contains laboratory panel codes (e.g., electrolyte panel), which bundle several laboratory tests into one code number. Some payers prefer to receive claims that contain individual code numbers for each laboratory test performed as part of the panel (e.g., carbon dioxide, chloride, potassium, and sodium). The payer's rationale is that a provider could order a series of tests and call it a panel, which is reimbursed at a higher rate than individual tests, even if not all of the panel tests were actually performed.

During the adjudication process, the status location of a claim can be monitored and providers can track claims within a health plan's internal claims processing, adjudication, and payment systems. (HIPAA standardized the status locations for all healthcare claims transactions.) Providers can even verify, through a batch transmission, the status of multiple claims. Providers can also verify patients' insurance coverage and eligibility for services, and they can find out when to expect reimbursement for claims processed.

> **EXAMPLE:** As part of Heather's job as a health insurance specialist for Dr. Miller's office, she queries the status of any claim that is 60 days or older. A typical onscreen display appears as follows:
>
> ```
> ABC1234 MEDICARE B ONLINE SYSTEM
> SC CLAIM SUMMARY INQUIRY
>
> HIC PROVIDER 123456 S/LOC TOB
> OPERATOR ID ABCDE FROM DATE TO DATE DDE SORT
> MEDICAL REVIEW SELECT
>
> HIC PROV/MRN S/LOC TOB ADM DT FRM DT THRU DT
> REC DT
> SEL LAST NAME FIRST INIT TOT CHG PROV REIMB PD DT
> CAN DT REAS NPC #DAYS
> 449999999A 179999 T B9997 131 0726YY 0726YY
> SMITH M R 250.00 F1
> ```
>
> Heather verifies that she is viewing the Medicare Part B claim status for M. R. Smith, a patient who was seen in the office on July 26, YY for a service that was billed for $250. She notes that the claim has been paid, which is the interpretation of the F1 code on the last line. Because Heather queried the status of the claim, thinking that it was 60 days or older, she will need to investigate whether the provider actually received the payment.

Payment of Claims

Once the adjudication process has been finalized, the claim is either denied or approved for payment. A remittance advice (Figure 4-16) is sent to the provider, and an explanation of benefits (EOB) (Figure 4-17) is mailed to the policyholder and/or patient. A remittance advice submitted to the provider electronically is called an **electronic remittance advice (ERA)**. It contains the same information as a paper-based remittance advice, but the provider receives ERAs more quickly. Providers use remittance advice information to process payments and adjustments to patient accounts. The remittance advice should be reviewed to make sure there are no processing errors (e.g., code changes, denial of benefits, and so on). (Patients should review EOBs to find out whether claims were paid; if denied, the patient should contact the provider's office to determine whether the claim was resubmitted, requested information was sent to the payer, and so on.) After reviewing the remittance advice and posting payments and adjustments, any code changes, denials, and partial payments should be followed up on. The payer may need additional information to make a determination about a claim, and prompt compliance with such requests will expedite payment.

> **NOTE:** Medicare calls the remittance advice a **Provider Remittance Notice (PRN)** and the explanation of benefits a Medicare Summary Notice (MSN).

It is common for payers to include multiple patients on one remittance advice and to send the provider one check for multiple claims. Providers also have the option of arranging for **electronic funds transfer (EFT)**, which means that payers deposit funds to the provider's account electronically.

```
From:                                          | To:
Medicare Administrative Contract # 09999       | Medicare Provider # 987ABC654
---------------------------------------------- | Medical Associates
EDI Exchange # 000000999                       | 100 Main Street
Jun 16, YYYY @ 9:00 AM                          | Suite B
EDI Receiver ID: PAYER                          | Alfred, NY 14802
```

Adjustment applied: $0.00
Payment of $200.00 by CHECK #999999 dated Jun 16, YYYY

Patient Ref #	12345SANDERS	Internal Control #	99S7654321
Patient Name:	Jane Sanders	Paid as:	PRIMARY
Patient HIC #	98765432	Claim Total:	$ 500.00
Date of Claim:	May 08, YYYY	Amount Paid:	$ 200.00

Service # 1

Date of Service:	May 08, YYYY	Allowable:	$ 200.00
Place of Service:	11	Deductible:	$ 0.00
Procedure Code:	10040	Coinsurance:	$ 0.00
Units:	1	Copayment:	$ 0.00
Charge:	$ 300.00	Paid:	$ 200.00
Provider ID:	987ABC654	Reasons:	Amount above fee schedule

Service # 2

Date of Service:	May 15, YYYY	Allowable:	$ 100.00
Place of Service:	11	Deductible:	$ 100.00
Procedure Code:	99213	Coinsurance:	$ 0.00
Units:	1	Copayment:	$ 0.00
Charge:	$ 200.00	Paid:	$ 0.00
Provider ID:	987ABC654	Reasons:	Deductible applies

FIGURE 4-16 Sample remittance advice for one patient (two office visits) (Courtesy Delmar/Cengage Learning)

THE KEYSTONE PLAN

P.O. BOX 900
ALFRED NY 14802-0900
(800) 555-9000

DATE: 04/05/YY
ID #: BLS123456789
ENROLLEE: MARY SUE PATIENT
CONTRACT: 300500
BENEFIT PLAN: STATE OF NEW YORK

MARY SUE PATIENT
100 MAIN ST
ALFRED NY 14802

EXPLANATION OF BENEFITS

SERVICE DETAIL

PATIENT/RELAT CLAIM NUMBER	PROVIDER/ SERVICE	DATE OF SERVICE	AMOUNT CHARGED	AMOUNT NOT COVERED	AMOUNT ALLOWED	COPAY/ DEDUCTIBLE	%	PLAN BENEFITS	REMARK CODE
ENROLLEE 5629587	D MILLER OFFICE VISITS	04/05/YYYY	40.25		40.25	8.00	100	32.25*	D1
						PLAN PAYS		32.25	

*THIS IS A COPY OF INFORMATION SENT TO THE PROVIDER. THANK YOU FOR USING THE PARTICIPATING PROVIDER PROGRAM.

REMARK CODE(S) LISTED BELOW ARE REFERENCED IN THE *SERVICE DETAIL* SECTION UNDER THE HEADING *REMARK CODE*
(D1)   THANK YOU FOR USING A NETWORK PROVIDER. WE HAVE APPLIED THE NETWORK CONTRACTED FEE. THE MEMBER IS NOT RESPONSIBLE FOR THE DIFFERENCE BETWEEN THE AMOUNT CHARGED AND THE AMOUNT ALLOWED BY THE CONTRACT.

BENEFIT PLAN PAYMENT SUMMARY INFORMATION
D MILLER $32.25

PATIENT NAME	MEDICAL/SURGICAL DEDUCTIBLE		MEDICAL/SURGICAL OUT OF POCKET		PHYSICAL MEDICINE DEDUCTIBLE	
	ANNUAL DEDUCT	YYYY YEAR TO-DATE	ANNUAL MAXIMUM	YYYY YEAR TO-DATE	ANNUAL DEDUCT	YYYY YEAR TO-DATE
ENROLLEE	$249.00	$0.00	$1804.00	$121.64	$250.00	$0.00

THIS CLAIM WAS PROCESSED IN ACCORDANCE WITH THE TERMS OF YOUR EMPLOYEE BENEFITS PLAN. IN THE EVENT THIS CLAIM HAS BEEN DENIED, IN WHOLE OR IN PART, A REQUEST FOR REVIEW MAY BE DIRECTED TO THE KEYSTONE PLAN AT THE ALFRED ADDRESS OR PHONE NUMBER SHOWN ABOVE. THE REQUEST FOR REVIEW MUST BE SUBMITTED WITHIN 60 DAYS AFTER THE CLAIM PAYMENT DATE, OR THE DATE OF THE NOTIFICATION OF DENIAL OF BENEFITS. WHEN REQUESTING A REVIEW, PLEASE STATE WHY YOU BELIEVE THE CLAIM DETERMINATION OR PRE-CERTIFICATION IMPROPERLY REDUCED OR DENIED YOUR BENEFITS. ALSO, SUBMIT ANY DATA OR COMMENTS TO SUPPORT THE APPEAL.

THIS IS NOT A BILL.

FIGURE 4-17 Sample explanation of benefits (EOB) (Courtesy Delmar/Cengage Learning)

INTERPRETING A REMITTANCE ADVICE (REMIT) AND AN EXPLANATION OF BENEFITS (EOB)

Third-party payers review submitted claims to determine whether services are covered by the patient's insurance plan (e.g., cosmetic surgery is usually not covered) and for coordination of benefits to determine which payer is responsible for reimbursement (e.g., services provided to a patient treated for a work-related injury are reimbursed by the employer's workers' compensation payer). Once a payer has completed the claims adjudication (decision-making) process, the claim is denied or approved for payment. The provider receives a remittance advice (remit), and the patient receives an explanation of benefits (EOB). (Some payers send providers an EOB instead of a remittance advice.) The remit and EOB each contains information about denied services, reimbursed services, and the patient's responsibility for payment (e.g., copayment). The remittance advice typically includes the following items:

- Third-party payer's name and contract number
- Electronic data interchange (EDI) information, including EDI exchange number, date and time remittance advice was generated, and EDI receive identifier
- Provider's name and mailing address
- Adjustments applied to the submitted claim (e.g., reduced payment, partial payment, zero payment, and so on)

- Amount and date of payment
- Patient's reference number, name and health insurance contract number, claim date, internal control number, paid status (e.g., primary, secondary, supplemental), claim total, and amount paid
- Date and place of service, procedure/service code, units, charge(s), provider identification number, allowable charges, deductible and coinsurance amounts, amount paid, and reasons (to explain payment amount)

The explanation of benefits typically includes the following items:

- Third-party payer's name, mailing address, and telephone number
- Date the EOB was generated, payer's identification number, contract number, and benefit plan
- Patient's name and mailing address
- Details of services reported on claim, including claim number, name of provider, date of service, amount charged, amount not covered by plan, amount allowed by plan, copayment and/or deductible amounts (that are the responsibility of the patient), amount paid under plan's benefits, and any remark codes (e.g., reason for denied claim).
- Benefit plan payment summary information, including provider's name and amount paid under plan's benefits
- Summary information about plan deductible and out-of-pocket amounts (paid by patient)
- Statement (at the bottom or top) that says THIS IS NOT A BILL

State Prompt Payment Laws and Regulations

The Prompt Payment Act of 1982 requires federal agencies to pay their bills on time or risk paying penalty fees if payments are late. Many states have also enacted prompt pay laws that apply to health insurance plans, requiring them to either pay or deny claims within a specified time frame (e.g., electronic claims must typically be paid within 30 days). In addition, many states apply penalty fees for late payments.

A federal regulation requires that Medicare Advantage organizations (previously called Medicare Choice, M+C, or Medicare Part C) make prompt payments for services provided by nonparticipating providers. Such organizations must pay 95 percent of clean claims within 30 days of submission, and the organization must pay interest on clean claims not paid within 30 days. (All other claims must be paid or denied within 60 days from the date of the receipt.)

Medicare claims must also be paid promptly by Medicare administrative contractors. Clean claims must be paid or denied within 30 days from receipt, and interest must be paid on claims that are paid after 30 days. The count starts on the day after the receipt date and ends on the date payment is made.

> **EXAMPLE:** For a clean claim received October 1 of this year and paid within 30 days, the requirement has been met.

OUT WITH THE OLD AND IN WITH THE NEW

The Old Days: Traditional Claims Processing

Payers receive health claim forms by mail, and they are opened, date-stamped, sorted, and grouped according to physician specialty. Data from the claim forms are keyed into a claims database, and the validity of the claim is determined. If valid, payment is mailed to the physician. If not valid, an exception report is printed, the claim is manually retrieved from the file system, and it is faxed to a review panel of physicians. The physician may receive a request for information from the payer so that further review can occur prior to approval for payment.

The New Way: Electronic Claims Processing

Paper claims are scanned for image archiving and sent to a database for electronic routing and processing. Tracking of claims is automated, and when a claim has to be retrieved for review, instead of searching through paper files, the image is quickly located and viewed onscreen or routed to a printer. Medicare is now enforcing mandatory submission of electronic claims, which means paper claims will be denied (except for those submitted by physician offices with fewer than 10 full-time equivalents, or FTEs).

MAINTAINING INSURANCE CLAIM FILES

> **NOTE:** Medicare *Conditions of Participation* require providers to maintain medical records for at least five years, and state retention laws are sometimes stricter (e.g., New York State requires medical records to be maintained for least six years).

CMS requires providers to retain copies of any government insurance claims and copies of all attachments filed by the provider for a period of six years (unless state law stipulates a longer period). (The provider could be audited during that period.)

CMS stipulated in March 1992 that providers and billing services filing claims electronically can comply with this federal regulation by retaining the financial **source document** (routing slip, charge slip, encounter form, or superbill) from which the insurance claim was generated. In addition, the provider should keep the e-mailed report of the summary of electronic claims received from the insurance company.

It is recommended that electronic and manual claim files be set up as follows:

> **NOTE:** If a patient requests a copy of the remittance advice received by the provider, all patient identification except that of the requesting patient must be removed.

1. **Open claims** are organized by month and insurance company and have been submitted to the payer, but processing is not complete. Open claims include those that were rejected due to an error or omission (because they must be reprocessed).

2. **Closed claims** are filed according to year and insurance company and include those for which all processing, including appeals, has been completed.

3. *Remittance advice files* are organized according to date of service because payers often report the results of insurance claims processed on different patients for the same date of service and provider. This mass report is called a *batched remittance advice.*

> **EXAMPLE:** Samantha Bartlett contacts the office to request a copy of the transmittal notice for her last date of service, explaining that she did not receive her copy. Because the information is on a batched remittance advice, the insurance specialist makes a copy of the page on which Samantha's information is found. Using the copy, the insurance specialist removes patients' information other than Samantha's, and mails the redacted (edited) copy to Samantha. The rest of the copy, which contains other patients' information, is shredded.

> **NOTE:** For offices that submit electronic claims, create folders on your computer to store these types of claims and files. Offices that submit manual claims should label folders according to the preceding guidelines, and file them in a secure filing cabinet.

4. **Unassigned claims** are organized by year and are generated for providers who do not accept assignment; the file includes all unassigned claims for which the provider is not obligated to perform any follow-up work.

Tracking Submitted Claims

CO-Pay

The insurance specialist is responsible for tracking insurance claims submitted to third-party payers and clearinghouses, ensuring that claims are processed and reimbursed in a timely manner. Effective claims tracking requires the following activities:

- Maintaining a paper or electronic copy of each submitted claim.
- Logging information about claims submitted in a paper-based insurance claims registry or by using medical practice management software.
- Reviewing the remittance advice (remit) to ensure that accurate reimbursement was received.

The remittance advice contains reason codes for "denied claims" (e.g., incorrect policy number, invalid CPT code), which are interpreted by the insurance specialist. If the claim was denied because the service is not covered by the payer, the claim is not resubmitted. (A bill is mailed to the patient, who receives an explanation of benefits from the payer that indicates the reason for the denial.) If the claim was denied due to errors, a corrected claim is submitted to the payer. The insurance specialist should carefully review the entire claim prior to resubmission, because processing of the original claim was halted by the payer (or clearinghouse) upon activation of a reason for denial. Other errors may exist in that claim, which need to be corrected prior to resubmission.

Remittance Advice Reconciliation

When the remittance advice and payment are received, retrieve the claim(s) and review and post payments to the patient accounts. Be sure to post the date payment was received, amount of payment, processing date, and any applicable transmittal notice number. Claims containing no errors are moved to the *closed claims* file. (Single-payment notices are attached to paper claims before filing in the *closed claims* file. Batched remittance advices are placed in the *batched remittance advice* file.)

Appeals Process

> **NOTE:** Medicare appeals are now called redeterminations or reconsiderations, per BIPA-mandated changes.

An **appeal** is documented as a letter (Figure 4-18) signed by the provider explaining why a claim should be reconsidered for payment. If appropriate, include copies of medical record documentation. Be sure the patient has signed a release-of-information authorization.

Appealing Denied Claims

> **NOTE:** When questioning the payer about a remittance advice that includes multiple patients, circle the pertinent patient information. Do not use a highlighter, because payer scanning equipment does not recognize highlighted information.

A remittance advice may indicate that payment was denied for a reason other than a processing error. The reasons for denials may include (1) procedure or service not medically necessary, (2) pre-existing condition not covered, (3) non-covered benefit, (4) termination of coverage, (5) failure to obtain preauthorization, (6) out-of-network provider used, or (7) lower level of care could have been provided. The following steps should be taken to appeal each type of denial.

> **NOTE:** If the medical record does not support medical necessity, discuss the case with the office manager and provider.

1. *Procedure or service not medically necessary:* The payer has determined that the procedure performed or service rendered was not medically necessary based on information submitted on the claim. To respond, first review the original source document (e.g., patient record) for the claim to determine whether significant diagnosis codes or other important information have been clearly documented or may have been overlooked.

Doctors Group
Main Street
Anywhere NY 12345
March 15, YYYY

Medicare B Review Department
P.O. Box 1001
Anywhere, US 12345

NAME OF PATIENT: _____
MEDICARE HICN*: _____
I do not agree with the determination you made on HICN* _____.

The reason I disagree with this determination is/are: (Check all that apply.)
☐ Service/Claim underpaid/reduced   ☐ Service/Claim overpaid   ☐ Service(s) overutilized
☐ Services not medically necessary   ☐ Duplicate claim submitted   ☐ Other: _____

Services in question are delineated as follows:

Date(s) of Service:	Quantity Billed:	Modifier:	Procedure Code(s):
_____	_____	_____	_____
_____	_____	_____	_____
_____	_____	_____	_____
_____	_____	_____	_____

Additional information to consider, including specific diagnosis, illness and/or condition:
_____
_____
_____

Attachments to consider: (Check all that apply)
☐ Medical Records   ☐ Ambulance Run Sheet   ☐ Copy of Claim   ☐ Certificate of Medical Necessity
☐ Other: _____

_____   _____
Signature of Claimant or Representative   Telephone Number

* HICN = Health Insurance Claim Number

FIGURE 4-18 Sample Medicare appeal letter (Courtesy Delmar/Cengage Learning)

Next, write an appeal letter to the payer providing the reasons the treatment is medically necessary.

> **NOTE:** A payer can cancel a patient's policy or deny payment on a claim if the patient failed to disclose a pre-existing condition. It is also likely that a payer would simply refuse to process the claim.

2. *Pre-existing condition:* The payer has denied this claim based on the wording of the pre-existing condition clause in the patient's insurance policy. A **pre-existing condition** is any medical condition that was diagnosed and/or treated within a specified period of time immediately preceding the enrollee's effective date of coverage. The wording associated with these clauses varies from policy to policy (e.g., length of time pre-existing condition clause applies). It is possible for an insurance company to cancel a policy (or at least deny payment on a claim) if the patient failed to disclose pre-existing conditions. Respond to this type of denial by determining whether the condition associated with treatment for which the claim was submitted was indeed pre-existing. If it is determined that an

incorrect diagnosis code was submitted on the original claim, for example, correct the claim and resubmit it for reconsideration of payment.

3. *Noncovered benefit:* The claim was denied based on a list developed by the insurance company that includes a description of items covered by the policy as well as those excluded. Excluded items may include procedures such as cosmetic surgery. Respond to this type of denial by determining whether the treatment submitted on the claim for payment is indeed excluded from coverage. If it is determined that an incorrect procedure code was submitted, for example, correct the claim and resubmit it for reconsideration of payment along with a copy of medical record documentation to support the code change.

4. *Termination of coverage:* The payer has denied this claim because the patient is no longer covered by the insurance policy. Respond to this type of denial by contacting the patient to determine appropriate coverage, and submit the claim accordingly. For example, a patient may have changed jobs and may no longer be covered by his former employer's health insurance plan. The office needs to obtain correct insurance payer information and submit a claim accordingly. This type of denial reinforces the need to interview patients about current address, telephone number, employment, and insurance coverage each time they come to the office for treatment.

5. *Failure to obtain preauthorization:* Many health plans require patients to call a toll-free number located on the insurance card to obtain prior authorization for particular treatments. Problems can arise during an emergency situation when there is a lack of communication between provider and health plan (payer), because treatment cannot be delayed while awaiting preauthorization. Although such a claim is usually paid, payment might be less and/or penalties may apply because preauthorization was not obtained. If failure to obtain preauthorization was due to a medical emergency, it is possible to have penalties waived. Respond to this situation by requesting a retrospective review of a claim, and be sure to submit information explaining special circumstances that might not be evident from review of the patient's chart.

EXAMPLE: The patient was admitted to the labor and delivery unit for an emergency cesarean section. The patient's EOB contained a $250 penalty notice (patient's responsibility) and a reduced payment to the provider (surgeon). The remittance advice stated that preauthorization for the surgical procedure (cesarean section) was not obtained. The provider appealed the claim, explaining the circumstances of the emergency surgery, and the payer waived the $250 penalty and reimbursed the provider at the regular rate.

6. *Out-of-network provider used:* The payer has denied payment because treatment was provided outside the provider network. Respond to this denial by writing a letter of appeal explaining why the patient sought treatment from outside the provider network (e.g., medical emergency when patient was out of town). Payment received could be reduced and penalties could also apply.

7. *Lower level of care could have been provided:* This type of denial applies when (a) care rendered on an inpatient basis is normally provided on an outpatient basis, (b) outpatient surgery could have been performed in a provider's office, or (c) skilled nursing care could have been performed by

a home health agency. Respond to this type of denial by writing a letter of appeal explaining why the higher level of care was required. Be prepared to forward copies of the patient's chart for review by the insurance payer.

CREDIT AND COLLECTIONS

Healthcare providers establish patient billing policies to routinely collect payments from patients that are due at the time services are delivered (e.g., copayments). Because most of a provider's fees are reimbursed by insurance plans, implementing consistent credit and collection practices is crucial to the operation of the organization.

Credit

Ideally, all payments are collected at the time the patient receives healthcare services. The reality is that alternate payment options are offered to patients (e.g., credit card billing, payment plans, and so on) to improve the organization's accounts receivable and reduce the need for collection practices. (Accounts receivable are the amounts owed to a business for services or goods provided.) If credit arrangements are available for patients, they must be consistently offered to all patients in accordance with the following federal laws:

- **Consumer Credit Protection Act of 1968** (or **Truth in Lending Act**) which requires providers to make certain written disclosures concerning all finance charges and related aspects of credit transactions (including disclosing finance charges expressed as an annual percentage rate).
- **Electronic Funds Transfer Act** which establishes the rights, liabilities, and responsibilities of participants in electronic fund transfer systems. Financial institutions are required to adopt certain practices respecting such matters as transaction accounting, preauthorized transfers, and error resolution. The act also sets liability limits for losses caused by unauthorized transfers. (This law applies to financial institutions that partner with providers to process electronic funds transfers.)
- **Equal Credit Opportunity Act** which prohibits discrimination on the basis of race, color, religion, national origin, sex, marital status, age, receipt of public assistance, or good-faith exercise of any rights under the Consumer Credit Protection Act.
- **Fair Credit and Charge Card Disclosure Act** which amended the Truth in Lending Act and requires credit and charge card issuers to provide certain disclosures in direct mail, telephone, and other applications and solicitations for open-end credit and charge accounts and under other circumstances (Figure 4-19). (This law applies to providers that accept credit cards.)
- **Fair Credit Billing Act** which amended the Truth in Lending Act and requires prompt written acknowledgment of consumer billing complaints and investigation of billing errors by creditors.
- **Fair Credit Reporting Act** which protects information collected by consumer reporting agencies such as credit bureaus, medical information companies, and tenant screening services. Organizations that provide information to consumer reporting agencies also have specific legal obligations, including the duty to investigate disputed information.
- **Fair Debt Collection Practices Act (FDCPA)** which states that third-party debt collectors are prohibited from employing deceptive or abusive conduct in the collection of consumer debts incurred for personal, family, or household purposes. Such collectors may not, for example, contact debtors at odd hours, subject them to repeated telephone calls, threaten legal action that is not actually contemplated, or reveal to other persons the existence of debts.

NOTE: The provider is also responsible for adhering to any state laws that affect credit and collection policies.

Forest Hills Medical Center
Forest Hills, NY 10001

TRUTH-IN-LENDING STATEMENT

Account Number _____   Date _____

Name of Patient (or Responsible Party) _____

Address _____

ANNUAL PERCENTAGE RATE (cost of your credit as a yearly rate)	FINANCE CHARGE (dollar amount credit will cost you)	AMOUNT FINANCED (amount of credit provided to you or on your behalf)	TOTAL OF PAYMENTS (amount you will have paid if you make all of the payments as scheduled)
_____ %	$ _____	$ _____	$ _____

Your payment schedule is as follows:

NUMBER OF PAYMENTS	AMOUNT OF PAYMENTS	WHEN PAYMENTS ARE DUE

Late Charge: If a payment is late, you may be charged $ _____

Repayment: If you pay off early, there will be no penalty.

Itemization of the amount financed of $ _____

$ _____ Amount given to you directly.

$ _____ Amount paid to the institution on your behalf.

I have received a copy of this statement.

_____
Signature of Patient (or Responsible Party)

FIGURE 4-19 Sample Truth-in-Lending statement (Courtesy Delmar/Cengage Learning)

Collections

As important as it is for a provider's employees to adhere to billing policies (e.g., verify current insurance information for each patient at the time of visit), following up on past-due accounts is crucial to the success of the business. A **past–due account** (or **delinquent account**) is one that has not been paid within a certain time frame (e.g., 120 days). Providers also track the status of **delinquent claims**, which have not been paid within a certain time frame (also about 120 days) (Table 4-1). The **delinquent claim cycle** advances through aging periods (e.g., 30 days, 60 days, 90 days, and so on), and providers typically focus internal recovery efforts on older delinquent claims (e.g., 120 days or more). As a result, many accounts in the earlier stages of the delinquency cycle are overlooked as they begin to age.

The best way to deal with delinquent claims is to prevent them by:

- Verifying health plan identification cards on all patients.
- Determining each patient's healthcare coverage (e.g., to ensure that a pre-existing condition is not submitted for reimbursement on the claim).
- Electronically submitting a *clean claim* that contains no errors.
- Contacting the payer to determine that the claim was received.
- Reviewing records to determine whether the claim was paid, denied, or is in **suspense** (pending) (e.g., subject to recovery of benefits paid in error on another patient's claim).
- Submitting supporting documentation requested by the payer to support the claim.

NOTE: Delinquent claims awaiting payer reimbursement are never outsourced. They are resolved with the payer.

NOTE: Payers establish time frames after which they will not process a claim, such as 180 days from the date of service. Once the claims submission date has passed, it is extremely difficult to obtain reimbursement from the payer, and *the provider is prohibited from billing the patient for payment.*

TABLE 4-1   Reasons to track claims

PROBLEM	DESCRIPTION
Coding errors	• Downcoding (assigning lower-level codes than documented in the record)
	• Incorrect code reported (e.g., incomplete code)
	• Incorrect coding system used (e.g., CPT code reported when HCPCS level II national code should have been reported)
	• Medical necessity does not correspond with procedure and service codes
	• Unbundling (submitting multiple CPT codes when just one code should have been submitted)
	NOTE: Unbundling is associated with the National Correct Coding Initiative (NCCI), which is further explained in Chapter 7 of this textbook.
	• Unspecified diagnosis codes are reported
Delinquent	• Payment is overdue, based on practice policy
Denied	• Medical coverage cancelled
	• Medical coverage lapsed beyond renewal date
	• Medical coverage policy issues prevent payment (e.g., pre-existing condition, noncovered benefit)
	• No-fault, personal injury protection (PIP), automobile insurance applies
	• Payer determines that services were not medically necessary
	• Procedure performed was experimental and therefore not reimbursable
	• Services should have been submitted to workers' compensation payer
	• Services were not preauthorized, as required under the health plan
	• Services were provided before medical coverage was in effect
Lost	• Claim was not received by payer
Overpayment	• Payer may apply offsets to future provider payments to recoup funds
	• Payer overpays provider's fee or managed care contract rate
	• Provider receives payment intended for patient
	• Provider receives duplicate payments from multiple payers
	• Payment is received on a claim not submitted by the provider
Payment errors	• Patient is paid directly by the payer when the provider should have been paid
	• Patient cashes a **two-party check** in error (check made out to both patient and provider)
Pending (suspense)	• Claim contains an error
	• Need for additional information
	• Review required by payer (e.g., high reimbursement, utilization management, complex procedures)
Rejected	• Also called *soft denials*
	• Claim contains a technical error (e.g., transposition of numbers, missing or incorrect data, duplicate charges or dates of service)
	• Payer instructions when submitting the claim were not followed
	• Resubmitted claim is returned (consider submitting a review request to payer)

> **NOTE:** Litigation (legal action) to recover a debt is usually a last resort for a medical practice. If legal action is taken, it usually occurs in small claims court where individuals can sue for money only without a lawyer. (Each state establishes limits for small claims, ranging from $2,000 to $25,000.)

To determine whether a claim is delinquent, generate an **accounts receivable aging report** (Figure 4-20), which shows the status (by date) of outstanding claims from each payer, as well as payments due from patients. At this point many practices **outsource** (contract out) delinquent accounts to a full-service collections agency that utilizes collection tactics, including written contacts and multiple calls from professional collectors. (Collection agencies are regulated by federal laws, such as the FDCPA, which specifies what a collection source may or may not do when pursuing payment of past-due accounts.) Agencies that collect past-due charges directly from patients can add a fee to the delinquent account balance *if the practice originally notified the patient that a fee would be added if the account was sent to an outside collection source for resolution.*

> **NOTE:** The *largest* past-due charges from the aging report are sent to collections first, followed by past-due charges in descending order. In Figure 4-20, the collections order would be MCD, BCBS, AG, and AETNA5.

An account receivable that cannot be collected by the provider or a collection agency is called a bad debt. To deduct a **bad debt**, the amount must have been previously included in the provider's income. Providers cannot deduct bad debts for money they expected to receive but did not (e.g., for money owed for services performed) because that amount was never included in their income.

1500 A/R Aging All
SOFTAID DEMO DATA
03/19/YYYY   16:11:34

Options
Entry Date 03/01/YYYY to 03/10/YYYY

Status Payer Code	Claim ID	Last Bill	Current	31 to 60	61 to 90	91 to 120	>120
CLAIM STATUS: PRIMARY							
AETNA OF CALIFORNIA – AETNA5						510	382-8563
PETERS, GEORGE 58698775501	135741	03/05/YYYY	160.00	0.00	0.00	0.00	0.00
AETNA OF CALIFORNIA			160.00	0.00	0.00	0.00	0.00
HOME HEALTH AGENCY – AG						958	855-4454
REYNOLDS, SAMUEL 56969885625	135740	03/04/YYYY	60.00	0.00	0.00	0.00	0.00
HOME HEALTH AGENCY			60.00	0.00	0.00	0.00	0.00
BLUE CROSS BLUE SHIELD OF FLOR – BCBS						305	336-3727
LANGE, MATTHEW 12536521588	135735	03/01/YYYY	160.00	0.00	0.00	0.00	0.00
MAJORS, MARTIN 56236598541	135736	03/01/YYYY	240.00	0.00	0.00	0.00	0.00
NEVERETT, WILLIAM 56213598471	135738	03/10/YYYY	80.00	0.00	0.00	0.00	0.00
SANDERS, JOHN 56236985214	135739	03/04/YYYY	113.00	0.00	0.00	0.00	0.00
BLUE CROSS BLUE SHIELD OF FLOR			593.00	0.00	0.00	0.00	0.00
TOTAL: PRIMARY			813.00	0.00	0.00	0.00	0.00
CLAIM STATUS: SECONDARY							
MEDICAID – MCD							
TINDER, VERONICA 52623659814	135737	03/03/YYYY	1,580.00	0.00	0.00	0.00	0.00
MEDICAID			1,580.00	0.00	0.00	0.00	0.00
TOTAL: SECONDARY			1,580.00	0.00	0.00	0.00	0.00

Current	31 to 60	61 to 90	91 to 120	>120	Grand Total
2,393.000	0.00	0.00	0.00	0.00	2,393.00
100.00%	0.00%	0.00%	0.00%	0.00%	

FIGURE 4-20 Sample accounts receivable aging report (Permission to reuse granted by Soft-Aid, Inc.)

EXAMPLE: An insurance company mails a check in the amount of $350 to the patient because the physician who treated the patient is a nonparticipating provider (nonPAR) for that health plan. The check is reimbursement for CRNA anesthesia services provided to the patient during outpatient surgery. The patient cashes the check and spends it on a weekend vacation. When he receives the bill for CRNA anesthesia services, he no longer has the money to pay it. That account becomes delinquent and is outsourced to a collection agency, which attempts to collect the payment. The collection agency is unable to obtain payment from the patient, and the amount is considered a "bad debt" for the provider's practice.

TEN STEPS TO AN EFFECTIVE COLLECTION PROCESS

Step 1: Call the patient within one week after providing services to determine patient satisfaction, and mention that an invoice for the outstanding balance is payable upon receipt.

Step 2: Mail a duplicate invoice ten days after the due date with "past due" stamped on it to alert the patient that the due date has passed.

Step 3: Mail a reminder letter with a duplicate invoice as the second overdue notice to remind the patient that the account needs attention.

Step 4: Make the first collection call, determine the reason for nonpayment, and obtain a promise to pay.

Step 5: Mail the first collection letter to the patient.

Step 6: Make the second collection call to the patient to request full payment, and obtain a promise to pay.

Step 7: Mail the second collection letter.

Step 8: Make the third collection phone call, and explain that the account will be submitted to a collection agency if payment is not made.

Step 9: Mail the final collection letter, and state that the account is being turned over to a collection agency.

Step 10: Submit the account to a collection agency.

State Insurance Regulators

Insurance is regulated by the individual states, not the federal government. State regulatory functions include registering insurance companies, overseeing compliance and penalty provisions of the state insurance code, supervising insurance company formation within the state, and monitoring the reinsurance market. State regulators ascertain that all authorized insurance companies meet and maintain financial, legal, and other requirements for doing business in the state. Regulators also license a number of insurance-related professionals, including agents, brokers, and adjusters.

If the practice has a complaint about an insurance claim, contact the state insurance regulatory agency (e.g., state insurance commission) for resolution. Although the commissioner will usually review a healthcare policy to determine whether the claims denial was based on legal provisions, the commissioner does not have legal authority to require a payer to reimburse a specific claim.

Improper Payments Information Act (IPIA) of 2002

IPIA legislated the Comprehensive Error Rate Testing (CERT) program, which was implemented in 2003 to assess and measure improper payments in the Medicare fee-for-service program. CERT produces a national *paid claims error rate,* which is used to target improvement efforts.

SUMMARY

The insurance claim used to report professional and technical services is called the CMS-1500 claim. The processing of an insurance claim begins when the new or established patient contacts the medical practice to schedule an appointment for health care. New patients should be pre-registered so that identification and health insurance information can be obtained prior to the scheduled office visit. Established patients are usually rescheduled at checkout of a current appointment.

The life cycle of a claim includes four stages: claims submission, claims processing, claims adjudication, and payment. Remittance advice reconciliation is an essential medical practice function that allows providers to determine the status of outstanding claims. Insurance claims processing problems arise as the result of a variety of issues, including coding errors, delinquent claims, denied claims, lost claims, overpayment, payment errors, pending (suspense) claims, and rejected claims.

INTERNET LINKS

- A.M. Best Company
  Go to **www.ambest.com,** locate the Popular Links heading, and click on the Support & Resources link. Then, scroll down and click on the State Insurance Regulators link to view a list of government regulators organized by state.

- HIPAA-Related Code Lists
  Go to **www.wpc-edi.com,** and click on HIPAA and then Code Lists to view healthcare EDI code lists (e.g., claim adjustment reason codes). The code lists contain narrative descriptions that assist in the interpretation of claims status data and information included on a remittance advice.

- Medicare Remit Easy Print (MREP) software
  Go to **www.cms.hhs.gov,** click on the Research, Statistics, Data and Systems link, click on the Access to CMS Data & Application link, and click on the Medicare Remit Easy Print (MREP) link to learn how to download the free (to Medicare providers and suppliers) software that is used to access and print remittance advice information, including special reports.

STUDY CHECKLIST

- ☐ Read this textbook chapter and highlight key concepts.
- ☐ Create an index card for each key term.
- ☐ Access the chapter Internet links to learn more about concepts.
- ☐ Answer the chapter review questions, verifying answers with your instructor.
- ☐ Complete WebTutor assignments and take online quizzes.
- ☐ Complete Workbook chapter, verifying answers with your instructor.
- ☐ Complete the StudyWare activities to receive immediate feedback.
- ☐ Form a study group with classmates to discuss chapter concepts in preparation for an exam.

REVIEW

MULTIPLE CHOICE Select the most appropriate response.

1. **Which means that the patient and/or insured has authorized the payer to reimburse the provider directly?**
   a. accept assignment
   b. assignment of benefits
   c. coordination of benefits
   d. medical necessity

2. **Providers who do not accept assignment of Medicare benefits do not receive information included on the _____, which is sent to the patient.**
   a. electronic flat file
   b. encounter form
   c. ledger
   d. Medicare Summary Notice

3. **The transmission of claims data to payers or clearinghouses is called claims**
   a. adjudication.
   b. assignment.
   c. processing.
   d. submission.

4. **Which facilitates processing of nonstandard claims data elements into standard data elements?**
   a. clearinghouse
   b. EHNAC
   c. payer
   d. provider

5. **A series of fixed-length records submitted to payers to bill for healthcare services is an electronic**
   a. flat file format.
   b. funds transfer.
   c. remittance advice.
   d. source document.

6. **Which is considered a covered entity?**
   a. EHNAC, which accredits clearinghouses
   b. private-sector payers that process electronic claims
   c. provider that submits paper-based CMS-1500 claims
   d. small self-administered health plan that processes manual claims

7. **A claim that is rejected because of an error or omission is considered a(n)**
   a. clean claim.
   b. closed claim.
   c. delinquent claim.
   d. open claim.

8. **An electronic claim is submitted using _____ as its transmission media.**
   a. facsimile machine
   b. magnetic tape
   c. scanning device
   d. software that prints claims

9. **Which supporting documentation is associated with submission of an insurance claim?**
   a. accounts receivable aging report
   b. claims attachment
   c. common data file
   d. electronic remittance advice

10. **Which is a group health insurance policy provision that prevents multiple payers from reimbursing benefits covered by other policies?**

    a. accept assignment

    b. assignment of benefits

    c. coordination of benefits

    d. pre-existing condition

11. **The sorting of claims upon submission to collect and verify information about the patient and provider is called claims**

    a. adjudication.

    b. authorization.

    c. processing.

    d. submission.

12. **Which of the following steps would occur first?**

    a. Clearinghouse converts electronic claims into electronic flat file format.

    b. Clearinghouse verifies claims data and transmits to payers.

    c. Health insurance specialist batches and submits claims to clearinghouse.

    d. Health insurance specialist completes electronic or paper-based claim.

13. **Comparing the claim to payer edits and the patient's health plan benefits is part of claims**

    a. adjudication.

    b. processing.

    c. submission.

    d. transmission.

14. **Which describes any procedure or service reported on a claim that is not included on the payer's master benefit list?**

    a. medically unnecessary

    b. noncovered benefit

    c. pre-existing condition

    d. unauthorized service

15. **Which is an abstract of all recent claims filed on each patient, used by the payer to determine whether the patient is receiving concurrent care for the same condition by more than one provider?**

    a. common data file

    b. encounter form

    c. patient ledger

    d. remittance advice

16. **Which is the fixed amount patients pay each time they receive healthcare services?**

    a. coinsurance

    b. copayment

    c. deductible

    d. insurance

17. **Which of the following steps would occur first?**

    a. Clearinghouse transmits claims data to payers.

    b. Payer approves claim for payment.

    c. Payer generates remittance advice.

    d. Payer performs claims validation.

18. **Which must accept whatever a payer reimburses for procedures or services performed?**
    a. nonparticipating provider
    b. out-of-network provider
    c. participating provider
    d. value-added provider

19. **Which is an interpretation of the birthday rule regarding two group health insurance policies when the parents of a child covered on both policies are married to each other and live in the same household?**
    a. The parent whose birth month and day occurs earlier in the calendar year is the primary policyholder.
    b. The parent who was born first is the primary policyholder.
    c. Both parents are primary policyholders.
    d. The parent whose income is higher is the primary policyholder.

20. **Which is the financial record source document usually generated by a hospital?**
    a. chargemaster
    b. day sheet
    c. encounter form
    d. superbill

21. **Refer to Figure 4-20 in this chapter. Which payer's claim should be followed up first to obtain reimbursement?**
    a. Aetna of California
    b. Blue Cross Blue Shield of Florida
    c. Home Health Agency
    d. Medicaid

22. **Which requires providers to make certain written disclosures concerning all finance charges and related aspects of credit transactions?**
    a. Equal Credit Opportunity Act
    b. Fair Credit Reporting Act
    c. Fair Debt Collection Practices Act
    d. Truth in Lending Act

23. **Which protects information collected by consumer reporting agencies?**
    a. Equal Credit Opportunity Act
    b. Fair Credit Reporting Act
    c. Fair Debt Collection Practices Act
    d. Truth in Lending Act

24. **Which is the best way to prevent delinquent claims?**
    a. Attach supporting medical documentation on all claims.
    b. Enter all claims data in the practice's suspense file.
    c. Submit closed claims to all third-party payers.
    d. Verify health plan identification information on all patients.

25. **Which is a characteristic of delinquent commercial claims awaiting payer reimbursement?**
    a. Delinquent claims are outsourced to a collection agency.
    b. The delinquent claims are resolved directly with the payer.
    c. The accounts receivable aging report was not submitted.
    d. The provided remittance notice was delayed by the payer.

Legal and Regulatory Issues

CHAPTER OUTLINE

Introduction to Legal and Regulatory
Considerations

Federal Laws and Events That Affect
Health Care

Retention of Records

Health Insurance Portability and
Accountability Act (HIPAA)

OBJECTIVES

Upon successful completion of this chapter, you should be able to:

1. Define key terms.
2. Provide examples of a statute, regulation, and case law, and explain the use of the *Federal Register*.
3. Summarize federal legislation and regulations affecting health care.
4. Explain retention of records laws.
5. List and explain HIPAA's provisions.

KEY TERMS

abuse
ANSI ASC X12N 837
authorization
black box edit
breach of confidentiality
case law
Comprehensive Error Rate Testing
(CERT) program
check digit
civil law
Clinical Data Abstracting Center (CDAC)
code pairs
common law

confidentiality
criminal law
Current Dental Terminology (CDT)
decrypt
Deficit Reduction Act of 2005
deposition
digital
edit pairs
electronic transaction standards
encrypt
False Claims Act (FCA)
Federal Claims Collection Act

Federal Register
First-look Analysis for Hospital Outlier
Monitoring (FATHOM)
fraud
Hospital Payment Monitoring Program
(HPMP)
Improper Payments Information Act of
2002 (IPIA)
interrogatory
listserv
Medicaid Integrity Program (MIP)
medically unlikely edits (MUEs)
Medicare administrative contractor (MAC)

message digest
modifier
National Drug Code (NDC)
National Health PlanID
    (PlanID)
National Individual Identifier
National Plan and Provider
    Enumeration System
    (NPPES)
National Provider Identifier
    (NPI)
National Standard Employer
    Identification Number
    (EIN)
National Standard Format (NSF)
overpayment
Patient Safety and Quality
    Improvement Act
Payment Error Prevention
    Program (PEPP)

payment error rate
Payment Error Rate
    Measurement (PERM)
    program
physician self-referral law
Physicians at Teaching
    Hospitals (PATH)
precedent
privacy
Privacy Act of 1974
privacy rule
privileged communication
Program for Evaluating
    Payment Patterns
    Electronic Report (PEPPER)
Program Safeguard Contracts
    (PSCs)
program transmittal
protected health information
    (PHI)

qui tam
record retention
Recovery Audit Contractor
    (RAC) program
regulations
security
security rule
Stark I
statute
statutory law
subpoena
subpoena duces tecum
Tax Relief and Health Care
    Act of 2006 (TRHCA)
UB-04
unique bit string
upcoding
Zone Program Integrity
    Contractor (ZPIC)

INTRODUCTION

The health insurance specialist must be knowledgeable about laws and regulations for maintaining patient records and processing health insurance claims. This chapter defines legal and regulatory terminology and summarizes laws and regulations that affect health insurance processing. Internet links are also included as a resource for remaining up to date and obtaining clarification of legal and regulatory issues.

Complete StudyWare practice quizzes and activities using the CD-ROM located inside the back cover of your textbook.

INTRODUCTION TO LEGAL AND REGULATORY CONSIDERATIONS

Federal and state **statutes** (or **statutory law**) are laws passed by legislative bodies (e.g., federal Congress and state legislatures). These laws are then implemented as **regulations**, which are guidelines written by administrative agencies (e.g., CMS). **Case law** (or **common law**) is based on court decisions that establish a **precedent** (or standard).

Federal laws and regulations affect health care in that they govern programs such as Medicare, Medicaid, TRICARE, and the Federal Employees Health Benefit Plans (FEHBP). State laws regulate insurance companies, recordkeeping practices, and provider licensing. State insurance departments determine coverage issues for insurance policies (contracts) and state workers' compensation plans.

Civil law deals with all areas of the law that are not classified as criminal. **Criminal law** is public law (statute or ordinance) that defines crimes and their prosecution. A **subpoena** is an order of the court that requires a witness to appear at a particular time and place to testify. A **subpoena duces tecum** requires documents (e.g., patient record) to be produced. A subpoena is used to obtain witness testimony at trial and at **deposition**, which is testimony under oath taken outside of court (e.g., at the provider's office). In civil cases (e.g., malpractice), the provider might be required to complete an **interrogatory**, which is a document containing a list of questions that must be answered in writing.

Qui tam is an abbreviation for the Latin phrase *qui tam pro domino rege quam pro sic ipso in hoc parte sequitur*, meaning "who as well for the king as for himself sues in this matter." It is a provision of the Federal False Claims Act, which allows a private citizen to file a lawsuit in the name of the U.S. government, charging fraud by government contractors and other entities that receive or use government funds, and to share in any money recovered. Common defendants in *qui tam* actions involving Medicare/Medicaid fraud include physicians, hospitals, HMOs, and clinics.

To accurately process health insurance claims, especially for government programs like Medicare and Medicaid, you should become familiar with the *Code of Federal Regulations* (Figure 5-1). Providers and health insurance specialists can locate legal and regulatory issues found in such publications as the *Federal Register* and *Medicare Bulletin*. The *Federal Register* (Figure 5-2) is a legal newspaper published every business day by the National Archives and Records Administration (NARA). It is available in paper form, on microfiche, and online.

EXAMPLE 1: FEDERAL STATUTE, IMPLEMENTED AS STATE PROGRAM

Congress passed Title XXI of the Social Security Act as part of the Balanced Budget Act of 1997, which called for implementation of the State Children's Health Insurance Program. In response, New York implemented Child Health Plus, which expanded insurance eligibility to children under age 19 who are not eligible for Medicaid and have limited or no health insurance. Even if family income is high, children can be eligible to enroll in Child Health Plus; an insurance premium in the form of a monthly family contribution may be required (e.g., a family of two with an income ranging from $24,977 to $25,920 pays $15 per month per child).

Title 42--Public Health

CHAPTER IV--CENTERS FOR MEDICARE & MEDICAID SERVICES, DEPARTMENT OF HEALTH AND HUMAN SERVICES

PART 405--FEDERAL HEALTH INSURANCE FOR THE AGED AND DISABLED

405.201	Scope of subpart and definitions.
405.203	FDA categorization of investigational devices.
405.205	Coverage of a non-experimental/investigational (Category B) device.
405.207	Services related to a noncovered device.
405.209	Payment for a non-experimental/investigational (Category B) device.
405.211	Procedures for Medicare contractors in making coverage decisions for a non-experimental/investigational (Category B) device.
405.213	Re-evaluation of a device categorization.
405.215	Confidential commercial and trade secret information.
405.301	Scope of subpart.
405.350	Individual's liability for payments made to providers and other persons for items and services furnished the individual.
405.351	Incorrect payments for which the individual is not liable.

FIGURE 5-1 Portion of table of contents from *Code of Federal Regulations*, Title 42, Public Health, Chapter IV, Centers for Medicare & Medicaid Services (Reprinted according to National Archives and Records Administration permissions notice.)

69840   Federal Register/Vol. 68, No. 240/Monday, December 15, 2003/Rules and Regulations

DEPARTMENT OF HEALTH AND HUMAN SERVICES

Centers for Medicare & Medicaid Services

42 CFR Parts 402 and 408
[CMS–0463–IFC]
RIN 0938–AM71

Medicare Program; Medicare Prescription Drug Discount Card

Agency: Centers for Medicare & Medicaid Services (CMS), HHS.
ACTION: Interim final rule with comment period.

SUMMARY: Section 101, subpart 4 of the Medicare Prescription Drug, Improvement, and Modernization Act of 2003, codified in section 1860D—31 of the Social Security Act, provides for a voluntary prescription drug discount card program for Medicare beneficiaries entitled to benefits, or enrolled, under Part A or enrolled under Part B, excluding beneficiaries entitled to medical assistance for outpatient prescription drugs under Medicaid, including section 1115 waiver demonstrations. Eligible beneficiaries may access negotiated prices on prescription drugs by enrolling in drug discount card programs offered by Medicare-endorsed sponsors.

Eligible beneficiaries may enroll in the Medicare drug discount card program beginning no later than 6 months after the date of enactment of the Medicare Prescription Drug, Improvement, and Modernization Act of 2003 and ending December 31, 2005. After December 31, 2005, beneficiaries enrolled in the program may continue to use their drug discount card during a short transition period beginning January 1, 2006 and ending upon the effective date of a beneficiary's outpatient drug coverage under Medicare Part D, but no later than the last day of the initial open enrollment period under Part D.

Beneficiaries with incomes no more than 135 percent of the poverty line applicable to their family size who do not have outpatient prescription drug coverage under certain programs— Medicaid, certain health insurance coverage or group health insurance (such as retiree coverage), TRICARE, and Federal Employees Health Benefits Program (FEHBP)—also are eligible for transitional assistance, or payment of $600 in 2004 and up to $600 in 2005 of the cost of covered discount card drugs obtained under the program. In most case, any transitional assistance

remaining available to a beneficiary on December 31, 2004 may be rolled over to 2005 and applied toward the cost of covered discount card drugs obtained under the program during 2005. Similarly, in most cases, any transitional assistance remaining available to a beneficiary on December 31, 2005 may be applied toward the cost of covered discount card drugs obtained under the program during the transition period.

The Centers for Medicare & Medicaid Services will solicit applications from entities seeking to offer beneficiaries negotiated prices on covered discount card drugs. Those meeting the requirements described in the authorizing statute and this rule, including administration of transitional assistance, will be permitted to offer a Medicare-endorsed drug discount card program to eligible beneficiaries. Endorsed sponsors may charge beneficiaries enrolling in their endorsed programs an annual enrollment fee for 2004 and 2005 of nor more than $30; CMS will pay this fee on behalf of enrollees entitled to transitional assistance.

To ensure that eligible Medicare beneficiaries take full advantage of the Medicare drug discount card program and make informed choices, CMS will educate beneficiaries about the existence and features of the program and the availability of transitional assistance for certain low-income beneficiaries; and publicize information that will allow Medicare beneficiaries to compare the various Medicare-endorsed drug discount card programs.

DATES: *Effective Date:* The provisions of this interim final rule with comment period are effective December 15, 2003.

Comment date: Comments will be considered if we receive them no later than 5 p.m. on January 14, 2004, at the appropriate address, as provided below.

ADDRESSES: In commenting, please refer to file code CMS–4063–IFC. Because of staff and resource limitations, we cannot accept comments by facsimile (FAX) transmission.

Mail written comments (1 original and 3 copies) to the following address ONLY: Centers for Medicare & Medicaid Services, Department of Health and Human Services, Attention: CMS–4063–FC, P.O. Box 8013, Baltimore, MD 21244–8012.

Please allow sufficient time for mailed comments to be timely received in the event of delivery delays.

If you prefer, you may deliver (by hand or courier) your written comments (1 original and 3 copies) to one of the following addresses: Room 445–G,

Hubert H. Humphrey Building, 200 Independence Avenue, SW., Washington, DC 20201, or Room C5–14–03, 7500 Security Boulevard, Baltimore, MD 21244–1850.

(Because access to the interior of the Hubert H. Humphrey Building is not readily available to persons without Federal Government identification, commenters are encouraged to leave their comments in the CMS drop slots located in the main lobby of the building. A stamp-in clock is available for commenters wishing to retain a proof of filing by stamping in and retaining an extra copy of the comments being filed.)

Comments mailed to the addresses indicated as appropriate for hand or courier delivery may be delayed and could be considered late.

For information on viewing public comments, see the beginning of the **SUPPLEMENTARY INFORMATION** section.

FOR FURTHER INFORMATION CONTACT: Teresa DeCaro, (410) 786-6604.

SUPPLEMENTARY INFORMATION: Copies: To order copies of the **Federal Register** containing this document, send your request to: New Orders, Superintendent of Documents, P.O. Box 371954, Pittsburgh, PA 15250–7954. Specify the date of the issue requested an enclose a check or money order payable to the Superintendent of Documents, or enclose your Visa or Master Card number and expiration date. Credit card orders can also be placed by calling the order desk at (202) 512–1800 (or toll free at 1–888–293–6498) or by faxing to (202) 512–2250. The cost for each copy is $10. As an alternative, you can view and photocopy the **Federal Register** document at most libraries designated as Federal Depository Libraries and at many other public and academic libraries throughout the country that receive the **Federal Register**. This **Federal Register** document is also available from the **Federal Register** online database through GPO Access, a service of the U.S. Government Printing Office. The Web site address is: *http://www.access.gpo.gov/nara/index.html.*

Inspection of Public Comments: Comments received timely will be available for public inspection as they are received, generally beginning approximately 3 weeks after publication of a document, at the headquarters of the Centers for Medicare & Medicaid Services, 7500 Security Boulevard, Baltimore, Maryland 21244, Monday through Friday of each week from 8:30 a.m. to 4 p.m. To schedule an appointment to view public comments, please call: (410) 786-7197.

FIGURE 5-2 Sample page from the *Federal Register* (Reprinted according to National Archives and Records Administration permissions notice.)

EXAMPLE 2: FEDERAL STATUTE, IMPLEMENTED AS A FEDERAL REGULATION, AND PUBLISHED IN THE *FEDERAL REGISTER*

Congress passed the Balanced Budget Refinement Act of 1999 (Public Law No. 106-113), which called for a number of revisions to Medicare, Medicaid, and the State Children's Health Insurance Program. On May 5, 2000, the Department of Health and Human Services published a proposed rule in the *Federal Register* to revise the Medicare hospital inpatient prospective payment system for operating costs. This proposed rule was entitled "Medicare Program; Changes to the Hospital Inpatient Prospective Payment Systems and Fiscal Year 2001 Rates; Proposed Rule." The purpose of publishing the proposed rule is to allow for comments from healthcare providers. Once the comment period has ended, the final rule is published in the *Federal Register.*

EXAMPLE 3: CASE LAW

When originally passed, New York State Public Health Law (PHL) sections 17 and 18 allowed a *reasonable charge* to be imposed for copies of patient records. Healthcare facilities, therefore, charged fees for locating the patient's record and making copies. These fees were later challenged in court, and reasonable charge language in the PHL was interpreted in *Hernandez v. Lutheran Medical Center* (1984), *Ventura v. Long Island Jewish Hillside Medical Center* (1985), and *Cohen v. South Nassau Communities Hospital* (1987). The interpretation permitted charges of $1.00 to $1.50 per page, plus a search and retrieval fee of $15.

NOTE: Sections 17 and 18 of the PHL were amended in 1991 when the phrase, "the reasonable fee for paper copies shall not exceed seventy-five cents per page" was added to the law.

NOTE: All 17 *carriers* (process Medicare Part B claims) and 23 *fiscal intermediaries (FI)* (process Medicare Part A claims) were eliminated in 2010 to create 23 Medicare administrative contractors (MACs). (*Durable Medical Equipment Carriers [DMERCs]* that process durable medical equipment, prosthetics, orthotics, and supplies [DMEPOS] were replaced with DME MACs. Home health and hospice claims are processed by HH & H MACs.) New jurisdictions were created for administration by MACs, which consolidate the administration of Medicare Part A and B benefits so that Medicare beneficiaries have claims processed by one contractor.

Program transmittals (Figure 5-3) contain new and changed Medicare policies and/or procedures that are to be incorporated into a specific CMS program manual (e.g., *Medicare Claims Processing Manual*). The cover page (or transmittal page) summarizes new and changed material, and subsequent pages provide details. The transmittals are sent to each **Medicare administrative contractor (MAC)**, which is an organization (e.g., insurance company) that contracts with CMS to process fee-for-service healthcare claims and perform program integrity tasks for both Medicare Part A and Part B. Each contractor makes program coverage decisions and publishes a newsletter, which is sent to providers who receive Medicare reimbursement.

EXAMPLE: HGS Administrators is a Medicare administrative contractor that processes Pennsylvania claims and publishes the following newsletters at its Web site (**www.hgsa.com**):

EDI Xchange, a quarterly newsletter that contains information about technical changes and issues related to electronic data interchange (EDI).

Medicare Report, a monthly newsletter for healthcare professionals and their office staff that contains information about Medicare policy, reimbursement updates, specialty billing information, claims reporting tips, and so on. The *EDI Xcellence* is a centerfold insert in the *Medicare Report* that disseminates information about EDI technical changes and EDI products and services available to Medicare providers.

Medicare Special Bulletin, a periodic newsletter that contains information about multiple topics (e.g., Medicare fee schedule and updates, anesthesia conversion factors).

Medicare Special Notice, a periodic newsletter that contains information about just one topic (e.g., CMS announces NPI deadline extension).

The Pulse of CMS, a quarterly regional newsletter for healthcare professionals.

CMS Manual System

Pub. 100-08 Program Integrity Manual

Department of Health & Human Services (DHHS) Centers for Medicare & Medicaid Services (CMS)

Transmittal 91	Date: DECEMBER 10, YYYY
	CHANGE REQUEST 3560

SUBJECT: Revision of Program Integrity Manual (PIM), Section 3.11.1.4

I. SUMMARY OF CHANGES: Revising the PIM to correct inconsistencies with section 3.4.1.2.

NEW/REVISED MATERIAL – EFFECTIVE DATE*: January 1, YYYY
IMPLEMENTATION DATE: January 3, YYYY

MANUALIZATION/CLARIFICATION – EFFECTIVE/IMPLEMENTATION DATES: Not Applicable.

Disclaimer for manual changes only: The revision date and transmittal number apply to the red italicized material only. Any other material was previously published and remains unchanged. However, if this revision contains a table of contents, you will receive the new/revised information only, and not the entire table of contents.

II. CHANGES IN MANUAL INSTRUCTIONS:
(R = REVISED, N = NEW, D = DELETED)

R/N/D	CHAPTER/SECTION/SUBSECTION/TITLE
R	3/11.1.4/Requesting Additional Documentation

III. FUNDING: Medicare contractors shall implement these instructions within their current operating budgets.

IV. ATTACHMENTS:

X	**Business Requirements**
X	**Manual Instruction**
	Confidential Requirements
	One-Time Notification
	Recurring Update Notification

*Unless otherwise specified, the effective date is the date of service.

FIGURE 5-3 Sample Medicare program transmittal (Reprinted in accordance with CMS Content Reuse Policy.)

Membership in professional associations can also prove helpful in accessing up-to-date information about the health insurance industry (refer to Chapter 1 for information on joining professional associations). Newsletters and journals published by professional associations routinely include articles that clarify implementation of new legal and regulatory mandates. They also provide resources for obtaining the most up-to-date information about such issues. Another way to remain current is to subscribe to a listserv, a subscriber-based question-and-answer forum available through e-mail.

FEDERAL LAWS AND EVENTS THAT AFFECT HEALTH CARE

The healthcare industry is heavily regulated by federal and state legislation. Table 5-1 summarizes major federal laws and events that affect health care. (Because state laws vary, it is recommended that they be researched individually.)

TABLE 5-1   Federal laws that affect health care

YEAR	FEDERAL LAW	DESCRIPTION
1863	False Claims Act (FCA)	• Regulated fraud associated with military contractors selling supplies and equipment to the Union Army • Used by federal agencies to regulate the conduct of any contractor that submits claims for payment to the federal government for any program (e.g., Medicare) • Amended in 1986 to increase civil monetary penalties (CMPs) to impose a maximum of $10,000 per false claim, plus three times the amount of damages that the government sustains; civil liability on those who submit false or fraudulent claims to the government for payment; and exclusion of violators from participation in Medicare and Medicaid **NOTE:** Control of fraud and abuse has been of great interest since implementation of DRGs. Prior to DRGs, the cost-based reimbursement system for Medicare claims made fraud almost unnecessary, because the system rewarded high utilization of services. The implementation of DRGs resulted in the first serious "gaming" of the system to find ways to maximize revenues for hospitals. Because the diagnosis and procedure codes reported affect the DRG selected (and resultant payment), some hospitals engaged in a practice called upcoding, which is the assignment of an ICD-9-CM diagnosis code that does not match patient record documentation for the purpose of illegally increasing reimbursement (e.g., assigning the ICD-9-CM code for heart attack code when angina was actually documented in the record). As a result, upcoding became a serious fraud concern under DRGs.
1906	Food and Drug Act	• Authorized federal government to monitor the purity of foods and the safety of medicines • Now a responsibility of the Food and Drug Administration (FDA)
1935	Social Security Act	• Included unemployment insurance, old-age assistance, aid to dependent children, and grants to states to provide various forms of medical care • Amended in 1965 to add disability coverage and medical benefits
1946	Hill-Burton Act (or Hospital Survey and Construction Act)	• Provided federal grants to modernize hospitals that had become obsolete due to lack of capital investment throughout the period of the Great Depression and World War II (1929 to 1945) • Required facilities to provide free or reduced-charge medical services to persons who were unable to pay, in return for federal funds • Program now addresses other types of infrastructure needs, and it is managed by the Health Resources and Services Administration (HRSA), within the Department of Health and Human Services (DHHS)
1962	Migrant Health Act	• Provided medical and support services to migrant and seasonal farm workers and their families

(continues)

TABLE 5-1   (continued)

YEAR	FEDERAL LAW	DESCRIPTION
1965	Social Security Amendments	• Created Medicare and Medicaid programs, making comprehensive health care available to millions of Americans • Established *Conditions of Participation (CoP)* and *Conditions for Coverage (CfC)*, which are federal regulations that healthcare facilities must comply with to participate in (receive reimbursement from) the Medicare and Medicaid programs; physicians must comply with billing and payment regulations published by CMS
1966	Federal Claims Collection Act	• Required carriers (process Medicare Part B claims) and fiscal intermediaries (process Medicare Part A claims), both of which were replaced by Medicare administrative contractors) (that administer the Medicare fee-for-program), to attempt the collection of overpayments (funds a provider or beneficiary receives in excess of amounts due and payable under Medicare and Medicaid)
1970	Occupational Safety and Health Act	• Created the Occupational Safety and Health Administration (OSHA), whose mission is to ensure safe and healthful workplaces in America • Since the agency was created in 1971, workplace fatalities have been cut in half and occupational injury and illness rates have declined 40 percent; at the same time, U.S. employment has doubled from 56 million workers at 3.5 million work sites to 111 million workers at 7 million sites
1971	National Cancer Act	• Amended the Public Health Service Act of 1798 to more effectively carry out the national effort against cancer • Part of President Nixon's "War on Cancer," which centralized research at the National Institutes of Health (NIH)
1972	Federal Anti-Kickback Law	• Protect patients and federal healthcare programs from fraud and abuse by curtailing the corrupting influence of money on healthcare decisions • Violations of the law are punishable by up to 5 years in prison, criminal fines up to $25,000, administrative civil money penalties up to $50,000, and exclusion from participation in federal healthcare programs • In 1987 DHHS published regulations designating specific "safe harbors" for various payment and business practices that, while potentially prohibited by the law, would not be prosecuted (e.g., investments in group practices)
	Drug Abuse and Treatment Act	• Required that drug and alcohol abuse patient records be kept confidential and not subject to disclosure except as provided by law • Applied to federally assisted alcohol or drug abuse programs, which are those that provide diagnosis, treatment, and referral for treatment of drug and/or alcohol abuse **NOTE:** General medical care facilities are required to comply with this legislation *only* if they have an identified drug/alcohol abuse treatment unit or their personnel provide drug/alcohol diagnosis, treatment, or referral.
	Social Security Amendments	• Strengthened utilization review process by creating professional standards review organizations (PSROs), which were independent peer review organizations that monitored the appropriateness, quality, and outcome of the services provided to beneficiaries of the Medicare, Medicaid, and Maternal and Child Health Programs • PSROs are now called quality improvement organizations (QIOs)

(continues)

TABLE 5-1 (continued)

YEAR	FEDERAL LAW	DESCRIPTION
1974	Employment Retirement Income Security Act (ERISA)	• Ensured that pension and other benefits were provided to employees as promised by employers
	Privacy Act of 1974	• Implemented to protect the privacy of individuals identified in information systems maintained by federal government hospitals (e.g., military hospitals) and to give individuals access to records concerning themselves • Does not preempt state laws that are more restrictive **NOTE:** Although this law has no effect on records maintained by nonfederal hospitals, effective April 14, 2003, the Health Insurance Portability and Accountability Act of 1996 (HIPAA) requires *all* health plans, healthcare clearinghouses, and healthcare providers that conduct electronic financial or administrative transactions (e.g., electronic billing) to comply with national patient privacy standards, which contain safeguards to protect the security and confidentiality of patient information.
1975	Consolidated Omnibus Budget Reconciliation Act (COBRA)	• Amended ERISA to include provisions for continuation of healthcare coverage, which apply to group health plans of employers with two or more employees • Participants maintain, at their own expense, healthcare plan coverage that would have been lost due to a triggering event (e.g., termination of employment); cost is comparable to what it would be if they were still members of the employer's group
1977	Utilization Review Act	• Facilitated ongoing assessment and management of healthcare services • Required hospitals to conduct continued-stay reviews to determine the medical necessity and appropriateness of Medicare and Medicaid inpatient hospitalizations
1979	Department of Education Organization Act	• Established a separate Department of Education • Health, Education and Welfare (HEW) became known as the Department of Health and Human Services (DHHS) on May 4, 1980
1982	Peer Review Improvement Act	• Replaced PSROs with peer review organizations (PROs) (now called QIOs), which were statewide utilization and quality control peer review organizations • In 1985, PROs incorporated a focused second-opinion program, which referred certain cases for diagnostic and treatment verification
	Tax Equity and Fiscal Responsibility Act (TEFRA)	• Established the first Medicare prospective payment system, which was implemented in 1983 • Diagnosis related groups (DRGs) required acute care hospitals to be reimbursed a predetermined rate according to discharge diagnosis (instead of a *per diem* rate, which compensated hospitals retrospectively based on charges incurred for the total inpatient length of stay, usually 80 percent of charges) **NOTE:** Additional prospective payment systems were implemented in subsequent years for other healthcare settings, as discussed in Chapter 9.
1985	Consolidated Omnibus Budget Reconciliation Act (COBRA)	• Allowed former employees, retirees, spouses, domestic partners, and eligible dependent children who lose coverage due to certain qualifying events the right to temporary continuation of health coverage at group rates; benefits can continue for 18 or 36 months, depending on the qualifying event, and premiums are calculated at 102 percent of the total premium rate, payable by the enrollee on a monthly basis directly to the payer • Also allowed HCFA (now called CMS) to deny reimbursement for substandard healthcare services provided to Medicare and Medicaid patients
1986	Omnibus Budget Reconciliation Act (OBRA 1986)	• Required PROs to report cases of substandard care to licensing and certification agencies

(continues)

TABLE 5-1   (continued)

YEAR	FEDERAL LAW	DESCRIPTION
1987	Nursing Home Reform Act (part of the Omnibus Budget Reconciliation Act of 1987)	• Ensured that residents of nursing homes receive quality care, required the provision of certain services to each resident, and established a Resident's Bill of Rights • Allowed nursing homes to receive Medicaid and Medicare payments for long-term care of residents if the homes were certified by the state in which they were located and were in substantial compliance with the requirements of the Nursing Home Reform Act
1988	McKinney Act	• Provided health care to the homeless
1989	Omnibus Budget Reconciliation Act (OBRA 1989)	• Enacted a physician self-referral law (or Stark I) to respond to concerns about physicians' conflicts of interest when referring Medicare patients for a variety of services • Stark I prohibited physicians from referring Medicare patients to *clinical laboratory services* in which the physicians or their family members had a financial ownership/investment interest and/or compensation arrangement • In 1994, because some providers routinely waived coinsurance and copayments, the DHHS Office of Inspector General (OIG) issued the following fraud alert: "Routine waiver of deductibles and copayments by charge-based providers, practitioners or suppliers is unlawful because it results in (1) false claims, (2) violations of the anti-kickback statute, and (3) excessive utilization of items and services paid for by Medicare"
1990	Omnibus Budget Reconciliation Act (OBRA 1990)	• Required PROs to report adverse actions to state medical boards and licensing agencies
1995	Physicians at Teaching Hospitals (PATH)	• Audits implemented by DHHS that examine the billing practices of physicians at teaching hospitals • Focus was on two issues: (1) compliance with the Medicare rule affecting payment for physician services provided by residents (e.g., whether a teaching physician was present for Part B services billed to Medicare between 1990 and 1996), and (2) whether the level of the physician service was coded and billed properly
1995	Stark II Physician Self-Referral Law	• Stark II (physician self-referral laws) expanded Stark I by including referrals of Medicare and Medicaid patients for the following designated healthcare services (DHCS): clinical laboratory services, durable medical equipment and supplies, home health services, inpatient and outpatient hospitalization services, occupational therapy services, outpatient prescription drugs, parenteral and enteral nutrients, equipment and supplies, physical therapy services, prosthetics, orthotics and prosthetic devices and supplies, radiation therapy services and supplies, and radiology services, including MRIs, CAT scans, and ultrasound services • Hospitals must also comply with Stark II regulations because of relationships they establish with physicians • In 2001 new regulations clarified what a *designated health service* was and under what circumstances physicians can have a financial relationship with an organization and still make referrals of Medicare patients for services or products provided by that organization **EXAMPLE:** Home care physicians who served as home health agency medical directors were prohibited from making in excess of $25,000/year if they wanted to make referrals to that agency. That cap was removed in the revised Stark II regulations.
1996	National Correct Coding Initiative (NCCI)	• Developed by CMS to reduce Medicare program expenditures by detecting inappropriate codes on claims and denying payment for them

(continues)

TABLE 5-1   (continued)

YEAR	FEDERAL LAW	DESCRIPTION
1996	Health Insurance Portability and Accountability Act (HIPAA)	• Mandated administrative simplification regulations that govern privacy, security, and electronic transaction standards for healthcare information • Amended ERISA and COBRA to improve portability and continuity of health insurance coverage in connection with employment; protects health insurance coverage for workers and their families when they change or lose their jobs • Created the Healthcare Integrity and Protection Data Bank (HIPDB), which combats fraud and abuse in health insurance and healthcare delivery by alerting users to conduct a comprehensive review of a practitioner's, provider's, or supplier's past actions • Established the Medicare integrity program (MIP)
1997	State Children's Health Insurance Program (SCHIP)	• Established a health insurance program for infants, children, and teens that covers healthcare services such as doctor visits, prescription medicines, and hospitalizations
1999	Payment Error Prevention Program (PEPP)	• Initiated by DHHS to require facilities to identify and reduce improper Medicare payments and, specifically, the Medicare payment error rate (number of dollars paid in error out of the total dollars paid for inpatient prospective payment system services) • Established Clinical Data Abstracting Centers (CDACs), which became responsible for initially requesting and screening medical records for PEPP surveillance sampling for medical review, DRG validation, and medical necessity; medical review criteria were developed by peer review organizations (now called quality improvement organizations or QIOs)
	Ticket to Work and Work Incentives Improvement Act	• Made it possible for millions of Americans with disabilities to join the workforce without fear of losing their Medicaid and Medicare coverage • Modernized employment services system for people with disabilities • Initiative on combating bioterrorism was launched
	Program Safeguard Contracts (PSCs)	CMS transferred responsibility for fraud and abuse detection from fiscal intermediaries (FIs) and carriers to Program Safeguard Contracts, PSCs. In 2009, the Zone Program Integrity Contractor (ZPIC) program replaced PSCs.
2002	Improper Payments Information Act of 2002 (IPIA)	• Established the Payment Error Rate Measurement (PERM) program to measure improper payments in the Medicaid program and the State Children's Health Insurance Program (SCHIP) • Established the Comprehensive Error Rate Testing (CERT) program to assess and measure improper Medicare fee-for-service payments (based on reviewing selected claims and associated medical record documentation) • Established the Hospital Payment Monitoring Program (HPMP) to measure, monitor, and reduce the incidence of Medicare fee-for-service payment errors for short-term, acute care, inpatient PPS hospitals, which included development of the: • First–look Analysis for Hospital Outlier Monitoring (FATHOM) data analysis tool, which provides administrative hospital and state-specific data for specific CMS target areas. • Program for Evaluating Payment Patterns Electronic Report (PEPPER), which contains hospital-specific administrative claims data for a number of CMS-identified problem areas (e.g., specific DRGs, types of discharges). A hospital uses PEPPER data to compare their performance with that of other hospitals.
2003	Medicare Prescription Drug, Improvement, and Modernization Act (MMA)	• Mandated implementation of the recovery audit contractor (RAC) program to find and correct improper Medicare payments paid to healthcare providers participating in fee-for-service Medicare. CMS created the Zone Program Integrity Contractor (ZPIC) program to review billing trends and patterns, focusing on providers whose billings for Medicare services are higher than the majority of providers in the community. CMS programs for detecting fraud and abuse were originally assigned to fiscal intermediaries (FIs) and carriers, all of which were replaced by Medicare administrative contractors (MACs) by 2009. ZPICs are assigned to the MAC jurisdictions, replacing CMS's Program Safeguard Contracts (PSCs). (The RAC and ZPIC programs were implemented in 2009.)

(continues)

TABLE 5-1   (continued)

YEAR	FEDERAL LAW	DESCRIPTION
2005	Patient Safety and Quality Improvement Act	• Amends Title IX of the Public Health Service Act to provide for improved patient safety by encouraging voluntary and confidential reporting of events that adversely affect patients • Creates Patient Safety Organizations (PSOs) to collect, aggregate, and analyze confidential information reported by healthcare providers • Designates information reported to PSOs as privileged and not subject to disclosure (except when a court determines that the information contains evidence of a criminal act or each provider identified in the information authorizes disclosure)
2005	Deficit Reduction Act of 2005	• Created Medicaid Integrity Program (MIP), which increased resources available to CMS to combat abuse, fraud, and waste in the Medicaid program. Congress requires annual reporting by CMS about the use and effectiveness of funds appropriated for the MIP.
2006	Tax Relief and Health Care Act of 2006 (TRHCA)	• Created Physician Quality Reporting Initiative (PQRI) system that establishes a financial incentive for eligible professionals who participate in a *voluntary* quality reporting program.

RETENTION OF RECORDS

Record retention is the storage of documentation for an established period of time, usually mandated by federal and/or state law. (The state in which the healthcare provider practices determines whether federal or state law mandates the retention period.) Its purpose is to ensure the availability of records for use by government agencies and other third parties (e.g., insurance audit, quality of care review). It is acceptable to store medical records and insurance claims (including attachments submitted to third-party payers) in a format other than original hard copy if the storage medium (e.g., microfilm, scanned images) accurately reproduces all original documents.

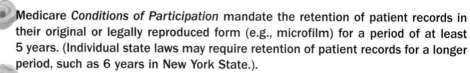

- Medicare *Conditions of Participation* mandate the retention of patient records in their original or legally reproduced form (e.g., microfilm) for a period of at least 5 years. (Individual state laws may require retention of patient records for a longer period, such as 6 years in New York State.).
- The Health Insurance Portability and Accountability Act (HIPAA) mandates the retention of health insurance claims and accounting records for a minimum of 6 years, unless state law specifies a longer period.
- HIPAA also mandates that health insurance claims be retained for a minimum of 2 years after a patient's death.

> **EXAMPLE 1:** Community Hospital is located in North Carolina (NC), which mandates that hospital medical records be retained for a minimum of 11 years following the discharge of an adult, and for a minor the record must be retained until the patient's 30th birthday. Because NC law is stricter than the HIPAA mandate regarding retention of records, Community Hospital must retain adult patient records for a period of 11 years and minor patient records until the patient's 30th birthday.

> **EXAMPLE 2:** Dr. Smith practices in Delaware (DE), which mandates that medical records be retained for 5 years. Because the HIPAA mandate is stricter than DE state law, Dr. Smith must retain patient records for a period of 6 years. For any patient who has died, Dr. Smith must retain the record for a period of 2 years after the date of death.

HEALTH INSURANCE PORTABILITY AND ACCOUNTABILITY ACT (HIPAA)

In 1996 Congress passed the Health Insurance Portability and Accountability Act (HIPAA) because of concerns about fraud (e.g., coding irregularities, medical necessity issues, and waiving of copays and deductibles). While the Federal False Claims Act provides CMS with regulatory authority to enforce fraud and abuse statutes for the Medicare program, HIPAA extends that authority to all federal and state healthcare programs.

The Health Insurance Portability and Accountability Act of 1996 (HIPAA), Public Law No. 104-191, amended the Internal Revenue Code of 1986 to:

- Improve the portability and continuity of health insurance coverage in the group and individual markets.
- Combat waste, fraud, and abuse in health insurance and healthcare delivery.
- Promote the use of medical savings accounts.
- Improve access to long-term care services and coverage.
- Simplify the administration of health insurance by creating unique identifiers for providers, health plans, employers, and individuals.
- Create standards for electronic health information transactions.
- Create privacy standards for health information.

A discussion on each HIPAA component follows. Although HIPAA standards are still being finalized, healthcare organizations should develop and implement a response to each component.

HIPAA legislation is organized according to five titles (Figure 5-4):

- Title I—Health Care Access, Portability, and Renewability.
- Title II—Preventing Health Care Fraud and Abuse, Administrative Simplification, and Medical Liability Reform.
- Title III—Tax-Related Health Provisions.
- Title IV—Application and Enforcement of Group Health Plan Requirements.
- Title V—Revenue Offsets.

Content in this chapter concerns itself with Title I and II provisions.

Healthcare Access, Portability, and Renewability

HIPAA provisions were designed to improve the portability and continuity of health coverage by:

- Limiting exclusions for pre-existing medical conditions.
- Providing credit for prior health coverage and a process for transmitting certificates and other information concerning prior coverage to a new group health plan or issuer.
- Providing new rights that allow individuals to enroll for health coverage when they lose other health coverage, change from group to individual coverage, or gain a new dependent.
- Prohibiting discrimination in enrollment and premiums against employees and their dependents based on health status.

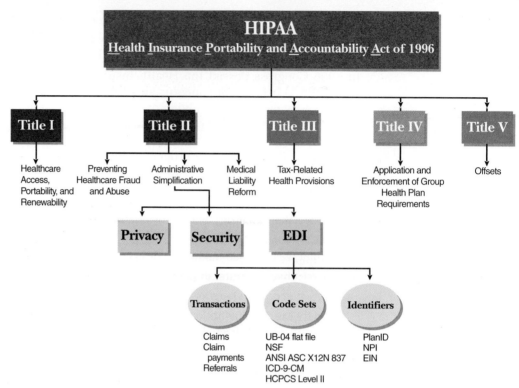

FIGURE 5-4 HIPAA provisions (Courtesy Delmar/Cengage Learning)

- Guaranteeing availability of health insurance coverage for small employers and renewability of health insurance coverage in both the small and large group markets.
- Preserving, through narrow preemption provisions, the states' traditional role in regulating health insurance, including state flexibility to provide greater protections.

Preventing Healthcare Fraud and Abuse

HIPAA defines fraud as "an intentional deception or misrepresentation that someone makes, knowing it is false, that could result in an unauthorized payment." The attempt itself is considered fraud, regardless of whether it is successful. Abuse "involves actions that are inconsistent with accepted, sound medical, business, or fiscal practices. Abuse directly or indirectly results in unnecessary costs to the program through improper payments." The difference between fraud and abuse is the individual's intent; however, both have the same impact in that they steal valuable resources from the healthcare industry. The most common forms of Medicare fraud include

- Billing for services not furnished.
- Misrepresenting the diagnosis to justify payment.
- Soliciting, offering, or receiving a kickback.
- Unbundling codes (reporting multiple CPT codes to increase reimbursement, when a single combination code should be reported).
- Falsifying certificates of medical necessity, plans of treatment, and medical records to justify payment.

Examples of abuse include:

- Excessive charges for services, equipment, or supplies.
- Submitting claims for items or services that are not medically necessary to treat the patient's stated condition.

- Improper billing practices that result in a payment by a government program when the claim is the legal responsibility of another third-party payer.
- Violations of participating provider agreements with insurance companies.

When a Medicare provider commits fraud, an investigation is conducted by the Department of Health and Human Services (DHHS) Office of the Inspector General (OIG). The OIG Office of Investigations prepares the case for referral to the Department of Justice for criminal and/or civil prosecution. A person found guilty of Medicare fraud faces criminal, civil, and/or administrative sanction penalties, including:

- Civil penalties of $5,000 to $10,000 per false claim plus triple damages under the False Claims Act. (The provider pays an amount equal to three times the claim submitted, in addition to the civil penalties fine.)
- Criminal fines and/or imprisonment of up to 10 years if convicted of the crime of healthcare fraud as outlined in HIPAA or, for violations of the Medicare/Medicaid Anti-Kickback Statute, imprisonment of up to 5 years and/or a criminal penalty fine of up to $50,000.
- Administrative sanctions, including up to a $10,000 civil monetary penalty per line item on a false claim, assessments of up to triple the amount falsely claimed, and/or exclusion from participation in Medicare and state healthcare programs.

In addition to these penalties, those who commit healthcare fraud can also be tried for mail and wire fraud.

> **EXAMPLE:** Medical review of claims submitted to Medicare by a physician group practice that contains mental health providers identified a pattern of psychiatric services billed on behalf of nursing facility patients with a medical history of dementia. Review of patient records revealed no mental healthcare physician orders or plans of treatment. This is an example of billing for services not furnished.

The DHHS Office of Inspector General (OIG) published the final *Compliance Program Guidance for Individual and Small Group Physician Practices* in the October 5, 2000, *Federal Register*. The intent of the guidance document is to help physicians in individual and small group practices design voluntary compliance programs that best fit the needs of their individual practices. By law, physicians are not subject to civil, administrative, or criminal penalties for innocent errors, or even negligence. The civil False Claims Act covers only offenses that are committed with *actual knowledge* of the falsity of the claim, or *reckless disregard* or *deliberate ignorance* of the truth or falsity of a claim. (The False Claims Act does not cover mistakes, errors, or negligence.) The OIG has stated that it is mindful of the difference between innocent errors (e.g., erroneous claims) and reckless or intentional conduct (e.g., fraudulent claims).

A voluntary compliance program can help physicians avoid generating erroneous and fraudulent claims by ensuring that submitted claims are true and accurate, expediting and optimizing proper payment of claims, minimizing billing mistakes, and avoiding conflicts with self-referral and antikickback statutes. Unlike other guidance previously issued by the OIG (e.g., *Third-Party Medical Billing Company Compliance Program Guidance*), the final physician guidance does not require that physician practices implement all seven standard components of a full-scale compliance program. (Although the seven components provide a solid basis upon which a physician practice can create a compliance program, the OIG acknowledges that full implementation of all components may not be feasible for smaller physician practices.) Instead, the guidance emphasizes a step-by-step approach for those practices to follow in developing and implementing a voluntary compliance program.

As a first step, physician practices can begin by identifying risk areas which, based on a practice's specific history with billing problems and other compliance issues, might benefit from closer scrutiny and corrective/educational measures. The step-by-step approach is as follows:

1. Perform periodic audits to internally monitor billing practices.

2. Develop written practice standards and procedures.

3. Designate a compliance officer to monitor compliance efforts and enforce practice standards.

4. Conduct appropriate training and education about practice standards and procedures.

5. Respond appropriately to detected violations by investigating allegations and disclosing incidents to appropriate government entities.

6. Develop open lines of communication (e.g., discussions at staff meetings regarding erroneous or fraudulent conduct issues) to keep practice employees updated regarding compliance activities.

7. Enforce disciplinary standards through well-publicized guidelines.

The final guidance further identifies four specific compliance risk areas for physicians: (1) proper coding and billing; (2) ensuring that services are reasonable and necessary; (3) proper documentation; and (4) avoiding improper inducements, kickbacks, and self-referrals. These risk areas reflect areas in which the OIG has focused its investigations and audits related to physician practices. The final guidance also provides direction to larger practices in developing compliance programs by recommending that they use both the physician guidance and previously issued guidance, such as the *Third-Party Medical Billing Company Compliance Program Guidance* or the *Clinical Laboratory Compliance Program Guidance*, to create a compliance program that meets the needs of the larger practice.

Medicaid Integrity Program (MIP)

The *Medicaid Integrity Program (MIP)* was mandated by the Deficit Reduction Act of 2005, which provides funds ($5 million in 2007 to $75 million by 2009 and each year thereafter) to combat fraud, waste, and abuse. Contractors will review the actions of those seeking payment from Medicaid (e.g., providers), perform audits, identify overpayments, and educate providers and others about program integrity and quality of care. Congress mandated that CMS devote at least 100 full-time staff members to the project, who will collaborate with state Medicaid officials. The MIP is based on four key principles:

- Accountability for the MIP's activities and those of its contractors and the states.
- Collaboration with internal and external partners and stakeholders.
- Flexibility to address the ever-changing nature of Medicaid fraud.
- National leadership in Medicaid program integrity.

The major strategies will include:

- Balancing the role of the MIP between providing training and technical assistance to states while conducting oversight of their activities; and between supporting criminal investigations of suspect providers while concurrently seeking administrative sanctions.

- Collaborating and coordinating with internal and external partners.
- Consulting with interested parties in the development of the comprehensive Medicaid integrity plan.
- Developing effective return on investment strategies.
- Employing lessons learned in developing guidance and directives aimed at fraud prevention.
- Targeting vulnerabilities in the Medicaid program.

Recovery Audit Contractor (RAC) Program

NOTE: Medicare processes more than 1.2 billion Medicare claims annually, submitted by more than one million healthcare providers, including hospitals, skilled nursing facilities, physicians, and medical equipment suppliers. Errors in claims submitted by these healthcare providers for services provided to Medicare beneficiaries can account for billions of dollars in improper payments each year.

The *Recovery Audit Contractor (RAC) program* is mandated by the Medicare Prescription Drug, Improvement, and Modernization Act of 2003 (MMA) to find and correct improper Medicare payments paid to healthcare providers participating in fee-for-service Medicare. The goal of the RAC program is to identify improper payments made on claims of healthcare services provided to Medicare beneficiaries. *Improper payments* include:

- *Overpayments* (e.g., submitted claims do not meet Medicare's National Correct Coding Initiative or medical necessity policies, documentation in the patient record does not support codes reported on the claim, Medicare administrative contractors reimburse providers more than once for the same patient encounter or calculate reimbursement using an incorrect fee schedule).
- *Underpayments* (e.g., submitted claims report codes simple procedures, when review of the record indicates a more complicated procedure was performed).

Healthcare providers subject to review include hospitals, physician practices, nursing homes, home health agencies, durable medical equipment suppliers and any other provider or supplier that bills Medicare Parts A and B.

Overpayments

Overpayments are funds a provider or beneficiary receives in excess of amounts due and payable under Medicare and Medicaid statutes and regulations. Once a determination of overpayment has been made, the amount so determined is a debt owed to the United States government. The Federal Claims Collection Act of 1966 requires Medicare administrative contractors (MACs) (as agents of the federal government) to attempt the collection of overpayments. Examples of overpayments include:

- Payment based on a charge that exceeds the reasonable charge.
- Duplicate processing of charges/claims.
- Payment to a physician on a nonassigned claim or to a beneficiary on an assigned claim (payment made to wrong payee).
- Payment for non covered items and services, including medically unnecessary services.
- Incorrect application of the deductible or coinsurance.
- Payment for items or services rendered during a period of nonentitlement.
- Primary payment for items or services for which another entity is the primary payer.
- Payment for items or services rendered after the beneficiary's date of death (post-payment reviews are conducted to identify and recover payments with a billed date of service that is after the beneficiary's date of death).

[Insert Medicare administrative contractor letterhead here]

May 15, YYYY

Doug M. Smith, M.D.
393 Main St
Anywhere US 12345

RE: SSN: 123-45-6789
      PATIENT: Nathan A. Sanders
      CLAIM #:   939395SLD0005

Dear Provider:

Please be advised that an overpayment of benefits has been made for the above named patient. In order to resolve this matter we are asking you to make reimbursement. Please make your check payable to:

EMPIRE STATE HEALTH PLAN

in the amount of

$675.00

and forward it to:

EMPIRE STATE HEALTH PLAN
P.O. BOX 93902
ANYWHERE US 12345

We are requesting this refund due to the following reason:

CLAIM WAS PROCESSED UNDER THE WRONG PATIENT FOR DATES OF SERVICE 4/15 & 4/20/YYYY.

If you have any questions, please feel free to contact us.

Sincerely,

Mary Louise Smith
Claims Analyst (39-392)

FIGURE 5-5 Sample overpayment recovery letter (Courtesy Delmar/Cengage Learning)

When a Medicare administrative contractor determines that an overpayment was made, it proceeds with recovery by issuing an overpayment demand letter (Figure 5-5) to the provider. The letter contains information about the review and statistical sampling methodology used as well as corrective actions to be taken. (An explanation of the sampling methodology that was followed is included.) Corrective actions include payment suspension, imposition of civil money penalties, institution of pre- or post-payment review, additional edits, and so on.

Providers and beneficiaries can receive a waiver of recovery of overpayments if one or more of the following provisions apply:

- **Overpayment was discovered subsequent to the third calendar year after the year of payment.**
- **If an overpaid physician is found to be without fault or is deemed without fault, overpayment shifts to the beneficiary (e.g., medically unnecessary services).**
- **When both provider and beneficiary are without fault with respect to an overpayment on an assigned claim for medically unnecessary services, liability is waived for the overpayment (e.g., no action is taken to recover the overpayment).**
- **If a beneficiary is liable for an incorrect payment, CMS or SSA may waive recovery if the beneficiary was without fault with respect to the overpayment and recovery would cause financial hardship or would be against equity and good conscience.**

Medicare administrative contractors are prohibited from seeking overpayment recovery when the following two time limitations apply:

- Overpayment is not reopened within 4 years (48 months) after the date of payment, unless the case involves fraud or similar fault.
- Overpayment is discovered later than three full calendar years after the year of payment, unless there is evidence that the provider or beneficiary was at fault with respect to the overpayment.

Provider Liability for Overpayments

Providers are liable for refunding an overpayment in the following situations:

- Overpayment resulted from incorrect reasonable charge determination (because providers are responsible for knowing Medicare reasonable charges for services).
  Exception: If the provider's reasonable charge screen was increased and the physician had no reason to question the amount of the increase, the physician is not liable and the case is referred to CMS for review.
- Provider received duplicate payments from the Medicare administrative contractor (because the claim was processed more than once, or the provider submitted duplicate claims).
- Provider received payment after agreeing to accept assignment (the provider agreed to accept as payment whatever the payer deemed a reasonable charge), and a beneficiary received payment on an itemized bill and submitted that payment to the provider.

NOTE: If the provider has reason to believe the increase was excessive, the provider is liable unless the question was brought promptly to the attention of the Medicare administrative contractor and that entity assured the physician that the increase was correct.

NOTE: The provider does not have a reasonable basis for assuming that the total payment received was correct, and thus should have questioned it. The provider is, therefore, at fault and liable for the overpayment.

NOTE: The provider is liable for the portion of the total amount paid in excess of the reasonable charge (including any copayment paid by the beneficiary). The beneficiary is liable for the balance of the overpayment. If the provider protests recovery of the overpayment on the ground that all or part of the check received from the beneficiary was applied to amounts the beneficiary owed for other services, the beneficiary, rather than the physician, is liable for refunding such amounts.

> **EXAMPLE:** Mary Sue Patient underwent office surgery on May 15, performed by Dr. Smith. Medicare determined the reasonable charge for the office surgery to be $375. In July, Dr. Smith and Mary Sue Patient each received a check from Medicare in the amount of $300. Mary Sue Patient then signed her $300 over to Dr. Smith. Thus, Dr. Smith received a total of $600 for services provided on May 15, an overpayment of $225 (the amount received in excess of the reasonable charge). Mary Sue Patient is liable for the remaining $75 of the duplicate payment. (If Mary Sue Patient had also previously paid Dr. Smith the $75 as coinsurance, Dr. Smith would be liable for the entire $300 overpayment.) *Dr. Smith is responsible for contacting the Medicare administrative contractor (MAC) to report the overpayment and make arrangements to provide a refund.*

- Provider received duplicate payments from Medicare and another payer directly or through the beneficiary, which happens to be the primary payer (e.g., automobile medical or no-fault insurer, liability insurer, or workers' compensation).
- Provider was paid but does not accept assignment.
- Provider furnished erroneous information, or provider failed to disclose facts known or that should have been known and that were material to payment of benefit.

NOTE: The provider is liable for the portion of the Medicare payment in excess of the amount Medicare is obligated to pay as a secondary payer. However, if the provider signs the other insurance payment over to the beneficiary, the beneficiary is liable.

NOTE: The provider is liable whether or not the beneficiary was also paid.

> **EXAMPLE 1:** A beneficiary is referred to a provider by an employer for a fracture that occurred during a fall at work. The physician billed Medicare and neglected to indicate on the claim that the injury was work related (although that information had been provided by the patient). If Medicare benefits are paid to the provider for services and the injury would have been covered by workers' compensation, the provider is liable for an overpayment because of failure to disclose that the injury was work-related.

EXAMPLE 2: A provider submitted an assigned claim showing total charges of $1,000. The provider did not indicate on the claim that any portion of the bill had been paid by the patient. The MAC determined the reasonable charge to be $600 and paid the physician $480 (80 percent of $600) on the assumption that no other payment had been received. The MAC later learned that the beneficiary had paid the physician $200 before the provider submitted his claim. Thus, the payment should have been split between provider and beneficiary, with $400 paid to the provider and $80 to the beneficiary. The provider is liable for causing the $80 overpayment, as the amount received from the beneficiary was not reported on the claim.

- Provider submitted a claim for services other than medically necessary services, but should have known they would not be covered (e.g., conversation with a relative of a beneficiary).
- Provider submitted a claim for medically unnecessary services.
- Items or services were furnished by a provider or supplier not qualified for Medicare reimbursement.

EXAMPLE 1: A lab test is performed by a nonqualified independent laboratory.

EXAMPLE 2: Services are rendered by a naturopath (practitioner who uses natural remedies instead of drugs and surgery).

- Overpayment was due to a mathematical or clerical error.
- Provider does not submit documentation to substantiate services billed, or there is a question as to whether services were actually performed (e.g., fraud is suspected).
- Overpayment was for rental of durable medical equipment, and supplier billed under the one-time authorization procedure.

Absence of Provider Liability for Overpayments

A provider is liable for overpayments received unless found to be *without fault* as determined by the Medicare administrative contractor (MAC). A provider can be considered without fault if reasonable care was exercised in billing for and accepting payment, and the provider had a reasonable basis for assuming that payment was correct. In addition, if the provider had reason to question the payment and promptly brought the question to the attention of the MAC, she may be found without liability.

These criteria are always met in the case of overpayments due to an error with respect to the beneficiary's entitlement to Medicare benefits and the MAC's failure to properly apply the deductible. Normally, it is clear from the circumstances of the overpayment whether the provider was without fault in causing the overpayment. When this is not clear from the record, the MAC must review the issue (as long as the review occurs within three calendar years after the year in which the overpayment was made).

National Correct Coding Initiative

The Centers for Medicare and Medicaid Services (CMS) developed the *National Correct Coding Initiative (NCCI)* in 1996 to reduce Medicare program expenditures by detecting inappropriate codes submitted on claims and denying payment for them, promote national correct coding methodologies, and eliminate improper coding practices. (Table 5-2 contains a list of NCCI terms, definitions, and examples.) There are more than 140,000 NCCI **code pairs** (or **edit pairs**) that cannot

TABLE 5-2   Medicare's NCCI terms and definitions

TERM	DEFINITION	EXAMPLE
CCI edits	Pairs of CPT and/or HCPCS level II codes, which are not separately payable except under certain circumstances (e.g., reporting appropriate modifier). The edits are applied to services billed by the same provider for the same beneficiary on the same date of service.	The surgeon intends to perform laparoscopic cholecystectomy; upon visualization of gallbladder, it is determined that an open cholecystectomy is required. If the surgeon reports CPT codes for removal of an organ through an open incision as well as with laparoscopy, the NCCI edit results in claims denial. **NOTE:** If a laparoscopic procedure becomes an open procedure, report only the open procedure code.
Column 1 code	The major procedure or service when reported with another code. The *column 1 code* represents greater work, effort, and time than to the other code reported. (Previously called *comprehensive codes*.) Higher payments are associated with column 1 codes.	The patient undergoes deep biopsy as well as superficial biopsy of the same site. If the surgeon reports CPT codes for both the deep and superficial biopsies, the NCCI edit results in claims denial. **NOTE:** Report only the deep biopsy when both deep and superficial biopsies are performed at the same location.
Column 2 code	The lesser procedure or service when reported with another code. The *column 2 code* is part of a major procedure or service and is often represented by a lower work relative value unit (RVU) under the Medicare Physician Fee Schedule as compared to the other code reported. (Previously called *component codes*.) Lower payments are associated with column 2 codes.	If the surgeon determines that the superficial biopsy code should be reported in addition to the deep biopsy code, supporting documentation must appear in the patient's record. **NOTE:** A modifier must be added to the code. A modifier is a two-digit code added to the main code to indicate a procedure/service has been altered (e.g., bilateral procedure).
Column 1/ Column 2 edit table (Figure 5-6)	Code combinations (or edit pairs), where one of the codes is a component (column 2) of the more comprehensive (column 2) code and only the comprehensive code is paid. (If clinical circumstances justify appending an NCCI-associated modifier to either code of a code pair edit, payment of both codes may be allowed.)	Figure 5-6 contains a sample listing of column 1/column 2 codes. Refer to Column 1 code 10040. If code 10040 is reported on a CMS-1500 claim, none of the codes from Column 2 can be reported on the same claim (unless a modifier is attached and supporting documentation is found in the patient's record).
Mutually exclusive codes	Procedures or services that could not reasonably be performed at the same session by the same provider on the same beneficiary.	A claim that contains codes for cystourethroscopy, with internal urethrotomy of a female (CPT code 52270) and that of a male (CPT code 52275), will result in denial as a result of this NCCI edit.
Mutually exclusive edit table (Figure 5-7)	Code combinations (or edit pairs), where one of the procedures/services would not reasonably be performed with the other. (If clinical circumstances justify adding an NCCI modifier to either code of a code pair edit, payment of both codes may be allowed.)	Figure 5-7 contains a partial listing of mutually exclusive codes. Refer to Column 1 code 10060. If code 10060 is reported on a CMS-1500 claim, none of the codes from Column 2 can be reported on the same claim (unless a modifier is attached and supporting documentation is found in the patient's record).

NATIONAL CORRECT CODING INITIATIVE COLUMN 1 / COLUMN 2 EDITS

Column 1	Column 2	* = In existence prior to 1996	Effective Date	Deletion Date * = no data	Modifier 0 = not allowed 1 = allowed 9 = not applicable
10021	J2001		20040701	*	1
10021	19290		20020101	*	1
10021	36000		20021001	*	1
10021	36410		20021001	*	1
10021	37202		20021001	*	1
10021	62318		20021001	*	1
10021	62319		20021001	*	1
10021	64415		20021001	*	1
10021	64416		20030101	*	1
10021	64417		20021001	*	1

FIGURE 5-6 Sample national correct coding initiative (NCCI) edits for column 1/column 2 codes (previously called comprehensive/component codes) (CPT copyright 2010 American Medical Association. All rights reserved.)

NOTE: When codes from columns 1 and 2 are reported on the same claim for the same date of service, payment is denied for the column 2 code(s). For example, codes 10021 and 19290 cannot be reported on the same claim for the same date of service.

NATIONAL CORRECT CODING INITIATIVE MUTUALLY EXCLUSIVE EDITS

Column 1	Column 2	* = In existence prior to 1996	Effective Date	Deletion Date * = no data	Modifier 0 = not allowed 1 = allowed 9 = not applicable
10060	11401		19960101	*	1
10060	11402		19960101	*	1
10060	11403		19960101	*	1
10060	11404		19960101	*	1
10060	11406		19960101	*	1

FIGURE 5-7 Sample national correct coding initiative (NCCI) edits for mutually exclusive codes (CPT copyright 2010 American Medical Association. All rights reserved.)

NOTE: The meaning of column 1 and column 2 in Figure 5-7 is not the same as for Figure 5-6, NCCI Edits for Column 1/Column 2 Codes. In Table 10-2, column 1 codes are payable (selected as first-listed code) when reported with column 2 code(s). When codes from columns 1 and 2 are reported on the same claim for the same date of service, payment is made for all codes (e.g., codes 10060 and 11401 can be reported on the same claim for the same date of service).

NOTE: The provider must make full disclosure to the MAC of all material facts and the basis on which information was made available, including, but not limited to, Medicare regulations.

be reported on the same claim for the same date of service, and they are based on coding conventions defined in CPT, current standards of medical and surgical coding practice, input from specialty societies, and analysis of current coding practices. CMS contracts with Correct Coding Solutions, LLC, to develop, maintain and refine the NCCI and medically unlikely edits (MUEs) (discussed below), which are published by the National Technical Information Service (NTIS).

In 2007, CMS incorporated **medically unlikely edits (MUEs)** into the NCCI program, which are units of service edits. An MUE for a CPT or HCPCS level II code is the maximum number of units of service (UOS) under most circumstances allowable by the same provider for the same beneficiary on the same date of service.

NOTE: Under a previous CMS contract, a private company refused to publish code edits it developed because it considered them proprietary; these nonpublished code edits were called **black box edits**. Use of these edits was discontinued when CMS did not renew its contract with the company, and future CMS contracts do not allow for such restrictions.

> **EXAMPLE:** Mary Jones underwent a cataract extraction in her left eye. The claim submitted by the provider contained a 3 in the units column of Block 24, which means the patient underwent cataract extraction surgery on three left eyes. The *medically unlikely edit* process rejected the claim (because the patient has just one left eye). If 1 had been entered in the units column of Block 24, the claim would have passed the *medically unlikely edit* and payment would have been processed.

NCCI edits (Table 5-3) are used to process Medicare Part B claims, and NCCI coding policies are based on the:

- Analysis of standard medical and surgical practice.
- Coding conventions included in CPT.
- Coding guidelines developed by national medical specialty societies (e.g., CPT advisory committee, which contains representatives of major medical societies).
- Local and national coverage determinations.
- Review of current coding practices.

The NCCI was initially developed for use by Medicare administrative contractors (MACs) that process Medicare Part B claims for physician office services. NCCI edits were added to the Outpatient Code Editor (OCE) in August 2000, and they are used by MACs to process Medicare Part B claims for outpatient hospital services. (Some OCE edits that apply to outpatient hospital services claims differ from comparable edits in the NCCI used to process physician office services claims.)

Carefully review parenthetical notes below CPT code descriptions to locate procedures that are separately reported (in addition to the major procedure performed). When reporting codes for outpatient hospital services and physician office services, make sure you use OCE software or NCCI software, respectively, to identify bundled codes for procedures and services considered necessary to accomplish the major procedure. Bundled procedure codes are *not* separately coded and reported with the major procedure code. Reporting bundled procedure codes in addition to the major procedure code is characterized as unbundling (fraud).

NOTE: OCE edits are packaged with commercial software, such as Ingenix's Encoder Pro Expert.

TABLE 5-3   Partial listing of National Correct Coding Initiative (NCCI) edits

NCCI EDIT	DESCRIPTION	DISPOSITION OF CLAIM
1	Invalid diagnosis code	Return to Provider
2	Diagnosis and age conflict	Return to Provider
3	Diagnosis and sex conflict	Return to Provider
4	Medicare secondary payer alert	Suspend

EXAMPLE: Code 67911 describes the "Correction of lid retraction." A parenthetical note below the code description advises that if autogenous graft materials are used during the same operative session, tissue graft codes 20920, 20922, or 20926 are reported in addition to code 67911.

According to the Medicare Code Editor (MCE), *other procedures necessary to accomplish* the "correction of lid retraction" are included in code 67911, such as full-thickness graft placement (15260). Other such procedures are not separately coded and reported when performed during the same operative session as the "correction of lid retraction."

CMS POSTS CORRECT CODING INITIATIVE (CCI) EDITS ON INTERNET
(Permission to reuse in accordance with **www.cms.hhs.gov** Web site Content Reuse Policy.)

The Centers for Medicare & Medicaid Services (CMS) has made it easier for physicians and other providers to bill properly and be paid promptly for their services to people with Medicare coverage. CMS has posted on its Web site **(cms.hhs.gov)** the automated edits used to identify questionable claims and adjust payments to reflect what would have been paid if the claim had been filed correctly. The edits, known as the National Correct Coding Initiative (NCCI), identify pairs of services that normally should not be billed by the same physician for the same patient on the same day. The NCCI also promotes uniformity among the contractors that process Medicare claims in interpreting Medicare payment policies.

The posting of NCCI edits is the most recent in a series of steps CMS has taken to use the Internet creatively to reduce the regulatory burden on physicians and make it easier for them to work with Medicare to improve services to beneficiaries. CMS has also added a feature to its Web site (**cms.hhs.gov**) that makes it possible for physicians to determine in advance what they will be paid for a particular service or range of services. The Medicare Physician Fee Schedule Look-Up provides the unadjusted payment rates as well as the payment rates by geographic location. While the NCCI is a cornerstone of efforts to ensure that Medicare and beneficiaries do not pay twice for the same service or for duplicative services, CMS believes physicians should have easy access to the edits used to identify incorrect claims. The NCCI includes two types of edits:

- Column 1/Column 2 edits (previously called comprehensive/component edits) (code pairs that should not be billed together because one service inherently includes the other)

- Mutually exclusive edits (code pairs that, for clinical reasons, are unlikely to be performed on the same patient on the same day; e.g., two different types of testing that yield equivalent results)

CPT codes representing services denied, based on NCCI edits, may not be billed to Medicare beneficiaries. Since these denials are based on incorrect coding rather than medical necessity, the provider cannot submit an Advance Beneficiary Notice (ABN) to seek payment from a Medicare beneficiary. An Advance Beneficiary Notice (ABN) is a form completed and signed by a Medicare beneficiary each time a provider believes a normally covered service will not be covered *and* the provider wants to bill the beneficiary directly for the service. In addition, because the denials are based on incorrect coding (rather than a legislated Medicare benefit exclusion), the provider

(continues)

(continued)

cannot seek payment from the beneficiary even if a Notice of Exclusions from Medicare Benefits (NEMB) was obtained.

A Notice of Exclusions from Medicare Benefits (NEMB) is a form completed and signed by a Medicare beneficiary before items, procedures, and services excluded from Medicare benefits are provided; it alerts Medicare beneficiaries in advance that Medicare does not cover certain items and services because they do not meet the definition of a Medicare benefit or because they are specifically excluded by law. NEMB is completed when an ABN is not appropriate.

The NCCI edits, which are updated quarterly, were previously available to physicians and other providers on a paid subscription basis; but they are now available to anyone with a computer. The NCCI edits are posted as a spreadsheet that allows users to sort by procedural code and effective date. A Find feature allows users to look for a specific code. The NCCI edit files are also indexed by procedural code ranges to allow for easy navigation.

The new Web page also includes links to documents that explain the edits, including the following:

- Medicare Claims Processing Manual.
- NCCI Edits Program Transmittals.
- NCCI FAQs (frequently asked questions).
- NCCI Policy Manual for Part B MACs.

Unbundling CPT Codes

Providers are responsible for reporting the CPT (and HCPCS level II) code that most comprehensively describes the services provided. NCCI edits determine the appropriateness of CPT code combinations for claims submitted to MACs. NCCI edits are designed to detect *unbundling*, which involves reporting multiple codes for a service when a single column 1 code should be assigned. The practice of unbundling occurs because:

- **Provider's coding staff unintentionally reports multiple codes based on misinterpreted coding guidelines.**
- **The reporting of multiple codes is intentional and is done to maximize reimbursement.**

Unbundling occurs when one service is divided into its component parts and a code for each component part is reported as if they were separate services.

> **EXAMPLE:** A 64-year-old female patient undergoes total abdominal hysterectomy with bilateral salpingectomy and oophorectomy. Review CPT Surgery code descriptions for 58150, 58700, and 58720. Reporting codes 58700 and 58720 in addition to 58150 is considered unbundling. If all three codes were submitted on a claim, reimbursement for codes 58700 and 58720 would be disallowed (and the provider might be subject to allegations of fraud and abuse).

Unbundling occurs when a code for the separate surgical approach (e.g., laparotomy) is reported in addition to a code for the surgical procedure. Procedures performed to gain access to an area or organ system are not separately reported.

> **EXAMPLE:** A 54-year-old female patient underwent excision of ileoanal reservoir with ileostomy, which required lysis of adhesions to gain access to the site of surgery. Review CPT Surgery code descriptions for 45136 and 44005. Report CPT code 45136 only because code 44005 is considered a component part of the total procedure (45136). Reporting both codes would be considered unbundling.

Administrative Simplification

HIPAA was part of a congressional attempt at incremental healthcare reform, with the *Administrative Simplification* aspect requiring DHHS to develop standards for maintenance and transmission of health information required to identify individual patients. These standards are designed to

- Improve efficiency and effectiveness of the healthcare system by standardizing the interchange of electronic data for specified administrative and financial transactions.
- Protect the security and confidentiality of electronic health information.

NOTE: California implemented a regulation that prohibits the use of social security numbers on health plan ID cards and health-related correspondence.

The requirements outlined by law and the regulations implemented by DHHS require compliance by *all* healthcare organizations that maintain or transmit electronic health information (e.g., health plans; healthcare clearinghouses; and healthcare providers, from large integrated delivery networks to individual physician offices).

The law also establishes significant financial penalties for violations.

General penalty for failure to comply:

- Each violation: $100.
- Maximum penalty for all violations of an identical requirement may not exceed $25,000.

Wrongful disclosure of individually identifiable health information:

- Wrongful disclosure offense: $50,000; imprisonment of not more than 1 year; or both.
- Offense under false pretenses: $100,000; imprisonment of not more than 5 years; or both.
- Offense with intent to sell information: $250,000; imprisonment of not more than 10 years; or both.

NOTE: The Centers for Medicare & Medicaid Services (CMS) developed the **National Plan and Provider Enumeration System (NPPES)** to assign unique identifiers to healthcare providers and health plans. Providers can apply for the national provider identifier (NPI) online (**nppes.cms.hhs.gov**), on paper, or through an organization (e.g., professional association). When applying for the NPI, it is important to remember that providers must:

- Apply just once because every health plan, including Medicare and Medicaid, will use the same NPI for the provider.

- Obtain an NPI even if they use a billing agency to prepare standard insurance transactions.

- Continue to participate in health plan enrollment and/or credentialing processes.

- Safeguard the NPI because it is a private identification number.

(Health plans also use NPPES to apply for their national health PlanID.)

Unique Identifiers

The administrative simplification (AS) provision of HIPAA requires establishment of standard identifiers for third-party payers (e.g., insurance companies, Medicare, and Medicaid), providers, and employers, as follows:

- **National Health PlanID (PlanID)** (formerly called **PAYERID**) is assigned to third-party payers; it has 10 numeric positions, including a check digit as the tenth position. (A check digit is a one-digit character, alphabetic or numeric, used to verify the validity of a unique identifier.)
- **National Individual Identifier** (patient identifier) has been put on hold. Several bills in Congress would eliminate the requirement to establish a National Individual Identifier.

- **National Provider Identifier (NPI)** is assigned to healthcare providers as a **10-digit** numeric identifier, including a check digit in the last position.
- **National Standard Employer Identification Number (EIN)** is assigned to employers who, as sponsors of health insurance for their employees, must be identified in healthcare transactions. It is the federal employer identification number (EIN) assigned by the Internal Revenue Service (IRS) and has nine digits with a hyphen (00-0000000). EIN assignment by the IRS began in January 1998.

Electronic Healthcare Transactions

HIPAA requires payers to implement **electronic transaction standards** (or transactions rule), which is a uniform language for electronic data interchange. Electronic data interchange (EDI) is the process of sending data from one party to another using computer linkages. The CMS Standard EDI Enrollment Form must be completed prior to submitting electronic media claims (EMC) to Medicare. The agreement must be executed by each provider of healthcare services, physician, or supplier that intends to submit EMC.

> **EXAMPLE:** Healthcare providers submit electronic claims data to payers on computer tape, diskette, or by computer modem. The payer receives the claim, processes the data, and sends the provider the results of processing electronic claims (an electronic remittance advice).

> **NOTE:** Computer-generated paper claims are not categorized as EDI.

The final rule on transactions and code sets was effective October 16, 2002, for large plans and October 16, 2003, for small plans. It requires the following to be used by health plans, healthcare clearinghouses (which perform centralized claims processing for providers and health plans), and healthcare providers who participate in electronic data interchanges:

> **NOTE:** The UB–04 flat file is a series of fixed-length records that is used to bill institutional services, such as services performed in hospitals. The **National Standard Format (NSF)** flat file format is used to bill physician and noninstitutional services, such as services reported by a general practitioner on a CMS-1500 claim. The **ANSI ASC X12N 837** variable-length file format is used to bill institutional, professional, dental, and drug claims. (The UB-04 is discussed in Chapter 9.)

- **Three electronic formats are supported for healthcare claim transactions, including the UB-04 flat file format, the National Standard Format (NSF), and the ANSI ASC X12N 837** (American National Standards Institute [ANSI], Accredited Standards Committee [ASC], Insurance Subcommittee [X12N], Claims validation tables [837]).
- **Dental services are using** *Current Dental Terminology (CDT)* **codes.** *Current Dental Terminology (CDT)* is a medical code set maintained and copyrighted by the American Dental Association.
- **Diagnoses and inpatient hospital services are reported using** *International Classification of Diseases, 9th Revision, Clinical Modification (ICD-9-CM)* **codes.**
- **Physician services are reported using** *Current Procedural Terminology (CPT)* **codes.**
- **Procedures are reported using: ICD-9-CM (Index to Procedures and Tabular List of Procedures) and the** *Healthcare Common Procedure Coding System (HCPCS),* *level I (CPT)*, and *level II (national)* **codes.**
- **Institutional and professional pharmacy transactions are reported using** *HCPCS level II (national)* **codes.**
- **Retail pharmacy transactions are reported using the** *National Drug Code* **manual. No standard code set was adopted for nonretail pharmacy drug claims.**

> **NOTE:** ICD-9-CM will be replaced by ICD-10-CM and ICD-10-PCS when the 10th edition is adopted for implementation in 2013.

The *National Drug Code (NDC)*, maintained by the Food and Drug Administration (FDA), identifies prescription drugs and some over-the-counter products. Each drug product is assigned a unique 11-digit, 3-segment number, which identifies the vendor, product, and trade package size. The Deficit Reduction

Act (DRA) of 2005 requires states to collect Medicaid rebates for physician-administered medications. Effective 2007, National Drug Codes (NDC) are reported on Medicaid CMS-1500 claims (in addition to the HCPCS level II codes) when physicians administer medication(s) to a patient during an encounter.

> **EXAMPLE:** During an office encounter, a physician administered 4 milligrams of Zofran intravenously (IV) to a Medicaid patient. Enter the following codes on the CMS-1500 claim:
>
> - J2405 as the HCPCS level II code for "ondansetron hydrochloride, per 1 mg. " (Also enter the number 4 in the Units field of the CMS-1500 claim.)
>
> - 00173044202 as the National Drug Code for "Zofran 2 mg/ml in solution form. " (The NDC is located on the medication container.)

Privacy and Security Standards

Any information communicated by a patient to a healthcare provider is considered **privileged communication**, and HIPAA provisions address the privacy and security of protected health information. **Protected health information (PHI)** is information that is identifiable to an individual (individual identifiers) such as name, address, telephone numbers, date of birth, Medicaid ID number and other medical record numbers, social security number (SSN), and name of employer. In most instances, covered entities (providers, payers, and clearinghouses) are required to obtain an individual's **authorization** prior to disclosing the individual's health information, and HIPAA has established specific requirements for an authorization form. **Privacy** is the right of individuals to keep their information from being disclosed to others. Once information is disclosed (e.g., for the purpose of obtaining health care), it is essential that confidentiality of the information be maintained. **Confidentiality** involves restricting patient information access to those with proper authorization and maintaining the security of patient information. **Security** involves the safekeeping of patient information by:

- **Controlling access to hard copy and computerized records (e.g., implementing password protection for computer-based patient records).**
- **Protecting patient information from alteration, destruction, tampering, or loss (e.g., establishing office policies).**
- **Providing employee training in confidentiality of patient information (e.g., conducting annual in-service education programs).**
- **Requiring employees to sign a confidentiality statement that details the consequences of not maintaining patient confidentiality (e.g., employee termination).**

Because patient information is readily available through computerized databases and other means, it is essential to take steps to maintain confidentiality. **Breach of confidentiality**, often unintentional, involves the unauthorized release of patient information to a third party, as in the following examples:

- **Discussing patient information in public places (e.g., elevators).**
- **Leaving patient information unattended (e.g., computer screen display).**
- **Communicating patient information to family members without the patient's consent.**
- **Publicly announcing patient information in a waiting room or registration area.**
- **Accessing patient information without a job-related reason.**

NOTE: Healthcare providers are required to notify patients when the security of their protected health information has been breached. (A *breach* occurs when protected health information (PHI) is acquired, accessed, used, or disclosed in a way that poses "significant risk of financial, reputational, or other harm to the individual.")

- Providers must notify individuals to whom the PHI pertains within 60 days after discovery of the breach.

- Providers also have a duty to notify the media of any breach that affects more than 500 individuals residing in one state or jurisdiction.

Some situations of unauthorized disclosure, access or use of unsecured PHI do *not* constitute a breach requiring notification. Examples include:

- Employee who unintentionally accesses PHI within the scope of his authority.

- PHI inadvertently disclosed to employee who normally has access to certain types of PHI.

- Individual to whom PHI was disclosed cannot readily retain the information.

NOTE: Computerized practices must obtain the patient's signature on the special release form and provide a copy to the patient's insurance company upon request. With this method, the CMS-1500 claim generated will contain "SIGNATURE ON FILE" in Block 12 (Figure 5-9).

NOTE: A dated, signed special release form is generally considered valid for 1 year. Be sure to obtain the patient's signature on the special release form each year. Undated signed forms are assumed to be valid until revoked by the patient or guardian. CMS regulations permit government programs to accept both dated and undated authorizations. Established medical practices must update patient information and obtain the necessary authorization forms. Patients who regularly seek care must sign a new authorization each year.

Although HIPAA privacy regulations do not require providers to obtain patient authorization for the release of healthcare information to payers for processing insurance claims, many providers continue to obtain patient authorization. The best practice is to advise patients that they have the right to restrict the release of their healthcare information (e.g., patient writes a letter informing the provider that medical records are not to be released to insurance companies). When a patient restricts the release of healthcare information, the provider should obtain the patient's signature on a consent form accepting financial responsibility for the cost of treatment. An insurance company that is prohibited from reviewing patient records will probably refuse to reimburse the provider for a submitted claim. The signed consent form accepting financial responsibility allows the provider to collect payment from the patient.

If patient authorization is obtained, be sure the patient has signed an "authorization for release of medical information" statement before completing the claim. The release can be obtained in one of two ways:

- Ask the patient to sign a special release form that is customized by each practice and specifically names the patient's insurance company (Figure 5-8) or
- Ask the patient to sign Block 12, "Patient's or Authorized Person's Signature," on the CMS-1500 claim (Figure 5-9).

NOTE: Patients who undergo screening for the human immun-odeficiency virus (HIV) or AIDS infection should sign an additional authorization statement for release of information regarding their HIV/AIDS status (Figure 5-11). Several states require very specific wording on this form. Be sure to determine if your state requires a special form.

When third parties (e.g., attorneys, family members, and others) request copies of patient information, be sure to obtain the patient's signature on an authorization to release medical information (Figure 5-10). Exceptions to the expectation of privacy include information released via subpoena duces tecum and according to statutory reporting requirements (e.g., communicable disease reporting).

The HIPAA **privacy rule** creates national standards to protect individuals' medical records and other personal health information. This rule also gives patients greater access to their own medical records and more control over how their personal health information is used. The rule addresses the obligations of healthcare providers and health plans to protect health information, requiring doctors, hospitals, and other healthcare providers to obtain a patient's written consent and an authorization before using or disclosing the patient's protected health information to carry out *treatment, payment, or healthcare operations (TPO)*.

NOTE: Privacy violations are subject to a penalty of no more than $100 per person per violation, not to exceed $25,000 per person per year per violation of a single standard. More serious violations are subject to more severe penalties, including the following:

- $50,000 and/or up to 1 year in prison for persons who knowingly obtain and disclose protected health information.

- $100,000 and/or up to 5 years in prison for persons who under "false pretense" obtain and disclose protected health information.

- $250,000 and up to 10 years in prison for persons with intent to sell, transfer, or use PHI for malicious reasons or personal gain.

HIPAA ALERT!

Patient access to records. The HIPAA privacy rule states that "an individual has the right to inspect and obtain a copy of the individual's protected health information (PHI) in a designated record set," except for the following:

- Psychotherapy notes.

- Information compiled in anticipation of use in a civil, criminal, or administration action or proceeding.

- PHI subject to the Clinical Laboratory Improvements Amendments (CLIA) of 1988, which is the federal law that delineates requirements for certification of clinical laboratories.

- PHI exempt from CLIA (e.g., information generated by facilities that perform forensic testing procedures).

The HIPAA **security rule** adopts standards and safeguards to protect health information that is collected, maintained, used, or transmitted *electronically*. Covered entities affected by this rule include health plans, healthcare clearinghouses, and certain healthcare providers.

[Insert letterhead]

Authorization for Release of Medical Information to the Payer and Assignment of Benefits to Physician

COMMERCIAL INSURANCE

I hereby authorize release of medical information necessary to file a claim with my insurance company and ASSIGN BENEFITS OTHERWISE PAYABLE TO ME TO _____ *(fill in provider's name)* _____

I understand that I am financially responsible for any balance not covered by my insurance carrier. A copy of this signature is as valid as the original.

Signature of patient or guardian_____   Date _____

MEDICARE

BENEFICIARY _____   Medicare Number _____

I request that payment of authorized Medicare benefits be made on my behalf to ____ *(fill in provider's name)* ____ for any service furnished to me by that provider. I authorize any custodian of medical information about me to release to the Centers for Medicare & Medicaid Services and its agents any information needed to determine these benefits or the benefits payable for related services.

Beneficiary Signature _____   Date _____

MEDICARE SUPPLEMENTAL INSURANCE

BENEFICIARY _____   Medicare Number _____

Medigap ID Number _____

I hereby give _____ *(Name of Physician or Practice)* _____ permission to bill for Medicare Supplemental Insurance payments for my medical care.

I understand that _____ *(Name of Medicare Supplemental Insurance Carrier)* _____ needs information about me and my medical condition to make a decision about these payments. I give permission for that information to go to _____ *(Name of Medicare Supplemental Insurance Company)* _____ .

I request that payment of authorized Medicare Supplemental benefits be made either to me or on my behalf to _____ *(Name of Physician or Practice)* _____ for any services furnished me by that physician. I authorize any holder of medical information about me to release to _____ *(Name of Medicare Supplemental Insurance Company)* _____ any information required to determine and pay these benefits.

Beneficiary Signature _____   Date _____

FIGURE 5-8 Sample authorization form for release of medical information and assignment of benefits (Courtesy Delmar/Cengage Learning)

READ BACK OF FORM BEFORE COMPLETING & SIGNING THIS FORM.
12. PATIENT'S OR AUTHORIZED PERSON'S SIGNATURE I authorize the release of any medical or other information necessary to process this claim. I also request payment of government benefits either to myself or to the party who accepts assignment below.

SIGNED _____ **SIGNATURE ON FILE** _____   DATE _____

FIGURE 5-9 Release of medical information (Block 12 on a CMS-1500 claim) (Courtesy Delmar/Cengage Learning)

[Insert letterhead]

AUTHORIZATION FOR DISCLOSURE OF PROTECTED HEALTH INFORMATION (PHI)

(1) I hereby authorize Alfred Medical Center to disclose/obtain information from the health records of:

_____	_____	_____
Patient Name	Date of Birth (mmddyyyy)	Telephone (w/ area code)
_____	_____	
Patient Address		Medical Record Number

(2) Covering the period(s) of healthcare:

_____	_____	_____	_____
From (mmddyyyy)	To (mmddyyyy)	From (mmddyyyy)	To (mmddyyyy)

(3) I authorize the following information to be released by (Name of Provider) (check applicable reports):

❑ Face Sheet	❑ Doctors Orders	❑ Scan Results	❑ Mental Health Care	❑ Other:
❑ Discharge Summary	❑ Progress Notes	❑ Operative Report	❑ Alcohol Abuse Care	_____
❑ History & Physical Exam	❑ Lab Results	❑ Pathology Report	❑ Drug Abuse Care	_____
❑ Consultation	❑ X-ray Reports	❑ HIV Testing Results	❑ Nurses Notes	_____

This information is to be disclosed to or obtained from:

_____	_____	_____
Name of Organization	Address of Organization	Telephone Number

for the purpose of: _____

Statement that information used or disclosed may be subject to redisclosure by the recipient and may no longer be protected by this rule. I understand that I have a right to revoke this authorization at any time. I understand that if I revoke this authorization I must do so in writing and present my written revocation to the Health Information Management Department. I understand that the revocation will not apply to information that has already been released in response to this authorization. I understand that the revocation will not apply to my insurance company when the law provides my insurer with the right to contest a claim under my policy. Unless otherwise revoked, this authorization will expire on the following date, event, or condition:

_____	_____	_____
Expiration Date	Expiration Event	Expiration Condition

If I fail to specify an expiration date, event or condition, this authorization will expire within six (6) months.

Signature of individual and date. I understand that authorizing the disclosure of this health information is voluntary. I can refuse to sign this authorization. I need not sign this form in order to ensure treatment. I understand that I may inspect or copy the information to be used or disclosed, provided in CFR 164.534. I understand that any disclosure of information carries with it the potential for an unauthorized redisclosure and may not be protected by federal confidentiality rules. If I have questions about disclosure of my health information, I can contact the Privacy Officer at Alfred Medical Center.

Signed:

_____	_____
Signature of Patient or Legal Representative	Date

If signed by legal representative:

_____	_____
Relationship to Patient	Signature of Witness

FIGURE 5-10 Sample authorization to release medical information (Courtesy Delmar/Cengage Learning)

[Insert letterhead]
Name and address of facility/provider obtaining release:
Name of person whose HIV related information will be released:
Name(s) and address(es) of person(s) signing this form (if other than above):
Relationship to person whose HIV information will be released:
Name(s) and address(es) of person(s) who will be given HIV related information:
Reason for release of HIV related information:
Time during which release is authorized: From: To:
The Facility/Provider obtaining this release must complete the following:
Exceptions, if any, to the right to revoke consent for disclosure: (for example, cannot revoke if disclosure has already been made)
Description of the consequences, if any, of failing to consent to disclosure upon treatment, payment, enrollment, or eligibility for benefits:
(Note: Federal privacy regulations may restrict some consequences.) My questions about this form have been answered. I know that I do not have to allow release of HIV related information, and that I can change my mind at any time and revoke my authorization by writing the facility/provider obtaining this release.
Date   Signature

FIGURE 5-11 Sample authorization for release of confidential HIV related information (This form and any updates to it are available to the public on the New York State Department of Health Web site at **www.health.state.ny.us**.)

In general, security provisions should include the following policies and procedures:

NOTE: Individual states (e.g., New York) may have passed laws or established regulations for patient access to records; providers must follow these laws or regulations if they are stricter than HIPAA provisions.

- **Define authorized users of patient information to control access.**
- **Implement a tracking procedure to sign out records to authorized personnel.**
- **Limit record storage access to authorized users.**
- **Lock record storage areas at all times.**
- **Require the original medical record to remain in the facility at all times.**

Telephone Inquiries

One area of concern regarding breach of confidentiality involves the clarification of insurance data by telephone. A signed release statement from the patient may be on file, but the office has no assurance of the identity or credentials of a telephone inquirer. It is very simple for a curious individual to place a call to a physician's office and claim to be an insurance company benefits clerk. The rule to follow is, *always require written requests for patient information.* (The only circumstance that would allow the release of information over the

NOTE: The proposed standard for electronic signature is **digital**, which applies a mathematical function to the electronic document resulting in a **unique bit string** (computer code) called a **message digest** that is encrypted and appended to the electronic document. **(Encrypt** means to encode a computer file, making it safe for electronic transmission so that unauthorized parties cannot read it.) The recipient of the transmitted electronic document **decrypts** (decodes) the message digest and compares the decoded digest with the transmitted version. If they are identical, the message is unaltered and the identity of the signer is proven.

telephone is an emergency situation that involves patient care. In this situation, be sure to authenticate the requesting party by using the "call-back method," which involves calling the facility's switchboard and asking to be connected to the requesting party.)

Facsimile Transmission

Great care must be taken to ensure that sensitive information sent by fax reaches the intended receiver and is handled properly. It is recommended that health information be faxed only when there is:

1. an urgent need for the health record and mailing the record will cause unnecessary delays in treatment, or

2. immediate authorization for treatment is required from a primary care physician or other third-party case manager.

In such cases, information transmitted should be limited only to the information required to satisfy the immediate needs of the requesting party. Each transmission of sensitive material should have a cover sheet including the following information:

NOTE: It is usually acceptable to submit a copy of the medical record for legal proceedings. If the original record is required, obtain a receipt from the court clerk and retain a copy of the record in the storage area. Be sure to properly protect the original record when transporting it to court by placing the record in a locked storage container. Make sure that the original record remains in the custody of the healthcare personnel transporting the record until the record is entered into evidence.

- **Name of the facility to receive the facsimile.**
- **Name and telephone number of the person authorized to receive the transmission.**
- **Name and telephone number of the sender.**
- **Number of pages being transmitted.**
- **A confidentiality notice or disclaimer (Figure 5-12).**
- **Instructions to authorized recipient to send verification of receipt of transmittal to the sender.**

The practice should keep a dated log of the transmission of all medically sensitive facsimiles and copies of all "receipt of transmittal" verifications signed and returned by the authorized recipient. Special care must be taken to ensure that proper facsimile destination numbers are keyed into the fax machine prior to transmission.

Confidentiality and the Internet

NOTE: Although *security* and *privacy* are linked, be sure you do not confuse the purpose of each rule. The *security rule* defines administrative, physical, and technical safeguards to protect the availability, confidentiality, and integrity of electronic protected health information (PHI). The *privacy rule* establishes standards for *how* PHI should be controlled, by indicating authorized uses (e.g., continuity of care) and disclosures (e.g., third-party reimbursement) and patients' rights with respect to their health information (e.g., patient access).

At present there is no guarantee of confidentiality when patient records are transmitted via the Internet. If time constraints prevent sending sensitive information through a more secure delivery system, special arrangements may be made with the requesting party to transmit the document after deleting specific patient identification information. It is best to call the party requesting the documents to arrange for an identifier code to be added to the document so that the receiving party is assured that the information received is that which was requested. This transmission should be followed by an official unedited copy of the record, sent by overnight delivery, that includes specific patient material that was deleted from the previous transmission. In 1998 the *HCFA Internet Security Policy* issued guidelines for the security and appropriate use of the Internet for accessing and transmitting sensitive information (e.g., Medicare beneficiary information). The information must be encrypted so that information is converted to a secure language format for transmission, and authentication or identification procedures must be implemented to ensure that the sender and receiver of data are known to each other and are authorized to send and/or receive such information.

> If you have received this transmittal in error, please notify the sender immediately.
>
> The material in this transmission contains confidential information that is legally privileged. This information is intended only for the use of the individual or entity named above.
>
> If you are not the intended recipient, you are hereby notified that any disclosure, copying, distribution, or action taken based on the contents of this transmission is strictly prohibited.

FIGURE 5-12 Sample fax confidentiality notice (Courtesy Delmar/Cengage Learning)

> **NOTE:** The *Patient Safety and Quality Improvement Act* allows providers to report healthcare errors on a voluntary and confidential basis. Patient safety organizations (PSOs) analyze the problems, identify solutions, and provide feedback to avoid future errors. A database tracks national trends and reoccurring problems.

Medical Liability

The threat of excessive awards in medical liability cases has increased providers' liability insurance premiums and resulted in increased healthcare costs. As a result, some providers stop practicing medicine in areas of the country where liability insurance costs are highest, and the direct result for individuals and communities across the country is reduced access to quality medical care. Although medical liability reform was included in HIPAA legislation, no final rule was published. Individual states, such as Ohio, have passed medical liability reform, and the U.S. Congress is also formulating separate federal medical liability reform legislation.

SUMMARY

Federal and state statutes are laws passed by legislative bodies and implemented as regulations (guidelines written by administrative agencies). The *Federal Register* is a legal newspaper published every business day by the federal government. Medicare program transmittals are legal notices about Medicare policies and procedures, and they are incorporated into the appropriate CMS program manual (e.g., *Medicare Claims Processing Manual*). Federal and state legislation have regulated the healthcare industry since 1863, when the False Claims Act (FCA) was enacted.

Record retention is the storage of documentation for an established period of time, usually mandated by federal and/or state law. HIPAA mandates the retention of health insurance claims for a minimum of 6 years, unless state law specifies a longer period. HIPAA also mandates that patient records and health insurance claims be retained for a minimum of 2 years after a patient's death.

The Health Insurance Portability and Accountability Act (HIPAA) includes the following provisions: health insurance reform, administrative simplification, fraud and abuse guidelines, use of medical savings accounts, improved access to long-term care services and coverage, electronic health information transaction standards, and privacy and security standards for health information.

INTERNET LINKS

- Federal Register
  www.archives.gov

- Administrative Simplification in the Health Care Industry (HIPAA)
  Go to **aspe.hhs.gov,** scroll down to the Often Requested heading, and click on the Administrative
  Simplification in the Health Care Industry (HIPAA) link.

- ANSI ASC X12N 837 implementation guides
  www.wpc-edi.com

- Centers for Medicare and Medicaid Services
  www.cms.hhs.gov

- DHHS OIG Prevention and Detection program
  oig.hhs.gov

- Healthcare policy and regulatory resources
  hippo.findlaw.com

- HIPAA Privacy
  Go to **www.hhs.gov,** scroll down to the Other Highlights heading, and click on the Privacy of Health
  Information/HIPAA link.

- *HIPAA Weekly Advisor* by HCPro, Inc.
  Go to **www.HCPro.com,** click on the "Subscribe to one of our free newsletters" link, and select HIPAA
  Weekly Advisor (or any other free newsletter) to subscribe.

- Medical liability reform
  Go to **thomas.loc.gov,** and enter "medical liability reform" in the search box to review federal
  legislation under consideration by the House and/or Senate.

- Medicare Claim Review Programs booklet
  Go to **http://www.cms.gov**, click on the MLN Products link, click on MLN Publications, enter
  "Medicare Claim Review Programs" in the "Show only items containing the following word"
  Search box, click Show Items, click on the October 2008 link, and click on the "Medicare Claim
  Review Programs: MUE, CCI, CERT, RAC [PDF 2MB]" link.

- Medicare newsletters
  Go to **www.trailblazerhealth.com,** and click on the Publications link.

- National Correct Coding Initiative Edits Manual
  www.ntis.gov

- National Plan and Provider Enumeration System (NPPES)
  nppes.cms.hhs.gov

- *The RAC Report* by HCPro, Inc.
  Go to **www.hcmarketplace.com,** click on the "Sign up for our FREE e-newsletter" link, and select The
  RAC Report (and other topics) to receive free e-newsletter(s).

- Retail pharmacy standards implementation guide
  www.ncpdp.org

- State and local government information
  Go to **thomas.loc.gov,** click on the Government Resources link, scroll down to the General
  Government Resources heading, and click on the Local Government Resources or the State
  Government Resources link.

STUDY CHECKLIST

☐ Read this textbook chapter and highlight key concepts.

☐ Create an index card for each key term.

☐ Access the chapter Internet links to learn more about concepts.

☐ Answer the chapter review questions, verifying answers with your instructor.

☐ Complete WebTutor assignments and take online quizzes.

☐ Complete Workbook chapter, verifying answers with your instructor.

☐ Complete the StudyWare activities to receive immediate feedback.

☐ Form a study group with classmates to discuss chapter concepts in preparation for an exam.

REVIEW

MULTIPLE CHOICE Select the most appropriate response.

1. **A commercial insurance company sends a letter to the physician requesting a copy of a patient's entire medical record in order to process payment. No other documents accompany the letter. The insurance specialist should**

   a. contact the patient via telephone to alert him about the request.

   b. let the patient's physician handle the situation personally.

   c. make a copy of the record and mail it to the insurance company.

   d. require a signed patient authorization from the insurance company.

2. **An attorney calls the physician's office and requests that a copy of his client's medical record be immediately faxed to the attorney's office. The insurance specialist should**

   a. call the HIPAA hotline number to report a breach of confidentiality.

   b. explain to the attorney that the office does not fax or copy patient records.

   c. instruct the attorney to obtain the patient's signed authorization.

   d. retrieve the patient's medical record and fax it to the attorney.

3. **An insurance company calls the office to request information about a claim. The insurance specialist confirms the patient's dates of service and the patient's negative HIV status. The insurance specialist**

   a. appropriately released the dates of service, but not the negative HIV status.

   b. breached patient confidentiality by confirming the dates of service.

   c. did not breach patient confidentiality because the patient's HIV status was negative.

   d. was in compliance with HIPAA provisions concerning release of dates of service and HIV status.

4. **A patient's spouse comes to the office and requests diagnostic and treatment information about his wife. The spouse is the primary policyholder on which his wife is named on the policy as a dependent. The insurance specialist should**

   a. allow the patient's spouse to review the actual record in the office, but not release a copy.

   b. inform the patient's spouse that he must request the information from his insurance company.

   c. obtain a signed patient authorization from the wife before releasing patient information.

   d. release a copy of the information to the patient's spouse, because he is the primary policyholder.

5. **Which is considered Medicare fraud?**

   a. billing for services that were not furnished and misrepresenting diagnoses to justify payment

   b. charging excessive fees for services, equipment, or supplies provided by the physician

   c. submitting claims for services that are not medically necessary to treat a patient's condition

d. violating participating provider agreements with insurance companies and government programs

6. **Which is considered Medicare abuse?**

   a. falsifying certificates of medical necessity, plans of treatment, and medical records to justify payment

   b. improper billing practices that result in Medicare payment when the claim is the legal responsibility of another third-party payer

   c. soliciting, offering, or receiving a kickback for procedures and/or services provided to patients in the physician's office

   d. unbundling codes; that is, reporting multiple CPT codes on a claim to increase reimbursement from a payer

7. **A patient received services on April 5, totaling $1,000. He paid a $90 coinsurance at the time services were rendered. (The payer required the patient to pay a 20 percent coinsurance at the time services were provided.) The physician accepted assignment, and the insurance company established the reasonable charge as $450. On July 1 the provider received $360 from the insurance company. On August 1 the patient received a check from the insurance company in the amount of $450. The overpayment was _____, and the _____ must reimburse the insurance company.**

   a. $450, patient

   b. $450, physician

   c. $550, patient

   d. $640, physician

8. **The patient underwent office surgery on October 10, and the third-party payer determined the reasonable charge to be $1,000. The patient paid the 20 percent coinsurance at the time of the office surgery. The physician and patient each received a check for $500, and the patient signed the check over to the physician. The overpayment was _____, and the _____ must reimburse the insurance company.**

   a. $200, patient

   b. $200, physician

   c. $500, patient

   d. $500, physician

9. **The 66-year-old patient was treated in the emergency department (ED) for a fractured arm. The patient said, "I was moving a file cabinet for my boss when it tipped over and fell on my arm." The facility billed Medicare and received reimbursement of $550. The facility later determined that Medicare was not the payer because this was a workers' compensation case.**

   a. is guilty of both fraud and abuse according to HIPAA because of accepting the $550.

   b. must give the $550 check to the patient, who should contact workers' compensation.

   c. should have billed the employer's workers' compensation payer for the ED visit.

   d. was appropriately reimbursed $550 by Medicare for the emergency department visit.

10. **The physician submitted a claim on which he had accepted assignment to the third-party payer. The patient signed an assignment-of-benefits statement for the office. The payer determined that the reasonable charge for services provided to the patient was $500 and reimbursed the physician $400. The patient paid $200 at the time services were provided. (The payer required the patient to pay a 20 percent coinsurance amount when services were provided.) The insurance specialist should**

   a. charge the patient an additional $100.

   b. refund the patient a $100 overpayment.

   c. return the $400 check to the payer.

   d. submit the patient's name to collections.

ICD-9-CM Coding

CHAPTER OUTLINE

OBJECTIVES

Upon successful completion of this chapter, you should be able to:

1. Define key terms.
2. Explain the purpose of reporting diagnosis codes on insurance claims, including the concept of medical necessity.
3. List and apply CMS outpatient guidelines in coding diagnoses.
4. Identify and properly use ICD-9-CM's coding conventions.
5. Accurately code diagnoses according to ICD-9-CM.
6. Explain the differences between ICD-9-CM and ICD-10-CM/PCS.

KEY TERMS

adverse effect

adverse reaction

axis of classification

benign

carcinoma (Ca) *in situ*

Classification of Drugs by AHFS List

Classification of Industrial Accidents
According to Agency

coding conventions

comorbidity

complication

computer-assisted coding (CAC)

congenital anomaly

contiguous site

131

Diagnostic Coding and Reporting Guidelines for Outpatient Services: Hospital-Based and Physician Office

E code

encoder

first-listed diagnosis

general equivalency mapping (GEM)

iatrogenic illness

Index to Diseases (ICD-9-CM)

    coding conventions

        code in slanted brackets

        eponym

        essential modifier

        main term

        NEC (not elsewhere classifiable)

        nonessential modifier

        notes

        qualifier

        see

        see also

        see also condition

        see category

        subterm

Index to Diseases (Volume 2)

Index to Procedures

    coding conventions (ICD-9-CM)

        code also any synchronous procedures

        omit code

Index to Procedures and Tabular List of Procedures (Volume 3)

indexing

injury

International Classification of Diseases, 10th Edition, Clinical Modification/Procedure Coding System, (ICD-10-CM/PCS)

late effect

lesion

List of Three-Digit Categories

malignant

metastasize

metastatic

morbidity

morphology

Morphology of Neoplasms (M codes)

mortality

National Center for Health Statistics (NCHS)

neoplasm

outpatient

overlapping site

perinatal condition

perinatal period

poisoning

preadmission testing (PAT)

primary malignancy

principal diagnosis

principal procedure

qualified diagnosis

qualifiers

re-excision

secondary diagnosis

secondary malignancy

secondary procedure

sequelae

Tabular List of Diseases (ICD-9-CM)

    coding conventions

        and

        bold type

        braces

        brackets

        categories

        code first underlying disease

        colon

        excludes

        format

        fourth and fifth digits

        includes

        major topic heading

        not otherwise specified (NOS)

        parentheses

        subcategory

        subclassification

        use additional code

        with

Tabular List of Diseases (Volume 1)

uncertain behavior

unspecified nature

V code

INTRODUCTION

There are two related classifications of diseases with similar titles. The *International Classification of Diseases (ICD)* is published by the World Health Organization (WHO) and is used to code and classify mortality (death) data from death certificates. The *International Classification of Diseases, Ninth Revision, Clinical Modification (ICD-9-CM)* was developed in the United States and is used to code and classify morbidity (disease) data from inpatient and outpatient records, including physician office records. The health insurance specialist employed in a physician's office assigns ICD-9-CM codes to diagnoses, signs, and symptoms documented by the healthcare provider. Entering ICD-9-CM codes on insurance claims results in uniform reporting of medical reasons for healthcare services provided.

Complete StudyWare practice quizzes and activities using the CD-ROM located inside the back cover of your textbook.

NOTE: Be sure to clarify the definition of *medical necessity* by insurance companies (other than Medicare), because the definition can vary.

NOTE: An *injury* is a traumatic wound or some other damage to an organ. In ICD-9-CM, injuries are initially classified in the Injury and Poisoning chapter by type (e.g., all open wounds are classified in the same chapter).

OVERVIEW OF ICD-9-CM

ICD-9-CM was sponsored in 1979 as the official system for assigning codes to diagnoses (inpatient and outpatient care, including physician offices) and procedures (inpatient care). The ICD-9-CM is organized into three volumes:

- **Volume 1 (Tabular List of Diseases).**
- **Volume 2 (Index to Diseases).**
- **Volume 3 (Index to Procedures and Tabular List of Procedures).**

The National Center for Health Statistics (NCHS) and CMS are U.S. Department of Health and Human Services agencies that comprise the ICD-9-CM Coordination and Maintenance Committee, which is responsible for overseeing all changes and modifications to the ICD-9-CM diagnosis (NCHS) and procedure (CMS) codes. The NCHS works with the World Health Organization (WHO) to coordinate official disease classification activities for ICD-9-CM (Index to Diseases and Tabular List of Diseases), which includes the use, interpretation, and periodic revision of the classification system. CMS is responsible for creating annual procedure classification updates for ICD-9-CM (Index to Procedures and Tabular List of Procedures). Updates are available from the official ICD-9-CM Web sites of the CMS and NCHS. A CD-ROM version that contains official coding guidelines as well as the complete, official version of the ICD-9-CM is available for purchase from the U.S. Government Bookstore (**bookstore.gpo.gov**).

ICD-9-CM coding books are also available from commercial publishing companies and are helpful in manual coding because they contain color-coded entries that identify required additional digits, nonspecific and unacceptable principal diagnoses, and more.

Mandatory Reporting of ICD-9-CM Codes

The Medicare Catastrophic Coverage Act of 1988 mandated the reporting of ICD-9-CM diagnosis codes on Medicare claims. Private payers adopted similar diagnosis coding requirements for claims submission in subsequent years (reporting procedure and service codes is discussed in Chapters 7 and 8). Requiring diagnosis codes to be reported on submitted claims establishes the medical necessity of procedures and services rendered to patients (e.g., inpatient care, office visit, outpatient visit, or emergency department visit). Medical necessity is defined by Medicare as "the determination that a service or procedure rendered is reasonable and necessary for the diagnosis or treatment of an illness or injury." If it is possible that scheduled tests, services, or procedures may be found "medically unnecessary" by Medicare, the patient must sign an *advance beneficiary notice (ABN)*, which acknowledges patient responsibility for payment if Medicare denies the claim. (Chapter 14 contains a complete explanation about the ABN, including a sample form.)

> **EXAMPLE:** A patient with insulin-dependent diabetes is treated at the physician's office for a leg injury sustained in a fall. When the physician questions the patient about his general health status since the last visit, the patient admits to knowing that a person on insulin should perform a daily blood sugar level check. The patient also admits to usually skipping this check one or two times a week, and he has not performed this check today. The physician orders an x-ray of the leg, which proves to be positive for a fracture, and a test of the patient's blood glucose level.

If the only stated diagnosis on the claim is a fractured tibia, the blood glucose test would be rejected for payment by the insurance company as an unnecessary medical procedure. The diagnostic statements reported on the claim should include both the fractured tibia and insulin-dependent diabetes to permit reimbursement consideration for both the x-ray and the blood glucose test.

ICD-9-CM Annual Updates

CMS enforces regulations pursuant to the Medicare Prescription Drug, Improvement, and Modernization Act (MMA), which require that all code sets (e.g., ICD-9-CM) reported on claims be valid at the time services are provided. To be compliant, this means that traditional mid-year (April 1) and end-of-year (October 1) coding updates must be immediately implemented so that accurate codes are reported on submitted claims.

It is crucial that updated coding manuals be purchased and/or billing systems be updated with coding changes so that billing delays (e.g., due to waiting for new coding manuals to arrive) and claims rejections are avoided. If outdated codes are submitted on claims, providers and healthcare facilities will incur administrative costs associated with resubmitting corrected claims and delayed reimbursement for services provided.

NOTE: The MMA now requires new, revised, and deleted ICD-9-CM codes to be implemented each October 1 and updated each April.

- Coders should consider using updateable coding manuals, which publishers offer as a subscription service. These coding manuals are usually stored in a three-ring binder so that coders can remove outdated pages and add new pages provided by the publisher.

- Another option is to purchase encoder software, also offered as a subscription service. Coders routinely download the most up-to-date encoder software, containing edits for new, revised, and discontinued codes. An encoder automates the coding process using computerized or Web-based software; instead of manually looking up conditions (or procedures) in the coding manual index, the coder uses the software's search feature to locate and verify diagnosis and procedure codes.

- Automating the medical coding process is the goal of computer–assisted coding (CAC), which uses a natural language processing engine to "read" patient records and generate ICD-9-CM and HCPCS/CPT codes. Because of this process, coders become coding auditors, responsible for ensuring the accuracy of codes reported to payers. (CAC can be compared to speech recognition technology that has transitioned the role of medical transcriptionists in certain fields, such as radiology, to that of medical editors.)

MEDICAL NECESSITY

Today's concept of medical necessity determines the extent to which individuals with health conditions receive healthcare services. (The concept was introduced in the 1970s when health insurance contracts intended to exclude care, such as voluntary hospitalizations, prescribed primarily for the convenience of the provider or patient.) *Medical necessity* is the measure of whether a healthcare procedure or service is appropriate for the diagnosis and/or treatment of a condition. This decision-making process is based on the payer's contractual language and the treating provider's documentation. Generally, the following criteria are used to determine medical necessity:

- *Purpose:* the procedure or service is performed to treat a medical condition.
- *Scope:* the most appropriate level of service is provided, taking into consideration potential benefit and harm to the patient.

- *Evidence:* the treatment is known to be effective in improving health outcomes.
- *Value:* the treatment is cost-effective for this condition when compared to alternative treatments, including no treatment.

OVERVIEW OF ICD-10-CM AND ICD-10-PCS

The *International Classification of Diseases, 10th Revision, Clinical Modification (ICD-10-CM)* and the *International Classification of Diseases, 10th Revision, Procedure Coding System (ICD-10-PCS)*, also abbreviated as ICD-10-CM/PCS, will replace ICD-9-CM on October 1, 2013. ICD-10-CM/PCS includes many more codes and applies to more users than ICD-9-CM because it is designed to collect data on every type of healthcare encounter (e.g., inpatient, outpatient, hospice, home health care, and long-term care). ICD-10-CM/PCS also enhances accurate payment for services rendered and facilitates evaluation of medical processes and outcomes.

To prepare for implementation of ICD-10-CM/PCS, healthcare professionals should assess their coding staff to determine whether they require education and training to:

- Apply advanced knowledge of anatomy and physiology, medical terminology, and pathophysiology.
- Effectively communicate with members of the medical staff.
- Interpret patient record documentation (e.g., operative reports).
- Interpret and apply coding guidelines to assign ICD-10-CM/PCS codes.

History of the ICD

The World Health Organization (WHO) originally intended for ICD to serve as a statistical tool for the international collection and exchange of mortality (death) data. A subsequent revision was expanded to accommodate data collection for morbidity (disease) statistics. The seventh revision of ICD, published by WHO in 1955, was clinically modified for use in the United States after a joint study was conducted to evaluate the efficiency of indexing (cataloging diseases and procedures by code number) hospital diseases. In 1959, the *International Classification of Diseases, Adapted for Indexing Hospital Records, Seventh Revision (ICDA-7)* was released by the federal Public Health Service, and provided the United States with a way to classify patient operations and treatments. The *Eighth Revision of the International Classification of Diseases, Adapted for Use in the United States (ICDA-8)* and the *Hospital Adaptation of ICDA (H-ICDA)* were subsequently published for use in the United States, followed by the *International Classification of Diseases, Ninth Revision, Clinical Modification (ICD-9-CM)* in 1979. This time the incentive for creating a clinical modification of the ICD resulted from a process, initiated in 1977 by the National Center for Hospital Statistics (NCHS), for hospital indexing and retrieval of case data for clinical studies. More than 30 years since its adoption in the United States, ICD has proven to be indispensable to anyone interested in payment schedules for the delivery of healthcare services to patients.

ICD-10

The WHO published ICD-10 in 1994 with a new name *(International Statistical Classification of Diseases and Related Health Problems)* and reorganized its three-digit categories (list following). Although the title was amended to clarify content and purpose and to reflect development of codes and descriptions beyond diseases and injuries, the familiar abbreviation "ICD" was kept. ICD-10 contains clinical detail, expands information about previously classified diseases, and classifies diseases discovered since the last revision. Though ICD-10 incorporates organizational changes and new features, its format and conventions remain largely unchanged. Chapter titles, organization and Includes and Excludes notes are similar to ICD-9. The biggest difference is that the new codes are alphanumeric, and there is more detail in ICD-10-CM than in ICD-9-CM.

A number of other countries have already adopted ICD-10, including the United Kingdom (1995), France (1997), Australia (1998), Germany (2000), and Canada (2001). ICD-10-CM and ICD-10-PCS provide more detailed information (than ICD-9-CM) and the ability to expand codes so that additional advancements in clinical medicine can be captured. The change from ICD-9-CM to the NCHS-developed ICD-10-CM and the CMS-developed ICD-10-PCS (Procedure Coding System) will occur on October 1, 2013. Information about each coding system is included below, and ICD-10-CM alerts appear throughout the remainder of this chapter (and in chapters 11 through 17 of this textbook) to assist with the transition to the new classification system.

ICD-10-CM AND ICD-10-PCS (ICD-10-CM/PCS)

ICD-10-CM is the United States' clinical modification of the ICD-10, developed by the National Center for Health Statistics (NCHS), and it will replace Volumes 1 and 2 of ICD-9-CM on October 1, 2013. The term *clinical* emphasizes the modification's intent, which is to:

- Serve as a useful tool in the area of classification of morbidity data for indexing of medical records, medical care review, and ambulatory and other medical care programs, as well as for basic health statistics.
- Describe the clinical picture of the patient, which means the codes must be more precise than those needed only for statistical groupings and trend analysis.
- *ICD-10-CM* is the diagnosis classification system developed by the Centers for Disease Control and Prevention (CDC) for use in *all* U.S. healthcare treatment settings. ICD-10-CM codes require up to seven characters, are entirely alphanumeric, and have new coding conventions (e.g., Excludes1 and Excludes2 notes). However, the format of ICD-10-CM is very similar to ICD-9-CM (e.g., index to diseases, tabular list of diseases, external causes of diseases).

ICD-10-PCS is an entirely new procedure classification system developed by the Centers for Medicare & Medicaid Services (CMS) for use in the United States for inpatient hospital settings *only*, and will replace Volume 3 of ICD-9-CM on October 1, 2013. ICD-10-PCS uses a multiaxial 7-character alphanumeric code structure (e.g., 047K04Z) that provides a unique code for all substantially different procedures. It also allows new procedures to be easily incorporated as new codes. ICD-10-PCS contains more than 87,000 7-character alphanumeric procedure codes. (ICD-9-CM has about 4,000 3- to 4-digit numeric procedure codes.)

ICD-10-CM and ICD-10-PCS (or ICD-10-CM/PCS) incorporate much greater specificity and clinical information, resulting in:

- Improved ability to measure healthcare services.
- Increased sensitivity when refining grouping and reimbursement methodologies.
- Enhanced ability to conduct public health surveillance.
- Decreased need to include supporting documentation with claims.

ICD-10-CM/PCS also includes updated medical terminology and classification of diseases, provides codes to allow comparison of mortality and morbidity data, and provides better data for:

NOTE: The *International Classification of Diseases, 9th Edition, Clinical Modification (ICD-9-CM)* does not provide the necessary detail about patients' medical conditions or the procedures performed on hospitalized inpatients. ICD-9-CM is over 30 years old, has outdated and obsolete terminology, uses outdated codes that produce inaccurate and limited data, and is inconsistent with current medical practice. It cannot accurately describe diagnoses or inpatient procedures of care delivered in the 21st century.

NOTE: In ICD-10-PCS, *multiaxial* means the codes contain independent characters, with each axis retaining its meaning across broad ranges of codes (to the extent possible). (There is no decimal used in ICD-10-PCS codes). ICD-9-CM procedure codes contain 3–4 digits, including a decimal (e.g., 39.50).

- Measuring care furnished to patients.
- Designing payment systems.
- Processing claims.
- Making clinical decisions.
- Tracking public health.
- Identifying fraud and abuse.
- Conducting research.

ICD-10-CM far exceeds ICD-9-CM in the number of codes provided, having been expanded to (1) include health-related conditions, (2) provide much greater specificity at the sixth digit level, and (3) add a seventh digit extension (in some cases). Assigning the sixth and seventh characters when available for ICD-10-CM codes is mandatory because they report information documented in the patient record.

EXAMPLE: The diagnosis is stage III pressure ulcer of the right lower back. In ICD-9-CM, two separate codes are reported for location and stage, but laterality (e.g., right sidedness) cannot be classified. In ICD-10-CM, a combination code is reported, and the right side (laterality) is classified.

- **ICD-9-CM:**   707.03, 707.23
- **ICD-10-CM:**   L89.133

ICD-9-CM contains just 15 codes to classify pressure ulcers according to location and depth. ICD-10-CM contains greater specificity because 125 codes are available to classify pressure ulcers according to location, depth, and laterality.

ICD-9-CM TABULAR LIST OF DISEASES	ICD-10-CM TABULAR LIST OF DISEASES

707.0   Pressure ulcer
Bed sore
Decubitus ulcer
Plaster ulcer
Use additional code to identify pressure ulcer
    stage (707.20–707.25)
707.03 Lower back
Coccyx
Sacrum
707.2   Pressure ulcer stages
Code first site of pressure ulcer
    (707.00–707.09)
707.23 Pressure ulcer stage III
Healing pressure ulcer, stage III
Pressure ulcer with full thickness skin loss
    involving damage or necrosis of subcuta-
    neous tissue
	L89.13 Pressure ulcer of right lower back
	L89.131 Pressure ulcer of right lower back, stage I
	Pressure area of right lower back
	Pressure ulcer of right lower back limited to
	    erythema only
	L89.132 Pressure ulcer of right lower back, stage II
	Pressure ulcer of right lower back with abra-
	    sion, blister, partial thickness skin loss
	    involving epidermis and dermis
	Pressure ulcer of right lower back with skin
	    loss NOS
	L89.133 Pressure ulcer of right lower back, stage III
	Pressure ulcer of right lower back with full
	    thickness skin loss involving damage or
	    necrosis of subcutaneous tissue extending
	    to underlying fascia
	L89.134 Pressure ulcer of right lower back, stage IV
	Pressure ulcer of right lower back with necrosis
	    of muscle, bone, and supporting structures
	    (i.e., tendon or joint capsule)
	L89.139 Pressure ulcer of right lower back,
	    unspecified stage

EXAMPLE: The diagnosis is "mechanical breakdown of femoral arterial graft." In ICD-9-CM, just one code is available for any mechanical complication of a vascular graft. In ICD-10-CM, a combination code is reported, and the right side is classified.

- **ICD-9-CM:**   996.1
- **ICD-10-CM:**   T82.312

In ICD-9-CM, just one code classifies mechanical complications of vascular grafts. ICD-10-CM contains a greatly expanded number of codes, with over 150 codes available to classify mechanical complications of vascular grafts, according to type of complication and type of graft (which also indicates the location of the graft)

ICD-9-CM TABULAR LIST OF DISEASES	ICD-10-CM TABULAR LIST OF DISEASES

996.1 Mechanical complication of other vascular device, implant, or graft
Mechanical complications involving:
aortic (bifurcation) graft (replacement)
arteriovenous:
  dialysis catheter ⎱
  fistula   ⎰ surgically created
  shunt
balloon (counterpulsation) device, intra-aortic
carotid artery bypass graft
femoral-popliteal bypass graft
umbrella device, vena cava
EXCLUDES *atherosclerosis of biological graft (440.30-440.32)*
embolism [occlusion NOS] [thrombus] of (biological) (synthetic) graft (996.74)
peritoneal dialysis catheter (996.56)
	T82.3 Mechanical complication of other vascular grafts
	T82.31 Breakdown (mechanical) of other vascular grafts
	T82.310 Breakdown (mechanical) of aortic (bifurcation) graft (replacement)
	T82.311 Breakdown (mechanical) of carotid arterial graft (bypass)
	T82.312 Breakdown (mechanical) of femoral arterial graft (bypass)
	T82.318 Breakdown (mechanical) of other vascular grafts
	T82.319 Breakdown (mechanical) of unspecified vascular grafts

General Equivalence Mappings (GEMs)

The National Center for Health Statistics (NCHS) and Centers for Medicare and Medicaid Services (CMS) annually publish **general equivalence mappings (GEMs)**, which are translation dictionaries or crosswalks of codes which can be used to roughly identify ICD-10-CM/PCS codes for their ICD-9-CM equivalent codes (and vice versa). General equivalence mappings (GEMs) facilitate the location of corresponding diagnosis codes between two code sets. In some areas of the classification, the correlation between codes is close and since the sets share the conventions of organization and formatting common to both revisions of ICD, translating between them is straightforward.

EXAMPLE: There is straightforward correspondence between the two code sets for infectious diseases, neoplasms, eye diseases, and ear diseases.

GENERAL EQUIVALENCE MAPPING	
ICD-9-CM Diagnosis Code and Description	**ICD-10-CM Diagnosis Code and Description**
003.21 Salmonella meningitis	A02.21 Salmonella Meningitis
205.01 Acute myeloid leukemia in remission	C92.01 Acute myeloid leukemia, in remission

EXAMPLE: In other areas, such as obstetrics, entire chapters are organized according to a different axis of classification and translating between them offers a series of possible codes that must be verified in the appropriate tabular list (ICD-9-CM or ICD-10-CM) or table of codes (ICD-10-PCS) to identify the correct code. (Think about translating the English language into Chinese or any other foreign language, and you will see the problems inherent in such translation.)

GENERAL EQUIVALENCE MAPPING	
ICD-9-CM Diagnosis Code and Description	**ICD-10-CM Diagnosis Code and Description**
649.50 Spotting complicating pregnancy, unspecified as to episode of care or not applicable	026.851 Spotting complicating pregnancy, first trimester 026.852 Spotting complicating pregnancy, second trimester 026.853 Spotting complicating pregnancy, third trimester 026.859 Spotting complicating pregnancy, unspecified trimester

OUTPATIENT CODING GUIDELINES

The **Diagnostic Coding and Reporting Guidelines for Outpatient Services: Hospital–Based and Physician Office** were developed by the federal government for use in reporting diagnoses for claims submission. Four cooperating parties are involved in the continued development and approval of the guidelines:

1. American Hospital Association (AHA).

2. American Health Information Management Association (AHIMA).

3. Centers for Medicare and Medicaid Services (CMS, formerly HCFA).

4. National Center for Health Statistics (NCHS).

Although the guidelines were originally developed for use in submitting government claims, insurance companies have also adopted them (sometimes with variation).

NOTE:

- Because variations may contradict the official guidelines, be sure to obtain each insurance company's official coding guidelines.

- When reviewing the guidelines, remember that the terms *encounter* and *visit* are used interchangeably in describing outpatient and physician office services.

> **CODING TIP:**
>
> Begin the search for the correct code by referring to the Index to Diseases. Never begin searching for a code in the Tabular List of Diseases because this will lead to coding errors.

A. Selection of First-listed Condition

In the outpatient setting, the term **first-listed diagnosis** is used (instead of the inpatient setting's *principal diagnosis*), and it is determined in accordance with ICD-9-CM's *coding conventions* (or rules) as well as general and disease-specific coding guidelines (below). Because diagnoses are often not established at the time of the patient's initial encounter or visit, two or more visits may be required before the diagnosis is confirmed. An **outpatient** is a person treated in one of four settings:

- Ambulatory surgery center (ASC) where the patient is released prior to a 24-hour stay (length of stay must be 23 hours, 59 minutes, and 59 seconds or less).
- Healthcare provider's office (e.g., physician).
- Hospital clinic, emergency department, outpatient department, same-day surgery unit (length of stay must be 23 hours, 59 minutes, and 59 seconds or less).
- Hospital observation where the patient's length of stay is: ■ 23 hours, 59 minutes, and 59 seconds or less (commercial insurance) (unless documentation for additional observation is medically justified). ■ 24–48 hours (Medicare).

> **CODING TIP:**
>
> - *Outpatient Surgery.* When a patient presents for outpatient surgery, code the reason for the surgery as the first-listed diagnosis (reason for the encounter), even if the surgery is not performed due to a contraindication.
>
> - *Observation Stay.* When a patient is admitted for observation for a medical condition, assign a code for the medical condition as the first-listed diagnosis.
>
> - *Outpatient Surgery that Requires Observation Stay.* When a patient presents for outpatient surgery and develops complications requiring admission to observation, code the reason for the surgery as the first reported diagnosis (reason for the encounter), followed by codes for the complications as secondary diagnoses.

An *inpatient* is a person admitted to a hospital or long-term care facility (LTCF) for treatment (or residential care, if LTCF) with the expectation that the patient will remain in the hospital for a period of 24 hours or more. The inpatient status is stipulated by the admitting physician.

You may see *principal diagnosis* referred to as *first-listed diagnosis* in medical literature. Remember! The outpatient setting's first-listed diagnosis is *not* the principal diagnosis. (The outpatient first-listed diagnosis used to be called the *primary diagnosis* because it was the most significant condition for which services and/or procedures were provided.) The outpatient first-listed diagnosis code is reported in Block 21 of the CMS-1500 claim. The inpatient **principal diagnosis** is defined as "the condition determined *after study* which resulted in the patient's admission to the hospital." The principal diagnosis code is reported in Form Locator 67 of the UB-04 (CMS-1450) claim.

Secondary diagnoses include comorbidities and complications. A **comorbidity** is a *concurrent condition* that coexists with the first-listed diagnosis (outpatient care) or principal diagnosis (inpatient care), has the potential to affect treatment of the first-listed diagnosis (outpatient care) or principal diagnosis (inpatient care), and is an active condition for which the patient is treated and/or monitored. (Insulin dependent diabetes mellitus is an example of a comorbidity.) A **complication** is a condition that develops after outpatient care has been provided (e.g., ruptured sutures after office surgery) or during an inpatient admission (e.g., inpatient develops postoperative wound infection). Secondary diagnoses are reported in Block 21 of the CMS-1500 claim and Form Locators 67A-67Q of the UB-04.

> **NOTE:** The outpatient *first-listed diagnosis* was previously called the *primary diagnosis.*

EXAMPLE 1: A patient seeks care at the healthcare provider's office for an injury to the right leg that, upon x-ray in the office, is diagnosed as a fractured tibia. While in the office, the physician also reviews the current status and treatment of the patient's type II diabetes.

- What is the first-listed diagnosis?
- What is the secondary diagnosis?
- Which diagnosis justifies medical necessity of the leg x-ray?
- Which diagnosis justifies medical necessity of the office visit?

Answer: The first-listed diagnosis is "fracture, shaft, right tibia"; the secondary diagnosis is "type II diabetes mellitus." On the CMS-1500 claim, report the diagnoses codes in Block 21 and enter the diagnosis link in Block 24E for the corresponding service or procedure.

DIAGNOSIS	LINK TO SERVICE OR PROCEDURE
Fracture, shaft, right tibia	x-ray of leg
Insulin-dependent diabetes mellitus	Office visit

EXAMPLE 2: The patient has a history of arteriosclerotic heart disease and was admitted to the hospital because of severe shortness of breath. After study, a diagnosis of congestive heart failure is added. What is the principal diagnosis?

Answer: The principal diagnosis is congestive heart failure. (This diagnosis was determined after study to be the cause of the patient's admission to the hospital. Arteriosclerosis alone would not have caused the hospitalization. Shortness of breath is not coded because it is a symptom of congestive heart failure.)

EXAMPLE 3: A patient was admitted with hemoptysis. The following procedures were performed: upper GI series, barium enema, chest x-ray, bronchoscopy with biopsy of the left bronchus, and resection of the upper lobe of the left lung. The discharge diagnosis was bronchogenic carcinoma. What is the principal diagnosis?

Answer: The principal diagnosis is bronchogenic carcinoma, left lung. (The hemoptysis precipitated the need for hospitalization, but is a symptom of the underlying problem, bronchogenic carcinoma. After admission to the hospital and after study, the diagnostic tests revealed the carcinoma.)

ICD-10-CM ALERT!

In guideline B., the range of codes will change to A00.0 through Z99.89, effective October 1, 2013.

ICD-10-CM ALERT!

Reference to "ICD-9-CM" in guideline C. will change to "ICD-10-CM" effective October 1, 2013.

ICD-10-CM ALERT!

Guideline D. will be eliminated on October 1, 2013, because all of the ICD-10-CM codes in the classification of diseases and injuries are alphanumeric.

B. ICD-9-CM Tabular List of Diseases (Codes 001.0 through V89.09)

The appropriate code or codes from 001.0 through V89.09 must be used to identify diagnoses, symptoms, conditions, problems, complaints, or any other reason for the encounter/visit.

C. Accurate Reporting of ICD-9-CM Diagnosis Codes

For accurate reporting of ICD-9-CM diagnosis codes, the documentation should describe the patient's condition using terminology that includes specific diagnoses as well as symptoms, problems, or reasons for the encounter. There are ICD-9-CM codes to describe all of these.

D. Selection of Codes 001.0 through 999.9

Codes 001.0 through 999.9 will frequently be used to describe the reason for the encounter. These codes are from the section of ICD-9-CM for the classification of diseases and injuries (e.g., infectious and parasitic diseases; neoplasms; symptoms, signs, and ill-defined conditions).

E. Codes that Describe Signs and Symptoms

Codes that describe signs and symptoms, as opposed to definitive diagnoses, are acceptable for reporting purposes when the physician has not documented an established or confirmed diagnosis. ICD-9-CM Chapter 16 "Symptoms, Signs, and Ill-defined Conditions" (780.0-799.9), contains many, but not all, codes for symptoms. Some symptom codes are located in other ICD-9-CM chapters that can be found by using the ICD-9-CM Index to Diseases.

ICD-10-CM ALERT!

Effective October 1, 2013, "Chapter 18 of ICD-10-CM, Symptoms, Signs, and Abnormal Clinical and Laboratory Findings Not Elsewhere Classified (codes R00-R99) contains many but not all codes for symptoms." (This means the guideline as it is written for ICD-9-CM will be edited to delete the statement, "Chapter 16 of ICD-9-CM, "Symptoms, Signs, and Ill-defined Conditions" (codes 780-799), contains many, but not all, codes for symptoms. Some symptom codes are located in other ICD-9-CM chapters, which can be found by properly using the ICD-9-CM Index to Diseases.")

ICD-10-CM ALERT!

"ICD-10-CM" will replace "ICD-9-CM" and "(Z00-Z99)" will replace "(V01.0-V89.09)" in guideline F., effective October 1, 2013.

F. Encounters for Circumstances Other Than Disease or Injury

ICD-9-CM provides codes to deal with encounters for circumstances other than a disease or injury. The Supplementary Classification of Factors Influencing Health Status and Contact with Health Services (V01.0–V89.09) is provided to deal with occasions when circumstances other than disease or injury are recorded as diagnoses or problems.

CODING TIP:

Coding guidelines require the assignment of a secondary code that identifies the underlying condition (e.g., abnormality of gait, 781.2) when rehabilitation codes, V57.0-V57.9, are reported as the first-listed code on an insurance claim.

Certain V codes can be reported as a first-listed or additional diagnosis for outpatient care. If a claim is denied due to a V code, contact your regional CMS office or the HIPAA enforcement office for resolution.

In some cases, the first-listed diagnosis may be a sign or symptom when a diagnosis has not been established (confirmed) by the physician.

G. Level of Detail in Coding

ICD-9-CM disease codes contain three, four, or five digits. Codes with three digits are included in ICD-9-CM as the heading of a category of disease codes that may be further subdivided by the assignment of fourth or fourth and fifth digits, which provide greater specificity.

A three-digit disease code is to be assigned only if it is not further subdivided. Where fourth-digit subcategories or fifth-digit subclassifications are provided, they must be assigned. A code is invalid if it has not been coded to the full number of digits required for that code.

ICD-10-CM ALERT!

Effective October 1, 2013, guideline G. will state, "ICD-10-CM is composed of codes with either 3, 4, 5, 6, or 7 digits. Codes with three digits are included in ICD-10-CM as the heading of a category of codes that may be further subdivided by the use of fourth, fifth, sixth, or seventh digits, which provide greater specificity.

A three-digit code is to be used only if it is not further subdivided. A code is invalid if it has not been coded to the full number of characters required for that code, including the 7th character extension, if applicable (requiring the use of x's as placeholders if necessary, such as code T16.1xxA).

H. ICD-9-CM Code for the Diagnosis, Condition, Problem, or Other Reason for Encounter/Visit

ICD-10-CM ALERT!

Effective October 1, 2013, "ICD-10-CM" will replace "ICD-9-CM" in both the heading and narrative of guideline H. The "note" (below) will also be eliminated effective October 1, 2013.

Report first the ICD-9-CM code for the diagnosis, condition, problem, or other reason for encounter/visit shown in the medical record to be chiefly responsible for the services provided. Then report additional codes that describe coexisting conditions that were treated or medically managed or that influenced the treatment of the patient during the encounter.

I. Uncertain Diagnoses

Do not code diagnoses documented as *probable, suspected, questionable, rule out,* or *working diagnosis,* because these are considered *uncertain (or qualified) diagnoses.* Instead, code condition(s) to the highest degree of certainty for that encounter/visit, such as symptoms, signs, abnormal test results, or other reasons for the visit.

Another difference in coding inpatient hospitalizations versus outpatient and/or provider office encounters involves the assignment of codes for qualified diagnoses. A **qualified diagnosis** is a working diagnosis that is not yet proven or established. Terms and phrases associated with qualified diagnoses include *suspected, rule out, possible, probable, questionable, suspicious for,* and *ruled out.* For office visits, do *not* assign an ICD-9-CM code to qualified diagnoses; instead, code the sign(s) and/or symptom(s) documented in the patient's chart.

EXAMPLE:

For Qualified Diagnosis:	Code the Sign or Symptom:
Suspected pneumonia	Shortness of breath, wheezing, rales, and/or rhonchi
Questionable Raynaud's	Numbness of hands
Ruled out wrist fracture	Wrist pain and/or swelling
Ruled out pneumonia	Influenza (flu)

NOTE: The rule in guideline I. differs from inpatient coding practices in acute care hospitals, where assigning codes to qualified diagnoses (e.g., probable) is permitted.

Qualified diagnoses are a necessary part of the hospital and office chart until a specific diagnosis can be determined. Although qualified diagnoses are routinely coded for hospital inpatient admissions and reported on the UB-04 claim, CMS *specifically prohibits the reporting of such diagnoses on the CMS-1500 claim submitted by healthcare provider offices.* CMS regulations permit the reporting of patients' signs and/or symptoms instead of the qualified diagnoses.

An additional incentive for not coding qualified diagnoses resulted from the Missouri case of *Stafford v. Neurological Medicine Inc.,* 811 F.2d 470 (8th

Cir. 1987). In this case, the diagnosis stated in the physician's office chart was "rule out brain tumor." The claim submitted by the office listed the diagnosis code for "brain tumor," although test results proved that a brain tumor did not exist. The physician assured the patient that although she had lung cancer, there was no metastasis to the brain. Sometime after the insurance company received the provider's claim, it was inadvertently sent to the patient. When the patient received the claim, she was so devastated by the diagnosis that she committed suicide. Her husband sued and was awarded $200,000 on the basis of "negligent paperwork" because the physician's office was responsible for reporting a qualified diagnosis.

J. Chronic Diseases

> **NOTE:** Payers review claims for "family history of" classification to determine reimbursement eligibility. Some plans reimburse for conditions that may not normally be eligible for payment when "family history of" a related condition is documented in the patient's record.

Chronic diseases treated on an ongoing basis may be coded and reported as many times as the patient receives treatment and care for the condition(s).

K. Code All Documented Conditions That Coexist

Code all documented conditions that coexist at the time of the encounter/visit and require or affect patient care treatment or management. Do not code conditions that were previously treated and no longer exist. However, history codes (V10–V19) may be reported as secondary codes if the historical condition or family history has an impact on current care or influences treatment.

> **ICD-10-CM ALERT!**
> Effective October 1, 2013, "(Z80-Z87)" will replace "(V10-V19)" in guideline K.

L. Patients Receiving Diagnostic Services Only

For patients receiving *diagnostic services only* during an encounter/visit, report first the diagnosis, condition, problem, or other reason for the encounter/visit that is documented in the patient record as being chiefly responsible for the outpatient services provided during the encounter/visit. (This is the *first-listed diagnosis.*)

> **NOTE:** The rule in guideline L. differs from coding practices in the acute care hospital inpatient setting because the physician establishes a confirmed or definitive diagnosis based on abnormal test result findings.

For outpatient encounters for diagnostic tests that have been interpreted by a physician *and* for which the final report is available at the time of coding, code any confirmed or definitive diagnoses documented in the interpretation. *Do not code related signs and symptoms as additional diagnoses.*

In addition, report code(s) for other diagnoses (e.g., chronic conditions) that are treated or medically managed or would affect the diagnostic services provided to the patient during this encounter/visit.

> **ICD-10-CM ALERT!**
> Effective October 1, 2013, the following statement will be added to guideline L. "For encounters for routine laboratory/radiology testing in the absence of any signs, symptoms, or associated diagnosis, assign Z01.89, Encounter for other specified special examinations. If routine testing is performed during the same diagnosis, it is appropriate to assign both the V code and the code describing the reason for the non-routine test." (Remember that V codes in ICD-10-CM classify signs and symptoms.).

M. Patients Receiving Therapeutic Services Only

> **ICD-10-CM ALERT!**
> Effective October 1, 2013, "... appropriate Z code ..." replaces "... appropriate V code ..." in guideline M.

For patients receiving *therapeutic services only* during an encounter/visit, sequence first the diagnosis, condition, problem, or other reason for the encounter/visit shown in the medical record to be chiefly responsible for the outpatient services provided during the encounter/visit.

Assign code(s) to other diagnoses (e.g., chronic conditions) that are treated or medically managed or would affect the patient's receipt of therapeutic services during this encounter/visit.

The only exception is when the reason for admission/encounter is for chemotherapy, radiation therapy, or rehabilitation. For these services, the appropriate V code for the service is reported first, and the diagnosis or problem for which the service is being performed is reported second.

N. Patients Receiving Preoperative Evaluations Only

For patients receiving *preoperative evaluation only*, assign the appropriate subclassification code located under subcategory V72.8, Other specified examinations, to describe the preoperative consultation.

Assign an additional code to the condition that describes the reason for the surgery. Also, assign additional code(s) to any findings discovered during the preoperative evaluation.

O. Ambulatory Surgery (or Outpatient Surgery)

For *ambulatory surgery* (or *outpatient surgery*), assign a code to the diagnosis for which the surgery was performed. If the postoperative diagnosis is different from the preoperative diagnosis when the diagnosis is confirmed, assign a code to the postoperative diagnosis instead (because it is more definitive).

P. Routine Outpatient Prenatal Visits

For routine outpatient prenatal visits when no complications are present, report code V22.0 (Supervision of normal first pregnancy) or V22.1 (Supervision of other normal pregnancy) as the first-listed diagnosis. *Do not report these codes in combination with ICD-9-CM Chapter 11 codes.*

ICD-9-CM CODING SYSTEM

The official version of ICD-9-CM was originally published in three volumes:

- **Volume 1 (Tabular List of Diseases).**
- **Volume 2 (Index to Diseases).**
- **Volume 3 (Index to Procedures and Tabular List of Procedures).**

Provider offices and healthcare facilities use the Tabular List of Diseases and Index to Diseases (Volumes 1 and 2 of ICD-9-CM) to code diagnoses. The

NOTE: Provider offices and outpatient healthcare settings use CPT and HCPCS level II to code procedures and services.

ICD-10-CM ALERT!

Effective October 1, 2013, provider offices and healthcare facilities will use ICD-10-CM to code diagnoses. Hospitals will use ICD-10-PCS to code inpatient procedures (Provider offices and outpatient healthcare settings will continue to use CPT and HCPCS level II to code procedures and services.)

ICD-10-CM ALERT!

The ICD-10-CM tabular list of diseases contains 21 chapters. There are no supplementary classifications because ICD-9-CM's V and E codes are incorporated into ICD-10-CM.

Index to Procedures and Tabular List of Procedures (Volume 3) is used by hospitals to code inpatient procedures. Many publishers offer their own versions of ICD-9-CM, and as a result, hospital (Volumes 1, 2, and 3) and outpatient (Volumes 1 and 2) editions of the coding manual are available. In addition, to make the coding procedure easier, publishers often place the Index to Diseases (Volume 2) in front of the Tabular List of Diseases (Volume 1).

Tabular List of Diseases (Volume 1)

The Tabular List of Diseases (Volume 1) contains 17 chapters that classify diseases and injuries, two supplemental classifications, and four appendices. The 17 chapters are organized as follows:

Chapter 1   Infectious and Parasitic Diseases (001–139)

Chapter 2   Neoplasms (140–239)

Chapter 3   Endocrine, Nutritional and Metabolic Diseases, and Immunity Disorders (240–279)

Chapter 4   Diseases of the Blood and Blood Forming Organs (280–289)

Chapter 5   Mental Disorders (290–319)

Chapter 6   Diseases of the Nervous System and Sense Organs (320–389)

Chapter 7   Diseases of the Circulatory System (390–459)

Chapter 8   Diseases of the Respiratory System (460–519)

Chapter 9   Diseases of the Digestive System (520–579)

Chapter 10   Diseases of the Genitourinary System (580–629)

Chapter 11   Complications of Pregnancy, Childbirth, and the Puerperium (630–679)

Chapter 12   Diseases of the Skin and Subcutaneous Tissue (680–709)

Chapter 13   Diseases of the Musculoskeletal System and Connective Tissue (710–739)

Chapter 14   Congenital Anomalies (740–759)

Chapter 15   Certain Conditions Originating in the Perinatal Period (760–779)

Chapter 16   Symptoms, Signs, and Ill-defined Conditions (780–799)

Chapter 17   Injury and Poisoning (800–999)

ICD-10-CM ALERT!

External Causes of Injury (E codes) and *Factors Influencing Health Status* (V codes) are incorporated into the core ICD-10-CM classification system as *External Causes of Morbidity* (Chapter 20) and *Factors Influencing Health Status and Contact with Health Services* (Chapter 21), respectively. They are no longer considered supplementary classifications.

The two supplemental classifications are:

V codes   Supplementary Classification of Factors Influencing Health Status and Contact with Health Services (V01–V89)

E codes   Supplementary Classification of External Causes of Injury and Poisoning (E000–E999)

ICD-10-CM ALERT!

The ICD-10-CM tabular list of diseases contains 21 chapters compared with 17 chapters and 2 supplementary classifications for V and E codes in the ICD-9-CM tabular list of diseases. (ICD-10, created by WHO, has 22 chapters; ICD-10-CM excludes the chapter entitled Codes for Special Purposes, U00-U99.)

ICD-10-CM CLASSIFICATION OF DISEASES AND INJURIES		
Chapter 1	A00-B99	Certain Infectious and Parasitic Diseases
Chapter 2	C00-D49	Neoplasms

Chapter 3	D50-D89	Diseases of the Blood and Blood-forming Organs and Certain Disorders Involving the Immune Mechanism
Chapter 4	E00-E90	Endocrine, Nutritional, and Metabolic Disorders
Chapter 5	F01-F99	Mental and Behavioral Disorders
Chapter 6	G00-G99	Diseases of the Nervous System
Chapter 7	H00-H59	Diseases of the Eye and Adnexa
Chapter 8	H60-H95	Diseases of the Ear and Mastoid Process
Chapter 9	I00-I99	Diseases of the Circulatory System
Chapter 10	J00-J99	Diseases of the Respiratory System
Chapter 11	K00-K94	Diseases of the Digestive System
Chapter 12	L00-L99	Diseases of the Skin and Subcutaneous Tissue
Chapter 13	M00-M99	Diseases of the Musculoskeletal System and Connective Tissue
Chapter 14	N00-N99	Diseases of the Genitourinary System
Chapter 15	O00-O99	Pregnancy, Childbirth, and the Puerperium
Chapter 16	P00-P96	Certain Conditions Originating in the Perinatal Period
Chapter 17	Q00-Q99	Congenital Malformations, Deformations, and Chromosomal Abnormalities
Chapter 18	R00-R99	Symptoms, Signs, and Abnormal Clinical and Laboratory Findings, Not Elsewhere Classified
Chapter 19	S00-T88	Injury, Poisoning, and Certain Other Consequences of External Causes
Chapter 20	V01-Y99	External Causes of Morbidity
Chapter 21	Z00-Z99	Factors Influencing Health Status and Contact with Health Services

NOTE: Appendix B was deleted as of October 1, 2004 (formerly the Glossary of Mental Disorders).

ICD-10-CM ALERT!

It remains to be seen whether ICD-10-CM will contain appendices similar to those in ICD-9-CM. The electronic files posted at www.cms.hhs.gov do not include appendices for ICD-10-CM.

ICD-10-CM ALERT!

In ICD-10-CM, "factors influencing health status and contact with health services" are incorporated into the tabular list as Chapter 21. It is no longer considered a supplementary classification.

The four appendices are:

Appendix A	Morphology of Neoplasms (M Codes)
Appendix C	Classification of Drugs by American Hospital Formulary Service List Number and Their ICD-9-CM Equivalents
Appendix D	Classification of Industrial Accidents According to Agency
Appendix E	List of Three-Digit Categories

Supplementary Classifications: V Codes and E Codes

V codes are located in the Tabular List of Diseases and are assigned for patient encounters when a circumstance other than a disease or injury is present. (V codes are indexed in the Index to Diseases.) Examples of V code assignment include:

- **Removal of a cast applied by another physician (V54.89).**
- **Exposure to tuberculosis (V01.1).**

- Personal history of breast cancer (V10.3).
- Well-baby checkup (V20.2).
- Annual physical examination (V70.0).

E codes, also located in the Tabular List of Diseases, describe external causes of injury, poisoning, or other adverse reactions affecting a patient's health. They are reported for environmental events, industrial accidents, injuries inflicted by criminal activity, and so on. Although assignment of these codes does not directly affect reimbursement to the provider, reporting E codes can expedite insurance claims processing because the circumstances related to an injury are indicated. (E codes are indexed in the Index to External Causes.)

> **EXAMPLE 1:** A patient who falls at home in the kitchen and breaks his leg would have place of occurrence code E849.0 reported on the insurance claim (in addition to the fracture code). This code indicates that the patient's health insurance policy, and not a liability policy, should cover treatment.

> **EXAMPLE 2:** A patient who falls at the grocery store and breaks his leg would have place of occurrence code E849.6 reported on the insurance claim (in addition to the fracture code). This code indicates that the store's liability insurance should be billed, not the patient's health insurance.

Appendices

ICD-9-CM appendices serve as a resource in coding neoplasms, adverse effects of drugs and chemicals, and external causes of disease and injury. In addition, the three digit disease category codes are listed as an appendix. Some publishers (e.g., *Ingenix's ICD-9-CM Experts for Hospitals Volumes 1, 2, & 3*) include adjunct appendices such as major diagnostic categories (MDCs) (associated with diagnosis related groups), diagnosis related groups (DRG) categories, valid three-digit ICD-9-CM codes (those that do not require a fourth or fifth digit), and differences and similarities between inpatient and outpatient coding guidelines.

Morphology of Neoplasms (M codes) (found in Appendix A of ICD-9-CM) contains a reference to the World Health Organization publication entitled *International Classification of Diseases for Oncology (ICD-O)*. The appendix also interprets the meaning of each digit of the morphology code number. Morphology indicates the tissue type of a neoplasm. M codes are *not reported on provider office claims,* but they are reported to state cancer registries. A basic knowledge of morphology coding can be helpful to a coder because the name of the neoplasm documented in the patient's chart does not always indicate whether the neoplasm is benign (not cancerous) or malignant (cancerous).

Referring to the morphology entry in the Index to Diseases helps determine which column in the neoplasm table should be referenced to select the correct code. In addition, coding should be delayed until the pathology report is available in the patient's chart for review.

> **EXAMPLE:** The patient's chart documents carcinoma of the breast. The Index to Diseases entry for *carcinoma* says "*see also* Neoplasm by site, malignant." This index entry directs the coder to the neoplasm table, and the code is selected from one of the first three columns (depending on whether the cancer is primary, secondary, or *in situ*—check the pathology report for documentation).

ICD-10-CM ALERT!

In ICD-10-CM, "external causes of injury, poisoning, or other adverse reactions affecting a patient's health" are incorporated into ICD-10-CM's tabular list as Chapter 20. It is no longer considered a supplemental classification.

ICD-10-CM ALERT!

ICD-10-CM code Y92.010 is assigned for the place of occurrence if a single-family house. ICD-10-CM's level of specificity results in different codes if the patient's home is an apartment or a mobile home.

ICD-10-CM ALERT!

ICD-10-CM Y92.512 is assigned for place of occurrence, grocery store. ICD-9-CM code E849.6 classifies place of occurrence as a public building, which includes grocery stores, movie theatres, restaurants, and so on. In ICD-10-CM, separate codes can be assigned for those places of occurrence.

ICD-10-CM ALERT!

Effective October 1, 2013, provider offices will report morphology codes as additional diagnoses on claims.

The *Glossary of Mental Disorders* (previously found in Appendix B of ICD-9-CM) corresponded to the psychiatric terms that appear in Chapter 5, "Mental Disorders," and consisted of an alphabetic listing of terms and definitions based on those contained in ICD-9-CM and input from the American Psychiatric Association's Task Force on Nomenclature and Statistics. Some definitions were based on those in *A Psychiatric Glossary, Dorland's Illustrated Medical Dictionary*, and *Stedman's Medical Dictionary, Illustrated*. This glossary has been permanently removed from ICD-9-CM and will not appear in future revisions. The mental health definitions it contained can be found in the DSM-IV manual published by the American Psychiatric Association.

> **EXAMPLE:** Diagnosis *chronic alcoholism* (303.9x) requires the addition of a fifth digit to completely code the condition. Often providers do not document the term necessary to assign the fifth digit (e.g., chronic alcoholism that is continuous, episodic, or in remission); therefore, the coder must assign a fifth digit for "unspecified" (0). The DSM-IV defines alcoholism according to *continuous, episodic,* and *in remission*—if the coder reviews these definitions, it is likely that the appropriate fifth digit will be assigned based on documentation in the patient's chart (even though the provider did not specify the term).

The **Classification of Drugs by AHFS List** (found in Appendix C of ICD-9-CM) contains the American Hospital Formulary Services List number and its ICD-9-CM equivalent code number, organized in numerical order according to AHFS List number. The List is published under the direction of the American Society of Hospital Pharmacists.

NOTE: The AHFS List can also be referenced within the Table of Drugs and Chemicals by looking up the word *Drug*. Because providers infrequently document the List number, it *may be* easier for coders to remember to reference the appendix.

> **EXAMPLE:** The patient's chart documents that the patient experienced a reaction to *substance 76:00*. By referring to the Classification of Drugs by AHFS List in Appendix C of ICD-9-CM, the coder can determine that *76:00* refers to *oxytocics*. The coder can then turn to the Table of Drugs and Chemicals in the Index to Diseases of ICD-9-CM and look up *oxytocics* (found in alphabetical order) to locate the reportable codes.

The **Classification of Industrial Accidents According to Agency** (found in Appendix D of ICD-9-CM) is based on employment injury statistics adopted by the Tenth International Conference of Labor Statisticians. Because it may be difficult to locate the E code entry in the ICD-9-CM Index to External Causes, coders may find the Industrial Accidents According to Agency appendix more helpful in identifying the category of equipment, and so on, for an external cause of injury.

> **EXAMPLE:** The patient sustained an injury as the result of a malfunctioning combine reaper. While the E code for "accident, caused by, combine" can be easily located in the Index to External Causes, if the coder does not know what a combine reaper is, the location of the accident cannot be properly coded. The Industrial Accidents According to Agency appendix can be referenced to determine that a combine reaper is categorized under agricultural machines. Thus, the coder can assign the location E code as "Accident, occurring (at), farm."

ICD-10-CM ALERT!

Each chapter in the ICD-10-CM tabular list contains a summary block of codes to provide an overview of codes in that chapter.

The **List of Three-Digit Categories** (found in Appendix E of ICD-9-CM) contains a breakdown of three-digit category codes organized beneath section headings.

EXAMPLE:

Acute rheumatic fever (390–392)

390   Rheumatic fever without mention of heart involvement

391   Rheumatic fever with heart involvement

392   Rheumatic chorea

Index to Diseases (Volume 2)

The Index to Diseases (Volume 2) contains three sections:

- *Index to Diseases.* This index includes two official tables that make it easier to code hypertension and neoplasms. Some publishers print special editions of ICD-9-CM manuals that contain additional tables to simplify the search for the correct code of other complex conditions.
- *Table of Drugs and Chemicals.* Adverse effects and poisonings associated with medicinal, chemical, and biological substances are coded by referring to this table.
- *Index to External Causes (E codes).* This separate index is often forgotten; it is helpful to mark it with a tab as a reminder of its usefulness.

Index to Procedures and Tabular List of Procedures (Volume 3)

The Index to Procedures and Tabular List of Procedures (Volume 3) is included in the hospital version of commercial ICD-9-CM books. It is a combined alphabetical index and numerical listing of inpatient procedures. Hospital outpatient departments and healthcare providers' offices use the *Current Procedural Terminology (CPT)* published by the American Medical Association (AMA), and/or additional codes created by CMS to augment CPT codes on Medicare claims. These special CMS codes are known as HCPCS level II codes. HCPCS stands for *Healthcare Common Procedure Coding System.* (CPT and HCPCS level II codes are further discussed in Chapters 7 and 8 of this textbook.)

ICD-9-CM INDEX TO DISEASES

The Index to Diseases is an alphabetical listing of main terms or conditions. The items are printed in boldface type and may be expressed as nouns, adjectives, or eponyms (Figure 6-1).

Main Terms

Main terms (conditions) are printed in boldface type and are followed by the code number. Main terms may or may not be followed by a listing of parenthetical terms that serve as nonessential modifiers of the main term (see the main term in Figure 6-1). Nonessential modifiers are supplementary words located in parentheses after a main term. They do not have to be included in the diagnostic statement for the code number to be assigned. Qualifiers are supplementary terms that further modify subterms and other qualifiers.

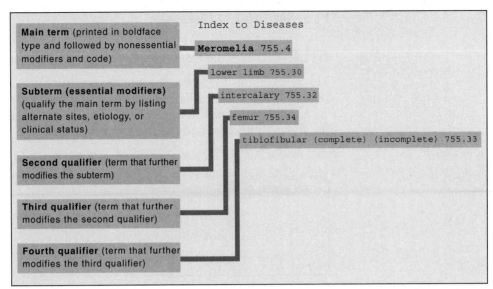

FIGURE 6-1 Display of main terms, subterms (essential modifiers) and qualifiers in the ICD-9-CM Index to Diseases (Courtesy Delmar/Cengage Learning)

START OF MAIN TERM IN INDEX TO DISEASES	
Main Term:	Deformity 738.9
Subterm:	aortic
2nd Qualifier:	arch 747.21
3rd Qualifier:	acquired 447.8

CONTINUATION OF MAIN TERM AT TOP OF NEXT COLUMN	
Main Term:	Deformity—*continued*
Subterm:	appendix 751.5
Subterm:	arm (acquired) 736.89
2nd Qualifier:	congenital 755.50

Subterms

Subterms (or essential modifiers) qualify the main term by listing alternate sites, etiology, or clinical status. A list of subterms is indented two spaces under the main term. Secondary qualifying conditions are indented two spaces under a subterm. Great care must be taken when moving from the bottom of one column to the top of the next column or when turning the page. The main term will be repeated and followed by "—*continued.*" Watch carefully to determine if the subterm has changed or new second or third qualifiers appear when moving from one column to another.

ICD-10-CM ALERT!

The ICD-10-CM Index to Diseases entries are also organized according to main terms, subterms, second qualifiers, and third qualifiers.

EXAMPLE: The ICD-9-CM Index to Diseases entries are organized according to main terms, subterms, second qualifiers, and third qualifiers. Refer to the index entry for "Deformity, aortic arch, acquired (447.8)" and review the indented subterm and qualifiers. Notice that when the main term continues at the top of a column (or on the next page of the Index to Diseases), the term "—*continued*" appears after the main term, and subterms and qualifiers are indented below the main term.

ICD-10-CM ALERT!

In ICD-10-CM, the code located after the main term is called the "default code."

CODING TIP:

1. A subterm or essential modifier provides greater specificity when included in the diagnosis. Select the code number stated after the essential modifier, not the one stated after the main condition. For example, the code to investigate in the Tabular List of Diseases for "acquired AC globulin deficiency" is 286.7.

2. Always consult the code description in the Tabular List of Diseases before assigning a code, because one or more instructional notes not included in the Index to Diseases may change the code selection.

Using the Index to Diseases

STEP 1 Locate the main term in the Index to Diseases (Volume 2).

This is accomplished by first locating the condition's boldfaced main term and then reviewing the subterms listed below the main term to locate the proper disorder.

Underlined terms in the following examples are the conditions to locate in the Index to find possible codes.

> **EXAMPLE:** Irritability of the bladder
>
> Impacted feces
>
> Comminuted fracture, left radius
>
> Upper respiratory infection

Table 6-1 is a list of special main terms that should be considered when the main condition is not obvious from the healthcare provider's diagnostic statement.

STEP 2 If the phrase "—see condition" is found after the main term, a descriptive term (an adjective) or the anatomic site has been referenced instead of the disorder or the disease (the condition) documented in the diagnostic statement.

> **EXAMPLE:** The provider's diagnostic statement is *myocardial infarction.*
>
> In the Index to Diseases, look up the word *myocardial.* Notice that the phrase "—see condition" appears next to the word *myocardial.*
>
> The phrase is instructing you to refer to the condition instead. In this case, the condition is *infarction.*

TABLE 6-1   Main terms to use when the condition is difficult to find in the Index to Diseases

Abnormal	Disease	Infection	Pregnancy
Admission	Disorder	Injury	Problem (with)
Aftercare	Examination	Late	Puerperal
Anomaly	Exposure to	Lesion(s)	Status (post)
Attention to	Foreign Body	Newborn	Syndrome
Complications	History (family) of	Observation	Vaccination
Delivery	History (personal) of	Outcome	

NOTE: Sometimes terms found in the Index to Diseases are not found in the Tabular List of Diseases when the code number is reviewed for verification. When this occurs, the coder should "trust the index," because, to save space in the tabular list, more terms are listed in the index than in the tabular list.

STEP 3 When the condition listed is not found, locate main terms such as *syndrome, disease, disorder, derangement of,* or *abnormal.* See Table 6-1, which lists special main terms for additional help.

> **EXAMPLE:** For the condition, *gum attrition,* main term *attrition* and subterm *gum* are found in the ICD-9-CM Index to Diseases. When code 523.20 is verified in the tabular list, the term *attrition* is not found; however, code 523.20 is still the correct code. (This is an example of "trust the index.")

If unsuccessful in finding a code using the main terms suggested in Table 6-1, turn to Appendix E—Three-Digit Categories—in the back of the ICD-9-CM code book. Review the categories listed under the chapter heading to determine which best fits the site of the patient's problem.

When you need a code that describes an external cause of injury, look for these conditions in the separate E code index located after the Table of Drugs and Chemicals at the back of the Index to Diseases.

EXERCISE 6-1

Finding the Condition in the Index to Diseases

Underline the condition in each of the following items, then, *using only the Index to Diseases,* locate the main term and the code number. Write the code number on the blank line provided.

> **NOTE:** Items 6 through 8 are rather uncommon disorders, but they are listed in the Index.

1. Bronchiole spasm   _____
2. Congenital candidiasis (age 3)   _____
3. Irritable bladder   _____
4. Earthquake injury   _____
5. Exposure to AIDS   _____
6. Ground itch   _____
7. Nun's knees   _____
8. Mice in right knee joint   _____
9. Contact dermatitis   _____
10. Ascending neuritis   _____

ICD-10-CM ALERT!
In ICD-10-CM, the majority of codes assigned to external causes of morbidity are located in chapter 20. Other conditions stated as due to external causes are also classified elsewhere in ICD-10-CM's Chapters 1–21. For these other conditions, ICD-10-CM codes from Chapter 20 are also reported to provide additional information regarding external cause of the condition (e.g., place of occurrence).

Coding Conventions

Coding conventions are rules that apply to the assignment of ICD-9-CM codes. They can be found in the Index to Diseases (Table 6-2), Tabular List of Diseases (Table 6-3), and Index to Procedures and Tabular List of Procedures (Table 6-4).

TABLE 6-2   Coding conventions for Index to Diseases

CODING CONVENTION & EXAMPLE	INDEX TO DISEASES ENTRY
CODES IN SLANTED BRACKETS are always listed as secondary codes because they are manifestations (results) of other conditions. **EXAMPLE:** Diabetic cataract.	**Diabetes, diabetic** (brittle) (congenital) (familial) (mellitus) (poorly controlled) (severe) (slight) (without complication) 250.0 cataract 250.5 *[366.41]*
EPONYMS are diseases (or procedures) named for an individual (e.g., physician who originally discovered the disease, first patient diagnosed with the disease). **EXAMPLE:** Barlow's Syndrome. ┌───┐ **ICD-10-CM ALERT!** The ICD-10-CM index contains "codes in brackets" (instead of "codes in slanted brackets"), which means italics have been removed in the formatting of this coding convention. "Codes in brackets" are always listed as secondary codes because they are manifestations (or results) of other conditions. └───┘	**Syndrome** *see also* Disease Barlow's (mitral valve prolapse) 424.0

ESSENTIAL MODIFIERS are **subterms** that are indented below the main term in alphabetical order (except for "with" and "without"). The essential modifier clarifies the main term and must be contained in the diagnostic statement for the code to be assigned.
 	
 EXAMPLE: Acute necrotizing encephalitis.
	Encephalitis (bacterial) (chronic) (hemorrhagic) (idiopathic) (nonepidemic) (spurious) (subacute) 323.9
	     acute—*see also* Encephalitis, viral
	         disseminated (postinfectious) NEC
	         136.9 *[323.6]*
	             postimmunization or postvaccination
	             323.5
	         inclusional 049.8
	         inclusional body 049.8
	         necrotizing 049.8

NEC (not elsewhere classifiable) identifies codes to be assigned when information needed to assign a more specific code cannot be located in the ICD-9-CM coding book.
 	
 EXAMPLE: Disseminated encephalitis.
	Encephalitis (bacterial) (chronic) (hemorrhagic) (idiopathic) (nonepidemic) (spurious) (subacute) 323.9
	     acute—*see also* Encephalitis, viral
	         disseminated (postinfectious) NEC
	         136.9 *[323.61]*

NONESSENTIAL MODIFIERS are subterms that are enclosed in parentheses following the main term. They clarify the code selection, but they do not have to be present in the provider's diagnostic statement.
 	
 EXAMPLE: Cerebral pseudomeningocele. In this example, cerebral pseudomeningocele and pseudomeningocele are both assigned code 349.2.
	Pseudomeningocele (cerebral) (infective) 349.2
	     postprocedural 997.01
	     spinal 349.2

NOTES are contained in boxes to define terms, clarify index entries, and list choices for additional digits (e.g., fourth and fifth digits). **EXAMPLE:** Spontaneous breech delivery. In this example, assign code 652.21.	**Delivery** ┌───┐ **NOTE:** Use the following fifth-digit subclassification with categories 640–649, 651–676 0 unspecified as to episode of care 1 delivered, with or without mention of antepartum condition 2 delivered, with mention of postpartum complication 3 antepartum condition or complication 4 postpartum condition or complication └───┘ **breech** (assisted) (buttocks) (complete) (frank) (spontaneous) 652.2

(continues)

TABLE 6-2   (continued)

CODING CONVENTION & EXAMPLE	INDEX TO DISEASES ENTRY

SEE directs the coder to a more specific term under which the code can be found.
 	
EXAMPLE: Traumatic delirium, with spinal cord lesion. The coder is directed to the index entry "injury, spinal, by site" and code 952.9 would be assigned.
	Delirium, delirious 780.09
	    traumatic–*see also* Injury, intracranial
	        with
	            lesion, spinal cord–*see* Injury, spinal,
	            by site
	Injury
	    spinal (cord) 952.9

SEE ALSO refers the coder to an index entry that may provide additional information to assign the code.
 	
EXAMPLE: Mucus inhalation.
 	
The coder is directed to the index entry "Asphyxia, mucus"; in this case, there is no added information that would change the code.
	Inhalation
	        mucus (*see also* Asphyxia, mucus) 933.1
	Asphyxia, asphyxiation (by) 799.01
	        mucus 933.1

SEE ALSO CONDITION refers the coder to the patient's condition for code assignment.
 	
EXAMPLE: Late pregnancy.
 	
Main term, "Late" directs the coder to "*see also* condition" because subterm "pregnancy" is not listed. (In this case, the coder would refer to main term "Pregnancy" as the condition.)
 	
SEE CATEGORY refers the coder directory to the Tabular List of Diseases three-digit code for code assignment.
 	
EXAMPLE: Late effect of intracranial abscess.
 	
The coder is directed to "*see category*" when main term "Late" and subterms "effect, abscess, intracranial" are located in the Index to Diseases.
	Late–*see also* condition
	effect(s) (of)– *see also* condition
	    abscess
	        intracranial or intraspinal (conditions
	            classifiable to 324) *see category*
	            326

EXERCISE 6-2

Working with Coding Conventions (Index to Diseases)

Underline the main term (condition) found in the Index to Diseases, and enter the ICD-9-CM code number and index convention on the blank lines.

CONDITION	ICD-9-CM CODE	INDEX CONVENTION USED
1. Acute purulent sinusitis	461.9	(purulent) is a nonessential modifier
2. Fracture, mandible	_____	_____
3. Actinomycotic meningitis	_____	_____
4. Psychomotor akinetic epilepsy	_____	_____
5. 3-cm laceration, right forearm	_____	_____
6. Contusion, abdominal organ	_____	_____
7. Pneumonia due to *H. influenzae*	_____	_____

(continues)

8. Delayed healing, open
   wound, abdomen   _____ _____

9. Bile duct cicatrix   _____ _____

10. Uncontrolled type II
    diabetes mellitus with
    osteomyelitis   _____ _____

ICD-9-CM TABULAR LIST OF DISEASES

ICD-9-CM codes for Chapters 1 through 17 (codes 001–999.9) are organized according to three-digit category codes. Specificity is achieved by assigning a decimal point and one or two digits, known as fourth (subcategory codes) and fifth (subclassification codes) digits, to the main three-digit code number (Figure 6-2). Two supplemental classifications also classify health status (V codes) and external causes of injuries and poisonings (E codes).

V codes (supplementary classification) are expressed as a three-character alphanumeric code (the letter V plus two digits) that can be subdivided with fourth and fifth digits to provide a more definitive description (Figure 6-3).

E codes (supplementary classification) are expressed as a four-character alphanumeric code (the letter E plus three digits). One additional decimal digit may be required to provide a more specific description of the external cause of the injury or poisoning (see Figure 6-3). E codes are always secondary diagnostic codes. *They are never reported as the first-listed diagnosis code on claims.*

Chapters

The chapter heading is printed in uppercase letters and is preceded by the chapter number. The instructional "Notes" that follow the chapter heading detail general guidelines for code selections within the entire chapter. If the note(s) include an **EXCLUDES** statement, the reference applies to the entire chapter (see Figure 6-2).

> **EXAMPLE:** Refer to Figure 6-2 and the Chapter 3 heading, "Endocrine, Nutritional and Metabolic Diseases, and Immunity Disorders" (240–279). Notice that an **EXCLUDES** statement is located just below the chapter heading along with a regular note. Both references apply to all codes contained within the chapter.

Major Topic Headings

ICD-9-CM chapters are subdivided into major topic headings printed in bold uppercase letters and followed by a range of codes enclosed in parentheses. Any note or **EXCLUDES** statement printed below a major topic heading applies only to the code numbers listed in parentheses after the major topic heading, not to the entire chapter.

> **EXAMPLE:**
>
> PSYCHOSES (290–299)
>
> **EXCLUDES** *mental retardation (317–319)*

ICD-10-CM ALERT!
The ICD-10-CM tabular list contains categories, subcategories, and codes. Category codes have 3, and subcategory codes are either 4 or 5 characters. Codes have 4, 5, 6, or 7 characters.

ICD-10-CM ALERT!
The ICD-10-CM Tabular List of Diseases includes 21 chapters, incorporating external causes of morbidity (V and Y codes) and factors influencing health status and contact with health service (Z codes). There are no supplementary classifications in ICD-10-CM.

ICD-10-CM ALERT!
In ICD-10-CM, anatomy is the primary axis of classification, which explains chapter titles like "Diseases of the Circulatory System" and "Diseases of the Genitourinary system." Some chapters are arranged according to condition (e.g., Neoplasms) or other criteria (e.g., External Causes of Morbidity).

Chapter heading

3. ENDOCRINE, NUTRITIONAL AND METABOLIC DISEASES, AND IMMUNITY DISORDERS (240–279)

Excludes note

EXCLUDES: *endocrine and metabolic disturbances specific to the fetus and newborn (775.0–775.9)*

Instructional note

Note: All neoplasms, whether functionally active or not, are classified in Chapter 2. Codes in Chapter 3 (i.e, 242.8, 246.0, 251–253, 255–259) may be used to identify such functional activity associated with any neoplasm, or by ectopic endocrine tissue.

Major topic heading

DISORDERS OF THYROID GLAND (240–246)

Category code

✓4th **240 Simple and unspecified goiter**

DEF: An enlarged thyroid gland often caused by an inadequate dietary intake of iodine.

Subcategory code

240.0 **Goiter, specified as simple**

Any condition classifiable to 240.9, specified as simple

240.9 **Goiter, unspecified**

Description statements

Enlargement of thyroid	Goiter or struma:
Goiter or struma:	hyperplastic
NOS	nontoxic (diffuse)
diffuse colloid	parenchymatous
endemic	sporadic

EXCLUDES: *congenital (dyshormonogenic) goiter (246.1)*

DISEASES OF OTHER ENDOCRINE GLANDS (249-259)

250 Diabetes mellitus

EXCLUDES: *gestational diabetes (648.8)*
hyperglycemia NOS (790.29)
neonatal diabetes mellitus (775.1)
nonclinical diabetes (790.29)
secondary diabetes (249.0–249.9)

The following fifth-digit subclassification is for use with category 250:

Subclassification codes for 5th digit assignment

0 type II or unspecified type, not stated as uncontrolled
Fifth-digit 0 is for use for type II patients, even if the patient requires insulin

Use additional code, if applicable, for associated long-term (current) insulin use V58.67

1 type I [juvenile type], not stated as uncontrolled

2 type II or unspecified type, uncontrolled
Fifth-digit 2 is for use for type II patients, even if the patient requires insulin
Use additional code, if applicable, for associated long-term (current) insulin use V58.67

3 type I [juvenile type], uncontrolled

DEF: Diabetes mellitus: Inability to metabolize carbohydrates, proteins, and fats with insufficient secretion of insulin. Symptoms may be unremarkable, with long-term complications, involving kidneys, nerves, blood vessels, and eyes.

DEF: Uncontrolled diabetes: A nonspecific term indicating that the current treatment regimen does not keep the blood sugar level of a patient within acceptable levels.

✓5th 250.0 **Diabetes mellitus without mention of complication**
(0–3) Diabetes mellitus without mention of complication or manifestation classifiable to 250.1–250.9
Diabetes (mellitus) NOS

✓5th 250.1 **Diabetes with ketoacidosis**
(0–3) Diabetic:
acidosis } without mention of coma
ketosis }

DEF: Diabetic hyperglycemic crisis causing ketone presence in body fluids.

FIGURE 6-2 ICD-9-CM Tabular List of Diseases (Permission to reprint granted by Ingenix.)

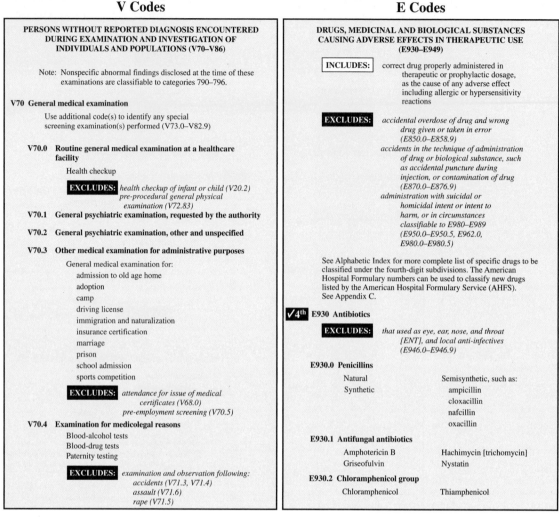

FIGURE 6-3 Sample pages from ICD-9-CM Supplementary Classifications, Tabular List of Diseases—V and E codes (Permission to reprint granted by Ingenix.)

Categories

Major topics are divided into three-digit categories. The **categories** are printed in bold upper- and lowercase type and are preceded by a three-digit code. Any **EXCLUDES** note that appears at this point applies to all three-, four-, or five-digit disease codes in the category.

EXAMPLE: Refer to Figure 6-2 and locate category code *250 Diabetes mellitus*. Notice the **EXCLUDES** statement below category 250. This reference applies to all codes classified within category 250 codes.

Subcategories

Fourth-digit **subcategories** are indented and printed in the same fashion as the major category headings (see Figure 6-2). An **EXCLUDES** note found at this level applies only to the specific fourth-digit code.

EXAMPLE: Refer to Figure 6-2 and locate subcategory codes *240.0 Goiter, specified as simple* and *240.9 Goiter, unspecified*. As this condition contains codes at the subcategory (fourth-digit) level, it is incorrect to report the three-digit code (240) on an insurance claim.

Subclassifications

Some fourth-digit subcategories are further subdivided into subclassifications, which require the assignment of a fifth digit. This requirement is indicated by the presence of a section mark (§), a red dot, or some other symbol, depending on the publisher of the code book. The placement and appearance of fifth digits are not standardized throughout ICD-9-CM. As you assign codes, you will notice varying fifth-digit placement.

REMEMBER!

Fifth digits are required when indicated in the code book.

Fifth-digit entries are associated with:

- chapters
- major topic headings
- categories
- subcategories

EXAMPLE 1: Fifth-Digit Entries Associated with Chapters

Refer to Chapter 13, Diseases of the Musculoskeletal System and Connective Tissue (710–739). The fifth-digit subclassification listed below the chapter heading is limited to certain categories (711–712, 715–716, 718–719, 730) in Chapter 13. The remaining categories in Chapter 13 either do not require the use of a fifth-digit subclassification (e.g., category 713) or the fifth-digit subclassification to be used is listed within specific subcategories (e.g., 714.3).

NOTE: Major topic heading *Other Pregnancy with Abortive Outcome (634-639)* lists fourth-digit subcategory codes that are used with categories 634-638. Do not confuse this subcategory listing with similarly styled fifth-digit subclassifications that are often associated with major topic headings. The fifth-digit subclassification for category codes 634-637 is located below each three-digit category code.

EXAMPLE 2: Fifth-Digit Entries Associated with Major Topic Headings

Refer to major topic heading, *Tuberculosis (010-018).* The fifth-digit subclassification listed below the major topic heading is to be used with codes 010 through 018.

EXAMPLE 3: Fifth-Digit Entries Associated with Categories

Refer to category code *250 Diabetes mellitus.* The fifth-digit subclassification listed below the category code is to be used with all subcategory codes.

NOTE: The E codes listing—Supplementary Classification of External Causes of Injury and Poisoning (E800–E999)—contains fourth-digit subcategories at the beginning of the following major section headings:

- Railway Accidents (E800–E807)
- Motor Vehicle Traffic Accidents (E810–E819)
- Motor Vehicle Nontraffic Accidents (E820–E825)
- Other Road Vehicle Accidents (E826–E829)
- Water Transport Accidents (E830–E838)
- Air and Space Transport Accidents (E840–E845)

EXAMPLE 4: Fifth-Digit Entries Associated with Subcategories

Refer to subcategory code 438.1. The fifth-digit subclassifications listed are to be used with subcategory 438.1 only. There are different fifth-digit subclassifications for subcategories 438.2, 438.3, and so on. Notice that subcategory codes 438.0, 438.6, 438.7, and 438.9 do not contain a fifth-digit subclassification list. They are considered complete as four-digit subcategory codes.

Using the Tabular List of Diseases

STEP 1 Locate the first possible code number after reviewing main terms and subterms in the Index to Diseases.

STEP 2 Locate the code number in the Tabular List of Diseases, and review the code descriptions. Review any **EXCLUDES** notes to determine whether the condition being coded is excluded.

If the condition is excluded, locate the code number listed as an alternative in the **EXCLUDES** note to determine whether it is the condition to be coded.

STEP 3 Assign any required fourth and fifth digits.

STEP 4 Check to be sure the code number is appropriate for the age and gender of the patient.

STEP 5 Return to the Index to Diseases for other possible code selections if the code description in the Tabular List of Diseases does not appear to fit the condition or reason for the visit.

STEP 6 Enter the final code selection.

EXERCISE 6-3

Confirming Codes in the Tabular List of Diseases

Using only the Tabular List of Diseases, verify the following code numbers to determine whether the code matches the stated diagnosis or an **EXCLUDES** statement applies.

- Place a "C" on the blank line if the code number is confirmed.
- Place an "E" on the blank line if the condition is excluded.
- Enter required fifth digits if applicable.

1. 515   Postinflammatory pulmonary fibrosis   _____
2. 250   Gestational diabetes   _____

(continues)

3.	727.67	Nontraumatic rupture of Achilles tendon	_____
4.	422.0	Acute myocarditis due to Coxsackie virus	_____
5.	813.22	Malunion, closed right radial fracture	_____
6.	483.0	Mycoplasmic pneumonia	_____
7.	795.71	Positive HIV test, asymptomatic	_____
8.	796.2	Elevated blood pressure	_____
9.	718.06	Old tear of right knee meniscus	_____
10.	383.1	Tuberculous mastoiditis	_____

Tabular List of Diseases Coding Conventions

Tabular List of Diseases coding conventions (Table 6-3) apply to disease and condition codes and to supplementary classification codes (e.g., factors influencing health status and contact with health services [V codes], and external causes of injury and poisoning [E codes]).

TABLE 6-3 Coding conventions for the Tabular List of Diseases

CODING CONVENTION	TABULAR LIST OF DISEASES ENTRY

AND is interpreted as "and/or" and indicates that either of the two disorders is associated with the category code.	**466** **Acute bronchitis and bronchiolitis**
	  466.0 **Acute bronchitis**
	  466.1 **Acute bronchiolitis**

BOLD TYPE is used for all category and sub-category codes and descriptions are printed in bold type.	**421** **Acute and subacute endocarditis**
	  421.0 **Acute and subacute bacterial endocarditis**
	  421.1 **Acute and subacute infective endocarditis in diseases classified elsewhere**

BRACES enclose a series of terms, each of which modifies the statement located to the right of the brace.	**478.5** **Other diseases of vocal cords**
	  Abscess
	  Cellulitis
	  Granuloma } **of vocal cords**
	  Leukoplakia
	  Singers' nodes

BRACKETS enclose synonyms, alternate wording, or explanatory phrases.	**482.2** **Pneumonia due to Hemophilus influenzae [H. influenzae]**

CODE FIRST UNDERLYING DISEASE appears when the code referenced is to be sequenced as a secondary code. The code, title, and instructions are italicized.	**366.42** **Tetanic cataract**
	  Code first underlying disease, as:
	    calcinosis (275.4)
	    hypoparathyroidism (252.1)

COLON is used after an incomplete term and is followed by one or more modifiers (additional terms)	**472.0** **Chronic rhinitis**
	  Ozena
	  Rhinitis:
	    NOS
	    atrophic
	    granulomatous
	    hypertrophic
	    obstructive
	    purulent
	    ulcerative

(continues)

TABLE 6-3   (continued)

CODING CONVENTION	TABULAR LIST OF DISEASES ENTRY

EXCLUDES note directs the coder to another location in the codebook for proper assignment of the code
 	
ICD-10-CM ALERT!
There are two types of excludes notes in ICD-10-CM:
 	
Excludes1 is a pure excludes note and means "not coded here!" The code excluded is never reported with the code above an Excludes1 note.
 	
Excludes2 means "not included here" and if the patient receives treatment for the excluded condition, an ICD-10-CM code is assigned to it.
	250 Diabetes mellitus
	       EXCLUDES *gestational diabetes (648.8)*
	                   hyperglycemia NOS (790.29)
	                   neonatal diabetes mellitus (775.1)
	                   nonclinical diabetes (790.29)
	                   secondary diabetes (249.0-249.9)

FORMAT is the way all additional terms are indented below the term to which they are linked, and if a definition or disease requires more than one line, that text is printed on the next line and further indented. (The additional terms are called *description statements*, which are located below the code description and include definitions, synonyms, types of complications, and so on.)	**455.2 Internal hemorrhoids with
	          other complication**
	       Internal hemorrhoids:
	          bleeding
	          prolapsed
	          strangulated
	          ulcerated

FOURTH & FIFTH DIGITS are indicated by an instructional note located below the category or subcategory description	**250 Diabetes mellitus**
	       EXCLUDES *gestational diabetes (648.8)*
	                   hyperglycemia NOS (790.29)
	                   neonatal diabetes mellitus (775.1)
	                   nonclinical diabetes (790.29)
	                   secondary diabetes (249.0-249.9)
	
	The following fifth-digit subclassification is for use with category 250:
	   0 type II or unspecified type, not stated as uncontrolled
	       Fifth-digit 0 is for use for type II patients, even if the patient requires insulin
	       Use additional code, if applicable, for associated long-term (current) insulin use V58.67
	   1 type I [juvenile type], not stated as uncontrolled
	   2 type II or unspecified type, uncontrolled
	       Fifth-digit 2 is for use for type II patients, even if the patient requires insulin
	       Use additonal code, if applicable, for associated long-term (current) insulin use V58.67
	   3 type I [juvenile type], uncontrolled

(continues)

TABLE 6-3 (continued)

CODING CONVENTION	TABULAR LIST OF DISEASES ENTRY
INCLUDES notes appear below a three-digit category code description to further define, clarify, or provide an example.	**244 Acquired hypothyroidism** **INCLUDES** athyroidism (acquired) hypothyroidism (acquired) myxedema (adult) (juvenile) thyroid (gland) insufficiency (acquired)

NEC is the abbreviation for "not elsewhere classifiable" and indicates a specific code is not available for a condition. NEC identifies the code as an "other" or "other specified" code.
    NOS is the abbreviation for "not otherwise specified" and indicates that the code is unspecified. Coders should ask the provider for a more specific diagnosis before assigning the code.
	008.8 Intestinal infection due to other organism, NEC
	Viral
	    enteritis NOS
	    gastroenteritis
	    EXCLUDES influenza with involvement of gastrointestinal tract
	    (487.8)

NOTES define terms, clarify information, and list choices for fourth and fifth digits.	**1. INFECTIOUS AND PARASITIC DISEASES (001–139)** NOTE: Categories for "late effects" of infectious and parasitic diseases are found at 137–139.
PARENTHESES enclose supplementary words that may be present or absent in the diagnostic statement, without affecting assignment of the code number.	**241.1 Nontoxic multinodular goiter** Multinodular goiter (nontoxic)
USE ADDITIONAL CODE indicates that a second code is to be reported to provide more information about the diagnosis.	**510 Empyema** Use additional code to identify infectious organism (041.0–041.9)
WITH is used when codes combine one disorder with another (e.g., code that combines primary condition with a complication), the provider's diagnostic statement must clearly indicate that both conditions are present and that a relationship exists between the conditions. NOTE: An exception to this rule is "chronic renal failure and hypertension," which assumes a relationship between the conditions.	**454 Varicose veins of lower extremities** **454.0 With ulcer**

EXERCISE 6-4

Working with Tabular List of Diseases Coding Conventions

Underline the main term (condition) to be referenced in the Index to Diseases, and apply index coding conventions in locating the code. Verify the code selected in the tabular list. Enter the ICD-9-CM code number(s) and tabular list coding convention used on the blank lines provided. If more than one code number is assigned, be sure to list the first-listed condition code first.

CONDITION	ICD-9-CM CODE(S)	INDEX CONVENTION(S) USED
1. <u>Pregnancy</u> complicated by chronic gonorrhea; chronic gonococcal <u>endometritis</u>	647.10 098.36	fifth digit required use additional code
2. Benign neoplasm, ear cartilage		
3. Cervicitis, tuberculous		
4. Uncontrolled type II diabetes with polyneuropathy		
5. Congenital hemangioma on face		
6. Hiss-Russell shigellosis		
7. Closed fracture, right leg		
8. Diabetic cataract		
9. Muscular atrophy, left leg		
10. Chronic smoker's bronchitis with acute bronchitis		

ICD-10-CM ALERT!

Effective October 1, 2013, the International Classification of Diseases, Tenth Revision, Procedure Coding System (ICD-10-PCS) will be implemented (replacing ICD-9-CM, Volume 3). ICD-10-PCS contains a multi-axial, seven-character alphanumeric code structure that provides a unique code for all substantially different procedures and allows new procedures to be easily incorporated as new codes. While ICD-10-PCS will be used to report codes for inpatient procedures, CPT and HCPCS level II will continue to be used to report codes for outpatient and physician office procedures and services.

ICD-9-CM INDEX TO PROCEDURES AND TABULAR LIST OF PROCEDURES

As mentioned previously, the Index to Procedures and Tabular List of Procedures (Volume 3) is included only in the hospital version of commercial ICD-9-CM books. It is a combined alphabetical index and numerical listing of inpatient procedures. Hospital outpatient departments and healthcare providers' offices report procedures and services using *Current Procedural Terminology (CPT)* and HCPCS level II national codes.

Principal versus Secondary Procedures

Hospital inpatient coders are required to differentiate between principal and secondary procedures rendered using the criteria discussed below. These criteria do not affect coding for healthcare providers' offices but are discussed here to introduce the full scope of ICD-9-CM diagnosis and procedure coding. Hospitals are required to rank all inpatient procedures according to specific criteria for selection of principal and secondary procedures and to code them using the ICD-9-CM procedure index and tabular list.

NOTE: Outpatient procedures and services, whether performed in the hospital or in the health-care provider's office, are coded using the CPT and HCPCS level II national coding systems.

A **principal procedure** is a procedure performed for definitive treatment rather than diagnostic purposes; one performed to treat a complication; or one that is most closely related to the principal diagnosis. There may be cases in which procedures performed are not directly related to the principal diagnosis, but are related to secondary conditions. In such cases, the principal procedure is considered to be the major definitive treatment performed. **Secondary procedures** are additional procedures performed during the same encounter as the principal procedure.

EXAMPLE 1: A patient was admitted to the hospital because of a fractured left hip. During the hospital stay, the patient developed a pulmonary embolism. The following procedures were performed: x-rays of the right and left hips, a lung scan, and a surgical pinning of the hip. Which is the principal procedure?

Answer: Pinning of the hip, also known as open reduction with internal fixation (ORIF), is the principal procedure; it is the major definitive treatment for the principal diagnosis of fractured hip. The lung scan was a necessary diagnostic procedure for confirmation of a pulmonary embolism. This diagnosis is the most life-threatening problem for the patient, but it does not meet the principal diagnosis criterion, which is the major cause, determined after study, for the hospitalization.

EXAMPLE 2: A patient entered the hospital with symptoms of profuse sweating, tremors, and polyuria. The patient has an existing problem with control of type I diabetes mellitus, as well as carpal tunnel syndrome. The diabetes was controlled within 18 hours by adjusting the patient's insulin dosage. A surgical carpal tunnel release was performed. The final diagnoses were carpal tunnel syndrome and uncontrolled type I diabetes mellitus. What is the principal procedure?

Answer: The principal procedure is the carpal tunnel release. The principal diagnosis is uncontrolled type II diabetes mellitus. (Carpal tunnel syndrome is not the principal diagnosis because it was not the problem that brought the patient to the hospital. Uncontrolled type II diabetes caused the admission in this case.)

Index to Procedures and Tabular List of Procedures Coding Conventions

Although the purpose of this textbook is to cover physician office coding (for which ICD-9-CM Index to Diseases and Tabular List of Procedures is used), Table 6-4 is included to provide comprehensive coverage of ICD-9-CM coding conventions.

TABLE 6-4 Coding conventions for the Index to Procedures and Tabular List of Procedures

CODING CONVENTION	INDEX TO PROCEDURES ENTRY
OMIT CODE is a term that identifies procedures or services that may be components of other procedures. The *omit code* instruction means that the procedure or service is not coded.	**Laparotomy** NEC 54.19 as operative approach–*omit code*

CODING CONVENTION	TABULAR LIST OF PROCEDURES ENTRY

CODE ALSO ANY SYNCHRONOUS PROCEDURES refers to operative procedures that are to be coded to completely classify a procedure.	**08.2 Excision or destruction of lesion or tissue of eyelid**
	  Code also any synchronous reconstruction
	  (08.61–08.74)

QUICK COMPARISON OF ICD-9-CM (PROCEDURE CODES) TO ICD-10-PCS

ICD-9-CM (procedure codes)	ICD-10-PCS
<ul><li>3-4 digit code structure</li><li>Decimal is entered after the second digit</li><li>All digits are numeric</li><li>Examples:<ul><li>56.2 (Ureterotomy)</li><li>76.11 (Biopsy of facial bone)</li></ul></li></ul>	<ul><li>7-character alphanumeric code structure</li><li>No decimal is used</li><li>Each character has up to 34 values (and include ten 0-9 digits and 24 letters A-H, J-N, and P-Z), is either alphabetic or numeric, and alphabetic digits are *not* case sensitive</li><li>Letters O and I are *not* used (to avoid confusion with numbers 0 and 1)</li><li>The first character of the procedure code specifies the section: 0 – Medical and Surgical 1 – Obstetrics 2 – Placement 3 – Administration 4 – Measurement and Monitoring 5 – Extracorporeal Assistance and Performance 6 – Extracorporeal Therapies 7 – Osteopathic 8 – Other Procedures 9 – Chiropractic B – Imaging C – Nuclear Medicine D – Radiation Oncology F – Physical Rehabilitation and Diagnostic Audiology G – Mental Health H – Substance Abuse Treatment</li><li>The second through seventh characters have a consistent meaning within each section, but may have different meanings across sections:<ul><li>In most sections, the third character specifies the type of procedure being performed</li><li>Other characters specify additional information, such as the body part on which the procedure is being performed</li></ul></li><li>A unique code is available for all substantially different procedures</li><li>As new procedures are implemented, ICD-10-PCS allows them to be easily included as unique codes</li><li>Multi-axial approach is used, which means independent characters each have an individual component that retains its meaning across broad ranges of codes, to the extent possible</li><li>Definitions of standardized terminology are included, which means each term is assigned a specific meaning</li><li>Diagnostic information is not included in procedure descriptions</li><li>Explicit *not otherwise specified (NOS)* code options are not included, which means documentation must be more comprehensive to specify the procedure site and/or operative approach</li><li>Limited use of *not elsewhere classified (NEC)*, except for classifying newly developed devices</li><li>Level of specificity is increased, which means all procedures currently performed can be specified using combinations of the seven alphanumeric characters</li><li>Examples:<ul><li>0FB03ZX (Excision of liver, percutaneous approach, diagnostic)</li><li>0DQ107Z (Repair, esophagus, upper, open with autograft)</li></ul></li></ul>

EXAMPLE: For the procedure "angioplasty of the right femoral artery using an open approach," in ICD-9-CM, just one code is available for any angioplasty procedure performed on peripheral vessels. In ICD-10-PCS, the code is "built" after referring to the term "angioplasty" in the Index to Procedures (to determine which section to go to in the Tables of Codes). As a result, there are 1,170 codes available, allowing for much greater specificity.

- **ICD-9-CM:**   39.50
- **ICD-10-PCS:**   047K0ZZ

ICD-9-CM Index to Procedures	ICD-10-PCS Index to Procedures
Angioplasty (laser) – *see also* Repair, blood vessel balloon (percutaneous transluminal) NEC 39.50	**Angioplasty** –*see* Dilation, Heart and Great Vessels 027. . . . –*see* Dilation, Lower Arteries 047. . . –*see* Dilation, Lower Veins 067. . . . –*see* Dilation, Upper Arteries 037. . . . –*see* Dilation, Upper Veins 057. . . . –*see* Repair, Heart and Great Vessels 02Q. . . . –*see* Repair, Lower Arteries 04Q. . . . –*see* Repair, Lower Veins 06Q. . . . –*see* Repair, Upper Arteries 03Q. . . . –*see* Repair, Upper Veins 05Q. . . . –*see* Replacement, Heart and Great Vessels 02R. . . . –*see* Replacement, Lower Arteries 04R. . . . –*see* Replacement, Lower Veins 06R. . . . –*see* Replacement, Upper Arteries 03R. . . . –*see* Replacement, Upper Veins 05R. . . .

ICD-9-CM Tabular List of Procedures	ICD-10-PCS Tables of Codes
39.50 Angioplasty or atherectomy of other non-coronary vessel(s) Percutaneous transluminal angioplasty (PTA) of non-coronary vessels: lower extremity vessels mesenteric artery renal artery upper extremity vessels Code also any: injection or infusion of thrombolytic agent (99.10) insertion of non-coronary stent(s) or stent graft(s) (390.90) number of vascular stents inserted (00.45-00.48) number of vessels treated (00.40-00.44) procedure on vessel bifurcation (00.44) **EXCLUDES:** *percutaneous angioplasty or atherectomy of precerebral or cerebral vessel(s) (00.61-00.62)*	Code 047K0ZZ is "built" using Table of Codes "047" in the Tables section of ICD-10-PCS.

047

0: MEDICAL AND SURGICAL
4: LOWER ARTERIES
7: DILATION: Expanding an orifice or the lumen of a tubular body part

Body Part Character 4	Approach Character 5	Device Character 6	Qualifier Character 7
0 Abdominal aorta 1 Celiac artery 2 Gastric artery 3 Hepatic artery 4 Splenic artery 5 Superior mesenteric artery 6 Colic artery, right 7 Colic artery, left 8 Colic artery, middle 9 Renal artery, right A Renal artery, left B Inferior mesenteric artery C Common Iliac artery, right D Common Iliac artery, left E Internal Iliac artery, right F Internal Iliac artery, left H External Iliac artery, right J External Iliac artery, left K Femoral artery, right L Femoral artery, left M Popliteal artery, right N Popliteal artery, left P Anterior tibial artery, right Q Anterior tibial artery, left R Posterior tibial artery, right S Posterior tibial artery, left T Peroneal artery, right U Peroneal artery, left V Foot artery, right W Foot artery, left Y Lower artery	0 Open 3 Percutaneous 4 Percutaneous endoscopic	4 Drug-eluting intraluminal device D Intraluminal device Z No device	Z No qualifier

ICD-9-CM INDEX TO DISEASES TABLES

Three tables appear in the Index to Diseases: Hypertension, Neoplasm, and Table of Drugs and Chemicals. The discussion that follows provides a basic understanding of how to use each table. Because the official tables consist of three to six columns, it will be helpful to use a ruler or paper guide when working with a specific diagnosis within a table, to ensure that you stay on the same horizontal line.

Hypertension/Hypertensive Table

The hypertension/hypertensive table contains a complete listing of hypertension codes and other associated conditions. Column headings are shown in Figure 6-4.

● **Malignant**—A severe form of hypertension with vascular damage and a diastolic pressure reading of 130 mm Hg or greater. (Hypertension is out of control or there was a rapid change from a benign state for a prolonged period.)

● **Benign**—Mild and/or controlled hypertension, with no damage to the patient's vascular system or organs.

● **Unspecified**—No notation of benign or malignant status is found in the diagnosis or in the patient's chart.

CODING TIP:

1. Always check the Tabular List of Diseases before assigning a code for hypertension/hypertensive conditions.

2. The table uses all three levels of indentations when the word "with" is included in the diagnostic statement. Be sure you review the subterms carefully. You may need to assign two codes when "with" separates two conditions in the diagnostic statement.

3. Secondary hypertension is a unique and separate condition listed on the table. In this case hypertension was caused by another primary condition (e.g., cancer).

4. Assign the fourth digit 9 sparingly.

Most insurance companies insist on conditions being coded to the highest degree of specificity known at the time of the encounter. They will not accept 401.9 Hypertension, unspecified, except during the first few weeks of treatment for hypertension. After that point, the physician usually knows whether the patient has benign (controlled by medication) or malignant (out-of-control) hypertension. If "benign" or "malignant" is not specified in the diagnosis, ask the physician to document the type of hypertension.

EXERCISE 6-5

Hypertension/Hypertensive Coding

Code the following conditions.

1. Essential hypertension   _____
2. Transient hypertension due to pregnancy   _____
3. Malignant hypertensive crisis   _____
4. Heart disease with hypertension   _____
5. Orthostatic hypertension, benign   _____

	Malignant	Benign	Unspecified
Hypertension, hypertensive (arterial) (arteriolar) (crisis) (degeneration) (disease) (essential) (fluctuating) (idiopathic) (intermittent) (labile) (low renin) (orthostatic) (paroxysmal) (primary) (systemic) (uncontrolled) (vascular)	401.0	401.1	401.9
with			
chronic kidney disease			
stage I through stage IV, or unspecified.	403.00	403.10	403.90
stage V or end stage renal disease	403.01	403.11	403.91
heart involvement (conditions classifiable to 429.0–429.3, 429.8, 429.9 due to hypertension) (*see also*			
Hypertension, heart)	402.00	402.10	402.90
with kidney involvement — *see* Hypertension, cardiorenal			
renal involvement (only conditions classifiable to 585, 586, 587) (excludes conditions classifiable to *584*) (*see also*			
Hypertension, kidney)	403.00	403.10	403.90
with heart involvement—*see* Hypertension, cardiorenal			
failure (and sclerosis) (*see also* Hypertension, kidney)	403.01	403.11	403.91
sclerosis without failure (*see also* Hypertension, kidney). . . .	403.00	403.10	403.90
accelerated (*see also* Hypertension, by type, malignant)	401.0	—	—
antepartum—*see* Hypertension, complicating pregnancy, childbirth, or the puerperium			

FIGURE 6-4 ICD-9-CM hypertension table (partial) (Permission to reprint granted by Ingenix.)

Neoplasm Table

Neoplasms are new growths, or tumors, in which cell reproduction is out of control. For coding purposes, the provider should specify whether the tumor is *benign* (noncancerous, nonmalignant, noninvasive) or *malignant* (cancerous, invasive, capable of spreading to other parts of the body). It is highly advisable that neoplasms be coded directly from the pathology report (generated by a hospital's or stand-alone laboratory's pathology department and mailed to the provider's office); however, until the diagnostic statement specifies whether the neoplasm is benign or malignant, coders should code the patient's sign (e.g., breast lump) or report a subcategory code from the "unspecified nature" column of the documented site using the Index to Diseases neoplasm table.

Another term associated with neoplasms is lesion, defined as any discontinuity of tissue (e.g., skin or organ) that may or may not be malignant. Disease index entries for "lesion" contain subterms according to anatomic site (e.g., organs or tissue), and that term should be referenced if the diagnostic statement does not confirm a malignancy. In addition, the following conditions are examples of benign lesions and are listed as separate Index to Diseases entries:

- **Mass (unless the word "neoplasm" is included in the diagnostic statement)**
- **Cyst**
- **Dysplasia**
- **Polyp**
- **Adenosis**

The neoplasm table (Figure 6-5) is indexed by anatomic site and contains four cellular classifications: malignant, benign, uncertain behavior, and unspecified nature. The malignant classification is subdivided into three divisions: primary, secondary, and carcinoma *in situ*. The six neoplasm classifications are defined as follows:

- Primary malignancy—**The original tumor site. All malignant tumors are considered primary unless otherwise documented as metastatic or secondary.**

Neoplasm, neoplastic	Malignant			Benign	Uncertain Behavior	Unspecified
	Primary	Secondary	Ca in situ			
Neoplasm, neoplastic...................	199.1	199.1	234.9	229.9	238.9	239.9

Notes— 1. The list below gives the code numbers for neoplasms by anatomic site. For each site there are six possible code numbers according to whether the neoplasm in question is malignant, benign, in situ, of uncertain behavior, or of unspecified nature. The description of the neoplasm will often indicate which of the six columns is appropriate; e.g., malignant melanoma of skin, benign fibroadenoma of breast, carcinoma in situ of cervix uteri.

Where such descriptors are not present, the remainder of the Index should be consulted where guidance is given to the appropriate column for each morphological (histological) variety listed; e.g., Mesonephroma — see Neoplasm, malignant; Embryoma — see also Neoplasm, uncertain behavior; Disease, Bowen's — see Neoplasm, skin, in situ. However, the guidance in the Index can be overridden if one of the descriptors mentioned above is present; e.g., malignant adenoma of colon is coded to 153.9 and not to 211.3 as the adjective "malignant" overrides the Index entry "Adenoma — see also Neoplasm, benign."

2. Sites marked with the sign * (e.g., face NEC*) should be classified to malignant neoplasm of skin of these sites if the variety of neoplasm is a squamous cell carcinoma or an epidermal carcinoma, and to benign neoplasm of skin of these sites if the variety of neoplasm is a papilloma (any type).

abdomen, abdominal	195.2	198.89	234.8	229.8	238.8	239.8
cavity	195.2	198.89	234.8	229.8	238.8	239.8
organ..............................	195.2	198.89	234.8	229.8	238.8	239.8
viscera	195.2	198.89	234.8	229.8	238.8	239.8
wall	173.5	198.2	232.5	216.5	238.2	239.2
connective tissue	171.5	198.89	—	215.5	238.1	239.2
abdominopelvic......................	195.8	198.89	234.8	229.8	238.8	239.8
accessory sinus — see Neoplasm, sinus						
acoustic nerve.......................	192.0	198.4	—	225.1	237.9	239.7
acromion (process)...................	170.4	198.5	—	213.4	238.0	239.2

FIGURE 6-5 ICD-9-CM neoplasm table (partial) (Permission to reprint granted by Ingenix.)

- Secondary malignancy—The tumor has metastasized (spread) to a secondary site, either adjacent to the primary site or to a remote region of the body.
- Carcinoma (Ca) *in situ*—A malignant tumor that is localized, circumscribed, encapsulated, and noninvasive (has not spread to deeper or adjacent tissues or organs).
- Benign—A noninvasive, nonspreading, nonmalignant tumor.
- Uncertain behavior—It is not possible to predict subsequent morphology or behavior from the submitted specimen. In order to assign a code from this column, the pathology report must specifically indicate the "uncertain behavior" of the neoplasm.
- Unspecified nature—A neoplasm is identified, but no further indication of the histology or nature of the tumor is reflected in the documented diagnosis. Assign a code from this column when the neoplasm was destroyed or removed and a tissue biopsy was performed and results are pending.

To go directly to the neoplasm table, you must know the classification and the site of the neoplasm. Some diagnostic statements specifically document "neoplasm" classification; others will not provide a clue.

If the diagnostic statement classifies the neoplasm, the coder can refer directly to the Index to Diseases neoplasm table to assign the proper code (verifying the code in the Tabular List of Diseases, of course). Because sufficient information is documented in the diagnostic statements in Example 1, coders can refer directly to the Index to Diseases neoplasm table.

EXAMPLE 1:

Diagnostic Statement	Neoplasm Table Reference
Tracheal carcinoma *in situ*	trachea, Malignant, Ca *in situ* (231.1)
Benign breast tumor, male	breast, male, Benign (217)
Cowper's gland tumor, uncertain behavior	Cowper's gland, Uncertain Behavior (236.99)
Metastatic carcinoma	unknown site or unspecified, Malignant—Secondary (199.1)
Cancer of the breast, primary	breast, Malignant—Primary (174.9)

If the diagnostic statement *does not* classify the neoplasm, the coder must refer to the Index to Diseases entry for the condition documented (instead of the neoplasm table). That entry will either contain a code number that can be verified in the Tabular List of Diseases or will refer the coder to the proper neoplasm table entry under which to locate the code.

EXAMPLE 2:

Diagnostic Statement	Index to Diseases Entry
non-Hodgkin's lymphoma	**Lymphoma (malignant)** (M9590/3) 202.8 non-Hodgkin's type NEC (M9591/3) 202.8
Adrenal adenolymphoma	**Adenolymphoma** (M8561/0) specified site—*see* Neoplasm, by site, benign
	Neoplasm (table) adrenal (cortex) (gland) (medulla) benign (227.0)

For non-Hodgkin's lymphoma, refer to code 202.8 in the Tabular List of Diseases to select the fifth digit (after referring to "lymphoma" in the Index to Diseases). There is no need to go to the neoplasm table. In fact, referencing the neoplasm table in this case would have been improper, and the coder would most likely have assigned an incorrect code (e.g., perhaps the coder would have referenced "lymph, lymphatic" within the neoplasm table and selected code 171.9 from the Malignant—Primary column, the wrong code).

For adrenal adenolymphoma, refer to "adenolymphoma" in the Index to Diseases. Because "adrenal" is the site specified in the diagnostic statement, the coder should follow the Index to Diseases instructions to "*see* Neoplasm, by site, benign." This instructional note refers the coder to the neoplasm table and the anatomic site for adrenal (cortex) (gland) (medulla). The coder would next refer to the "Benign" column and assign code 227.0 (after verifying the code in the Tabular List of Diseases).

CODING TIP:

1. Assigning codes from the neoplasm table is a two-step process. First, classify the neoplasm by its behavior (e.g., malignant, secondary) and then by its anatomic site (e.g., acoustic nerve).

2. To classify the neoplasm's behavior, review the provider's diagnostic statement (e.g., carcinoma of the throat), and look up "carcinoma" in the Index to Diseases. The entry will classify the behavior for you, directing you to the proper column in the neoplasm table. (If malignant, you will still need to determine whether primary, secondary, or *in situ* based on documentation in the patient's record.)

EXERCISE 6-6

Neoplasm Coding I

Underline the main term found in the Index to Diseases, and enter the code number (after verifying it in the Tabular List of Diseases) on the blank line.

1. Kaposi's sarcoma _____

2. Lipoma, skin, upper back _____

3. Carcinoma *in situ,* skin, left cheek _____

4. Scrotum mass _____

5. Neurofibroma _____

6. Cyst on left ovary _____

7. Ganglion right wrist _____

8. Yaws, frambeside _____

9. Breast, chronic cystic disease _____

10. Hürthle cell tumor _____

Primary Malignancies

A malignancy is coded as the primary site if the diagnostic statement documents:

- Metastatic *from* a site.
- Spread *from* a site.
- *Primary neoplasm* of a site.
- A malignancy for which no specific classification is documented.
- A *recurrent* tumor.

> **EXAMPLE:**
>
> Carcinoma of cervical lymph nodes, metastatic from the breast
>
> > Primary: breast
> >
> > Secondary: cervical lymph nodes
>
> Oat cell carcinoma of the lung with spread to the brain
>
> > Primary: lung
> >
> > Secondary: brain

Secondary Malignancies

Secondary malignancies are metastatic and indicate that a primary cancer has spread (metastasized) to another part of the body. Sequencing of neoplasm codes depends on whether the primary or secondary cancer is being managed and/or treated.

> **NOTE:** Examples in this section consistently sequence the primary malignancy first. In practice, the insurance specialist sequences reported codes based on documentation (e.g., treatment).

     To properly code secondary malignancies, consider the following:

- **Cancer described as *metastatic* from a site is *primary* of that site. Assign one code to the primary neoplasm and a second code to the secondary neoplasm of the specified site (if secondary site is known) or unspecified site (if secondary site is unknown).**

> **EXAMPLE 1:** Metastatic carcinoma from breast to lung
>
> > Assign two codes:
> >
> > > primary malignant neoplasm of breast (174.9)
> > >
> > > secondary neoplasm of lung (197.0)

> **EXAMPLE 2:** Metastatic carcinoma from breast
>
> > Assign two codes:
> >
> > > primary malignant neoplasm of breast (174.9)
> > >
> > > secondary neoplasm of unspecified site (199.1)

- **Cancer described as *metastatic* to a site is considered *secondary* of that site. Assign one code to the secondary site and a second code to the specified primary site (if primary site is known) or unspecified site (if primary site is unknown). In the following example, the metastatic site is listed first; in practice, the sequencing of codes depends on the reason for the encounter (e.g., whether the primary or secondary cancer site is being treated or medically managed).**

> **EXAMPLE 1:** Metastatic carcinoma from liver to lung
>
> > Assign two codes:
> >
> > > secondary neoplasm of lung (197.0)
> > >
> > > primary malignant neoplasm of liver (155.0)

EXAMPLE 2: Metastatic carcinoma to lung

Assign two codes as follows:

secondary neoplasm of lung (197.0)

primary malignant neoplasm of unspecified site (199.1)

- When anatomic sites are documented as *metastatic*, assign *secondary* neoplasm code(s) to those sites, and assign an *unspecified* site code to the primary malignant neoplasm.

EXAMPLE 1: Metastatic renal cell carcinoma of lung

Assign two codes:

secondary neoplasm of lung (197.0)

primary renal cell carcinoma (189.0)

EXAMPLE 2: Metastatic osteosarcoma of brain

Assign two codes:

secondary neoplasm of brain (198.3)

primary malignant neoplasm of bone (170.9)

EXAMPLE 3: Metastatic melanoma of lung and liver

Assign three codes:

secondary neoplasm of lung (197.0)

secondary neoplasm of liver (197.7)

primary malignant melanoma of unspecified site (172.9)

EXAMPLE 4: Metastatic adenocarcinoma of prostate and vertebra

Assign three codes:

primary adenocarcinoma of unspecified site (199.1)

secondary neoplasm of prostate (198.82)

secondary neoplasm of bone (198.5)

- If the diagnostic statement does not specify whether the neoplasm site is primary or secondary, code the site as *primary* unless the documented site is bone, brain, diaphragm, heart, liver, lymph nodes, mediastinum, meninges, peritoneum, pleura, retroperitoneum, spinal cord, or classifiable to 195. These sites are considered *secondary* sites unless the physician specifies that they are primary.

NOTE: Lung is not included in the above list of secondary (metastatic sites); therefore, this cancer is coded as primary.

> **EXAMPLE 1:** Lung cancer
>
> Assign one code:
>
> primary malignant neoplasm of lung (162.9)

> **EXAMPLE 2:** Brain cancer
>
> Assign two codes:
>
> secondary neoplasm of brain (198.3)
>
> primary malignant neoplasm of unspecified site (199.1)

> **EXAMPLE 3:** Metastatic cancer of hip
>
> Assign two codes:
>
> secondary neoplasm of hip NEC (198.89)
>
> primary malignant neoplasm of unspecified site (199.1)

Anatomic Site Is Not Documented

If the cancer diagnosis does not contain documentation of the anatomic site, but the term *metastatic* is documented, assign codes for "unspecified site" for both the primary and secondary sites.

> **EXAMPLE:** Metastatic chromophobe adenocarcinoma
>
> Assign two codes as follows:
>
> secondary neoplasm of unspecified site (199.1)
>
> primary chromophobe adenocarcinoma of unspecified site (194.3)

Primary Malignant Site Is No Longer Present

If the primary site of malignancy is no longer present, do not assign the code for primary of unspecified site. Instead, classify the previous primary site by assigning the appropriate code from category V10, "Personal history of malignant neoplasm."

> **EXAMPLE:** Metastatic carcinoma to lung from breast (left radical mastectomy performed last year)
>
> Assign two codes as follows:
>
> secondary neoplasm of lung (197.0)
>
> personal history of malignant neoplasm of breast (V10.3)

Contiguous or Overlapping Sites

Contiguous sites (or overlapping sites) occur when the origin of the tumor (primary site) involves two adjacent sites. Neoplasms with overlapping site boundaries are classified to the fourth-digit subcategory .8, "Other."

EXAMPLE: Cancer of the jejunum and ileum

Go to the Index to Diseases entry for "intestine, small, contiguous sites" in the neoplasm table. Locate code 152.8 in the Malignant—Primary column, and verify the code in the Tabular List of Diseases, which appears as:

152   Malignant neoplasm of small intestine, including duodenum

      152.8   Other specified sites of small intestine
               Duodenojejunal junction
               Malignant neoplasm of contiguous or
                    overlapping sites of small intestine whose
                    point of origin cannot be determined

Re-excision of Tumors

A re-excision of a tumor occurs when the pathology report recommends that the surgeon perform a second excision to widen the margins of the original tumor site. The re-excision is performed to ensure that all tumor cells have been removed and that a clear border (margin) of normal tissue surrounds the excised specimen. Use the diagnostic statement found in the report of the original excision to code the reason for the re-excision. The pathology report for the re-excision may not specify a malignancy at this time, but the patient is still under treatment for the original neoplasm.

CODING TIP:

1. Read all notes in the table that apply to the condition you are coding.

2. Never assign a code directly from the table or Index to Diseases.

3. Be certain you are submitting codes that represent the *current status of the neoplasm.*

4. Assign a neoplasm code if the tumor has been excised and the patient is still undergoing radiation or chemotherapy treatment.

5. Assign a V code if the tumor is no longer present or if the patient is not receiving treatment, but is returning for follow-up care.

EXAMPLE: V10–V15   Personal history of a malignancy

          V67.xx   Examination follow-up, no disease

---

6. Classification stated on a pathology report overrides the morphology classification stated in the Index to Diseases.

EXERCISE 6-7

Neoplasm Coding II

STEP 1 Review the notes located at the beginning of the neoplasm table and at the beginning of Chapter 2 in the Tabular List of Diseases.

STEP 2 Code the following diagnostic statements.

1. Ca (carcinoma) of the lung   _____

2. Metastasis from the lung   _____

3. Abdominal mass   _____

4. Carcinoma of the breast (female) with metastasis to the axillary lymph nodes   _____

5. Carcinoma of axillary lymph nodes and lungs, metastatic from the breast (female)   _____

Table of Drugs and Chemicals

NOTE: When coding an adverse effect, code first the adverse effect (or manifestation).

The Table of Drugs and Chemicals is used to identify drugs or chemicals that caused poisonings and adverse effects (Figure 6-6).

The official ICD-9-CM table contains a listing of the generic names of the drugs or chemicals, one column for poisonings, and five separate columns to indicate the external causes of adverse effects or poisonings. (Some publishers are now adding brand names to the list of drugs and chemicals.)

An **adverse effect** or **adverse reaction** is the appearance of a pathologic condition caused by ingestion or exposure to a chemical substance properly administered or taken.

Code first the adverse effect(s) (or manifestations) (e.g., coma) by referring to the Index to Diseases.

The chemical substance is coded by referring to the Therapeutic Use column of the Table of Drugs and Chemicals.

NOTE: An iatrogenic illness can result from a medical intervention, such as an adverse reaction to contrast material injected prior to a scan.

ICD-10-CM ALERT!

Iatrogenic illnesses (adverse effects or adverse reactions) are classified within individual ICD-10-CM chapters (e.g., E81.43, iatrogenic carnitine deficiency, in Chapter 4, Endocrine, nutritional and metabolic diseases (E00-E90).

CODING TIP:

Never assign a code from the Poisoning column with a code from the Therapeutic Use column. Consider highlighting the Therapeutic Use column (Figure 6-6) in your coding manual as a reminder that these codes are *not* assigned with any of the others in the Table of Drugs and Chemicals.

EXAMPLE: Gastritis due to prescribed tetracycline

In this statement, gastritis (535.50) is the adverse effect (or manifestation) of the properly administered drug, tetracycline (E930.4).

Poisonings occur as the result of an overdose, wrong substance administered or taken, or intoxication (e.g., combining prescribed drugs with nonprescribed

Substance	Poisoning	External Cause (E Code)				
		Accident	Therapeutic Use	Suicide Attempt	Assault	Undetermined
1-propanol	980.3	E860.4	—	E950.9	E962.1	E980.9
2-propanol	980.2	E860.3	—	E950.9	E962.1	E980.9
2, 4-D (dichlorophenoxyacetic acid)	989.4	E863.5	—	E950.6	E962.1	E980.7
2, 4-toluene diisocyanate	983.0	E864.0	—	E950.7	E962.1	E980.6
2, 4, 5-T (trichlorophenoxyacetic acid)	989.2	E863.5	—	E950.6	E962.1	E980.7
14-hydroxydihydromorphinone	965.09	E850.2	E935.2	E950.0	E962.0	E980.0
ABOB	961.7	E857	E931.7	E950.4	E962.0	E980.4
Abrus (seed)	988.2	E865.3	—	E950.9	E962.1	E980.9
Absinthe	980.0	E860.1	—	E950.9	E962.1	E980.9
beverage	980.0	E860.0	—	E950.9	E962.1	E980.9
Acenocoumarin, acenocoumarol	964.2	E858.2	E934.2	E950.4	E962.0	E980.4
Acepromazine	969.1	E853.0	E939.1	E950.3	E962.0	E980.3
Acetal	982.8	E862.4	—	E950.9	E962.1	E980.9
Acetaldehyde (vapor)	987.8	E869.8	—	E952.8	E962.2	E982.8
liquid	989.89	E866.8	—	E950.9	E962.1	E980.9
Acetaminophen	965.4	E850.4	E935.4	E950.0	E962.0	E980.0
Acetaminosalol	965.1	E850.3	E935.3	E950.0	E962.0	E980.0
Acetanilid(e)	965.4	E850.4	E935.4	E950.0	E962.0	E980.0
Acetarsol, acetarsone	961.1	E857	E931.1	E950.4	E962.0	E980.4
Acetazolamide	974.2	E858.5	E944.2	E950.4	E962.0	E980.4
Acetic						
acid	983.1	E864.1	—	E950.7	E962.1	E980.6
with sodium acetate (ointment)	976.3	E858.7	E946.3	E950.4	E962.0	E980.4
irrigating solution	974.5	E858.5	E944.5	E950.4	E962.0	E980.4
lotion	976.2	E858.7	E946.2	E950.4	E962.0	E980.4
anhydride	983.1	E864.1	—	E950.7	E962.1	E980.6
ether (vapor)	982.8	E862.4	—	E950.9	E962.1	E980.9

FIGURE 6-6 ICD-9-CM Table of Drugs and Chemicals (partial) (Permission to reprint granted by Ingenix.)

drugs or alcohol). The Table of Drugs and Chemicals categorizes poisonings according to accident, suicide attempt, assault, or undetermined.

Poisonings are coded by referring first to the Poisoning column of the Table of Drugs and Chemicals and then the External Cause (E code) columns within the table (with the exception of the Therapeutic Use column).

> **EXAMPLE:** Accidental overdose of tetracycline
>
> In this statement, the poisoning code is listed first (960.4), followed by the accidental overdose E code (E856).

Review the patient's record to determine the manifestations of the poisoning (e.g., headache, coma); refer to the Index to Diseases and sequence these codes *after* the codes for the poisoning and external cause.

The Table of Drugs and Chemicals contains six columns of codes:

- **Poisoning** (codes 960–989) is assigned according to classification of the drug or chemical.

- **Accident** (codes E850–E869) is used for accidental overdosing, wrong substance given or taken, drug inadvertently taken, or accidents in the use of drugs and chemical substances during medical or surgical procedures, and to show external causes of poisonings classifiable to 960–989.

- **Therapeutic use** (codes E930–E949) is used for the external effect caused by correct substance properly administered in therapeutic or prophylactic dosages.
- **Suicide attempt** (codes E950–E952) is a self-inflicted poisoning.
- **Assault** (codes E961–E962) is a poisoning inflicted by another person who intended to kill or injure the patient.
- **Undetermined** (codes E980–E982) is used if the record does not state whether the poisoning was intentional or accidental.

CODING TIP:

The term *intoxication* often indicates that alcohol was involved (e.g., alcohol intoxication) or that an accumulation effect of a medication in the patient's bloodstream occurred (e.g., Coumadin intoxication). When *alcohol intoxication* occurs, assign a code from the Poisoning column along with the appropriate E code. When an accumulation effect of a medication occurs, assign the manifestation code first (e.g., dizziness) and an E code from the Therapeutic Use column (e.g., daily Coumadin use).

E codes are used to explain the cause of the poisoning or the adverse effect. They are external causes or results of injury codes (not diagnosis codes). Therefore, *E codes are always reported as secondary codes, never first-listed or principal diagnosis, codes.*

EXAMPLE 1: Hives, due to prescribed penicillin

Answer: 708.9 (hives NOS), E930.0 (therapeutic use of penicillin)

EXAMPLE 2: Coma due to overdose of barbiturates, attempted suicide

Answer: 967.0 (poisoning by barbiturates), E950.1 (suicide by barbiturates), 780.01 (coma)

EXERCISE 6-8

Using the Table of Drugs and Chemicals

Code the following statements using ICD-9-CM.

1. Adverse reaction to pertussis vaccine   _____
2. Cardiac arrhythmia caused by interaction
   between prescribed ephedrine and nonprescribed alcohol   _____
3. Stupor, due to overdose of Nytol (suicide attempt)   _____
4. High blood pressure due to prescribed Albuterol   _____
5. Rash due to combining prescribed Amoxicillin
   with nonprescribed Benadryl.   _____

ICD-9-CM SUPPLEMENTARY CLASSIFICATIONS

ICD-9-CM contains two supplementary classifications:

- **V codes: factors influencing health status and contact with health services (V01–V89).**
- **E codes: external causes of injury and poisoning (E800–E999).**

V Codes

V codes are contained in a supplementary classification of factors influencing the person's health status (Table 6-5A). These codes are used when a person seeks health care but does not have active complaints or symptoms, or when it is necessary to describe circumstances that could influence the patient's health care. These services fall into one of three categories:

1. Problems—issues that could affect the patient's health status.

2. Services—Person is seen for treatment that is not caused by illness or injury.

3. Factual reporting—used for statistical purposes (e.g., outcome of delivery or referral of patient without examination).

Refer to Table 6-5B for a list of main terms found in the ICD-9-CM Index to Diseases.

CODING TIP:

Consult Appendix E (List of Three-Digit Categories) if you have trouble locating a V code category in the Index to Diseases.

EXERCISE 6-9

Exploring V Codes

Code the following statements using ICD-9-CM.

1. Family history of epilepsy with no evidence of seizures   _____

2. Six-week postpartum checkup   _____

3. Premarital physical   _____

4. Consult with dietitian for patient with diabetes mellitus   _____

5. Rubella screening   _____

TABLE 6-5A ICD-9-CM V code sections, descriptions, and code categories and uses

SECTION	DESCRIPTION	CODE CATEGORY AND USE
V01-V06	Persons with potential health hazards related to communicable diseases	• V01—Patients who have been exposed to communicable diseases but have not been diagnosed • V02—Patients who have been identified as or are suspected of being infectious disease carriers • V03-V06—Patients who are seeking immunization against disease
V07-V09	Persons with need for isolation, other potential health hazards and prophylactic measures	• V07—Patients who are placed in an isolation area or who are receiving prophylactic measures (e.g., prophylactic fluoride administration by a dentist) • V08—Asymptomatic HIV infection status **NOTE:** *Do not report code V08 if the patient is diagnosed with:* • *AIDS (042)* • *Exposure to HIV (V01.79)* • *Nonspecific serologic evidence of HIV (795.71)* • V09—Patient's infection is drug-resistant; these are reported as a secondary code(s)
V10-V19	Persons with potential health hazards related to personal and family history	• V10-V15—Patient has personal history of malignant neoplasm, mental disorder, disease, allergy, hazard to health, or having undergone certain surgeries • V16-V19—Patient has family history of malignant neoplasm or other diseases/conditions **CODING TIP:** • Codes from categories V10-V15 are reported when the patient's condition no longer exists. • Verify history of codes in the tabular list before reporting. • Do not confuse *personal history of* with *family history of* codes.
V20-V29	Persons encountering health services in circumstances related to reproduction and development	• V20-V21—Patient is seen for a well-baby or well-child office visit **CODING TIP:** If documentation supports treatment of a condition during the well-baby/child visit, report a code for the condition in addition to a code from category V20-V21. • V22-V23—Patient is supervised during pregnancy, whether normal or high-risk • V24—Patient is treated after having given birth • V25-V26—Patient is seen for contraceptive or procreative management • V27—Outcome of delivery is coded on the mother's insurance claim **CODING TIP:** V27.x is never reported as the first code on the insurance claim. Report a code from 650-659 first. • V28—Patient is screened during pregnancy • V29—Newborn is observed/evaluated, but no condition is diagnosed
V30-V39	Liveborn infants according to type of birth	• V30-V39—Type of birth is coded on the baby's insurance claim **CODING TIP:** V3x.xx is always reported as the first code on the insurance claim. If documented, also report congenital, perinatal, and other conditions.

(continues)

TABLE 6-5A   (continued)

SECTION	DESCRIPTION	CODE CATEGORY AND USE
V40–V49	Persons with a condition influencing their health status	• V40–V49—Patients who have not been diagnosed, but who have conditions that influence their health status **EXAMPLE:** Patient undergoes colostomy as the result of colon cancer, which was successfully treated. Patient is seen for hay fever, and the provider documents that the patient is adjusting to having a colostomy. Code V44.3 is reported in addition to hay fever (477.9).
V50–V59	Persons encountering health services for specific procedures and aftercare	• V50—Patient undergoes elective surgery (most payers will not provide reimbursement) • V51—Patient undergoes plastic surgery as aftercare **EXAMPLE:** Patient receives breast implant following mastectomy. Assign code V51.0 • V52–V54—Patient is fitted for prosthesis or implant or has device adjusted or removed • V55—Patient receives attention to artificial opening, such as colostomy cleansing • V56—Patient undergoes dialysis and dialysis catheter care **CODING TIP:** When reporting V56.xx, code also the associated condition (e.g., renal failure). • V57—Patient undergoes rehabilitation procedures **CODING TIP:** When reporting V57.xx, code also the associated condition (e.g., dysphasia). • V58—Patient receives other treatment or aftercare **EXAMPLE:** Patient is diagnosed with breast cancer, undergoes mastectomy, and is admitted for chemotherapy. Assign V58.1 as well as the appropriate breast cancer code. • V59—Individual is donating an organ or tissue **CODING TIP:** Do not report V59.x on the recipient's insurance claim.
V60–V69	Persons encountering health services in other circumstances	• V60–V69—Individuals are seen for reasons other than resulting from illness or injury **NOTE:** Payers usually do not reimburse for these services. **EXAMPLE:** Patient pretends to be in pain so a narcotic will be prescribed, and the provider is alerted to the pretense by another provider (V65.2).

(continues)

TABLE 6-5A   (continued)

SECTION	DESCRIPTION	CODE CATEGORY AND USE
V70-V88	Persons without reported diagnosis encountered during examination and investigation of individuals and populations	• V70—Patient seen for routine examination, such as annual physical **CODING TIP:** V70.x may be reported with other ICD codes when documentation supports the exam as well as treatment of a condition. • V71—Patient is observed and evaluated for a suspected condition, which is ruled out **CODING TIP:** Before reporting a V71 code, review the record to determine whether a sign or symptom can be coded instead. • V72-V82—Patient undergoes special investigations, examinations, or screenings **EXAMPLE:** Patient has extensive family history of ovarian cancer (e.g., mother, aunts, sisters) and elects to undergo screening as a preventive measure (V76.46). • V83—Patient has genetic carrier status determined • V84—Patient has genetic susceptibility to disease • V85—Patient has body mass index determined • V86—Patient has Estrogen receptor status determined • V87—Patient was exposed to or has history of other hazard to health • V88—Patient underwent surgery to have organs or other tissue removed • V89—Patient has other suspected condition that was not found

TABLE 6-5B   Main terms to use when the V code is difficult to find

Admission	Donor	Outcome of delivery
Aftercare	Encounter for	Pregnancy
Attention to	Examination	Procedure (surgical) not done
Carrier (suspected) of	Exposure	Prophylactic
Checking	Fitting	Removal
Checkup	Follow-up	Resistance, resistant
Closure	History, family	Routine postpartum follow-up
Contact	History (personal) of	Screening
Contraception, contraceptive	Maladjustment	Status
Counseling	Newborn	Test(s)
Dialysis	Observation	Vaccination

CAUTION:

Before entering codes on a claim or any other official document that leaves the office, check to ensure that a signed "Authorization for Release of HIV Status" form was obtained from the patient. (See Figure 5-11 in Chapter 5 for a sample authorization.)

CODING SPECIAL DISORDERS ACCORDING TO ICD-9-CM

HIV/AIDS

Code 042 is assigned when a documented diagnosis states that the patient is HIV-positive and exhibits manifestations associated with AIDS. Secondary codes are assigned to classify the manifestations such as Kaposi's sarcoma, candidiasis, coccidiosis, hemolytic anemia, and so on.

Assign code 079.53 in addition to 042 when HIV type 2 is identified by the provider.

Assign code 795.71 when screening for HIV was reported as nonspecific. For example, this code is used when a newborn tests positive upon HIV screening, but it cannot be determined whether the positive result reflects the true status of the baby or the seropositive status of the mother.

V01.71-V01.79 are assigned for patients who were exposed to the virus but not tested for infection.

V08 is assigned when the patient is HIV-positive, asymptomatic, and does not exhibit manifestations of AIDS. Once the patient presents with symptoms, V08 can never again be reported.

Assign V65.44 when the reason for the encounter is counseling of a patient who has been tested for HIV. It does not matter whether the patient's HIV status is positive or negative.

Fracture Cases

CODING TIP:

Study the fifth-digit subclassification note at the beginning of the Musculoskeletal System chapter before coding fractures. This information is extremely helpful in selecting the correct code.

Distinction is required between closed and open fractures. If the diagnostic statement does not specify closed or open, select the appropriate closed fracture code. (It is important to realize that an open fracture does not always require an open reduction.) A list of common types of fractures appears in Table 6-6.

When a patient has suffered multiple injuries, list the injuries in descending order of severity on the claim.

TABLE 6-6   Common types of fracture

COMMON CLOSED FRACTURE TERMS	COMMON OPEN FRACTURE TERMS
Comminuted	Compound
Linear	Missile
Spiral	Puncture
Impacted	Fracture with a foreign body
Simple	Infected fracture
Greenstick	
Compressed	

EXERCISE 6-10

Coding HIV/AIDS and Fracture Cases

Code the following statements.

1. Patient is HIV-positive with no symptoms _____

2. AIDS patient treated for candidiasis _____

3. Open fracture, maxilla _____

4. Greenstick fracture, third digit, right foot _____

5. Multiple fractures, right femur, distal end _____

NOTE: Sequelae (singular form is sequela) are late effects of injury or illness. In ICD-9-CM, these are classified within sections 990-995, which are located at the end of the injury and Poisoning chapter.

ICD-10-CM ALERT!

In ICD-10-CM, late effects of injury or illness (sequelae) codes appear at the end of each anatomic chapter, as appropriate.

Late Effect

A late effect is a residual effect or sequela of a previous acute illness, injury, or surgery. The patient is currently dealing with long-term chronic effects of the disorder or trauma. The underlying acute condition no longer exists (Table 6-7).

In most cases, two codes will be required to classify diagnostic statements specifying residual conditions of an original illness or injury. The primary code is the residual (condition currently affecting the patient). The secondary code represents the original condition or etiology of the late effect. Locate the appropriate code by referencing the Index to Diseases under the main term, "Late." If the late effect is also due to an external cause, reference the Index to External Causes under the word, "Late." Occasionally, one combination code is used to classify the diagnostic statement.

EXAMPLE: For dysphasia due to CVA 6 months ago, the combination code is 438.12.

Occasionally, there will be a reversal of the primary and secondary positions. This occurs when the index references the late effect first followed by a slanted bracketed residual code.

TABLE 6-7 Common late effects

ORIGINAL CONDITION/ETIOLOGY	LATE EFFECT/SEQUELA
Fracture	Malunion
CVA	Hemiplegia
Third-degree burn	Deep scarring
Polio	Contractures
Laceration	Keloid
Breast implant	Ruptured implant

EXAMPLE: Scoliosis due to childhood polio

Index entry is: Scoliosis (acquired) (postural) 737.30

due to or associated with

poliomyelitis 138 [737.43]

The first-listed code is 138. The secondary code is 737.43 (as indicated by the slanted bracketed code in the index convention).

Burns

Burns require two codes: one for the site and degree and a second for the percentage of body surface (not body part) affected.

The percentage of total body area or surface affected follows the "rule of nines":

Head and neck	=	9%
Back (trunk)	=	18%
Chest (trunk)	=	18%
Leg (each)	=	18%
		18%
Arm (each)	=	9%
		9%
Genitalia	=	1%
Total body surface (TBS)		100%

NOTE: To find the total percentage affected, health professionals add the affected extremities or regions together and state the combined total.

EXERCISE 6-11

Coding Late Effects and Burns

1. Malunion due to fracture, right ankle, 9 months ago _____

2. Brain damage due to subdural hematoma, 18 months previously _____

3. Second degree burn, anterior chest wall _____

4. Scalding with erythema, right forearm and hand _____

5. Third-degree burn, back, 18 percent body surface _____

Congenital versus Perinatal Conditions

Congenital anomalies (codes 740–759) are disorders diagnosed in infants at birth. (Adults can also be diagnosed with congenital anomalies because such disorders may have been previously undetected.)

EXAMPLE: Congenital heart disease (746.xx) describes heart defects that develop prior to birth and result from a failure of the heart or the blood vessels near the heart to develop normally. The causes are mostly unknown, but in some cases the disorder is due to alcohol consumption during pregnancy, heredity (genetics), or an infection during pregnancy. The disorder may be diagnosed before birth, or it may not be detected until birth (and even weeks or years after birth).

Perinatal conditions (codes 760–779) occur before birth, during birth, or within the **perinatal period**, or the first 28 days of life. Think of these conditions as something that happens to the patient.

> **EXAMPLE:** Drug withdrawal syndrome in a newborn (779.5) results when a mother is dependent on narcotics during the pregnancy. The narcotics taken by the mother pass from the mother's bloodstream through the placenta to the fetus, resulting in fetal addiction. At birth the baby's dependence continues, but the narcotics are no longer available, and the baby's central nervous system becomes overstimulated, causing withdrawal symptoms. The infant may also develop related problems, such as low birth weight (765.xx).

Use of E Codes

An E code consists of a four-character number (an E followed by three digits) and one digit after a decimal point. The Index to External Causes (E codes) is located separately in the Index to Diseases, after the Table of Drugs and Chemicals.

Although many states require the reporting of E codes, provider office insurance claims do not. However, reporting E codes on claims can expedite payment by health insurance carriers when no third-party liability for an accident exists. In such cases, it is necessary to report two E codes in addition to the appropriate injury codes. *(E codes are never reported as first-listed codes.)*

> **EXAMPLE:** Patient is seen for treatment of a fractured pelvis, which was sustained when he fell from a ladder while repairing his house. The fractured pelvis is coded and sequenced first on the claim followed by two E codes, one for the external cause and another for the place of occurrence: 808.8, E881.0, and E849.0.
>
> | | | |
> |---|---|---|
> | Injury: | Fracture | |
> | | pelvis | 808.8 |
> | External Cause: | Fall (falling) | |
> | | from, off ladder | E881.0 |
> | Place of Occurrence: | Accident (to) | |
> | | occurring (at) (in) | |
> | | home (private) (residential) | E849.0 |
>
> (Homeowners insurance covers injuries sustained by visitors, but not family members living in the home.)

CODING TIP:

Review the note at the beginning of the E-Code tabular list before coding external causes of injuries and poisonings.

At the end of the Index to External Causes is a section entitled: "Fourth-Digit Subdivisions for the External Cause (E) Codes."

It may be necessary to consult the Appendix E List of Three-Digit Categories for assistance in locating possible main terms in the E code index.

EXERCISE 6-12

Coding External Cause of Injury

Code the following statements.

1. Automobile accident, highway, passenger   _____
2. Employee injured by fall from ladder at work   _____
3. Accidental drowning, fell from power boat located on lake   _____
4. Soft tissue injury, right arm, due to snowmobile accident in patient's yard   _____
5. Fall from playground equipment   _____

REMINDERS TO ENSURE ACCURATE ICD-9-CM CODING

1. Preprinted diagnosis codes on encounter forms, routing slips, and coding lists should be reviewed to verify accuracy.
2. The latest edition code books should be purchased because codes are updated (added/deleted/revised).
3. Providers and insurance specialists should be kept informed of coding changes (e.g., newsletter subscription).
4. Diagnosis codes should be reviewed for accuracy when updates are installed in office management software.
5. A policy should be established to address assignment of codes when the office is awaiting the results of laboratory and pathology reports.
6. Reports of diagnostic tests performed at other facilities should be reviewed to ensure accurate coding.
7. The postoperative diagnosis should be coded (not the preoperative diagnosis).
8. Some computer programs automatically generate insurance claims for each encounter. Office staff should intercept these claims to verify the diagnosis code(s) assigned (e.g., review for definitive diagnosis).
9. M codes (morphology codes) should *not* be reported on the CMS-1500 claim.
10. Diagnosis codes should be proofread to ensure proper entry in the permanent record (e.g., onscreen, paper, and electronic claims).

QUICK COMPARISON OF ICD-9-CM (DIAGNOSIS CODES) TO ICD-10-CM	
ICD-9-CM (diagnosis codes)	**ICD-10-CM**
• Divided into an index and a tabular list	• Divided into an index and a tabular list
• Index is divided into two parts: 　◦ Index to Diseases (includes Hypertension Table, Neoplasm Table, and a Table of Drugs and Chemicals) 　◦ Index to External Causes	• Index is divided into two parts: 　◦ Index to Diseases (includes Neoplasm table and a Table of Drugs and Chemicals) 　◦ Index to External Causes of Injury ICD-10-CM does *not* contain a Hypertension Table because codes for "benign" and "malignant" hypertension were eliminated from the classification system.

QUICK COMPARISON OF ICD-9-CM (DIAGNOSIS CODES) TO ICD-10-CM

ICD-9-CM (diagnosis codes)	ICD-10-CM
• Tabular List of Diseases includes 17 chapters, and approximately 13,600 codes plus a Supplemental Classification of Factors Influencing Health Status and Contact with Health Services (V codes) and a Supplementary Classification of External Causes of Injury and Poisoning (E codes) ◊ ICD-9-CM has limited space to add new codes and lacks detail ◊ Data is difficult to analyze due to number of nonspecific codes ◊ Cannot support data exchange with other countries	• Tabular List of Diseases includes 21 chapters, and approximately 120,000 codes incorporating *external causes of morbidity* (V and Y codes) and *factors influencing health status and contact with health service* (Z codes), and each chapter lists a summary block of codes to provide an overview of the codes in that chapter ◊ Primary axis of classification for most chapters is anatomy ◊ Some chapters are arranged by etiology (e.g., Neoplasms) or other criteria (e.g., External Causes of Morbidity)
• Valid codes can be 3–5 characters	• Valid codes can be 3, 4, 5, 6, or 7 alphanumeric characters
• First character is numeric, except for E and V codes	• First character is always alphabetic
• Second and third digits are always numeric	• Second and third digits are always numeric
• Three-digit categories remain vacant to allow for code revisions and future additions	• Three-digit categories remain vacant to allow for code revisions and future additions
• Decimal is entered after third digit (e.g., 250.00)	• Decimal is entered after third character (e.g., A69.21)
• Fourth-digit subcategory and fifth-digit subclassification codes are always numeric	• Fourth-digit subcategory codes are either alphanumeric or numeric, as are fifth- and sixth-digit subclassification codes, and seventh characters are either alphabetic or numeric, seventh character is assigned only to certain codes, and alphabetic digits are *not* case sensitive • Fourth character, if present, indicates etiology • Fifth character, if present, indicates anatomic site • Sixth character, if present, indicates intent of drug poisoning (e.g., intentional, self-harm, assault), laterality (e.g., right, left), nature of an injury, severity (e.g., depth of skin ulcer), trimester of a pregnancy, or "with" or "without" a given manifestation • Seventh character, if present, is a mandatory "extension" for classification of injuries, obstetrics, and external causes of injuries (e.g., fracture codes require a seventh character to indicate initial versus subsequent encounter, routine versus delayed healing, open versus closed fracture, or late effect of fracture) **NOTE:** In ICD-10-CM, the fourth through sixth characters can also serve as placeholders, which means an "x" is entered when a seventh character is required for classification of injuries, obstetrics, and external causes of injuries. The "x" placeholder: • is applicable to selected codes (that would otherwise have just five digits) so that the code has the potential for expanded meaning while not altering the significance and placement of code extensions. • allows for future expansion of a code. • allows for consistent format of an "extension" code to facilitate entry of a character in the seventh position and to retain the meaning of the extension code.
• Coding conventions assist in the accurate assignment of codes ◊ Instructions (e.g., excludes and includes notes) ◊ Punctuation (e.g., brackets, colons, parentheses) ◊ Words and phrases (e.g., and, with, without, other specified, unspecified, not elsewhere classified, not otherwise specified, use additional code)	• Coding conventions assist in the accurate assignment of codes, and many are similar to those found in ICD-9-CM ◊ Instructions ◊ Punctuation ◊ Words and phrases (Refer to the "Major Changes in ICD-10-CM" shaded box, to learn about new coding conventions.)

QUICK COMPARISON OF ICD-9-CM (DIAGNOSIS CODES) TO ICD-10-CM

ICD-9-CM (diagnosis codes)	ICD-10-CM
• ICD-9-CM coding guidelines are published by the Centers for Medicare and Medicaid Services (CMS)	• ICD-10-CM coding guidelines are published by CMS, and many of them are similar to the ICD-9-CM coding guidelines (e.g., principal diagnosis, first-listed diagnosis, principal procedure, first-listed procedure, and so on)

SUMMARY OF MAJOR CHANGES IN ICD-10-CM

- CHANGES APPLICABLE TO ALL OF ICD-10-CM:
  ◊ Code descriptions are complete for each code, which means there is no need to refer to the description of a category code when assigning a subcategory or subclassification code.
  ◊ Combination codes are used for symptom/diagnosis (e.g., N30.01, acute cystitis with hematuria) and etiology/manifestation (e.g., E11.21, type 2 diabetes with diabetic nephropathy).
  ◊ Conditions with new treatment protocols and/or that were recently discovered are classified in appropriate chapters.
  ◊ Certain conditions are reassigned to a different ICD-10-CM chapter because of new medical knowledge. For example, "gout" was relocated from ICD-9-CM's Chapter 3, *Endocrine, Nutritional, and Metabolic Diseases and Immunity Disorders*, to ICD-10-CM's Chapter 13, *Diseases of the Musculoskeletal System and Connective Tissue*.
  ◊ Postoperative complications are located in the procedure-specific body system chapter (instead of having their own chapter as in ICD-9-CM).
  ◊ There are two types of excludes notes:
    ■ *Excludes1* indicates codes listed elsewhere are mutually exclusive, which means they are *never* reported together.
    ■ *Excludes2* indicates both codes may be reported together if the excluded condition is not classified by the code in question *and* if the patient is treated for both conditions.
  ◊ *Diseases of the Genitourinary System* (Chapter 14), *Pregnancy, Childbirth and the Puerperium* (Chapter 15), *Certain Conditions Originating in the Perinatal Period* (Chapter 16), and *Congenital Malformations, Deformations, and Chromosomal Abnormalities* (Chapter 17) are sequential in ICD-10-CM.
  ◊ ICD-9-CM's *External Causes of Injury* (E codes) and *Factors Influencing Health Status* (V codes) are incorporated into the core ICD-10-CM classification system as *External Causes of Morbidity* (Chapter 20) and *Factors Influencing Health Status and Contact with Health Services* (Chapter 21), respectively. They are no longer considered supplementary classifications.

- CHAPTER 1, CERTAIN INFECTIOUS AND PARASITIC DISEASES:
  ◊ Chapter title is revised in ICD-10-CM to stress the fact that localized infections are classified to the pertinent body system (e.g., urinary tract infection is classified to ICD-10-CM Chapter 14, Diseases of the Genitourinary System).
  ◊ Diagnosis of "severe sepsis" requires assignment of three codes:
    ■ infection code.
    ■ severe sepsis code (R65.2, located in Chapter 18 of ICD-10-CM).
    ■ associated organ dysfunction code, if documented (e.g., renal failure).
  ◊ Nosocomial infections (or hospital-acquired infections) are classified with a code from the Y95 category located in Chapter 20 of ICD-10-CM (in addition to a code for the infection). For example, hospital-acquired pneumonia is assigned two codes, J18.9 and Y95.

- CHAPTER 2, NEOPLASMS:
  ◊ Codes are expanded to include gender and laterality.
  ◊ Morphology codes are assigned as additional diagnoses.

- CHAPTER 3, DISEASES OF THE BLOOD AND BLOOD-FORMING ORGANS AND CERTAIN DISORDERS INVOLVING THE IMMUNE MECHANISM:
  Classifies disorders of the immune mechanism. (Disorders of the immune mechanism were included in Chapter 3, Endocrine, Nutritional, and Metabolic Diseases, of ICD-9-CM.)

(continues)

SUMMARY OF MAJOR CHANGES IN ICD-10-CM

- CHAPTER 4, ENDOCRINE, NUTRITIONAL, AND METABOLIC DISORDERS: Diabetes codes were extensively revised, and the chapter now differentiates among type 1 and 2 diabetes mellitus and:
  - ◊ diabetes due to underlying condition.
  - ◊ drug- or chemical-induced diabetes.

- CHAPTER 5, MENTAL AND BEHAVIORAL DISORDERS:
  - ◊ Chapter title is revised to add "and Behavioral."
  - ◊ Alcohol- and substance-abuse codes are expanded.
  - ◊ Combination codes are used for some conditions (e.g., F11.250, opioid dependence with opioid-induced psychotic disorder with delusions).

- CHAPTER 6, DISEASES OF THE NERVOUS SYSTEM: Sense organs codes are relocated to the following new chapters in ICD-10-CM:
  - ◊ Chapter 7, Diseases of the Eye and Adnexa.
  - ◊ Chapter 8, Diseases of the Ear and Mastoid Process.

- CHAPTER 9, DISEASES OF THE CIRCULATORY SYSTEM: Hypertension is not classified as "benign" or "malignant," which means the hypertension table found in ICD-9-CM does *not* exist in ICD-10-CM.

- CHAPTER 15, PREGNANCY, CHILDBIRTH, AND THE PUERPERIUM:
  - ◊ Obstetric codes identify trimester (and the ICD-9-CM fifth digit for "episode of care" was eliminated).
  - ◊ Early and late vomiting of pregnancy are assessed against the criteria of "before or after 20 weeks gestation" as time delineation.

- CHAPTER 17, CONGENITAL MALFORMATIONS, DEFORMATIONS, AND CHROMOSOMAL ABNORMALITIES: "Deformations, and chromosomal abnormalities" are added to the chapter title.

- CHAPTER 19, INJURY, POISONING, AND CERTAIN OTHER CONSEQUENCES OF EXTERNAL CAUSES:
  - ◊ Injury codes are expanded in number and grouped according to site (instead of type of injury):
  - ◊ fifth character defines type of injury.
  - ◊ sixth character defines laterality (unspecified, right or left).
  - ◊ seventh character defines type of encounter.
  - ◊ Seventh-character code extensions are assigned to most categories in the for Injuries, Poisoning and Certain Other Consequences of External Causes chapter. For example, "A" (or "a") indicates initial encounter for treatment of injury.

- CHAPTER 20, EXTERNAL CAUSES OF MORBIDITY:
  - ◊ The following are more specifically classified: causes of injury (e.g., accident, assault), place of injury (e.g., apartment), and activity in which engaged when injury occurred (e.g., work, nonwork, student, military).
  - ◊ The place of occurrence for treatment of external causes is expanded to include ambulatory (outpatient), hospice, and nursing home facilities and the patient's home (in addition to hospital).

SUMMARY

The United States adopted the *International Classification of Diseases, 9th Revision, Clinical Modification (ICD-9-CM)* to facilitate the coding and classification of morbidity (disease) data from inpatient and outpatient records, physician office records, and statistical surveys. The Medicare Catastrophic Coverage Act of 1988 mandated the reporting of ICD-9-CM diagnosis codes on Medicare claims. (Private insurers adopted similar requirements in subsequent years.) (ICD-10-CM and ICD-10-PCS will be implemented on October 1, 2013, to replace ICD-9-CM.)

Medical necessity is the measure of whether a healthcare procedure or service is appropriate for the diagnosis and/or treatment of a condition. Third-party payers use medical necessity measurements to make a decision about whether to pay a claim.

Diagnostic Coding and Reporting Guidelines for Outpatient Services: Hospital-Based and Physician Office-Based were developed by the federal government for use in reporting diagnoses for claims submission. Outpatient claims (CMS-1500) require reporting of the patient's first-listed diagnosis, secondary diagnoses, procedures, and services. Diagnoses are assigned ICD-9-CM codes, and procedures or services are assigned CPT and HCPCS national (level II) codes. Inpatient claims (UB-04) require reporting of the principal diagnosis, secondary diagnoses, principal procedure, and secondary procedures.

ICD-9-CM consists of Volume 1 (Tabular List of Diseases), Volume 2 (Index to Diseases), and Volume 3 (Index to Procedures and Tabular List of Procedures). The ICD-9-CM Index to Diseases is organized according to alphabetical main terms (boldfaced conditions), nonessential modifiers (in parentheses), and subterms (essential modifiers that are indented below main terms). It also contains a hypertension table, neoplasm table, and table of drugs and chemicals. To properly assign an ICD-9-CM code, locate the main term in the Index to Diseases, apply coding conventions, and verify the code in the Tabular List of Diseases (applying additional coding conventions).

INTERNET LINKS

- Computer-assisted coding (CAC)
  www.coderyte.com
  www.platocode.com
- ICD-9-CM encoders (free)
  www.ICD9coding.com
- ICD-9-CM encoders (subscription-based)
  www.EncoderPro.com (free trial available)
- ICD-9-CM searchable indexes and tabular lists (free)
  icd9cm.chrisendres.com
  www.eICD.com
- ICD-9-CM coding updates and ICD-10-CM/PCS information
  Go to **www.cdc.gov** and click on the Publications and Products link. Scroll down and click on the National Center for Health Statistics link; then scroll down and click on the ICD Information link.
- *Federal Register* listserv
  At **listserv.access.gpo.gov,** click on the Online mailing list archives link, click on the FEDREGTOC-L link, and click on the Join or leave the list (or change settings) link to register to receive the daily *Federal Register* table of contents via e-mail. The document will contain the Centers for Medicare and Medicaid Services final rule about implementation of ICD-10-CM and ICD-10-PCS.
- ICD-9 Special Updates and ICD-10 Corner: Latest News
  Go to **www.ingenixonline.com** and click on the related link below Quick Access Resources.
- Official version of ICD-9-CM from the U.S. Government Bookstore
  bookstore.gpo.gov
- ICD-10
  Go to **www.who.int,** enter "ICD-10" in the Search box, and click Search to locate information about the World Health Organization's ICD-10.

STUDY CHECKLIST

- ☐ Read this textbook chapter and highlight key concepts.
- ☐ Create an index card for each key term.
- ☐ Access the chapter Internet links to learn more about concepts.

☐ Complete the chapter review, verifying answers with your instructor.
☐ Complete WebTutor assignments and take online quizzes.
☐ Complete Workbook chapter assignments, verifying answers with your instructor.
☐ Complete the StudyWare activities to receive immediate feedback.
☐ Form a study group with classmates to discuss chapter concepts in preparation for an exam.

NOTE: Although the review is organized by chapter and supplemental classification, codes from outside a particular chapter or supplemental classification may be required to completely classify a case. Also, ICD-10-CM answer keys to the chapter review are available at the textbook's online companion (discussed in the preface).

The ICD-9-CM coding review is organized according to the ICD-9-CM chapters and supplemental classifications. To properly code, refer first to the Index to Diseases (to locate main term and subterm entries) and then to the Tabular List of Diseases (to review notes and verify the code selected).

Underline the main term in each item; then use Index to Diseases and Tabular List of Diseases coding rules and conventions to assign the code(s). Enter the code(s) on the line next to each diagnostic statement. Be sure to list the primary code first.

INFECTIOUS AND PARASITIC DISEASES (INCLUDING HIV)

1. Aseptic meningitis due to AIDS _____

2. Asymptomatic HIV infection _____

3. Septicemia due to streptococcus _____

4. Dermatophytosis of the foot _____

5. Measles; no complications noted _____

6. Nodular pulmonary tuberculosis; confirmed histologically _____

7. Acute cystitis due to *E. coli* _____

8. Tuberculosis osteomyelitis of lower leg; confirmed by histology _____

9. Gas gangrene _____

NEOPLASMS

10. Malignant melanoma of skin of scalp _____

11. Lipoma of face _____

12. Glioma of the parietal lobe of the brain _____

13. Adenocarcinoma of prostate _____

14. Carcinoma *in situ* of vocal cord _____

15. Hodgkin's granuloma of intra-abdominal lymph nodes and spleen _____

16. Paget's disease with infiltrating duct carcinoma of breast, nipple, and areola _____

17. Liver cancer _____

18. Metastatic adenocarcinoma from breast to brain (right mastectomy performed 5 years ago) _____

19. Cancer of the pleura (primary site) _____

ENDOCRINE, NUTRITIONAL AND METABOLIC DISEASES, AND IMMUNITY DISORDERS

20. Cushing's Syndrome _____

21. Hypokalemia _____

22. Type II diabetes mellitus, uncontrolled, with malnutrition _____

23. Hypogammaglobulinemia _____

24. Hypercholesterolemia _____

25. Nephrosis due to type II diabetes _____

26. Toxic diffuse goiter with thyrotoxic crisis _____

27. Cystic fibrosis _____

28. Panhypopituitarism _____

29. Rickets _____

DISEASES OF THE BLOOD AND BLOOD-FORMING ORGANS

30. Sickle cell disease with crisis _____

31. Iron deficiency anemia secondary to blood loss _____

32. Von Willebrand's disease _____

33. Chronic congestive splenomegaly _____

34. Congenital nonspherocytic hemolytic anemia _____

35. Essential thrombocytopenia _____

36. Malignant neutropenia _____

37. Fanconi's anemia _____

38. Microangiopathic hemolytic anemia _____

39. Aplastic anemia secondary to antineoplastic medication for breast cancer _____

MENTAL DISORDERS

40. Acute exacerbation of chronic undifferentiated schizophrenia _____

41. Reactive depressive psychosis due to the death of a child _____

42. Hysterical neurosis _____

43. Anxiety reaction manifested by fainting _____

44. Alcoholic gastritis due to chronic alcoholism (episodic) _____

45. Juvenile delinquency; patient was caught shoplifting _____

46. Depression _____

47. Hypochondria; patient also has continuous laxative habit _____

48. Acute senile dementia with Alzheimer's disease _____

49. Epileptic psychosis with generalized grand mal epilepsy _____

DISEASES OF THE NERVOUS SYSTEM AND SENSE ORGANS

50. *Neisseria* meningitis   _____

51. Intracranial abscess   _____

52. Postvaricella encephalitis   _____

53. Hemiplegia due to old CVA   _____

54. Encephalitis   _____

55. Retinal detachment with retinal defect   _____

56. Congenital diplegic cerebral palsy   _____

57. Tonic-clonic epilepsy   _____

58. Infantile glaucoma   _____

59. Mature cataract   _____

DISEASES OF THE CIRCULATORY SYSTEM

60. Congestive rheumatic heart failure   _____

61. Mitral valve stenosis with aortic valve insufficiency   _____

62. Acute rheumatic heart disease   _____

63. Hypertensive cardiovascular disease, malignant   _____

64. Congestive heart failure; benign hypertension   _____

65. Secondary benign hypertension; stenosis of renal artery   _____

66. Malignant hypertensive nephropathy with uremia   _____

67. Acute renal failure; essential hypertension   _____

68. Acute myocardial infarction of inferolateral wall, initial episode of care   _____

69. Arteriosclerotic heart disease (native coronary artery) with angina pectoris   _____

DISEASES OF THE RESPIRATORY SYSTEM

70. Aspiration pneumonia due to regurgitated food   _____

71. Streptococcal Group B pneumonia   _____

72. Respiratory failure due to myasthenia gravis   _____

73. Intrinsic asthma in status asthmaticus   _____

74. COPD with emphysema   _____

DISEASES OF THE DIGESTIVE SYSTEM

75. Supernumerary tooth   _____

76. Unilateral femoral hernia with gangrene   _____

77. Cholesterolosis of gallbladder   _____

78. Diarrhea   _____

79. Acute perforated peptic ulcer   _____

80. Acute hemorrhagic gastritis with acute blood loss anemia   _____

81. Acute appendicitis with perforation and peritoneal abscess   _____

82. Acute cholecystitis with cholelithiasis   _____

83. Aphthous stomatitis   _____

84. Diverticulosis and diverticulitis of colon   _____

85. Esophageal reflux with esophagitis   _____

DISEASES OF THE GENITOURINARY SYSTEM

86. Vesicoureteral reflux with bilateral reflux nephropathy   _____

87. Acute glomerulonephritis with necrotizing glomerulolitis   _____

88. Actinomycotic cystitis   _____

89. Subserosal uterine leiomyoma, cervical polyp, and endometriosis of uterus   _____

90. Dysplasia of the cervix   _____

DISEASES OF PREGNANCY, CHILDBIRTH, AND THE PUERPERIUM

91. Defibrination syndrome following termination of pregnancy procedure 2 weeks ago   _____

92. Miscarriage at 19 weeks gestation   _____

93. Incompetent cervix resulting in miscarriage and fetal death   _____

94. Postpartum varicose veins of legs   _____

95. Spontaneous breech delivery   _____

96. Triplet pregnancy, delivered spontaneously   _____

97. Retained placenta without hemorrhage, delivery this admission   _____

98. Pyrexia of unknown origin during the puerperium (postpartum), delivery during previous admission   _____

99. Late vomiting of pregnancy, undelivered   _____

100. Pre-eclampsia complicating pregnancy, delivered this admission   _____

DISEASES OF THE SKIN AND SUBCUTANEOUS TISSUE

101. Diaper rash   _____

102. Acne vulgaris   _____

103. Post-infectional skin cicatrix   _____

104. Cellulitis of the foot; culture reveals staphylococcus   _____

105. Infected ingrowing nail   _____

DISEASES OF THE MUSCULOSKELETAL SYSTEM AND CONNECTIVE TISSUE

106. Displacement of thoracic intervertebral disc   _____

107. Primary localized osteoarthrosis of the hip   _____

108. Acute juvenile rheumatoid arthritis   _____

109. Chondromalacia of the patella   _____

110. Pathologic fracture of the vertebra due to metastatic carcinoma of the bone from the lung   _____

CONGENITAL ANOMALIES

111. Congenital diaphragmatic hernia   _____

112. Single liveborn male (born in the hospital) with polydactyly of fingers   _____

113. Unilateral cleft lip and palate   _____

114. Patent ductus arteriosus   _____

115. Congenital talipes equinovalgus   _____

CERTAIN CONDITIONS ORIGINATING IN THE PERINATAL PERIOD

116. Erythroblastosis fetalis   _____

117. Hyperbilirubinemia of prematurity, prematurity (birthweight 2,000 grams)   _____

118. Erb's palsy   _____

119. Hypoglycemia in infant with diabetic mother   _____

120. Premature "crack" baby born in hospital to cocaine-dependent mother (birthweight 1,247 grams)   _____

SYMPTOMS, SIGNS, AND ILL-DEFINED CONDITIONS

121. Abnormal cervical Pap smear   _____

122. Sudden infant death syndrome   _____

123. Sleep apnea with insomnia   _____

124. Fluid retention and edema   _____

125. Elevated blood pressure reading   _____

INJURY AND POISONING
FRACTURES, DISLOCATIONS, AND SPRAINS

126. Open frontal fracture with subarachnoid hemorrhage with brief loss of consciousness   _____

127. Supracondylar fracture of right humerus and fracture of olecranon process of the right ulna   _____

128. Anterior dislocation of the elbow   _____

129. Dislocation of the first and second cervical vertebrae   _____

130. Sprain of lateral collateral ligament of knee   _____

OPEN WOUNDS AND OTHER TRAUMA

131. Avulsion of eye   _____

132. Traumatic below-the-knee amputation with delayed healing   _____

133. Open wound of buttock   _____

134. Open wound of wrist involving tendons   _____

135. Laceration of external ear   _____

136. Traumatic subdural hemorrhage with open intracranial wound; loss of consciousness, 30 minutes   _____

137. Concussion without loss of consciousness   _____

138. Traumatic laceration of the liver, moderate   _____

139. Traumatic hemothorax with open wound into thorax and concussion with loss of consciousness   _____

140. Traumatic duodenal injury   _____

BURNS

141. Third-degree burn of lower leg and second-degree burn of thigh   _____

142. Deep third-degree burn of forearm   _____

143. Third-degree burns of back involving 20 percent of body surface   _____

144. Thirty percent body burns with 10 percent third-degree   _____

145. First- and second-degree burns of palm   _____

FOREIGN BODIES

146. Coin in the bronchus with bronchoscopy for removal of the coin   _____

147. Foreign body in the eye   _____

148. Marble in colon   _____

149. Bean in nose   _____

150. Q-tip stuck in ear   _____

COMPLICATIONS

151. Infected ventriculoperitoneal shunt   _____

152. Displaced breast prosthesis   _____

153. Leakage of mitral valve prosthesis   _____

154. Postoperative superficial thrombophlebitis of the right leg   _____

155. Dislocated hip prosthesis   _____

V CODES

156. Exposure to tuberculosis   _____

157. Family history of colon carcinoma   _____

158. Status post unilateral kidney transplant, human donor   _____

159. Encounter for removal of cast   _____

160. Admitted to donate bone marrow   _____

161. Encounter for chemotherapy for patient with Hodgkin's lymphoma   _____

162. Reprogramming of cardiac pacemaker   _____

163. Replacement of tracheostomy tube   _____

164. Encounter for renal dialysis for patient in chronic renal failure   _____

165. Encounter for speech therapy for patient with dysphasia secondary to an old CVA   _____

166. Encounter for fitting of artificial leg   _____

167. Encounter for observation of suspected malignant neoplasm of the cervix   _____

168. Visit to radiology department for barium swallow to rule out ulcer; findings are negative; barium swallow performed and the findings are negative   _____

169. Follow-up examination of colon adenocarcinoma resected 1 year ago, no recurrence found   _____

170. Routine general medical examination   _____

171. Examination of eyes   _____

172. Encounter for laboratory test to rule out tuberculosis   _____

173. Encounter for physical therapy; status post below-the-knee amputation 6 months ago   _____

174. Kidney donor   _____

175. Encounter for chemotherapy; breast carcinoma   _____

CODING LATE EFFECTS

Place an X on the line in front of each diagnostic statement that identifies a late effect of an injury/illness.

176. _____ Hemiplegia due to previous cerebrovascular accident

177. _____ Malunion of fracture, right femur

178. _____ Scoliosis due to infantile paralysis

179. _____ Keloid secondary to injury 9 months ago

180. _____ Gangrene, left foot, following third-degree burn of foot 2 weeks ago

181. _____ Cerebral thrombosis with hemiplegia

182. _____ Mental retardation due to previous viral encephalitis

183. _____ Laceration of tendon of finger 2 weeks ago. Admitted now for tendon repair

Code the following:

184. Residuals of poliomyelitis   _____

185. Sequela of old crush injury to left foot   _____

186. Cerebrovascular accident 2 years ago with late effects   _____

187. Effects of old gunshot wound, left thigh   _____

188. Disuse osteoporosis due to previous poliomyelitis   _____

189. Brain damage following cerebral abscess 7 months ago   _____

190. Hemiplegia due to old cerebrovascular accident   _____

ADVERSE REACTIONS AND POISONINGS

191. Ataxia due to interaction between prescribed carbamazepine and erythromycin   _____

192. Vertigo as a result of dye administered for a scheduled IVP   _____

193. Accidental ingestion of mother's oral contraceptives (no signs or symptoms resulted)   _____

194. Hemiplegia; patient had an adverse reaction to prescribed Enovid 1 year ago   _____

195. Stricture of esophagus due to accidental lye ingestion 3 years ago   _____

196. Listlessness resulting from reaction between prescribed Valium and ingestion of a six-pack of beer   _____

197. Lead poisoning (child had been discovered eating paint chips)   _____

198. Allergic reaction to unspecified drug   _____

199. Theophylline toxicity   _____

200. Carbon monoxide poisoning from car exhaust (suicide attempt)   _____

CHAPTER 7

CPT Coding

CHAPTER OUTLINE

Overview of CPT

CPT Sections, Subsections, Categories, and Subcategories

CPT Index

CPT Modifiers

Coding Procedures and Services

Evaluation and Management Section

Anesthesia Section

Surgery Section

Radiology Section

Pathology and Laboratory Section

Medicine Section

National Correct Coding Initiative

OBJECTIVES

Upon successful completion of this chapter, you should be able to:

1. Define key terms.
2. Explain the format used in CPT.
3. Locate main terms and subterms in the CPT index.
4. Select appropriate modifiers to add to CPT codes.
5. Assign CPT codes to procedures and services.

KEY TERMS

care plan oversight services
case management services
Category I codes
Category II codes
Category III codes
comprehensive assessment
concurrent care
consultation
contributory components

coordination of care
counseling
CPT-5
CPT-5 Project
CPT Coding Conventions
   boldface type
   cross-reference *(See)*
   descriptive qualifier
   guidelines

inferred words
instructional notes
italicized type
separate procedure
CPT Symbols
   ●
   ▲
   ►◄
   ;

201

+

∅

⊙

𝒩

\#

critical care services

direct patient contact

emergency department services

established patient

Evaluation and Management Documentation Guidelines

Evaluation and Management (E/M) section

extent of examination (CPT)

comprehensive

detailed

expanded problem focused

problem focused

extent of history (CPT)

comprehensive

detailed

expanded problem focused

problem focused

face-to-face time

global period

global surgery

history

home services

hospital discharge services

initial hospital care

key components

level of service

medical decision making

moderate (conscious) sedation

monitored anesthesia care (MAC)

multiple surgical procedures

nature of the presenting problem

new patient

newborn care

nursing facility services

observation or inpatient care services

observation services

organ- or disease-oriented panel

partial hospitalization

physical examination

physical status modifier

physician standby services

place of service (POS)

preoperative clearance

preventive medicine services

professional component

prolonged services

qualifying circumstances

radiologic views

referral

special report

subsequent hospital care

surgical package

technical component

transfer of care

type of service (TOS)

unit/floor time

unlisted procedure

unlisted service

without direct patient contact

INTRODUCTION

This chapter introduces the assignment of *Current Procedural Terminology (CPT)* service and procedure codes reported on insurance claims. CPT is published by the American Medical Association and includes codes for procedures performed and services provided to patients. It is level I of the Healthcare Common Procedure Coding System (HCPCS), which also contains level II (national codes). Because of the introductory nature of this chapter, you are encouraged to obtain a comprehensive textbook that covers CPT principles and practice (e.g., Delmar's *3-2-1 Code It!* by Michelle A. Green).

Complete StudyWare practice quizzes and activities using the CD-ROM located inside the back cover of your textbook.

OVERVIEW OF CPT

Current Procedural Terminology (CPT) is a listing of descriptive terms and identifying codes for reporting medical services and procedures. It provides a uniform language that describes medical, surgical, and diagnostic services to facilitate communication among providers, patients, and insurers. The American Medical Association (AMA) first published CPT in 1966, and subsequent editions expanded its descriptive terms and codes for diagnostic and therapeutic procedures. Five-digit codes were introduced in 1970, replacing the four-digit classification. In 1983 CPT was adopted as part of the Healthcare Common Procedure Coding System (HCPCS), and its use was mandated for reporting Medicare Part B services. In 1986 HCPCS was required for reporting to Medicaid agencies, and in July 1987, as part of the Omnibus Budget Reconciliation Act (OBRA), CMS mandated that CPT codes be reported for outpatient hospital surgical procedures.

HIPAA ALERT!

HIPAA named CPT and HCPCS as the procedure code set for physician services, physical and occupational therapy services, radiological procedures, clinical laboratory tests, other medical diagnostic procedures, hearing and vision services, and transportation services, including ambulance. HIPAA also named ICD-9-CM as the code set for diagnosis codes and inpatient hospital services, CDT for dental services, and NDC for drugs. It eliminated HCPCS level III local codes effective December 2003.

> **NOTE:** The MMA requires that new, revised, and deleted ICD-9-CM codes be implemented each October 1 and updated each April, and changes to CPT and HCPCS level II national codes be implemented each January 1.

CMS enforced regulations resulting from the Medicare Prescription Drug, Improvement, and Modernization Act (MMA) on October 1, 2004, which required that new, revised, and deleted CPT codes be implemented each January 1. In the past, a 90-day grace period (from January 1 through March 31) had been allowed so providers and healthcare facilities had time to update billing systems and coders had an opportunity to undergo training regarding new, revised, and deleted codes. Be sure to purchase updated coding manuals to avoid billing delays and claims rejections. If outdated codes are submitted on claims, providers and healthcare facilities will incur administrative costs associated with resubmitting corrected claims and delayed reimbursement for services provided.

CPT codes are used to report services and procedures performed on patients:

- By providers in offices, clinics, and private homes.
- By providers in institutional settings such as hospitals, nursing facilities, and hospices.
- When the provider is employed by the healthcare facility (e.g., many of the physicians associated with Veterans Administration Medical Centers are employees of that organization).
- By a hospital outpatient department (e.g., ambulatory surgery, emergency department, and outpatient laboratory or radiographic procedures).

Procedures and services submitted on a claim must be linked to the ICD-9-CM code that justifies the need for the service or procedure. That ICD-9-CM code must demonstrate medical necessity for the service or procedure to receive reimbursement consideration by insurance payers.

The assignment of CPT codes simplifies reporting and assists in the accurate identification of procedures and services for third-party payer consideration. CPT codes and descriptions are based on consistency with contemporary medical practice as performed by clinical providers throughout the country.

In response to the electronic data interchange requirements of the Health Insurance Portability and Accountability Act of 1996 (HIPAA), the American Medical Association reviewed and revised the *Current Procedural Coding* system. Among HIPAA's requirements is that code sets and classification systems be implemented in a cost-effective manner that includes low-cost, efficient distribution, and application to all users. Although CPT was identified as the procedure coding standard for the reporting of physician services in 2000, the May 7, 1998 *Federal Register* reported that "CPT is not always precise or unambiguous. . . ."

CPT codes remained five digits in length, and code descriptions continued to reflect healthcare services and procedures performed in modern medical practice. In addition, the process of periodically reviewing and updating codes and descriptions has continued.

Changes to CPT

CPT supports electronic data interchange (EDI), the computer-based patient record (CPR) or electronic medical record (EMR), and reference/research databases. CPT can also be used to track new technology and performance measures. Code descriptors were improved to eliminate ambiguous terms, and guidelines and notes underwent revision to make them more comprehensive, easier to interpret, and more specific. A CPT glossary was created to standardize definitions and differentiate the use of synonymous terms; and a searchable, electronic CPT index is under development, along with a computerized database to delineate relationships among CPT code descriptions.

Improvements to CPT are underway to address the needs of hospitals, managed care organizations, and long-term care facilities. In 2000, the AMA completed the CPT- 5 Project (with changes phased in starting with CPT 2000 and concluding with CPT 2003), resulting in the establishment of three categories of CPT codes:

- **Category I codes:** procedures/services identified by a five-digit CPT code and descriptor nomenclature; these are codes traditionally associated with CPT and organized within six sections.
- **Category II codes:** contain "performance measurements" tracking codes that are assigned an alphanumeric identifier with a letter in the last field (e.g., 1234A); these codes will be located after the Medicine section, and *their use is optional.*
- **Category III codes:** contain "emerging technology" temporary codes assigned for data collection purposes that are assigned an alphanumeric identifier with a letter in the last field (e.g., 0001T); these codes are located after the Medicine section, and they will be archived after five years unless accepted for placement within Category I sections of CPT.

CPT Sections

CPT organizes Category I procedures and services within six sections:

- **Evaluation and Management (E/M) (99201–99499).**
- **Anesthesia (00100–01999, 99100–99140).**
- **Surgery (10021–69990).**
- **Radiology (70010–79999).**
- **Pathology and Laboratory (80047–89398).**
- **Medicine (90281–99199, 99500–99607).**

CPT Code Number Format

A five-digit code number and a narrative description identify each procedure and service listed in CPT. Most procedures and services contain stand-alone descriptions. To save space, some descriptions are not printed in their entirety

> **NOTE:**
>
> · The E/M section is located at the beginning of CPT because these codes are reported by all specialties.
>
> · Medicine section codes (99100–99140) that classify *Qualifying Circumstances for Anesthesia Services* are explained in the Anesthesia section guidelines; they are to be reported with Anesthesia codes.

next to a code number. Instead, the entry is indented and the coder must refer back to the common portion of the code description that is located before the semicolon.

EXAMPLE 1: Stand-alone code description

27870   Arthrodesis, ankle, open

EXAMPLE 2: Indented code description

27780   Closed treatment of proximal fibula or shaft fracture; without manipulation

27781   with manipulation

The code description for 27781 is *closed treatment of proximal fibula or shaft fracture with manipulation*.

CPT Appendices

CPT contains appendices that are located between the Medicine section and the index. Insurance specialists should carefully review these appendices to become familiar with coding changes that affect the practice annually:

CPT APPENDIX	DESCRIPTION
Appendix A	Detailed descriptions of each CPT modifier. **CODING TIP:** Place a marker at the beginning of Appendix A because you will refer to this appendix often.
Appendix B	Annual CPT coding changes (added, deleted, revised CPT codes). **CODING TIP:** Carefully review Appendix B because it will serve as the basis for updating encounter forms and chargemasters.
Appendix C	Clinical examples for Evaluation and Management (E/M) section codes. **NOTE:** The AMA halted the project to revise E/M code descriptions using clinical examples (or vignettes) in 2004. However, previously developed clinical examples are still included in Appendix C.
Appendix D	Add-on codes. **CODING TIP:** Add-on codes are identified in CPT with the **+** symbol.
Appendix E	Codes exempt from modifier -51 reporting rules. **CODING TIP:** Exempt codes are identified in CPT with the $\emptyset$ symbol.

(continues)

(continued)

CPT APPENDIX	DESCRIPTION
Appendix F	CPT codes exempt from modifier -63 reporting rules.
Appendix G	Summary of CPT codes that include moderate (conscious) sedation.
	CODING TIP:
	Codes that include moderate (conscious) sedation are identified in CPT with the ⊙ symbol.
Appendix H	Alphabetic index of performance measures by clinical condition or topic, which serves as a crosswalk to the Category II codes section. A *crosswalk* links data (e.g., Category II codes) to elements (e.g., performance measures.)
Appendix I	Genetic testing code modifiers, which are reported with molecular laboratory procedures related to genetic testing.
Appendix J	Electrodiagnostic medicine listing of sensory, motor, and mixed nerves that are reported for motor and nerve studies codes. There is also a table that indicates the "type of study and maximum number of studies" generally performed for needle electromyogram (EMG), nerve conduction studies, and other EMG studies. The AMA's *CPT Changes 2006: An Insider's View* calls this table a " . . . tool to detect outliers."
Appendix K	Appendix K contains a list of products that are pending Food and Drug Administration (FDA) approval but that have been assigned a CPT code. In the CPT manual, these codes are preceded by the flash symbol (✗).
Appendix L	List of vascular families that is intended to assist in the selection of first-, second-, third-, and beyond third-order branch arteries.
Appendix M	Crosswalk of deleted to new CPT codes.
Appendix N	Summary of resequenced CPT codes.

> **NOTE:** Examples of CPT symbols are included for illustrative purposes only and may not match the current CPT manual. Refer to your CPT coding manual to locate current uses of the bullet, triangle, and horizontal triangles.

CPT Symbols

Symbols located throughout the CPT coding book include the following:

- A bullet located to the left of a code number identifies new procedures and services added to CPT.

> **EXAMPLE:** CPT code 84145 was added.
>
> ● **84145**   Procalcitonin (PCT)

▲ A triangle located to the left of a code number identifies a code description that has been revised.

> **EXAMPLE:** CPT code 24150 was revised to change "for" to "of."
>
> ▲ 24150   Radical resection of tumor; shaft, or distal humerus

▶◀   Horizontal triangles surround revised guidelines and notes. *This symbol is not used for revised code descriptions.*

> **EXAMPLE:** The "special report" guideline in each section of CPT.
>
> ▶ Concurrent Care and Transfer of Care ◀

A complete list of code additions, deletions, and revisions is found in Appendix B of CPT. Revisions marked with horizontal triangles (▶ ◀) are *not* included in Appendix B, and coders need to carefully review all CPT guidelines and notes in the new edition of CPT.

; A semicolon is used to save space in CPT, and some code descriptions are not printed in their entirety next to a code number. Instead, the entry is indented and the coder must refer back to the common portion of the code description that is located before the semicolon. The common portion begins with a capital letter, and the abbreviated (or subordinate) descriptions are indented and begin with lower-case letters.

EXAMPLE: The code description for 67255 is *scleral reinforcement with graft.*

67250	Scleral reinforcement (separate procedure); without graft
67255	with graft

CPT is printed using proportional spacing, and careful review of code descriptions to locate the semicolon may be necessary.

+ The plus symbol identifies add-on codes (Appendix D of CPT) for procedures that are commonly, but not always, performed at the same time and by the same surgeon as the primary procedure. Parenthetical notes, located below add-on codes, often identify the primary procedure to which add-on codes apply.

EXAMPLE:

22210	Osteotomy of spine, posterior or posterolateral approach, one vertebral segment; cervical
+ 22216	each additional vertebral segment (List separately in addition to primary procedure) (Use 22216 in conjunction with codes 22210, 22212, 22214)

Codes identified with **+** are *never* reported as stand-alone codes; they are reported with primary codes. Also, *do not* append add-on codes with modifier -51.

∅ The forbidden symbol identifies codes that are *not* to be used with modifier -51. These codes are reported in addition to other codes, but they are *not* classified as add-on codes.

> **EXAMPLE:** The patient underwent closed treatment of sternum fracture with noninvasive electrical stimulation procedure to promote bone healing.
>
> ⊘ **20974**   Electrical stimulation to aid bone healing; noninvasive (nonoperative)
>
> **21820**   Closed treatment of sternum fracture
>
> Both codes (21820 and 20974, in that order) are reported on the claim, but neither is assigned modifier -51. Because both are required to completely describe the procedure performed, payers automatically reduce reimbursement for the second code. If modifier -51 is reported with 20974, the payer further reduces reimbursement and the provider receives less money than it is entitled to.

NOTE: A complete list of codes that are exempt from modifier -51 is found in Appendix E of CPT.

⊙   The bull's-eye symbol indicates a procedure that includes moderate (conscious) sedation.

Moderate (conscious) sedation is the administration of moderate sedation or analgesia, which results in a drug-induced depression of consciousness. CPT established a package concept for moderate (conscious) sedation, and the bull's-eye (⊙) symbol located next to the code number identifies moderate (conscious) sedation as an inherent part of providing specific procedures. Because these codes include moderate (conscious) sedation, it is inappropriate for a physician to report a separate moderate (conscious) sedation code from the CPT Medicine section (99143-99150).

If, however, the patient undergoes a procedure for which the CPT code has a bull's-eye symbol and the patient does *not* receive moderate (conscious) sedation, report the CPT procedure code only (e.g., 33208). Do *not* assign modifier -52 (reduced services) to the procedure code. If the patient receives general anesthesia, the anesthesiologist reports an anesthesia code.

NOTE: A complete list of codes that include moderate (conscious) sedation is located in Appendix G of CPT.

> **EXAMPLE:** Patient undergoes insertion of permanent pacemaker with atrial transvenous electrodes. Moderate (conscious) sedation was administered. Report code 33206 only.
>
> **33206** ⊙   Insertion or replacement of permanent pacemaker with transvenous electrode(s); atrial

⚡   The flash symbol (⚡) indicates codes that classify products that are pending FDA approval but have been assigned a CPT code (e.g., code 90663).

\#   The number symbol (#) precedes CPT codes that appear out of numerical order (e.g., code 51797).

CPT SECTIONS, SUBSECTIONS, CATEGORIES, AND SUBCATEGORIES

CPT Category I codes are organized according to six sections that are subdivided into subsections, categories, and subcategories (Figure 7-1).

Guidelines

Guidelines are located at the beginning of each CPT section, and *should be carefully reviewed before attempting to code*. **Guidelines** define terms and explain

NOTE: CPT is inconsistent in
its use of subsection, category,
and subcategory terminology.
For example, Table 1 in the CPT
Evaluation and Management
section guidelines lists categories and subcategories (instead
of the more logical subsections
and categories). Remaining
CPT section guidelines include
lists of subsections except for
the Radiology section, which
includes some subcategories
in the list of subsections.
To make matters even more
complicated, CPT refers to
headings and subheadings in
some section guidelines and
categories and subcategories
in other section guidelines. In
addition, the Surgery guidelines
include "Subsection Information"
that refers to "subheadings or
subsections." It would be more
logical if the latter phrase had
been written as "subheadings or
subcategories."

SYMBOL / CONVENTION	CPT ENTRY:	
Section	**Surgery**	
Subsection	**Integumentary System**	
Category / Heading	**Skin, Subcutaneous and Accessory Structures**	
Subcategory / Subheading	**Incision and Drainage**	
Note	(For excision, see 11400, et seq)	
Code number / Description	10040	Acne surgery (eg, marsupialization, opening or removal of multiple milia, comedones, cysts, pustules)
Use of semicolon	11000	Debridement of extensive eczematous or infected skin; up to 10% of body surface
Use of plus symbol	+11001	each additional 10% of the body surface, or part thereof (List separately in addition to code for primary procedure)
Use of -51 modifier exemption symbol	⊘ 93503	Insertion and placement of flow directed catheter (eg, Swan-Ganz) for monitoring purposes

FIGURE 7-1 Selection from CPT that illustrates symbols and conventions (CPT copyright 2009 American Medical Association. All rights reserved.)

the assignment of codes for procedures and services located in a particular section (Figure 7-2). This means that guidelines in one section do not apply to another section in CPT.

Unlisted Procedures/Services

An **unlisted procedure** or **unlisted service** code is assigned when the provider performs a procedure or service for which there is no CPT code. When an unlisted procedure or service code is reported, a **special report** (e.g., copy of procedure report) must accompany the claim to describe the nature, extent, and need for the procedure or service along with the time, effort, and equipment necessary to provide the service.

Notes

Instructional notes appear throughout CPT sections to clarify the assignment of codes. They are typeset in two patterns (Figure 7-3):

1. A *blocked unindented note* is located below a subsection title and contains instructions that apply to all codes in the subsection.

2. An *indented parenthetical note* is located below a subsection title, code description, or code description that contains an example.

Parenthetical notes that contain the abbreviation "eg" are examples.

NOTE: Medicare and other third party payers often require providers to report HCPCS level II (national) codes instead of unlisted procedure or service CPT codes.

NOTE:
· Terminology in the CPT code example need not appear in the procedural statement documented by the provider.
· Parenthetical notes within a code series provide information about deleted codes.

Surgery Guidelines

Items used by all physicians in reporting their services are presented in the **Introduction**. Some of the commonalities are repeated here for the convenience of those physicians referring to this section on **Surgery**. Other definitions and items unique to Surgery are also listed.

Physicians' Services

Physicians' services rendered in the office, home, or hospital, consultations, and other medical services are listed in the section entitled **Evaluation and Management Services** (99201-99499) found in the front of the book, beginning on page 9. "Special Services and Reports" (99000 series) is presented in the **Medicine** section.

Materials Supplied by Physician

Supplies and materials provided by the physician (eg, sterile trays/drugs), over and above those usually included with the procedure(s) rendered are reported separately. List drugs, trays, supplies, and materials provided. Identify as 99070 or specific supply code.

FIGURE 7-2 Portion of CPT Surgery Guidelines (CPT copyright 2009 American Medical Association. All rights reserved.)

Cardiovascular System

Blocked unindented note

Selective vascular catheterizations should be coded to include introduction and all lesser order selective catheterizations used in the approach (eg, the description for a selective right middle cerebral artery catheterization includes the introduction and placement catheterization of the right common and internal carotid arteries).

Additional second and/or third order arterial catheterizations within the same family of arteries supplied by a single first order artery should be expressed by 36218 or 36248. Additional first order or higher catheterizations in vascular families supplied by a first order vessel different from a previously selected and coded family should be separately coded using the conventions described above.

Indented parenthetical note located below subsection title

(For monitoring, operation of pump and other nonsurgical services, *see* 99190-99192, 99291, 99292, 99354-99360)

(For other medical or laboratory related services, see appropriate section)

(For radiological supervision and interpretation, see 75600-75978)

Heart and Pericardium

Pericardium

⊙ 33010   Pericardiocentesis; initial

Parenthetical note located below code description

(For radiological supervision and interpretation, use 76930)

FIGURE 7-3 Selection from CPT that illustrates types of instructional notes (CPT copyright 2009 American Medical Association. All rights reserved.)

Descriptive Qualifiers

Descriptive qualifiers are terms that clarify the assignment of a CPT code. They can occur in the middle of a main clause or after the semicolon and may or may not be enclosed in parentheses. Be sure to read all code descriptions very carefully to properly assign CPT codes that require descriptive qualifiers.

EXAMPLE: 17000   Destruction (eg, laser surgery, electrosurgery, cryosurgery, chemosurgery, surgical curettement), premalignant lesions (eg, actinic keratoses); first lesion

+ 17003   <u>second through 14 lesions, each</u> (List separately in addition to code for first lesion)

The underlining identifies descriptive qualifiers in the code description for 17003.

CODING TIP:

Coders working in a provider's office should highlight descriptive qualifiers in CPT that pertain to the office's specialty. This will help ensure that qualifiers are not overlooked when assigning codes.

EXERCISE 7-1

Working with CPT Symbols and Conventions

Instructions: If the statement is true, place a T in front of the number. If the statement is false, enter an F and correct the statement.

_____ **1.** The major sections of CPT are surgery, pathology and laboratory, radiology, and medicine.

_____ **2.** The triangle indicates a new procedure code number.

_____ **3.** CPT requires a two- or five-digit modifier to be attached to the five-digit CPT code.

_____ **4.** "Notes" should be applied to all codes located under a heading.

_____ **5.** Semicolons save space in CPT where a series of related codes are found.

_____ **6.** Qualifiers for a particular code are always found in an indented code description.

_____ **7.** Parenthetical statements beginning with "eg" provide examples of terms that must be included in the healthcare provider's documentation of services/procedures performed.

_____ **8.** Horizontal triangles (►◄) surround revised guidelines, notes, and procedure descriptions.

_____ **9.** The bullet (●) located to the left of a CPT code indicates a code new to that edition of CPT.

_____ **10.** Upon review of the CPT tabular listing below, code 50620 would be reported for a *ureterolithotomy performed on the upper or middle one-third of the ureter.*

50610   Ureterolithotomy; upper one-third of ureter

50620   middle one-third of ureter

50630   lower one-third of ureter

CPT INDEX

The CPT index (Figure 7-4) is organized by alphabetical main terms printed in boldface. The main terms represent procedures or services, organs, anatomic sites, conditions, eponyms, or abbreviations. The main term is followed by subterms that modify the main term. The subterms are followed by additional subterms that are indented.

Single Codes and Code Ranges

Index code numbers for specific procedures may be represented as a single code number, a range of codes separated by a dash, a series of codes separated by commas, or a combination of single codes and ranges of codes. All listed numbers should be investigated before assigning a code for the procedure or service.

Boldface Type

Main terms in the CPT index are printed in **boldface type**, along with CPT categories, subcategories, headings, and code numbers.

EXAMPLE:

Repair

  Liver

    Abscess 47300

    Cyst 47300

    Wound 47350–47361

N

Cross-referenced term

Main term
Subterm (not indented)

Range of codes to investigate

Subterm (indented)

N. Meningitidis
See Neisseria Meningitidis

Nails
Avulsion...11730-11732
Biopsy..11755
Debridement..............................11720-11721
Evacuation
    Hematoma, Subungual.......................11740

FIGURE 7-4 Selection from CPT index (CPT copyright 2009 American Medical Association. All rights reserved.)

Cross-Reference Term

See is a **cross-reference** that directs coders to an index entry under which codes are listed. No codes are listed under the original entry.

> **EXAMPLE: AV Shunt**
> *See* Arteriovenous Shunt
>
> In this example, the coder is directed to the index entry for Arteriovenous Shunt because no codes are listed for AV Shunt.

Italicized Type

Italicized type is used for the cross-reference term, *See*, in the CPT Index.

Inferred Words

To save space in the CPT index when referencing subterms, inferred words are used.

> **EXAMPLE: Abdomen**
> Exploration (of) 49000-49002
>
> In this example, the word in parentheses, (of), is inferred and does not appear in the CPT index.

EXERCISE 7-2

Working with the CPT Index

Instructions: Answer each item below.

1. Turn to code number 47300 and review all procedural descriptions through code 47362. What does the term *marsupialization* mean? If you don't know the meaning, look it up in your medical dictionary.

   _____

   _____

2. How do codes 47350, 47360–47362 differ?

   47350 _____

   _____

   47360 _____

   _____

   47361 _____

   _____

   47362 _____

   _____

3. The cross-reference that directs coders to refer to a different index entry because no codes are found under the original entry is called *See*. TRUE or FALSE.

4. Main terms appear in *italics* in the CPT index. TRUE or FALSE.

5. Inferred words appear in the CPT index to assist coders in assigning appropriate codes. TRUE or FALSE.

CODING TIP:

The descriptions of *all* codes listed for a specific procedure must be carefully investigated before selecting a final code. As with ICD-9-CM, CPT coding must *never* be performed solely from the index.

NOTE: The CMS-1500 electronic claim format requires entry of two-digit or two-character modifiers.

CPT MODIFIERS

CPT modifiers clarify services and procedures performed by providers. Although the CPT code and description remain unchanged, modifiers indicate that the description of the service or procedure performed has been altered. CPT modifiers are reported as two-digit numeric codes added to the five-digit CPT code.

EXAMPLE: 30630-77.

A patient undergoes repair of a deviated nasal septum (code 30630), which was unsuccessful. The patient undergoes repeat repair of the deviated nasal septum by a different surgeon (modifier -77). The same CPT code is assigned, and a modifier is added to indicate the repeat repair.

CPT modifiers have always been reported on claims submitted for provider office services and procedures. In April 2000, hospitals also began reporting CPT and HCPCS level II (national) modifiers for outpatient services.

CODING TIP:

A list of all CPT modifiers with brief descriptions is located inside the front cover of the coding manual. CPT and HCPCS level II national modifiers approved for hospital outpatient reporting purposes are also identified. Appendix A of the CPT coding manual contains a list of modifiers with descriptions.

NOTE: HCPCS level II national modifiers are detailed in Chapter 8.

NOTE: In an attempt to simplify the explanation of modifiers, the wording in this textbook does not correspond word-for-word with descriptions found in CPT.

Not all CPT modifiers apply to each section of CPT. Software (e.g., Ingenix's *Encoder Pro*) can be used to select modifiers associated with a CPT (or HCPCS level II) code.

The AMA develops new modifiers on a continuous basis, and next available numbers are assigned. This means there is no relationship among groups of modifier numbers. Reviewing modifiers in strict numerical order does not allow for comparison of those that are related to one other in terms of content; therefore, Table 7-1 organizes modifiers according to reporting similarity.

TABLE 7-1 Organization of CPT modifiers according to reporting similarity

	SPECIAL EVALUATION AND MANAGEMENT (E/M) CASES	
MODIFIER	**DESCRIPTION**	**INTERPRETATION**
-24	Unrelated Evaluation and Management Service by the Same Physician During a Postoperative Period	Assign to indicate that an E/M service was performed during the standard postoperative period for a condition unrelated to the surgery. The procedure to which the modifier is attached *must be* linked to a diagnosis that is *unrelated* to the surgical diagnosis previously submitted. Be sure to submit a copy of documentation with the claim to explain the circumstances.
	EXAMPLE: One week after the surgical release of a frozen shoulder, a patient fell and severely sprained his ankle, which required strapping immobilization for support and comfort. Report 29540-24.	
-25	Significant, Separately Identifiable Evaluation and Management Service by the Same Physician on the Same Day of the Procedure or Other Services	Assign when a documented E/M service was performed on the same day as another procedure because the patient's condition required the assignment of significant, separately identifiable, additional E/M services normally not a part of the other procedure. **NOTE:** The documented history, examination, and medical decision making must "stand on its own" to justify reporting modifier -25 with the E/M code. The E/M service provided must be "above and beyond" what is normally performed during a procedure. Many payers restrict the reporting of modifier -25. Be sure to obtain payer reporting guidelines.
	EXAMPLE: During routine annual examination, it was discovered that a 65-year-old established patient had an enlarged liver, necessitating expansion of the scope of level 4 E/M services. Report 99397 and 99214-25. (Be sure to submit supporting documentation to the payer.)	
-57	Decision for Surgery	Assign when the reported E/M service resulted in the *initial* decision to perform surgery on the day before *or* the day of surgery, to exempt it from the global surgery package.
	EXAMPLE: The patient received level 4 E/M services for chest pain in the emergency department, and a decision was made to insert a coronary arterial stent. Report 99284-57.	
	GREATER, REDUCED, OR DISCONTINUED SERVICES	
MODIFIER	**DESCRIPTION**	**INTERPRETATION**
-22	Increased Procedural Services	Assign when a procedure *requires greater than usual service(s)*. Documentation that would support using this modifier includes difficult, complicated, extensive, unusual, or rare procedure(s). **NOTE:** This modifier has been overused. Be sure special circumstances are documented, and send a copy of documentation with the claim.
	EXAMPLE: Procedure report documents blood loss of 600 cc or greater. Operative report documents prolonged operative time due to . . .	

(continues)

TABLE 7-1   (continued)

GREATER, REDUCED, OR DISCONTINUED SERVICES (continued)		
MODIFIER	**DESCRIPTION**	**INTERPRETATION**
-52	Reduced Services	Report when a service has been partially reduced at the physician's discretion and does not completely match the CPT code description. **NOTE:** Attach a copy of documentation to the claim.
	EXAMPLE: A 28-year-old new female patient presented with complaints of dyspareunia. During a level 4 E/M service, the provider began a gynecologic exam, but discontinued it when it became apparent that the patient was experiencing extreme discomfort. Report 99204-52.	
-53	Discontinued Procedure	Report when a provider elects to terminate a procedure because of extenuating circumstances that threaten the well-being of the patient. **NOTE:** This modifier applies only to provider office settings *and only if* surgical prep has begun or induction of anesthesia has been initiated. Do *not* report for procedures electively canceled prior to induction of anesthesia and/or surgical prep.
	EXAMPLE: Record documented that the procedure was started and terminated due to equipment failure.	
-73	Discontinued Outpatient Hospital/Ambulatory Surgery Center (ASC) Procedure Prior to Anesthesia Administration	Report to describe procedures discontinued *prior to the administration of any anesthesia* because of extenuating circumstances threatening the well-being of the patient. Do not report for elective cancellations. **NOTE:** Report a code from ICD-9-CM category V64 to document reason procedure was halted.
	EXAMPLE: Patient developed heart arrhythmia prior to anesthesia administration for left breast biopsy, and surgery was halted. Report 19103-73.	
-74	Discontinued Outpatient Hospital/Ambulatory Surgery Center (ASC) Procedure After Anesthesia Administration	Report to describe procedures discontinued *after the administration of anesthesia* due to extenuating circumstances. **NOTE:** Report a code from ICD-9-CM category V64 to document reason procedure was halted.
	EXAMPLE: Patient was prepped and draped, and general anesthesia administered prior to performance of a laparoscopic cholecystectomy. Anesthesiologist noted a sudden increase in blood pressure, and the procedure was terminated. Report 47562-74.	
GLOBAL SURGERY		

NOTE: · These modifiers apply to the four areas related to the CPT surgical package (Figure 7-5), which includes the procedure; local infiltration, metacarpal/digital block or topical anesthesia when used; and normal, uncomplicated follow-up care.

· These modifiers do not apply to obstetric coding where the CPT description of specific codes clearly describes separate antepartum, postpartum, and delivery services for both vaginal and cesarean deliveries.

(continues)

TABLE 7-1   (continued)

GLOBAL SURGERY (continued)

MODIFIER	DESCRIPTION	INTERPRETATION

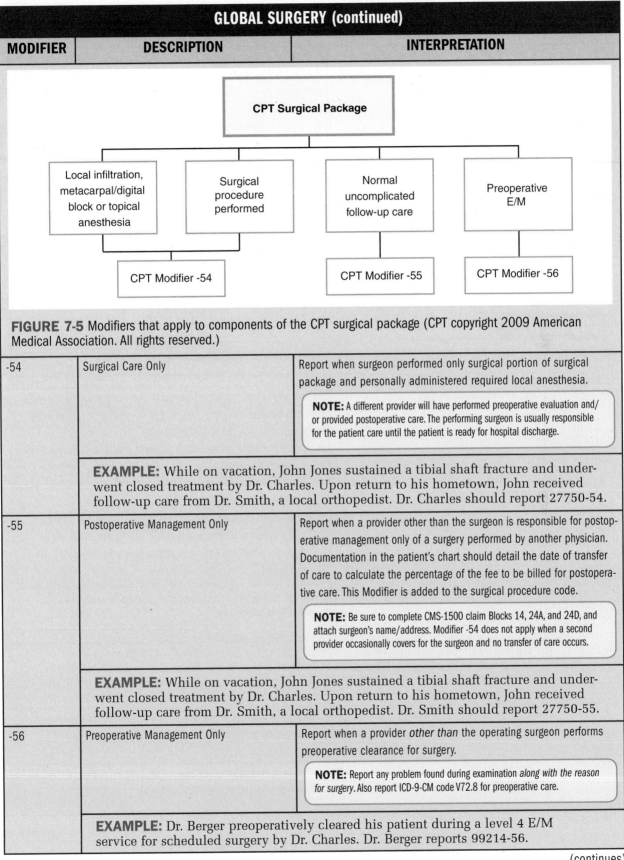

FIGURE 7-5 Modifiers that apply to components of the CPT surgical package (CPT copyright 2009 American Medical Association. All rights reserved.)

-54	Surgical Care Only	Report when surgeon performed only surgical portion of surgical package and personally administered required local anesthesia.
		NOTE: A different provider will have performed preoperative evaluation and/or provided postoperative care. The performing surgeon is usually responsible for the patient care until the patient is ready for hospital discharge.
	EXAMPLE: While on vacation, John Jones sustained a tibial shaft fracture and underwent closed treatment by Dr. Charles. Upon return to his hometown, John received follow-up care from Dr. Smith, a local orthopedist. Dr. Charles should report 27750-54.	
-55	Postoperative Management Only	Report when a provider other than the surgeon is responsible for postoperative management only of a surgery performed by another physician. Documentation in the patient's chart should detail the date of transfer of care to calculate the percentage of the fee to be billed for postoperative care. This Modifier is added to the surgical procedure code.
		NOTE: Be sure to complete CMS-1500 claim Blocks 14, 24A, and 24D, and attach surgeon's name/address. Modifier -54 does not apply when a second provider occasionally covers for the surgeon and no transfer of care occurs.
	EXAMPLE: While on vacation, John Jones sustained a tibial shaft fracture and underwent closed treatment by Dr. Charles. Upon return to his hometown, John received follow-up care from Dr. Smith, a local orthopedist. Dr. Smith should report 27750-55.	
-56	Preoperative Management Only	Report when a provider *other than* the operating surgeon performs preoperative clearance for surgery.
		NOTE: Report any problem found during examination *along with the reason for surgery.* Also report ICD-9-CM code V72.8 for preoperative care.
	EXAMPLE: Dr. Berger preoperatively cleared his patient during a level 4 E/M service for scheduled surgery by Dr. Charles. Dr. Berger reports 99214-56.	

(continues)

TABLE 7-1 (continued)

SPECIAL SURGICAL AND PROCEDURAL EVENTS		
MODIFIER	**DESCRIPTION**	**INTERPRETATION**
-58	Staged or Related Procedure or Service by the Same Physician During the Postoperative Period	Report to indicate that additional related surgery was required during the postoperative period of a previously completed surgery and was performed by the same physician. Documentation should include one of the following: • Original plan for surgery included additional stages to be performed within postoperative period of first stage of procedure. • Underlying disease required performance of a second related, but unplanned, procedure. • Additional related therapy is required after the performance of a diagnostic surgical procedure.
	EXAMPLE: A surgical wound is not healing properly because of the patient's underlying diabetes. Patient was told prior to the original surgery that if this happened, additional surgery would be required for full-thickness debridement of the wound. Report 11041-58 for debridement surgery.	

CODING TIP:

Do not report modifier -58 if the CPT code description describes multiple sessions of an event.

-59	Distinct Procedural Service	Report when same physician performs one or more *distinctly independent procedures* on the same day as other procedures or services, according to the following criteria: • Procedures are performed at different sessions or during different patient encounters. • Procedures are performed on different sites or organs and require a different surgical prep. • Procedures are performed for multiple or extensive injuries, using separate incisions/excisions; for separate lesions; or for procedures not ordinarily encountered/performed on the same day. **NOTE:** Modifier -51, multiple procedures, may also be added to reported secondary procedures codes.
	EXAMPLE: Patient has two basal cell carcinomas removed, one from the forehead with a simple closure (11640) and the other from the nose requiring adjacent tissue transfer (14060). Report as 14060, 11640-51 (forehead), 11640-59-51 (nose).	
-63	Procedure Performed on Infants Less Than 4 kg	Report when infant weights less than 4 kilograms (kg) because procedures performed may require increased complexity and provider work.
	EXAMPLE: Baby Girl Markel's weight was 3.5 kg at the time she underwent radio frequency catheter ablation (RFCA) for ventricular tachycardia. Report 93652-63.	

(continues)

TABLE 7-1 (continued)

SPECIAL SURGICAL AND PROCEDURAL EVENTS (continued)		
MODIFIER	**DESCRIPTION**	**INTERPRETATION**
-78	Return to Operating Room for a Related Procedure During the Postoperative Period	Report for unplanned circumstances that require return to operating room for complications of initial operation.
	EXAMPLE: Surgical sutures of the axilla did not hold, and 12 cm layer closure of axillary wound was performed. Report 12034-78.	

CODING TIP:

To ensure payment, medical necessity for the return to operating room must reflect the surgical complication.

-79	Unrelated Procedure or Service by the Same Physician During the Postoperative Period	Report when a new procedure or service is performed by a surgeon during the normal postoperative period of a previously performed but unrelated surgery.
	EXAMPLE: Six weeks following cataract surgery performed on the left eye, the patient underwent diathermic repair of retinal detachment, right eye. Report 67101-79.	

BILATERAL AND MULTIPLE PROCEDURES		
MODIFIER	**DESCRIPTION**	**INTERPRETATION**
-50	Bilateral Procedure	Report when a procedure was performed bilaterally *during the same session and when the code description does not specify that the procedure is bilateral.*
	EXAMPLE: Patient underwent bilateral athrodesis, knees. Report 27580-50 (or report HCPCS level II national modifiers as codes 27580-LT and 27580-RT.)	

CODING TIP:

- Although CPT modifier -50 refers to *operative session,* both diagnostic and therapeutic procedures can be reported with the bilateral modifier *if the anatomic structures are found bilaterally and the identical procedure is performed on both sides.*

- Reporting HCPCS modifiers -LT (left side) and -RT (right side) with procedure codes will remove any doubt that a bilateral procedure was performed. Documentation should accompany the submitted claim. *Do not report modifier -50 with HCPCS modifiers -LT and -RT.*

-27	Multiple Outpatient Hospital E/M Encounters on the Same Date	Report for patients who receive multiple E/M services performed by *different providers* on the same day. **NOTE:** Do *not* report for multiple E/M services performed by the same provider on the same day.
	EXAMPLE: A patient was seen in the hospital's emergency department and received level 4 evaluation and management services due to a fractured ankle. The patient was seen later the same day in the urgent care center and received level 3 evaluation and management services due to a migraine that did not respond to prescribed medication taken at home. Report codes 99284-27 and 99213-27.	

(continues)

TABLE 7-1   (continued)

\multicolumn{3}{c}{**BILATERAL AND MULTIPLE PROCEDURES (continued)**}
MODIFIER	**DESCRIPTION**	**INTERPRETATION**
-51	Multiple Procedures	Report when multiple procedures *other than E/M services* are performed at the same session by the same provider. The procedures performed are characterized as: • Multiple, related surgical procedures performed at the same session. • Surgical procedures performed in combination, whether through the same or another incision, or involving the same or different anatomy. • Combination medical and surgical procedures performed at the same session. **NOTE:** This modifier is reported with the secondary or lesser procedure(s).
	\multicolumn{2}{l}{**EXAMPLE:** Patient underwent right tibial shaft fracture repair and arthrodesis of left knee. Report codes 27750 and 27580-51.}

CODING TIP:

Do not report modifier -51 if:

• Notes at the beginning of a category instruct the coder to *report additional codes in addition to . . .* (see note before code 22305).

• The code description states *List separately in addition to the code for primary procedure* (see code 22116).

• The code description includes the words *each or each additional segment* (e.g., code 22103).

• The symbol **+** precedes a code; this designates an add-on code.

• Codes are reported from the Laboratory and Pathology 80000 series.

\multicolumn{3}{c}{**REPEAT SERVICES**}
MODIFIER	**DESCRIPTION**	**INTERPRETATION**
-76	Repeat Procedure by Same Physician	Report when a procedure was repeated because of special circumstances involving the original service, and the same physician performed the repeat procedure.
	\multicolumn{2}{l}{**EXAMPLE:** A repeat EKG is performed because of changes in the patient's condition or the need to assess the effect of therapeutic procedures. Report 93041-76.}
-77	Repeat Procedure by Another Physician	Report when a physician *other than the original physician* performs a repeat procedure because of special circumstances involving the original study or procedure.
	\multicolumn{2}{l}{**EXAMPLE:** Patient underwent sterilization procedure (e.g., tubal ligation), but became pregnant. After C-section delivery, she underwent a second sterilization procedure. Report code 59510 and 58611-77.}

(continues)

TABLE 7-1   (continued)

MODIFIER	DESCRIPTION	INTERPRETATION
	MULTIPLE SURGEONS	
-62	Two Surgeons	Report when two primary surgeons are required during an operative session, each performing distinct parts of a reportable procedure. Ideally, the surgeons represent different specialties.
	EXAMPLE: A spinal surgeon and a general surgeon work together as primary surgeons to perform an anterior spinal fusion of L5–S1; the spinal surgeon also inserts an intervertebral synthetic cage and performs iliac bone grafting. Each surgeon reports code 22558-62. The spinal surgeon also reports codes 22851-51 and 20937-51. **NOTE:** Surgeons should document the procedure(s) they performed in individual operative reports.	

CODING TIP:

Report modifiers -62 and -50 (bilateral procedure) when co-surgery is done by surgeons of the same specialty (e.g., bilateral knee replacement that required two surgeons to operate on both knees at the same time due to the patient's condition or risk).

CODING TIP:

If either surgeon acts as the assistant surgeon for additional unrelated procedure(s) performed during the same operative session, report modifier -80 or -81 with the additional procedures code(s).

MODIFIER	DESCRIPTION	INTERPRETATION
-66	Surgical Team	Report when surgery performed is highly complex and requires the services of a skilled team of three or more physicians. The procedure reported on the claim for each participating physician must include this modifier. The operative reports must document the complexity of the surgery and refer to the actions of each team member.
	EXAMPLE: Reattachment of severed forearm. Each surgeon reports 20805-66.	
-80	Assistant Surgeon	Report when one physician assists another during an operative session. The assistant surgeon reports the same CPT code as the operating physician.
	EXAMPLE: Dr. Landry assisted Dr. Bartron during single CABG surgery. Dr. Landry reports code 33510-80.	
-81	Minimum Assistant Surgeon	Report when primary operating physician planned to perform a surgical procedure alone, but circumstances arise that require the services of an assistant surgeon for a short time. The second surgeon reports the same CPT code as the operating physician.
	EXAMPLE: Dr. Kelly begins an invasive cholecystectomy procedure on a patient and discovers that the gallbladder is the size of a hot dog bun, which necessitates calling Dr. Pietro to assist for a short time. Dr. Pietro reports 47600-81. (A gallbladder is supposed to be the size of your little finger.)	

(continues)

TABLE 7-1 (continued)

MULTIPLE SURGEONS (continued)		
MODIFIER	**DESCRIPTION**	**INTERPRETATION**
-82	Assistant Surgeon (when qualified resident surgeon not available)	Report when a qualified resident surgeon is unavailable to assist with a procedure. In teaching hospitals, the physician acting as the assistant surgeon is usually a qualified resident surgeon. If circumstances arise (e.g., rotational changes) and a qualified resident surgeon is not available, another surgeon may assist with a procedure. The nonresident-assistant surgeon reports the same CPT code as the operating physician.
	EXAMPLE: Resident surgeon Dr. Smith was to assist surgeon Dr. Manlin with a routine laparoscopic appendectomy. Dr. Smith was temporarily reassigned to the emergency department due to a staffing problem. Therefore, Dr. Manlin's partner, Dr. Lando, assisted with the procedure. Dr. Lando reports 44970-82.	

CODING TIP:

Do not report modifiers -80, -81, and -82 for non-physician surgical assistant services (e.g., physician assistant, nurse practitioner) *unless the payer authorizes this reporting.*

PROFESSIONAL AND TECHNICAL COMPONENTS		
MODIFIER	**DESCRIPTION**	**INTERPRETATION**
-26	Professional Component	Report when the physician either interprets test results or operates equipment for a procedure. *Do not report this modifier when a specific separately identifiable code describes the professional component of a procedure (e.g., 93010).*
	EXAMPLE: Independent radiologist Dr. Minion interprets a stereo frontal chest x-ray that was performed on Mary Sue Patient by another provider. Dr. Minion reports code 71021-26.	

MANDATED SERVICES		
MODIFIER	**DESCRIPTION**	**INTERPRETATION**
-32	Mandated Services	Report when services (e.g., second or third opinion for a surgical procedure) provided were mandated by a third party (e.g., attorney, payer).
	EXAMPLE: Mary Sue Patient is seen by her primary care provider who recommends respiratory therapy. Before the payer will approve reimbursement for respiratory therapy, Mary Sue Patient receives a level 3 E/M service by respiratory specialist Dr. Powell. Dr. Powell reports code 99243-32.	

UNUSUAL ANESTHESIA		
MODIFIER	**DESCRIPTION**	**INTERPRETATION**
-23	Unusual Anesthesia	Report when circumstances (e.g., extent of service, patient's physical condition) require anesthesia for procedures that usually require either no anesthesia or local anesthesia.
	EXAMPLE: The 30-year-old patient is mentally handicapped and extremely apprehensive and requires general anesthesia for sliding hernia repair. Report 49525-23.	
-47	Anesthesia by Surgeon	Report when the surgeon provides regional or general anesthesia in addition to performing the surgical procedure.
	EXAMPLE: Instead of calling in an anesthesiologist to assist with a surgical case, Dr. Borja administers regional anesthesia and performs the spigelian hernia repair. Dr. Borja reports code 49590-47.	

(continues)

TABLE 7-1 (continued)

UNUSUAL ANESTHESIA (continued)		
MODIFIER	**DESCRIPTION**	**INTERPRETATION**

> **CODING TIP:**
> Modifier -47 is added to the CPT surgery code. It is not reported with Anesthesia codes 00100-01999.

LABORATORY SERVICES		
MODIFIER	**DESCRIPTION**	**INTERPRETATION**
-90	Reference (Outside) Laboratory	Report when a laboratory test is performed by an outside or reference laboratory.
	EXAMPLE: The provider orders a complete blood count (CBC). Because the office does not perform lab testing, arrangements are made with an outside laboratory to perform the CBC and bill the physician. The physician reports the CBC as code 85025-90. Code 36415 is also reported for routine venipuncture.	
-91	Repeat Clinical Diagnostic Laboratory Test	Report when a clinical diagnostic laboratory test is repeated on the same day to obtain subsequent (multiple) test results. *This modifier is not reported when lab tests are repeated to confirm initial results* (e.g., due to equipment problems).
	EXAMPLE: The patient was in the emergency department for 18 hours for observation of chest pain. He underwent serial (repeated) lab tests for cardiac enzyme testing every 6 hours. Report codes 82657, 82657-91, 82657-91.	
-92	Alternative Laboratory Platform Testing	When a single-use disposable kit or transportable instrument is used to perform HIV laboratory testing (CPT codes 86701-86703), add modifier -92 to the reported code.
	EXAMPLE: During the annual physical examination of a 30-year-old single male by his primary care provider, the established patient stated that he had had multiple sexual partners during the past year. The provider obtained an HIV rapid test kit from the clinic's laboratory department, performed venipuncture on the patient to obtain a blood sample, and completed an HIV-1 and HIV-2, single assay, antibody test. Report code 86703-92 (in addition to CPT codes 99395 and 36415).	

MULTIPLE MODIFIERS		
MODIFIER	**DESCRIPTION**	**INTERPRETATION**
-99	Multiple Modifiers	Report to alert third-party payers that more than three modifiers are being added to a procedure/service code.
	EXAMPLE: The CMS-1500 claim allows up to four modifiers to be listed after a CPT or HCPCS level II code. If more than four modifiers are required to report a procedure or service, enter the first three modifiers and modifier 99 on line 1 of Block 24D. On line 2, report the same CPT or HCPCS level II code and enter the remaining modifiers.	

24. A DATE(S) OF SERVICE		B. PLACE OF	C.	D. PROCEDURES, SERVICES, OR SUPPLIES	E. DIAGNOSIS	F.	G. DAYS OR	H. EPSDT	I. ID.	J. RENDERING
From	To	SERVICE	EMG	(Explain Unusual Circumstances)	POINTER	$ CHARGES	UNITS	Family Plan	QUAL.	PROVIDER ID. #
MM DD YY	MM DD YY			CPT/HCPCS MODIFER						
1				32615 51 54 77 80					NPI	

(continues)

TABLE 7-1   (continued)

MULTIPLE MODIFIERS (continued)		
MODIFIER	**DESCRIPTION**	**INTERPRETATION**
	NOTE: The UB-04 claim allows up to two modifiers to be listed after a CPT or HCPCS level II code in Form Locator 44. If more than two modifiers are required to report a procedure or service, enter the first modifier and modifier 99 on the first line. On the subsequent line(s), enter the same CPT or HCPCS level II code and enter the remaining modifiers.	

42 REV CD.	43 DESCRIPTION	44 HCPSC / RATE /HIPPS CODE	45 SERV DATE	46 SERV UNITS	47 TOTAL CHARGES	48 NON COVER CHARGES	49
		19100 50 80					

EXAMPLE: An assistant surgeon (-80) reports an unusual service (-22), bilateral (-50), surgeon provided general anesthesia services (-47) for lumbar hernia repair procedure (49540). On the CMS-1500 claim, report as 49540 22 47 50 99 and 49540 80. (On the UB-04, report as 49540 22 99, 49540 47 50, and 49540 80.)

EXAMPLE: Mrs. T has a history of gallbladder disease. After several hours of acute pain, she was referred to Dr. S for an evaluation of her condition. Dr. S performed a complete history and physical examination and decided to admit the patient to the hospital for an immediate work-up for cholecystitis. When the results of the laboratory tests and sonogram were received, the patient was scheduled for an emergency laparoscopic cholecystectomy.

The surgeon was Dr. S and the assistant surgeon was Dr. A. The surgery was successful, and the patient was discharged the next day and told to return to the office in seven days. Four days later, Mrs. T returned to Dr. S's office complaining of chest pains. Dr. S performed another examination and ordered the necessary tests. After reviewing the test results and confirming with the patient's primary care physician, it was determined that the patient was suffering from mild angina.

Dr. S submitted a claim (Figure 7-6) for the following services:

- Initial hospital visit, comprehensive, with medical decision making of high complexity (99223-57) (modifier -57 indicates that the decision to perform surgery was made during the hospital evaluation).

- Laparoscopic cholecystectomy (47562).

- Office visit, established patient, expanded problem focused, with medical decision making of low complexity (99213-24) (modifier -24 indicates that the reexamination of the patient revealed the problem to be unrelated to the normal postoperative care provided to a cholecystectomy patient. The diagnosis linked to this visit is angina).

Dr. A submits a claim (Figure 7-7) for the following service: Laparoscopic cholecystectomy 47562-80 (modifier -80 indicates that Dr. A is the assistant surgeon).

FIGURE 7-6 Completed Block 24D on CMS-1500 claim (Courtesy Delmar/Cengage Learning.)

FIGURE 7-7 Completed Block 24D on CMS-1500 claim (Courtesy Delmar/Cengage Learning.)

EXERCISE 7-3

Assigning CPT Modifiers

Instructions: Assign appropriate modifier(s) to each statement below.

___ 1. Assistant surgeon reporting patient's cesarean section, delivery only.

___ 2. Cholecystectomy reported during postoperative period for treatment of leg fracture.

___ 3. Treatment for chronic conditions at same time preventive medicine is provided.

___ 4. Inpatient visit performed by surgeon, with decision to perform surgery tomorrow.

___ 5. Office consultation as preoperative clearance for surgery.

___ 6. Postoperative management of vaginal hysterectomy.

___ 7. Repeat gallbladder x-ray series, same physician.

___ 8. Arthroscopy of right elbow and closed fracture reduction of left wrist.

___ 9. Needle core biopsy of right and left breast.

___10. Consultation required by payer.

CODING PROCEDURES AND SERVICES

STEP 1 Read the introduction in the CPT coding manual.

STEP 2 Review guidelines at the beginning of each section.

STEP 3 Review the procedure or service listed in the source document (e.g, charge slip, progress note, operative report, laboratory report, or pathology report). Code only what is documented in the source document; do not make assumptions about conditions, procedures, or services not stated. If necessary, obtain clarification from the provider.

STEP 4 Refer to the CPT index, and locate the main term for the procedure or service documented. Main terms can be located by referring to the:

    a. *Procedure or service* documented.
        EXAMPLE: Arthroscopy
                 Consultation

    b. *Organ or anatomic site.*
        EXAMPLE: Arm

    c. *Condition documented in the record.*
        EXAMPLE: Hernia

    d. *Substance being tested.*
        EXAMPLE: Blood

    e. *Synonym* (terms with similar meanings).
        EXAMPLE: Pyothorax is abscess, thorax; both are found in the index.

    f. *Eponym* (procedures and diagnoses named for an individual).
        EXAMPLE: Babcock Operation is ligation, saphenous vein. Both are found in the index.

    g. *Abbreviation*
        EXAMPLE: CBC

STEP 5 Locate subterms and follow cross references.

HINT:

If the main term is located at the bottom of a CPT index page, turn the page and check to see if the main term and subterm(s) continue.

STEP 6 Review descriptions of service/procedure codes, and compare all qualifiers to descriptive statements.

STEP 7 Assign the applicable code number and any add-on (+) or additional codes needed to accurately classify the statement being coded.

CODING TIP:

You may have to refer to synonyms, translate medical terms to ordinary English, or substitute medical words for English terms documented in the provider's statement to find the main term in the index. Some examples are:

Procedure Statement	Word Substitution
Placement of a shunt	Insertion of shunt
Pacemaker implantation	Pacemaker insertion
Resection of tumor	Excision or removal of tumor
Radiograph of the chest	X-ray of chest
Suture laceration	Repair open wound
Placement of nerve block	Injection of nerve anesthesia

EXERCISE 7-4

Finding Procedures in the Index

Instructions: Using only the CPT index, find the code or range of codes to be investigated. Note the code or range of codes and any word substitution you made that led to selected code numbers.

1. Closed treatment of wrist dislocation   _____
2. Dilation of cervix   _____
3. Placement of upper GI feeding tube   _____
4. Radiograph and fluoroscopy of chest, four views   _____
5. Magnetic resonance imaging (MRI), lower spine   _____
6. Darrach procedure   _____
7. Automated CBC   _____
8. Electrosurgical removal, skin tags   _____
9. Molar pregnancy excision   _____
10. Muscle denervation, hip joint   _____

EVALUATION AND MANAGEMENT SECTION

The **Evaluation and Management (E/M) section** (codes 99201–99499) is located at the beginning of CPT because these codes describe services most frequently provided by physicians. Accurate assignment of *E/M codes* is essential to the success of a physician's practice because most of the revenue generated by the office is based on provision of these services. Before assigning E/M codes, make sure you review the guidelines (located at the beginning of the E/M section) and apply any notes (located below category and subcategory titles).

Most E/M services are cognitive services—this means that the provider must acquire information from the patient, use reasoning skills to process the information, interact with the patient to provide feedback, and respond by creating an appropriate plan of care. E/M services do not include significant procedural services (e.g., diagnostic tests or surgical procedures), which are coded separately. However, some services that arise directly from the E/M service provided are included (e.g., cleansing traumatic lesions, closing lacerations with adhesive strips, applying dressings, and providing counseling and educational services).

Overview of Evaluation and Management Section

CPT 1992 introduced the E/M level of service codes, replacing the brief, limited office visit codes included in the Medicine section of past CPT revisions. The E/M section is organized according to place of service (POS) (e.g., office, hospital, home, nursing facility [NF], emergency department [ED], or critical care), type of service (TOS) (e.g., new or initial encounter, follow-up or subsequent encounter, or consultation), and miscellaneous services (e.g., prolonged physician service or care plan oversight service). The E/M **level of service** reflects the amount of work involved in providing health care to a patient, and correct coding requires determining the extent of history and examination performed as well as the complexity of medical decision making.

Between three and five levels of service are included in E/M categories, and documentation in the patient's chart must support the level of service reported. CMS often refers to E/M codes by level numbers, and the level often corresponds to the last digit of the CPT code (e.g., 99204 is a level 4 E/M service).

> **EXAMPLE:** Refer to the Office or Outpatient Services category in the E/M section, and notice that it contains two subcategories:
>
> - New patient (contains 5 codes)
> - Established patient (contains 5 codes)
>
> Each code represents a level of E/M service, ranked from lowest to highest level. CMS would consider E/M code 99201 a level 1 code.

Accurate assignment of E/M codes depends on (1) identifying the place of service (POS) and/or type of service (TOS) provided to the patient, (2) determining whether the patient is new or established to the practice, (3) reviewing the patient's record for documentation of level of service components, (4) applying CMS's *Documentation Guidelines for Evaluation and Management Services,* and (5) determining whether E/M guidelines (e.g., unlisted service) apply.

Place of Service (POS)

Place of service (POS) refers to the physical location where health care is provided to patients (e.g., office or other outpatient settings, hospitals, NFs, home health care, or EDs).

EXAMPLE 1: The provider treated the patient in her office.

Place of Service: Office

E/M Category: Office or Other Outpatient Services

EXAMPLE 2: The patient received care in the hospital's ED.

Place of Service: Hospital ED

E/M Category: Emergency Department Services

Type of Service (TOS)

Type of service (TOS) refers to the kind of healthcare services provided to patients. It includes critical care, consultation, initial hospital care, subsequent hospital care, and confirmatory consultation.

EXAMPLE 1: The patient underwent an annual physical examination in the provider's office.

Type of Service: Preventive care

E/M Category: Preventive Medicine Services

EXAMPLE 2: The hospital inpatient was transferred to the regular medical-surgical unit where he was recovering from surgery. He suddenly stopped breathing and required respirator management by his physician.

Type of Service: Critical care

E/M Category: Critical Care Services

Sometimes *both the TOS and POS* must be identified before the proper code can be assigned.

EXAMPLE 1: Dr. Smith completed Josie Black's history and physical examination on the first day of her inpatient admission.

Place of Service: Hospital

Type of Service: Initial inpatient care

E/M Category: Hospital Inpatient Services

E/M Subcategory: Initial Hospital Care

EXAMPLE 2: Dr. Charles saw Josie Black in her office to render a second opinion.

Place of Service: Office

Type of Service: Consultation

E/M Category: Consultations

E/M Subcategory: Office or Other Outpatient Consultations

CODING TIP:

Refer to the CPT Medicine section for codes that describe specialty services (e.g., ophthalmologic services, psychiatric services) that require evaluation and management. When codes for specialty services are reported from the Medicine section, a code from the CPT E/M section is *not* reported on the same date *unless a significant, separately identifiable E/M service was provided (and modifier -25 is attached).*

New and Established Patients

A **new patient** is one who has *not* received any professional services from the physician, or from another physician of the same specialty who belongs to the same group practice, within the past three years. An **established patient** is one who *has* received professional services from the physician, or from another physician of the same specialty who belongs to the same group practice, within the past three years.

CODING TIP:

- Professional services may not require a face-to-face encounter with a provider.

- Definitions of new and established patients include professional services rendered by other physicians of the same specialty in the same group practice.

EXAMPLE 1: Sally Dunlop had a prescription renewed by Dr. Smith's office on January 1, 2005, but she did not see the physician. She has been Dr. Smith's patient since her initial office visit on March 15, 2002. On December 1, 2005, Dr. Smith treated Sally during an office visit.

New Patient: March 15, 2002.

Established Patient: January 1, 2005, and December 1, 2005.

Because she received professional services (the prescription renewal) on January 1, 2005, Sally Dunlop is considered an established patient for the December 1, 2005, visit.

EXAMPLE 2: Dr. Charles and Dr. Black share a practice. Dr. Charles is a general surgeon who treated Mary Smith in the office on July 1, 2005. Mary was first seen by the practice on February 15, 2002, when Dr. Black provided preventive care services to her. Mary returned to the practice on November 1, 2005, for her annual physical examination conducted by Dr. Black.

New Patient: February 15, 2002, and July 1, 2005.

Established Patient: November 1, 2005.

> **EXAMPLE 3:** Dr. Corey left Alfred Medical Group to join Buffalo Physician Group as a family practitioner. At Buffalo Physician Group, when Dr. Corey provides professional services to patients, are those patients considered new or established?
>
> **Answer:** Patients who have not received professional services from Dr. Corey or another physician of the same specialty at Buffalo Physician Group are considered new. Patients who have been treated by another family practitioner at Buffalo Physician Group within the past three years are considered established. If any of Dr. Corey's patients from the Alfred Medical Group choose to seek care from him at the Buffalo Physician Group, they will be considered established patients.

Concurrent Care and Transfer of Care

Concurrent care is the provision of similar services, such as hospital inpatient visits, to the same patient by more than one provider on the same day. Effective October 1995, CMS published new regulations that permit concurrent care by two or more providers on the same day even if the providers are of the same specialty. To avoid reimbursement denials by third-party payers and Medicare administrative contracts, the provider should report different ICD-9-CM diagnosis codes from those reported by other providers who see the patient on the same day. Transfer of care occurs when a physician who is managing some or all of a patient's problems releases the patient to the care of another physician who is not providing consultative services.

> **EXAMPLE:** Laurie Birch was admitted to the hospital on October 5 for an acute myocardial infarction. On October 7, her attending physician (a cardiologist) wrote a physician's order requesting a psychiatrist to consult with the patient regarding her anxiety and depression. The cardiologist's insurance specialist should report the ICD code for "acute myocardial infarction" to justify inpatient E/M services provided to the patient. The psychiatrist's insurance specialist should report the ICD codes for "anxiety and depression" to justify inpatient consultation E/M services provided to the patient. If each provider reported the ICD code for "acute myocardial infarction," the provider who submitted the claim first would be reimbursed (and the other provider's claim would be denied).

Evaluation and Management Guidelines

Evaluation and management guidelines clarify that an *unlisted service* code is assigned when the provider furnishes an E/M service for which there is no CPT code. When an unlisted procedure or service code is reported, a special report (e.g., copy of documented encounter note record) must accompany the claim to describe the nature of, extent of, and need for the procedure or service.

CODING TIP:

> Medicare and third-party payers often require providers to report HCPCS level II national codes instead of unlisted procedure or service CPT codes. (HCPCS level II national codes are discussed in Chapter 8 of this textbook.)

When an unlisted service code is reported, a *special report* must be submitted with the insurance claim to demonstrate medical appropriateness. The provider should document the following elements in the special report:

- Complexity of patient's symptoms.
- Description of, nature of, extent of, and need for service.

- **Diagnostic and therapeutic procedures performed.**
- **Follow-up care.**
- **Patient's final diagnosis and concurrent problems.**
- **Pertinent physical findings.**
- **Time, effort, and equipment required to provide the service.**

Appendix C of the CPT coding manual contains clinical examples of E/M service codes. Along with a careful review of the E/M code descriptions, they assist providers in selecting the appropriate code for documented E/M services. The AMA cautions providers that the clinical examples "do not encompass the entire scope of medical practice." They can be used in addition to documented key components (history, examination, and/or medical decision making) that are required to determine a particular level of service.

Levels of Evaluation and Management Services

Evaluation and management (E/M) categories and subcategories contain codes that are classified according to level of services for reporting to third-party payers. Although the last number of some E/M codes represents the level of service (e.g., code 99213 is a level 3 E/M service), the levels within categories and subcategories are not interchangeable. Levels of E/M services include conferences with or about patients, evaluations, examinations, preventive adult and pediatric health supervision, treatments, and other medical services (e.g., determining the need for and/or location of appropriate care, such as hospice care for a terminally ill patient).

> **EXAMPLE:** CPT code 99201 classifies a level 1 office or other outpatient service reported for new patients, and it includes a problem focused history and examination and straightforward medical decision making. CPT code 99211 classifies a level 1 office or other outpatient service reported for established patients, but it is reported when the physician's presence may not be required (e.g., office nurse takes patient's blood pressure and records it in the record).

Typically, just one E/M code is reported each day by a provider for a patient. When a separately identifiable E/M service is provided in addition to a surgical procedure, the E/M code is reported with modifier -25.

> **EXAMPLE 1:** A physician sutured a patient's 2.5 centimeter scalp wound in the ED and performed a comprehensive neurological history and exam of the patient. The patient had sustained head trauma as the result of a car accident, and EMT personnel documented that he had been unconscious at the scene. Medical decision making was of high complexity. Report code 12001 for the simple repair of the scalp wound, and report code 99285-25 for the E/M service provided.

> **EXAMPLE 2:** A physician sutured a 5 centimeter laceration of a patient's left hand and confirmed that the patient was up to date regarding tetanus toxoids immunization status. Report code 12002 for the simple repair of the skin laceration, hand. Do not report an E/M code because the patient was not evaluated other than confirmation of her tetanus immunization status.

NOTE: Because they were believed to be insufficient to guarantee consistent coding by providers and reliable medical review by payers, CMS developed Evaluation and Management Documentation Guidelines, which explain how E/M codes are assigned according to elements associated with comprehensive multisystem and single-system examinations. The first set of guidelines created by CMS in 1995 was criticized by providers as containing unclear criteria for single-system specialty examinations. Therefore, CMS created an alternate set of guidelines in 1997, which was also criticized as being confusing and requiring extensive counting of services and other elements. In response, CMS instructed Medicare administrative contractors to use both sets of guidelines when reviewing records. Providers could use whichever set of guidelines was most advantageous to their practice reimbursement.

The levels of E/M services code descriptions include seven components, six of which determine the level of E/M service code to be assigned:

- History
- Examination
- Medical decision making
- Counseling
- Coordination of care
- Nature of presenting problem
- Time

The **key components** of history, examination, and medical decision making are required when selecting an E/M level of service code. **Contributory components** include counseling, coordination of care, nature of presenting problem, and time; and they are used to select the appropriate E/M service code when patient record documentation indicates that they were the focus of the visit.

Key Components

E/M code selection is based on three key components:

- **Extent of history**
- **Extent of examination**
- **Complexity of medical decision making**

NOTE:
· When assigning codes for new patients, all three key components must be considered.
· For established patients, two of three key components must be considered.

All three key components must be considered when assigning codes for new patients. For established patients, two of the three key components must be considered. This means that documentation in the patient's chart must support the key components used to determine the E/M code selected. The E/M code reported to a payer must be supported by documentation in the patient's record (e.g., office progress note, diagnostic test results, operative findings). Although providers are responsible for selecting the E/M code at the time patient care is rendered, insurance specialists audit records to make sure that the appropriate level of E/M code was reported to the third-party payer.

Extent of History

A history is an interview of the patient that includes the following elements: history of present illness (HPI) (including the patient's chief complaint, CC), a review of systems (ROS), and a past/family/social history (PFSH). The **extent of history (CPT)** (Figure 7-8A) is categorized according to four levels:

- **Problem focused history (chief complaint, brief history of present illness or problem).**
- **Expanded problem focused history (chief complaint, brief history of present illness, problem pertinent system review).**
- **Detailed history (chief complaint, extended history of present illness, problem pertinent system review extended to include a limited number of additional systems, pertinent past/family/social history directly related to patient's problem).**
- **Comprehensive history (chief complaint, extended history of present illness, review of systems directly related to the problem(s) identified in the history of the present illness in addition to a review of all additional body systems, complete past/family/social history).**

SELECTING EXTENT OF HISTORY: To select extent of history, review the following elements documented in the patient record. If an element is not documented, it cannot be considered when selecting the level of E/M service code.
- History of Present Illness (HPI)
- Review of Systems (ROS)
- Past, Family, and Social History (PFSH)

HISTORY OF PRESENT ILLNESS (HPI): Review the patient's record, and for each documented HPI element listed below place an **x** in the box located in front of the element on this form. Then, count the number of **x**'s, and enter that number in the box located in front of the Total Score (below). Select the level of history based on the total number of elements documented, and place an **x** in the appropriate box.

☐ **Duration:** of pain/discomfort: length of the time condition has persisted (e.g., pain began three days ago)
☐ **Location:** of pain/discomfort (e.g., is pain diffuse/localized, unilateral/bilateral, does it radiate or refer?)
☐ **Quality:** a description of the quality of the symptom (e.g., is pain described as sharp, dull, throbbing, stabbing, constant, intermittent, acute or chronic, stable, improving or worsening?)
☐ **Severity:** use of self-assessment scale to measure subjective levels (e.g., "on a scale of 1–10, how severe is the pain?"), or comparison of pain quantitatively with previously experienced pain
☐ **Timing:** establishing onset of pain and chronology of pain development (e.g., migraine in the morning)
☐ **Context:** where was the patient and what was he doing when pain begins (e.g., was patient at rest or involved in an activity; was pain aggravated or relieved, or does it recur, with a specific activity; did situational stress or some other factor precede or accompany the pain?)
☐ **Modifying factors:** what has patient attempted to do to relieve pain (e.g., heat vs. cold; does it relieve or exacerbate pain; what makes the pain worse; have over-the-counter drugs been attempted - with what results?)
☐ **Associated signs/symptoms:** clinician's impressions formulated during the interview may lead to questioning about additional sensations or feelings (e.g., diaphoresis associated with indigestion or chest pain, blurred vision accompanying a headache, etc.)

_____ **Total Score:** Enter the number of **x**'s entered above. Place an **x** in front of the HPI type below.
☐ BRIEF HPI (1-3 elements)
☐ EXTENDED HPI (4 or more elements)

REVIEW OF SYSTEMS (ROS): Review the clinic or SOAP note in the patient's record, and for each documented ROS element listed below, place an **x** in the box located in front of the element on this form. Then, total the **x**'s and enter that number in the box located in front of the Total Score (below). Finally, select the level of ROS based on the total number of elements documented, and place an **x** in the appropriate box.

☐ Allergic / Immunologic   ☐ Eyes   ☐ Musculoskeletal
☐ Constitutional symptoms   ☐ Gastrointestinal   ☐ Neurologic
☐ Cardiovascular   ☐ Genitourinary   ☐ Psychiatric
☐ Ears, nose, mouth, throat   ☐ Hematologic/Lymphatic   ☐ Respiratory
☐ Endocrine   ☐ Integumentary
                                      (including skin and breast)

_____ **Total Score:** Enter the number of **x**'s entered above. Place an **x** in front of the ROS type below.
☐ NONE
☐ PROBLEM PERTINENT ROS (1 body system documented)
☐ EXTENDED ROS (2-9 body systems documented)
☐ COMPLETE ROS (all body systems documented)

PAST, FAMILY AND/OR SOCIAL HISTORY (PFSH): Review the clinic or SOAP note in the patient's record, and for each documented PFSH element (below), place an **x** in the box located in front of the element on this form. Then, total the **x**'s entered and enter that number in the box located in front of the Total Score (below). Finally, select the level of PFSH based on the total number of elements documented, and place an **x** in the appropriate box.

☐ Past history (current medications, drug allergies, immunizations, and prior illnesses/ injuries, hospitalizations, surgeries)
☐ Family history (health status/cause of death of relatives, specific disease related to CC, HPI, ROS, hereditary diseases for which patient is at risk)
☐ Social history (alcohol use, current employment, illicit drug use, level of education, nutritional status, occupational history, sexual history, tobacco use)

_____ **Total Score:** Enter the number of **x**'s selected. Place an **x** in front of the PFSH type below.
☐ NONE
☐ PERTINENT PFSH (1 history area documented)
☐ COMPLETE PFSH (2 or 3 history areas documented)

Circle the type of HPI, ROS and PFSH. Select the Extent of History. (3 of 3 elements must be met or exceeded.)

HPI	Brief	Brief	Extended	Extended
ROS	None	Problem Pertinent	Extended	Complete
PFSH	None	None	Pertinent	Complete
EXTENT OF HISTORY	PROBLEM FOCUSED	EXPANDED PROBLEM FOCUSED	DETAILED	COMPREHENSIVE

FIGURE 7-8A Extent of history (Courtesy Delmar/Cengage Learning.)

NOTE: Physicians and providers can use either the 1995 or 1997 documentation guidelines for evaluation and management services, which were jointly developed by CMS and the American Medical Association. Each set of guidelines define documentation elements that determine the level of examination.

· The 1995 guidelines are typically used by general practitioners and others who do not perform single-system examinations.

· The 1997 guidelines are often used by specialists who perform organ- or body area specific examinations.

Regardless of guidelines used, documentation in the patient record must support the level of examination selected.

Extent of Examination

A **physical examination** is an assessment of the patient's organ (e.g., extremities) and body systems (e.g., cardiovascular). The **extent of examination (CPT)** (Figure 7-8B) is categorized according to four levels:

- **Problem-focused examination** (limited examination of the affected body area or organ system).
- **Expanded problem-focused examination** (limited examination of the affected body area or organ system and other symptomatic or related organ system(s)).
- **Detailed examination** (extended examination of the affected body area(s) and other symptomatic or related organ system(s)).
- **Comprehensive examination** (general multisystem examination or a complete examination of a single organ system).

Complexity of Medical Decision Making

Medical decision making (Figure 7-8C) refers to the complexity of establishing a diagnosis and/or selecting a management option as measured by the:

- **Number of diagnoses or management options.**
- **Amount and/or complexity of data to be reviewed.**
- **Risk of complications and/or morbidity or mortality.**

SELECTING EXTENT OF EXAMINATION: To select the level of examination, first determine whether a *single organ examination* (e.g., specialist exam, such as ophthalmologist) or a *general multisystem examination* (e.g., family practitioner) was completed.

SINGLE ORGAN SYSTEM EXAMINATION: Refer to single organ system examination requirements in CMS's *Documentation Guidelines for Evaluation and Management Services*. Place an **x** in front of the appropriate exam type below.

☐ PROBLEM FOCUSED EXAMINATION (1–5 elements identified by a bullet)

☐ EXPANDED PROBLEM FOCUSED EXAMINATION (at least 6 elements identified by a bullet)

☐ DETAILED EXAMINATION (at least 12 elements identified by a bullet)

☐ COMPREHENSIVE EXAMINATION (all elements identified by a bullet; document every element in each box with a shaded border and at least 1 element in each box with an unshaded border)

NOTE: for eye and psychiatric examinations, at least 9 elements in each box with a shaded border and at least 1 element in each box with a shaded or unshaded border is documented.

GENERAL MULTISYSTEM EXAM: Refer to the general multisystem examination requirements in CMS's *Documentation Guidelines for Evaluation and Management Services*. Place an **x** in front of the organ system or body area for up to the total number of allowed elements (e.g., up to 2 marks can be made for the Neck exam.)

☐ Constitutional (2)   ☐ Gastrointestinal (5)   ☐ Psychiatric (4)
☐ Cardiovascular (7)   ☐ Genitourinary (M–3; F–6)   ☐ Respiratory (4)
☐ Chest (Breasts) (2)   ☐ Musculoskeletal (6)   ☐ Skin (2)
☐ Eyes (3)   ☐ Neck (2)
☐ Ears, nose, mouth, throat (6) ☐ Neurologic (3)

_____ **Total Score:** Enter the number of **x**'s entered above. Place an **x** in front of the Examination type below.

☐ PROBLEM FOCUSED EXAMINATION (1-5 elements identified by a bullet on CMS's *E/M Documentation Guidelines*)

☐ EXPANDED PROBLEM FOCUSED EXAMINATION (at least 6 elements identified by a bullet on CMS's *E/M Documentation Guidelines*)

☐ DETAILED EXAMINATION (at least 2 elements identified by a bullet from each of 6 organ systems or body areas or at least 12 elements identified by a bullet in 2 or more systems or areas, on CMS's *E/M Documentation Guidelines*)

☐ COMPREHENSIVE EXAMINATION (documentation of all elements identified by a bullet in at least 9 organ systems or body areas, and documentation of at least 2 elements identified by a bullet from each of 9 organ systems or body areas, on CMS's *E/M Documentation Guidelines*)

FIGURE 7-8B Extent of examination (Courtesy Delmar/Cengage Learning.)

CRITERIA to DETERMINE COMPLEXITY OF MEDICAL DECISION MAKING			
Number of Diagnoses or Management Options	Amount/Complexity of Data to Be Reviewed	Risk of Complications and/or Morbidity/Mortality	Complexity of Medical Decision Making
minimal	minimal or none	minimal	Straightforward
limited	limited	low	Low complexity
multiple	moderate	moderate	Moderate complexity
extensive	extensive	high	High complexity

FIGURE 7-8C Criteria to determine complexity of medical decision making (CPT copyright 2009 American Medical Association. All rights reserved.)

Complexity of medical decision-making criteria reflects the provider's level of uncertainty, volume of data to review, and risk to the patient. Documentation in the patient's record includes:

- Laboratory, imaging, and other test results that are significant to the management of the patient's care.
- List of known diagnoses as well as those that are suspected.
- Opinions of other physicians who have been consulted.
- Planned course of action for the patient's treatment (plan of treatment).
- Review of patient records obtained from other facilities.

The physician is responsible for determining the complexity of medical decision making, and that decision must be supported by documentation in the patient's chart. CPT includes a table in the E/M guidelines that can assist in determining complexity of medical decision making. Once the key components for extent of history and examination are determined, the type of medical decision making can be selected as follows:

- Straightforward
- Low complexity
- Moderate complexity
- High complexity

Assigning the E/M Code

Once the extent of history, extent of examination, and complexity of medical decision making are determined, select the appropriate E/M code (Figure 7-8D).

Select the E/M code based on extent of history, extent of examination, and complexity of medical decision making:				
History	Problem focused	Expanded problem focused	Expanded problem focused	Detailed	Comprehensive
Examination	Problem focused	Expanded problem focused	Expanded problem focused	Detailed	Comprehensive
Medical Decision Making	Straightforward	Low complexity	Moderate complexity	Moderate complexity	High complexity
Go to the appropriate E/M category/subcategory, and select the code based upon the information above				

FIGURE 7-8D E/M code selection based on extent of history and examination and complexity of medical decision making (CPT copyright 2009 American Medical Association. All rights reserved.)

CODING TIP:

Use the E/M CodeBuilder located in Appendix III to select the correct E/M code.

EXAMPLE: Review the progress note below (documented using the SOAP format), and use Figures 7-8A, 7-8B, 7-8C, and 7-8D to determine extent of history and examination and complexity of medical decision making for a patient who is seen by his general practitioner.

SUBJECTIVE: The patient is a 35-year-old established male patient seen today with a chief complaint of severe snoring. He says that this has gone on for years and that he's finally ready to do something about it because it causes him to awaken during the night, and his wife to lose sleep as well. He says that he wakes up in the morning feeling very tired and notices that he gets very tired during the day. Review of systems reveals allergies. He denies smoking or alcohol use. He is on no medications.

OBJECTIVE: Blood pressure is 126/86. Pulse is 82. Weight is 185. EYES: Pupils equal, round, and reactive to light and accommodation; extraocular muscles intact. EARS & NOSE: Tympanic membranes normal; oropharynx benign. NECK: Supple without jugular venous distention, bruits, or thyromegaly. RESPIRATORY: Breath sounds are clear to percussion and auscultation. EXTREMITIES: Without edema; pulses intact.

ASSESSMENT: Possible sleep apnea.

PLAN: Patient to undergo sleep study in two weeks. Results to be evaluated by Dr. Jones, ENT specialist, to determine whether patient is candidate for laser-assisted uvuloplasty (LAUP) surgery.

To assign the E/M code, the following is determined:

NEW OR ESTABLISHED PATIENT: This is an established patient.

EXTENT OF HISTORY: HPI elements include quality, severity, timing, and context; extended HPI (four elements) is documented. ROS elements include allergic; problem pertinent ROS (one body system) is documented. PFSH elements include documentation of social history; pertinent PFSH (one history area) is documented for a score of 1. Because three out of three HPI/ROS/PFHS types must be selected to determine the higher-level extent of history, expanded problem focused history is assigned.

EXTENT OF EXAMINATION: Constitutional (1), Eyes (1), ENT (2), Neck (1), Respiratory (1), Cardiovascular (1); expanded problem focused examination (six elements) is documented.

COMPLEXITY OF MEDICAL DECISION MAKING:
Undiagnosed new problem with uncertain prognosis is documented (possible sleep apnea). Although "physiologic test not under stress" (sleep study) is documented as being ordered, results are not reviewed by this provider. In addition, this provider will not follow through on management options because the patient is referred to an ENT specialist. Therefore, complexity of medical decision making is straightforward because two of three elements are required and just one element is documented.

E/M CODE ASSIGNED: 99213 (Two of three key components are required.)

Contributory Components

The contributory components of counseling, coordination of care, nature of presenting illness, and time play an important role in selecting the E/M code when documentation in the patient record indicates that they were the focus of the visit. Counseling and/or coordination of care components drive CPT code selection only when they dominate the encounter (e.g., office visit), requiring that more than 50 percent of the provider's time be spent on such components. In such circumstances, the provider must be sure to carefully document these elements so as to support the higher-level code selected. (Some E/M code descriptions include notes about time and nature of the presenting problem to assist in determining the appropriate code number to report.)

Counseling

CPT defines counseling as it relates to E/M coding as a discussion with a patient and/or family concerning one or more of the following areas: diagnostic results, impressions, and/or recommended diagnostic studies; prognosis; risks and benefits of management (treatment) options; instructions for management (treatment) and/or follow-up; importance of compliance with chosen management (treatment) options; risk factor reduction; patient and family education.

Providers typically select the level of E/M code based on extent of history and examination and complexity of medical decision making. However, some patients require counseling services (e.g., nutrition instruction, smoking cessation, and weight management) during an E/M visit. If provided, such counseling should be properly documented and the appropriate level of E/M code selected.

Coordination of Care

When the physician makes arrangements with other providers or agencies for services to be provided to a patient, this is called coordination of care.

Nature of the Presenting Problem

CPT defines nature of the presenting problem as "a disease, condition, illness, injury, symptom, sign, finding, complaint, or other reason for the encounter, with or without a diagnosis being established at the time of the encounter." The *nature of the presenting problem* is considered when determining the number of diagnoses or management options for medical decision making complexity.

Five types of presenting problems are recognized:

- Minimal (problem may not require the presence of the physician, but service is provided under the physician's supervision, such as a patient who comes to the office once a week to have blood pressure taken and recorded).

- Self-limited or minor (problem that runs a definite and prescribed course, is transient in nature, and is not likely to permanently alter health status or that has a good prognosis with management/compliance, such as a patient diagnosed with adult-onset diabetes mellitus controlled by diet and exercise).

- Low severity (problem where the risk of morbidity without treatment is low; there is little to no risk of mortality without treatment; full recovery without functional impairment is expected, such as a patient who is diagnosed with eczema and who does not respond to over-the-counter medications).

- Moderate severity (problem where the risk of morbidity without treatment is moderate; there is moderate risk of mortality without treatment; uncertain prognosis; increased probability of prolonged functional impairment, such as a 35-year-old male patient diagnosed with chest pain on exertion).

- High severity (problem where the risk of morbidity without treatment is high to extreme; there is a moderate to high risk of mortality without treatment; high probability of severe, prolonged functional impairment, such as an infant hospitalized with a diagnosis of respiratory syncytial virus).

Time (Face-to-Face versus Unit/Floor)

Face-to-face time is the amount of time the office or outpatient care provider spends with the patient and/or family. Unit/floor time is the amount of time the provider spends at the patient's bedside and at management of the patient's care on the unit or floor (e.g., writing orders for diagnostic tests or reviewing test results). Unit/floor time applies to inpatient hospital care, hospital observation care, initial and follow-up inpatient hospital consultations, and nursing facility services.

As mentioned previously, although the key components of history, examination, and medical decision making usually determine the E/M code, visits consisting predominantly of counseling and/or coordination of care are the exception. When the physician spends more than 50 percent of the encounter providing counseling and/or coordination of care, it is considered dominant and can be considered a key factor in selecting a particular E/M code. The extent of counseling must be documented in the patient's chart to support the E/M code selected.

EXAMPLE: Anne Sider is seen by Dr. Cyrix in the office for her three-month check-up. (She has chronic hypertension controlled by diet and exercise.) During the visit, Dr. Cyrix notes that the patient seems distracted and stressed, and he asks her about these symptoms. Anne starts to cry and spends ten minutes telling Dr. Cyrix that her "life is falling apart" and that she wakes up in the middle of the night with a pounding heart, feeling as though she's going to die. Dr. Cyrix spends the next 45 minutes (of the 70-minute visit) counseling Anne about these symptoms. He determines that Anne is suffering from panic attacks, so he prescribes a medication and contacts ABC Counseling Associates to arrange an appointment for mental health counseling. In this example, a routine three-month check-up (for which code 99212 or 99213 would be selected) evolves into a higher-level service (for which code 99215 can be reported). The provider must carefully document all aspects of this visit, which includes the recheck for hypertension, provision of counseling, coordination of care provided, and length of time spent face-to-face with the patient. (The coder should report an ICD-9-CM disease code from subcategory V65.4, in addition to the hypertension disease code, when counseling and/or coordination of care dominates the patient encounter *and is documented by the provider.*)

To properly bill an E/M level of service for an encounter based on time, the provider must provide counseling and/or coordination of care *in the presence of the patient* and document the following:

- Total length of time of the encounter.
- Length of time spent coordinating care and/or counseling patient.
- Issues discussed.
- Relevant history, exam, and medical decision making (if performed).

Evaluation and Management Subsections

The E/M section (99201–99499) contains notes unique to each category and subcategory (Table 7-2). *Remember to review notes before assigning an E/M code.* (For a complete list of categories and subcategories, refer to Table 1, Categories and Subcategories of Service, in the E/M Services Guidelines of your CPT coding manual.) (CPT refers to E/M subsections and categories as categories and subcategories, respectively.)

> **EXAMPLE:** Lucy Moreno is a 45-year-old established female patient who was seen in the office on April 22 for problem focused history and examination as follow-up for her diagnosis of lower back pain. Patient states that she is having great difficulty managing her pain, and she says that she realizes part of the problem is that she needs to lose 50 pounds. A variety of weight-loss management options was discussed with the patient, including an appropriate exercise program; and she is scheduled to return in one month for recheck. Today's visit was 30 minutes in length, more than half of which was spent discussing weight loss management. Report code 99214.

TABLE 7-2   Evaluation and management subsections (categories)

SUBSECTION (CATEGORY)	DESCRIPTION
Office or Other Outpatient Services	E/M services provided in a physician's office, a hospital outpatient department, or another ambulatory care facility (e.g., standalone ambulatory care center). Before assigning an E/M level of service code from this category, make sure you apply the definition of *new* and *established* patient.
	NOTE: Code 99211 is commonly thought of as a "nurse visit" because it is typically reported when ancillary personnel provide E/M services. However, the code can be reported when the E/M service is rendered by any other provider (e.g., nurse practitioner, physician assistant, or physician).
	· CMS "incident to" guidelines apply when the 99211 E/M level of service is provided by ancillary personnel in the office. The guidelines state that the physician must be physically present in the suite of offices when the service is provided.
	· Documentation of a 99211 level of service includes a chief complaint and a description of the service provided. Because the presenting problem is considered of minimal severity, documentation of a history and examination is not required.
	· When prescription drug management services are provided during an office visit, report a minimum level 3 E/M code. Reporting a level 1 or 2 E/M code is considered under-coding.
Hospital Observation Services	**Observation services** are furnished in a hospital outpatient setting, and the patient is considered an outpatient. Services include use of a bed and at least periodic monitoring by a hospital's nursing or other staff that is reasonable and necessary to evaluate an outpatient's condition or determine the need for possible admission to the hospital as an inpatient. Observation services are reimbursed only when ordered by a physician (or another individual authorized by state licensure law and hospital staff bylaws to admit patients to the hospital or to order outpatient tests). Medicare requires the physician to order an inpatient admission if the duration of observation care is expected to be 48 hours or more. (Other payers require an inpatient admission order if the duration of observation care is expected to be 24 hours or more.) Subcategories include: ● Observation care discharge services ● Initial observation care

(continues)

TABLE 7-2   (continued)

SUBSECTION (CATEGORY)	DESCRIPTION
Hospital Inpatient Services	E/M services provided to hospital inpatients, including partial hospitalization services; they are indicated when the patient's condition requires services and/or procedures that cannot be performed in any other POS without putting the patient at risk. Subcategories include: ● **Initial hospital care** (covers first inpatient encounter) ● **Subsequent hospital care** (includes review of chart for changes in patient's condition, results of diagnostic studies, and/or reassessment of patient's condition since performance of last assessment) ● **Observation or inpatient care services** (assigned only if the patient is admitted to and discharged from observation/inpatient status on the same day) ● **Hospital discharge services** (include final examination of the patient, discussion of hospital stay with patient/caregiver, instructions for continued care, and preparation of discharge records, prescriptions, and referral forms) **NOTE:** A *hospital inpatient* is someone who is admitted and discharged and has a length of stay (LOS) of one or more days. **Partial hospitalization** is a short term, intensive treatment program where individuals who are experiencing an acute episode of an illness (e.g., geriatric, psychiatric, or rehabilitative) can receive medically supervised treatment during a significant number of daytime or nighttime hours. This type of program is an alternative to 24-hour inpatient hospitalization and allows the patients to maintain their everyday life without the disruption associated with an inpatient hospital stay.
Consultations	A **consultation** is an examination of a patient by a healthcare provider, usually a specialist, for the purpose of advising the referring or attending physician in the evaluation and/or management of a specific problem with a known diagnosis. Consultants may initiate diagnostic and/or therapeutic services as necessary during the consultation. **CODING TIP:** Do not confuse a *consultation* with a **referral**, which occurs when a patient reports that another provider "referred" the patient to the provider. Because the referring provider did not schedule the appointment or document a request for the referral, a referral is *not* a consultation. **Preoperative clearance** occurs when a surgeon requests a specialist or other physician (e.g., general practitioner) to examine a patient and provide an opinion about whether the patient can withstand the expected risks of a specific surgery. If the referring surgeon documents a written request for preoperative clearance, this service is considered a consultation, even when provided by the patient's primary care physician. **NOTE:** In 2010, CMS and the federal Office of Workers' Compensation Board eliminated reporting of CPT consultation codes. Providers are required to report codes from the "Office or Other Outpatient Services" or "Inpatient Hospital Services" subsections of CPT. For the hospital inpatient setting, the admitting or attending physician will attach modifier -A1 (Principal Physician of Record) to the initial visit code. This will distinguish the admitting or attending physician's service from those who provide consultation services. The OIG reported that most consultation services reported to Medicare in 2001 were inappropriate, and subsequent education efforts to improve reporting failed to produce desired results. Other third-party payers will likely adopt the elimination of CPT's consultation codes. It is unknown whether the AMA will eliminate the "Consultations" subsection from a future revision of CPT. **EXAMPLE:** On May 1, Mary Smith is seen in the hospital's emergency department (ED) and receives level 4 evaluation and management services from Dr. Axel (ED physician) for complaints of severe shortness of breath, chest pain radiating down the left arm, back pain, and extreme anxiety. The patient is admitted to the hospital, and Dr. Rodney (attending physician) provides level 3 initial hospital care. Dr. Axel reports code 99284, and Dr. Rodney reports code 92222-A1.

(continues)

TABLE 7-2 (continued)

SUBSECTION (CATEGORY)	DESCRIPTION
Emergency Department Services	**Emergency department services** are provided in a hospital, which is open 24 hours for the purpose of providing unscheduled episodic services to patients who require immediate medical attention. • While ED physicians employed by the facility usually provide ED services, any physician who provides services to a patient registered in the ED may report the ED services codes. The physician does not have to be assigned to the hospital's ED. • When services provided in the ED are determined not to be an actual emergency, ED services codes (99281-99288) are still reportable if ED services were provided. Typically, the hospital reports a lower level ED services code for nonemergency conditions. • If a physician provides emergency services to a patient in the office, it is *not* appropriate to assign codes from the Emergency Department Services category of E/M. If the patient's primary care provider asks the patient to meet him in the hospital's ED as an alternative to the physician's office and the patient is not registered as a patient in the ED, the physician should report a code from the Office or Other Outpatient Services category of E/M. ED services codes are reported only if the patient receives services in the hospital's ED. **NOTE:** Instead of developing national emergency department coding guidelines, CMS instructed hospitals to develop internal guidelines for reporting emergency department E/M visits. The guidelines must reflect hospital resources (not physician resources) used in providing the service. CMS reviews hospital claims to evaluate patterns associated with reporting different levels of emergency department E/M codes to: · Verify appropriate billing of Medicare services. · Ensure that hospitals follow their own internally developed guidelines. **NOTE:** · A medical emergency is the sudden and unexpected onset of a medical condition, or the acute exacerbation of a chronic condition that is threatening to life, limb, or sight and that requires immediate medical treatment or that manifests painful symptomatology requiring immediate palliative effort to relieve suffering. · A maternity emergency is a sudden unexpected medical complication that puts the mother or fetus at risk. · A psychiatric inpatient admission is an emergency situation in which, based on a psychiatric evaluation performed by a physician (or another qualified mental healthcare professional with hospital admission authority), the patient is at immediate risk of serious harm to self or others as a result of a mental disorder, and requires immediate continuous skilled observation at the acute level of care. **CODING TIP:** Code 99288 (Other Emergency Services) is reported when the physician is in two-way communication contact with ambulance or rescue crew personnel located outside the hospital.
Critical Care Services	*Critical care* is the direct delivery of medical care by a physician to a patient who is critically ill or injured. **Critical care services** are reported when a physician directly delivers medical care for a critically ill or critically injured patient. Critical care services can be provided on multiple days even if no changes are made to the treatment rendered to the patient, as long as the patient's condition requires the direct delivery of critical care services by the provider. *The provider should document the total time spent delivering critical care services.* **NOTE:** It is not necessary for a patient to be admitted to a critical care unit or an intensive care unit to receive critical care services. Patients can receive critical care services in the hospital emergency department, medical/surgical unit, and so on.

(continues)

TABLE 7-2 (continued)

SUBSECTION (CATEGORY)	DESCRIPTION
Critical Care Services (continued)	**EXAMPLE:** Dr. Smith delivers critical care services to his patient on June 15th from 8:00 to 9:00 a.m., 10:30 to 10:45 a.m., and 3:00 to 3:45 p.m. To assign codes to this case, total the minutes of critical care services directly delivered by the provider. (Refer to the table located in the CPT coding manual's Critical Care Services category to select the codes.) Report codes 99291 and 99292 x 2. **CODING TIP:** When critical care service codes are reported in addition to another E/M service code (e.g., ED care and initial hospital care), add modifier -25 to the E/M service code to report it as a separately identified service provided to the patient. Remember! Critical care services are reported based on the total time the physician spends in constant attendance, and the time need not be continuous.
Nursing Facility Services	**Nursing facility services** are provided at a nursing facility (NF), skilled nursing facility (SNF), intermediate care facility/mentally handicapped (ICF), long-term care facility (LTCF), or psychiatric residential treatment facility. NFs provide convalescent, rehabilitative, or long-term care for patients. A comprehensive assessment must be completed on each patient upon admission, and then annually (unless the patient's condition requires more frequent assessments). Subcategories include: • Initial nursing facility care • Subsequent nursing facility care • Nursing facility discharge services • Other nursing facility services **NOTE:** The **comprehensive assessment** documents the patient's functional capacity, identification of potential problems, and nursing plan to enhance (or at least maintain) the patient's physical and psychosocial functions. The assessments are written when the patient is admitted or readmitted to the facility or when a reassessment is necessary because of a substantial change in the patient's status. The nursing facility assessment code (99318) is reported when the nursing facility patient's attending physician conducts an annual assessment.
Domiciliary, Rest Home, or Custodial Care Services	Provided to residents of a facility that offers room, board, and other personal assistance services, usually on a long-term basis. Medical services (e.g., 24-hour nursing care) are *not* provided to residents.
Domiciliary, Rest Home (e.g., Assisted Living Facility), or Home Care Plan Oversight Services	**Care plan oversight services** cover the physician's time supervising a complex and multidisciplinary care treatment program for a specific patient who is under the care of a domiciliary or rest home, or who resides at home.
Home Services	**Home services** provided to individuals in their place of residence to promote, maintain, or restore health and/or to minimize the effects of disability and illness, including terminal illness.
Prolonged Services	Physicians' services involving patient contact that are considered beyond the usual service in either an inpatient or outpatient setting may be reported as **prolonged services**. Subcategories include: • Prolonged physician service with direct (face-to-face) patient content (**direct patient contact** refers to face-to-face patient contact on an inpatient or outpatient basis, and these codes are reported in addition to other E/M services provided). • Prolonged physician service without direct (face-to-face) patient contact (**without direct patient contact** refers to *non*-face-to-face time spent by the physician on an inpatient or outpatient basis *and occurring before and/or after direct patient care*)

(continues)

TABLE 7-2   (continued)

SUBSECTION (CATEGORY)	DESCRIPTION
	Physician standby services cover physicians who spend prolonged periods of time without direct patient contact, until physician's services are required.
Case Management Services	**Case management services** include "processes in which a physician is responsible for direct care of a patient, and for coordinating and controlling access to or initiating and/or supervising other health-care services needed by the patient." Subcategories include: ● Team conferences ● Anticoagulant management
Care Plan Oversight Services	Cover the physician's time supervising a complex and multidisciplinary care treatment program for a specific patient who is under the care of a home health agency, hospice, or nursing facility. These codes are classified separately from other E/M codes when the physician is involved in direct patient examinations. The billing covers a 30-day period, and only one physician in a group practice may bill for this service in any given 30-day period.
Preventive Medicine Services	**Preventive medicine services** include routine examinations or risk management counseling for children and adults who exhibit no overt signs or symptoms of a disorder while presenting to the medical office for a preventive medical physical. Such services are also called wellness visits. Discussion of risk factors such as diet and exercise counseling, family problems, substance abuse counseling, and injury prevention are an integral part of preventive medicine. Care must be taken to select the proper code according to the age of the patient and the patient's status (new or established). Subcategories include: ● New patient ● Established patient ● Counseling and/or risk factor reduction intervention ● Preventive medicine, individual counseling ● Preventive medicine, group counseling ● Other preventive medicine services
Non-Face-to-Face Physician Services	Non-face-to-face physician services include telephone services and online medical evaluation.
Special Evaluation and Management Services	Provided for establishment of baseline information prior to life or disability insurance certificates being issued and for examination of a patient with a work-related or medical disability problem. During special evaluation and management services, the examining provider does *not* assume active management of the patient's health problems.
Newborn Care Services	**Newborn care** includes services provided to newborns in a variety of healthcare settings (e.g., hospital, birthing center, and home birth).
Inpatient Neonatal Intensive Care Services and Pediatric and Neonatal Critical Care Services	Provided to critically ill neonates and infants by a physician. A neonate is a newborn, up to 28 days old. An infant is a very young child, up to one year old. (The same definitions for critical care services codes apply to adult, child, and neonate.) Subcategories include: ● Inpatient pediatric critical care ● Inpatient neonatal critical care ● Continuing intensive care services Pediatric patient transport includes the physical attendance and direct face-to-face care provided by a physician during the interfacility transport of a critically ill or critically injured patient, aged 24 months or less.
Other Evaluation and Management Services	Code 99499 is assigned when the E/M service provided is not described in any other listed E/M codes. The use of modifiers with this code is not appropriate. In addition, a special report must be submitted with the CMS-1500 claim.

EXERCISE 7-5

Evaluation and Management Section

Instructions: Review each statement, and use your CPT coding manual to assign the appropriate level-of-service E/M code.

1. Home visit, problem focused, established patient _____

2. ED service, new patient, low complexity _____

3. Hospital care, new patient, initial, high complexity _____

4. Hospital care, subsequent, detailed _____

5. ED care, problem focused, counseling 15 minutes _____

6. Patient requested consultation, new patient, moderate complexity _____

7. Office consultation, high complexity, established patient _____

8. Follow-up consultation, office, problem focused, counseling 15 minutes, encounter was 25 minutes _____

9. Follow-up consultation, inpatient, detailed, 35 minutes _____

10. Blood pressure check by nurse (established patient) _____

11. New patient, routine preventive medicine, age 11. Risk factor discussion, 20 minutes. _____

12. Critical care, 1.5 hours _____

13. Nursing facility visit, subsequent visit, expanded problem focused H&PE _____

14. Medical team conference, 50 minutes, nurse practitioner and discharge planner _____

15. Follow-up visit, ICU patient, stable, expanded problem focused H&PE _____

16. Resuscitation of newborn in delivery room _____

17. Telephone E/M service by physician to established patient, 10 minutes _____

18. Custodial care, established patient, detailed H&PE, high complexity _____

19. Pediatrician on standby, high-risk birth, 65 minutes _____

20. Heart risk factor education, group counseling, asymptomatic attendees, 65 minutes _____

ANESTHESIA SECTION

Anesthesia services are associated with the administration of analgesia and/or anesthesia as provided by an anesthesiologist (physician) or certified registered nurse anesthetist (CRNA). Services include the administration of local, regional, epidural, general anesthesia, monitored anesthesia care (MAC), and/or the administration of anxiolytics (drug that relieves anxiety) or amnesia-inducing medications. The patient's physiological parameters are also monitored during the administration of local or peripheral block anesthesia with sedation (when medically necessary), and other supportive services are provided when the anesthesiologist deems them necessary during any procedure.

Anesthesia care requires the preoperative evaluation of a patient, which includes documenting the history and physical examination to minimize the risk of adverse reactions, planning alternative approaches to administering anesthesia, and answering all questions asked by the patient about the anesthesia procedure. The anesthesiologist or CRNA is responsible for the patient's post-anesthesia recovery period until patient care is assumed by the surgeon or another physician; this occurs when the patient is discharged from the post-anesthesia recovery area.

> **NOTE: Monitored anesthesia care (MAC)** is the provision of local or regional anesthetic services with certain conscious altering drugs when provided by a physician, anesthesiologist, or medically-directed CRNA. MAC involves sufficiently monitoring the patient to anticipate the potential need for administration of general anesthesia, and it requires continuous evaluation of vital physiologic functions as well as recognition and treatment of adverse changes.

Assigning Anesthesia Codes

Anesthesia codes describe a general anatomic area or service that is associated with a number of surgical procedures, often from multiple CPT sections.

- Codes 00100–01860 are reported for anesthesia services administered during surgical interventions.
- Codes 01905–01933 are reported when anesthesia is administered during interventional radiology.
- CPT codes 01990–01999 are reported for miscellaneous anesthesia services.

A one-to-one correspondence for Anesthesia to Surgery codes does not exist, and one anesthesia code is often reported for many different surgical procedures that share similar anesthesia requirements. Anesthesia section guidelines also include four codes (99100-99140) that are located in the Medicine section, which are used to report qualifying circumstances for anesthesia.

Qualifying Circumstances for Anesthesia

When anesthesia services are provided during situations or circumstances that make anesthesia administration more difficult, report a qualifying circumstances code from the CPT Medicine section (in addition to the anesthesia code). Difficult circumstances depend on factors such as extraordinary condition of patient, notable operative conditions, or unusual risk factors. These code(s) are reported in addition to the anesthesia code(s). Qualifying circumstances codes include:

- 99100 (Anesthesia for patient of extreme age, under one year and over 70).
- 99116 (Anesthesia complicated by utilization of total body hypothermia).
- 99135 (Anesthesia complicated by utilization of controlled hypotension).
- 99140 (Anesthesia complicated by emergency conditions [specify]). (An *emergency condition* results when a delay in treatment of the patient would lead to a significant increase in threat to life or body part.)

> **EXAMPLE:** A 92-year-old female patient received general anesthesia services from a CRNA, who was monitored by an anesthesiologist, during total left hip arthroplasty. Report codes 01214-P2-QX and 99100.

Anesthesia Modifiers

All anesthesia services require the following types of modifiers to be reviewed for assignment with reported anesthesia codes:

- Physical status modifiers
- HCPCS level II modifiers
- CPT modifiers

Physical Status Modifiers

A physical status modifier is added to each reported anesthesia code to indicate the patient's condition at the time anesthesia was administered. The modifier also serves to identify the complexity of services provided. (The physical status modifier is determined by the anesthesiologist or CRNA and is documented as such in the patient record). Physical status modifiers are represented by the letter "P" followed by a single digit, from 1 to 6, as indicated below:

- -P1 (normal healthy patient; e.g., no biochemical, organic, physiologic, psychiatric disturbance).
- -P2 (patient with mild systemic disease; e.g., anemia, chronic asthma, chronic bronchitis, diabetes mellitus, essential hypertension, heart disease that only slightly limits physical activity, obesity).
- -P3 (patient with moderate systemic disease; e.g., angina pectoris, chronic pulmonary disease that limits activity, history of prior myocardial infarction, heart disease that limits activity, poorly controlled essential hypertension, morbid obesity; diabetes mellitus, type I and/or with vascular complications).
- -P4 (patient with severe systemic disease that is a constant threat to life; e.g., advanced pulmonary/renal/hepatic dysfunction, congestive heart failure, persistent angina pectoris, unstable/rest angina).
- -P5 (moribund patient who is not expected to survive without the operation; e.g., abdominal aortic aneurysm).
- -P6 (declared brain-dead patient whose organs are being removed for donor purposes).

> **EXAMPLE:** An anesthesiologist provided general anesthesia services to a 65-year-old male with mild systemic disease who underwent total knee replacement. Report code 01402-P2.

HCPCS Level II Anesthesia Modifiers

When applicable, the following HCPCS level II modifiers are added to reported anesthesia codes:

- -AA (anesthesia services performed personally by anesthesiologist).
- -AD (medically supervised by a physician for more than 4 concurrent procedures).
- -G8 (monitored anesthesia care (MAC) for deep complex, complicated, or markedly invasive surgical procedure).
- -G9 (monitored anesthesia care (MAC) for patient who has history of severe cardiopulmonary condition).
- -QK (medical direction of 2, 3, or 4 concurrent anesthetic procedures involving qualified individuals).

NOTE: Report modifier -G8 with CPT codes 00100, 00400, 00160, 00300, 00532, 00920 only. Do not report modifier -G8 modifier with modifier -QS.

- -QS (monitored anesthesia care service).
- -QX (CRNA service, with medical direction by physician).
- -QY (medical direction of one Certified Registered Nurse Anesthetist (CRNA) by an anesthesiologist).
- -QZ (CRNA service, without medical direction by physician).

> **EXAMPLE:** A CRNA provided general anesthesia services to an otherwise healthy patient who underwent a vaginal hysterectomy due to uterine fibroids. The CRNA received medical direction from an anesthesiologist. Report code 00944-P1-QX.

CPT Modifiers

The following CPT modifiers should be reviewed to determine whether they should be added to the reported anesthesia codes:

- -23 (unusual anesthesia) (When a patient's circumstances warrant the administration of general or regional anesthesia instead of the usual local anesthesia, add modifier -23 to the anesthesia code [e.g., extremely apprehensive patients, mentally handicapped individuals, patients who have a physical condition, such as spasticity or tremors]).
- -53 (discontinued procedure).
- -59 (distinct procedural service).
- -74 (discontinued outpatient hospital/ambulatory surgery center procedure after anesthesia administration).
- -99 (multiple modifiers).

> **EXAMPLE:** An anesthesiologist provided general anesthesia services to a 49-year-old male patient with chronic obstructive pulmonary disease who underwent extracorporeal shock wave lithotripsy, with water bath. The patient was extremely anxious about the procedure, which normally does not require general anesthesia. Report code 00872-P2-23-AA.

Anesthesia Time Units

NOTE: Anesthesia time is calculated as the continuous actual presence of the anesthesiologist or CRNA during the administration of anesthesia. Anesthesia time begins when the anesthesiologist or CRNA begins to prepare the patient for anesthesia care in the operating room or equivalent area and ends when the anesthesiologist or CRNA is no longer in personal attendance.

When reporting Anesthesia codes, be sure to report the time units in Block 24G of the CMS-1500. (An *anesthesia time unit* is one 15-minute increment.) Reimbursement for anesthesia services is based on the reported time units, which represents the continuous actual presence of the anesthesiologist or CRNA during the administration of anesthesia. Anesthesia time starts when the anesthesiologist or CRNA begins to prepare the patient for anesthesia care in the operating room or equivalent area (e.g., patient's room) and ends when the anesthesiologist or CRNA is no longer in personal attendance (e.g., patient is released for postoperative supervision by the surgeon).

When calculating anesthesia time units, do *not* include:

- Examination and evaluation of the patient by the anesthesiologist or CRNA prior to administration of anesthesia (e.g., reviewing patient records prior to the administration of anesthesia). (If surgery is canceled, report an appropriate code from the CPT evaluation and management section. Usually, a consultation code is reported.)
- Non-monitored interval time (e.g., period of time when patient does not require monitored anesthesia care, period of time during which anesthesiologist or CRNA leaves operating room to assist with another procedure).

- Recovery room time. (The anesthesiologist or CRNA is responsible for monitoring the patient in the recovery room as part of the anesthesia service provided.)
- Routine postoperative evaluation by the anesthesiologist or CRNA. (When postoperative evaluation and management services are significant, separately identifiable services, such as postoperative pain management services or extensive unrelated ventilator management, report an appropriate code from the CPT evaluation and management section. In addition, the management of epidural or subarachnoid medication administration is reported with CPT code 01996 because it is separately payable on dates of service subsequent to surgery *but not on the date of surgery.*)

EXAMPLE: A patient undergoes cataract extraction surgery, which requires monitored anesthesia care by the CRNA. At 9:45 a.m., the CRNA administered a sedative and then performed a retrobulbar injection to administer regional block anesthesia. From 10:00 a.m. until 10:30 a.m., the patient did not require monitored anesthesia care. The CRNA began monitored anesthesia care again at 10:30 a.m. during the cataract extraction procedure, and monitored anesthesia care ended at 10:45 a.m. The patient was released from the recovery room to the surgeon for postoperative care at 11:30 a.m.

Carefully read the procedure outlined in the operative report. Sometimes the discriminating factor between one code and another will be the surgical approach or type of procedure documented.

The total time calculated for monitored anesthesia care is 30 minutes, or 2 time units. (Total time calculated does not include the 30 minutes of non-monitored interval time [9:00–9:30 a.m.] and the 45 minutes of recovery room time [10:00–10:45 a.m.]).

EXERCISE 7-6

Anesthesia Section

Instructions: Review each statement, and use your CPT coding manual to assign the appropriate Anesthesia code, including CPT and HCPCS level II modifiers.

1. Anesthesiologist provided anesthesia services to a 77-year-old female patient who received a corneal transplant. The patient has a history of prior stroke.

    _____

2. Anesthesiologist provided anesthesia services to a 50-year-old diabetic patient who underwent direct coronary artery bypass grafting.

    _____

3. Anesthesiologist provided anesthesia services for hernia repair in the lower abdomen of an otherwise healthy 9-month-old infant.

    _____

4. CRNA provided anesthesia services under physician direction during an extensive procedure on the cervical spine of an otherwise healthy patient.

    _____

5. CRNA provided anesthesia services to a morbidly obese female patient who underwent repair of malunion, humerus.

    _____

SURGERY SECTION

The surgery section contains subsections that are organized by body system. Each subsection is subdivided into categories by specific organ or anatomic site. Some categories are further subdivided by procedure subcategories in the following order:

- Incision
- Excision
- Introduction or Removal
- Repair, Endoscopy
- Revision or Reconstruction
- Destruction
- Grafts
- Suture
- Other procedures

To code surgeries properly, three questions must be asked:

1. What body system was involved?

2. What anatomic site was involved?

3. What type of procedure was performed?

Carefully read the procedure outlined in the operative report. Sometimes the discriminating factor between one code and another will be the surgical approach or type of procedure documented.

EXAMPLE 1: Surgical approach

57540	Excision of cervical stump, abdominal approach;
57545	with pelvic floor repair
57550	Excision of cervical stump, vaginal approach;
57556	with repair of enterocele

When reporting the code number for the excision of cervical stump, code 57540 would be reported for an abdominal approach, and code 57550 would be reported for a vaginal approach.

EXAMPLE 2: Type of procedure

11600	Excision, malignant lesion including margins, trunk, arms, or legs; excised diameter 0.5 cm or less
17260	Destruction, malignant lesion (eg, laser surgery, electro-surgery, cryosurgery, chemosurgery, surgical curettement), trunk, arms, or legs; lesion diameter 0.5 cm or less

When reporting the code for removal of a 0.5 cm malignant lesion of the arm, code 11600 would be reported for a surgical excision, and code 17260 would be reported for a destruction procedure (e.g., laser ablation).

Surgical Package

The **surgical package** (or **global surgery**) includes a variety of services provided by a surgeon (Figure 7-9), including:

- Surgical procedure performed.
- Local infiltration, metacarpal/metatarsal/digital block, or topical anesthesia.
- One related Evaluation and Management (E/M) encounter on the date immediately prior to *or* on the date of the procedure (including history and physical).
- Immediate postoperative care, including dictating operative notes, talking with family and other physicians, writing postoperative orders, and evaluating the patient in the postanesthesia recovery area.
- Typical postoperative follow-up care, including pain management, suture removal, dressing changes, local incisional care, removal of operative packs/cutaneous sutures/staples/lines/wires/tubes/drains/casts/splints (however, casting supplies can usually be billed separately).

The **global period** is the number of days associated with the surgical package (or global surgery) and is designated by the payer as 0, 10, or 90 days. During the global period, all postoperative services are included in the procedure code; postoperative services (except services provided to treat complications) cannot be separately reported and billed. (Obtain global period information from each payer.) The following designations are also associated with the surgical package:

- MMM (global period policy does not apply).
- XXX (global period policy does not apply).
- YYY (payer-determined global period).
- ZZZ (procedure/service is related to another service; falls within the global period of another service).

> **NOTE:** The surgical package does *not* apply to treatment of patients for surgical complications. Procedures and/or services provided to treat complications are reported in addition to the surgical package CPT code.

When different physicians in a same-specialty group practice participate in the pre- and postoperative care of a patient, the physician who performs the surgery reports the CPT code, patient care is shared by the physicians, and reimbursement is distributed within the group. Do *not* bill separately for services included in the global package, even though a different physician in a same-specialty group practice provides the service.

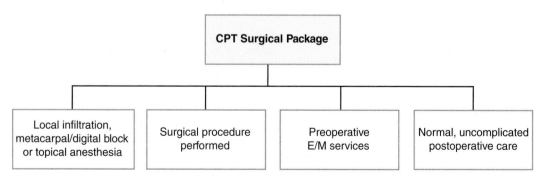

FIGURE 7-9 Components of the surgical package (Courtesy Delmar/Cengage Learning.)

Coders must be aware that *unbundling* is not allowed; unbundling means assigning multiple codes to procedures/services when just one comprehensive code *should be* reported. Examples of procedures that are bundled (included) with the surgical package code include:

- Local infiltration of medication.
- Closure of surgically created wounds.
- Minor debridement.
- Exploration of operative area.
- Fulguration of bleeding points.
- Application of dressings.
- Application of splints with musculoskeletal procedures.

Read the descriptions of surgical procedures carefully, and remember that the main clause—the narrative to the left of the semicolon (;)—of an indented surgical description is stated only once in a series of related intraoperative procedures. The complexity of the related intraoperative procedures increases as you proceed through the listings of indented code descriptions. *Always report the comprehensive code rather than codes for individual components of a surgery.*

EXAMPLE:

35001	Direct repair of aneurysm, pseudoaneurysm, or excision (partial or total) and graft insertion, with or without patch graft; for aneurysm and associated occlusive disease, carotid, subclavian artery, by neck incision
35002	for ruptured aneurysm, carotid, subclavian artery, by neck incision
35005	for aneurysm, pseudoaneurysm, and associated occlusive disease, vertebral artery
35011	for aneurysm and associated occlusive disease, axillary-brachial artery, by arm incision
35013	for ruptured aneurysm, axillary-brachial artery, by arm incision

Only one code from this series of five codes is assigned *if the procedures performed and reported were rendered during the same operative session.* Note the increasing complexity of procedures as code numbers increase within a series.

Exceptions to reporting one combination code occur either when the code number is marked by a **+** symbol (add-on code) or when a parenthetical note indicates that a code should be reported in addition to the primary code. The following statements appear in CPT code descriptions or as parenthetical notes when it is appropriate to report additional codes:

- List separately in addition to code for primary procedure.
- Use . . . in conjunction with. . .
- Each additional. . .
- Each separate/additional. . .

EXERCISE 7-7

Working with the Surgical Package

Instructions: Review each statement, and use your CPT coding manual to assign the appropriate Surgery code.

1. Incision and drainage (I&D), finger abscess   _____

2. Percutaneous I&D, abscess, appendix   _____

3. Therapeutic agent injection, L-5 paravertebral nerve, with image guidance   _____

4. Laparoscopic cholecystectomy with cholangiography   _____

5. Flexible esophagoscopy with removal of foreign body and radiologic supervision and interpretation (S&I)   _____

Separate Procedure

The parenthetical note, **separate procedure**, follows a code description identifying procedures that are an integral part of another procedure or service. In addition, a *separate procedure* code is reported if the procedure or service is performed independently of the comprehensive procedure or service or is unrelated to or distinct from another procedure or service performed at the same time. The *separate procedure* code is *not* reported if the procedure or service performed is included in the description of another reported code.

EXAMPLE: The patient undergoes only a cystourethroscopy (passage of an endoscope through the urethra to visualize the urinary bladder). CPT codes for cystourethroscopy include:

52000	Cystourethroscopy (separate procedure)
52001	Cystourethroscopy, with irrigation and evacuation of multiple obstructing clots
52005	Cystourethroscopy, with ureteral catheterization, with or without irrigation, instillation, or ureteropyelography, exclusive of radiologic service;
52007	with brush biopsy of ureter and/or renal pelvis
52010	Cystourethroscopy, with ejaculatory duct catheterization, with or without irrigation, instillation, or duct radiography, exclusive of radiologic service

Report code 52000, because only the cystourethroscopy was performed. A code from 52001–52010 would be reported *only* if the operative report documented additional procedures that were included in the code description.

The placement of the phrase "separate procedure" is critical to correct coding. When it appears after the semicolon, it applies to that specific code.

EXAMPLE:

38100	Splenectomy; total (separate procedure)

The phrase that appears to the left of the semicolon applies to all indented code descriptions.

> **EXAMPLE:**
>
> 32601   Thoracoscopy, diagnostic (separate procedure); lungs and pleural space, without biopsy
>
> 32602   lungs and pleural space, with biopsy

Multiple Surgical Procedures

Great care must be taken when billing multiple surgical procedures (two or more surgeries performed during the same operative session). The major surgical procedure (the procedure reimbursed at the highest level) should be reported first on the claim, and the lesser surgeries listed on the claim in descending order of expense. Modifier -51 is added to the CPT number for each lesser surgical procedure that does not have the symbol X or + in front of the code. (Appendix E in the CPT coding manual provides a complete list of modifier -51 exemptions.)

The ranking into major and minor procedures is done to accommodate the fact that most insurance companies will reduce the fee for the second surgery by 50 percent of the regular fee and for the third, fourth, and so on, by 50 to 75 percent. If a lesser procedure is listed first, it may be paid at 100 percent and the major or most expensive surgery reduced by 50 to 75 percent, resulting in a lower payment for the combined surgeries. Insurance companies reason that when multiple surgical procedures are performed during the same operative session, they share the same pre- and postoperative session; therefore, the fee is reduced because the pre- and postoperative portions are covered in the full payment for the major procedure.

> **BILLING TIP:**
>
> Computerized practices must be sure that *multiple surgeries performed during the same operative session are entered into the computer in the proper order* to ensure that they will print correctly on the computer-generated claim.

EXERCISE 7-8

Coding Separate and Multiple Procedures

Instructions: Review each statement, and use your CPT coding manual to assign the appropriate Surgery code.

1. Diagnostic arthroscopy, right wrist, with synovial biopsy   _____
2. Simple vaginal mucosal biopsy   _____
3. Diagnostic nasal endoscopy, bilateral, and facial chemical peel   _____
4. Diagnostic thoracoscopy, lungs and pleural space, with right lung biopsy   _____
5. Needle biopsy of testis   _____
6. Total abdominal hysterectomy with removal of ovaries and anterior colporrhaphy   _____
7. Laparoscopic appendectomy and lumbar hernia repair   _____
8. Biopsy of larynx (indirect) via laryngoscopy and laryngoplasty   _____
9. Excision of chest wall lesion with removal of ribs and plastic reconstruction   _____
10. Partial-thickness facial skin debridement and full-thickness leg skin debridement   _____

RADIOLOGY SECTION

The Radiology section includes subsections (Table 7-3) for diagnostic radiology (imaging), diagnostic ultrasound, radiation oncology, and nuclear medicine. These subsections are further subdivided into anatomic categories.

The number of **radiologic views** (studies taken from different angles) described in the report or on the charge slip determines the code selection for many diagnostic radiologic procedures. The term "complete" in the discussion of views is a reference to the number of views required for a full study of a designated body part. Carefully review code descriptions to understand how many views constitute a "complete study" for a specific type of radiologic procedure.

> **EXAMPLE:**
>
> 70120   Radiologic examination, mastoids; less than three views per side
>
> 70130   complete, minimum of three views per side

TABLE 7-3   Radiology subsections

SUBSECTION (CATEGORY)	DESCRIPTION
Diagnostic Radiology (Diagnostic Imaging)	Codes for noninvasive (noninterventional) and invasive (interventional) diagnostic and therapeutic procedures, in addition to CT, MRI, and magnetic resonance angiography (MRA). These diagnostic procedures can be as simple as a routine chest x-ray or as complex as a carotid angiography, which requires selective vascular catheterization. To code diagnostic radiology procedures accurately, identify the following: ● Anatomic site ● Type of procedure ● Number of views ● Laterality of the procedure (e.g., unilateral or bilateral) ● Use of contrast media **EXAMPLE 1:** Patient underwent complete x-ray of facial bones. Report code 70150. **EXAMPLE 2:** Patient underwent CT of the cervical spine. Report code 72125. (There is no mention of "contrast material" in this example.)
Diagnostic Ultrasound	Use of high-frequency sound waves (e.g., mechanical oscillations) to produce an image. Codes are organized according to anatomic site, and procedures are often performed as follow-up studies for inconclusive diagnostic radiology procedures, intraoperatively (e.g., during endoscopic procedures), and as guidance for biopsies, cyst localization, invasive procedures, paracentesis, pericardiocentesis, placement of radiation therapy fields, and thoracentesis. **EXAMPLE:** Patient underwent ultrasound of the spinal canal and contents. Report code 76800.
Radiologic Guidance	Performed during a procedure to visualize access to an anatomic site; contains four headings: fluoroscopic guidance, computed tomography guidance, magnetic resonance guidance, and other radiologic guidance. **EXAMPLE:** Patient underwent fluoroscopic guidance for needle placement prior to biopsy procedure. Report code 77002.

(continues)

TABLE 7-3   (continued)

SUBSECTION (CATEGORY)	DESCRIPTION
Breast Mammography	Radiological examination of the soft tissue and internal structures of the breast. Screening mammography is performed when a patient presents *without* signs and symptoms of breast disease (e.g., routine annual screening for early detection of unsuspected breast cancer). Diagnostic mammography includes an assessment of suspected disease (e.g., suspicious mass is palpated on physical examination) and is reported when an abnormality is found or suspected. **EXAMPLE:** Patient underwent bilateral screening mammography, which was reviewed and interpreted by the radiologist. Report code 77057.
Bone/Joint Studies	CPT codes 77071-77084 classify bone and joint studies. **EXAMPLE:** Female patient, age 51, underwent complete osseous survey. Report code 77075.
Radiation Oncology	Uses high-energy ionizing radiation to treat malignant neoplasms and certain nonmalignant conditions. Therapeutic modalities (methods) directed at malignant and benign lesions include brachytherapy, hyperthermia, stereotactic radiation, and teletherapy. **EXAMPLE:** Radiation oncologist provided intermediate therapeutic radiology treatment planning services to a 49-year-old male patient. Report code 77262.
Nuclear Medicine	Use of radioactive elements (e.g., radionuclides and radioisotopes) for diagnostic imaging (e.g., scan) and radiopharmaceutical therapy (destroys diseased tissue, such as a malignant neoplasm). The isotope emits gamma rays as it deteriorates, which enables the radiologist to visualize internal abnormalities (e.g., tumors). The images created by the contrast media (radioactive element) are detected by a gamma camera. Nuclear medicine codes do not include the provision of radium, which means that the nuclear medicine report must be reviewed to identify the diagnostic or therapeutic radiopharmaceutical provided. Then an appropriate HCPCS level II code is reported for the radiopharmaceutical administered. (The injection of the radionuclide is included as part of the procedure, and a separate injection code is not reported.) Common diagnostic nuclear medicine procedures include bone scans, cardiac scans (e.g., thallium scan and MUGA), renal scans, thyroid scans, and hepatobiliary scans (e.g., HIDA scans). Therapeutic nuclear medicine procedures are used to treat diseases such as chronic leukemia, hyperthyroidism, and thyroid cancer. **EXAMPLE:** Patient underwent particulate pulmonary perfusion imaging, which required venous injection of 10 mc of radioactive Technetium Tc-99m macroaggregated albumin. Report codes 78580, 36000, and A9540.

Complete Procedure

Do not confuse use of the term "complete" in the code description with its use in a parenthetical note. When the word "complete" is found in the code description, one code is reported to "completely" describe the procedure performed.

> **EXAMPLE:** For a clavicle x-ray, one code is reported (by the radiologist).
>
> **73000**   Radiologic examination; clavicle, complete

When the word "complete" is found in a parenthetical note below a code, it may be necessary to report more than one code to "completely" describe the procedure performed. In this case, when each component is performed by the same physician (e.g., radiologist), that physician reports all codes. However, when multiple physicians (e.g., radiologist and surgeon or other physician) perform each component of the procedure, each physician reports an appropriate code.

> **EXAMPLE:** For a cervical/thoracic myelography via cervical contrast injection procedure, two codes are reported to completely describe the procedure performed.
>
> - Code 72270 is reported for the myelography procedure with radiological supervision and interpretation.
> - The parenthetical note located below code 72270 indicates that codes 61055, 62284, and 72270 should be reviewed to determine whether additional code(s) need to be reported. Thus, code 61055 is reported for the cervical contrast injection procedure.
>
> **72270**   Myelography, two or more regions (eg, lumbar/thoracic, cervical/thoracic, lumbar/cervical, lumbar/thoracic/cervical), radiological supervision and interpretation
>
>   (For complete myelography of entire spinal canal, see 61055, 62284, 72270)
>
> **61055**   Cisternal or lateral cervical (C1-C2) puncture; with injection of medication or other substance for diagnosis or treatment (eg, C1-C2)
>
>   (For radiological supervision and interpretation, see Radiology)
>
> **62284**   Injection procedure for myelography and/or computed tomography, spinal (other than C1-C2 and posterior fossa)
>
>   (For injection procedure at C1-C2, see 61055)
>
>   (For radiological supervision and interpretation, see Radiology)

Professional versus Technical Component

Another consideration in radiology coding involves determining which physician is responsible for the professional and technical components of an examination.

- The professional component of a radiologic examination covers the supervision of the procedure and the interpretation and writing of a report describing the examination and its findings.
- The technical component of an examination covers the use of the equipment, supplies provided, and employment of the radiologic technicians.

When the examination takes place in a clinic or private office that owns the equipment, and professional services are performed by a physician employed by the clinic or private office, both professional and technical components are billed on the same claim. If, however, the equipment and supplies are owned by a hospital or other corporation and the radiologist performs only the professional component of the examination, two separate billings are generated: one by the physician for the professional component and one by the hospital for the technical component.

When two separate billings are required, the professional component is billed by adding the modifier -26 to the CPT code number. (HCPCS level II modifier -TC, Technical Component, is added to the Radiology code reported by the provider who performs the radiologic procedure.)

An exception to this rule is when the code description restricts the use of the code to "supervision and interpretation."

CODING TIP:

Report code 76140 when physician consultation is requested to review x-rays produced in another facility and the consultant generates a written report.

Special care must be taken when coding interventional diagnostic procedures that involve injection of contrast media, local anesthesia, or needle localization of a mass. CPT assigns two separate codes to these interventional procedures: a 70000 series Supervision and Interpretation code, and a Surgery code. This is done because these procedures may be performed by two physicians, each billing separately. If only one physician is involved, the claim should still include both codes.

EXAMPLE:

75710   Angiography, extremity, unilateral, radiologic supervision and interpretation

EXERCISE 7-9

Radiology Coding

Instructions: Review each statement, and use your CPT coding manual to assign the appropriate Radiology code.

1. GI series (x-ray), with small bowel and air studies, without KUB   _____

2. Chest x-ray, frontal & left lateral   _____

3. Cervical spine x-ray, complete, with flexion and extension (spine)   _____

4. X-ray pelvis, AP   _____

5. Abdomen, flat plate, AP (x-ray)   _____

6. BE, colon, with air (x-ray colon)   _____

7. Postoperative radiologic supervision and interpretation of cholangiography by radiologist   _____

8. Bilateral screening mammography   _____

9. Retrograde pyelography with KUB (Urography) via cystourethroscopy   _____

10. SPECT liver imaging   _____

PATHOLOGY AND LABORATORY SECTION

This section is organized according to the type of pathology or laboratory procedure performed (Table 7-4). Within each subsection, procedures are listed alphabetically.

NOTE: The Clinical Laboratory Improvement Act (CLIA) established quality standards for all laboratory testing to ensure the accuracy, reliability, and timeliness of patient test results regardless of where the test was performed.

TABLE 7-4   Pathology and Laboratory subsections

SUBSECTION(S)	DESCRIPTION
Organ or Disease Oriented Panels	Single code numbers assigned to **organ- or disease-oriented panels**, which consist of a series of blood chemistry studies routinely ordered by providers at the same time for the purpose of investigating a specific organ or disorder. The composition of the panel is very specific, and no substitutions are allowed. **EXAMPLE:** Report code 80061 when the physician orders a "lipid panel." The following tests are performed on the blood sample: cholesterol, serum, total (82465); lipoprotein, direct measurement, high-density cholesterol (HDL cholesterol) (83718); and triglycerides (84478). NOTE: Refer to "Blood Tests, Panels" in the CPT Index to locate organ- or disease-oriented panel codes.
Drug Testing	Codes for laboratory tests that determine whether a drug or a specific classification of drugs is present in blood or urine. **EXAMPLE:** Report code 80102 to confirm the presence of a single drug class (e.g., cocaine and metabolites).
Therapeutic Drug Assays	Codes for laboratory tests performed to determine how much of a specific prescribed drug is in the patient's blood. **EXAMPLE:** Report code 80162 when the physician orders a therapeutic drug assay to determine the patient's digoxin level. (Patient digoxin levels are routinely monitored for therapeutic purposes.)
Evocative/Suppression Testing	Codes for laboratory tests when substances are injected for the purpose of confirming or ruling out specific disorders. **EXAMPLE:** Report 80400 when the physician orders an adrenocorticotropic hormone (ACTH) stimulation panel to determine whether the patient has adrenal insufficiency.
Consultations (Clinical Pathology)	Codes reported by pathologists who perform clinical pathology consultations requested by attending physicians when a test result requires additional medical interpretive judgment. ● For face-to-face patient contact, assign codes 99241–99275. ● For consultative review of tissue specimen slides, report codes 88321–88325. ● For pathologic consultation during surgery, report codes 88329–88332. **EXAMPLE:** Report code 80500 when a pathologist reviews the patient's lab tests for a limited diagnosis problem, and prepares a report.
● Urinalysis ● Chemistry ● Hematology and Coagulation ● Immunology	Codes for laboratory tests performed on body fluids (e.g., urine, blood). Tests are ordered by physicians and performed by technologists under the supervision of a physician (usually a pathologist). **EXAMPLE:** Report code 81025 for a urine pregnancy test.
Transfusion Medicine	Codes reported for procedures associated with blood transfusions. **EXAMPLE:** Report code 86900 for ABO blood typing. (ABO refers to the four blood groups: A, B, AB, and O.) NOTE: Codes for transfusion of blood and blood components (e.g., packed cells) are located in the CPT Surgery section (36430–36460), except for "leukocyte transfusion," which is assigned code 86950).

(continues)

TABLE 7-4 (continued)

SUBSECTION(S)	DESCRIPTION
Microbiology	Codes reported for bacteriology, mycology, parasitology, and virology procedures. **EXAMPLE:** Report code 87086 for a urine culture that tests for bacteria.
Anatomic Pathology	Codes reported for postmortem examination (also called *autopsy* or *necropsy*). **EXAMPLE:** Report code 88027 for a gross and microscopic autopsy performed on an adult, which includes the central nervous system (CNS, brain, and spinal cord).
• Cytopathology • Cytogenetic Studies	Codes reported for pathology screening tests (cytopathology) and for tissue cultures and chromosome analysis studies (cytogenetic studies). **EXAMPLE:** Report code 88125 for forensic cytopathology on a sperm specimen.
Surgical Pathology	Codes reported when specimen(s) removed during surgery require pathologic diagnosis. Codes are organized according to level. (Refer to codes 88300–88309 for descriptions of levels and associated procedures.) **EXAMPLE 1:** Report code 88304 for a gallbladder specimen removed during cholecystectomy. This subsection also includes additional codes reported for histochemistry, consultation and report on referred material, and so on. **EXAMPLE 2:** Report code 88321 when a pathologist reviews tissue slides prepared elsewhere to render a second opinion regarding pathologic diagnosis.
In Vivo	Reported for *noninvasive* laboratory procedures that are performed transcutaneously, which means the measurement is obtained by pressing a laboratory instrument against the patient's skin or using visible and near-infrared optical bands to obtain a laboratory value.
Transcutaneous Procedures	Code reported for transcutaneous total bilirubin. **EXAMPLE:** Report code 88720 for transcutaneous total bilirubin.
Other Procedures	Codes reported for miscellaneous laboratory procedures, not elsewhere classified in the CPT Pathology and Laboratory section. **EXAMPLE:** Report code 89230 for sweat collection by iontophoresis.
Reproductive Medicine Procedures	Codes reported for oocyte or embryo procedures are coded for the female partner, and codes involving sperm alone are coded for the male partner. They address the coding needs in the evolving reproductive medicine area. (The AMA states that, alternatively, *all* "reproductive medicine procedures" codes may also be applied to the female.) **EXAMPLE:** Report code 89259 for cryopreservation of sperm. (Patient can be male or female because a male could have donated the sperm for purchase by a female who will arrange to have it stored.)

EXERCISE 7-10

Pathology and Laboratory Coding

Instructions: Review each statement, and use your CPT coding manual to assign the appropriate Pathology and Laboratory code.

1. Hepatic function panel   _____
2. Acute hepatitis panel   _____
3. TB skin test, PPD   _____
4. UA (Urinalysis) by dip stick with micro, automated _____
5. WBC count with Diff, automated   _____
6. Stool for occult blood   _____
7. Wet mount, vaginal smear   _____
8. Glucose/blood sugar, quantitative   _____
9. Sedimentation rate, automated   _____
10. Throat culture, bacterial   _____
11. Urine sensitivity, disk   _____
12. Microhematocrit blood count, spun   _____
13. Monospot test   _____
14. Strep test, group A, rapid   _____
15. One-year storage of sperm   _____

MEDICINE SECTION

The CPT Medicine section classifies *noninvasive* or *minimally invasive* diagnostic and therapeutic procedures and services.

- *Noninvasive* procedures require no surgical incision or excision, and they are not open procedures.
- *Minimally invasive* procedures include percutaneous access.

Medicine is the last section of CPT, and its codes are reported with those from all other sections. The Medicine section includes subsections (Table 7-5) that:

- Classify procedures and procedure-oriented services (e.g., immunizations).
- Apply to various medical specialties (e.g., gastroenterology, ophthalmology, otorhinolaryngology, and psychiatry).
- Apply to different types of healthcare providers (e.g., physical therapists and occupational therapists).

TABLE 7-5   Medicine subsections

MEDICINE SUBSECTION	DESCRIPTION
Immune Globulins	Reported for the *supply of the immune globulin product,* including broad-spectrum and anti-infective immune globulins, antitoxins, and other isoantibodies. (The *administration* of an immune globulin is reported separately with a code from the Therapeutic, Prophylactic, and Diagnostic Injections and Infusions subsection.)
Immunization Administration for Vaccines/Toxoids	Reported for intradermal, intramuscular, percutaneous, and subcutaneous injections and intranasal/oral administration.
Vaccines, Toxoids	Reported to identify the vaccine/toxoid product only, in addition to immunization administration for vaccines/toxoids codes.
Psychiatry	Reported by psychiatrists, psychologists, and licensed clinical social workers for provision of psychiatric diagnostic or evaluative interview procedures; psychiatric therapeutic procedures; insight-oriented, behavior-modifying, and/or supportive psychotherapy; interactive psychotherapy; other psychotherapy; and other psychiatric services or procedures.
Biofeedback	Reported for biofeedback services, including review of the patient's history; preparation of biofeedback equipment; placement of electrodes on patient; reading and interpreting responses; monitoring the patient; and control of muscle responses. (*Biofeedback* is a technique that trains the patient to gain some control over autonomic body functions.)
Dialysis	Reported for end-stage renal disease services, hemodialysis, and miscellaneous dialysis procedures.
Gastroenterology	Reported for gastric physiology services and other procedures.
Ophthalmology	Reported for general ophthalmological services, special ophthalmological services, contact lens services, and spectacle services (including prosthesis for aphakia).
Special Otorhinolaryngologic Services	Reported for vestibular function tests, with observation and evaluation by physician, without electrical recording; vestibular function tests, with recording (e.g., ENG, PENG), and medical diagnostic evaluation; audiologic function tests with medical diagnostic evaluation; and evaluative and therapeutic services. When otorhinolaryngologic services are performed during provision of an evaluation and management (E/M) service, do *not* code and report the component procedures separately (e.g., otoscopy, tuning fork test, whispered voice test). However, special otorhinolaryngologic services (92502–92700) that are *not* typically included in a comprehensive otorhinolaryngologic evaluation *are* reported separately.
Cardiovascular	Reported for therapeutic services, cardiography, echocardiography, cardiac catheterization, intracardiac electrophysiological procedures/studies, peripheral arterial disease rehabilitation, and other vascular studies.
Noninvasive Vascular Diagnostic Studies	Reported for cerebrovascular arterial studies, extremity arterial and venous studies, visceral and penile vascular studies, and extremity arterial-venous studies. Also reported for noninvasive vascular diagnostic studies (e.g., a duplex scan), which includes ultrasound scanning to display two-dimensional structure and motion. (A *duplex scan* is a noninvasive test that is performed to evaluate a vessel's blood flow.)
Pulmonary	Reported for lung function procedures, lung capacity testing and treatment, pulmonary laboratory procedures and interpretations (e.g., continuous positive airway pressure, intermittent positive pressure breathing, pulse oximetry, spirometry, ventilation assistance).
Allergy and Clinical Immunology	Reported for allergy testing and allergen immunotherapy.
Endocrinology	Reported for subcutaneous placement of a sensor for continual glucose (blood sugar) monitoring (up to 72 hours) and physician interpretation/report of results of monitoring.

(continues)

TABLE 7-5   (continued)

MEDICINE SUBSECTION	DESCRIPTION
Neurology and Neuromuscular Procedures	Reported for neurology and neuromuscular diagnostic and therapeutic services that do *not* require surgical procedures (e.g., sleep testing, EEG, EMG, motion analysis).
Medical Genetics and Genetic Counseling Services	Reported for counseling of an individual, couple, or family to investigate family genetic history and assess risks associated with genetic defects in offspring.
Central Nervous System Assessments/Tests	Reported for tests performed to measure cognitive function of the central nervous system (e.g., cognitive processes, visual motor responses, and abstractive abilities).
Health and Behavior Assessment/Intervention	Reported for tests that identify the psychological, behavioral, emotional, cognitive, and social elements involved in the prevention, treatment, or management of physical health problems.
Hydration, Therapeutic, Prophylactic, Diagnostic Injections and Infusions; and Chemotherapy and Other Highly Complex Biologic Administration	Reported for hydration IV infusion that consists of prepackaged fluid and electrolytes (but no drugs or other substances). Codes include the administration of local anesthesia; intravenous (IV) insertion; access to catheter, IV, or port; routine syringe, tubing, and other supplies; and flushing performed upon completion of infusion. Reported for the administration of chemotherapeutic agents by multiple routes (e.g., intravenously). These codes can be separately billed when an E/M service is rendered on the same day as the chemotherapy administration. *Chemotherapy* is the treatment of cancer with drugs that serve to destroy cancer cells or slow the growth of cancer cells, keep cancer from spreading to other parts of the body, and prevent recurrence of the cancer. Chemotherapy administered in addition to other cancer treatments, such as surgery and/or radiation therapy, is called *adjuvant chemotherapy*.
Photodynamic Therapy	Reported for the administration of light therapy to destroy premalignant/malignant lesions or ablate abnormal tissue using photosensitive drugs.
Special Dermatological Procedures	Reported for dermatology procedures that are typically performed in addition to an appropriate evaluation and management (E/M) service code.
Physical Medicine and Rehabilitation	Reported for services that focus on the prevention, diagnosis, and treatment of disorders of the musculoskeletal, cardiovascular, and pulmonary systems that may produce temporary or permanent impairment.
Medical Nutrition Therapy	Reported for medical nutrition therapy, which is classified according to type of assessment, individual or group therapy, and length of time.
Acupuncture	Reported for acupuncture treatment, which is classified as face-to-face patient contact for 15-minute increments of time and according to whether electrical stimulation was provided.
Osteopathic Manipulative Treatment	Reported for manual treatment applied by a physician to eliminate or alleviate somatic dysfunction and related disorders.
Chiropractic Manipulative Treatment	Reported for manual treatments that influence joint and neurophysiological function.
Education and Training for Patient Self-Management	Reported for education and training services provided for patient self-management by a qualified, non-physician healthcare professional using a standard curriculum. The codes are classified according to the length of time spent face-to-face with one or more patients.
Non-Face-to-Face Non-Physician Services	Reported for telephone services provided to an established patient, parent, or guardian; and online medical evaluation.
Special Services, Procedures, and Reports	Reported for special services, procedures, and reports (e.g., handling/conveyance of specimen for transfer from physician's office to laboratory).
Qualifying Circumstances for Anesthesia	Reported for situations that complicate the administration of anesthesia services (e.g., emergencies, extreme age, hypotension, and hypothermia). Codes 99100–99140 are add-on codes, which means they are reported in addition to a code from the Anesthesia section.

(continues)

TABLE 7-5   (continued)

MEDICINE SUBSECTION	DESCRIPTION
Moderate (Conscious) Sedation	Reported for a drug-induced depression of consciousness that requires no interventions to maintain airway patency or ventilation. • CPT specifies that moderate (conscious) sedation does not include minimal sedation (e.g., anxiolysis), deep sedation, or monitored anesthesia care (MAC). • Subsection notes specify services that are included in moderate (conscious) sedation codes (e.g., IV access, administration of agent, and monitoring oxygen saturation). • The surgeon who performs a surgical procedure usually provides moderate (conscious) sedation services. When another physician (e.g., an anesthesiologist) provides general anesthesia, regional anesthesia, or monitored anesthesia care, that other physician reports an appropriate Anesthesia code and its modifiers. • CPT's Appendix G lists procedures that include moderate (conscious) sedation as an inherent part of the procedure, identified with the bull's-eye symbol (()).
Other Services and Procedures	Reported for services and procedures that cannot be classified in another subsection of the Medicine section (e.g., anogenital examination, vision screening by nonoptical professionals, hypothermia treatment).
Home Health Procedures/ Services	Reported by non-physician healthcare professionals who perform procedures and provide services to the patient in the patient's residence (the patient's home, assisted living facility, or group home).
Medication Therapy Management Services	Reported when a pharmacist provides individual management of medication therapy with assessment and intervention.

EXERCISE 7-11

Medicine Section

Instructions: Review each statement, and use your CPT coding manual to assign the appropriate Medicine code, including modifiers.

1. Cardiac catheterization, right side only, with conscious sedation, IV   _____

2. Routine ECG, tracing only   _____

3. Spirometry   _____

4. CPR, in office   _____

5. Diagnostic psychiatric examination   _____

6. Influenza vaccine, age 18 months   _____

7. Whirlpool and paraffin bath therapy   _____

8. WAIS-R and MMPI psychological tests and report, 1 hour   _____

9. Office services on emergency basis   _____

10. Physical therapy evaluation (and management)   _____

NATIONAL CORRECT CODING INITIATIVE

The Centers for Medicare and Medicaid Services (CMS) implemented the National Correct Coding Initiative (NCCI) to promote national correct coding methodologies and to control the improper assignment of codes that result in inappropriate reimbursement of Medicare Part B claims. NCCI edits (Table 7-6) are used to process Medicare Part B claims, and NCCI coding policies are based on the:

- Analysis of standard medical and surgical practice.
- Coding conventions included in CPT.
- Coding guidelines developed by national medical specialty societies (e.g., CPT Advisory Committee, which contains representatives of major medical societies).
- Local and national coverage determinations.
- Review of current coding practices.

The NCCI was initially developed for use by Medicare administrative contractors (MACs) that process Medicare Part B claims for physician office services. NCCI edits were added to the Outpatient Code Editor (OCE) in August 2000, and they are used by MACs to process Medicare Part B claims for outpatient hospital services. (Some OCE edits that apply to outpatient hospital services claims differ from comparable edits in the NCCI used to process physician office services claims.)

Carefully review parenthetical notes below CPT code descriptions to locate procedures that are separately reported (in addition to the major procedure performed). When reporting codes for outpatient hospital services and physician office services, be sure to use outpatient code editor (OCE) software or NCCI software, respectively, to identify bundled codes for procedures and services considered necessary to accomplish the major procedure. Bundled procedure codes are *not* separately coded or reported with the major procedure code. Reporting bundled procedure codes in addition to the major procedure code is characterized as unbundling (fraud). The OCE edits are packaged with commercial software, such as Ingenix's Encoder Pro Expert. The NCCI edits are available at **www.cms.hhs.gov.** (The OCE and NCCI edits are available for purchase from the National Technical Information Service [NTIS] at **www.ntis.gov.**)

TABLE 7-6   Partial listing of National Correct Coding Initiative (NCCI) edits

NCCI EDIT	DESCRIPTION	DISPOSITION OF CLAIM
1	Invalid diagnosis code	Return to Provider
2	Diagnosis and age conflict	Return to Provider
3	Diagnosis and sex conflict	Return to Provider
4	Medicare secondary payer alert	Suspend
19	Mutually exclusive procedure that is not allowed by NCCI even if appropriate modifier is present	Line Item Rejection
20	Component of a comprehensive procedure that is not allowed by NCCI even if appropriate modifier is present	Line Item Rejection
39	Mutually exclusive procedure that would be allowed by NCCI if appropriate modifier were present	Line Item Rejection
40	Component of a comprehensive procedure that would be allowed by NCCI if appropriate modifier were present	Line Item Rejection

> **EXAMPLE:** Code 67911 describes the "Correction of lid retraction." A parenthetical note below the code description advises that, if autogenous graft materials are used during the same operative session, tissue graft codes 20920, 20922, or 20926 are reported in addition to code 67911.

According to the Medicare Code Editor (MCE), *other procedures necessary to accomplish* the "correction of lid retraction" are included in code 67911, such as full-thickness graft placement (15260). Such other procedures are not separately coded and reported when performed during the same operative session as the "correction of lid retraction."

NOTE: Locate Medlearn articles that contain OCE updates by going to **www.cms.hhs.gov**, clicking on the Outreach and Education link, and clicking on the MLN Matters Articles link.

CMS POSTS CORRECT CODING INITIATIVE (CCI) EDITS ON INTERNET

(Permission to reuse in accordance with **www.cms.hhs.gov** Web site Content Reuse Policy.)

The Centers for Medicare & Medicaid Services (CMS) today make it easier for physicians and other providers to bill properly and be paid promptly for their services to people with Medicare coverage. CMS has posted on its Web site (**www.cms.hhs.gov**) the automated edits used to identify questionable claims and adjust payments to reflect what would have been paid if the claim had been filed correctly. The edits, known as the National Correct Coding Initiative (NCCI), identify pairs of services that normally should not be billed by the same physician for the same patient on the same day. The NCCI also promotes uniformity among the contractors that process Medicare claims in interpreting Medicare payment policies.

The posting of NCCI edits is the most recent in a series of steps CMS has taken to use the Internet creatively to reduce the regulatory burden on physicians and make it easier for them to work with Medicare to improve services to beneficiaries. CMS has also added a feature to its Web site that makes it possible for physicians to determine in advance what they will be paid for a particular service or range of services. The Medicare Physician Fee Schedule look-up provides both the unadjusted payment rates, as well as the payment rates by geographic location. While the NCCI is a cornerstone of efforts to ensure that Medicare and beneficiaries do not pay twice for the same service or for duplicative services, CMS believes physicians should have easy access to the edits used to identify incorrect claims. The NCCI includes two types of edits:

- Comprehensive/component edits (code pairs that should not be billed together because one service inherently includes the other)

- Mutually exclusive edits (code pairs that, for clinical reasons, are unlikely to be performed on the same patient on the same day; for example, two different types of testing that yield equivalent results)

CPT codes representing services denied based on NCCI edits may not be billed to Medicare beneficiaries. Since these denials are based on incorrect coding rather than medical necessity, the provider cannot submit an Advance Beneficiary Notice (ABN) to seek payment from a Medicare beneficiary. An Advance Beneficiary Notice (ABN) is a form completed and signed by a Medicare beneficiary each time a provider believes a normally covered service will not be covered *and* the provider wants to bill the beneficiary directly for the service. In addition, because the denials are based on incorrect coding

(continues)

(continued)

> (rather than a legislated Medicare benefit exclusion) the provider *cannot* seek payment from the beneficiary even if a Notice of Exclusions from Medicare Benefits (NEMB) was obtained.
>
> A *Notice of Exclusions from Medicare Benefits (NEMB)* is a form completed and signed by a Medicare beneficiary before items, procedures, and services excluded from Medicare benefits are provided; alerts Medicare beneficiaries in advance that Medicare does not cover certain items and services because they do not meet the definition of a Medicare benefit or because they are specifically excluded by law; NEMB is completed when an ABN is not appropriate.
>
> The NCCI edits, which are updated quarterly, were previously available to physicians and other providers on a paid subscription basis, but they are now available to anyone with a personal computer. The NCCI edits are posted as a spreadsheet that will allow users to sort by procedural code and effective date. A "find" feature will allow users to look for a specific code. The NCCI edit files are also indexed by procedural code ranges for easy navigation.
>
> The new Web page also includes links to documents that explain the edits, including the:
>
> - Medicare Claims Processing Manual.
> - NCCI Edits Program Transmittals.
> - NCCI FAQs (frequently asked questions).
> - NCCI Policy Manual for Part B MACs.

Unbundling CPT Codes

Providers are responsible for reporting the CPT (and HCPCS level II) code that most comprehensively describes the services provided. NCCI edits determine the appropriateness of CPT code combinations for claims submitted to Medicare administrative contractors. NCCI edits are designed to detect unbundling, which involves reporting multiple codes for a service when a single comprehensive code should be assigned. The practice of unbundling occurs because:

- **Provider's coding staff unintentionally reports multiple codes based on misinterpreted coding guidelines.**
- **Reporting multiple codes is intentional and is done to maximize reimbursement.**

Unbundling occurs when one service is divided into its component parts, and a code for each component part is reported as if they were separate services.

> **EXAMPLE:** A 64-year-old female patient undergoes total abdominal hysterectomy with bilateral salpingectomy and oophorectomy. Review CPT Surgery code descriptions for 58150, 58700, and 58720. Reporting codes 58700 and 58720 in addition to 58150 is considered unbundling. If all three codes are submitted on a claim, reimbursement for codes 58700 and 58720 would be disallowed (and the provider might be subject to allegations of fraud and abuse).

Unbundling occurs when a code for the separate surgical approach (e.g., laparotomy) is reported in addition to a code for the surgical procedure. Procedures performed to gain access to an area or organ system are not separately reported.

> **EXAMPLE:** A 54-year-old female patient underwent excision of ileoanal reservoir with ileostomy, which required lysis of adhesions to gain access to the site of surgery. Review CPT Surgery code descriptions for 45136 and 44005. Report CPT code 45136 only because code 44005 is considered a component part of the total procedure (45136). Reporting both codes would be considered unbundling.

SUMMARY

CPT codes are reported for services and procedures provided by home health care and hospice agencies, outpatient hospital departments, physicians who are employees of a healthcare facility, and physicians who see patients in their offices or clinics and in patients' homes. CPT organizes Category I procedures and services into six sections:

- Evaluation and Management (E/M) (99201–99499).
- Anesthesia (00100–01999, 99100–99140).
- Surgery (10021–69990).
- Radiology (70010–79999).
- Pathology and Laboratory (80047–89356).
- Medicine (90281–99199, 99500–99607).

The CPT index is organized by alphabetical main terms printed in boldface; appendices are located between the Medicine section and the index. CPT Category I codes are organized according to six sections that are subdivided into subsections, categories, and subcategories. Guidelines, notes, and descriptive qualifiers are also organized according to sections, subsections, categories, and subcategories. Two-digit modifiers are added to five-digit CPT codes to clarify services and procedures performed by providers.

INTERNET LINKS

- American Medical Association
  www.ama-assn.org
- E/M Documentation Guidelines
  Go to **www.cms.hhs.gov,** click on the "Outreach and Education" link, and click on "Documentation Guidelines for E&M Services" link.
- Highmark Medicare Services
  www.highmarkmedicareservices.com
- *Family Practice Management*
  Go to **www.aafp.org,** and click on the "Family Practice Management" link to view past and current issues in this helpful journal.
- Decision Health billing, coding, and reimbursement e-zines (free)
  Go to **www.decisionhealth.com,** and click on the "7 free ezines - Sign-up here" link.
- Coding newsletters (free)
  ezines.decisionhealth.com

STUDY CHECKLIST

☐ Read this textbook chapter, and highlight key concepts.

☐ Create an index card for each key term.

☐ Access the chapter Internet links to learn more about concepts.

☐ Complete the chapter review, verifying answers with your instructor.

☐ Complete WebTutor assignments and take online quizzes.

☐ Complete Workbook chapter assignments, verifying answers with your instructor.

☐ Complete the StudyWare activities to receive immediate feedback.

☐ Form a study group with classmates to discuss chapter concepts in preparation for an exam.

REVIEW

EVALUATION AND MANAGEMENT SECTION

Refer to the CPT coding manual to answer each of the following items.

1. Which category is used to report services for patients seen in stand-alone ambulatory care centers?

2. Office or Other Outpatient Services is used to report services rendered by a physician to a patient in a hospital observation area. TRUE or FALSE.

3. Which category is used to report services provided to patients in a partial hospital setting?

4. What is the name of the service provided by a physician whose opinion is requested?

5. The service identified in question #4 must be requested by another physician (e.g., attending physician). TRUE or FALSE.

6. Consultations provided in a physician's office are reported using office or other outpatient services codes. TRUE or FALSE.

7. Only one initial consultation is to be reported by a consultant per hospital inpatient admission. TRUE or FALSE.

8. A consultant who participates in management of an inpatient after conducting an initial consultation will report services using codes from which subcategory?

9. Which modifier is reported for mandated services?

10. A distinction is made between new and established patients when reporting E/M emergency department services. TRUE or FALSE.

11. Which code would you assign to report for a physician who provides directed emergency care?

12. What is meant by the phrase *directed emergency care?*

13. Critical care services must be provided in a critical care unit area (e.g., ICU). TRUE or FALSE.

14. Which code(s) would be assigned to report 2-1/2 hours of critical care provided by the attending physician?

15. SNFs, ICFs, and LTCFs are classified in CPT as _____.

16. Which category would be used when reporting a physician's visit to a patient residing in a boarding home?

17. Services provided by a physician to patients in a private residence are reported using codes from which category? _____

18. Which code would be reported when a physician calls a patient about recent lab test results? _____

19. A physical examination was performed on an 18-year-old who is scheduled to attend college in the fall. Which code(s) would you assign? _____

20. Assign code(s) to well-baby care of a 9-month-old that includes the administration of DTP and oral polio vaccines. _____

HINT:

You'll also need to refer to the Medicine section of CPT.

21. Assign a code for preventive medicine service to a 56-year-old established patient. _____

22. Assign code(s) to a patient who was admitted to observation services on June 30th and also discharged from observation services on that date. _____

23. Assign code(s) to a patient who received critical care services for a total of 210 minutes on July 15th. On this date, the patient also underwent inpatient comprehensive history and examination with medical decision making of high complexity. _____

24. Identify the code to assign to a patient who underwent a medical disability evaluation by his own physician. _____

In questions 25–29, identify the E/M category and subcategory you would use to code each of the following cases. The key components of history, examination, and medical decision making are identified in each case, and you are required to assign the correct code based on that information.

25. Dr. Jones is an internist who performed a hospital admission, examination, and initiation of treatment program for a 67-year-old male with uncomplicated pneumonia who requires IV antibiotic therapy. Dr. Jones completed a comprehensive history and examination; the medical decision making is of low complexity. Minimal patient counseling was provided. The patient's problem was of low severity.

Identify the CPT category and subcategory _____.

Identify the appropriate CPT code _____.

26. Dr. Smith completed an office consultation for management of systolic hypertension in a 70-year-old male scheduled for elective prostate resection. Dr. Smith conducted an expanded problem-focused history and examination; medical decision making was straightforward. The patient's problem is of low severity. Dr. Smith spent 20 minutes counseling the patient.

Identify the CPT category and subcategory _____.

Identify the appropriate CPT code _____.

27. Dr. Choi conducted subsequent hospital care for the evaluation and management of a healthy newborn on the second day of inpatient stay.

Identify the CPT category _____.

Identify the appropriate CPT code _____.

28. Dr. Lange saw an established patient in the office for recent syncopal attacks. Comprehensive history and examination were performed. Medical decision making is of high complexity.

Identify the CPT category and subcategory _____.

Identify the appropriate CPT code _____.

29. Dr. Doolittle conducted a follow-up hospital visit for a 54-year-old patient, post myocardial infarction, who is out of the CCU but is now having frequent premature ventricular contractions on telemetry. Expanded problem-focused interval history and examination were completed. Medical decision making is of moderate complexity. Dr. Doolittle coordinated care with the patient's providers and discussed the case with the patient's immediate family.

Identify the CPT category and subcategory _____.

Identify the appropriate CPT code _____.

SURGERY SECTION

Use your CPT manual to assign procedure codes, adding appropriate modifier(s).

30. Pneumocentesis; assistant surgeon reporting _____

31. Electrodesiccation, basal cell carcinoma (1 cm), face _____

32. Complicated bilateral repair of recurrent inguinal hernia _____

33. Biopsy of anorectal wall via proctosigmoidoscopy _____

34. Mastectomy for gynecomastia, bilateral _____

35. Open reduction, right tibia/fibula shaft fracture, with insertion of screws _____

36. Excision, condylomata, penis _____

37. Replacement of breast tissue expander with breast prosthesis (permanent) _____

38. Closed reduction of closed fracture, clavicle _____

39. Incision and drainage of infected bursa, wrist _____

40. Cystourethroscopy with biopsy of urinary bladder _____

41. Endoscopic right maxillary sinusotomy with partial polypectomy _____

42. Insertion of non-tunneled Hickman catheter (short-term) (age 70) _____

43. Avulsion of four nail plates _____

RADIOLOGY, PATHOLOGY AND LABORATORY, AND MEDICINE SECTIONS

Use your CPT manual to assign procedure and service codes, adding appropriate modifier(s).

44. Arthrography of the shoulder, supervision and interpretation _____

45. Chest x-ray, frontal, single view (professional component only) _____

46. Transabdominal ultrasound of pregnant uterus, first pregnancy (real time with image documentation), fetal and maternal evaluation, second trimester _____

47. Application of radioactive needles (radioelement), intracavitary of uterus, intermediate _____

48. Lipid panel blood test _____

49. Drug screen for opiates (outside laboratory performed drug screen) _____

50. Hemogram (manual) (complete CBC) _____

51. Cervical cytopathology slides, manual screening under physician supervision _____

52. Gross and microscopic examination of gallbladder _____

53. Complete echocardiography, transthoracic (real-time with image documentation [2D] with M-mode recording) _____

54. Mumps vaccine immunization _____

55. Intermittent positive pressure breathing of a newborn _____

56. Gait training, first 30 minutes _____

57. Medical psychoanalysis _____

58. Ultraviolet light is used to treat a skin disorder _____

59. Chemotherapy, IV infusion technique, 10 hours, requiring use of portable pump (including refill) _____

60. Combined right cardiac catheterization and retrograde left heart catheterization _____

CATEGORY II CODES

Use your CPT manual to assign procedure and service codes, adding appropriate modifier(s).

61. Initial prenatal care visit _____

62. Assessment of tobacco use _____

63. Recording of vital signs _____

64. Documentation and review of spirometry results _____

65. Inhaled bronchodilator prescribed for COPD patient _____

CATEGORY III CODES

Use your CPT manual to assign procedure and service codes, adding appropriate modifier(s).

66. Destruction of macular drusen via photocoagulation _____

67. Antiprothrombin antibody IgA test _____

68. Remote real-time interactive video-conferenced critical care, evaluation and management of critically ill patient, 45 minutes _____

69. Pancreatic islet cell transplantation through portal vein, open approach _____

70. Surgical laparoscopy with implantation of gastric stimulation electrodes, lesser curvature of the stomach, for patient diagnosed with morbid obesity _____

HCPCS Level II Coding

CHAPTER OUTLINE

Overview of HCPCS

HCPCS Level II National Codes

Determining Payer Responsibility

Assigning HCPCS Level II Codes

OBJECTIVES

Upon successful completion of this chapter, you should be able to:

1. Define key terms.
2. Describe the HCPCS levels.
3. Assign HCPCS level II codes and modifiers.
4. Identify claims to be submitted to Medicare administrative contractors according to HCPCS level II code number.
5. List situations in which both HCPCS levels I and II codes are assigned.

KEY TERMS

durable medical equipment (DME)

durable medical equipment, prosthetics, orthotics, and supplies (DMEPOS)

durable medical equipment, prosthetics, orthotics, and supplies (DMEPOS) dealers

Pricing, Data Analysis and Coding (PDAC) Contractor

transitional pass-through payments

Types of HCPCS level II codes:
  dental codes
  miscellaneous codes
  permanent national codes
  temporary codes

INTRODUCTION

NOTE: HCPCS used to be called the HCFA Common Procedure Coding System when the Centers for Medicare and Medicaid Services (CMS) was titled the Health Care Financing Administration (HCFA). The change to Healthcare Common Procedure Coding System occurred in 2002 when CMS became the new name for HCFA.

This chapter presents the procedure/service coding reference developed by CMS, the *Healthcare Common Procedure Coding System* (HCPCS, pronounced "hick-picks"). HCPCS level II was introduced in 1983 after Medicare found that its payers used more than 100 different coding systems, making it difficult to analyze claims data. HCPCS furnishes healthcare providers and suppliers with a standardized language for reporting professional services, procedures, supplies, and equipment. Most state Medicaid programs and many commercial payers also use the HCPCS level II coding system.

273

> **NOTE:** Effective December 31, 2003, HCPCS level III codes were no longer required. They had the same structure as level II codes, but were assigned by the local Medicare carriers (LMCs), which process Medicare claims. HCPCS level III codes began with the letters W, X, Y, or Z.

OVERVIEW OF HCPCS

Two levels of codes are associated with HCPCS, commonly referred to as HCPCS level I and II codes:

- **HCPCS level I: Current Procedural Terminology (CPT).**
- **HCPCS level II: national codes.**

The majority of procedures and services are reported using CPT (HCPCS level I) codes. However, CPT does not describe durable medical equipment, prosthetics, orthotics, and supplies (DMEPOS), and certain other services reported on claims submitted for Medicare and some Medicaid patients. Therefore, the CMS developed HCPCS level II national codes to report DMEPOS and other services. (Medicare carriers previously developed HCPCS level III local codes, which were discontinued December 31, 2003. Medicare administrative contractors (MACs) replaced carriers, DMERCs, and fiscal intermediaries.

HCPCS Level I

HCPCS level I includes the five-digit CPT codes developed and published by the American Medical Association (AMA). The AMA is responsible for the annual update of this coding system and its two-digit modifiers. (CPT coding is covered in Chapter 7 of this textbook.)

HCPCS Level II

HCPCS level II (or HCPCS national codes) were created in 1983 to describe common medical services and supplies not classified in CPT. HCPCS level II national codes are five characters in length, and they begin with letters A–V, followed by four numbers. HCPCS level II codes identify services performed by physician and nonphysician providers (e.g., nurse practitioners and speech therapists), ambulance companies, and durable medical equipment (DME) companies (called durable medical equipment, prosthetics, orthotics, and supplies [DMEPOS] dealers).

- **Durable medical equipment (DME) is defined by Medicare as equipment that can withstand repeated use, is primarily used to serve a medical purpose, is used in the patient's home, and would not be used in the absence of illness or injury.**
- **Durable medical equipment, prosthetics, orthotics, and supplies (DMEPOS) include artificial limbs, braces, medications, surgical dressings, and wheelchairs.**
- **Durable medical equipment, prosthetics, orthotics, and supplies (DMEPOS) dealers supply patients with DME (e.g., canes, crutches, walkers, commode chairs, and blood-glucose monitors). DMEPOS claims are submitted to DME Medicare administrative contractors (DMEMACs) that replaced durable medical equipment regional carriers, or DMERCs) that were awarded contracts by CMS. Each DME MAC covers a specific geographic region of the country and is responsible for processing DMEPOS claims for its specific region.**

> **NOTE:** Originally, HCPCS level II codes were simply listed on a healthcare facility's *charge-master* (or *charge description master*) for selection by the healthcare professional who provided patient services. However, implementation of the outpatient prospective payment system (OPPS) resulted in more invasive procedures being assigned HCPCS level II codes for outpatient encounters, and coders must review patient records to assign the codes.

When an appropriate HCPCS level II code exists, it is often assigned instead of a CPT code (with the same or similar code description) for Medicare accounts and for some state Medicaid systems. (Other payers may not require the reporting of HCPCS level II codes instead of CPT codes, so coders should check with individual payers to determine their policies.) CMS creates HCPCS level II codes:

- **For services and procedures that will probably never be assigned a CPT code** (e.g., **medications, equipment, supplies**).
- **To determine the volumes and costs of newly implemented technologies.**

New HCPCS level II codes are reported for several years until CMS initiates a process to create corresponding CPT codes. When the CPT codes are published, they are reported instead of the original HCPCS level II codes. (HCPCS level II codes that are replaced by CPT codes are often deleted. If not deleted, they are probably continuing to be reported by another payer or government demonstration program.)

NOTE: Effective December 31, 2003, HCPCS level III codes were no longer required. They had the same structure as level II codes, but were assigned by the *local Medicare carriers (LMCs)* (replaced by *Medicare administrative contractors*), which process Medicare claims. HCPCS level III codes began with the letters W, X, Y, or Z.

> **EXAMPLE:** HCPCS level II device code C1725 is reported for the surgical supply of a "catheter, transluminal angioplasty, nonlaser method (may include guidance, infusion/perfusion capability)" during vascular surgery. Thus, when a CPT code from range 35450-35476 is reported for a transluminal balloon angioplasty procedure, HCPCS level II device code C1725 is also reported as the surgical supply of the catheter.

CODING TIP:

When people refer to HCPCS codes, they are most likely referring to HCPCS level II national codes. CMS is responsible for the annual updates to HCPCS level II codes and two-character alphanumeric modifiers.

HCPCS LEVEL II NATIONAL CODES

The HCPCS level II national coding system classifies similar medical products and services for the purpose of efficient claims processing. Each HCPCS level II code contains a description, and the codes are used primarily for billing purposes.

> **EXAMPLE:** DMEPOS dealers report HCPCS level II codes to identify items on claims billed to private or public health insurers.

HCPCS is *not* a reimbursement methodology or system, and it is important to understand that just because codes exist for certain products or services, coverage (e.g., payment) is not guaranteed. The HCPCS level II coding system has the following characteristics:

- **It ensures uniform reporting of medical products or services on claims forms.**
- **Code descriptors identify similar products or services (rather than specific products or brand/trade names).**
- **HCPCS is not a reimbursement methodology for making coverage or payment determinations. (Each payer makes determinations on coverage and payment outside this coding process.)**

REMEMBER!

Effective January 1, 2005, CMS no longer allows a 90-day grace period (traditionally, January 1 through March 31) for reporting discontinued, revised, and new HCPCS level II national codes on claims. There is also no 90-day grace period for implementing mid-year HCPCS level II national coding updates.

Responsibility for HCPCS Level II Codes

HCPCS level II codes are developed and maintained by CMS and do not carry the copyright of a private organization. They are in the public domain, and many publishers print annual coding manuals.

Some HCPCS level II references contain general instructions or guidelines for each section; an appendix summarizing additions, deletions, and terminology revisions for codes (similar to Appendix B in CPT); or separate tables of drugs or deleted codes. Others use symbols to identify codes excluded from Medicare coverage, codes where payment is left to the discretion of the payer, or codes with special coverage instructions. In addition, most references provide a complete appendix of current HCPCS level II national modifiers. CMS has stated that it is not responsible for any errors that might occur in or from the use of these private printings of HCPCS level II codes.

Types of HCPCS Level II Codes

HCPCS level II codes are organized by type, depending on the purpose of the codes and the entity responsible for establishing and maintaining them. The five types are:

- Permanent national codes.
- Dental codes.
- Miscellaneous codes.
- Temporary codes.
- Modifiers.

Permanent National Codes

HCPCS level II permanent national codes are maintained by the HCPCS National Panel, which is composed of representatives from the Blue Cross/Blue Shield Association (BCBSA), the Health Insurance Association of America (HIAA), and CMS. The HCPCS National Panel is responsible for making decisions about additions, revisions, and deletions to the permanent national alphanumeric codes. Decisions regarding changes to the permanent national codes are made only by unanimous consent of all three parties. As HCPCS level II is a national coding system, none of the parties, including CMS, can make unilateral decisions regarding permanent national codes. These codes are for the use of all private and public health insurers.

Dental Codes

HCPCS level II dental codes are actually contained in *Current Dental Terminology (CDT),* a coding manual copyrighted and published by the American Dental Association (ADA) that lists codes for billing for dental procedures and supplies. Decisions regarding the modification, deletion, or addition of CDT codes are made by the ADA rather than the HCPCS National Panel. The Department of Health and Human Services' agreement with the ADA is similar to its agreement with the AMA pertaining to the use of CPT codes. (CDT is discussed in Appendix IV.)

Miscellaneous Codes

HCPCS level II **miscellaneous codes** include *miscellaneous/not otherwise classified* codes that are reported when a DMEPOS dealer submits a claim for a product or service for which there is no existing HCPCS level II code. Miscellaneous codes allow DMEPOS dealers to submit a claim for a product or service as soon as it is approved by the Food and Drug Administration (FDA), even though there is no code that describes the product or service. The use of miscellaneous codes also helps avoid the inefficiency of assigning codes for items or services that are rarely furnished or for which payers expect to receive few claims.

Claims that contain miscellaneous codes are manually reviewed by the payer, and the following must be provided for use in the review process:

- **Complete description of product or service.**
- **Pricing information for product or service.**
- **Documentation to explain why the item or service is needed by the beneficiary.**

Before reporting a miscellaneous code on a claim, a DMEPOS dealer should check with the payer to determine if a specific code has been identified for use (instead of a miscellaneous code).

Temporary Codes

HCPCS level II **temporary codes** are maintained by the CMS and other members of the HCPCS National Panel, independent of permanent HCPCS level II codes. Permanent codes are updated once a year on January 1, but temporary codes allow payers the flexibility to establish codes that are needed before the next January 1 annual update. Approximately 35 percent of the HCPCS level II codes are temporary codes. Certain sections of the HCPCS level II codes were set aside to allow HCPCS National Panel members to develop temporary codes, and decisions regarding the number and type of temporary codes and how they are used are made independently by each HCPCS National Panel member. Temporary codes serve the purpose of meeting short-time-frame operational needs of a particular payer.

Although the HCPCS National Panel may decide to replace temporary codes with permanent codes, if permanent codes are not established, the temporary codes remain "temporary" indefinitely.

Categories of Temporary Codes

C codes permit implementation of section 201 of the Balanced Budget Refinement Act of 1999, and they identify items that may qualify for **transitional pass-through payments** under the hospital outpatient prospective payment system (OPPS). These are temporary additional payments (over and above the OPPS payment) made for certain innovative medical devices, drugs, and biologicals provided to Medicare beneficiaries. These codes are used exclusively for OPPS purposes and are only valid for Medicare claims submitted by hospital outpatient departments.

G codes identify professional healthcare procedures and services that do not have codes identified in CPT. G codes are reported to all payers.

H codes are reported to state Medicaid agencies that are mandated by state law to establish separate codes for identifying mental health services (e.g., alcohol and drug treatment services).

K codes are reported to MACs when existing permanent codes do not include codes needed to implement a MAC medical review coverage policy.

Q codes identify services that would not ordinarily be assigned a CPT code (e.g., drugs, biologicals, and other types of medical equipment or services).

S codes are used by the BCBSA and the HIAA when no HCPCS level II codes exist to report drugs, services, and supplies, but codes are needed to implement private payer policies and programs for claims processing.

T codes are reported to state Medicaid agencies when no HCPCS level II permanent codes exist, but codes are needed to administer the Medicaid program. (T codes are not reported to Medicare, but can be reported to private payers).

Modifiers

HCPCS modifiers clarify services and procedures performed by providers. Although the HCPCS level II code and description remain unchanged, modifiers indicate that the description of the service or procedure performed has been altered. HCPCS modifiers are reported as two-character alphabetic or alphanumeric codes added to the five-character HCPCS level II code.

> **EXAMPLE:** Modifier -UE indicates the product is "used equipment"
>
> Modifier -NU indicates the product is "new equipment"

HCPCS level II modifiers are either alphabetic (two letters) or alphanumeric (one letter followed by one number) (Figure 8-1).

> **EXAMPLE 1:** A patient sees a clinical psychologist for individual psychotherapy (CPT code 90804). Report:
>
> 90804-AH

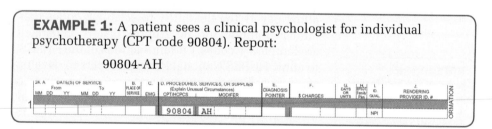

> **EXAMPLE 2:** A Medicare patient undergoes tendon excision, right palm (CPT code 26170) and left middle finger (CPT code 26180). Report:
>
> 26170-RT
>
> 26180-59-F2

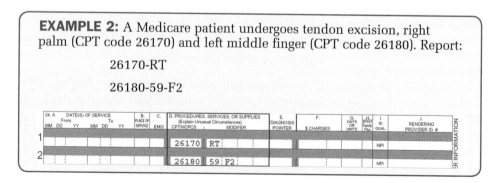

HCPCS Level II Modifiers

Bolded modifiers are reported under the Outpatient Prospective Payment System (OPPS).

NOTE: When CPT modifier -50 is reported, do not report modifiers -RT and -LT.

AA	Anesthesia services performed personally by anesthesiologist
AD	Medical supervision by a physician: more than four concurrent anesthesia procedures
AH	Clinical psychologist
AM	Physician, team member service
AP	Ophthalmological examination
AS	Physician assistant, nurse practitioner, or clinical nurse specialist services for assistant at surgery
AT	Acute treatment (this modifier should be used when reporting service 98940, 98941, 98942)
E1	Upper left, eyelid
E2	Lower left, eyelid
E3	Upper right, eyelid
E4	Lower right, eyelid

FIGURE 8-1 Sample HCPCS level II modifiers (Reprinted according to **www.cms.hhs.gov** Web site Content Reuse Policy.)

The alphabetic first character identifies the code sections of HCPCS level II. Some are logical, such as D for dental or R for radiology, whereas others, such as J for drugs, appear to be arbitrarily assigned. The HCPCS level II code ranges are as follows:

NOTE: C codes are reported for new drugs, biologicals, and devices that are eligible for transitional pass-through payments under the ambulatory payment classifications (APCs) under the outpatient prospective payment system.

NOTE: The Clinical Laboratory Improvement Act (CLIA) established quality standards for all laboratory testing to ensure the accuracy, reliability, and timeliness of patient test results regardless of where the test was performed.

A0000–A0999	Transport Services Including Ambulance
A4000–A8999	Medical and Surgical Supplies
A9000–A9999	Administrative, Miscellaneous and Investigational
B4000–B9999	Enteral and Parenteral Therapy
C1300–C9899	Outpatient PPS
D0000–D9999	Dental Procedures
E0100–E9999	Durable Medical Equipment
G0000–G9999	Procedures/Professional Services (Temporary)
H0001–H2037	Alcohol and/or Drug Abuse Treatment Services
J0000–J9999	Drugs Administered Other Than Oral Method
K0000–K9999	Temporary Codes (durable medical equipment)
L0000–L4999	Orthotic Procedures and Devices
L5000–L9999	Prosthetic Procedures
M0000–M0301	Medical Services
P0000–P9999	Pathology and Laboratory Services
Q0035–Q9968	Q Codes (Temporary) Diagnostic
R0000–R5999	Diagnostic Radiology Services
S0000–S9999	Temporary National Codes (non-Medicare)
T1000–T9999	National T Codes Established for State Medicaid Agencies
V0000–V2999	Vision Services
V5000–V5999	Hearing Services

Organization of Coding Manual

Because of the wide variety of services and procedures described in HCPCS level II, the alphabetical index (Figure 8-2) is very helpful in finding the correct code. The various publishers of the reference may include an expanded index that lists "alcohol wipes" and "wipes" as well as "Ancef" and "cefazolin sodium," making the search for codes easier and faster. Some references also include a Table of Drugs (Figure 8-3) that lists J codes assigned to medications. Some publishers print brand names beneath the generic description, and others provide a special expanded index of the drug codes. It is important never to code directly from the index and always to verify the code in the tabular section of the coding

---

Index

A

Abarelix, J0128
Abatacept, J0129
Abciximab, J0130
Abdomen/abdominal
  dressing holder/binder, A4462
  pad, low profile, L1270
Abduction
  control, each, L2624
  pillow, E1399
  rotation bar, foot L3140-L3170
Abortion, S2260-S2267
Abscess, incision and drainage,
    D7150-D7520
Absorption dressing, A6251-A6256
Abutments
  for implants, D6056-D6057
  retainers for resin bonded "Maryland
    bridge", D6545
Accession of brush biopsy sample,
    D0486
Accession of tissue, dental, D0472-
    D0474
Accessories
  ambulation devices, E0153-E0159
  artificial kidney and machine (*see*
    also ESRD), E1510-E1699
  beds, E0271-E0280, E0305-E0326
  oxygen, E1354-E1358
  wheelchairs E0950-E1010, E1050-
    E1298, E2201-E2231, E2295,
    E2300-E2367, K0001-K0108

2009 HCPCS

FIGURE 8-2 HCPCS level II index entries (portion) (Permission to reuse granted by Ingenix.)

manual. You may wish to review the HCPCS level II references from several publishers and select the one that best meets your needs and is the easiest for you to use.

If you have difficulty locating the service or procedure in the HCPCS level II index, review the contents of the appropriate section to locate the code (Figure 8-4). Read the code descriptions very carefully. You may need to ask the provider to help select the correct code.

Drug Name	Unit Per	Route	Code
10% LMD	500 ML	IV	J7100
5% DEXTROSE/NORMAL SALINE	5%	VAR	J7042
5% DEXTROSE/WATER	500 ML	IV	J7060
ABARELIX	10 MG	IM	J0128
ABATACEPT	10 MG	IV	J0129
ABCIXIMAB	10 MG	IV	J0130
ABELCET	50 MG	IV	J0285
ABILIFY	0.25 MG	IM	J0400
ABRAXANE	1 MG	IV	J9264
ACELLULAR PERICARDIAL TISSUE MATRIX NONHUMAN	SQ CM	OTH	C9365

FIGURE 8-3 HCPCS level II table of drugs (portion) (Permission to reuse granted by Ingenix.)

EXERCISE 8-1

HCPCS Index

Instructions: Using the HCPCS level II index, find and verify the following codes in the tabular section. Indicate the key word(s) used to search the index.

1. _____ Unclassified drug

   Key word(s): _____

2. _____ Fern test

   Key word(s): _____

3. _____ Benesch boot, pair, junior

   Key word(s): _____

4. _____ Safety belt for wheelchair

   Key word(s): _____

5. _____ Miscellaneous dialysis supplies

   Key word(s): _____

Contents

FIGURE 8-4 Sample of HCPCS level II table of contents (Reprinted according to **www.cms.hhs.gov** Web site Content Reuse Policy.)

NOTE: At one time the local Medicare carriers (LMCs) (replaced by Medicare administrative contractors) processed all claims for DME. The emphasis on keeping seniors in their own homes led to a rapid expansion in DME services and dealers. Also, many of the larger companies operated in several states and sent their claims to multiple Medicare carriers. Unfortunately, a few dealers formed for the sole purpose of collecting as much money as possible from the Medicare program and then closed down. When CMS began to investigate and pursue fraudulent claims, it became apparent that DME billings were out of control, so CMS decided to have all DME claims processed by only four regional MACs. This allowed the local MACs to concentrate on the familiar, traditional claims of providers billing for services, not equipment.

DETERMINING PAYER RESPONSIBILITY

The specific HCPCS level II code determines whether the claim is sent to the local Medicare administrative contractor (MAC) or the regional DME MAC. Annual lists of valid HCPCS level II codes give providers complete billing instructions for those services.

HCPCS level II codes that begin with:

- D, G, M, P, or F are reported to the local MAC.
- B, E, K, or L are reported to the regional DME MAC.
- A, J, Q, or V are reported to either the local MAC or regional DME MAC.

EXERCISE 8-2

Recognizing Payer Responsibility

Instructions: Using the above criteria and the codes assigned in Exercise 8-1, enter the codes reported to the local MAC, the regional DME MAC, or those possibly reported to either MAC.

local MAC: _____

regional DME MAC: _____

local MAC or regional DME MAC: _____

When the doctor treats a Medicare patient for a broken ankle and supplies the patient with crutches, two claims are generated. The one for the fracture care, or professional service, is sent to the local Medicare administrative contractor (MAC); the claim for the crutches is sent to the regional DME MAC. The physician must register with both, review billing rules, comply with claims instructions, and forward claims correctly to secure payment for both services. If the doctor is not registered with the regional DME MAC to provide medical equipment and supplies, the patient is given a prescription for crutches to take to a local DMEPOS dealer.

Some services, such as most dental procedures, are excluded as Medicare benefits by law and will not be covered by either MAC. Splints and casts for traumatic injuries have CPT numbers that would be used to report these supplies or services to the local MAC. Because the review procedure for adding new codes to level II is a much shorter process, new medical and surgical services may first be assigned a level II code and then incorporated into CPT at a later date.

ASSIGNING HCPCS LEVEL II CODES

Some services must be reported by assigning both a CPT and a HCPCS code. The most common scenario uses the CPT code for administration of an injection and the HCPCS code to identify the medication. Most drugs have qualifying terms such as dosage limits that could alter the quantity reported (Figure 8-3). If a drug stating "per 50 mg" is administered in a 70-mg dose, the quantity billed would be "2." If you administered only 15 mg of a drug stating "up to 20 mg," the quantity is "1." Imagine how much money providers lose by reporting only the CPT code for injections. Unless the payer or insurance plan advises the provider that it does not pay separately for the medication injected, always report this combination of codes.

It is possible that a particular service would be assigned a CPT code and a HCPCS level II code. Which one should you report? The answer is found in the instructions from the payer. Most commercial payers require the CPT code. Medicare gives HCPCS level II codes the highest priority if the CPT code is general and the HCPCS level II code is more specific.

Most supplies are included in the charge for the office visit or the procedure. CPT provides code 99070 for all supplies and materials exceeding those usually included in the primary service or procedure performed. However, this CPT code may be too general to ensure correct payment. If the office provides additional supplies when performing a service, the HCPCS level II codes may identify the supplies in sufficient detail to secure proper reimbursement.

Although CMS developed this system, some HCPCS levels I and II services are not payable by Medicare. Medicare may also place qualifications or conditions on payment for some services. As an example, an ECG is a covered service for a cardiac problem but is not covered when performed as part of a routine examination. Also, the payment for some services may be left to the payers discretion. Two CMS publications assist payers in correctly processing claims. The *Medicare National Coverage Determinations Manual* advises the MAC whether a service is covered or excluded under Medicare regulations. The *Medicare Benefit Policy Manual* directs the MAC to pay a service or reject it using a specific "remark" or explanation code.

There are more than 4,000 HCPCS level II codes, but you may find that no code exists for the procedure or service you need to report. Unlike CPT, HCPCS level II does not have a consistent method of establishing codes for reporting "unlisted procedure" services. If the MAC does not provide special instructions for reporting these services in HCPCS, report them with the proper "unlisted procedure" code from CPT. Remember to submit documentation explaining the procedure or service when using the "unlisted procedure" codes.

> **NOTE:** CMS developed the HCPCS level II codes for Medicare, but commercial payers also adopt them.

SUMMARY

Two levels of codes are associated with HCPCS, commonly referred to as HCPCS level I and II codes. (HCPCS level III codes were discontinued effective December 31, 2003.) HCPCS level I includes the five-digit Current Procedural Terminology (CPT) codes developed and published by the American Medical Association (AMA). HCPCS level II (or HCPCS national codes) were created in the 1980s to describe common medical services and supplies not classified in CPT.

The HCPCS level II national coding system classifies similar medical products and services for the purpose of efficient claims processing. Each code contains a description, and the codes are used primarily for billing purposes. The codes describe DME devices, accessories, supplies, and repairs; prosthetics; orthotics; medical and surgical supplies; medications; provider services; temporary Medicare codes (e.g., Q codes); and other items and services (e.g., ambulance services). Some services must be reported by assigning both a CPT and a HCPCS level II national code. The most common scenario uses the CPT code for the administration of an injection and the HCPCS code to identify the medication.

The specific HCPCS level II code determines whether the claim is sent to the primary Medicare administrative contractor (MAC) that processes provider claims or the DME MAC that processes DMEPOS dealer claims. Providers and DMEPOS dealers obtain annual lists of valid HCPCS level II national codes, which include billing instructions for services.

INTERNET LINKS

- HCPCS information
  Go to **www.cms.hhs.gov**, click on the Medicare link, and scroll down to the Coding heading and click on the HCPCS—General Information and HCPCS Release & Code Sets links.

- HCPCS/CPT drug and product reimbursement coding and pricing information
  www.reimbursementcodes.com

- HCPCS level II online coding manual
  Go to **www.eicd.com** and click on the eHCPCS Online link.

- Medicare Pricing, Data Analysis, and Coding (PDAC)
  www.dmepdac.com

STUDY CHECKLIST

- ☐ Read this textbook chapter and highlight key concepts.
- ☐ Create an index card for each key term.
- ☐ Access the chapter Internet links to learn more about concepts.
- ☐ Complete the chapter review, verifying answers with your instructor.
- ☐ Complete WebTutor assignments and take online quizzes.
- ☐ Complete Workbook chapter, verifying answers with your instructor.
- ☐ Complete the StudyWare activities to receive immediate feedback.
- ☐ Form a study group with classmates to discuss chapter concepts in preparation for an exam.

REVIEW

FILL-IN-THE-BLANK

1. **Using the current edition of a HCPCS level II coding manual, assign the correct codes, HCPCS modifier(s), and quantity to each of the following services.**

   a. B-12 injection not covered by Medicare, but patient agrees to pay.

   Code _____ Modifier(s) _____ Quantity _____

   b. Purchase of new rolling chair with six-inch wheels. Rental declined.

   Code _____ Modifier(s) _____ Quantity _____

   c. 100 reagent strips for home glucose monitor. Patient not on insulin.

   Code _____ Modifier(s) _____ Quantity _____

   d. Cervical cancer screening, including pelvic and clinical breast exam, at clinic in rural underserved area.

   Code _____ Modifier(s) _____ Quantity _____

   e. Third-month rental of oxygen concentrator.

   Code _____ Modifier(s) _____ Quantity _____

2. **Using the current editions of CPT and HCPCS level II coding manuals, assign the correct code and the HCPCS modifier(s) and quantity to each of the following scenarios.**

   a. Metatarsophalangeal synovectomy, third digit, left foot.

   Code _____ Modifier(s) _____ Quantity _____

   b. HemoCue 3 sample GTT.

   Code _____ Modifier(s) _____ Quantity _____

   c. Closed manipulation, left Potts fracture, by physician who has opted out of Medicare.

   Code _____ Modifier(s) _____ Quantity _____

   d. Anesthesiologist provides medical direction of her employee for radical nasal surgery (quantity not required).

   Code _____ Modifier(s) _____ Quantity _____

   e. Neuropsychological testing, two hours, by clinical psychologist.

   Code _____ Modifier(s) _____ Quantity _____

CMS Reimbursement Methodologies

CHAPTER OUTLINE

OBJECTIVES

Upon successful completion of this chapter, you should be able to:

1. Define key terms.
2. Explain the historical development of CMS reimbursement systems.
3. List and define each CMS payment system.
4. Apply special rules for the Medicare physician fee schedule payment system.
5. Interpret a chargemaster.
6. Explain hospital revenue cycle management.
7. Complete a UB-04 claim.

KEY TERMS

allowable charge

All Patient diagnosis-related group (AP-DRG)

All Patient Refined diagnosis-related group (APR-DRG)

ambulance fee schedule

ambulatory surgical center (ASC)

ambulatory surgical center payment rate

balance billing

case mix

chargemaster (charge description master [CDM])

clinical laboratory fee schedule

clinical nurse specialist (CNS)

CMS program transmittal

CMS Quarterly Provider Update (QPU)

conversion factor

Diagnostic and Statistical Manual (DSM)

disproportionate share hospital (DSH) adjustment

durable medical equipment, prosthetics/orthotics, and supplies (DMEPOS) fee schedule

employer group health plan (EGHP)

ESRD composite payment rate system

grouper software

health insurance prospective payment system (HIPPS) code set

Home Assessment Validation and Entry (HAVEN)

home health resource groups (HHRGs)

incident to

indirect medical education (IME) adjustment

inpatient prospective payment system (IPPS)

Inpatient Rehabilitation Validation and Entry (IRVEN)

intensity of resources

IPPS 3-day payment window

IPPS 72-hour rule

IPPS transfer rule

large group health plan (LGHP)

limiting charge

long-term (acute) care hospital prospective payment system (LTCPPS)

major diagnostic category (MDC)

Medicare physician fee schedule (MPFS)

Medicare Secondary Payer (MSP)

Medicare severity diagnosis-related groups (MS-DRGs)

Medicare Summary Notice (MSN)

nurse practitioner (NP)

Outcomes and Assessment Information Set (OASIS)

outlier

outpatient encounter (outpatient visit)

payment system

physician assistant (PA)

prospective cost-based rates

prospective price-based rates

relative value units (RVUs)

Resident Assessment Validation and Entry (RAVEN)

retrospective reasonable cost system

revenue code

revenue cycle management

risk of mortality (ROM)

severity of illness (SOI)

site of service differential

wage index

INTRODUCTION

NOTE:

· Content about the Medicare physician fee schedule (MPFS) begins later in this chapter. (Medical assistant academic programs often cover just the MPFS in this chapter.)

· Coding and health information management academic programs cover all content in this chapter.

Since the Medicare program was implemented in 1966, expenditures have increased at an unanticipated rate, and the news media frequently report that the program will be bankrupt in a few years. In 1983 the Health Care Financing Administration (HCFA, now called CMS) implemented the first prospective payment system (PPS) to control the cost of hospital inpatient care.

In subsequent years, similar reimbursement systems were implemented for alternate care (e.g., physician office, long-term care). This chapter details CMS's reimbursement systems and related issues, including the Medicare physician fee schedule (MPFS), UB-04 claim, and chargemaster.

StudyWARE

Complete StudyWare practice quizzes and activities using the CD-ROM located inside the back cover of your textbook.

HISTORICAL PERSPECTIVE OF CMS REIMBURSEMENT SYSTEMS

In 1964 the Johnson administration avoided opposition from hospitals for passage of the Medicare and Medicaid programs by adopting retrospective reasonable cost-basis payment arrangements previously established by Blue Cross.

Reimbursement according to a **retrospective reasonable cost system** meant that hospitals reported actual charges for inpatient care to payers after discharge of the patient from the hospital. Payers then reimbursed hospitals 80 percent of allowed charges. Although this policy helped secure passage of Medicare and Medicaid (by enticing hospital participation), subsequent spiraling reimbursement costs ensued.

Shortly after the passage of Medicare and Medicaid, Congress began investigating prospective payment systems (PPS) (Table 9-1), which established predetermined rates based on patient category or the type of facility (with annual increases based on an inflation index and a geographic wage index):

- **Prospective cost–based rates** are also established in advance, but they are based on reported healthcare costs (charges) from which a predetermined *per diem* (Latin meaning "for each day") rate is determined. Annual rates are usually adjusted using actual costs from the prior year. This method may be based on the facility's case mix (patient acuity), (e.g., resource utilization groups [RUGs] for skilled nursing care facilities).

- **Prospective price–based rates** are associated with a particular category of patient (e.g., inpatients), and rates are established by the payer (e.g., Medicare) prior to the provision of healthcare services (e.g., diagnosis-related groups [DRGs] for inpatient care).

> **EXAMPLE:** Prior to 1983, acute care hospitals generated invoices based on total charges for an inpatient stay. In 1982 an eight-day inpatient hospitalization at $225 per day (including ancillary service charges) would be billed $1,800. This *per diem* reimbursement rate actually discouraged hospitals from limiting inpatient lengths of stay. In 1983 the hospital would have been reimbursed a PPS rate of $950 for the same inpatient hospitalization, regardless of length of stay (unless the case qualified for additional reimbursement as an outlier). The PPS rate encourages hospitals to limit inpatient lengths of stay because any reimbursement received in excess of the actual cost of providing care is retained by the facility. (In this example, if the $950 PPS rate had been paid in 1980, the hospital would have absorbed the $850 loss.)

CMS PAYMENT SYSTEMS

The federal government administers several healthcare programs, some of which require services to be reimbursed according to a predetermined reimbursement methodology **(payment system)**. Federal healthcare programs (an overview of each is located in Chapter 2) include:

- **CHAMPVA.**
- **Indian Health Service (IHS).**
- **Medicaid (including the State Children's Health Insurance Program, or SCHIP).**
- **Medicare.**
- **TRICARE (formerly CHAMPUS).**
- **Workers' Compensation. (Also a state healthcare program.)**

Depending on the type of healthcare services provided to beneficiaries, the federal government requires that one of the payment systems listed in Table 9-1 be used for the CHAMPVA, Medicaid, Medicare, and TRICARE programs.

TABLE 9-1   Prospective payment systems, year implemented, and type

PROSPECTIVE PAYMENT SYSTEM	YEAR	TYPE
Ambulance Fee Schedule	2002	Cost-based
Ambulatory Surgical Center (ASC) Payment Rates	1994	Cost-based
Clinical Laboratory Fee Schedule	1985	Cost-based
Durable Medical Equipment, Prosthetics/Orthotics, and Supplies (DMEPOS) Fee Schedule	1989	Cost-based
End-Stage Renal Disease (ESRD) Composite Payment Rate System	2005	Price-based
Home Health Prospective Payment System (HH PPS) (Home Health Resource Groups [HHRG])	2000	Price-based
Hospital Inpatient Prospective Patient System (IPPS)	1983	Price-based
Hospital Outpatient Prospective Payment System (HOPPS)	2001	Price-based
Inpatient Psychiatric Facility Prospective Payment System (IPF PPS)	2004	Cost-based
Inpatient Rehabilitation Facility Prospective Payment System (IRF PPS)	2002	Price-based
Long-Term Care Hospital Prospective Payment System (LTCH PPS)	2001	Price-based
Resource-Based Relative Value Scale (RBRVS) System (or Medicare Physician Fee Schedule, [MPFS])	1992	Cost-based
Skilled Nursing Facility Prospective Payment System (SNF PPS)	1998	Cost-based

AMBULANCE FEE SCHEDULE

The Balanced Budget Act of 1997 required establishment of an **ambulance fee schedule** payment system for ambulance services provided to Medicare beneficiaries. Starting in April 2002, the ambulance fee schedule was phased in over a five-year period replacing a retrospective reasonable cost payment system for providers and suppliers of ambulance services (because such a wide variation of payment rates resulted for the same service). This schedule requires:

- Ambulance suppliers to accept Medicare assignment.
- Reporting of HCPCS codes on claims for ambulance services.
- Establishment of increased payment under the fee schedule for ambulance services furnished in rural areas based on the location of the beneficiary at the time the beneficiary is placed on board the ambulance.
- Revision of the certification requirements for coverage of nonemergency ambulance services.
- Medicare to pay for beneficiary transportation services when other means of transportation are contraindicated. Ambulance services are divided into different levels of ground (land and water transportation) and air ambulance services based on the medically necessary treatment provided during transport.

NOTE: For the purpose of this example, the charges and rates remain the same for each year. Medicare actually adjusts ambulance fee schedule rates according to an inflationary formula.

EXAMPLE: A patient was transported by ambulance from her home to the local hospital for care. Under the retrospective reasonable cost payment system, the ambulance company charged $600, and Medicare paid 80 percent of that amount, or $480. The ambulance fee schedule requires Medicare to reimburse the ambulance company $425, which is an amount equal to the predetermined rate or *fee schedule.*

AMBULATORY SURGICAL CENTER PAYMENT RATES

An **ambulatory surgical center (ASC)** is a state-licensed, Medicare-certified supplier (not provider) of surgical healthcare services that must *accept assignment* on Medicare claims. An ASC must be a separate entity distinguishable from any other entity or facility, and it must have its own employer identifier number (EIN) as well as processes for:

- **Accreditation.**
- **Administrative functions.**
- **Clinical services.**
- **Financial and accounting systems.**
- **Governance (of medical staff).**
- **Professional supervision.**
- **Recordkeeping.**
- **State licensure.**

> **NOTE:** An ASC can be physically located within a healthcare organization and still be considered separate for Medicare reimbursement purposes if all the preceding criteria are met.

> **NOTE:** Hospital outpatient departments that perform surgery are reimbursed under the outpatient prospective payment system (OPPS), which uses ambulatory payment classifications (APCs) as its reimbursement methodology, as discussed later in this chapter.

In 1980 Medicare authorized implementation of **ambulatory surgical center payment rates** as a fee to ambulatory surgery centers (ASCs) for facility services furnished in connection with performing certain surgical procedures. (Physician's professional services are separately reimbursed by the Medicare physician fee schedule, discussed later in this chapter.) Medicare identifies surgical procedures that are appropriately and safely performed on an ambulatory basis in an ASC, and that list of procedures is reviewed and updated at least every two years in consultation with appropriate trade and professional associations. Prior to 2008, procedures included on the ASC list were assigned to one of nine payment groups, based on an estimate of the costs incurred by the facility to perform the procedure. When procedures are added to the list, they are assigned to one of the existing payment groups.

Effective January 1, 2008, the outpatient prospective payment system (OPPS) payment amount substitutes the ASC standard overhead amount for surgical procedures performed at an ASC. (The Medicare Prescription Drug, Improvement, and Modernization Act of 2003 [MMA] mandated implementation of a revised payment system for ASC surgical services by no later than January 1, 2008.) Medicare has also proposed that under this revised ASC payment system, Medicare would allow payment of an ASC facility fee for any surgical procedure performed at an ASC, *except those surgical procedures that Medicare has determined are not eligible for the ASC facility fee.* This means that instead of maintaining and updating an "inclusive list of procedures," Medicare would maintain and update an "exclusionary list of procedures" for which an ASC facility fee would *not* be paid (e.g., any procedure included on the OPPS inpatient list).

Under the revised payment system (Table 9-2), Medicare will use the ambulatory payment classification (APC) groups and relative payment weights for surgical procedures established under the OPPS as the basis of the payment groups and the relative payment weights for surgical procedures performed at ASCs. These payment weights would be multiplied by an ASC conversion factor in order to calculate the ASC payment rates.

The ASC relative payment weights would be updated each year using the national OPPS relative payment weights for that calendar year and, for office-based procedures, the practice expense payments under the physician fee schedule for that calendar year. Medicare also plans to make the relative payment weights budget neutral to ensure that changes in the relative payment weights from year to year do not cause the estimated amount of expenditures to ASCs to increase or decrease as a function of those changes.

TABLE 9-2　Sample list of Medicare-approved ASC procedures under revised payment system

HCPCS CODE	HCPCS CODE DESCRIPTION	ASC RELATIVE PAYMENT WEIGHT	ASC FACILITY FEE PAYMENT	PATIENT COPAYMENT
G0104	Colorectal cancer screening; flexible sigmoidoscopy	1.7292	$68.63	$13.73
G0105	Colorectal cancer screening; colonoscopy on individual at high risk	7.8134	$310.10	$62.02
G0121	Colorectal cancer screening; colonoscopy on individual not meeting criteria for high risk	7.8134	$310.10	$62.02
G0127	Trimming of dystrophic nails, any number	0.2665	$10.58	$2.12
G0186	Destruction of localized lesion of choroid (for example, choroidal neovascularization); photocoagulation, feeder vessel technique (one or more sessions)	4.0750	$161.73	$32.35
G0260	Injection procedure for sacroiliac joint; provision of anesthetic, steroid and/or other therapeutic agent, with or without arthrography	5.5439	$220.03	$44.01
G0268	Removal of impacted cerumen (one or both ears) by physician on same date of service as audiologic function testing	0.5409	$21.47	$4.29
G0364	Bone marrow aspiration performed with bone marrow biopsy through the same incision on the same date of service	0.1293	$5.13	$1.03

CLINICAL LABORATORY FEE SCHEDULE

The Deficit Reduction Act of 1984 established the Medicare **clinical laboratory fee schedule** (Figure 9-1), which is a data set based on local fee schedules (for outpatient clinical diagnostic laboratory services). Medicare reimburses laboratory services according to the (1) submitted charge, (2) national limitation amount, or (3) local fee schedule amount, whichever is lowest. The local fee schedules are developed by Medicare administrative contractors who are:

NOTE: The clinical laboratory fee schedule contains approximately 1,000 separate clinical laboratory codes currently listed in the 80048–89399 CPT code series, along with a small number (less than 50) of HCPCS level II national codes.

- Local contractors that process Medicare Part B claims, including claims submitted by independent laboratories and physician office laboratories.
- Local contractors that process Medicare Part A claims, including outpatient laboratory tests performed by hospitals, nursing homes, and end-stage renal disease centers.

Clinical Diagnostic Laboratory Fee Schedule
12/10/YYYY

CPT code	Modifier	National Limit	Mid Point	N.Y.S. rate	Short Description of HCPCS code
78267		$10.98	$14.84	$10.98	Breath test attain/anal c-14
78268		$94.11	$127.18	$94.11	Breath test analysis, c-14
80048		$11.83	$15.98	$11.83	Basic metabolic panel
80051		$9.80	$13.24	$8.93	Electrolyte panel
80053		$14.77	$19.96	$14.77	Comprehensive metabolic panel
80061		$0.00	$0.00	$15.88	Lipid panel
80061	-QW	$0.00	$0.00	$15.88	Lipid panel
80069		$12.13	$16.39	$12.13	Renal function panel
80074		$0.00	$0.00	$64.46	Acute hepatitis panel
80076		$11.42	$15.43	$11.42	Hepatic function panel
80100		$20.32	$27.46	$20.32	Drug screen, qualitative/multi

FIGURE 9-1 Sample clinical lab fee schedule data (modifier -QW is reported for a CLIA-waived laboratory test) (CPT copyright 2009 American Medical Association. All rights reserved.)

DURABLE MEDICAL EQUIPMENT, PROSTHETICS/ ORTHOTICS, AND SUPPLIES FEE SCHEDULE

NOTE: A valid ICD-9-CM diagnosis code must be reported for each line item on electronically submitted claims. If an electronic claim that is submitted to a regional DME MAC does not contain a valid ICD-9-CM diagnosis code, it will be rejected.

The Deficit Reduction Act of 1984 also established the Medicare **durable medical equipment, prosthetics/orthotics, and supplies (DMEPOS) fee schedule** (Figure 9-2). Medicare reimburses DMEPOS either 80 percent of the actual charge for the item *or* the fee schedule amount whichever is lower. (Fee schedule amounts are annually updated and legislated by Congress.)

The Medicare Prescription Drug, Improvement, and Modernization Act of 2003 (MMA) authorized Medicare to replace the current durable medical equipment (DME) payment methodology for *certain items* with a competitive acquisition process to improve the effectiveness of its methodology for establishing DME payment amounts. The new bidding process will establish payment amounts for certain durable medical equipment, enteral nutrition, and off-the-shelf orthotics. Competitive bidding provides a way to create incentives for suppliers to provide quality items and services in an efficient manner and at reasonable cost.

Durable Medical Equipment, Prosthetics, Orthotics, and Supplies (DMEPOS)
8/16/YYYY

HCPCS code	Modifier	Jurisdiction[1]	Category[2]	Ceiling[3]	Floor[4]	N.Y.S. rate	Short Description of HCPCS code
A4217		D	SU	$3.13	$2.66	$2.66	Sterile water/saline, 500 ml
A4217	-AU	D	OS	$3.13	$2.66	$2.66	Sterile water/saline, 500 ml
A4221		D	SU	$22.64	$19.24	$22.64	Supplies for maint drug infus cath, per wk.
A4222		D	SU	$46.73	$39.72	$46.73	External drug infusion pump supplies, per cassette or bag
A4253	-NU	D	IN	$38.52	$32.74	$38.52	Blood glucose/reagent strips, per 50
A4255		D	SU	$4.11	$3.49	$4.11	Glucose monitor platforms, 50 per box

[1]**Jursidiction**
D (Regional DME MAC jurisdiction)
L (Local Part B administrative contractor jurisdiction)
J (Joint regional DME MAC/local MAC jurisdiction)

[2]**Category**
IN (inexpensive and other routinely purchased items)
FS (frequently serviced items)
CR (capped rental items)
OX (oxygen and oxygen equipment)
OS (ostomy, tracheostomy & urological items)
SD (surgical dressings)
PO (prosthetics & orthotics)
SU (supplies)
TE (transcutaneous electrical nerve stimulators)

[3]**Ceiling** (maximum fee schedule amount)

[4]**Floor** (minimum fee schedule amount)

FIGURE 9-2 Sample DMEPOS fee schedule data (Courtesy Delmar/Cengage Learning)

END-STAGE RENAL DISEASE (ESRD) COMPOSITE PAYMENT RATE SYSTEM

Medicare's ESRD benefit allows patients to receive dialysis treatments, which remove excess fluids and toxins from the bloodstream. Patients also receive items and services related to their dialysis treatments, including drugs to treat conditions resulting from the loss of kidney function, such as anemia and low blood calcium. CMS traditionally divided ESRD items and services into two groups for payment purposes:

- Dialysis and associated routine services (e.g., nursing, supplies, equipment, certain drugs, and certain laboratory tests) are reimbursed according to a composite rate (one rate for a defined set of services). Paying according to a composite rate (or fixed) is a common form of Medicare payment, also known as *bundling*.

- Injectable drugs and certain laboratory tests that were either not routine or not available in 1983, when Medicare implemented the ESRD composite rate, are reimbursed separately on a per-service basis. They were referred to as "separately billable." Drugs that were separately billable were paid based on the average wholesale price (AWP).

While Medicare's composite rate was not automatically adjusted for inflation (and covered less of the costs associated with providing routine dialysis services), reimbursement for separately billable drugs usually exceeded the providers' costs to obtain the drugs. Thus, dialysis facilities relied on reimbursement for separately billable drugs to subsidize composite rate payments, and as the use of separately billable drugs became routine, reimbursement for these drugs increased substantially.

The Medicare Prescription Drug, Improvement and Modernization Act (MMA) of 2003 required Medicare to change the way it pays facilities for dialysis treatments and separately billable drugs. A key purpose of the MMA was to eliminate the cross-subsidization of composite rate payments by drug payments. These revisions also resulted in more accurate reimbursement for drugs and the composite rate. Medicare spends the same amount of money as would have been spent under the prior system, but the cross-subsidy was eliminated. The ESRD composite payment rate system bundles ESRD drugs and related laboratory tests with the composite rate payments, resulting in one reimbursement amount paid for ESRD services provided to patients. The rate is case-mix adjusted to provide a mechanism to account for differences in patients' utilization of healthcare resources (e.g., patient's age, documentation and reporting of comorbidities) (Table 9-3).

> **NOTE:** A facility's **case mix** is a measure of the types of patients treated, and it reflects patient utilization of varying levels of healthcare resources. Patients are classified according to age, gender, health status, and so on.
>
> For example, elderly patients usually require more complex care than teenage patients, which means a greater amount of money is spent on patient care provided to the elderly.)

TABLE 9-3   Case-mix adjustments to composite rates based on patient age

AGE RANGE	CASE-MIX INDEX MULTIPLIER
18–44	1.223
45–59	1.055
60–69	1.000
70–79	1.094
80+	1.174

> **EXAMPLE:** A healthcare facility's composite rate is $128.35, which means that Medicare reimburses the facility $128.35 for an ESRD service. According to Table 9-3, that rate applies only to patients whose ages range from 60 to 69. When a 58-year-old patient receives ESRD services, the facility's reimbursement increases to $135.41 because the composite rate ($128.35) is multiplied by the case-mix index (1.055).

HOME HEALTH PROSPECTIVE PAYMENT SYSTEM

The BBA of 1997 called for implementation of a Medicare *home health prospective payment system* (HH PPS), which uses a classification system called *home health resource groups* (HHRGs) to establish prospective reimbursement rates for each 60-day episode of home health care. Home health resource groups (HHRGs) classify patients into one of 80 groups, which range in severity level. Each HHRG has an associated weight value that increases or decreases Medicare's payment for an episode of home health care. HHRGs are reported to Medicare on HH PPS claims (UB-04, discussed later in this chapter) using the health insurance prospective payment system (HIPPS) code set. Codes in this set are five-digit alphanumeric codes that represent case-mix groups about which payment determinations are made for the HH PPS. CMS originally created the HIPPS code set for the skilled nursing facility prospective payment system (SNF PPS) in 1998, and reporting requirements for the HH PPS (and inpatient rehabilitation facility PPS) were added later. HIPPS codes are determined after patient assessments using the Outcomes and Assessment Information Set (OASIS) are completed.

> **NOTE:** ICD-9-CM codes are used to determine the appropriate HH PPS payment level. One principal diagnosis and up to eight additional diagnosis codes are submitted.

Grouper software is used to determine the appropriate HHRG after Outcomes and Assessment Information Set (OASIS) data (Figure 9-3) is input on each patient (to measure the outcome of all adult patients receiving home health services). Home Assessment Validation and Entry (HAVEN) data entry software is then used to collect OASIS assessment data for transmission to state databases.

HOSPITAL INPATIENT PROSPECTIVE PAYMENT SYSTEM

Before 1983, Medicare payments for hospital inpatient care were based on a retrospective reasonable cost system, which meant hospitals received 80 percent of reasonable charges. Since 1983, when the inpatient prospective payment system (IPPS) was implemented, Medicare has reimbursed hospitals for inpatient hospital services according to a predetermined rate for each discharge. Each discharge is categorized into a *diagnosis-related group (DRG)*, which is based on the patient's principal and secondary diagnoses (including comorbidities and complications) as well as principal and secondary procedures (if performed) (Figure 9-4). The DRG determines how much payment the hospital receives. Diagnosis-related groups are organized into mutually exclusive categories called major diagnostic categories (MDCs), which are loosely based on body systems (e.g., nervous system).

> **NOTE:** ICD-9-CM codes directly affect DRG assignment. CPT codes play no role in DRG assignments.

> **NOTE:** Cancer hospitals are excluded from the IPPS and continue to be paid on a reasonable cost basis subject to per-discharge limits.

Because the IPPS payment is based on an adjusted average payment rate, some cases receive Medicare reimbursement in excess of costs (rather than billed charges), while other cases receive payment that is less than costs incurred. The system is designed to provide hospitals with an incentive to manage their operations more efficiently by finding areas in which increased efficiencies can be instituted without affecting the quality of care and by treating a mix of patients to balance cost and payments. Note that a hospital's payment is not affected by the length of stay prior to discharge (unless the patient is transferred). It is expected that some patients will stay longer than others and that hospitals will offset the higher costs of a longer stay with the lower costs of a reduced stay.

Each DRG has a payment weight assigned to it, based on the average resources used to treat Medicare patients in that DRG, and the reimbursement rate can be adjusted according to the following guidelines:

- Disproportionate share hospital (DSH) adjustment. **Hospitals that treat a high-percentage of low-income patients receive increased Medicare payments.**

DISCHARGE ASSESSMENT
(Page 1 of 11)

Client's Name: _____

Client Record No. _____

The *Outcome and Assessment Information Set (OASIS)* is the intellectual property of The Center for Health Services and Policy Research. Copyright ©2000 Used with Permission.

A. DEMOGRAPHIC/GENERAL INFORMATION

1. **(M0010) Agency Medicare Provider Number:**

   _ _ _ _ _ _

2. **(M0012) Agency Medicaid Provider Number:**

   _ _ _ _ _ _ _ _ _ _ _ _

Branch Identification (Optional, for Agency Use)

3. **(M0014) Branch State:** _ _

4. **(M0016) Branch ID Number:** _ _ _ _ _ _ _ _ _ _
   (Agency-assigned)

5. **(M0020) Patient ID Number:** _ _ _ _ _ _ _ _ _ _ _ _ _ _ _ _ _ _ _

6. **(M0030) Start of Care Date:**

   _ _ – _ _ – _ _ _ _
   m m   d d   y y y y

7. **(M0032) Resumption of Care Date:**

   _ _ – _ _ – _ _ _ _
   m m   d d   y y y y

   ☐ NA - Not Applicable

8. **(M0040) Patient Name:**

   _____ ____ _____ _____
   (First)   (MI) (Last)   (Suffix)

9. **Patient Address:**

   Street, Route, Apt. Number - not P.O. Box
   _____

   City _____ (M0050) State ____ (M0060) Zip Code

10. **Patient Phone:**

    (_ _ _) _ _ _ – _ _ _ _

11. **(M0063) Medicare Number:**

    _ _ _ _ _ _ _ _ _ _ _   ☐ NA - No Medicare
    (including suffix if any)

12. **(M0064) Social Security Number:**

    _ _ _ _ _ _ _ _ _   ☐ UK - Unknown or
                          Not Available

13. **(M0065) Medicaid Number:**

    _ _ _ _ _ _ _ _ _ _   ☐ NA - No Medicaid

14. **(M0066) Birth Date:**

    _ _ – _ _ – _ _ _ _
    m m   d d   y y y y

15. **(M0069) Gender:**   ☐ 1 - Male   ☐ 2 - Female

16. **(M0072) Primary Referring Physician ID:** _ _ _ _ _ _ _ _ _ _ (UPIN#)   ☐ UK - Unknown or Not Available

17. **(M0080) Discipline of Person Completing Assessment:**

    ☐ 1 - RN   ☐ 3 - SLP/ST
    ☐ 2 - PT   ☐ 4 - OT

18. **(M0090) Date Assessment Completed:**

    _ _ – _ _ – _ _ _ _
    m m   d d   y y y y

19. **(M0100) This Assessment is Currently Being Completed for the Following Reason:**

    Start/Resumption of Care
    1 - Start of care—further visits planned
    2 - Start of care—no further visits planned
    3 - Resumption of care (after inpatient stay)

    Follow-Up
    4 - Recertification (follow-up) reassessment
    5 - Other follow-up

    Transfer to an Inpatient Facility
    ☐ 6 - Transferred to an inpatient facility—patient not discharged from agency [Go to *M0150*]
    ☐ 7 - Transferred to an inpatient facility—patient discharged from agency [Go to *M0150*]

    Discharge from Agency—Not to an Inpatient Facility
    ☐ 8 - Death at home [Go to *M0150*]
    ☐ 9 - Discharge from agency [Go to *M0150*]
    ☐ 10 - Discharge from agency—no visits completed after start/resumption of care assessment [Go to *M0150*]

20. **(M0150) Current Payment Sources for Home Care:** (Mark all that apply.)

    ☐ 0 - None; no charge for current services
    ☐ 1 - Medicare (traditional fee-for-service)
    ☐ 2 - Medicare (HMO/managed care)
    ☐ 3 - Medicaid (traditional fee-for-service)
    ☐ 4 - Medicaid (HMO/managed care)
    ☐ 5 - Workers' compensation
    ☐ 6 - Title programs (e.g., Title III, V or XX)
    ☐ 7 - Other government (e.g., CHAMPUS, VA, etc.)
    ☐ 8 - Private insurance
    ☐ 9 - Private HMO/managed care
    ☐ 10 - Self-pay
    ☐ 11 - Other (specify) _____

    | If reason for assessment (RFA) for M0100 is 6 or 7, go to *M0830*. |
    | If RFA for M0100 is 8 or 10, go to *M0906*. |
    | If RFA for M0100 is 9, go to *M0200*. |

21. **(M0200) Medical or Treatment Regimen Change Within Past 14 Days:** Has this patient experienced a change in medical or treatment regimen (e.g., medication, treatment, or service change due to new or additional diagnosis, etc.) within the last 14 days?

    ☐ 0 - No [If No, go to *Section B - Therapies*]
    ☐ 1 - Yes

22. **(M0210)** List the patient's **Medical Diagnoses** and ICD code categories (three digits required; five digits optional) for those conditions requiring changed medical or treatment regimen (no surgical or V-codes):

    Changed Medical Regimen Diagnosis   ICD

    a. _____   (_ _ _ . _ _)

    b. _____   (_ _ _ . _ _)

    c. _____   (_ _ _ . _ _)

    d. _____   (_ _ _ . _ _)

OASIS-B1 DC (08/2000)

FIGURE 9-3 Page 1 of the discharge assessment form completed by home health agencies to capture OASIS data. (The Outcome and Assessment Information Set [OASIS] is the intellectual property of the Center for Health Services Research, Denver, Colorado. Used with permission.)

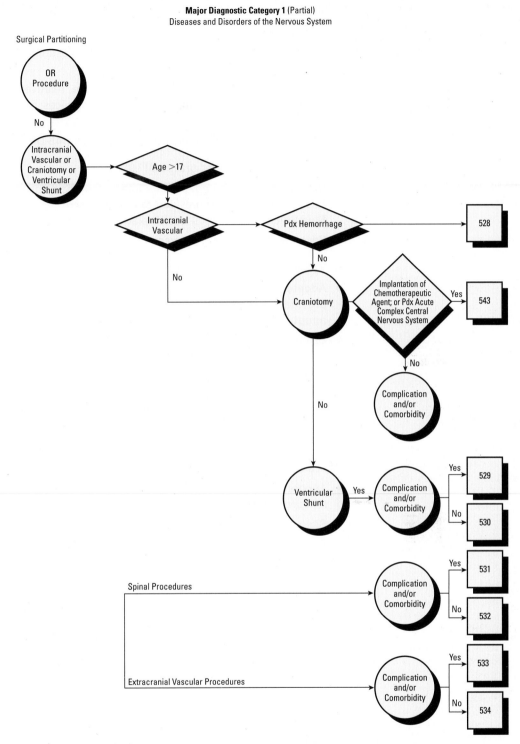

Major Diagnostic Category 1 (Partial)
Diseases and Disorders of the Nervous System

FIGURE 9-4 Sample DRG decision tree (Permission to reprint granted by Ingenix.)

- **Indirect medical education (IME) adjustment.** Approved teaching hospitals receive increased Medicare payments. The adjustment varies depending on the ratio of residents-to-beds (to calculate operating costs) and residents-to-average-daily-census (to calculate capital costs).

- **Outliers.** Hospitals that treat unusually costly cases receive increased medical payments. The additional payment is designed to protect hospitals from large financial losses due to unusually expensive cases. Outlier payments are added to DSH or IME adjustments, when applicable.

Several DRG systems were developed for use in the United States, including:

- *Diagnosis-related groups (DRGs)*
  - Original system used by CMS to reimburse hospitals for inpatient care provided to Medicare beneficiaries
  - Based on intensity of resources, which is the relative volume and types of diagnostic, therapeutic, and inpatient bed services used to manage an inpatient disease
  - Replaced in 2008 by Medicare severity DRGs (MS-DRGs) (discussed below)

- All-Patient diagnosis-related groups (AP-DRGs)
  - Original DRG system adapted for use by third-party payers to reimburse hospitals for inpatient care provided to *non*-Medicare beneficiaries (e.g., Blue Cross Blue Shield, commercial health plans, TRICARE)
  - Based on intensity of resources

- All-Patient Refined diagnosis-related groups (APR-DRGs)
  - Adopted by Medicare in 2007 to reimburse hospitals for inpatient care provided to Medicare beneficiaries (but discontinued when MS-DRGs were adopted in 2008)
  - Expanded original DRG system (based on intensity of resources) to add two subclasses to each DRG that adjusts Medicare inpatient hospital reimbursement rates for severity of illness (SOI) (extent of physiological decompensation or organ system loss of function) and risk of mortality (ROM) (likelihood of dying)
  - Each subclass, in turn, is subdivided into four areas: (1) minor, (2) moderate, (3) major, and (4) extreme.

- Medicare severity diagnosis-related groups (MS-DRGs)
  - Adopted by Medicare in 2008 to improve recognition of severity of illness and resource consumption and reduce cost variation among DRGs.
  - Bases DRG relative weights on hospital *costs* (instead of hospital charges that are associated with pre-2008 DRGs), and expanded number from 538 DRGs to over 750 MS-DRGs, but retained improvements and refinements made to DRGs since 1983.
  - Recognized approximately 335 "base" DRGs, which are further refined by *complications* (undesirable effect of disease or treatment that can change the patient's outcome and may require additional treatment), conditions that arise during hospitalization, and/or *comorbidities* (co-existing conditions treated during hospitalization) (CC).
  - Re-evaluated CC list to assign *all* ICD-9-CM codes as non-CC status (conditions that should not be treated as CCs for specific clinical conditions), CC status, *or* major CC status, which prevents Medicare from paying additional costs of treating patients who acquire conditions (e.g., infections) during hospitalization.
  - Assigned diagnoses closely associated with patient mortality (cardiogenic shock, cardiac arrest, other shock without mention of trauma, respiratory arrest, and ventricular fibrillation) to different CC subclasses, depending on whether the patient lived or expired.
  - Emphasized the importance of proper documentation of patient care, relating it to reimbursement optimization (e.g., increased diagnosis specificity to justify more severe illnesses, resulting in increased reimbursement)—facilities implemented clinical documentation improvement (CDI) programs to ensure thorough and accurate documentation in patient records.

CODING FOR DIAGNOSIS-RELATED GROUPS (DRGs)

Diagnoses and procedures are assigned ICD-9-CM codes, and they are sequenced according to CMS official coding guidelines and the Uniform Hospital Discharge Data Set (UHDDS). This means that hospitals are not required to assign codes to every diagnosis and procedure documented in the patient record. However, hospitals must evaluate their institutional data needs to develop coding policies, which will determine the assignment of ICD-9-CM codes to diagnoses and procedures.

When assigning codes to comorbidities (co-existing conditions) and complications (conditions that develop during inpatient admission), be sure to carefully review patient record documentation to assign the most specific code possible. Revisions to the MS-DRGs comorbidities and complications (CC) list eliminated many diagnoses that were considered CCs in the past. As a result, physicians must be educated about the importance of proper documentation practices.

EXAMPLE: Under MS-DRGs:

- Chronic obstructive pulmonary disease (COPD) (496) is not a CC. However, acute exacerbation of COPD (491.21) is a CC.

- Congestive heart failure (CHF) (428.0) is not a CC. However, chronic systolic heart failure (428.22) is a CC and acute systolic heart failure (428.21) is a major CC (MCC).

ICD-9-CM codes are assigned for documented OR (operating room) and non-OR procedures. (Non-OR procedures are performed in the patient's room, emergency department, radiology department, and so on.) Whether ICD-9-CM codes are assigned to other procedures, such as ancillary tests (e.g., EKG, laboratory tests, and so on), is dependent on the hospital's coding policy.

The *present on admission (POA) indicator* differentiates between patient conditions present upon inpatient admission and those that develop during the inpatient admission. Claims that do not report the POA indicator are returned to the facility for correction. Hospital-acquired conditions that are reported as not present at the time of admission are not considered when calculating the MS-DRG payment. This means that such conditions, even if included on the CC and MCC lists, are not considered a CC or MCC if diagnosed during the inpatient stay and the facility will not receive additional payment for such conditions.

To determine an IPPS payment, hospitals submit a UB-04 claim for each patient to a Medicare administrative contractor (MAC), which is a third-party payer that contracts with Medicare to carry out the operational functions of the Medicare program. Based on the information provided on the UB-04, the case is categorized into a DRG, which determines the reimbursement provided to the hospital. (DRG payments are adjusted as discussed previously.)

The IPPS 3-day payment window (or IPPS 72-hour rule) requires outpatient preadmission services provided by a hospital on the day of or during the three days prior to a patient's inpatient admission to be covered by the IPPS DRG payment and reported on the UB-04 with ICD-9-CM (or ICD-10-CM) procedure codes (*not* CPT codes) for:

- Diagnostic services (e.g., lab testing).

- Therapeutic (or nondiagnostic) services for which the inpatient principal diagnosis code (ICD-9-CM) exactly matches that for preadmission services.

NOTE: Services that are distinct from and unrelated to the inpatient admission are separately billed by the hospital *if documentation supports that the service is unrelated to the inpatient admission.*

not licensed for specialty care but that occasionally treat patients with behavioral health or chemical dependency diagnoses are exempt from the IPF PPS.)

Health information department coders will use ICD-9-CM to assign codes to inpatient behavioral health diagnoses and procedures and will enter data into DRG software to calculate the IPF PPS DRG. Inpatient psychiatric facilities are reimbursed according to a *per diem* payment that is calculated using DRG data, wage-adjusted rates, and facility-level adjusters (Figure 9-6). (IPPS MS-DRGs reimburse acute care hospitals a flat payment based on ICD-9-CM codes and other data.) Providers will use the **Diagnostic and Statistical Manual (DSM)** published by the American Psychiatric Association. Although DSM codes do not affect IPF PPS rates, the manual contains diagnostic assessment criteria that are used as tools to identify psychiatric disorders. The DSM includes psychiatric disorders and codes, provides a mechanism for communicating and recording diagnostic information, and is used in the areas of research and statistics.

INPATIENT REHABILITATION FACILITY PROSPECTIVE PAYMENT SYSTEM

The BBA of 1997 authorized the implementation of a per-discharge prospective payment system (PPS) for inpatient rehabilitation hospitals and rehabilitation units, also called inpatient rehabilitation facilities (IRFs). Implemented in 2002, the IRF PPS utilizes information from a patient assessment instrument to classify patients into distinct groups based on clinical characteristics and expected resource needs. Separate payments are calculated for each group, including the application of case- and facility-level adjustments.

A *patient assessment instrument* classifies patients into IRF PPS groups based on clinical characteristics and expected resource needs. Separate IRF PPS payments are calculated for each group and include case- and facility-level adjustments. Elements of the IRF PPS include:

- *Minimum Data Set for Post Acute Care (MDS-PAC)* (patient-centered assessment instrument completed by each Medicare patient that emphasizes the patient's care needs instead of the provider's characteristics; it classifies patients for Medicare payment and contains an appropriate quality-of-care monitoring system, including the use of quality indicators).

- *Case-mix groups (CMGs)* (classification of patients into 97 function-related groups, which predict resources needed to furnish patient care to different types of patients; data elements from the MDS-PAC are used to classify a patient into a CMG).

- *CMG relative weights* (weights that account for the variance in cost per discharge and resource utilization among CMGs; reimbursement is based on a national formula that adjusts for case mix).

- *CMG payment rates* (predetermined, per-discharge reimbursement amount that includes all operating and capital costs associated with providing covered inpatient rehabilitation services).

Inpatient Rehabilitation Validation and Entry (IRVEN) software (Figure 9-7) is the computerized data entry system used by inpatient rehabilitation facilities to create a file in a standard format that can be electronically transmitted to a national database. The data collected is used to assess the clinical characteristics of patients in rehabilitation hospitals and rehabilitation units in acute care hospitals. It provides agencies and facilities with a means to objectively measure and compare facility performance and quality. It will also provide researchers with information to support the development of improved standards.

Inpatient Psychiatric Hospital PPS Calculator

		Adjustment Factors
Patient Age	Patient is under age 65	1
Principal Diagnosis	DRG 12: Degenerative Nervous System Disorders (select as many comorbidities that apply below)	1.07
Comorbidity	Renal Failure, Chronic	1.14
Comorbidity	Arteriosclerosis of the Extremity with Gangrene	1.17
Comorbidity	Infectious Diseases	1.08
LOS (Days)	18	
Geographic Location	Rural	1.16
Teaching Adj.	0.6	1.28
Wage Area	Utah	0.9312

After making selections (above), scroll down for payment calculation information.

Budget Neutral Base Rate	**$530**

Calculate Wage Adjusted Rate	
The labor portion of the base rate	$386
Apply wage index factor of 0.9312 to the labor portion of $386	$359
The non-labor portion of the Federal base rate	$144
The total wage-adjusted rate	$503

Apply Facility Level Adjusters	
Teaching Adjustment	1.28
Rural Adjustment (if applicable)	1.16

Apply Patient Level Adjusters	
DRG 12: Degenerative Nervous System Disorders	1.07
Apply age adjustment	1
Apply comorbidity adjusters:	
Renal Failure, Chronic	1.14
Arteriosclerosis of the Extremity with Gangrene	1.17
Infectious Diseases	1.08

Total PPS Adjustment Factor	**2.2846**

The wage-adjusted and PPS-adjusted per diem amount is $1,150 (2.2846 * $503)

	Per Diem Amount	Unit	Extended
Apply variable per diem adjustment for 18 days:			
Day 1 (adjustment factor=1.26):	$1,150 * 1.26 = $1,449	1	$1,449
Days 2–4 (adjustment factor=1.12):	$1,150 * 1.12 = $1,288	3	$3,865
Days 5–8 (adjustment factor=1.05):	$1,150 * 1.05 = $1,208	4	$4,831
Days over 8 (adjustment factor=1.00):	$1,150 * 1.00 = $1,150	10	$11,502

Total Inpatient Psychiatric Hospital PPS Payment:	**$21,646**

FIGURE 9-6 Psychiatric hospital IPF PPS calculator worksheet (Permission to reuse in accordance with CMS Web site Content Reuse Policy.)

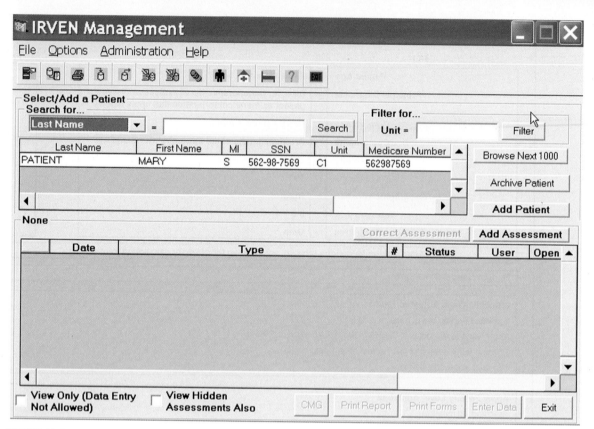

FIGURE 9-7 Opening screen from IRVEN software (Permission to reuse in accordance with CMS Web site Content Reuse Policy.)

LONG-TERM (ACUTE) CARE HOSPITAL PROSPECTIVE PAYMENT SYSTEM

The BBRA of 1999 authorized the implementation of a per-discharge DRG **long-term (acute) care hospital prospective payment system (LTCHPPS)** for cost reporting periods beginning on or after October 1, 2002. This new prospective payment system replaced the reasonable cost-based payment system under which long-term (acute) care hospitals (LTCHs) were previously paid. (In 2008, Medicare severity long term care diagnosis-related groups [MS-LTC-DRGs] were adopted for the LTCHPPS.) Long-term (acute) care hospitals are defined by Medicare as having an average inpatient length of stay of greater than 25 days.

Major elements of the LTCHPPS include:

- *Patient classification system* (patients are classified according to long-term [acute] care diagnosis related groups, LTC DRGs, based on clinical characteristics and average resource needs; the LTC DRGs are based on existing IPPS DRGs, which have been weighted to reflect the resources required to treat medically complex patients in long-term care hospitals).

- *Relative weights* (the MS-LTC-DRGs primary element that accounts for variations in cost per discharge, because the weights reflect severity of illness and resource consumption for each diagnosis).

- *Payment rate* (LTCHPPS payments for Medicare patients will be predetermined, per-discharge amounts for each MS-LTC-DRG).

- *Adjustments* (LTCHPPS payments are adjusted for short stay cases, interrupted stay cases, cases discharged and readmitted to co-located providers, and high-cost outlier cases. In addition, adjustments are made for differences in area wages and a cost-of living adjustment [COLA] for LTCHs in Alaska and Hawaii).

SKILLED NURSING FACILITY PROSPECTIVE PAYMENT SYSTEM

The BBA of 1997 modified reimbursement for Medicare Part A (inpatient) skilled nursing facility (SNF) services and, beginning in 1998, SNFs were no longer paid on a reasonable cost basis but rather on the basis of a prospective payment system.

Major elements of the SNF PPS include:

- *Payment rate* (federal rates are determined using allowable costs from facility cost reports, and data is aggregated nationally by urban and rural area to determine standardized federal *per diem* rates to which case-mix and wage adjustments apply).

- *Case mix adjustment* (*per diem* payments for each admission are case-mix adjusted using a resident classification system called Resource Utilization Groups, based on data from resident assessments and relative weights developed from staff time data).

- *Geographic adjustment* (labor portions of federal rates are adjusted for geographic variation in wages using the hospital wage index).

Computerized data entry software entitled Resident Assessment Validation and Entry (RAVEN) is used to enter MDS data about SNF patients and transmit those assessments in CMS-standard format to individual state databases. RAVEN also allows facilities to generate system reports (Figure 9-8).

```
RAVEN - Clinical Data Collection Design System Report

Assessment Data Entry


Date:     June 04, YYYY
Requested by:    MDS


ASSESSMENT DATA ENTRY REPORT FOR ASSESSMENT ID = 1-00001
Last entry Date:  05/23/YYYY    Dictionary Version:    MDS700
Data entry Time:  00:08:41      Data Entry Version:    MDS700
Data entry user:  MDS
MDS Module, Screen Set:
Full Assessment


Header Records


(Assessment Date)                        : 05/23/YYYY
Assessment Form Type                     : RAVEN Assessment
Facility Option AB and AC                : 5
Quarter type                             :
Include section t and u                  :
```

FIGURE 9-8 Sample report generated from RAVEN software (Permission to reuse in accordance with CMS Web site Content Reuse Policy.)

MEDICARE PHYSICIAN FEE SCHEDULE

As of 1992, physician services and procedures are reimbursed according to a payment system known as the *Resource-Based Relative Value Scale (RBRVS)*. The RBRVS replaced the Medicare physician payment system of "customary, prevailing, and reasonable" (CPR) charges under which physicians were reimbursed according to the historical record of the charge for the provision of each service. This system, now called the Medicare physician fee schedule (MPFS), reimburses providers according to predetermined rates assigned to services and is revised by CMS each year. All services are standardized to measure the value of a service as compared with other services provided. These standards, called relative value units (RVUs), are payment components consisting of:

- *Physician work*, **which reflects the physician's time and intensity in providing the service (e.g., judgment, technical skill, and physical effort).**
- *Practice expense*, **which reflects overhead costs involved in providing a service (e.g., rent, utilities, equipment, and staff salaries).**
- *Malpractice expense*, **which reflects malpractice expenses (e.g., costs of liability insurance).**

> **NOTE:** Most third-party payers, including state Medicaid programs, have adopted aspects of the MPFS.

Payment limits were also established by adjusting the RVUs for each locality by geographic adjustment factors (GAF), called *geographic cost practice indices (GCPIs)*, so that Medicare providers are paid differently in each state and also within each state (e.g., New York state has five separate payment localities). An annual conversion factor (dollar multiplier) converts RVUs into payments using a formula (Figure 9-9).

Although the Medicare physician fee schedule is used to determine payment for Medicare Part B (physician) services, other services, such as anesthesia, pathology/laboratory, and radiology, require special consideration.

> **NOTE:** The Medicare physician fee schedule may list fees for services not commonly provided to Medicare patients (e.g., obstetrical services) because private payers also adopt the schedule.

- **Anesthesia services payments are based on the actual time an Anesthesiologist spends with a partial and the American Society of Anesthesiologists' relative value system.**
- **Radiology services payments vary according to place of service (e.g., hospital radiology department vs. freestanding radiology center).**
- **Pathology services payments vary according to the number of patients served:**
  - **Pathology services that include clinical laboratory management and supervision of technologists are covered and paid as hospital services.**
  - **Pathology services that are directed to an individual patient in a hospital setting (e.g., pathology consultation) are paid under the physician fee schedule.**

Before 1992, Medicare required anesthesiologists to submit a CPT surgery code (instead of a code from the Anesthesia section of CPT) plus type of service (TOS) code "7" to denote anesthesia services. Medicare *discontinued* use of the TOS code for any service, replacing it with an expanded two-digit location, or place of service (POS), code. Anesthesiologists now submit the appropriate code from the Anesthesia section of CPT with a POS code.

Nonparticipating Physicians

> **NOTE:** NonPARs can accept assignment on a case-by-case basis, as discussed in Chapter 14.

When the nonparticipating provider (nonPAR) does not accept assignment from Medicare, the amount Medicare reimburses for services provided is subject to a 5 percent reduction of the Medicare physician fee schedule (MPFS) amount. In addition, Medicare requires the nonPAR to charge the patient

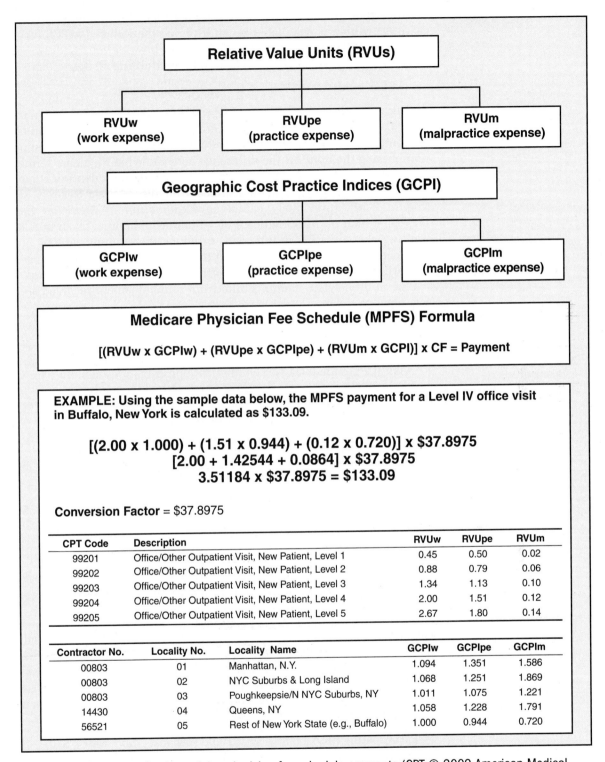

FIGURE 9-9 Formula for determining physician fee schedule payments (CPT © 2009 American Medical Association. All rights reserved.)

no more than the difference between what Medicare reimburses and the limiting charge, which is calculated by multiplying the reduced MPFS (or allowable charge) by 115 percent.

Use the following formula to calculate the limiting charge:

[MPFS − (MPFS × 5%)] × 115% = limiting charge.

For example, [$80 − ($80 × 5%)] × 115% = $76 × 115% = $87.40 (limiting charge). (Medicare reimburses the nonPAR based on the $76 reduced MPFS amount, such as 80 percent of that reduced MPFS. The patient is responsible for reimbursing the nonPAR the difference between what Medicare reimburses the nonPAR and the limiting charge, or $26.60, which includes any copayment.)

Limiting charge information appears on the **Medicare Summary Notice (MSN)** (Figure 9-10), (previously called an *Explanation of Medicare Benefits*, or *EOMB*), which notifies Medicare beneficiaries of actions taken on claims. The limiting charge policy is intended to reduce the amount patients enrolled in Medicare are expected to pay when they receive healthcare services. If a participating (PAR) and a nonparticipating (nonPAR) physician charge the same fee for an office visit, amounts billed and reimbursement received are different for each physician.

> **NOTE:** Medicare discounts its physician fee schedule 5 percent for nonPAR providers, which is called the **allowable charge** or allowed charge.

EXAMPLE: A PAR and nonPAR physician each charge $50 for an office visit (CPT code 99213). The Medicare physician fee schedule for CPT code 99213 is $40. The nonPAR is reimbursed a maximum of $38 by Medicare (because of the 5 percent reduction of the MPFS rate) and the limiting charge is $43.70 ($38 × 115%).

The PAR physician is reimbursed:

Medicare payment (80% of $40)	$32.00
Beneficiary coinsurance (20% of $40)	+ $8.00
TOTAL REIMBURSEMENT TO PAR	$40.00

The nonPAR physician is reimbursed:

Medicare payment (80% of $38)	$30.40
Beneficiary is billed the balance of the $43.70 limiting charge	+ $13.30
TOTAL REIMBURSEMENT TO NONPAR	$43.70

Generally, participating physicians report their actual fees to Medicare but adjust, or write off, the uncollectible portion of the charge when they receive payment. NonPAR doctors usually report only the *limiting charge* as their fee. Billing write-off or adjustment amounts to beneficiaries is called **balance billing** and is prohibited by Medicare regulations. In the preceding example, using CPT code 99213, the write-off amounts are:

Participating physician	$10.00 (because $50 − $40 = $10)
NonPAR physician	$6.30 (because $50 − $43.70 = $6.30)

The patient pays $5.30 more ($13.30 − $8 = $5.30) to the nonPAR, which can be significant for people living on a fixed income. Beneficiaries frequently ask, "Does the doctor participate in Medicare?" when calling for an appointment. With very few exceptions, people who qualify for Medicare are not allowed to purchase other primary health insurance. CMS must be certain that Medicare beneficiaries are not required to pay excessive out-of-pocket amounts for healthcare services. To protect Medicare enrollees financially, providers must comply with extensive rules and regulations.

Medicare Summary Notice

July 10, YYYY

JOHN Q. PUBLIC
10A SENATE ST.
ANYWHERE NY 12345

CUSTOMER SERVICE INFORMATION
Your Medicare Number: 112-34-9801A

If you have questions, write or call:
Medicare Part A
101 Main St
Anywhere NY 12345

Local: 1-800-555-4606 (Maryland)
Toll-free: 1-800-555-1636 (Others)

HELP STOP FRAUD: Read your Medicare Summary Notice carefully for accuracy of dates, services, and amounts billed to Medicare.

This is a summary of claims processed on 06/26/YYYY.

PART B MEDICAL INSURANCE - OUTPATIENT FACILITY CLAIMS

Dates of Service	Services Provided	Amount Charged	Non-Covered Charged	Deductible and Coinsurance	You May Be Billed	See Notes Section
Claim number 12345678901245						a, b
Goodmedicine Hospital						
Anywhere St.						
Anywhere US 12345						
Referred by: E Helper						
05/25/YY	CAT scan for therapy guide (76370)	$212.00	$0.00	$122.40	$0.00	c

Notes Section:

a. This information is being sent to your private insurer(s). Send any questions regarding your benefits to them.
b. $100.00 of the money approved by your primary insurer has been credited to your Medicare Part B deductible. You do not have to pay this amount.
c. $100.00 of this approved amount has been applied toward your deductible.

Your Medicare Number: 112-34-9801A

Deductible Information:

You have met the Part B deductible for YYYY .

General Information:

Who pays? You pay. Report Medicare fraud by calling 1-800-447-8477. An example of fraud would be claims for Medicare items or services you did not receive. If you have any other questions about your claim, please contact the Medicare contractor telephone number shown on this notice.

You can protect yourself from some pneumococcal infections by getting a pneumococcal vaccination. Medicare Part B will pay for your vaccination. One pneumococcal vaccination may be all you ever need.

Appeals Information - Part B (Outpatient)

If you disagree with any claims decision on this notice, you can request an appeal by **January 10, YYYY.**
Follow the instructions below:

1. Circle the item(s) you disagree with and explain why you disagree.
2. Send this notice, or a copy, to the address in the "Customer Service Information" box on Page 1.
3. Sign here _____ Phone number (_____) _____

THIS IS NOT A BILL - Keep this notice for your records.

FIGURE 9-10 Sample Medicare Summary Notice (MSN) (Courtesy Delmar/Cengage Learning)

Medicare Secondary Payer

Medicare Secondary Payer (MSP) refers to situations in which the Medicare program does not have primary responsibility for paying a beneficiary's medical expenses. The Medicare beneficiary may be entitled to other coverage that should pay before Medicare. From the time the Medicare program began in 1966, providers of health care grew accustomed to billing Medicare first for services to Medicare beneficiaries. The MSP program was initiated in 1980, and when a Medicare beneficiary also has coverage from one of the following groups, Medicare is a secondary payer:

- Automobile medical or no-fault insurance.
- Disabled individual covered by a large group health plan (LGHP) or who has coverage under the LGHP of a family member who is currently employed. A large group health plan (LGHP) is provided by an employer who has 100 or more employees *or* a multi-employer plan in which at least one employer has 100 or more full- or part-time employees.
- End-stage renal disease program.
- Federal black-lung program.
- Other liability insurance (e.g., general casualty insurance, homeowner's liability insurance, malpractice insurance, or product liability insurance).
- Veterans Administration benefits.
- Workers' compensation.
- Working aged coverage by an employer group health plan (EGHP), or an individual age 65 or older who is covered by a working spouse's EGHP. (The working spouse can be any age.) An employer group health plan (EGHP) is contributed to by an employer or employee pay-all plan and provides coverage to employees and dependents without regard to the enrollee's employment status (i.e., full-time, part-time, or retired). These provisions are applicable regardless of the size of the employer.

Upon claims submission, the amount of secondary benefits payable is the lowest of the:

- Actual charge by the physician or supplier minus the amount paid by the primary payer.
- Amount Medicare would pay if services were not covered by the primary payer.
- Higher of the Medicare physician fee schedule (or other amount payable under Medicare or the third-party payer's allowable charge) minus the amount actually paid by the primary payer.

To calculate the amount of Medicare secondary benefits payable on a given claim, the following information is required:

- Amount paid by the primary payer.
- Primary payer's allowable charge.

This information can be obtained from the primary payer's remittance advice or the patient's explanation of benefits (EOB).

EXAMPLE: An individual received treatment from a physician who charged $250. The individual's Medicare Part B deductible had previously been met. As primary payer, the employer group health plan's (EGHP) allowed charge was $200, and the EGHP paid 80 percent of this amount (or $160). The Medicare physician fee schedule amount is $150. The Medicare secondary payment is calculated as follows:

1. Physician charge minus EGHP payment ($250 − $160 = $90)

2. Medicare payment (determined in usual manner) (80% of $150 = $120)

3. EGHP allowable charge minus EGHP payment ($200 − $160 = $40)

4. Medicare pays $40 (lowest of amounts in steps 1, 2, or 3)

Some Medicare beneficiaries are covered by an employer plan if they are still working or if the spouse is employed and the health plan covers family members. Medicare has very specific rules about payment when another insurance is primary. This billing order is discussed in Chapter 14 of this text.

Nonphysician Practitioners

Medicare reimburses professional services provided by nonphysician practitioners, including nurse practitioners, clinical nurse specialists, and physician assistants. A **nurse practitioner (NP)** is a registered nurse licensed to practice as an NP in the state in which services are furnished, is certified by a national association (e.g., American Academy of Nurse Practitioners), and has a master's degree in nursing. NPs often work as primary care providers along with physicians, and they must *accept assignment* to receive reimbursement from Medicare. A **clinical nurse specialist (CNS)** is a registered nurse licensed by the state in which services are provided, has a master's degree in a defined clinical area of nursing from an accredited educational institution, and is certified as a CNS by the American Nurses Credentialing Center. A **physician assistant (PA)** must be legally authorized and licensed by the state to furnish services, have graduated from a physician assistant educational program that is accredited by the Accreditation Review Commission on Education for the Physician Assistant, and have passed the national certification examination of the National Commission on Certification of Physician Assistants (NCCPA). Some states (e.g., Texas) require PAs to work under a supervising physician who is approved by the state to direct and manage professional activities and who ensures that services provided are medically appropriate for the patient.

Nonphysician practitioner reimbursement rules include the following:

NOTE: Nonphysician practitioners that bill Medicare under an incident-to provision report the physician's provider number on the CMS-1500 claim (instead of their own provider number). This provision is based on the Medicare regulation that permits billing of ancillary personnel services under the physician's provider number (e.g., office EKG performed by a medical assistant).

- **Reimbursement for services provided by nonphysician practitioners is allowed *only* if no facility or other provider is paid in connection with such services.**

- **Payment is based on 80 percent of the actual charge or 85 percent of the Medicare physician fee schedule, whichever is less. Medicare reimburses 80 percent of the resultant payment, and the patient pays 20 percent.**

- **Direct payment can be made to the nonphysician practitioner, the employer, or the contractor (except for services provided by PAs, for which payment *must* be made to the employer).**

- **If nonphysician practitioners provide services outside of the office setting, they must obtain their own Medicare provider numbers.**

- Services provided by nonphysician practitioners may also be reported to Medicare as incident to the supervising physician's service. (Nonphysician practitioners *do not* have to have their own Medicare provider numbers when billing incident-to services.) *Incident-to* services are reimbursed at 100 percent of the Medicare physician fee schedule, and Medicare pays 80 percent of that amount directly to the physician.

- Reimbursement is available for services provided by nonphysician practitioners who work *in collaboration with* a physician (e.g., DO or MD), which means that a written agreement is in place specifying the services to be provided by the nonphysician practitioner, who must work with one or more physicians to deliver healthcare services, receiving medical direction and appropriate supervision as required by state law.

The types of services nonphysician practitioners provide include those traditionally reserved to physicians, such as physical examination, minor surgery, setting casts for simple fractures, interpreting x-rays, and other activities that involve independent evaluation or treatment of the patient's condition. Also, if authorized under the scope of their state licenses, nonphysician practitioners may furnish services billed under all levels of evaluation and management codes and diagnostic tests *if furnished in collaboration with a physician.*

Location of Service Adjustment

Physicians are usually reimbursed on a fee-for-service basis with payments established by the Medicare physician fee schedule (MPFS) based on RBRVS. When office-based services are performed in a facility, such as a hospital or outpatient setting, payments are reduced because the doctor did not provide supplies, utilities, or the costs of running the facility. This is known as the site of service differential. Other rules govern the services performed by hospital-based providers and teaching physicians. This chapter discusses rules that affect private practice physicians billing under the MPFS.

CMS Manual System

The Centers for Medicare and Medicaid Services (CMS) publish Internet-only manuals (IOMs) (e.g., Medicare Claims Processing Manual) on their Web site. The manuals include CMS program issuances (e.g., transmittal notices, national coverage determinations, and so on), day-to-day operating instructions, policies, and procedures that are based on statutes, regulations, guidelines, models, and directives. The CMS program components, providers, contractors, Medicare Advantage organizations and state survey agencies use the IOMs to administer CMS programs. They are also a good source of Medicare and Medicaid information for the general public.

CMS program transmittals communicate new or changed policies, and/or procedures that are being incorporated into a specific CMS Internet-only program manual. The CMS Quarterly Provider Update (QPU) is an online CMS publication that contains information about regulations and major policies currently under development, regulations and major policies completed or cancelled, and new or revised manual instructions.

CHARGEMASTER

The chargemaster (or charge description master, CDM) is a document that contains a computer-generated list of procedures, services, and supplies with charges for each. Chargemaster data are entered in the facility's patient accounting system, and charges are automatically posted to the patient's bill (UB-04). The bill is then submitted to the payer to generate payment for inpatient, ancillary and other services (e.g., emergency department, laboratory, radiology, and so on).

The chargemaster allows the facility to accurately and efficiently bill the payer for services rendered, and it usually contains the following:

- **Department code** (refers to the specific ancillary department where the service is performed).
- **Service code** (internal identification of specific service rendered).
- **Service description** (narrative description of the service, procedure, or supply).
- **Revenue code** (UB-04 revenue code that is assigned to each procedure, service, or product).
- **Charge amount** (dollar amount facility charges for each procedure, service, or supply).
- **Relative value units (RVUs)** (numeric value assigned to a procedure; based on difficulty and time consumed).

EXAMPLE: CHARGEMASTER

GOODMEDICINE HOSPITAL
ANYWHERE US 12345

Printed on:
04/15/YYYY

DEPARTMENT CODE: 01-855
DEPARTMENT: Radiology

SERVICE CODE	SERVICE DESCRIPTION	REVENUE CODE	CPT CODE	CHARGE	RVU
8550001	Chest x-ray, single view	0324	71010	74.50	0.70
8550002	Chest x-ray, two views	0324	71020	82.50	0.95
8550025	Bone scan, limited area	0350	72132	899.50	8.73
8550026	Bone scan, whole body	0350	72133	999.50	11.10

Personnel who render services to institutional patients (e.g., nursing, laboratory, radiology) enter data into the commercial software product. The data resides in the patient's computerized account, and upon discharge from the institution, the data is verified by billing office personnel and transmitted electronically (Figure 9-11) as a UB-04 claim to a third-party payer or a clearinghouse. When submitted directly to the payer, the claim is processed to authorize reimbursement to the facility. When submitted to a clearinghouse, electronic claims are edited and validated to ensure that they are error-free, reformatted to the specifications of the payer, and submitted electronically to the appropriate payer for further processing to generate reimbursement to the facility.

EXAMPLE: During an inpatient admission, the attending physician documents an order in the patient's record for a blood glucose level to be performed by the laboratory. The patient's nurse processes the order by contacting the laboratory (e.g., telephone or computer message), which sends a technician to the patient's room to perform a venipuncture (blood draw, or withdrawing blood from the patient's arm using a syringe). The blood specimen is transported to the laboratory by the technician where the blood glucose test is completed. The technician enters the results into the patient record information technology (IT) system using a computer terminal, and UB-04 data elements are input into the patient's account. This data resides in the patient's computerized account until it is verified by the billing office (at patient discharge) and is then transmitted to a clearinghouse that processes the claim and submits it to the third-party payer. The clearinghouse also uses the network to send an acknowledgment to the institution upon receipt of the submitted claim.

UB-04 data elements in ASC X12N format	Description of data elements
`ST*837*123456~` `BHT*0019*00*A98765*YYYY0504*0830~`	Header
`NM1*41*2*GOODMEDICINE HOSPITAL*****54*888229999~`	Submitter name
`NM1*40*2*CAPITAL BLUE CROSS*****54*16000~`	Receiver name
`HL*1**20*1~`	Service provider hierarchical level for submitter
`NM1*85*2*GOODMEDICINE HOSPITAL*****54*888229999~` `REF*1J*898989~`	Service provider name
`HL*2*1*22*1~` `SBR*P********BL~`	Subscriber (patient) hierarchical level

`NM1*IL*1*PUBLIC*JOHN*Q**MI*GRNESSC1234~`
`N3*1247 HILL STREET~`
`N4*ANYWHERE*US*12345~`
`DMG*D8*19820805*M**::RET:3::RET:2~`
`REF*SY*150259874~`
	Subscriber (patient) name

`NM1*PR*2*CAPITAL BLUE CROSS*****PI*00303~`	Payer name

`CLM*ABH123456*5015***11:A:1~`
`DTP*096*TM*1200~`
`DTP*434*RD8*YYYY0504-YYYY0510~`
`DTP*435*DT*YYYY05101100~`
`CL1*2*1*01~`
`HI*BK:66411*BJ:66411~`
`HI*BF:66331::::::::Y*BF:66111:::::::N*BF:V270:::::::N~`
`HI*BR:7569:D8:YYYY0510~`
	Claim information

`SE*91*123456~`	Trailer

FIGURE 9-11 Portion of UB-04 data submitted in ASC X12N electronic protocol format (Courtesy Delmar/Cengage Learning)

Revenue codes are four-digit codes preprinted on a facility's chargemaster to indicate the location or type of service provided to an institutional patient. (They are reported in FL42 of the UB-04.)

NOTE: Prior to 2002, revenue codes contained just three digits.

EXAMPLE: REVENUE CODES

CODE	COMPLETE DESCRIPTION	ABBREVIATED DESCRIPTION
0270	Medical/surgical supplies	MED SURG SUPPLIES
0450	Emergency department services	EMER/FACILITY CHARGE
0981	Emergency department physician fee	EMER/PHYSICIAN FEE

FIGURE 9-12 The revenue cycle (Courtesy Delmar/Cengage Learning)

REVENUE CYCLE MANAGEMENT

Revenue cycle management (Figure 9-12) is the process by which healthcare facilities and providers ensure their financial viability by increasing revenue, improving cash flow, and enhancing the patient's experience. Revenue cycle management includes the following features, typically in this order:

- *Physician ordering* (physician order for inpatient admission or outpatient services is documented by responsible physician).
- *Patient registration* (patient is admitted as an inpatient or scheduled for outpatient services).
  - Appropriate consents for treatment and release of information are obtained
  - Patient demographic and insurance information is collected
  - Patient's insurance coverage is validated and utilization management is performed (e.g., clinical reviews) to determine medical necessity
  - Preadmission clearance (e.g., precertification, preauthorization, screening for medical necessity)
- *Charge capture* (or *data capture*) (providers use chargemasters or encounter forms to select procedures or services provided) (ancillary departments, such as the laboratory, use automated systems that link to the chargemaster).
- *Diagnosis and procedure coding* (assignment of appropriate ICD-9-CM and/or CPT/HCPCS codes, typically performed by health information management personnel, to assign APCs, DRGs, and so on).

- *Patient discharge processing* (patient information is verified, discharge instructions are provided, patient follow-up visit is scheduled, consent forms are reviewed for signatures, and patient policies are explained to the patient).
- *Billing and claims processing* (all patient information and codes are input into the billing system, and CMS-1500 or UB-04 claims are generated and submitted to third-party payers).
- *Resubmitting claims* (before reimbursement is received from third-party payers, late charges, lost charges, or corrections to previously processed CMS-1500 or UB-04 claims are entered, and claims are resubmitted to payers—this may result in payment delays and claims denials).
- *Third-party payer reimbursement posting* (payment from third-party payers is posted to appropriate accounts, and rejected claims are resubmitted with appropriate documentation; this process includes *electronic remittance*, which involves receiving reimbursement from third-party payers electronically).
- *Appeals process* (analysis of reimbursement received from third-party payers identifies variations in expected payments or contracted rates and may result in submission of appeal letters to payers).
- *Patient billing* (self-pay balances are billed to the patient; these include deductibles, co-payments, and non-covered charges).
- *Self-pay reimbursement posting* (self-pay balances received from patients are posted to appropriate accounts).
- *Collections* (payments not received from patients in a timely manner results in collections letters being mailed to patients until payment is received; if payment is still not received, the account is turned over to an outside collections agency).
- *Collections reimbursement posting* (payments received from patients are posted to appropriate accounts).
- *Auditing process*
  - *Compliance monitoring* (level of compliance with established managed care contracts is monitored; provider performance per managed care contractual requirements is monitored; compliance risk is monitored)
  - *Denials management* (claims denials are analyzed to prevent future denials; rejected claims are resubmitted with appropriate documentation)
  - *Tracking of resubmitted claims and appeals for denied claims* (resubmitted claims and appealed claims are tracked to ensure payment by payers)
  - *Posting lost charges and late charges* (late claims are submitted)

NOTE: In a physician practice, revenue cycle management is also called *accounts receivable management*.

NOTE: UB-04 claims are not manually completed (unlike CMS-1500 claims that continue to be manually completed by many physician practices). Instead, the UB-04 claim is automatically generated when data is transmitted to the facility's billing department by providers who:
- Circle procedure/service CPT/HCPCS codes on a paper-based chargemaster (after which keyboarding specialists enter the codes into the facility's computer).
- Select codes using a hand-held computer, such as a personal digital assistant (PDA) (and click to transmit the codes).

UB-04 CLAIM

The UB-04 claim (Figure 9-13) (previously called the UB-92) contains data entry blocks called form locators (FLs) that are similar to the CMS-1500 claim blocks used to input information about procedures or services provided to a patient. Although some institutions manually complete the UB-04 claim and submit it to third-party payers for reimbursement, others perform data entry of UB-04 information using commercial software (Figure 9-14). However, most institutions do not complete the UB-04 because it is automatically generated from chargemaster data entered by providers (e.g., nurses, therapists, laboratory, and so on).

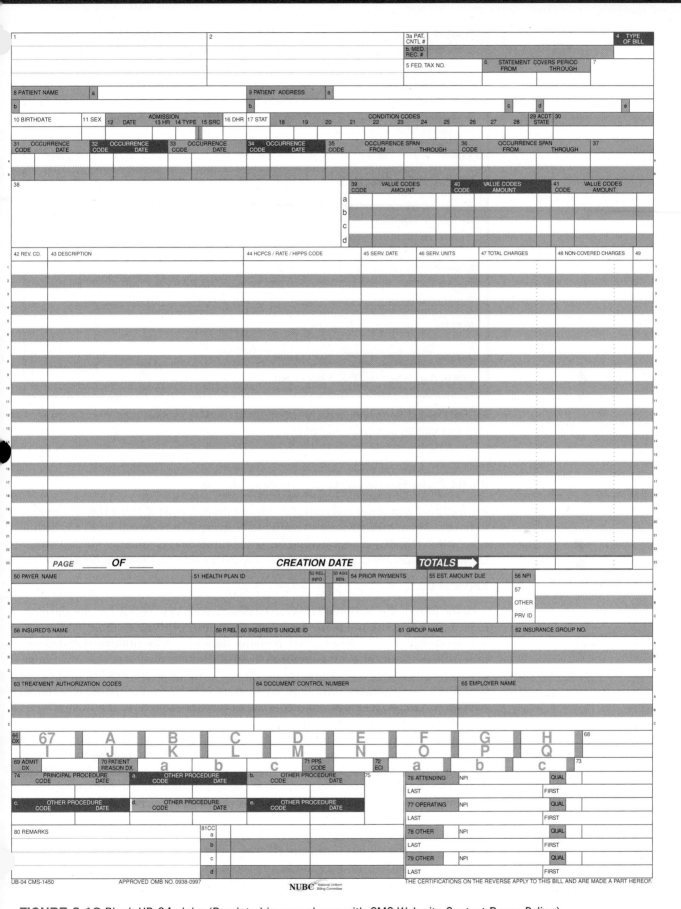

FIGURE 9-13 Blank UB-04 claim (Reprinted in accordance with CMS Web site Content Reuse Policy.)

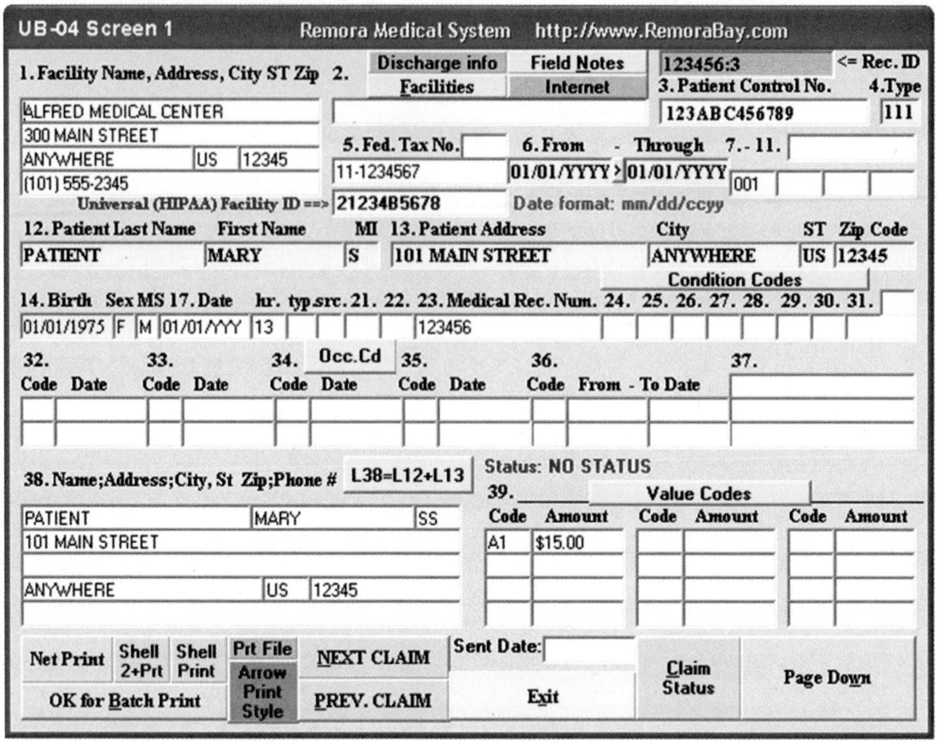

FIGURE 9-14 Sample data entry screen using UB-04 electronic data interchange software (Permission to reprint granted by Remora Software, Inc.)

UB-04 Claim Development and Implementation

Institutional and other selected providers submit UB-04 (CMS-1450) claim data to payers for reimbursement of patient services. The National Uniform Billing Committee (NUBC) is responsible for developing data elements reported on the UB-04 in cooperation with State Uniform Billing Committees (SUBCs).

National Uniform Billing Committee (NUBC)

Like the role of the National Uniform Claims Committee (NUCC) in the development of the CMS-1500 claim, the National Uniform Billing Committee (NUBC) is responsible for identifying and revising data elements (information entered into UB-04 form locators or submitted by institutions using electronic data interchange). (The claim was originally designed as the first uniform bill and called the UB-82 because of its 1982 implementation date. Then, the UB-92 was implemented in 1992.) The current claim is called the UB-04 because it was developed in 2004 (but implemented in 2007).

The NUBC was created by the American Hospital Association (AHA) in 1975 and is represented by major national provider (e.g., AHA state hospital association representatives) and payer (e.g., Blue Cross and Blue Shield Association) organizations. The intent was to develop a single billing form and standard data set that could be used by all institutional providers and payers for healthcare claims processing. In 1982 the NUBC voted to accept the UB-82 and its data set (a compilation of data elements that are reported on the uniform bill) for implementation as a national uniform bill. Once the UB-82 was adopted, the focus of the NUBC shifted to the state level, and a State Uniform Billing Committee (SUBC) was created in each state to handle implementation and distribution of state-specific UB-82 manuals (that contained national guidelines along with unique state billing requirements).

NOTE: UB-04 claims data for Medicare Part A reimbursement is submitted to Medicare administrative contractors (MACs, replacing carriers, DMERCs, and fiscal intermediaries), and other third-party payers. Payments are processed for hospitals, skilled nursing facilities, home health and hospice agencies, dialysis facilities, rehabilitation facilities, and rural health clinics.

When the NUBC established the UB-82 data set design and specifications, it also implemented an evaluation process through 1990 to determine whether the UB-82 data set was appropriate for third-party payer claims processing. The NUBC surveyed SUBCs to obtain suggestions for improving the design of the UB-82, and the UB-92 was implemented in 1992 to incorporate the best of the UB-82 with data set design improvements (e.g., providers no longer had to include as many attachments to UB-92 claims submitted). UB-04 revisions emphasize clarification of definitions for data elements and codes to eliminate ambiguity and to create consistency. The UB-04 also addresses emergency department (ED) coding and data collection issues to respond to concerns of state public health reporting systems. The NUBC continues to emphasize the need for data sources to continue to support public health data reporting needs.

Data Specifications for the UB-04

When reviewing data specifications for the UB-04, the NUBC balanced the payers' need to collect information against the burden of providers to report that information. In addition, the administrative simplification provisions of the Health Insurance Portability and Accountability Act of 1996 (HIPAA) are applied when developing data elements. Each data element required for reporting purposes is assigned to a unique UB-04 form locator (FL), which is the designated space on the claim identified by a unique number and title, such as the patient name in FL8 (Figure 9-13).

UB-04 Claims Submission

Whether completed manually (see Figure 9-13) or using onscreen software (see Figure 9-14), the UB-04 claim contains 81 form locators (Table 9-4). The data is entered according to third-party payer guidelines that contain instructions for completing the UB-04. Providers that submit the UB-04 claim (or UB-04 data elements in EDI format) include the following:

- Ambulance companies
- Ambulatory surgery centers
- Home healthcare agencies
- Hospice organizations
- Hospitals (emergency department, inpatient, and outpatient services)
- Psychiatric drug/alcohol treatment facilities (inpatient and outpatient services)
- Skilled nursing facilities
- Subacute facilities
- Stand-alone clinical/laboratory facilities
- Walk-in clinics

The UB-04 (CMS-1450) and its data elements serve the needs of many third-party payers. Although some payers do not collect certain data elements, it is important to capture all NUBC-approved data elements for audit trail purposes. In addition, NUBC-approved data elements are reported by facilities that have established coordination of benefits agreements with the payers.

TABLE 9-4 UB-04 (CMS-1450) form locator (FL) descriptions and Medicare claims completion instructions

FL	DESCRIPTION	INSTRUCTIONS
	NOTE: Form locator (FL) descriptions indicate whether data entry for Medicare claims is required (mandatory), not required (optional), not used (leave FL blank), or situational (dependent on circumstances clarified in the FL instructions). Payer-specific instructions can be located by conducting Internet searches.	
1	Provider name, street address, city, state, ZIP code, telephone number, country code, and fax number (REQUIRED)	Enter the provider name, city, state, and ZIP code. Either the provider's post office box number or street name and number may be included. The state can be abbreviated using standard post office abbreviations, and 5- or 9-digit ZIP codes are acceptable. Phone and/or fax numbers are desirable. NOTE: Payer compares FL1 information to data on file for provider number reported in FL51 (to verify provider identity).
2	Pay-to name, address, and secondary ID fields (SITUATIONAL)	Enter provider name, address, city, state, and ZIP code *if the pay-to name and address information is different from the Billing Provider information in FL1*. Otherwise, leave blank.
3a	Patient control number (unique claim number) (REQUIRED)	Enter the alphanumeric control number *if assigned by the provider and needed to facilitate retrieval of patient financial records and for posting payments.*
3b	Medical record number (or health record number) (SITUATIONAL)	Enter the medical record number *if assigned by the provider and needed to facilitate retrieval of patient records*. Otherwise, leave blank.
4	Type of bill (TOB) (REQUIRED)	NOTE: The 4-digit alphanumeric TOB code provides three specific pieces of information after a leading zero. Digit 1 (the leading 0) is ignored by CMS. Digit 2 identifies the type of facility. Digit 3 classifies the type of care provided. Digit 4 indicates the sequence of this bill for this particular episode of care, and it is called a *frequency code*.

Enter a valid 4-digit TOB classification number.
- Digit 1: Leading Zero
- Digit 2: Type of Facility
    1. Hospital
    2. Skilled nursing
    3. Home health (includes HH PPS claims, for which CMS determines whether services are paid from the Medicare Part A or Part B)
    4. Religious nonmedical (hospital)
    5. Reserved for national assignment (discontinued 10/1/05)
    6. Intermediate care
    7. Clinic or hospital-based renal dialysis facility (requires assignment of special information as Digit 3 below)
    8. Special facility or hospital ASC surgery (requires assignment of special information as Digit 3 below)
    9. Reserved for national assignment
- Digit 3 (Bill Classification, Except Clinics and Special Facilities)
    1. Inpatient (Medicare Part A)
    2. Inpatient (Medicare Part B)
    3. Outpatient
    4. Other (Medicare Part B)
    5. Intermediate Care - Level I
    6. Intermediate Care - Level II
    7. Reserved for national assignment (discontinued 10/1/05)
    8. Swing bed
    9. Reserved for national assignment

(continues)

TABLE 9-4 (continued)

FL	DESCRIPTION	INSTRUCTIONS
4	Type of bill (TOB) (REQUIRED)—continued	• Digit 3 (Clinics Only) 1 Rural health clinic (RHC) 2 Hospital-based or independent renal dialysis facility 3 Freestanding provider-based federally qualified health center (FQHC) 4 Other rehabilitation facility (ORF) 5 Comprehensive outpatient rehabilitation facility (CORF) 6 Community mental health center (CMHC) 7-8 Reserved for national assignment 9 Other • Digit 3 (Special Facilities Only) 1 Hospice (non-hospital-based) 2 Hospice (hospital-based) 3 Ambulatory surgical center services to hospital outpatients 4 Freestanding birthing center 5 Critical access hospital 6-8 Reserved for national assignment 9 Other • Digit 4 (Frequency - Definition) A Admission/election notice (hospice or religious non-medical healthcare institution) B Termination/revocation notice (hospice/Medicare coordinated care demonstration or religious non-medical healthcare institution) C Change of provider notice (hospice) D Healthcare institution void/cancel notice (hospice) E Change of ownership (hospice) F Beneficiary initiated adjustment claim G Common working file (CWF) initiated adjustment claim CMS initiated adjustment claim H Fiscal intermediary (FI) adjustment claim (other than quality improvement organization or provider) I Initiated adjustment claim (other entities) J OIG initiated adjustment claim M Medicare as secondary payer (MSP) initiated adjustment claim P Quality improvement organization (QIO) adjustment claim 0 Nonpayment/zero claims provider 1 Admit through discharge claim 2 Interim - first claim 3 Interim - continuing claim(s) 4 Interim - last claim 5 Late charge only (There is no code 6) 7 Replacement of prior claim 8 Void/cancel of a prior claim 9 Final claim for HHPPS episode • Sample Bill Type Codes 011X Hospital inpatient (Medicare Part A) 012X Hospital inpatient (Medicare Part B) 013X Hospital outpatient 014X Hospital other (Medicare Part B)

(continues)

TABLE 9-4   (continued)

FL	DESCRIPTION	INSTRUCTIONS
4	Type of bill (TOB) (REQUIRED)—continued	• Sample Bill Type Codes (continued) 018X Hospital swing bed 021X SNF inpatient 022X SNF inpatient (Medicare Part B) 023X SNF outpatient 028X SNF swing bed 032X Home health 033X Home health 034X Home health (Medicare Part B only) 041X Religious non-medical healthcare institutions 071X Clinical rural health 072X Clinic ESRD 073X Federally qualified health centers 074X Clinic outpatient physical therapy (OPT) 075X Clinic CORF 076X Community mental health centers 081X Non-hospital-based hospice 082X Hospital-based hospice 083X Hospital outpatient (ASC) 085X Critical access hospital
5	Federal tax number (REQUIRED)	Enter the facility's federal tax identification number in 00-0000000 format.
6	Statement covers period (from-through) (REQUIRED)	Enter beginning and ending dates of the period included on this bill as MMDDYY.
7	Unlabeled (NOT USED)	Leave blank.
8a	Patient identifier (SITUATIONAL)	Enter the patient's payer identification (ID) number *if different from the subscriber/insured ID number entered in FL60.* Otherwise, leave blank.
8b	Patient name (REQUIRED)	Enter patient's last name, first name, and middle initial (if any). Use a comma to separate the last name, first name, and middle initial. **NOTE:** When the patient's last name contains a prefix, do not enter a space after the prefix (e.g., VonSchmidt). When the patient's name contains a suffix, enter as LastName Suffix, FirstName (e.g., Smith III, James).
9a-e	Patient address (REQUIRED)	• Enter the patient's street address in 9a. • Enter the patient's city in 9b. • Enter the patient's state in 9c. • Enter the patient's 5- or 9-digit ZIP code in 9d. • Enter the patient's country code *if the patient resides outside of the United States.*
10	Patient birth date (REQUIRED)	Enter the patient's date of birth as MMDDCCYY. **NOTE:** If birth date is unknown, enter zeros for all eight digits.
11	Patient sex (REQUIRED)	Enter the patient's gender as a 1-character letter: M Male F Female
12	Admission date (REQUIRED for inpatient and home health)	Enter the inpatient date of admission (or home health start-of-care date) as MMDDYY.

(continues

TABLE 9-4 (continued)

FL	DESCRIPTION	INSTRUCTIONS
13	Admission hour (NOT REQUIRED)	Leave blank.
14	Type of admission/visit (REQUIRED FOR INPATIENT CLAIMS)	Enter 1-digit type of admission/visit code: 1 Emergency 2 Urgent 3 Elective 4 Newborn 5 Trauma center 6-8 Reserved for national assignment 9 Information not available
15	Source of referral for admission or visit (REQUIRED)	Enter 1-digit source of admission or visit code: 1 Physician referral 2 Clinic referral 3 Managed care plan referral 4 Transfer from a hospital 5 Transfer from a skilled nursing facility 6 Transfer from another healthcare facility 7 Emergency room 8 Court/law enforcement 9 Information not available A Transfer from a critical access hospital B Transfer from another home health agency C Readmission to same home health agency D Transfer from hospital inpatient in the same facility resulting in a separate claim to the payer E-Z Reserved for national assignment
16	Discharge hour (NOT REQUIRED)	Leave blank.
17	Patient discharge status (REQUIRED)	Enter 2-digit patient discharge status code: 01 Discharged to home or self care (routine discharge) 02 Discharged/transferred to a short-term general hospital for inpatient care 03 Discharged/transferred to SNF with Medicare certification in anticipation of covered skilled care (effective 2/23/05) 04 Discharged/transferred to an intermediate care facility (ICF) 05 Discharged/transferred to another type of institution not defined elsewhere in this code list (effective 2/23/05) (e.g., cancer hospitals excluded from Medicare PPS and children's hospitals) 06 Discharged/transferred to home under care of organized home health service organization in anticipation of covered skills care (effective 2/23/05) 07 Left against medical advice or discontinued care 08 Reserved for national assignment 09 Admitted as an inpatient to this hospital **NOTE:** For patient status code 09, in situations where a patient is admitted before midnight of the third day following the day of an outpatient diagnostic service or a service related to the reason for the admission, the outpatient services are considered inpatient. Therefore, code 09 would apply only to services that began longer than three days earlier or were unrelated to the reason for admission, such as observation following outpatient surgery, which results in admission.

(continues)

TABLE 9-4   (continued)

FL	DESCRIPTION	INSTRUCTIONS
17	Patient status (REQUIRED) (continued)	Enter 2-digit patient discharge status code: (continued) 10-19 Reserved for national assignment 21 Expired (or did not recover - religious non-medical healthcare patient) Discharged/transferred to court/law enforcement 22-29 Reserved for national assignment 30 Still patient or expected to return for outpatient services 31-39 Reserved for national assignment 40 Expired at home (Hospice claims only) 41 Expired in a medical facility (e.g., hospital, SNF, ICF or freestanding hospice) (Hospice claims only) 42 Expired - place unknown (Hospice claims only) 43 Discharged/transferred to a federal healthcare facility (effective 10/1/03) (e.g., Department of Defense hospital, Veteran's Administration hospital) 44-49 Reserved for national assignment 50 Discharged/transferred to Hospice (home) 51 Discharged/transferred to Hospice (medical facility) 52-60 Reserved for national assignment 61 Discharged/transferred within this institution to a hospital-based Medicare-approved swing bed 62 Discharged/transferred to an inpatient rehabilitation facility including distinct parts/units of a hospital 63 Discharged/transferred to long term care hospital 64 Discharged/transferred to a nursing facility certified under Medicaid *but not certified under Medicare* 65 Discharged/transferred to a psychiatric hospital or psychiatric distinct part/unit of a hospital 66 Discharged/transferred to a critical access hospital (effective 1/1/06) 67-99 Reserved for national assignment
18-28	Condition codes (SITUATIONAL)	Enter the 2-digit code (in numerical order) that describes any of the following conditions or events that apply to this billing period. Otherwise, leave blank. (*Sample of condition codes listed below.*) 02 Condition is employment-related 03 Patient covered by insurance not reflected here 04 Information only bill 05 Lien has been filed **NOTE:** For a comprehensive list of condition codes, refer to Chapter 25 of the *Medicare Claims Processing Manual* **(www.cms.hhs.gov).**
29	Accident State (NOT USED)	Leave blank.
30	Unlabeled (NOT USED)	Leave blank.
31-34	Occurrence code(s) and date(s) (SITUATIONAL)	Enter occurrence code(s) and associated date(s) (MMDDYY) to report specific event(s) related to this billing period *if condition code(s) were entered in FL18-28*. Otherwise, leave blank. (*Sample of occurrence codes listed below.*) 01 = Accident/medical coverage 02 = No Fault Insurance Involved 03 = Accident/Tort Liability 04 = Accident Employment Related 05 = Accident No Medical/Liability Coverage 06 - Crime Victim **NOTE:** For a comprehensive list of occurrence codes, refer to Chapter 25 of the *Medicare Claims Processing Manual* **(www.cms.hhs.gov).**

(continues)

TABLE 9-4 (continued)

FL	DESCRIPTION	INSTRUCTIONS
35-36	Occurrence span code and dates (SITUATIONAL FOR INPATIENT CLAIMS)	Enter occurrence span code(s) and beginning/ending dates defining a specific event relating to this billing period as MMDDYY. (*Sample of occurrence span codes listed below.*) 70 Qualifying stay dates (Medicare Part A SNF level of care only) or non-utilization dates (for payer use on hospital bills only) 71 Hospital prior stay dates 72 First/last visit (occurring in this billing period where these dates are different from those in FL6) 74 Non-covered level of care 75 SNF level of care **NOTE:** For a comprehensive list of occurrence span codes, refer to Chapter 25 of the *Medicare Claims Processing Manual* (**www.cms.hhs.gov**).
37	Untitled (NOT USED)	Leave blank.
38	Responsible party name and address (NOT REQUIRED)	Leave blank.
39-41	Value codes and amounts (REQUIRED)	Enter 2-character value code(s) and dollar/unit amount(s). Codes and related dollar or unit amounts identify data of a monetary nature necessary for processing the claim. Negative amounts are not allowed, except in FL41. If more than one value code is entered for the same billing period, enter in ascending numeric sequence. Line "a" through "d" allow for entry of up to four lines of data. Enter data in FL39A through 41A before FL39B through 41B, and so on. Codes 80-83 are only available for use on the UB-04. (*Sample of value codes listed below.*) 01 = Most Common Semi-Private Rooms 02 = Provider has no Semi-Private Rooms 08 = Lifetime reserve amount in the first calendar year 45 = Accident Hour 50 = Physical Therapy Visit A1 = Inpatient Deductible Part A A2 = Inpatient Coinsurance Part A A3 = Estimated Responsibility Part A B1 = Outpatient Deductible **NOTE:** For a comprehensive list of value codes, refer to Chapter 25 of the *Medicare Claims Processing Manual* (**www.cms.hhs.gov**).
42	Revenue code(s) (REQUIRED)	Enter 4-character revenue code(s) to identify accommodation and/or ancillary charges. **NOTE:** When completing UB-04 claims in this chapter, revenue codes are provided in case studies (Figure 9-14). *Revenue codes* entered in FL42 explain charges entered in FL47. They are entered in ascending numeric sequence, and do not repeat on the same bill. (*Sample revenue codes listed below.*) 010X All inclusive rate (e.g., 0100, 0101) 0 All-inclusive room and board plus ancillary 1 All-inclusive room and board **NOTE:** For a comprehensive list of revenue codes, refer to Chapter 25 of the *Medicare Claims Processing Manual* (**www.cms.hhs.gov**).

(continues)

TABLE 9-4 (continued)

FL	DESCRIPTION	INSTRUCTIONS
43	Revenue description (NOT REQUIRED)	Enter the narrative description (or standard abbreviation) for each revenue code, reported in FL42, on the adjacent line in FL43. (This information assists clerical bill review by the facility/provider and payer.)
44	HCPCS/Rates/HIPPS Rate Codes (REQUIRED)	• For outpatient claims, enter the HCPCS (CPT and/or HCPCS level II) code that describes outpatient services or procedures. • For inpatient claims, enter the accommodation rate. • For SNF claims, enter the Health Insurance Prospective Payment System (HIPPS) rate code (obtained from resource utilization groups, RUGs, grouper software) and the 2-digit assessment indicator (AI) to specify the type of assessment associated with the RUG code obtained from the grouper.
45	Service date (REQUIRED FOR OUTPATIENT CLAIMS)	Enter line item dates of service, including claims where "from" and "through" dates are the same.
46	Units of service (REQUIRED)	Enter the number of units that quantify services reported as revenue codes (FL42) (e.g., number of days for type of accommodation, number of pints of blood). When HCPCS codes are reported for procedures/services, units equal the number of times the procedure/service reported was performed.
47	Total charges (REQUIRED)	• Enter charges for procedures/services reported as revenue codes (FL42) *on each line*. Be sure to consider the units of service (FL46) in your calculations. • Enter the sum of all charges reported on the last line (same line as revenue code 0001).
48	Non-covered charges (REQUIRED)	Enter non-covered charge(s) (e.g., copayment, day after active care ended) *if related revenue codes were entered in FL42.* (Do not enter negative charges.)
49	Untitled (NOT USED)	Leave blank.

NOTE: Enter appropriate data in the PAGE _____ OF _____ (e.g., 1 OF 1) and CREATION DATE (e.g., date UB-04 was submitted to payer) fields.

FL	DESCRIPTION	INSTRUCTIONS
50A-C	Payer name (REQUIRED)	Enter the name of the health insurance payer as follows: • Line A (Primary Payer) • Line B (Secondary Payer) • Line C (Tertiary Payer)
51A-C	Health plan ID (REQUIRED)	Report the payer's 10-digit national health plan identifier.
52A-C	Release of information certification indicator (REQUIRED)	Enter the appropriate identifier for release of information certification, which is needed to permit the release of data to other organizations to adjudicate (process) the claim. I Informed consent to release medical information for conditions or diagnoses regulated by federal statutes Y Provider has on file a signed statement permitting the release of medical/billing date related to a claim
53A-C	Assignment of benefits certification indicator (NOT USED)	Leave blank.
54A-C	Prior payment(s) (SITUATIONAL)	Enter the sum of payments collected from the patient toward payer deductibles/coinsurance or blood deductibles.
		EXAMPLE: The first three pints of blood are treated as non-covered by Medicare. If total inpatient hospital charges were $350, including $50 for a deductible pint of blood, the hospital would enter $300 (toward the Part A deductible) and $50 (toward the blood deductible) in 54A and 54B, respectively.
55A-C	Estimated amount due from patient (NOT REQUIRED)	Leave blank.

(continues)

TABLE 9-4   (continued)

FL	DESCRIPTION	INSTRUCTIONS
56	National provider identifier (NPI) (REQUIRED)	Enter the billing provider's NPI.
57A-C	Other provider ID (NOT USED)	Leave blank.
58A-C	Insured's name (REQUIRED)	Enter the insured's name (last, first, middle initial), as verified on the patient's health insurance card, *on the same lettered line (A, B, or C) that corresponds to the line on which payer information was entered in FL50A-C.*

59A-C	Patient's relationship to insured (REQUIRED)	Enter the "patient's relationship to subscriber/insured" code to indicate the relationship of the patient to the insured.
		    01 Spouse
		    18 Self
		    19 Child
		    20 Employee
		    21 Unknown
		    39 Organ Donor
		    40 Cadaver Donor
		    53 Life Partner
		    G8 Other Relationship

60A-C	Insured's unique identification number (REQUIRED)	Enter the patient's health insurance claim number *on the same lettered line (A, B, or C) that corresponds to the line on which payer information was entered in FL50A-C.*
61A-C	Insured's group name (SITUATIONAL)	Enter the name of the health insurance group *on the same lettered line (A, B, or C) if workers' compensation or an employer group health plan (EGHP) was entered in FL50A-C.*
62A-C	Insured's group number (SITUATIONAL)	Enter the group number (or other identification number) of the health insurance group *on the same lettered line (A, B, or C) if workers' compensation or an employer group health plan (EGHP) was entered in FL50A-C.*
63A-C	Treatment authorization code (SITUATIONAL)	Enter the treatment authorization code or referral number assigned by the payer *if procedures/services reported on this claim were preauthorized or a referral was required.* **NOTE:** When quality improvement organization (QIO) review is performed for Medicare outpatient preadmission, pre-procedure, or home IV therapy services, enter the treatment authorization number for all approved admissions or services.
64A-C	Document control number (SITUATIONAL)	Enter the control number assigned to the original bill by the health plan or the health plan's fiscal agent as part of their internal control *if this is not the original UB-04 submitted for procedures/ services provided* (e.g., this UB-04 is a corrected claim).
65A-C	Employer name (SITUATIONAL)	Enter the name of the employer that provides healthcare coverage for the insured (identified on the same line in FL58) *if workers' compensation or an employer group health plan (EGHP) was entered in FL50A-C.*

66	Diagnosis version qualifier (REQUIRED)	Enter the indicator to designate which version of ICD was used to report diagnosis codes.
		    9 Ninth revision
		    0 Tenth revision

67	Principal diagnosis code (REQUIRED)	Enter the ICD code for the principal diagnosis (hospital inpatient) *or* the first-listed diagnosis (hospital outpatient). **NOTE:** • Do *not* enter the decimal in the reported ICD code because it is implied (e.g., 25000 instead of 250.00). • Do *not* report ICD diagnosis codes on nonpatient claims for laboratory services, where the hospital functions as an independent laboratory.

(continues)

TABLE 9-4   (continued)

FL	DESCRIPTION	INSTRUCTIONS
67A-H	Other diagnosis code(s) (REQUIRED)	Enter ICD codes for up to eight additional diagnoses *if they co-existed (in addition to the principal diagnosis) at the time of admission or developed subsequently, and which had an effect upon the treatment or the length of stay* (hospital inpatient) or *if they co-existed in addition to the first-listed diagnosis* (hospital outpatient). **NOTE:** • Do *not* enter the decimal in the reported ICD code because it is implied (e.g., 25000 instead of 250.00). • Do *not* report ICD diagnosis codes on *nonpatient claims for laboratory services* when the hospital functions as an independent laboratory.
67I-Q	Other diagnosis code(s) (NOT REQUIRED)	Leave blank.
68	Untitled (NOT USED)	Leave blank.
69	Admitting diagnosis code (REQUIRED FOR HOSPITAL INPATIENT CLAIMS)	Enter the ICD code for the admitting diagnosis, which is the condition identified by the physician at the time of the patient's admission to the hospital.
70a-c	Patient's reason for visit diagnosis code (SITUATIONAL)	Enter the ICD code for the patient's reason for visit (e.g., sign, symptom, diagnosis) *if the patient received care for an unscheduled outpatient visit* (e.g., emergency department).
71	Prospective payment system (PPS) code (NOT USED)	Leave blank.
72a-c	ECI (external cause of injury) (E-codes)	Leave blank. **NOTE:** Check to determine if your state (e.g., New York) requires entry of E-codes for data capture purposes (e.g., statistical analysis).
73	Untitled (NOT USED)	Leave blank.
74	Principal procedure code and date (SITUATIONAL FOR INPATIENT CLAIMS)	Enter the ICD code for the principal procedure *if an inpatient procedure was performed.* Enter the date as MMDDYY. (Leave blank for outpatient claims.) **NOTE:** Do *not* enter the decimal in the reported ICD code because it is implied (e.g., 1471 instead of 14.71).
74a-e	Other procedure code(s) and date(s) (SITUATIONAL)	Enter the ICD code *if additional inpatient procedure(s) were performed.* Enter the date as MMDDYY. (Leave blank for outpatient claims.) **NOTE:** Do *not* enter the decimal in the reported ICD code because it is implied (e.g., 1471 instead of 14.71).
75	Untitled (NOT USED)	Leave blank.
76	Attending provider name and identifiers (SITUATIONAL)	• Enter the name and NPI of the attending provider for all claims *except those submitted for nonscheduled transportation services.* • Leave the QUAL field blank. **NOTE:** The *attending provider* is the individual who has overall responsibility for the patient's medical care and treatment reported on this claim.
77	Operating physician name and NPI (SITUATIONAL)	Enter the name and NPI of the operating physician *if a surgical procedure ICD code is reported on this claim.* (Leave the QUAL field blank.)

(continues)

TABLE 9-4   (continued)

FL	DESCRIPTION	INSTRUCTIONS
78-79	Other provider name and NPI (SITUATIONAL)	Enter the name and NPI number of the provider that corresponds to the following qualifier codes: DN Referring Provider (The provider who sends the patient to another provider for services. Required on outpatient claims when the referring provider is different from the attending provider.) ZZ Other Operating Physician (The individual who performs a secondary surgical procedure or assists the operating physician. Required when another operating physician is involved.) 82 Rendering Provider (The healthcare professional who delivers or completes a particular medical service or non-surgical procedure. Required when state or federal regulations call for a combined claim, such as a claim that includes both facility and professional fee components.)
80	Remarks (SITUATIONAL)	Enter remarks for the following situations: • DME billings (provider enters rental rate, cost, and anticipated months of usage so that payer may determine whether to approve the rental or purchase of the equipment) • Medicare is not primary payer (because workers' compensation, EGHP, automobile medical, no-fault, or liability insurer is primary) • Renal Dialysis Facilities (provider enters first month of the 30-month period during which Medicare benefits are secondary to benefits payable under an EGHP) • Other information not entered elsewhere on the UB-04, which is necessary for proper payment
81a-d	Code-Code (SITUATIONAL)	Enter the code qualifier (from the list below) and additional codes (e.g., occurrence codes) as related to a form locator or to report from the external code list approved by the NUBC for inclusion in the institutional data set. 01-A0 Reserved for national assignment A1 National Uniform Billing Committee condition codes – not used for Medicare A2 National Uniform Billing Committee occurrence codes – not used for Medicare A3 National Uniform Billing Committee occurrence span codes – not used for Medicare A4 National Uniform Billing Committee value codes – not used for Medicare A5-B0 Reserved for national assignment B3 Healthcare provider taxonomy code B4-ZZ Reserved for national assignment CODE SOURCE: ASC X12 External Code Source 682 (National Uniform Claim Committee)

UB-04 Case Study

> **NOTE:** Many form locators will remain blank on the completed UB-04 claim.

Use the blank UB-04 claim (Figure 9-13) to enter data from the outpatient case study (Figure 9-15). Codes (e.g., ICD, CPT/HCPCS, revenue) required for completion of the UB-04 claim are included in the case study. Refer to Table 9-4 (above) in your textbook for instructions on completing the UB-04 claim. Then, compare your completed claim to answer key in Figure 9-16.

Alfred Medical Center • 548 N Main St • Alfred NY 14802

(607) 555-1234   **EIN:** 87-1349061   **NPI:** 987654321   **TOB:** 0131

OUTPATIENT CASE

PATIENT NAME	DATE & START/END TIME OF VISIT		SOURCE OF ADMISSION
John Q Public	0505YY 0900 1300		Physician referral

PATIENT ADDRESS	PATIENT TELEPHONE NUMBER	BIRTH DATE	GENDER
15 Main St Alfred NY 14802	(607)555-1234	08-05-70	M (Male)

MARITAL STATUS	MEDICAL RECORD #	PATIENT CONTROL #	PATIENT DISCHARGE STATUS
Widowed	987654	859ABC451562	01 (Discharged home)

PAYER	HEALTH INSURANCE ID NUMBER (HICN)
Aetna	524856254

PRIMARY PAYER MAILING ADDRESS	Health Plan ID
Aetna, P.O. Box 650, Canandaigua NY 14424	3429872450

PATIENT RELATIONSHIP TO INSURED	EMPLOYMENT STATUS	NAME OF EMPLOYER
18 (Self)	Employed full time	Alstom, Hornell NY

RESPONSIBLE PHYSICIAN	RESPONSIBLE PHYSICIAN N.P.I.	TYPE OF ADMISSION
John Smith, M.D.	1265891895	Elective

RELEASE OF INFORMATION FORM	ASSIGNMENTS OF BENEFITS FORM
Signed by patient	Signed by patient

CASE SUMMARY	DIAGNOSES	ICD CODES
Patient was registered in the outpatient clinic and underwent single view chest x-ray for chronic obstructive pulmonary disease (COPD). Patient discharged home, to be followed by primary care physician.	COPD	496

CHARGE DESCRIPTION MASTER (PARTIAL)

ALFRED MEDICAL CENTER
548 N MAIN ST
ALFRED NY 14802

Printed on 05/05/YY

DEPARTMENT CODE: 01.855   DEPARTMENT: Radiology

SERVICE CODE		SERVICE DESCRIPTION	REVENUE CODE	CPT CODE	CHARGE	RVU
X	8550001	Chest x-ray, single view	0324	71010	74.50	0.70
	8550002	Chest x-ray, two views	0324	71020	82.50	0.95

FIGURE 9-15 Outpatient case (Courtesy Delmar/Cengage Learning)

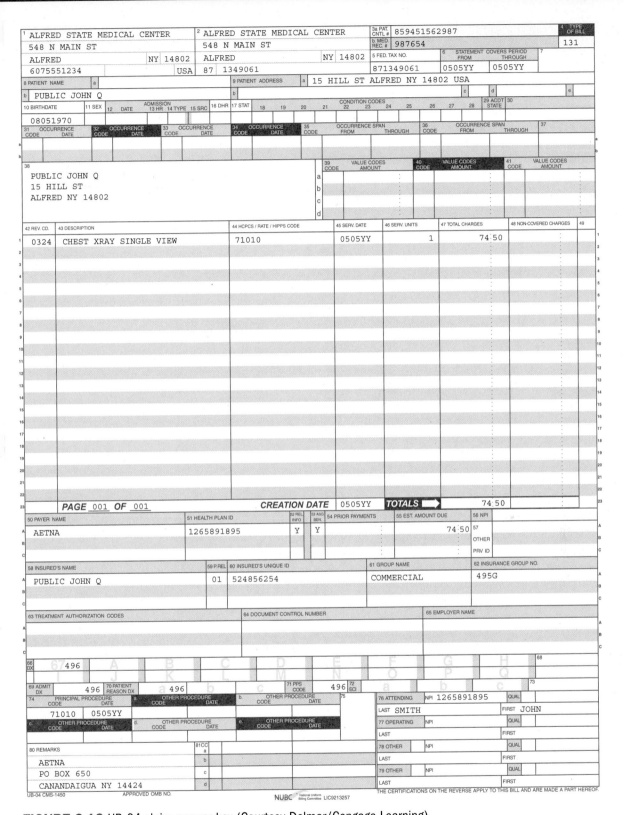

FIGURE 9-16 UB-04 claim answer key (Courtesy Delmar/Cengage Learning)

SUMMARY

Healthcare costs increased dramatically with the implementation of government-sponsored health programs in 1965. This led to the creation and implementation of prospective payment systems and fee schedules for government health programs as a way to control costs by reimbursing facilities according to predetermined rates based on patient category or type of facility (with annual increases based on an inflation index and a geographic wage index). The Centers for Medicare and Medicaid Services (CMS) manage implementation of Medicare PPS, fee schedules, and exclusions according to prospective cost-based rates and prospective price-based rates.

Prospective cost-based rates are based on reported healthcare costs (e.g., charges) from which a prospective *per diem* rate is determined. Annual rates are usually adjusted using actual costs from the prior year. This method may be based on the facility's *case mix* (types and categories of patients that reflect need for different levels of service based on acuity). Prospective payment systems based on this reimbursement methodology include resource utilization groups (RUGs) for skilled nursing care.

Prospective price-based rates are associated with a particular category of patient (e.g., inpatients), and rates are established by the payer (e.g., Medicare) prior to the provision of healthcare services. Prospective payment systems based on this reimbursement methodology include Medicare severity diagnosis-related groups (MS-DRGs) for inpatient care.

Typically, third-party payers adopt prospective payment systems, fee schedules, and exclusions after Medicare has implemented them; payers modify them to suit their needs.

- A fee schedule is cost-based, fee-for-service reimbursement methodology that includes a list of maximum fees and corresponding procedures/services, which payers use to compensate providers for healthcare services delivered to patients.

- Exclusions are "Medicare PPS Excluded Cancer Hospitals" (e.g., Roswell Park Memorial Institute in Buffalo, New York) that applied for and were granted waivers from mandatory participation in the hospital inpatient PPS.

The UB-04 claim contains data entry blocks called form locators (FLs) that are similar to the CMS-1500 claim blocks used to input information about procedures or services provided to a patient. Revenue codes are four-digit codes preprinted on a facility's chargemaster to indicate the location or type of service provided to an institutional patient, and they are reported on the UB-04. The chargemaster (or charge description master, CDM) is a document that contains a computer-generated list of procedures, services, and supplies with charges for each. Chargemaster data are entered in the facility's patient accounting system, and charges are automatically posted to the patient's bill (UB-04). Although some institutions actually complete the UB-04 claim and submit it to third-party payers for reimbursement, most perform data entry of UB-04 information using commercial software.

INTERNET LINKS

- CMS manuals
  Go to **www.cms.hhs.gov,** click on the Regulations & Guidance link, click on the Manuals link (below the Guidance heading), and click on the Internet-Only Manuals (IOMs) or Paper-Based Manuals link to access CMS manuals.

- *Diagnostic Statistical Manual*
  www.appi.org

- HIPPS rate codes
  Go to **www.cms.hhs.gov,** click on Medicare, and click on the Prospective Payment Systems—General Information link, and click on the HIPPS Codes link.

- *Medicare Claims Processing Manual,* Chapter 25
  Go to **www.cms.hhs.gov,** click on the Regulations & Guidance link, click on the Manuals link (below the Guidance heading), click on the Internet-Only Manuals (IOMs) link, click on the 100-04 (Medicare Claims Processing Manual) link, and click on the Chapter 25—Completing and Processing the Form CMS-1450 Data Set link.

- Medicare payment systems
  Go to **www.cms.hhs.gov,** click on the Medicare link, scroll to the Medicare Fee-for-Service Payment heading, and click on any payment system link.
- NUBC
  Go to **www.nubc.org** and click on What's New to learn more about the implementation of the UB-04.
- PatientFriendlyBilling® Project
  Go to **www.patientfriendlybilling.org** to view patient-friendly financial communications and resources (e.g., brochures, case studies, reports, and so on).
- Quarterly Medicare provider updates
  Go to **www.cms.hhs.gov,** click on the Regulations and Guidance link, scroll down to the Regulations & Policies heading, and click on the Quarterly Provider Updates—Regulations link. (Click on the CMS-QPU listserv link to join and receive email updates.)
- SageHealth revenue cycle management tools
  Go to **www.sagehealth.com,** and scroll down to click on the Revenue Cycle Management link to access free tools.
- UBEditor Pro
  Go to **www.ubeditorpro.com** to try Ingenix's web-based UB editing subscription service.

STUDY CHECKLIST

- ☐ Read this textbook chapter and highlight key concepts.
- ☐ Create an index card for each key term.
- ☐ Access the chapter Internet links to learn more about concepts.
- ☐ Complete the chapter review.
- ☐ Complete WebTutor assignments and take online quizzes.
- ☐ Complete the Workbook chapter, verifying answers with your instructor.
- ☐ Complete the StudyWare activities to receive immediate feedback.
- ☐ Form a study group with classmates to discuss chapter concepts in preparation for an exam.

REVIEW

SHORT ANSWER Complete the following.

1. Calculate the following amounts for a participating provider who bills Medicare:

Submitted charge (based on provider's regular fee for office visit)	$ 75
Medicare physician fee schedule (PFS)	$ 60
Coinsurance amount (paid by patient or supplemental insurance)	$ 12
Medicare payment (80 percent of the allowed amount)	_____
Medicare write-off (not to be paid by Medicare or the beneficiary)	_____

2. Calculate the following amounts for a nonPAR who bills Medicare:

Submitted charge (based on provider's regular fee)	$ 650
NonPAR Medicare physician fee schedule allowed amount	$ 450
Limiting charge (115 percent of MPFS allowed amount)	_____
Medicare payment (80 percent of the MPFS allowed amount)	_____
Beneficiary is billed 20 percent plus the balance of the limiting charge	$ 157.50
Medicare write-off (*not* to be paid by Medicare or the beneficiary)	_____

3. Calculate the following amounts for a nurse practitioner who bills Medicare:

Submitted charge (based on provider's regular fee for office visit)	$ 75
Medicare allowed amount (according to the Medicare physician fee schedule)	$ 60
Nurse practitioner allowed amount (100 percent of MPFS)	_____
Medicare payment (80 percent of the allowed amount)	_____

MATCHING   Match the type of rate with the prospective payment system.

____ 4.   Ambulance fee schedule   a. cost-based

____ 5.   Ambulatory surgical center payment rates   b. price-based

____ 6.   IPPS

____ 7.   Inpatient psychiatric facility PPS

____ 8.   SNF PPS

MULTIPLE CHOICE   Select the most appropriate response.

9. Which PPS provides a predetermined payment that depends on the patient's principal diagnosis, comorbidities, complications, and principal and secondary procedures?

   a. OPPS

   b. IPPS

   c. MPFS

   d. SNF PPS

10. Which is the abbreviation for the numeric codes reported on the CMS-1500 claim that indicate where services were provided to beneficiaries?

   a. ABN

   b. MSP

   c. POS

   d. TOS

11. The chargemaster is a(n)

   a. computer-generated list used by facilities, which contains procedures, services, supplies, revenue codes, and charges.

   b. data entry screen used by coders to assign diagnosis and procedure codes to generate a diagnosis-related group.

   c. document used by third-party payers and government plans to generate national provider identification numbers.

   d. encounter form used by physicians and other providers to collect data about office procedures provided to patients.

12. Resource utilization groups (RUGs) is a _____ reimbursement methodology used by skilled nursing facilities.

   a. fee-for-service based

   b. cost-based

   c. managed care

   d. price-based

13. Which legislated implementation of the long-term (acute) care hospital inpatient prospective payment system?

   a. BBA

   b. BBRA

   c. OBRA

   d. TEFRA

14. **The resource-based relative value scale (RBRVS) system is more commonly called the**
    a. clinical laboratory fee schedule.
    b. long-term care prospective payment system.
    c. Medicare physician fee schedule.
    d. outpatient prospective payment system.

15. **Reimbursement rates based on the anticipated care needs of patients result in reduced risks to facilities and to payers. The process by which healthcare facilities and payers determine anticipated care needs by reviewing types and/or categories of patients treated by a facility is called its**
    a. capitation.
    b. case mix.
    c. chargemaster.
    d. claims.

16. **Diagnosis-related groups are organized into mutually exclusive categories called _____, which are loosely based on body systems.**
    a. ambulatory payment classifications
    b. major diagnostic categories
    c. outcomes and assessment information sets
    d. resource utilization groups

17. **Physician work, practice expense, and malpractice expense are components in computing _____ for the resource-based relative value scale system.**
    a. conversion factors
    b. limiting charges
    c. relative-value units
    d. site of service differentials

18. **Four-digit _____ codes are preprinted on a facility's chargemaster to indicate the location or type of service provided to an institutional patient.**
    a. disease and procedure
    b. place of service
    c. revenue
    d. type of service

19. **The type of bill (TOB) is a required element that is entered in FL4 on the UB-04, and it contains _____ digits.**
    a. 3
    b. 4
    c. 5
    d. 10

20. **Which is responsible for developing data elements reported on the UB-04?**
    a. AHA
    b. CMS
    c. NUBC
    d. NUCC

Coding for Medical Necessity

CHAPTER OUTLINE

Applying Coding Guidelines

Coding and Billing Considerations

Coding from Case Scenarios

Coding from Patient Reports

OBJECTIVES

Upon successful completion of this chapter, you should be able to:

1. Define key terms.
2. Select and code diagnoses and procedures from case studies and sample reports.
3. Research local coverage determinations.

KEY TERMS

assessment

auditing process

local coverage determination (LCD)

medically managed

Medicare coverage database (MCD)

narrative clinic note

national coverage determination (NCD)

objective

operative report

outpatient code editor (OCE)

plan

SOAP note

subjective

INTRODUCTION

In Chapters 7 through 9, coding practice exercises consisted of statements for which diagnosis or procedure/service codes were assigned. The next step in learning to code properly is to select diagnoses and procedures/services from a case and link each procedure/service with the diagnosis code that justifies the medical necessity for performing it. (Medical necessity of procedures/services is required by payers for reimbursement consideration.) This chapter requires you to review case scenarios and patient reports to determine diagnoses and procedures/services to be coded, and medical necessity issues.

Coding for medical necessity requires a background in patient record documentation practices and the ability to interpret provider documentation. Delmar Learning's *Essentials of Health Information Management,* by Michelle A. Green and Mary Jo Bowie, contains detailed content about patient record documentation practices.

This chapter includes case studies that will allow you to practice interpreting provider documentation to select appropriate diagnoses and procedures/services for coding purposes and medical necessity determination.

APPLYING CODING GUIDELINES

In Chapters 6 through 8, diagnosis and procedure statements were coded according to ICD-9-CM, CPT, or HCPCS level II. In preparation for entering codes in the diagnosis blocks on the CMS-1500 claim, it is necessary to apply the CMS established *Official Coding Guidelines for Physician and Outpatient Hospital Services* (Chapter 6), and to understand the limitations of the CMS-1500 claim when billing payers.

Coding may not be a problem when you are reviewing short, one-line diagnosis or procedures/service statements such as those that appeared in most of the earlier exercises. When working with case scenarios, sample reports, or patient records, however, you must select the diagnosis and procedures/service to code based on provider documentation.

Be sure to code and report only those diagnoses, conditions, procedures, and/or services that are documented in the patient record as having been *treated* or *medically managed*. Medically managed means that even though a diagnosis (e.g., hypertension) may not receive direct treatment during an encounter, the provider has to consider that diagnosis when determining treatment for other conditions. It is appropriate to code and report medically-managed diagnoses and conditions. Questions that should be considered before coding and reporting a diagnosis or condition include:

1. Does the diagnosis or condition support a procedure or service provided during this encounter?

2. Did the provider prescribe a new medication or change a prescription for a new or existing diagnosis or condition?

3. Are positive diagnostic test results documented in the patient record to support a diagnosis or condition?

4. Did the provider have to consider the impact of treatment for chronic conditions when treating a newly diagnosed condition?

Up to four diagnosis codes can be reported on one CMS-1500. When reporting procedure/service codes on the CMS-1500, it is important to carefully match the appropriate diagnosis code with the procedure or service provided. Providers often document past conditions that are not active problems for the patient, and these conditions are not coded or reported on the claim. (For data capture purposes, a V code can be assigned to past conditions.)

NOTE: A diagnosis or condition code is linked with each procedure or service code reported on the CMS-1500 claim. Up to four ICD-9-CM codes are entered next to numbers 1–4 in Block 21 of the CMS-1500 claim. The appropriate diagnosis pointer (number) from Block 21 is reported in Block 24E to justify medical necessity of the procedure or service code reported in Block 24D.

> **EXAMPLE:** Do not code or report the following conditions:
>
> Status post left ankle fracture
>
> Strep throat, six months ago

Report ICD-9-CM codes on the claim, beginning with the *first-listed diagnosis* and followed by any secondary diagnoses (e.g., coexisting conditions) that were treated or medically managed. Then, link the code for each procedure or service provided with the diagnosis or condition that proves the *medical necessity* for performing the procedure or service.

EXAMPLE: Tim Johnson's primary care provider performed a level 3 E/M service (99213) in the office on June 1 to evaluate Tim's symptoms of upset stomach (536.8) and vomiting (787.03). Tim's diabetes mellitus (250.00) was medically managed during the encounter when venipuncture (36415) and a blood glucose test (82947) were performed; test results were within normal limits. Table 10-1 demonstrates how diagnoses and conditions are linked with procedures or services performed during the encounter. Figure 10-1 illustrates completion of Blocks 21 and 24A-E on the CMS-1500 claim. Note that Block 24E, line 1, contains just one diagnosis code link from Block 21. If a payer allows multiple diagnosis codes to be linked to procedure/services in Block 24, enter 1 2 or 1 2 3 in Block 24E, line 1.

TABLE 10-1 Linking diagnosis and procedure/service codes from Block 21 with Block 24E of the CMS-1500 claim

DIAGNOSES DOCUMENTED ON PATIENT'S CHART	ICD-9-CM CODE (ENTER IN BLOCK 21 OF CMS-1500 CLAIM)	PROCEDURE OR SERVICE RENDERED TO PATIENT	CPT CODE (ENTER IN BLOCK 24D OF CMS-1500 CLAIM)	DIAGNOSIS POINTER (ENTER IN BLOCK 24E OF CMS-1500 CLAIM)
Upset stomach	536.8	Office visit	99213	1
Vomiting	787.03	Office visit	99213	2
Diabetes mellitus	250.00	Venipuncture	36415	3
		Blood-sugar test	82947	3

FIGURE 10-1 Completed Blocks 21, 24A, 24D, and 24E of the CMS-1500 claim (Courtesy Delmar/Cengage Learning)

EXERCISE 10-1

Choosing the First-Listed Diagnosis

Review the list of symptoms, complaints, and disorders in each case and underline the first-listed diagnosis, which is reported in Block 21 of the CMS-1500 claim.

1. Occasional bouts of urinary frequency, but symptom-free today
   Sore throat with swollen glands and enlarged tonsils
   Acute pharyngitis with negative rapid strep test
   Urinalysis test negative

(continues)

EXERCISE 10-1 (continued)

2. Edema, left lateral malleolus
   Limited range of motion due to pain
   Musculoligamentous sprain, left ankle
   X-ray negative for fracture

3. Distended urinary bladder
   Benign prostatic hypertrophy (BPH) with urinary retention
   Enlarged prostate

4. Pale, diaphoretic, and in acute distress
   Bacterial endocarditis
   Limited chest expansion, scattered bilateral wheezes
   Pulse 112 and regular, respirations 22 with some shortness of breath

5. Right leg still weak
   Partial drop foot gait, right
   Tightness in lower back

EXERCISE 10-2

Linking Diagnoses with Procedures/Services

Link the diagnosis with the procedure/service by entering just one number in the DIAGNOSIS POINTER column.

REMEMBER!

To link the diagnosis with the procedure/service means to match up the appropriate diagnosis with the procedure/service that was rendered to treat or manage the diagnosis.

EXAMPLE: The patient was treated by the doctor in the office for a fractured thumb, and x-rays were taken. The following diagnoses and procedures were documented in the patient's chart:

1. diabetes mellitus, non-insulin-dependent, controlled
2. benign essential hypertension
3. simple fracture, right thumb

DIAGNOSIS POINTER	PROCEDURE/SERVICE
3	Office visit
3	X-ray, right thumb

Based on the procedure performed and service delivered, the patient was seen for the thumb fracture. Because the diabetes and hypertension are under control, they require no treatment or management during this visit. Therefore, only the fracture is linked to the procedure and service.

(continues)

EXERCISE 10-2 (continued)

CASE 1

The patient was treated in the office for abdominal cramping. A hemoccult test was positive for blood in the stool. The patient was scheduled for proctoscopy with biopsy two days later, and Duke C carcinoma of the colon was diagnosed. The patient was scheduled for proctectomy to be performed in seven days. The following diagnoses were documented on the patient's chart:

1. abdominal cramping

2. blood in the stool

3. Duke C carcinoma, colon

DIAGNOSIS POINTER	PROCEDURE/SERVICE
	Hemoccult lab test
	Proctoscopy with biopsy
	Proctectomy

CASE 2

The patient was treated in the office for urinary frequency with dysuria, sore throat with cough, and headaches. The urinalysis was negative, and the rapid strep test was positive for streptococcus infection. The patient was placed on antibiotics and was scheduled to be seen in 10 days. The following diagnoses were documented on the patient's chart:

1. urinary frequency with dysuria

2. sore throat with cough

3. headaches

4. strep throat

DIAGNOSIS POINTER	PROCEDURE/SERVICE
	Office visit
	Urinalysis
	Rapid strep test

CASE 3

The patient was treated in the office to rule out pneumonia. She had been experiencing wheezing and congestion, and her respirations were labored. The chest x-ray done in the office was positive for pneumonia. The following diagnoses were documented on the patient's chart:

1. pneumonia

2. wheezing

3. congestion

4. labored respirations

DIAGNOSIS POINTER	PROCEDURE/SERVICE
	Office visit
	Chest x-ray

(continues)

EXERCISE 10-2 (continued)

CASE 4

The doctor treated the patient in the nursing facility for the second time since she was admitted. The patient complained of malaise. It was noted that the patient had a cough as well as a fever of 103°F and that her pharynx was injected (abnormally red in appearance, which is a sign of infection). The following diagnoses were documented on the patient's chart:

1. malaise

2. cough

3. fever of 103°F

4. injected pharynx

DIAGNOSIS POINTER	PROCEDURE/SERVICE
	Nursing facility visit

CASE 5

The patient was treated in the emergency department for chills and fever. The physician noted left lower abdominal quadrant pain and tenderness. The physician diagnosed *acute diverticulitis.* The following diagnoses were documented on the patient's chart:

1. chills

2. fever

3. acute diverticulitis

DIAGNOSIS POINTER	PROCEDURE/SERVICE
	Emergency department visit

CODING AND BILLING CONSIDERATIONS

In addition to applying coding guidelines and rules to accurately assign and report codes on insurance claims, you should also incorporate the following as part of practice management:

- Completion of an Advance Beneficiary Notice (ABN) when appropriate.
- Implementation of an auditing process.
- Review of local coverage determinations (LCDs) and national coverage determinations (NCDs).
- Complete and timely patient record documentation.
- Use of Outpatient Code Editor (OCE) software (for outpatient hospital claims).

Patient record documentation must justify and support the medical necessity of procedures and services reported to payers. The following characteristics are associated with patient record documentation in all healthcare settings:

- Documentation should be generated at the time of service or shortly thereafter.
- Delayed entries within a reasonable time frame (24 to 48 hours) are acceptable for purposes of clarification, correction of errors, addition of information not initially available, and when certain unusual circumstances prevent documentation at the time of service. Delayed entries cannot be used to authenticate services or substantiate medical necessity for the purpose of reimbursement.

NOTE: It is recommended that an *authentication legend* be generated that contains the word-processed provider's name and, next to it, the provider's signature.

- The patient record cannot be altered. Doing so is considered tampering with documentation. This means that errors must be legibly corrected so that a reviewer can determine the origin of the corrections, and the use of correction fluid (e.g., Wite-Out™) is prohibited.

- Corrections or additions to the patient record must be dated, timed, and legibly signed or initialed.

- Patient record entries must be legible.

- Entries should be dated, timed, and authenticated by the author.

An *Advance Beneficiary Notice (ABN)* (Figure 14-2) is a waiver required by Medicare for all outpatient and physician office procedures/services that are not covered by the Medicare program. Before providing a procedure or service that is not medically necessary and/or that Medicare will not cover, the patient must be informed and required to sign the waiver. (Even though a provider considers a procedure or service medically necessary, Medicare may not cover that procedure or service.) Patients sign the waiver to indicate that they understand the procedure or service is not covered by Medicare and that they will be financially responsible for reimbursing the provider for the procedure or service performed. If the waiver is not signed before the procedure/service is provided *and* Medicare denies coverage, the perception is that the provider is providing free services to Medicare patients—this is considered *fraud* by the Office of the Inspector General for CMS!

> **EXAMPLE:** A Medicare patient is seen by her healthcare provider for severe left shoulder pain. There is no history of trauma, and in the office the patient has full range of motion with moderate pain. The patient insists that she wants the shoulder scanned to make sure she does not have cancer. Her physician explains that Medicare will reimburse for a scanning procedure *only if medically necessary* and that her symptoms and past history do not justify his ordering the scan. The patient insists again that she wants the scan even if she has to pay for it herself. The physician explains that this is an option for her and that she can sign the facility's ABN so that if Medicare denies the claim, the facility can bill her for the scan. The patient signs the ABN, which the physician keeps on file in the office, and the scan is ordered. The claim is submitted to Medicare, but it is denied due to lack of medical necessity to justify the scan. The patient is billed for the scan and is responsible for reimbursing the facility.

Medical practices and healthcare facilities should routinely participate in an **auditing process**, which involves reviewing patient records and CMS-1500 or UB-04 claims to assess coding accuracy and completeness of documentation. Medical practices should also review encounter forms to ensure the accuracy of ICD-9-CM and HCPCS/CPT codes, and healthcare facilities should audit chargemasters to ensure the accuracy of HCPCS/CPT and UB-04 revenue codes. Physicians use an *encounter form* (or *superbill*) to select diagnoses treated or medically managed and procedures, services, and supplies provided to patients during an office visit. Physicians and other personnel use *chargemasters* to select procedures, services, and supplies provided to hospital emergency department patients and outpatients. (No diagnosis codes are included on chargemasters because diagnoses are documented in the patient record, coded by health information personnel, entered using an automated abstracting system, and reported on the UB-04 by billing office personnel. Nursing and other personnel typically use automated order-entry software to capture procedures, services, and supplies provided to healthcare facility inpatients.)

NOTE: Appendix III contains an E/M CodeBuilder that can be used to audit patient record documentation to ensure that codes submitted to payers are accurate.

EXAMPLE: Upon routine audit of outpatient records and UB-04 claims submitted to payers, a claim for $4,890 submitted to a commercial payer was paid based on 80 percent of total billed charges, or $3,912. Review of the patient record revealed that the patient was actually treated in the hospital for 36 hours—this case should have been billed as an inpatient at a DRG rate of $1,500 (based on the patient's diagnosis). The result of the audit was an overpayment of $2,412, which the facility has an obligation to refund to the payer.

The **Medicare coverage database (MCD)** is used by Medicare administrative contractors, providers, and other healthcare industry professionals to determine whether a procedure or service is reasonable and necessary for the diagnosis or treatment of an illness or injury. The MCD contains:

● National coverage determinations (NCDs), including draft policies and proposed decisions

● Local coverage determinations (LCDs), including policy articles

The MCD also includes other types of national coverage analyses (NCAs), coding analyses for labs (CALs), Medicare Evidence Development & Coverage Advisory Committee (MedCAC) proceedings, and Medicare coverage guidance documents.

CMS develops **national coverage determinations (NCDs)** on an ongoing basis, and Medicare administrative contractors create edits for NCD rules, called local coverage determinations (LCDs) (discussed below). NCDs (and LCDs) link ICD-9-CM diagnosis codes with procedures or services that are considered reasonable and necessary for the diagnosis or treatment of an illness or injury. When review of NCDs (or LCDs) indicates that a procedure or service is not medically necessary, the provider is permitted to bill the patient only if an Advance Beneficiary Notice (ABN) is signed by the patient prior to providing the procedure or service.

● Claims submitted with diagnosis and procedure/service codes that fail NCD or LCD edits may be denied.

● When an LCD and an NCD exist for the same procedure or service, the NCD takes precedence.

EXAMPLE: The Centers for Medicare and Medicaid Services (CMS) published national coverage determinations (NCDs) that will prevent Medicare from paying for the following surgical errors:

● Wrong surgical or other invasive procedures performed on a patient

● Surgical or other invasive procedures performed on the wrong body part

● Surgical or other invasive procedures performed on the wrong patient

Local coverage determinations (LCDs) (formerly called *local medical review policies,* LMRPs) specify under what clinical circumstances a service is covered (including under what clinical circumstances it is considered to be reasonable and necessary) and coded correctly. They list covered and noncovered codes, but they do not include coding guidelines. LCDs assist Medicare administrative contractors (MACs) (previously called carriers and fiscal intermediaries) and providers (e.g., hospitals, physicians, and suppliers) by outlining how contractors will review claims to ensure that they meet Medicare coverage requirements. MACs publish LCDs to provide guidance to the public and medical community within a specified geographic area. CMS requires that LCDs be consistent with national guidance (although they can be more detailed or specific), developed with scientific evidence and clinical practice, and created using specified federal guidelines. If a MAC develops an LCD, it applies only within the area serviced by that contractor. Although another MAC may come to a similar decision, CMS does not require it to do so.

EXAMPLE: A Medicare administrative contractor (MAC) established an *LCD for Chest X-ray (L6097)*, which defines indications and limitations of coverage and/or medical necessity, reasons for denials, documentation requirements, and a list of ICD-9-CM codes that support medical necessity. Before submitting a claim for payment of a chest x-ray to the MAC, the insurance specialist should review this LCD to make sure the procedure is covered, that the ICD-9-CM codes reported are accurate, and that the patient record documentation supports medical necessity of the procedure.

The **outpatient code editor (OCE)** is software that edits outpatient claims submitted by hospitals, community mental health centers, comprehensive outpatient rehabilitation facilities, and home health agencies. The software assigns ambulatory payment classifications (APCs) and reviews submissions for coding validity (e.g., missing fifth digits) and coverage (e.g., medical necessity). OCE edits result in one of the following dispositions: rejection, denial, return to provider (RTP), or suspension.

EXAMPLE: The OCE reviews data elements submitted on the UB-04 claim such as from/through dates, ICD-9-CM diagnosis codes, type of bill, age, gender, HCPCS/CPT codes, revenue codes, service units, and so on.

EXERCISE 10-3

National Coverage Determinations

Assign ICD (diagnosis) and CPT/HCPCS (procedure/service) codes to each of the following outpatient scenarios. (Do *not* assign ICD procedure codes.) Then go to **www.cms.hhs.gov,** scroll to the Top 10 Links, click on the Medicare Coverage Database, click the **Indexes** link, and click on the **Alphabetical Listing** link to locate the procedure/service and carefully review its contents to determine whether Medicare covers that procedure/service.

(continues)

EXERCISE 10-3 (continued)

> **EXAMPLE:** A 67-year-old black female, status post menopause, underwent ultrasound bone density measurement for osteoporosis screening.
>
> **Answer:** 76977 (ultrasound bone density measurement); V49.81 (status post menopause); and V82.81 (osteoporosis screening). Upon review of the NCD entitled *Bone (Mineral) Density Studies,* it is noted that conditions for coverage of "bone mass measurements" are located in the *Medicare Benefit Policy Manual,* which indicates that "bone mass measurement" (BMM) is covered under certain conditions (e.g., BMM is ordered by the treating physician, is reasonable and necessary for treating patient's condition, and so on).

1. A 72-year-old male undergoes left heart cardiac catheterization by cutdown for coronary artery disease and angina pectoris. The patient is status post myocardial infarction four weeks ago.

2. A 66-year-old female undergoes cardiac rehabilitation with continuous ECG monitoring for status post coronary angioplasty, status post coronary bypass, and unstable angina.

3. An 81-year-old female undergoes diagnostic colonoscopy through stoma for history of colon cancer (treatment complete), Crohn's disease, blood in stool, and abdominal pain.

4. A 94-year-old male undergoes CT scan of head for laceration of scalp, closed head trauma, contusion of scalp, suspected brain lesion, and suspected brain metastasis.

CODING FROM CASE SCENARIOS

Case scenarios summarize medical data from patient records and, in this text, they introduce the student to the process of selecting (or abstracting) diagnoses and procedures. Once this technique is learned, it will be easier to move on to selecting diagnoses and procedures from patient records.

STEP 1 Read the entire case scenario to obtain an overview of the problems presented and procedures/service performed. Research any word or abbreviation not understood.

NOTE: Do *not* use a highlighter or other marker on an original document because copies of the document will be illegible. Highlighting marks photocopy as a thick, black or gray line. Instead, make a copy of the original document for mark-up purposes, and then destroy the copy after the coding process has been completed.

STEP 2 Reread the problem and highlight the diagnoses, symptoms, or health status that supports, justifies, and/or proves the medical necessity of any procedure or service performed.

STEP 3 Code the documented diagnoses, symptoms, procedure(s), signs, health status, and/or service(s).

STEP 4 Assign modifiers, if applicable.

STEP 5 Identify the primary condition.

STEP 6 Link each procedure or service to a diagnosis, symptom, or health status to communicate medical necessity.

Case 1

Patient returned to the surgeon's office <u>during postoperative period</u> because of symptoms of <u>shortness of breath, dizzy spells, and pain in the left arm</u>. A Level 3 re-examination (detailed history and examination was documented) of the patient was performed. The wound is healing nicely. There is no abnormal redness or abnormal pain from the incision. A 3-lead ECG rhythm strip was performed, which revealed an <u>inversion of the T wave</u>. The <u>abnormal ECG</u> was discussed with the patient and he agreed to an immediate referral to Dr. Cardiac for a cardiac work-up.

Answer

Procedure(s) performed	Code	Diagnosis(es)
1. Office visit, established patient, level 3	99213-24	1. Postoperative status (V45.89)
2. 3-lead ECG rhythm strip	93040	2. Shortness of breath (786.05) and dizziness (780.4)
		3. Pain, left arm (729.5)
		4. Abnormal ECG-inverted T wave (794.31)

Rationale

1. The service provided is a level 3 office visit, established patient.
2. The words "re-examination" and "during postoperative period, by same surgeon" justify the use of the -24 modifier because this examination was conducted during the postoperative period.
3. Abnormal ECG illustrates inversion of T wave, the documented problem.
4. "Shortness of breath, dizzy spells, and pain in the left arm" are symptoms of the abnormal ECG.

Case 2

This 72-year-old man with multiple chronic conditions registered for hospital outpatient surgery and was scheduled for repair of an initial, uncomplicated left <u>inguinal hernia</u>. The patient was cleared for surgery by his primary care physician. General anesthesia was administered by the anesthesiologist, after which the incision was made. At this point the patient went into <u>shock</u>, the surgery was halted, and the wound was closed. Patient was sent to Recovery.

Answer

Procedure(s) performed	Code	Diagnosis(es)
1. Hernia repair, initial	49505-74	1. Inguinal hernia (550.90)
		2. Shock due to surgery (998.0)
		3. Surgery cancelled (V64.1)

Rationale

1. Procedure initiated for repair of uncomplicated, inguinal hernia.
2. Modifier -74 indicates surgery was stopped after anesthesia had been administered because of the threat to the patient's well-being from the shock.
3. First-listed diagnosis is inguinal hernia, which is the reason the patient sought health care.
4. Secondary diagnoses include shock resulting from surgery (explains the discontinuation of the surgery) and cancelled surgery.

EXERCISE 10-4

Coding Case Scenarios

A. List and code the procedures, services, and diagnosis(es) for each of the following case scenarios.

B. Be sure to include all necessary CPT and/or HCPCS modifiers.

C. Underline the first-listed condition.

1. A 66-year-old Medicare patient came to the office for his annual physical. He has past history of hypertension, controlled by medication, and new complaints of dizziness and tiredness. During the course of the examination the physician found BP of 160/130. A detailed history and exam of this established patient was performed in addition to the preventive medicine encounter.

    Procedures/Services　　　　**Diagnoses**

    _____　_____

    _____　_____

    _____　_____

2. A 67-year-old woman came to the surgery center for a scheduled diagnostic arthroscopy of her right shoulder because of constant pain on rotation of the shoulder. Prior to entering the operating room she told the nurse, "I have been feeling weak, depressed, and tired ever since my last visit." The surgeon performs a re-examination with a detailed history, expanded problem focused physical, and moderate-complexity decision making prior to the surgery. The findings were negative and the procedure was performed uneventfully.

    Procedures/Services　　　　**Diagnoses**

    _____　_____

    _____　_____

    _____　_____

3. The patient was seen in the emergency department (ED) at 10:00 a.m. for right lower quadrant pain; the ED physician performed an expanded problem-focused history and exam. Ultrasound revealed an inflamed appendix. A surgeon was called in, who evaluated the patient (conducting a level 3 new patient E/M service) and performed outpatient laparoscopic appendectomy at 1:00 p.m. for ruptured appendix with abscess. The patient was discharged at 9:00 a.m. the next morning.

    Procedures/Services　　　　**Diagnoses**

    _____　_____

    _____　_____

    _____　_____

4. An emergency department (ED) physician performed a level 3 evaluation on a patient who was seen for complaints of severe abdominal pain, nausea, and vomiting. An ultrasound revealed enlarged gallbladder. A surgeon was called in, evaluated the patient (conducting a level 3 new patient E/M service) and performed a laparoscopic cholecystectomy, which revealed acute cholecystitis. The patient's stay was less than 24 hours.

(continues)

EXERCISE 10-4 (continued)

Procedures/Services   Diagnoses

_____

_____

_____

5. Dr. B performed an expanded problem-focused, postoperative examination on an established patient. He also removed the sutures from an open appendectomy that the patient underwent while on vacation in another part of the country.

Procedures/Services   Diagnoses

_____

_____

_____

Additional scenarios are found at the end of this chapter and in the Workbook that accompanies this text.

CODING FROM PATIENT REPORTS

A patient record serves as the business record for a patient encounter, and is maintained in a manual record or automated format (e.g., electronic medical record). The patient record contains documentation of all healthcare services provided to a patient to support diagnoses, justify treatment, and record treatment results. The primary purpose of the patient record is to provide *continuity of care* (documentation of patient care services so that others who treat the patient have a source of information from which to base additional care and treatment). Secondary purposes of the patient record do not relate directly to patient care, and they include

NOTE: Health insurance specialists review the patient record when assigning codes to diagnosis, procedures, and services. In addition, copies of reports from the patient record may be requested from third-party payers to process insurance claims.

- Evaluating the quality of patient care.
- Providing information to third-party payers for reimbursement.
- Serving the medico-legal interests of the patient, facility, and providers of care.
- Providing data for use in clinical research, epidemiology studies, education, public policy making, facilities planning, and healthcare statistics.

VETERANS HEALTH INFORMATION SYSTEMS AND TECHNOLOGY ARCHITECTURE (VistA®)

The Veterans Health Information Systems and Technology Architecture (VistA®) electronic health record was developed by the United States Department of Veterans Affairs (VA) and is used by VA medical centers and outpatient clinics to document health care provided to military veterans. (An electronic health record allows for immediate access to information such as laboratory data, office notes, radiology reports, and so on.) Originally called the Decentralized Hospital Computer Program (DHCP), which was introduced in 1985 when all VA computers were operational, the software was renamed "VistA" in 1994. (VistA's origins predate its programming to that of its conception and design,

(continues)

when President Lyndon Johnson signed the Social Security Amendments Act [or Medicare Act] into law on July 30, 1965.)

The CMS (Centers for Medicare and Medicaid Services) has made VistA-Office EHR (VOE) software available to physician offices, and it includes the following features:

- Patient registration

- Progress note templates (including customization)

- Graphing (e.g., lab test results can be viewed as a graph)

- Clinical reminders (e.g., assist in clinical decision-making)

- Report generation (e.g., patient treatment profile)

- HIPAA compliance (e.g., role-based access security controls, electronic signature, audit capabilities)

- Codified data (e.g., allows assignment of ICD-9 codes)

- Risk, social, and medical factors (e.g., alcohol and drug use, marital status)

- Hospitalization functionality (e.g., document inpatient hospital discharge summary)

- Immunization history

- Laboratory functionality (e.g., order lab tests and view results)

- Pharmacy functionality (e.g., order medications, print prescriptions for signature, fax prescriptions to a local pharmacy with electronic signature)

- Laboratory interface

- Billing/practice management interface

Diagnoses, procedures, and services are selected and coded from clinic notes, consultation reports, and diagnostic reports. This process is the same as that used for case scenarios. The major difference is that clinic notes, consultations, and diagnostic reports contain more detail.

NOTE: Abbreviations are commonly used by providers when documenting patient care. The Joint Commission has implemented a patient safety goal to help reduce the numbers of medical errors related to incorrect use of terminology. To facilitate compliance with the goal, the Joint Commission issued a list of abbreviations, acronyms, and symbols that should no longer be used by providers.

To locate the list, go to **www.jointcommission.org**, click on the Patient Safety link, and click on the "Do Not Use" List link.

Clinic Notes

Healthcare providers use two major formats for documenting clinic notes:

- **Narrative clinic notes.**

- **SOAP notes.**

Diagnoses, procedures, and services can be selected and coded from either format. Both require documentation to support the level of Evaluation and Management (E/M) service coded and reported on the CMS-1500 claim, even if the provider selects the E/M code from a preprinted encounter form (e.g., superbill).

> **EXAMPLE:** Portion of encounter form containing E/M service, date, code, and charge
>
> | New Patient E/M Service | 01-01-YYYY | ☑99203 | $70.00 |

Narrative Clinic Note

A **narrative clinic note** is written in paragraph format.

> **EXAMPLE:** Narrative clinic note
>
> A 21-year-old female patient comes to the office today, having been referred by Dr. Bandaid for pain in the RLQ of the abdomen, 2 days' duration. Temp: 102°F. Detailed history and physical examination revealed rebound tenderness over McBurney's point with radiation to the RUQ and RLQ. The remainder of the physical examination is normal. For additional information see the complete history and physical in this chart. Laboratory data ordered by Dr. Bandaid (oral report given by Goodtechnique Lab) is as follows: WBC 19.1; RBC 4.61; platelets 234,000; hematocrit 42; hemoglobin 13.5; bands 15%, and PMNs 88%. UA and all other blood work were within normal limits. Patient is to be admitted to Goodmedicine Hospital for further work-up and possible appendectomy.
>
> *T.J. Stitcher, M.D.*

SOAP Notes

SOAP notes are written in outline format ("SOAP" is an acronym derived from the first letter of the topic headings used in the note: Subjective, Objective, Assessment, and Plan).

The **subjective** part of the note contains the chief complaint and the patient's description of the presenting problem. It can also include the response to treatment prescribed earlier, past history, review of symptoms, and relevant family and social history. The documentation may appear in quotes because it represents the patient's statement verbatim.

The **objective** part of the note contains documentation of measurable or objective observations made during physical examination and diagnostic testing. Some healthcare providers may also include historical information obtained from previous encounters in this section.

The **assessment** contains the diagnostic statement and may include the physician's rationale for the diagnosis. If this section is missing from the report, look for positive diagnostic test results documented in the objective data or code the symptoms presented in either the subjective or objective data.

The **plan** is the statement of the physician's future plans for the work-up and medical management of the case. This includes plans for medications, diet, and therapy, future diagnostic tests to be performed, suggested lifestyle changes, items covered in the informed consent discussions, items covered in patient education sessions, and suggested follow-up care.

EXAMPLE: SOAP note

3/29/YYYY

S:　Pt states "no complaints, no new symptoms since last visit, which was seven days ago."

O:　Patient seen today, on 10th day postop. T 98.6°F; P 80; R 20; BP 120/86, right arm, sitting, WT 120 lb.
Incision, inner aspect of left breast, healing well. No sign of inflammation or infection.

A:　Papilloma with fibrocystic changes, no malignancy.
Size 3.0 x 1.5 x 0.2 cm.

P:　1.　Suture removal today.
　　2.　Return visit, 3 months for follow-up.

Janet B. Surgeon, M.D.

In this example, the chief complaint (S:) and the vital signs (O:) were documented by the medical assistant (or nurse). The provider then performed an examination (O:), documented her findings (A:), and established a plan for the patient (P:). Because this note documents a postoperative follow-up office visit within the global period, no diagnoses or procedures/services are selected or coded. Neither the third-party payer nor the patient is billed for this postoperative visit. However, when the patient returns in three months for follow-up, that visit is billed to the payer (because it is not within the postoperative global period).

Diagnostic Test Results

Diagnostic test results are documented in two locations:

- **Clinic notes**
- **Laboratory reports**

Laboratory reports quantify data, and diagnostic implications are summarized in *clinic notes* documented by the provider. Other diagnostic tests (e.g., x-ray and pathology reports) include an interpretation by the responsible physician (e.g., radiologist or pathologist).

The laboratory report in Figure 10-2 documents a high glucose level (denoted by the **H** on the report). Upon review of the clinic note, if the insurance specialist finds documentation of signs and symptoms like a high glucose level, the provider should be asked whether a definitive diagnosis is to be coded instead.

The x-ray in Figure 10-3 was justified by the diagnosis of mild fibrocystic changes of the breast. (If the diagnosis is not documented in the patient's record, be sure to check with the provider before coding this as the diagnosis.)

MILLION, IMA	Patient No. 12345		PROVIDER: Erin Helper, M.D.
Specimen: Blood (collected 03/03/YYYY).	Test completed: 03/03/YYYY at 04:50 P.M.		Technician: 099
Test	**Result**		**Normal Values**
Sodium	142 mEq/L		(135–148)
Potassium	4.4 mEq/L		(3.5–5.1)
Chloride	105 mEq/L		(97–107)
Glucose	176 mg/dL	**H**	(70–110)
BUN	14 mg/dL		(5–20)
Creatinine	1.0 mg/dL		(0.8–1.5)

FIGURE 10-2 Sample laboratory report with abnormal glucose level (Courtesy Delmar/Cengage Learning)

MILLION, IMA   **Patient No.** 12345   **PROVIDER:** Erin Helper, M.D.

Baseline Mammogram

There are mild fibrocystic changes in both breasts but without evidence of a dominant mass, grouped microcalcifications, or retractions. Density on the left side is slightly greater and thought to be simply asymmetric breast tissue. There are some small axillary nodes bilaterally.

IMPRESSION: Class 1 (normal or clinically insignificant findings).

Follow-up in 1 year is suggested to assess stability in view of the fibrocystic asymmetric findings. Thereafter, biannual follow-up if stable. No dominant mass is present particularly in the upper inner quadrant of the left breast.

Maryanne Iona, M.D.

FIGURE 10-3 Sample radiology report (Courtesy Delmar/Cengage Learning)

EXERCISE 10-5

Coding SOAP Notes

Review the following SOAP notes, then select and code the diagnoses.

1. S: Patient complains of stomach pain, 3 days' duration. She also stated that her legs still get painful from the knees down.

   O: Ht 5'6"; Wt 164; BP 122/86; pulse 92 and regular; temp 97.0°F, oral; chest normal; heart normal. The Doppler arteriogram of lower extremities taken last week at the hospital is reported as within normal limits bilaterally.

   A: Another episode of atrophic gastritis. Leg pain.

   P: Carafate 1 g. Take 1 tablet qid before meals and at bedtime, #120 tabs.

(continues)

EXERCISE 10-5 (continued)

DIAGNOSES	ICD-9-CM CODES

2. **S:** Patient seems to be doing quite well, postop cholecystectomy; however, the pain that he had prior to his surgery is not gone.

   O: Incision is well healed. Abdomen is soft and nontender.

   A: Pathology report revealed chronic cholecystitis and cholelithiasis.

   P: 1. Lengthy discussion with patient and his wife about treatment in the future. Asked that they call any time they have questions.

   2. Return visit here on a prn basis.

DIAGNOSES	ICD-9-CM CODES

3. **S:** Patient complains of generalized stiffness and being tired. She also notes that her left knee was swollen and felt hot to the touch last week. She was last seen 18 months ago on Penicillamine and 2 mg prednisone bid. Her other meds are loperamide for loose stool and Tagamet 300 mg bid.

   O: Examination reveals some swelling of the left knee with active synovitis and minimal fluid. Her present weight is 134 lb, BP 116/72. The hematocrit performed today is 37.5 and her sed rate is 65.

   A: This patient has active rheumatoid arthritis.

   P: 1. Increase prednisone to 5 mg bid, and Penicillamine to 500 mg bid.

   2. X-ray of left knee tomorrow.

   3. Recheck CBC, sed rate, and urinalysis in 4 weeks.

   4. Discussed with her the possibility of injecting steroids into the knee if she shows no improvement.

DIAGNOSES	ICD-9-CM CODES

(continues)

EXERCISE 10-5 (continued)

4. S: Patient returns today for follow-up of chronic angina and dyspnea. She says the angina still appears mainly when she is resting, and particularly just as she is waking up in the morning. This is accompanied by some dyspnea and pain occasionally radiating into the left jaw, but no palpitations. The angina is relieved by nitroglycerin. She continues to take Inderal 40 mg qid.

O: BP, left arm, sitting, 128/72; weight is 150 lb. Chest is clear. No wheezing or rales.

A: Unstable angina. Patient again refused to consider a heart catheterization.

P: New RX: Isordil Tembids 40 mg.
Refill nitroglycerin.

DIAGNOSES	ICD-9-CM CODES

5. S: This 17-year-old, single, white female presents to the office with a sore throat, fever, and swollen glands, 2 days' duration.

O: Oral temp 102.4°F; pulse 84; respirations 18; BP 118/78; wt 138 lb. The throat is markedly erythematous with evidence of exudative tonsillitis. Ears show normal TMs bilaterally. Few tender, submandibular nodes, bilaterally.

A: Acute tonsillitis.

P: 1. Obtained throat culture that was sent to the lab.
2. Patient started on an empiric course of Pen Vee K 250 mg #40 to be taken qid × 10 days
3. Encouraged patient to increase oral fluid intake.
4. Patient to call office in 48 hours to obtain culture results and report her progress.

DIAGNOSES	ICD-9-CM CODES

6. S: This is a 50-year-old widow who comes to the office following a possible seizure. Her friend reports she was seated at her desk, and after a crash was heard, they found her lying on the floor. She had urinary incontinence, and now complains of confusion and headache. Patient says this was her first episode and denies ever having chest pain, palpitations, or paresthesias. She cannot recall any recent head trauma or auras. She reports no allergies to medication and currently denies taking a medication.

(continues)

EXERCISE 10-5 (continued)

She does have a history of well-differentiated nodular lymphoma, which was treated successfully by a course of radiation at the Goodmedicine Hospital in Anywhere, US. She has had no clinical evidence of recurrence. She reports no hospitalizations except for normal delivery of her son 25 years ago. She does admit to mild COPD. Her family history is negative for seizures.

O: Review of systems is noncontributory. Wt 155 lb; BP 116/72, both arms; pulse 72 and regular; respirations 18 and unlabored. Head is normocephalic and atraumatic. PERRLA. EOMs are intact. The sclerae are white. Conjunctivae are pink. Funduscopic examination is benign. The ears are normal bilaterally. No evidence of Battle sign. Mouth and throat are normal; tongue is midline and normal. The neck is supple and negative. Chest is clear. Heart rate and rhythm are regular with a grade II/IV systolic ejection murmur along the left sternal border without gallop, rub, click, or other adventitious sounds. Abdomen is soft, nontender, and otherwise negative. Bowel sounds are normal. Pelvic was deferred. There is good rectal sphincter tone. No masses are felt. Hemoccult test was negative. Extremities and lymphatics are noncontributory.

Neurologic exam shows normal mental status. Cranial nerves II–XII are intact. Motor, sensory, cerebellar function, and Romberg are normal. Babinski is absent. Reflexes are 2+ and symmetric in both upper and lower extremities.

A: New-onset seizure disorder. Rule out metabolic versus vascular etiologies.

P: The patient will be scheduled for MRI of the brain and EEG at Goodmedicine Hospital. Obtain electrolytes, calcium, albumin, LFTs, and CBC with platelet and sed rate at the same visit.

DIAGNOSES	ICD-9-CM CODES

Operative Reports

Operative reports will vary from a short narrative description of a minor procedure that is performed in the physician's office (Figure 10-4) to more formal reports dictated by the surgeon in a format required by hospitals and ambulatory surgical centers (ASCs) (Figure 10-5).

Hospital and ASC formats may vary slightly, but all contain the following information in outline form:

- Date of the surgery
- Patient identification
- Pre- and postoperative diagnosis(es)

MILLION, IMA   **Patient No.** 12345   **PROVIDER:** Erin Helper, M.D.

12/5/YYYY

Reason for Visit: Postpartum exam and colposcopy.

Vital Signs: Temperature 97.2F. Blood pressure 88/52. Weight 107.

Labs: Glucose negative; Albumin, trace.

Patient seems to be doing fine, thinks the bleeding has just about stopped at this point. Her daughter is apparently doing fine; she is to get back chromosomal analysis in a couple of days. No other system defects have been found yet.

Examination: *Breasts:* Negative. Patient is breastfeeding. *Abdomen:* Soft, flat, no masses, nontender. *Pelvic:* Cervix appeared clear, no bleeding noted. Uterus anteverted, small, nontender. Adnexa negative. Vagina appeared atrophic. Episiotomy healing well.

Procedure: Colposcopy of cervix performed with staining of acetic acid. Entire squamocolumnar junction could not be visualized even with aid of endocervical speculum. Exam was made more difficult because of very thick cervical mucus, which could not be completely removed, and because the vagina and cervix were somewhat atrophic appearing. Whitening of epithelium around entire circumference of cervix noted, but no abnormal vasculature noted. Numerous biopsies were taken from posterior and anterior lip of cervix. Endocervical curettage done. Repeat Pap smear of cervix also done.

Plan: Patient to call at the end of this week for biopsy results. Patient told she could have intercourse after five days, to use condoms, or to come back to office first to have size of diaphragm checked.

Erin Helper, M.D.

FIGURE 10-4 Sample physician's office operative report (Courtesy Delmar/Cengage Learning)

MILLION, IMA   **Patient No.** 12345   **PROVIDER:** Gail R. Bones, M.D.
Room #: 101B   **DATE OF SURGERY:** 01/01/YYYY

Preoperative Diagnosis:	Displaced supracondylar fracture, left humerus
Postoperative Diagnosis:	Same
Procedure:	Closed reduction and casting, left humeral fracture
Surgeon:	Gail R. Bones, M.D.
Assistant Surgeon:	T.J. Stitcher, M.D.

Findings and Procedure:

After adequate general anesthesia, the patient's left elbow was gently manipulated and held at 110 degrees of flexion, at which point continued to maintain a good radial pulse. X-rays revealed a good reduction; therefore, a plaster splint was applied, care being taken not to put any constriction in the antecubital fossa. X-rays were taken again, and showed excellent reduction has been maintained. Patient maintained good radial pulse, was awake, and was taken to Recovery in good condition.

Gail R. Bones, M.D.

FIGURE 10-5 Sample hospital outpatient surgery or ambulatory surgery center operative report (Courtesy Delmar/Cengage Learning)

- List of the procedure(s) performed
- Name of primary and secondary surgeons who performed surgery

The body of the report contains a detailed narrative of:

- Positioning and draping of the patient for surgery
- Achievement of anesthesia
- Detailed description of how the procedure(s) was performed; identification of the incision made; and instruments, drains, dressings, special packs, and so on used during surgery
- Identification of abnormalities found during the surgery
- Description of how hemostasis was obtained and the closure of the surgical site(s)
- Condition of the patient when (s)he left the operating room
- Signature of surgeon

Procedure for Coding Operative Reports

STEP 1 Make a copy of the operative report.

This will allow you to freely make notations in the margin and highlight special details without marking up the original (which must remain in the patient's record).

STEP 2 Carefully review the list of procedures performed.

STEP 3 Read the body of the report and make a note of procedures to be coded.

Key words to look for include:

    Simple versus complicated
    Partial, complete, total, or incomplete
    Unilateral versus bilateral
    Initial versus subsequent
    Incision versus excision
    Open versus closed treatment, surgery, or fracture
    Reconstructive surgery, ___ plasty,
    ___ plastic repair
    Repair, ___ pexy
    Endoscopy
    Biopsy
    Ligation
    Debridement
    Complex, simple, intermediate, repair
    Micronerve repair
    Reconstruction
    Graft (bone, nerve, or tendon requires additional code)
    Diagnostic versus surgical procedure

Be alert to the following:

1. Additional procedures documented in the body of the report that are not listed in the heading of the report (e.g., Procedures Performed) should be coded.

EXAMPLE:

Postoperative Diagnosis: Chronic cholecystitis and cholelithiasis without obstruction

Procedures Performed: Laparoscopic cholecystectomy with cholangiography

In the body of the operative report the surgeon describes the laparoscopic cholecystectomy and a cholangiogram. The surgeon also documents the operative findings and a biopsy of a suspicious liver nodule. The insurance specialist should contact the surgeon so that the liver biopsy is added to the *Procedures Performed* statement and then assign a CPT code to it (in addition to the laparoscopic cholecystectomy and cholangiogram).

---

2. When the *Procedures Performed* heading lists procedures performed that are not described in the body of the operative report, the surgeon will have to add a written addendum to the operative report documenting the performance of any listed procedure that should be coded.

EXAMPLE:

Procedures Performed: Arthroscopy, right knee. Open repair, right knee, collateral and cruciate ligaments

Upon review of the body of the report, the insurance specialist notes that the surgeon did not document removal of the scope. Even though the removal of a scope is not coded, the insurance specialist should instruct the surgeon to document this as an addendum to the operative report.

STEP 4 Identify main term(s) and subterms for the procedure(s) to be coded.

STEP 5 Underline and research any terms in the report that you cannot define.

Many coding errors are made when the coder does not understand critical medical terms in the report.

STEP 6 Locate the main term(s) in the CPT index.

Check for the proper anatomic site or organ.

STEP 7 Research all suggested codes.

Read all notes and guidelines pertaining to the codes you are investigating. Watch for add-on procedures described in any notes/guidelines.

STEP 8 Return to the CPT index and research additional codes if you cannot find a particular code(s) that matches the description of the procedure(s) performed in the operative report.

Because a monetary value is associated with each CPT code, and to avoid bundling, never assign multiple, separate codes to describe a procedure if CPT has a single code that classifies all the individual components of the procedure described by the physician.

REMEMBER!

Global surgery includes preoperative assessment, the surgery, and normal uncomplicated postoperative care. Key words associated with global surgeries:

Exploratory	Anastomosis
Exploration of _____	Transection
Minor lysis of adhesions	Bisection
Temporary _____	Blunt bisection (dissection)
Electrocautery	Sharp dissection
Simple closure	Take down (to take apart)
Minor debridement	Undermining of tissue (to
Wound culture	cut at a horizontal angle)
Intraoperative photo	

Never assign a code number described in CPT as a "separate procedure" when it is performed within the same incision as the primary procedure and is an integral part of a larger procedure.

STEP 9 Investigate the possibility of adding modifiers to a specific code description to fully explain the procedure(s) performed.

EXAMPLE: Key word indicators for use of modifier -22

Extensive debridement/lysis or adhesions

Excessive bleeding (>500 cc)

Friable tissue

Prolonged procedure due to _____

Unusual anatomy, findings, or circumstances

Very difficult

STEP 10 Code the postoperative diagnosis. This should explain the medical necessity for performing the procedure(s). If the postoperative diagnosis does not support the procedure performed, be sure the patient's chart contains documentation to justify the procedure.

> **EXAMPLE:** Patient seen in the emergency department (ED) with right lower quadrant pain, and evaluation reveals elevated temperature and increased white blood count. Preoperative diagnosis is *appendicitis*, and the patient undergoes *appendectomy;* however, the postoperative diagnosis is *normal appendix.* In this situation the documentation of the patient's signs and symptoms in the ED chart justifies the surgery performed even though the postoperative diagnosis does not support the surgery performed.

Look for additional findings in the body of the report if the postoperative diagnosis listed on the operative report does not completely justify the medical necessity for the procedure.

Compare the postoperative diagnosis with the biopsy report on all excised neoplasms to determine whether the tissue is benign or malignant.

When doing the exercises in this text and the Workbook, use any stated pathology report to determine whether excised tissue is benign or malignant if it is not covered in the postoperative diagnosis(es).

When working in a medical practice, do not code an excision until the pathology report is received.

STEP 11 Review code options with the physician who performed the procedure if the case is unusual.

Before assigning an "unlisted CPT procedure" code, review HCPCS level II codes. Remember that a description of the procedure performed must accompany the claim if an unlisted CPT code is reported.

STEP 12 Assign final code numbers for procedures verified in steps 3 and 4 and any addendum the physician added to the original report.

STEP 13 Properly sequence the codes, listing first the most significant procedure performed during the episode.

STEP 14 Be sure to destroy the copy of the operative report (e.g., shred it) after the abstracting and coding process is completed.

EXERCISE 10-6

Coding Operative Reports

When working with the case studies in this text, code procedures as listed in the case. When working in a medical practice, refer to the Medicare physician fee schedule or the payer's fee schedule to determine which surgical procedure receives the highest reimbursement.

CASE 1

Preoperative Diagnosis:	Questionable recurrent basal cell carcinoma, frontal scalp
Postoperative Diagnosis:	Benign lesion, frontal scalp
Operation:	Biopsy of granulating area with electrodessication of possible recurrent basal cell carcinoma of frontal scalp

(continues)

EXERCISE 10-6 (continued)

History: About 1 year ago, the patient had an excision and grafting of a very extensive basal cell carcinoma of the forehead at the edge of the scalp. The patient now has a large granular area at 12 o'clock on the grafted area. This may be a recurrence of the basal cell carcinoma.

Procedure: The patient was placed in the dorsal recumbent position and draped in the usual fashion. The skin and subcutaneous tissues at the junction of the skin grafts of the previous excision and the normal scalp were infiltrated with 1/2% xylocaine containing epinephrine. An elliptical excision of the normal skin and the granulating area was made. After hemostasis was obtained, the entire area of granulating tissue was thoroughly electrodesiccated.

Pathology Report: The entire specimen measures $0.7 \times 0.4 \times 0.3$ cm depth. Part of the specimen is a slightly nodular hemorrhagic lesion measuring 0.3 cm in diameter.

Resected piece of skin shows partial loss of epithelium accompanied by acute and chronic inflammation of granulation tissue from a previous excision of basal cell carcinoma.

Diagnosis: This specimen is benign; there is no evidence of tumor.

CASE 2

Preoperative Diagnosis:	Tumor of the skin of the back with atypical melanocyte cells
Postoperative Diagnosis:	Same
Operation Performed:	Wide excision
Anesthesia:	General

Indications: The patient had a previous biopsy of a nevus located on the back. The pathology report indicated atypical melanocyte cells in the area close to the margin of the excision. The pathologist recommended that a wide re-excision be performed. The patient was informed of the situation during an office visit last week, and he agreed to be readmitted for a wider excision of the tumor area.

Procedure: The patient was placed on his left side, and general anesthesia was administered. The skin was prepped and draped in a usual fashion. A wide excision, 5.0 cm in length and 4.0 cm wide, was made. The pathologist was alerted, and the specimen was sent to the lab. The frozen section was reported as negative for melanocytes on the excisional margin at this time. After the report was received, the wound was closed in layers and a dressing was applied. The patient tolerated the procedure well and was sent to Recovery in good condition.

CASE 3

Preoperative Diagnosis:	Colonic polyps
Postoperative Diagnosis:	Benign colonic polyps Melanosis coli
Operation Performed:	Colonoscopy
Anesthesia:	An additional 25 mg of Demerol and 2.5 mg of Valium were administered for sedation.

(continues)

EXERCISE 10-6 (continued)

Procedure: The Olympus video colonoscope was passed into the rectum and slowly advanced. The cecum was identified by the ileocecal valve. The prep was suboptimal.

The colonic mucosa had diffuse dark pigmentation suggestive of melanosis coli. The ascending colon, transverse colon, and proximal descending colon appeared unremarkable. There were two polyps which were about 8 mm in size adjacent to each other in the sigmoid colon. One was removed for biopsy, and the other was fulgurated with hot wire biopsy forceps. After this, the colonoscope was gradually withdrawn. The patient tolerated the procedure well and was sent to Recovery.

Because of the suboptimal prep, small polyps or arteriovenous malformations could have been missed.

CASE 4

Preoperative Diagnosis:	Serous otitis media
Postoperative Diagnosis:	Same
Operation Performed:	Bilateral myringotomy with insertion of ventilating tubes
Anesthesia:	General

Procedure: The patient was placed in a supine position and induction of general anesthesia was achieved by face mask. The ears were examined bilaterally using an operating microscope. An incision was made in the anteroinferior quadrants. A large amount of thick fluid was aspirated from both ears, more so from the left side. Ventilating tubes were introduced with no difficulties. Patient tolerated the procedure well and was sent to Recovery in satisfactory condition.

CASE 5

Preoperative Diagnosis:	Lesion, buccal mucosa, left upper lip
Postoperative Diagnosis:	Same
Operation Performed:	Excisional biopsy of lesion, left buccal mucosa
Anesthesia:	Local

Procedure: The patient was placed in the supine position, and a 3 × 4 mm hard lesion could be felt under the mucosa of the left upper lip. After application of 1% xylocaine with 1:1000 epinephrine, the lesion was completely excised. The surgical wound was closed using #4-00 chromic catgut.

The patient tolerated the procedure well and returned to the Outpatient Surgery Unit in satisfactory condition.

CASE 6

Preoperative Diagnosis:	Pilonidal cyst
Postoperative Diagnosis:	Same
Operation Performed:	Pilonidal cystectomy

(continues)

EXERCISE 10-6 (continued)

Anesthesia:	Local with 4 cc of 1/2% xylocaine
Estimated Blood Loss:	Minimal
Fluids:	550 cc intraoperatively

Procedure: The patient was brought to the operating room and placed in a jackknife position. After sterile prepping and draping, 40 cc of 1/2% xylocaine was infiltrated into the surrounding tissue of the pilonidal cyst that had a surface opening on the median raphe over the sacrum. After adequate anesthesia was obtained and 1 gram of IV Ancef administered intraoperatively, the surface opening was probed. There were no apparent tracks demonstrated upon probing. Next, a scalpel was used to make an approximately 8 × 8 cm elliptical incision around the pilonidal cyst. The incision was carried down through subcutaneous tissue to the fascia and the tissue was then excised. Attention was turned to achieving hemostasis with Bovie electrocautery. The pilonidal cyst was then opened and found to contain fibrous tissue. The wound was closed with 0 Prolene interrupted vertical mattress. Estimated blood loss was minimal, and the patient received 550 cc of crystalloid intraoperatively. The patient tolerated the procedure well and was sent to the Recovery Room in stable condition.

CASE 7

Preoperative Diagnosis:	Incarcerated right femoral hernia
Postoperative Diagnosis:	Same
Operation Performed:	Right femoral herniorrhaphy
Anesthesia:	General

Procedure: Patient is a 37-year-old male. Initially, the patient was placed in the supine position, and the abdomen was prepped and draped with Betadine in the appropriate manner. Xylocaine (1%) was infiltrated into the skin and subcutaneous tissue. Because of the patient's reaction to pain, general anesthesia was also administered. An oblique skin incision was performed from the anterior superior iliac spine to the pubic tubercle. The skin and subcutaneous tissues were sharply incised. Dissection was carried down until the external oblique was divided in the line of its fibers with care taken to identify the ilioinguinal nerve to avoid injury. Sharp and blunt dissection were used to free the inguinal cord. The cremasteric muscle was transected. Attempts at reduction of the incarcerated femoral hernia from below were unsuccessful.

The femoral canal was opened in an inferior to superior manner, and finally this large incarcerated hernia was reduced. The conjoint tendon was then sutured to Cooper's ligament with 0 Prolene interrupted suture. The conjoint tendon was somewhat attenuated and of poor quality. A transition suture was placed from the conjoint tendon to Cooper's ligament and then to the inguinal ligament with care taken to obliterate the femoral space without stenosis of the femoral vein. The conjoint tendon was then sutured laterally to the shelving border or Poupart's ligament. The external oblique was closed over the cord with 0 chromic running suture. 3-0 plain was placed in the subcutaneous tissue and the skin was closed with staples. Sterile dressings were applied. The patient tolerated the operative procedure well and was gently taken to Recovery in satisfactory condition.

SUMMARY

Medically managed means that even though a diagnosis may not receive direct treatment during an encounter, the provider has to consider that diagnosis when determining treatment for other conditions. Up to four diagnosis codes can be reported on one CMS-1500, and the appropriate diagnosis code must be linked to the procedure or service provided. Patient record documentation must justify and support the medical necessity of procedures and services reported to payers for reimbursement. Medical practices and healthcare facilities should routinely participate in an auditing process, which involves reviewing patient records and CMS-1500 or UB-04 claims to assess coding accuracy and completeness of documentation. Medical practices should also review encounter forms to ensure the accuracy of ICD-9-CM and HCPCS/CPT codes, and healthcare facilities should audit chargemasters to ensure the accuracy of HCPCS/CPT and UB-04 revenue codes.

National coverage determinations (NCDs) and local coverage determinations (LCDs) specify under what clinical circumstances a service is covered, and they list covered and noncovered codes (but they do not include coding guidelines). The outpatient code editor (OCE) is software that edits outpatient claims, assigns ambulatory payment classifications (APCs), and reviews submissions for coding validity and coverage. NCDs and LCDs comprise the Medicare coverage database (MCD).

Healthcare providers document narrative clinic note and SOAP note, and diagnostic test results are documented in clinic notes and laboratory reports. Operative reports can include a short narrative description of a minor procedure or dictated reports as typically required by hospitals and ambulatory surgical centers (ASCs).

INTERNET LINKS

- MedicalNecessityPro.com
  Go to **www.MedicalNecessityPro.com** to register for a 30-day online trial of Ingenix's Web-based subscription service for LCDs/LMRPs for Medicare Part A and Part B items, services, and procedures. The subscription also includes national coverage decisions (NCDs) and detailed code crosswalk information to help hospitals, physicians, and payers accurately determine medical necessity criteria for coverage.

- Medicare Coverage Database (MCD)
  Go to **www.cms.hhs.gov,** click on the Regulations & Guidance link, click on the Medicare Coverage Center link (located at the bottom of the page), and click on the Medicare Coverage Database (MCD) link. (To locate a Medicare coverage database PowerPoint presentation, click on the Help link.)

- My Family Health Portrait
  Go to **familyhistory.hhs.gov** to create a personalized family health history report.

- The FPM Toolbox
  Go to **www.aafp.org,** click on the Family Practice Management (FPM) link, and click on The FPM Toolbox to view coding guides, flow sheets, and forms that can be used for physician practices.

- VistA-Office EHR (VOE)
  Go to **www.worldvista.org,** and click on the WorldVistA EHR link.

STUDY CHECKLIST

- ☐ Read this textbook chapter and highlight key concepts.
- ☐ Create an index card for each key term.
- ☐ Complete the chapter review.
- ☐ Complete WebTutor assignments and take online quizzes.
- ☐ Complete the Workbook chapter, verifying answers with your instructor.
- ☐ Complete the StudyWare activities to receive immediate feedback.
- ☐ Form a study group with classmates to discuss chapter concepts in preparation for an exam.

REVIEW

COMPREHENSIVE CODING PRACTICE

A. Code all diagnoses, procedures, and services in the following case scenarios, and link the diagnoses to the appropriate procedure/service.

1. A 42-year-old white male was referred to a gastroenterologist by his primary care physician because of a two-month history of gross rectal bleeding. The new patient was seen, and the doctor performed a comprehensive history and exam. Medical decision making was of moderate complexity. The patient was scheduled for a complete diagnostic colonoscopy four days later. The patient was given detailed instructions for the bowel prep that was to be started at home on Friday at 1:00 p.m. On Friday, conscious sedation was administered and the colonoscopy started. The examination had to be halted at the splenic flexure because of inadequate bowel preparation. The patient was rescheduled for Monday and given additional instructions for bowel prep to be performed starting at 3:00 p.m. on Sunday. On Monday, conscious sedation was again administered and a successful total colonoscopy was performed. Diverticulosis was noted in the ascending colon and two polyps were excised from the descending colon using snare technique. The pathology report indicated the polyps were benign.

2. Patient underwent an upper GI series, which included both a KUB and delayed films. The request form noted severe esophageal burning daily for the past six weeks. The radiology impression was Barrett's esophagus.

3. Patient was referred to a cardiologist for transesophageal echocardiography. Patient suffered a stroke three days after a three-hour session of cardiac arrhythmia. The cardiologist supervised and interpreted the echocardiography, which included probe placement and image acquisition. The report stated the "transesophageal echocardiogram showed normal valvular function with no intra-atrial or intraventicular thrombus, and no significant aortic atherosclerosis."

4. The patient had been seen in the office for a level 2 E/M service on the morning of May 5, and a diagnosis of sinusitis was made. Her husband called at 8:00 p.m. that same evening to report his wife had become very lethargic and her speech was slightly slurred. The patient was admitted to the hospital at 8:30 p.m. by the primary care physician. The doctor performed a comprehensive history and examination, and medical decision making was of high complexity. At 9:00 a.m. the next day, the patient was comatose and was transferred to the critical care unit. The doctor was in constant attendance from 8:10 a.m. until the patient expired at 9:35 a.m. The attending physician listed CVA as the diagnosis.

B. Determining Medical Necessity

5. Make several copies of the Coding Case Study Form located in Appendix III.

6. Review the case studies located in Appendix I.

7. In the appropriate column, enter each case study number (e.g., 1-1), procedure/service code(s), and diagnosis code(s).

8. Link the appropriate diagnosis code with procedure/service code to establish medical necessity for each.

C. Coding and Determining Medical Necessity

9. Make several copies of the Coding Case Studies worksheet located in Appendix III.

10. Review the case studies located in Appendix II.

11. In the appropriate column, enter each case study number (e.g., 2-1), procedure/service code(s), and diagnosis code(s).

12. Link the appropriate diagnosis code with procedure/service code to establish medical necessity for each.

EVALUATION AND MANAGEMENT CODING PRACTICE

Review each case, and select the appropriate level of history, examination, and medical decision making (key components) before referring to the CPT E/M section to assign the code. To assist in the process of assigning E/M codes, use the E/M CodeBuilder in Appendix III.

15. Mary Adams was initially seen by her physician, Dr. Thompson, as an inpatient on May 1 with the chief complaint of having taken an overdose of Ornade. She had been suffering from flu-like symptoms for one week and had been taking the prescribed drug, Ornade, for several days. She states that she apparently took too many pills this morning and started exhibiting symptoms of dizziness and nausea. She called the office complaining of these symptoms and was told to meet Dr. Thompson at the hospital emergency department. From the emergency department, she was admitted to the hospital.

Past History revealed no history of hypertension, diabetes, or rheumatic fever. The patient denies any chest pain or past history of previously having taken an overdose of Ornade as mentioned above. Social history reveals she does not smoke or drink. She has two healthy children. Family history is unremarkable.

Systemic Review revealed HEENT within normal limits. Review of the CNS revealed headache and dizziness. She had a fainting spell this morning. No paresthesias. Cardiorespiratory revealed cough but no chest pain or hemoptysis. GI revealed nausea; she had one episode of vomiting early this morning. No other abdominal distress noted. GU revealed no frequency, dysuria, or hematuria.

Physical Examination revealed the patient to be stable without any major symptoms upon arrival to the telemetry area. Head & Neck Exam revealed pupil reaction normal to light and accommodation. Fundoscopic examination is normal. Thyroid is not palpable. ENT normal. No lymphadenopathy noted. Cardiovascular Exam revealed the point of maximum impulse is felt in the left fifth intercostal space in the midclavicular line. No S_3 or S_4 gallop. Ejection click was heard and grade 2/6 systolic murmur in the left third and fourth intercostal space was heard. No diastolic murmur. Chest is clear to auscultation. Abdomen reveals no organomegaly. Neurologic Exam is normal. Peripheral Vascular System is intact.

ECG reveals a sinus tachycardia, and there was no evidence of myocardial ischemia. A pattern of early repolarization syndrome was noted.

Assessment: Will be briefly observed in the telemetry area to rule out any specific evidence of cardiac arrhythmia. She will also have a routine biochemical and hematologic profile, chest x-ray, and cardiogram. Estimated length of stay will be fairly short.

Impression: Rule out dizziness. Rule out cardiac arrhythmias.

Identify the E/M category/subcategory _____

Determine the extent of history obtained _____

Determine the extent of examination performed _____

Determine the complexity of medical decision making _____

CPT E/M code number: _____

16. Sandy White is a 52-year-old white female who was seen in the office by Dr. Kramer on January 15 with the chief complaint of low back pain. The patient has complained of lumbosacral pain off and on for many months, but it has been getting worse for the last two to three weeks. The pain is constant and gets worse with sneezing and coughing. There is no radiation of the pain to the legs.

Past History reveals no history of trauma, no history of urinary symptoms and no history of weakness or numbness in the legs. Had measles during childhood. She's had high blood pressure for a few years. Also has a previous history of rectal bleeding from hemorrhoids. She had appendectomy and cholecystectomy in 1975. She also has diabetes mellitus, controlled by diet alone.

Family History: Mother died postoperatively at age 62 of an abdominal operation, the exact nature of which is not known. She had massive bleeding. Father died at the age of 75 of a myocardial infarction. He also had carcinoma of the bladder and diabetes mellitus. One sister has high blood pressure.

Social History: She is widowed. Smokes and drinks just socially. Job at the *Evening Tribune* involves heavy lifting.

Systemic Review reveals no history of cough, expectoration, or hemoptysis. No history of weight loss or loss of appetite. No history of thyroid or kidney disease. The patient has been overweight for many years. HEENT is unremarkable; hearing and vision are normal. Cardiorespiratory reveals *no known murmurs.* GI reveals no food allergies or chronic constipation. GU reveals no nocturia, enuresis, or GI infection. Neuromuscular reveals no history of paralysis or numbness in the past.

Physical Examination in the office reveals a slightly obese, middle-aged female in acute distress with lower back pain. Pulse is 80, blood pressure is 140/85, respirations 16, temperature 98.4°F. HEENT: PERRLA. Conjunctivae are not pale. Sclerae not icteric. Fundi show arteriolar narrowing. Neck: No thyroid or lymph node palpable. No venous engorgement. No bruit heard in the neck. Chest: PMI is not palpable. S_1, S_2 normal. No gallop or murmur heard. Chest moves equally on both sides with respirations. Breath sounds are diminished. No adventitious sounds heard. Abdomen: She has scars from her previous surgery. There is no tenderness. Liver, spleen, kidneys not palpable. Bowel sounds normal. Extremities: Leg-raising sign is negative on both sides. Both femorals and dorsalis pedis are palpable and equal bilaterally. There is no ankle edema. Central Nervous System: Speech is normal. Cranial nerves are intact. Motor system is normal. Sensory system is normal. Reflexes are equal bilaterally.

Impression: The impression is lumbosacral pain. The patient is being referred for physical therapy treatment twice per week. Darvocet-N will be prescribed for the pain.

Identify the E/M category/subcategory _____

Determine the extent of history obtained _____

Determine the extent of examination performed _____

Determine the complexity of medical decision making _____

CPT E/M code number: _____

17. S: Monica Sullivan was seen in the office by Dr. White on 12/13 for the second time. She presented with a chief complaint of dizziness and weakness; she stated that she wanted to have her blood pressure checked.

   O: Patient has been on Vasotec 5 mg and Hydrodiuril 25 mg. B/P has been going up at home. Patient has felt ill, weak, and dizzy, with headache for three days. Cardiovascular exam reveals a B/P of 130/110 and pulse rate of 84. Her temperature is 98.6°F and normal.

   A: Accelerated hypertension. Bell's palsy.

   P: Increase Vasotec to 5 mg a.m. and 2.5 mg p.m. SMA & CBC.

Identify the E/M category/subcategory _____

Determine the extent of history obtained _____

Determine the extent of examination performed _____

Determine the complexity of medical decision making _____

CPT E/M code number: _____

18. Ginny Tallman is a 73-year-old female who is followed in the Alfred State Medical Clinic for COPD. Her medications include Theo-Dur 300 mg p.o. q a.m. History of present illness reveals that she seems to have adequate control of bronchospasm using this medication. She also uses an albuterol inhaler two puffs p.o. q6h. She has no recent complaints of acute shortness of breath, no chest tightness. She has a chronic, dry cough, productive of scanty sputum. At this time she is complaining of shortness of breath.

PE reveals an elderly female in no real distress. BP in the left arm sitting is 110/84, pulse 74 per minute and regular, respiratory rate 12 per minute and somewhat labored. Lungs reveal scattered wheezes in both lung fields. There is also noted an increased expiratory phase. CV exam reveals no S_3, S_4, or murmurs.

The impression is COPD with asthmatic bronchitis. The patient will have present medications increased to Theo-Dur 300 mg p.o. q a.m. and 400 mg p.o. q p.m. She should receive follow-up care in the clinic in approximately two months time.

Identify the E/M category/subcategory _____

Determine the extent of history obtained _____

Determine the extent of examination performed _____

Determine the complexity of medical decision making _____

CPT E/M code number: _____

19. Dr. Linde telephoned established patient Mark Jones at 8:00 a.m. to discuss the results of his blood-glucose level test. The doctor concluded the call at 9:00 a.m. after discussing the test results and proposed therapy regimen. Mr. Jones had numerous questions that Dr. Linde took the time to answer completely.

Identify the E/M category/subcategory _____

Identify the appropriate code(s) _____

CORRECTING CLAIMS SUBMISSION ERRORS

Review each case scenario, identify the coding error(s), and enter the corresponding letter to describe the error.

- **a.** Code is inappropriate for patient's age
- **b.** Code is incomplete (e.g., missing digits)
- **c.** Code reported is incorrect (e.g., wrong code)
- **d.** Medical necessity not met
- **e.** Procedure codes are unbundled

EXAMPLE: A patient was treated for excision of a 1-cm skin lesion on her arm. The pathology diagnosis was benign nevus. The physician documented benign nevus as the final diagnosis.

Coding Error	Procedure Code	Diagnosis Code
c	11401	709.9

Select "c" because the coder referred to Lesion, Skin in the ICD-9-CM Index to Diseases to assign 709.9, which is incorrect. The pathology diagnosis documents "benign nevus." The Index to Diseases term "Nevus" instructs the coder to "*see also* Neoplasm, skin, benign." The Neoplasm Table entry for "skin, benign" assigns code 216.6 to the "benign nevus" pathology diagnosis.

20. The physician performed an automated urinalysis without microscopy in the office on a patient who complained of dysuria. The urinalysis revealed more than 100,000 white cells and was positive for bacteria.

Coding Error	Procedure Code	Diagnosis Code
	81003	599.0
		041.4

21. An office single-view frontal chest x-ray was performed on a patient referred for shortness of breath. The radiologist reported no acute findings, but an incidental note was made of a small hiatal hernia.

Coding Error	Procedure Code	Diagnosis Code
	71010	553.3

22. A healthy 20-year-old male underwent a physical examination performed by his family physician, prior to starting soccer training.

Coding Error	Procedure Code	Diagnosis Code
	99394	V70.3

23. The patient was diagnosed with incipient cataract, and on March 5 underwent extracapsular cataract removal that required phacoemulsification, with insertion of intraocular lens prosthesis.

Coding Error	Procedure Code	Diagnosis Code
	66984	366.12
	66985-51	

24. Patient underwent physical therapy evaluation for hemiplegia due to CVA.

Coding Error	Procedure Code	Diagnosis Code
	97001	438.2

Essential CMS-1500 Claim Instructions

CHAPTER OUTLINE

OBJECTIVES

Upon successful completion of this chapter, you should be able to:

1. Define key terms.
2. List and define general insurance billing guidelines.
3. Apply optical scanning guidelines when completing claims.
4. Enter patient and policyholder names, provider names, mailing addresses, and telephone numbers according to claims completion guidelines.
5. Describe how funds are recovered from responsible payers.
6. Explain the use of the national provider identifier (NPI).
7. Differentiate between assignment of benefits and accept assignment.
8. Report ICD-9-CM, HCPCS level II, and CPT codes according to claims completion guidelines.
9. Explain the use of the national standard employer identifier.

10. Explain when the signature of a physician or supplier is required on a claim.

11. Enter the billing entity according to claims completion guidelines.

12. Explain how secondary claims are processed.

13. List and describe common errors that delay claims processing.

14. State the final steps required in claims processing.

15. Establish insurance claim files for a physician's practice.

KEY TERMS

billing entity

diagnosis pointer number

medically unlikely edits (MUE) project

Medigap

National Plan and Provider Enumeration System (NPPES)

optical character reader (OCR)

optical scanning

supplemental plan

INTRODUCTION

Complete StudyWare practice quizzes and activities using the CD-ROM located inside the back cover of your textbook.

This chapter presents universal instructions that must be considered before entering data on the CMS-1500 claim. In addition, there is a discussion of common errors made on claims, guidelines for maintaining the practice's insurance claim files, processing assigned claims, and the Federal Privacy Act of 1974.

REMEMBER!

To prevent breach of patient confidentiality, all healthcare professionals involved in processing insurance claims should check to be sure the patient has signed an "Authorization for Release of Medical Information" statement before completing the claim. The release can be obtained in one of two ways:

- Ask the patient to sign Block 12, Patient's or Authorized Person's Signature, of the CMS-1500 claim.

- Ask the patient to sign a special release form that is customized by each practice and specifically names the patient's health plan and to enter SIGNATURE ON FILE (or SOF) in Block 12 of the CMS-1500 claim.

Don't forget! HIPAA privacy standards require providers to notify patients about their right to privacy, and providers should obtain their patients' written acknowledgment of receipt of this notice. Patients will also be required to authorize in advance the nonroutine use or disclosure of information. In addition, state or other applicable laws govern the control of health information about minor children and provide parents with new rights to control that information.

EXAMPLE: Before Aetna will pay the claim submitted for Mary Sue Patient's office visit, the provider is required to submit a copy of the patient's entire medical record. HIPAA regulations specify that providers can disclose protected health information for payment activities. Typically, this information includes just the patient's diagnosis and procedures/services rendered. Therefore, the provider should require Mary Sue Patient to sign an authorization to release medical information before sending a copy of her record to Aetna.

Distinguishing between a patient's primary and secondary insurance policies as determined during the pre-clinical interview and check-in procedures is discussed in Chapter 4.

REMEMBER!

The development of an insurance claim begins when the patient contacts a health-care provider's office and schedules an appointment. At this time, it is important to determine whether the patient is requesting an initial appointment or is returning to the practice for additional services. (The preclinical interview and check-in of a new patient are more extensive than that of an established patient.)

> **EXAMPLE:** Section 1862 of Title XVIII—Health Insurance for the Aged and Disabled of the Social Security Act specifies that for an individual covered by both workers' compensation (WC) and Medicare, WC is primary. For an individual covered by both Medicare and Medicaid, Medicare is primary.

INSURANCE BILLING GUIDELINES

General billing guidelines common to most payers include:

1. Provider services for *inpatient care* are billed on a fee-for-service basis. Each physician service results in a unique and separate charge designated by a CPT/HCPCS service/procedure code. (Hospital inpatient charges are reported on the UB-04, discussed in Chapter 9.)

> **EXAMPLE:** The patient was admitted on June 1 with a diagnosis of bronchopneumonia. The doctor sees the patient each morning until the patient is discharged on June 5. Billing for this inpatient includes:
>
> | 6/1 | Initial hospital visit (99xxx) |
> | 6/2–6/4 | Three subsequent hospital visits (99xxx × 3) |
> | 6/5 | Discharge visit (99xxx) |

> **EXAMPLE:** Dr. Adams and Dr. Lowry are partners in an internal medicine group practice. Dr. Adams' patient, Irene Ahearn, was admitted on May 1 with a chief complaint of severe chest pain, and Dr. Adams provided E/M services at 11:00 a.m. at which time the patient was stable. (Dr. Lowry is on call as of 5:00 p.m. on May 1.) At 7:00 p.m., Dr. Lowry was summoned to provide critical care because the patient's condition became unstable. Dr. Adams reports an initial hospital care CPT code, and Dr. Lowry reports appropriate E/M critical care code(s) with modifier -25 attached.

2. Appropriately report observation services. The Medicare Benefit Policy manual (PUB 100-02), Section 20.5—Outpatient Observation Services, defines *observation care* as "a well-defined set of specific, clinically appropriate services, which include ongoing short-term treatment, assessment, and reassessment before a decision can be made regarding whether patients will require further treatment as hospital inpatients or if they are able to be discharged from the hospital. Observation status is commonly assigned to patients who present to the emergency department and who then require a significant period of treatment or monitoring before a decision is made concerning their admission or discharge. Observation services are covered only when provided by the order of a

physician or another individual authorized by state licensure law and hospital staff bylaws (policies) to admit patients to the hospital or to order outpatient tests. In the majority of cases, the decision whether to discharge a patient from the hospital following resolution of the reason for the observation care or to admit the patient as an inpatient can be made in less than 48 hours, usually in less than 24 hours. In only rare and exceptional cases do reasonable and necessary outpatient observation services span more than 48 hours. Hospitals may bill for patients who are direct admissions to observation. A *direct admission* occurs when a physician in the community refers a patient to the hospital for observation, bypassing the clinic or emergency department (ED)."

EXAMPLE: A 66-year-old male experiences three or four annual episodes of mild lower substernal chest pressure after meals. The condition is unresponsive to nitroglycerin and usually subsides after 15 to 30 minutes. The patient's physician has diagnosed stable angina versus gastrointestinal pain. On one occasion, while in recovery following outpatient bunion repair, the patient experiences an episode of lower substernal chest pressure. The patient's physician is contacted and seven hours of observation services are provided, after which the patient is released.

3. The surgeon's charges for inpatient and outpatient surgery are billed according to a global fee (or global surgery package), which means that one charge covers presurgical evaluation and management, initial and subsequent hospital visits, surgical procedure, the discharge visit, and uncomplicated postoperative follow-up care in the surgeon's office.

4. Postoperative complications requiring a return to the operating room for surgery related to the original procedure are billed as an additional procedure. (Be sure to use the correct modifier, and link the additional procedure to a new diagnosis that describes the complication.)

5. *Combined medical/surgical cases* in which the patient is admitted to the hospital as a medical case but, after testing, requires surgery, are billed according to the instructions in items 3–4.

EXAMPLE: Patient is admitted on June 1 for suspected pancreatic cancer. Tests are performed on June 2 and 3. On June 4 the decision is made to perform surgery. Surgery is performed on June 5. The patient is discharged on June 10.

This case begins as a medical admission.

The billing will show:

6/1	Initial hospital visit (99xxx)
6/2 and 6/3	Two subsequent hospital visits (99xxx × 2)
6/4	One subsequent hospital visit with modifier -57 (99xxx-57) (indicating the decision for surgery was made on this day)

At this point this becomes a surgery case.

The billing continues with:

6/5	Pancreatic surgery (48xxx)

6. Some claims require attachments, such as operative reports, discharge summaries, clinic notes, or letters, to aid in determination of the fee to be paid by the insurance company. Attachments are also required when CPT unlisted codes are reported. Each claims attachment (medical report substantiating the medical condition) should include patient and policy identification information. Instructions for submitting *electronic media claims (EMC)* and paper-generated claims are discussed in Chapter 4.

Any *letter* written by the provider should contain clear and simple English rather than "medicalese." The letter can describe an unusual procedure, special operation, or a patient's medical condition that warranted performing surgery in a setting different from the CMS-stipulated site for that surgery. A letter should be used in any of the following circumstances:

- **Surgery defined as an inpatient procedure that is performed at an** *ambulatory surgical center (ASC)* **or physician's office.**
- **Surgery typically categorized as an office or outpatient procedure that is performed in an ASC or on a hospital inpatient.**
- **A patient's stay in the hospital is prolonged because of medical or psychological complications.**
- **An outpatient or office procedure is performed as an inpatient procedure because the patient is a high-risk case.**
- **Explanation of why a fee submitted to an insurance company is higher than the healthcare provider's normal fee for the coded procedure. (Modifier -22 should be added to the procedure code number.)**
- **A procedure is submitted with an "unlisted procedure" CPT code number or an explanation or report of a procedure is required before reimbursement can be determined.**

7. For paper-generated claims, great care must be taken to ensure that the data prints well within the boundaries of the properly designated blocks on the form. Data that run over into the adjacent blocks or appear in the wrong block will cause rejection of claims.

> **NOTE:** HIPAA regulations require all payers to accept electronic attachments (e.g., notes, reports, referrals).

> **NOTE:** Most computer programs have a claim form test pattern to assist with the alignment of paper in printers. Print this test pattern before printing claims. If claims must be completed on a typewriter, each must be meticulously aligned in both the horizontal and vertical planes.

> **NOTE:** If entering patient claim data directly into practice management software, such as Medical Manager®, the software may require that all data be entered using upper- and lowercase and other data to be entered without regard to OCR guidelines. In these cases, the computer program converts the data to the OCR format when claims are printed or electronically transmitted to a payer.

OPTICAL SCANNING GUIDELINES

The CMS-1500 paper claim was designed to accommodate optical scanning of paper claims. This process uses a device (e.g., scanner) to convert printed or handwritten characters into text that can be viewed by an optical character reader (OCR) (a device used for optical character recognition). Entering data into the computer using this technology greatly increases productivity associated with claims processing because the need to manually enter data from the claim into a computer is eliminated. OCR guidelines were established when the HCFA-1500 (now called CMS-1500) claim was developed and are now used by all payers that process claims using the official CMS-1500 claim.

All claims for case studies in this text are prepared according to OCR standards.

- **All data must be entered on the claim within the borders of the data field. "X"s must be contained completely within the boxes, and no letters or numbers should be printed on vertical solid or dotted lines (Figure 11-1).**

FIGURE 11-1 Examples of correct (1) and incorrect (2) placement of the X within a box on the CMS-1500 claim (Courtesy Delmar/Cengage Learning)

Computer-generated paper claims: Software programs should have a test pattern program that fills the claim with "X"s so that you can test the alignment of forms. This is a critical operation with a pin-fed printer. Check the alignment and make any necessary adjustments each time a new batch of claims is inserted into the printer.

Typewritten claims: Proper alignment in the typewriter is critical. The claim has two test strips printed at the right and left margins. To check the horizontal alignment, it is necessary to type "X"s in both the left and the right test patterns.

- Use pica type (10 characters per inch). The equivalent computer font is Courier 10 or OCR 10.
- Enter all alpha characters in uppercase (capital letters).
- Do not enter the alpha character "O" for a zero (0).
- *Enter a space* for the following, which are preprinted on the claim:
  - Dollar sign or decimal in all charges or totals
  - Decimal point in a diagnosis code number (except when entering E Codes)
  - Parentheses surrounding the area code in a telephone number
- Do *not* enter a hyphen between the CPT or HCPCS code and modifier. Enter a space between the code and modifier. If multiple modifiers are reported for one CPT or HCPCS code, enter spaces between modifiers.
- Do *not* enter hyphens or spaces in the social security number, in the employer identification number (EIN) or in the patient Plan ID number.
- Enter commas between the patient or policyholder's last name, first name, and middle initial.
- *Do not* use any other punctuation in a patient's or policyholder's name, except for a hyphen in a compound name.

> **EXAMPLE:** GARDNER-BEY

- *Do not* enter a person's title or other designations, such as Sr., Jr., II, or III, unless printed on the patient's insurance ID card.

> **EXAMPLE:** The name on the ID card states:
>
> Wm F. Goodpatient, IV
>
> Name on claim is entered as:
>
> GOODPATIENT IV, WILLIAM, F

- Enter two zeroes in the cents column when a fee or a monetary total is expressed in whole dollars. *Do not* enter any leading zeroes in front of the dollar amount.

EXAMPLES:

Six dollars is entered as 6 00

Six thousand dollars is entered as 6000 00

- Birth dates are entered as eight digits with spaces between the digits representing the month, day, and the *four-digit year (MM DD YYYY)* except for Blocks 24A and 31 (MMDDYYYY). Care should be taken to ensure that none of the digits fall on the vertical separations within the block (Figure 11-2). Two-digit code numbers for the months are:

Jan—01	Apr—04	July—07	Oct—10
Feb—02	May—05	Aug—08	Nov—11
Mar—03	June—06	Sept—09	Dec—12

- All corrections to typewriter-generated claims must be made using permanent, not removable or lift-off, correction tape and should be typed/printed using pica type. If a paper claim with insufficient or incorrect data is returned by the payer or contains payer processing numbers or markings, corrections should be made by typewriter directly on the returned form. For an electronic media claim, all corrections must be made within the computer data set. On a computer-generated paper claim, for errors caught before mailing, correct the data in the computer and reprint the form. Errors should then be corrected in the computer database.

- *Handwritten claims:* Claims that contain handwritten data, with the exception of the blocks that require signatures, must be manually processed because they cannot be processed by scanners. This will cause a delay in payment of the claim.

- Extraneous data, such as handwritten notes, printed material, or special stamps, should be placed on an attachment to the claim.

- The borders of pin-fed claims should be removed evenly at the side perforations, and the claim forms should be separated.

- Nothing should be written or typed in the upper right-hand half of the claim. Place the name and address of the insurance company in the upper left-hand corner of the form.

- List only one procedure per line, starting with line one of Block 24. Do not skip lines between dates of service in Blocks 24A–K. (To report more than six procedures or services for the same date of service, generate a new claim.)

- Photocopies of claims are not allowed because they cannot be optically scanned. All resubmissions must also be prepared on an original (red-print) CMS-1500 claim. (In addition, information located on the reverse of the claim must be present.)

NOTE: Typewritten and handwritten claims have higher error rates, resulting in payment delays.

FIGURE 11-2 Proper entry for birth date (Courtesy Delmar/Cengage Learning)

EXERCISE 11-1

Applying Optical Scanning Guidelines

On a blank sheet of paper, enter the following items according to optical scanning guidelines.

1. Patient name: Jeffrey L. Green, D.D.S.
2. Total charge of three hundred dollars.
3. Procedure code 12345 with modifiers -22 and -51.
4. ID number 123-45-6789.
5. Illustrate improper marking of boxes.
6. Enter the birth date for a person who was born on March 8, 2000.

Answer the following questions.

7. Your computer always enters the name of the payer and its mailing address on the claim. Where should this be placed?
8. Your computer uses pin-fed paper. You just ran a batch of 50 claims that will be mailed to one insurance company. All claims are properly processed. What must be done to the claims before they are placed in the envelope for mailing?
9. What is the rule for placing handwritten material on the claim?
10. Name the computer/typewriter font style and print size requirements acceptable for optical scanning of claims.

NOTE:

- When entering the name of the patient and/or policyholder on the CMS-1500 claim, it is acceptable to enter a last name suffix (e.g., JR, SR) after the last name (e.g., DOE JR, JOHN, S) and/or a hyphen for hyphenated names (e.g., BLUM-CONDON, MARY, T).

It is *unacceptable* to enter periods, titles (e.g., Sister, Capt, Dr), or professional suffixes (e.g., PhD, MD, Esq.) within a name.

NOTE: In Block 31, some third-party payers allow providers to:

- Use a signature stamp and handwrite the date.
- Sign and date a printed CMS-1500 claim.
- Enter SIGNATURE ON FILE or SOF for electronic claims transmissions if a certification letter is filed with the payer; the date is entered as MMDDYYYY (without spaces).

ENTERING PATIENT AND POLICYHOLDER NAMES

When entering the patient's name in Block 2, separate the last name, first name, and middle initial with commas (e.g., DOE, JOHN, S). When entering the policyholder's name in Block 4, separate the last name, first name, and middle initial with commas (e.g., DOE, JOHN, S). If the patient is the policyholder, enter the patient's name last name, first name, and middle initial (separated by commas).

ENTERING PROVIDER NAMES

When entering the name of a provider on the CMS-1500 claim, enter the first name, middle initial (if known), last name, and credentials (e.g., MARY SMITH MD). *Do not enter any punctuation.*

ICD-10-CM ALERT!

In ICD-10-CM, the majority of codes assigned to external causes of morbidity are located in Chapter 20. Other conditions stated as due to external causes are also classified elsewhere in ICD-10-CM's Chapters 1–25. For these other conditions, ICD-10-CM codes from Chapter 20 are also reported to provide additional information regarding external cause of the condition (e.g., place of occurrence).

NOTE: Entering an X in any of the YES boxes in Block 10 of the CMS-1500 alerts the commercial payer that another insurance company might be liable for payment. The commercial payer will not consider the claim unless the provider submits a remittance advice from the liable party (e.g., automobile policy) indicating that the claim was denied. For employment-related conditions, another option is to attach a letter from the workers' compensation payer that documents rejection of payment for an on-the-job injury.

ENTERING MAILING ADDRESSES AND TELEPHONE NUMBERS

When entering a patient's and/or policyholder's (Blocks 5 and 7) mailing address and telephone number, enter the street address on line 1. Enter the city and state on line 2. Enter the 5- or 9-digit zip code and telephone number on line 3.

The patient's address refers to the patient's permanent residence. Do not enter a temporary address or a school address.

When entering a provider's name, mailing address, and telephone number (Block 33), enter the provider's name on line 1, enter the provider's billing address on line 2, and enter the provider's city, state, and 5- or 9-digit zip code on line 3. Enter the phone number in the area next to the Block title.

RECOVERY OF FUNDS FROM RESPONSIBLE PAYERS

Payers flag claims for investigation when an X is entered in one or more of the YES boxes in Block 10 of the CMS-1500 claim or an ICD-9-CM E code is reported in Block 21. Such an entry is an indication that payment might be the responsibility of a workers' compensation payer (Block 10a); automobile insurance company (Block 10b); or homeowners, business, or other liability policy insurance company (Block 10c). Some payers reimburse the claim and outsource (to a vendor that specializes in "backend recovery") the pursuit of funds from the appropriate payer. Other payers deny payment until the provider submits documentation to support reimbursement processing by the payer (e.g., remittance advice from workers' compensation or other liability payer denying the claim).

```
10. IS PATIENT'S CONDITION RELATED TO:


a. EMPLOYMENT? (CURRENT OR PREVIOUS)

        [ ] YES        [ ] NO

b. AUTO ACCIDENT?              PLACE (State)

        [ ] YES        [ ] NO
                               |_____|
c. OTHER ACCIDENT?

        [ ] YES        [ ] NO
```

NATIONAL PROVIDER IDENTIFIER (NPI)

The *national provider identifier (NPI)* is a unique 10-digit number issued to individual providers (e.g., physicians, dentists, pharmacists) and healthcare organizations (e.g., group physician practices, hospitals, nursing facilities). The NPI replaced healthcare provider identifiers (e.g., PIN, UPIN) previously generated by health plans and government programs. Submission of the NPI has been required on the CMS-1500 claim for:

● **Large health plans (e.g., private payers, Medicare, Medicaid) and all healthcare clearinghouses, effective May 23, 2007.**

● **Small health plans, effective May 23, 2008.**

Even if an individual provider moves, changes specialty, or changes practices, the provider will keep the same NPI (but must notify CMS to supply the new information). *The NPI will identify the provider throughout his or her career.*

The NPI issued to a healthcare organization is also permanent *except in rare situations when a healthcare provider does not wish to continue an association with a previously used NPI.*

NPI Application Process

The **National Plan and Provider Enumeration System (NPPES)** was developed by CMS to assign the unique healthcare provider and health plan identifiers and to serve as a database from which to extract data (e.g., health plan verification of provider NPI). Each health plan will develop a process by which NPI data will be accessed to verify the identity of providers who submit HIPAA transactions.

Providers apply for an NPI by submitting the following:

- **Web-based application**
- **Paper-based application**
- **Electronic file (e.g., hospital submits an electronic file that contains information about all physician employees, such as emergency department physicians, pathologists, and radiologists)**

Practices That Bill "Incident To"

When a nonphysician practitioner (NPP) (e.g., nurse practitioner, physician assistant) in a group practice bills "incident to" a physician, but that physician is out of the office on the day the NPP provides services to the patient, another physician in the same group can provide direct supervision to meet the "incident to" requirements. In that situation, the following entries are made on the CMS-1500:

- Enter the ordering physician's name in Block 17 (*not* the supervising physician's name).
- Enter the ordering physician's NPI in Block 17b.
- Enter the supervising physician's NPI in Block 24I.
- Enter the supervising physician's name (or signature) in Block 31.

17. NAME OF REFERRING PHYSICIAN OR OTHER SOURCE	17a.	
	17b.	NPI

ASSIGNMENT OF BENEFITS VERSUS ACCEPT ASSIGNMENT

An area of confusion for health insurance specialists is differentiating between *assignment of benefits* and *accept assignment*. Patients sign Block 13 of the CMS-1500 claim to instruct the payer to directly reimburse the provider. This is called *assignment of benefits*. If the patient does not sign Block 13, the payer sends reimbursement to the patient. The patient is then responsible for reimbursing the provider.

When the YES box in Block 27 contains an X, the provider agrees to accept as payment in full whatever the payer reimburses. This is called *accept assignment*. The provider can still collect deductible, copayment, and coinsurance amounts from the patient. If the NO box in Block 27 contains an X, the provider does not accept assignment. The provider can bill the patient for the amount not paid by the payer.

---

13. INSURED'S OR AUTHORIZED PERSON'S SIGNATURE I authorize payment of medical benefits to the undersigned physician or supplier for services described below.

SIGNED _____

---

27. ACCEPT ASSIGNMENT?
(for govt. claims, see back)
☐ YES   ☐ NO

REPORTING DIAGNOSES: ICD-9-CM CODES

Block 21

Diagnosis codes are entered in Block 21 on the claim. A maximum of *four* ICD-9-CM codes may be entered on a single claim.

If more than four diagnoses are required to justify the procedures and/or services on a claim, generate additional claims. In such cases, be sure that the diagnoses justify the medical necessity for performing the procedures/services reported on each claim. Diagnoses must be documented in the patient's record to validate medical necessity of procedures or services billed.

> **NOTE:**
>
> - Enter a space instead of the decimal point because the decimal point is preprinted on the claim (e.g., 401 9, not 401.9).
>
> - When entering an ICD-9-CM code that contains more than three digits in front of the decimal point, enter the fourth digit on top of the decimal point (e.g., E8000, not E800.0).
>
> - When a payer allows more than one diagnosis pointer to be entered in Block 24E of the CMS-1500 claim, enter a space between each number (e.g., 1 2 3 4). *Do not enter commas between pointer numbers.*

21. DIAGNOSIS OR NATURE OF ILLNESS OR INJURY (Relate Items 1, 2, 3 or 4 to Item 24E by Line)

1. 250 00   3. V70 0
2. 401 9   4. E8490

21. DIAGNOSIS OR NATURE OF ILLNESS OR INJURY (Relate Items 1, 2, 3 or 4 to Item 24E by Line)

1. E11 8   3. Z00 00
2. I10   4. Y92 099

E.
DIAGNOSIS
POINTER

Sequencing Multiple Diagnoses

The first-listed code reported is the major reason the patient was treated by the healthcare provider. *Secondary diagnoses codes are entered in numbers 2 through 4 of Block 21 and should be included on the claim only if they are necessary to justify procedures/services reported in Block 24.* Do not enter any diagnoses stated in the patient record that were not treated or medically managed during the encounter.

Be sure code numbers are placed within the designated field on the claim. The decimal point needed to separate the third and fourth digits is preprinted on the form. Enter a space; do not enter decimal points.

> **ICD-10-CM ALERT!**
>
> All ICD-10-CM codes contain three alphanumeric characters in front of the decimal and up to four characters after the decimal) (e.g., I20.1, R94.30, V00.311, M123.456F).

Accurate Coding

For physician office and outpatient claims processing, *never* report a code for diagnoses that include such terms as "rule out," "suspicious for," "probable," "ruled out," "possible," or "questionable." Code either the patient's symptoms or complaints, or do not complete this block until a definitive diagnosis is determined.

Be sure all diagnosis codes are reported to the highest degree of specificity known at the time of the treatment. Verify fourth and fifth digits in the coding manual. Do not assign unspecified codes (xxx.9).

If the computerized billing system displays a default diagnosis code (e.g., condition last treated) when entering a patient's claim information, determine if the code validates the current procedure/service reported. It may frequently be necessary to edit this code because, although the diagnosis may still be present, it may not have been treated or medically managed during the subject encounter.

> **NOTE:** Coders should be aware that some chronic conditions always affect patient care because they require medical management and should, therefore, be coded and reported on the CMS-1500 claim. Examples include diabetes mellitus and hypertension.

REPORTING PROCEDURES AND SERVICES: HCPCS/CPT CODES

Instructions in this section are for those blocks that are universally required. All other blocks are discussed individually in Chapters 12 through 17.

Block 24A—Dates of Service

When the claim form was designed, space was allotted for a six-digit date pattern with spaces between the month, day, and two-digit year (MM DD YY). No allowance was made for the year 2000 or beyond and the need for a four-digit year. Therefore, an eight-digit date is entered *without spaces* in Blocks 24A and 31 (MMDDYYYY).

All other blocks that require dates have room for the OCR required MM DD YYYY pattern, as illustrated in Figure 11-2.

> **NOTE:** All third-party payers require entry of the eight-digit date in the *From* column of Block 24A. A few payers (e.g., Blue Cross/Blue Shield) require entry of the eight-digit date in both the *From* and *To* columns, even when a service was performed on one date.

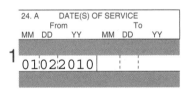

Block 24B—Place of Service

All payers require entry of a place of service (POS) code on the claim. The POS code reported must be consistent with the CPT procedure/service code description, and it will be one or two digits, depending on the payer. (Refer to Appendix II for POS codes.)

BLUE SHIELD POS CODES	MEDICARE POS CODES	DESCRIPTION
1	21	Hospital Inpatient
2	22	Hospital Outpatient
3	11	Physician's Office
4	12	Parent's Home

Block 24C–EMG

Check with the payer for their definition of emergency (EMG) treatment. If the payer requires completion of Block 24C, and EMG treatment was provided, enter a Y (for YES). Otherwise, leave blank.

Block 24D–Procedures and Services

> **NOTE:** Do not report procedure and/or service codes if no fee was charged.

> **NOTE:** Shaded lines were added to Block 24 because:
> - Blocks 24I and 24J were split to accommodate reporting of the NPI (effective May 2007) and other identification numbers (prior to May 2007).
> - Input from the health insurance industry indicated a need to report supplemental information about services reported.
>
> The completely shaded area across lines 1-6 in Block 24 will be used to report supplemental information for each reported service (e.g., anesthesia, National Drug Codes, product numbers).

Procedure codes and modifiers are reported in Block 24D. A maximum of six procedures and/or services may be reported on one claim. If the reporting of additional procedure and/or service codes is necessary, generate additional CMS-1500 claim(s).

Below the heading in Block 24D is a parenthetical instruction that says *(Explain Unusual Circumstances)*, which means to report official CPT or HCPCS modifiers, attach documentation from the patient's record, or include a letter written by the provider.

When reporting more than one code on a CMS-1500 claim, enter the code with the highest fee in line 1 of Block 24, and then enter additional codes (and modifiers) in descending order of charges. Be sure to completely enter data on each horizontal line before beginning to enter data on another line.

Identical procedures or services can be reported on the same line *if* the following circumstances apply:

- **Procedures were performed on consecutive days in the same month.**
- **The same code is assigned to the procedures/services reported.**
- **Identical charges apply to the assigned code.**
- **Block 24G (Days or Units) is completed.**

Modifiers

To accurately report a procedure or service, up to four CPT/HCPCS modifiers can be entered to the right of the solid vertical line in Block 24D on the claim. The first modifier is entered between the solid vertical line and the dotted line.

> **EXAMPLE:** Patient is admitted to the hospital on June 1. The doctor reports detailed subsequent hospital visits on June 2, 3, and 4.
>
> Date of service 06012008 (no spaces) is entered on a separate line in Block 24 because the CPT code assigned for initial inpatient care (on the day of admission) is different from subsequent hospital visits (reported for June 2, 3, and 4 as 0602008 through 06042008).
>
>
>
> If identical consecutive procedures fall within a two-month span, use two lines, one for the first month and one for the second.

EXAMPLE: Patient is admitted to the hospital on May 29. The doctor reports an initial E/M service on May 29 and subsequent E/M services on May 30, May 31, June 1, June 2, and June 3.

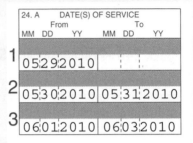

When reporting consecutive days on one line, the first date is reported in 24A in the *From* column and the last day in the *To* column. The *DAYS OR UNITS* column (24G) should reflect the number of days reported in 24A.

If additional modifier(s) are added, enter one blank space between modifiers. *Do not* enter a hyphen in front of the modifier. (CPT © 2009 American Medical Association. All rights reserved.)

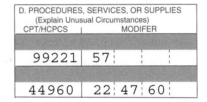

Block 24E–Diagnosis Pointer

Diagnosis pointer numbers 1 through 4 are preprinted in Block 21 of the CMS-1500 claim, and they are reported in Block 24E. Although reporting of diagnosis pointer numbers rather than ICD code numbers is required, some payers require just one pointer number to be entered in Block 24E; others allow multiple pointer numbers (separated by one blank space) to be entered in Block 24E. Be sure to consult individual payers for specific instructions on how many pointer numbers can be reported in Block 24E.

ICD-10-CM ALERT!

When implemented on October 1, 2013, ICD-10-CM codes will be entered in Block 21. A maximum of four ICD-10-CM codes may be entered on a single claim.

REMEMBER!

If more than one pointer number is reported, the first-listed code is the reason the patient sought care from the provider.

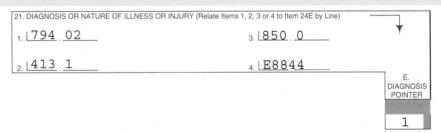

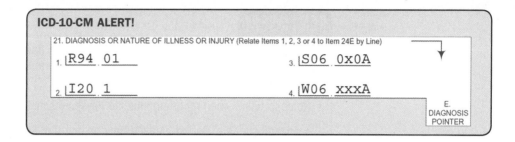

ICD-10-CM ALERT!

21. DIAGNOSIS OR NATURE OF ILLNESS OR INJURY (Relate Items 1, 2, 3 or 4 to Item 24E by Line)

1. R94 . 01

2. I20 . 1

3. S06 . 0x0A

4. W06 . xxxA

E.
DIAGNOSIS
POINTER

Block 24F Charges

Careful alignment of the charges in Block 24F, as well as the totals in Blocks 28 through 30, is critical. Precise entry of dollars and cents is also critical. The block has room for five characters in the dollar column and three in the cents column. Dollar amounts and cents must be entered in their own blocks with only one blank space between them (Figure 11-3).

Block 24G Days or Units

Block 24G requires reporting of the number of encounters, units of service or supplies, amount of drug injected, and so on, for the procedure reported on the same line in Block 24D. This block has room for only three digits.

The most common number entered in Block 24G is "1" to represent the delivery of a single procedure/service.

The entry of a number greater than "1" is required if identical procedures are reported on the same line. Do not confuse the number of units assigned on one line with the number of days the patient is in the hospital.

> **EXAMPLE:** Patient is in the hospital for three days following an open cholecystectomy. The number of units assigned to the line reporting the surgery is "1" (only one cholecystectomy was performed).

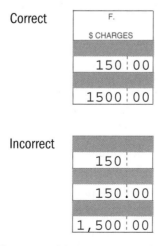

Correct

F.
$ CHARGES
150 : 00
1500 : 00

Incorrect

150 :
150 : 00
1,500 : 00

FIGURE 11-3 Correct and incorrect entry of charges in Blocks 24F and 28–30 (Courtesy Delmar/Cengage Learning)

REMEMBER!

When a procedure is performed more than once a day, enter appropriate modifier(s) in Block 24D and attach a copy of supporting documentation to the claim.

Rules to follow when reporting multiple days/units include:

- *Anesthesia time:* Report elapsed time as one unit for each 15 minutes (or fraction thereof) of anesthesia time. Convert hours to minutes, first.

> **EXAMPLE:** Elapsed time 3 hours and 15 minutes, reported as 13 units (195 minutes divided by 15 minutes equals 13).

- *Multiple procedures:* Enter the procedure code that will be reimbursed highest first, and then enter secondary procedure codes in descending order of charges. Enter a "1" in the units column for each procedure entered. Then enter any required modifiers to the secondary procedures in Block 24D (e.g., modifier 51 for multiple procedures).

- *Inclusive dates of similar services:* Report the number of days indicated in the *From* and *To* blocks (Block 24A); the number of days is reported in Block 24G.

> **EXAMPLE:** Physician treated Mr. Greenstalk on 01/02 through 01/04 and performed a detailed inpatient subsequent exam each day. The same E/M code is reported on one line in Block 24 and a 3 is entered as the units in Block 24G.

- *Radiology services:* Enter a number greater than "1" when the same radiology study is performed more than once on the same day. *Do not report the number of x-ray views taken for a specific study.*

> **EXAMPLE:** 71030 Chest, four views
>   Enter 1 in Block 24G.

MEDICALLY UNLIKELY EDITS (MUE) PROJECT

In 2007 CMS implemented the medically unlikely edits (MUE) project to improve the accuracy of Medicare payments by detecting and denying unlikely Medicare claims on a prepayment basis. The project is CMS's response to the May 2006 Office of Inspector General (OIG) report, entitled *Excessive Payments for Outpatient Services Processed by Mutual of Omaha,* which reported errors due to inappropriate units of service, accounting for $2.8 million in outpatient service overpayments (2003) from one third-party payer. The OIG determined that the payer made these overpayments because sufficient edits were not in place during year 2003 to detect billing errors related to units of service.

The following examples illustrate ways providers overstated the units of service on individual claims:

- A provider billed 10,001 units of service for 1 CT scan as the result of a typing error. The payer was overpaid approximately $958,000.

- A provider billed 141 units of service (the number of minutes in the operating room) for 1 shoulder arthroscopy procedure. The payer was overpaid approximately $97,000.

(continues)

(continued)

- A provider billed 8 units of service (the number of 15-minute time increments in the operating room) for 1 cochlear implant procedure. The payer was overpaid approximately $67,000.

MUEs are used to compare units of service with code numbers as reported on submitted claims:

NOTE: If the EIN is unavailable, enter the provider's SSN.

- **CMS-1500:** Block 24G (units of service) is compared with Block 24D (code number) on the same line.

- **UB-04:** Form Locator 46 (service units) is compared with Form Locator 44 (HCPCS/RATE/HIPPS CODE).

NATIONAL STANDARD EMPLOYER IDENTIFIER

NOTE: Reporting correct EIN and/or SSN information is crucial because payers report reimbursement to the Internal Revenue Service (IRS) according to EIN or SSN.

Block 25 requires entry of either the social security number (SSN) or the employer tax identification number (EIN). Enter the practice's EIN in this block. Do not enter the hyphen (e.g., 111234567). The SSN is also entered without hyphens or spaces.

25. FEDERAL TAX I.D. NUMBER	SSN	EIN
111233412		X

EXERCISE 11-2

Entering Procedures in Block 24

Review the following unrelated scenarios and enter the data into columns A, D, F, and G of Block 24. If a procedure is performed on consecutive dates enter on one line. (CPT © 2009 American Medical Association. All rights reserved.)

1. 10/10   OV, est pt, detailed history and physical exam   99214 $65.00

2. 10/10   Subsequent hosp visit, expanded problem focused   99232 $45.00

NOTE: The physician visited the patient twice in the hospital on 10/10.

    10/12   Subsequent hosp visit, problem focused   99231 $35.00

3. 10/15   X-ray, pelvis, 4 views   72190 $150.00

4. 11/09   Cholecystectomy, open   47600 $900.00

    11/09   Diagnostic arthroscopy, knee   29870-51 $500.00

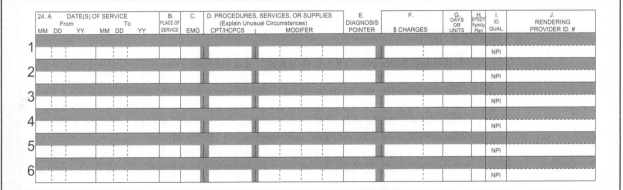

NOTE: When a nonphysician practitioner bills incident to a physician in the same group, but that physician is out of the office on a day the nonphysician practitioner treats the physician's patient, another physician in the same group can provide direct supervision to meet the incident-to requirements. The ordering physician's name is entered in Block 17 of the CMS-1500 claim. The supervising physician's NPI is entered in Block 24K, and the supervising physician authenticates the claim in Block 31.

SIGNATURE OF PHYSICIAN OR SUPPLIER

The provider signature in Block 31 of the CMS-1500 provides attestation (confirmation) that the services were billed properly. This means that the provider is responsible for claims submitted in their name, even if they did not have actual knowledge of a billing impropriety.

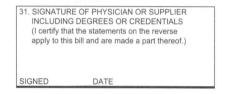

REPORTING THE BILLING ENTITY

Block 33 requires entry of the name, address, and telephone number of the billing entity. The **billing entity** is the legal business name of the practice (e.g., Goodmedicine Clinic). In the case of a solo practitioner, the name of the practice may be entered as the name of the physician followed by initials that designate how the practice is incorporated (e.g., Irvin M. Gooddoc, M.D., PA). The phone number, including area code, should be entered on the same line as the printed words "& phone #." Below this line is a blank space for a three-line billing entity mailing address.

The last line of Block 33 is for entering the provider and/or group practice numbers, if one is assigned by the payer.

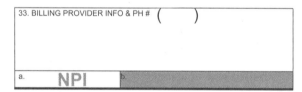

EXERCISE 11-3

Completing Block 33

What is the name of the billing entity in these cases?

1. Dr. Cardiac is employed by Goodmedicine Clinic.
2. Dr. Blank is a solo practitioner. The official name of his practice is Timbuktu Orthopedics.
3. Dr. Jones shares office space with Dr. Blank at Timbuktu Orthopedics; Dr. Jones, PA, and Timbuktu Orthopedics have separate EIN numbers.

PROCESSING SECONDARY CLAIMS

The secondary insurance claim is filed only after the remittance advice generated as a result of processing the primary claim has been received by the medical practice. As a general rule, the secondary claim cannot be filed electronically because the remittance advice must be attached to the claim sent to the secondary payer.

When primary and secondary information is entered on the same CMS-1500 claim, primary insurance policy information is entered in Block 11 through 11c, and an X is entered in the YES box in Block 11d. The secondary insurance policy information is entered in Blocks 9–9d of the same claim (Figure 11-4).

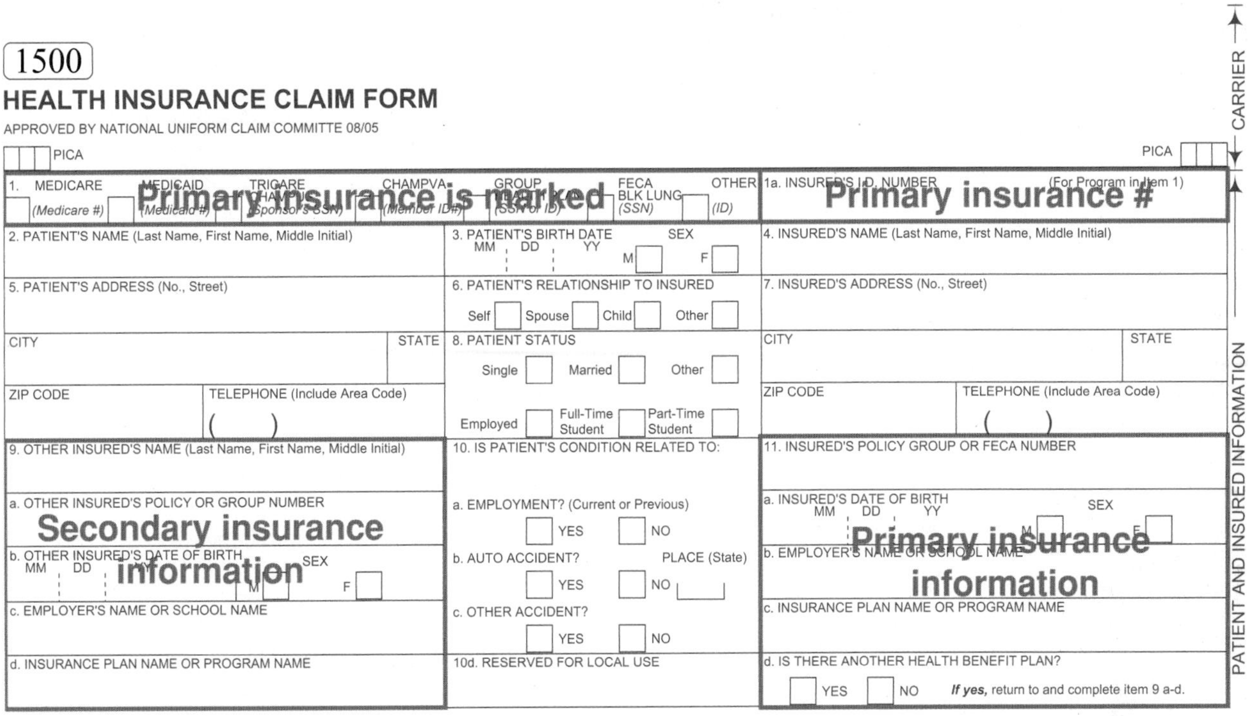

FIGURE 11-4 Entry of secondary policy information in Block of primary CMS-1500 claim (primary policy information is entered in Blocks 1, 1a, and 11) (Courtesy Delmar/Cengage Learning)

When generating claims from this text and the Workbook, a single CMS-1500 claim is generated when the patient's primary and secondary insurance policies are with the same payer (e.g., Blue Cross and Blue Shield). Multiple claims are generated when the patient is covered by multiple insurance policies with different companies (e.g., Aetna and United Healthcare). For example, if the patient has both primary and secondary insurance with different payers, two claims are generated. The primary claim is completed according to step-by-step instructions, and the secondary claim is completed by following special instructions included in each chapter.

Supplemental Plans

Supplemental plans usually cover the deductible and copay or coinsurance of a primary health insurance policy. Some plans may also cover additional benefits not included in the primary policy. The best known supplemental plans are the Medigap plans, which are supplemental plans designed by the federal government but sold by private commercial insurance companies to "cover the gaps in Medicare." Supplemental plan information is entered in Blocks 9-9d on the primary insurance claim (Figure 11-5).

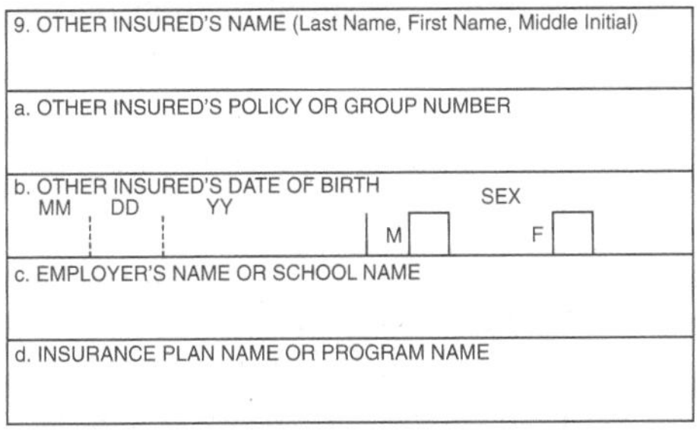

FIGURE 11-5 Supplemental plan information is entered in Block 9 (Courtesy Delmar/Cengage Learning)

REMEMBER!

Block 10 (Figure 11-6) indicates whether the condition treated is related to employment, auto accident, or other accident. Information reported in this block affects which payer is considered primary.

```
10. IS PATIENT'S CONDITION RELATED TO:


a. EMPLOYMENT? (Current or Previous)
              [ ] YES      [ ] NO

b. AUTO ACCIDENT?                    PLACE (State)
              [ ] YES      [ ] NO  |____|

c. OTHER ACCIDENT?
              [ ] YES      [ ] NO
```

FIGURE 11-6 Block 10 of CMS-1500 claim (Courtesy Delmar/Cengage Learning)

COMMON ERRORS THAT DELAY PROCESSING

NOTE: Because the first character of each ICD-10-CM code is alphabetic *and letters I and O are used,* carefully enter ICD-10-CM I and O codes (so that numbers 1 and 0 are not mistakenly entered as first characters).

After the claim has been completed, check for these common errors:

1. Keyboarding errors or incorrectly entered information, as follows:
   - **Procedure code number**
   - **Diagnosis code number**
   - **Policy identification numbers**
   - **Dates of service**
   - **Federal employer tax ID number (EIN)**
   - **Total amount due on a claim**
   - **Incomplete or incorrect name of the patient or policyholder (name must match the name on the policy; no nicknames)**

2. Omission of the following:
   - **Current diagnosis (because of failure to change the patient's default diagnosis in the computer program)**
   - **Required fourth and/or fifth ICD-9-CM digits (Required fourth, fifth, and/or sixth ICD-10-CM digits)**
   - **Procedure service dates**
   - **Hospital admission and/or discharge dates**
   - **Name and NPI of the referring provider**
   - **Required prior treatment authorization numbers**
   - **Units of service**

3. Attachments without patient and policy identification information on each page.

4. Failure to properly align the claim form in the printer to ensure that each item fits within the proper field on the claim.

5. Handwritten items or messages on the claim other than required signatures.

6. Failure to properly link each procedure with the correct diagnosis (Block 24E).

FINAL STEPS IN PROCESSING CLAIMS

STEP 1 Double check each claim for errors and omissions.

STEP 2 Add any necessary attachments.

STEP 3 If required by the payer, obtain the provider's signature on claims.

STEP 4 Post submission of the claim on the patient's account/ledger.

STEP 5 Place a copy of the claim in the practice's claims files.

STEP 6 Submit the claim to the payer.

MAINTAINING INSURANCE CLAIM FILES FOR THE PRACTICE

Medicare *Conditions of Participation (CoP)* require providers to keep copies of any government insurance claims and copies of all attachments filed by the provider for a period of five years, unless state law specifies a longer period. "Providers and billing services filing claims electronically can comply with the federal regulation by retaining the source documents (routing slip, charge slip, encounter form, superbill) from which they generated the claim and the daily summary of claims transmitted and received for" these years.

Although there are no specific laws covering retention of commercial or Blue Cross/Blue Shield claims, healthcare provider contracts with specific insurance carriers may stipulate a specific time frame for all participating providers. It is good business practice to keep these claims until you are sure all transactions have been completed.

Insurance File Set-up

Files should be organized in the following manner:

1. File *open assigned cases* by month and payer. (These claims have been sent to the payer, but processing is not complete.)

2. File *closed assigned cases* by year and payer.

3. File *batched remittance advice notices*.

4. File *unassigned or non-participating claims* by year and payer.

Processing Assigned Paid Claims

When the remittance advice arrives from the payer, pull the claim(s) and review the payment(s). Make a notation of the amount of payment, remittance advice notice processing date, and applicable batch number on the claim. Claims with no processing errors and payment in full are marked "closed." They are moved to the closed assigned claims file. Single-payment remittance advice notices may be stapled to the claim before filing in the closed assigned claims file. Batched remittance advice notices are refiled and if, after comparing the remittance advice notices and the claim, an error in processing is found, the following steps should be taken:

STEP 1 Write an immediate appeal for reconsideration of the payment.

STEP 2 Make a copy of the original claim, the remittance advice notices, and the written appeal.

STEP 3 Generate a new CMS-1500 claim, and attach it to the remittance advice notices and the appeal. (Black-and-white copies cannot be read by the payer's optical scanner.) Make sure the date in Block 31 matches the date on the original claim.

STEP 4 Mail the appeal and claim to the payer.

STEP 5 Make a notation of the payment (including the check number) on the office copy of the claim.

STEP 6 Refile the claim and attachments in the assigned open claims file.

Federal Privacy Act

The Federal Privacy Act of 1974 prohibits a payer from notifying the provider about payment or rejection of unassigned claims or payments sent directly to the patient/policyholder. If the provider is to assist the patient with the appeal of a claim, the patient must provide a copy of the explanation of benefits (EOB) received from the payer and a letter that explains the error. The letter is to be signed by the patient and policyholder, to give the payer permission to allow the provider to appeal the unassigned claim. The EOB and letter must accompany the provider's request for reconsideration of the case. If the policyholder writes the appeal, the provider must supply the policyholder with the supporting documentation required to have the claim reconsidered.

In recent years Congress has increased efforts to prevent submission of fraudulent claims to government programs. Congress is now considering repealing the legislation that prohibits sending EOBs to the provider on unassigned claims. This would allow the provider to appeal processing errors on unassigned government claims.

SUMMARY

The CMS-1500 paper claim was designed to accommodate optical scanning of paper claims, which requires use of a scanner to convert printed or handwritten characters into text that can be viewed by an optical character reader (OCR). Entering data into the computer using this technology greatly increases productivity associated with claims processing because the need to manually enter data from the claim into a computer is eliminated. The 10-digit *national provider identifier (NPI)* is issued to individual providers and healthcare organizations, and replaces healthcare provider identifiers (e.g., PIN, UPIN) previously generated by health plans and government programs. The NPI has been submitted on CMS-1500 claims for large health plans and all healthcare clearinghouses effective May 23, 2007, and small health plans effective May 23, 2008.

INTERNET LINKS

- Consumer guides for getting and keeping health insurance
  www.healthinsuranceinfo.net
- Insure Kids Now!
  www.insurekidsnow.gov
- National Plan and Provider Enumeration System (NPPES)
  nppes.cms.hhs.gov

STUDY CHECKLIST

- ☐ Read this textbook chapter and highlight key concepts.
- ☐ Create an index card for each key term.
- ☐ Complete the chapter review, verifying answer with your instructor.
- ☐ Complete WebTutor assignments and take online quizzes.
- ☐ Complete the Workbook chapter, verifying answers with your instructor.
- ☐ Complete the StudyWare activities to receive immediate feedback.
- ☐ Form a study group with classmates to discuss chapter concepts in preparation for an exam.

REVIEW

MULTIPLE CHOICE Select the most appropriate response.

1. Physician services for inpatient care are billed on a fee-for-service basis, and physicians submit
   _____ service/procedure codes to payers.
   a. CPT/HCPCS level II
   b. DSM-IV-TR
   c. HCPCS level III
   d. ICD-9-CM (or ICD-10-CM)

2. A patient develops surgical complications and returns to the operating room to undergo surgery
   related to the original procedure. The return surgery is
   a. billed as an additional surgical procedure.
   b. coded for office data capture purposes only.
   c. included as part of the original procedure.
   d. not reported on the CMS-1500 or UB-04.

3. Outpatient surgery and surgeon charges for inpatient surgery are billed according to a global
   fee, which means that the presurgical evaluation and management, initial and subsequent hospital visits, surgical procedure, discharge visit, and uncomplicated postoperative follow-up care
   in the surgeon's office are billed as
   a. DRG payments.
   b. multiple charges.
   c. one charge.
   d. separate charges.

4. When one charge covers presurgical evaluation and management, initial and subsequent hospital
   visits, surgical procedure, the discharge visit, and uncomplicated postoperative follow-up care in
   the surgeon's office, this is called a(n)
   a. combined medical/surgical case.
   b. fee-for-service charge.
   c. global fee.
   d. itemized list of separate charges.

5. **Which situation requires the provider to write a letter explaining special circumstances?**
   a. A patient's inpatient stay was prolonged because of medical or psychological complications.
   b. Charges submitted to the payer are lower than the provider's normal fee (e.g., -22 added to code).
   c. Surgery defined as an inpatient procedure was performed while the patient was in the hospital.
   d. Surgery typically categorized as an office procedure was performed in a hospital outpatient setting.

6. **The optical character reader (OCR) is a device that is used to**
   a. convert CMS-1500 claims.
   b. enter CMS-1500 claims.
   c. scan CMS-1500 claims.
   d. view CMS-1500 text.

7. **When entering patient claims data onto the CMS-1500 claim, enter alpha characters using**
   a. lower case.
   b. sentence case.
   c. title case.
   d. upper case.

8. **Which statement is an accurate interpretation of the phrase "assignment of benefits"? If signed by the patient on the CMS-1500 claim**
   a. the payer is instructed to reimburse the provider directly.
   b. the payer sends reimbursement for services to the patient.
   c. the provider accepts as payment what the payer reimburses.
   d. the provider cannot collect copayments from the patient.

9. **When an X is entered in one or more of the YES boxes in Block 10 of the CMS-1500 claim, payment might be the responsibility of a _____ insurance company.**
   a. disability
   b. homeowner's
   c. life
   d. managed care

10. **The billing entity, as reported in Block 33 of the CMS-1500 claim, includes the legal business name of the**
    a. acute care hospital.
    b. insurance company.
    c. medical practice.
    d. patient (or spouse).

Commercial Insurance

CHAPTER OUTLINE

Commercial Health Insurance

Automobile, Disability, and Liability
  Insurance

Commercial Claims

Claims Instructions

Commercial Secondary Coverage

Commercial Group Health Plan
  Coverage

OBJECTIVES

Upon successful completion of this chapter, you should be able to:

1. Define key terms.
2. Explain the characteristics of commercial insurance plans.
3. Differentiate among automobile, disability, and liability insurance.
4. Differentiate between primary and secondary commercial claims.
5. Complete commercial primary and secondary fee-for-service claims.

KEY TERMS

automobile insurance policy
base period
commercial health insurance

disability insurance
liability insurance

lien
subrogation

INTRODUCTION

This chapter contains instructions for completing fee-for-service claims that are generally
accepted nationwide by most commercial health insurance companies, including Aetna,
United Health Care, Prudential, Cigna, and others. (Instructions for filing Blue Cross/Blue
Shield, Medicare, Medicaid, TRICARE, CHAMPVA, and workers' compen-
sation claims are found in later chapters.)

> **NOTE:** Information
> presented in this chapter
> builds on the claims
> completion instructions
> presented in Chapter 11.

These instructions apply to *all primary commercial and HMO fee-for-
service (noncapitated) claims.* Separate instructions are provided when the
patient has secondary and/or supplemental health insurance coverage.

395

To assist you in learning how to process commercial claims, this chapter includes:

- Separate instructions for primary, secondary, and supplemental commercial insurance plans.
- Instructions in a table format for completing claims.
- A case study and completed claim to illustrate the instructions.
- A case-study exercise, a blank claim, and the completed claim that allows the student to practice completing a claim. The completed claim allows the student to receive immediate feedback. (Additional case-study claims-completion exercises are located in Appendices I and II.)

COMMERCIAL HEALTH INSURANCE

Commercial health insurance covers the medical expenses of individuals (e.g., private health insurance) and groups (e.g., employer group health insurance). Premiums and benefits vary according to the type of plan offered, but group health insurance usually costs less than individual private health insurance. Individual health insurance policies are regulated by individual states and include the following:

- *Fee-for-service* (or *indemnity*) *insurance* (traditional health insurance that covers a portion of services, such as inpatient hospitalizations or physician office visits, with the patient paying the remaining costs)
- *High-risk pools* ("last resort" health insurance for individuals who cannot obtain coverage due to a serious medical condition; certain eligibility requirements apply, such as refusal by at least one or two insurance companies)
- *Managed care* (e.g., health maintenance organization, preferred provider organization) (Review chapter 3 of this textbook for comprehensive information about managed care.)
- *Association health insurance* (offered to members of a professional association and marketed to small business owners as a way to provide coverage to employees; however, these plans are not subject to the same regulations as group health insurance plans and, therefore, are more risky)

Group health insurance is available through employers and other organizations (e.g., labor unions, rural and consumer health cooperatives), and all or part of premium costs are paid by employers. Employer-based group health insurance:

- Covers all employees, regardless of health status, and cannot be cancelled if an employee becomes ill.
- Limits exclusions for pre-existing conditions, which means the payer *can* exclude an employee from coverage for a pre-existing condition but only for 12–18 months, depending on the circumstances.
- Is portable, which means if an employee had insurance before enrolling in employer group health insurance, the payer must reduce the pre-existing condition exclusion period by the amount of time covered on the previous plan.
- Offers COBRA continuation coverage, which means when an employee resigns (or has another qualifying event), the employee must be offered COBRA continuation coverage that lasts for 18–36 months, depending on the employee's situation.
- Has employer-limited plan options (e.g., prescription drug plan that covers a certain list of medications, called a *formulary*).

AUTOMOBILE, DISABILITY, AND LIABILITY INSURANCE

Automobile Insurance

An automobile insurance policy is a contract between an individual and an insurance company whereby the individual pays a premium and, in exchange, the insurance company agrees to pay for specific car-related financial losses during the term of the policy. Available coverage typically includes the following:

- **Collision (pays for damage to a covered vehicle caused by collision with another object or by an automobile accident; a deductible is required);**
- **Comprehensive (pays for loss of or damage to a covered vehicle, such as that caused by fire, flood, hail, impact with an animal, theft, vandalism, or wind; a deductible may apply);**
- **Emergency road service (pays expenses incurred for having an automobile towed as a result of a breakdown);**
- **Liability (pays for accidental bodily injury and property damage to others, including medical expenses, pain and suffering, lost wages, and other special damages; property damage includes damaged property and may include loss of use);**
- **Medical payments (reimburses medical and funeral expenses for covered individuals, regardless of fault, when those expenses are related to an automobile accident);**
- **Personal injury protection (PIP) (reimburses medical expenses for covered individuals, regardless of fault, for treatment due to an automobile accident; also pays for funeral expenses, lost earnings, rehabilitation, and replacement of services such as child care if a parent is disabled);**
- **Rental reimbursement (pays expenses incurred for renting a car when an automobile is disabled because of an automobile accident);**
- **Underinsured motorist (pays damages when a covered individual is injured in an automobile accident caused by another driver who has insufficient liability insurance—not available in every state).**

Medical payments and PIP coverage usually reimburses, up to certain limits, the medical expenses of an injured driver and any passengers in a vehicle that was involved in an automobile accident. (Coverage might also be available for pedestrians injured by a vehicle.) The automobile insurance company's *medical adjuster* reviews healthcare bills submitted to the insurance company for treatment of injuries sustained as the result of a motor vehicle accident to determine coverage. Medical expenses that may be reimbursed include ambulance services; emergency department care; laboratory services; medical supplies (e.g., crutches); physical therapy; prescription drugs; services provided by chiropractors, dentists, physicians, and specialists; x-rays; and so on. (In addition, nonautomobile health insurance policies may include coverage that pays medical bills regardless of who was at fault during an automobile accident.)

Disability Insurance

Disability insurance is defined as reimbursement for income lost as a result of a temporary or permanent illness or injury. When patients are treated for disability diagnoses and other medical problems, separate patient records must be maintained. It is also a good idea to organize the financial records separately for these patients. Offices that generate one patient record for the treatment of disability diagnoses as well as other medical problems often confuse the submission of diagnostic and procedural data for insurance processing. This can

NOTE: Disability insurance generally does not pay for healthcare services, but provides the disabled person with financial assistance.

result in payment delays and claims denials. For example, under certain circumstances, other insurance coverage (e.g., workers' compensation) is primary to basic medical coverage.

Disability benefits are usually paid if an individual

- **Has been unable to do regular or customary work for a certain number of days (number of days depends on the policy);**
- **Was employed when disabled (e.g., individuals must have lost wages because of a disability);**
- **Has disability insurance coverage;**
- **Was under the care and treatment of a licensed provider during initial disability; to continue receiving benefits, the individual must remain under care and treatment;**
- **Processes a claim within a certain number of days after the date the individual was disabled (number of days depends on the policy);**
- **Has the licensed provider complete the disability medical certification document(s).**

Individuals may be found ineligible for disability benefits if they

- **Are claiming or receiving unemployment insurance benefits;**
- **Became disabled while committing a crime that resulted in a felony conviction;**
- **Are receiving workers' compensation benefits at a weekly rate equal to or greater than the disability rate;**
- **Are in jail, prison, or a recovery home (e.g., halfway house) because of being convicted of a crime;**
- **Fail to have an independent medical examination when requested to do so.**

> **NOTE:** The federal Social Security Disability Insurance (SSDI) and Supplemental Security Income (SSI) disability programs provide assistance to people with disabilities. Both programs are administered by the federal Social Security Administration, and only individuals who have a disability and meet medical criteria qualify for benefits under either program. Social Security Disability Insurance pays benefits to you and certain members of your family if you are "insured," meaning that you worked long enough and paid Social Security taxes. Supplemental Security Income pays benefits based on financial need.

A disability claim begins on the date of disability, and the disability payer calculates an individual's weekly benefit amount using a base period. The base period usually covers 12 months and is divided into 4 consecutive quarters. It includes taxed wages paid approximately 6 to 18 months before the disability claim begins. The base period does not include wages being paid at the time the disability began.

A final payment notice is sent when records show that an individual has been paid through the doctor's estimated date of recovery. If the individual is still disabled, the doctor must submit appropriate documentation so that the case can be reviewed. When an individual has recovered or returned to work and becomes disabled again, a new claim should be submitted along with a report of the dates worked.

Liability Insurance

Although processing of liability insurance claims is not covered in this text, it is important to understand how it influences the processing of health insurance claims. Liability insurance is a policy that covers losses to a third party caused by the insured, by an object owned by the insured, or on premises owned by the insured. Liability insurance claims are made to cover the cost of medical care for traumatic injuries and lost wages, and, in many cases, remuneration (compensation) for the "pain and suffering" of the injured party. Most health insurance contracts state that health insurance benefits are secondary to liability insurance. In this situation, the patient is *not* the insured. This means that the insured (e.g., employer) is responsible for payment, and the patient's health insurance plan is billed as secondary (and reimburses only the remaining costs of health care *not* covered by the insured). When negligence by another party is suspected in an injury claim, the health insurance company will not reimburse the patient for medical treatment of the injury until one of two factors is established: (1) it is determined that there was no third-party negligence, or (2) in cases in which third-party negligence did occur, the liability payer determines that the incident is not covered by the negligent party's liability contract.

NOTE: Third-party payers implement a "pay and chase" method to aggressively pursue the recovery and coordination of payment for healthcare expenses from liability payers (e.g., malpractice cases, public property injuries, and automobile accidents). Third-party payers review diagnosis codes reported on claims (e.g., trauma) to determine whether a liability payer should be considered primary. Once this initial determination has been made, third-party payers often outsource the recovery and coordination of payment for healthcare expenses from liability payers to *subrogation vendors,* which further screen data to identify potential liability claims and recover reimbursement paid on claims by third-party payers. **Subrogation** refers to the contractual right of a third-party payer to recover healthcare expenses from a liable party. (For example, if a patient is injured on the job, the workers' compensation payer is responsible for reimbursing for the patient's healthcare expenses.) Third-party recovery standards for investigation of liability coverage and the process for filing a **lien** (securing a debtor's property as security or payment for a debt) in a potential liability case vary on a federal and state basis.

EXAMPLE: Dr. Small treats Jim Keene in the office for scalp lacerations (cuts) from a work-related injury. Mr. Keene is covered by an employer-sponsored group health plan called HealthCareUSA, and his employer provides workers' compensation insurance coverage for on-the-job injuries.

The insurance claim for treatment of Mr. Keene's lacerations should be submitted to the employer's workers' compensation insurance payer.

If the claim were submitted to HealthCareUSA, it would be subject to review because the diagnosis code submitted would indicate trauma (injury), which activates the review of patient records by an insurance company. Upon reviewing requested copies of patient records, HealthCareUSA would determine that another insurance plan should have been billed for this treatment. HealthCareUSA would deny payment of the claim, and Dr. Small's office would then submit the claim to the workers' compensation carrier payer. In this scenario, a delay in payment for treatment results.

To file a claim with a liability payer, a regular patient billing statement is often used rather than an insurance claim. Be sure to include the name of the policyholder and the liability policy identification numbers. If the liability payer denies payment, a claim is then filed with the patient's health insurance plan. *A photocopy of the written denial of responsibility from the liability payer must accompany the health insurance claim.*

EXAMPLE: California's Medical Care Services operates Medi-Cal, which is California's Medicaid program, and its Third Party Liability Branch is responsible for ensuring that Medi-Cal complies with state and federal laws relating to the legal liability of third parties to reimburse healthcare services to beneficiaries. The Branch ensures that all reasonable measures are taken to ensure that the Medi-Cal program is the *payer of last resort.* As a result, in 2003, the Branch recovered more than $202 million, which was recycled back into the Medi-Cal program.

COMMERCIAL CLAIMS

The commercial claims completion instructions in this chapter are generally recognized nationwide. Some payers may require variations in a few of the blocks, and their requirements should be followed accordingly. Throughout the year, commercial payers implement changes to claims completion requirements that are discovered by providers when claims are denied—commercial payers do not typically make available their billing manual or updates.

NOTE: As you review the CMS-1500 claims instructions in Table 12-1, refer to the John Q. Public case study (Figure 12-1) and completed CMS-1500 claim (Figure 12-2). The completed claim will also assist you when you begin work on Exercise 12-1.

Primary claims submission is covered in this chapter's claims completion instructions (Table 12-1), as determined by *one* of the following criteria:

- **The patient is covered by just one commercial plan.**
- **The patient is covered by a large employer group health plan (EGHP),** *and* **the patient is also a Medicare beneficiary (EGHP is primary).**
- **The patient is covered by a small** *or* **large employer group health plan on which the patient is designated as policyholder (or insured),** *and* **the patient is also listed as a dependent on another EGHP.**
- **The patient is a child covered by two or more plans. The primary policyholder is the parent whose birthday occurs first in the year.**

REMEMBER!

The birthday rule states that the policyholder whose birth month and day occurs earlier in the calendar year holds the primary policy when each parent subscribes to a different health insurance plan.

Before working with commercial claims, complete the Review at the end of this chapter.

CLAIMS INSTRUCTIONS

TABLE 12-1   CMS-1500 claims completion instructions for commercial payers

NOTE: Refer to Chapter 11 for clarification of claims completion (e.g., entering names, mailing addresses, ICD codes, diagnosis pointer numbers, NPI, and so on).

BLOCK	INSTRUCTIONS
1	Enter an X in the *Other* box if the patient is covered by an individual or family health plan. Or, enter an X in the *Group Health Plan* box if the patient is covered by a group health plan.
	NOTE: The patient is covered by a group health plan if a group number is printed on the patient's insurance identification card (or a group number is included on case studies located in this textbook, workbook, and SimClaim software).
1a	Enter the health insurance identification number as it appears on the patient's insurance card. *Do not enter hyphens or spaces in the number.*
2	Enter the patient's last name, first name, and middle initial (separated by commas) (e.g., DOE, JANE, M.).
3	Enter the patient's birth date as MM DD YYYY (with spaces). Enter an X in the appropriate box to indicate the patient's gender. If the patient's gender is unknown, leave blank.
4	Enter the policyholder's last name, first name, and middle initial (separated by commas) (e.g., DOE, JANE, M).
5	Enter the patient's mailing address and telephone number. Enter the street address on line 1, enter the city and state on line 2, and enter the 5- or 9-digit zip code and phone number on line 3.
6	Enter an X in the appropriate box to indicate the patient's relationship to the policyholder. If the patient is an unmarried domestic partner, enter an X in the *Other* box.
7	Enter the policyholder's mailing address and telephone number. Enter the street address on line 1, enter the city and state on line 2, and enter the 5- or 9-digit zip code and phone number on line 3.
8	Enter an X in the appropriate box to indicate the patient's marital status. If the patient is an unmarried domestic partner, enter an X in the *Other* box. Enter an X in the appropriate box to indicate the patient's employment or student status. If the patient is unemployed and/or not a full- or part-time student, leave blank.

(continues)

TABLE 12-1 (continued)

BLOCK	INSTRUCTIONS
9, 9a–9d	Leave blank. Blocks 9 and 9a–9d are completed if the patient has secondary insurance coverage (*discussed later in this chapter*). **NOTE:** When the patient is covered by a primary commercial health insurance plan and another health insurance plan (e.g., another commercial health insurance plan, Medicaid, Medicare, and so on), complete Blocks 9 and 9a–9d.
10a–c	Enter an X in the appropriate boxes to indicate whether the patient's condition is related to employment, an automobile accident, and/or another type of accident. If an X is entered in the YES box for auto accident, enter the 2-character state abbreviation of the patient's residence.
10d	Leave blank.
11	Enter the policyholder's commercial group number if the patient is covered by a group health plan. *Do not enter hyphens or spaces in the group number.* Otherwise, leave blank. **NOTE:** The policyholder's group number refers to the alphanumeric or numeric identifier for group health plan coverage. (The FECA number is the 9-digit alphanumeric identifier assigned to a patient claiming work-related condition(s) under the Federal Employees Compensation Act. The FECA number is discussed in Chapter 17 of this textbook.)
11a	Enter the policyholder's birth date as MM DD YYYY (with spaces). Enter an X in the appropriate box to indicate the policyholder's gender. If the policyholder's gender is unknown, leave blank.
11b	Enter the name of the policyholder's employer (if policyholder is employed) or school (if policyholder is unemployed and considered a full- or part-time student). Otherwise, leave blank.
11c	Enter the name of the policyholder's commercial health insurance plan.
11d	Enter an X in the NO box (if the patient does not have secondary insurance coverage). **NOTE:** When the patient is covered by a primary commercial health insurance plan and another health insurance plan (e.g., another commercial health insurance plan, Medicaid, Medicare, and so on), enter an X in the YES box (discussed later in this chapter).
12	Enter SIGNATURE ON FILE. Leave the date field blank. (The abbreviation SOF is also acceptable.) **NOTE:** Entering SIGNATURE ON FILE means that the patient has previously signed an authorization to release medical information to the payer, and it is maintained "on file" by the provider. If the patient has not signed an authorization, the patient must sign and date the Block.
13	Enter SIGNATURE ON FILE to authorize direct payment to the provider for benefits due the patient. (The abbreviation SOF is also acceptable.)
14	Enter the date as MM DD YYYY (with spaces) to indicate when the patient first experienced signs *or* symptoms of the present illness or injury *or* the date of the last menstrual period (LMP) for obstetric visits. *If the date is not documented in the patient's record, but the history indicates an appropriate date (e.g., three weeks ago), simply count back to the approximate date and enter it on the claim.* **EXAMPLE:** For encounter date 06/08/YYYY, when the record documents that the patient was "injured three months ago," enter 03 08 YYYY in Block 14.
15	Enter the date as MM DD YYYY (with spaces) to indicate that a prior episode of the same or similar illness began, *if documented in the patient's record. Previous pregnancies are not a similar illness.* Otherwise, leave blank.
16	Enter dates as MM DD YYYY (with spaces) to indicate the period of time the patient was unable to work in his current occupation, *if documented in the patient's record. An entry in this Block might indicate employment-related insurance coverage.* Otherwise, leave blank.
17	Enter the first name, middle initial (if known), last name, and credentials of the professional who referred or ordered healthcare service(s) or supply(s) reported on the claim. *Do not enter any punctuation.* Otherwise, leave blank.

(continues)

TABLE 12-1   (continued)

BLOCK	INSTRUCTIONS
17a	Leave blank.
17b	Enter the 10-digit national provider identifier (NPI) of the provider entered in Block 17. Otherwise, leave blank.
18	Enter the admission date and discharge date as MM DD YYYY (with spaces) if the patient received inpatient services (e.g., hospital, skilled nursing facility). *If the patient has not been discharged at the time the claim is completed, leave the discharge date blank.* Otherwise, leave blank.
19	Leave blank (except when entering information to describe a procedure code reported in Block 24D, such as CPT supply code 99070).
20	Enter an X in the NO box if all laboratory procedures reported on the claim were performed in the provider's office. Enter an X in the YES box if laboratory procedures reported on the claim were performed by an outside laboratory and billed to the provider. Enter the total amount charged by the outside laboratory in $ CHARGES, and enter the outside laboratory's name, mailing address, and NPI in Block 32. (Charges are entered *without* punctuation. For example, $1,100.00 is entered as 110000 below $ CHARGES.)
21	Enter the ICD code for up to four diagnoses or conditions treated or medically managed during the encounter. Lines 1, 2, 3, and 4 in Block 21 will relate to CPT/HCPCS service/procedure codes reported in Block 24E.
22	Leave blank. Reserved for Medicaid claims.
23	Enter prior authorization number, referral number, mammography pre-certification number, or Clinical Laboratory Improvement Amendments (CLIA) number, as assigned by the payer for the current service. *Do not enter hyphens or spaces in the number.* Otherwise, leave blank.
24A	Enter the date the procedure or service was performed in the FROM column as MMDDYYYY (without spaces). Enter a date in the TO column *if the procedure or service was performed on consecutive days during a range of dates. Then, enter the number of consecutive days in Block 24G.* **NOTE:** The shaded area in each line is used to enter supplemental information to support reported services *if instructed by the payer to enter such information.* Data entry in Block 24 is limited to reporting six services. *Do not use the shaded lines to report additional services.* If additional services were provided, generate new CMS-1500 claim(s) to report the additional services.
24B	Enter the appropriate 2-digit Place of Service (POS) code to identify the location where the reported procedure or service was performed. (Refer to Appendix II for POS codes.)
24C	Leave blank.
24D	Enter the CPT or HCPCS level II code and applicable required modifier(s) for procedures or services performed. *Separate the CPT/HCPCS code and first modifier with one space. Separate additional modifiers with one space each. Up to four modifiers can be entered.*
24E	Enter the diagnosis pointer number from Block 21 that relates to the procedure/service performed on the date of service.
24F	Enter the fee charged for each reported procedure or service (e.g., 55 00). When multiple procedures or services are reported on the same line, enter the total fee charged. *Do not enter commas, periods, or dollar signs. Do not enter negative amounts. Enter 00 in the cents area if the amount is a whole number.*
24G	Enter the number of days or units for procedures or services reported in Block 24D. *If just one procedure or service was reported in Block 24D, enter a 1 in Block 24G.*
24H	Leave blank. Reserved for Medicaid claims.
24I	Leave blank. (The NPI abbreviation is preprinted on the CMS-1500 claim.)

(continues)

TABLE 12-1   (continued)

BLOCK	INSTRUCTIONS
24J	Enter the 10-digit NPI for the: • provider who performed the service *if the provider is a member of a group practice.* (Leave blank if the provider is a solo practitioner.) • supervising provider *if the service was provided "incident to" the service of a physician or nonphysician practitioner* **and** *the physician or practitioner who ordered the service did not supervise the provider.* (Leave blank if the "incident to" service was performed under the supervision of the physician or nonphysician practitioner.) • DMEPOS supplier or outside laboratory *if the physician submits the claim for services provided by the DMEPOS supplier or outside laboratory.* (Leave blank if the DMEPOS supplier or outside laboratory submits the claim.) Otherwise, leave blank. **EXAMPLE:** Dr. Sanderlee evaluates Mary Smith during a three-month recheck of her chronic anemia. He performs venipuncture and sends the patient's blood sample to an outside laboratory where a complete blood count test will be performed. Dr. Sanderlee's insurance specialist enters the outside laboratory's NPI in Block 24J because the complete blood count test is reported in Block 24D on that line.
25	Enter the provider's social security number (SSN) or employer identification number (EIN). *Do not enter hyphens or spaces in the number.* Enter an X in the appropriate box to indicate which number is reported. **EXAMPLE:** • Dr. Brilliant is a solo practitioner. Enter Dr. Brilliant's EIN in Block 25. • Dr. Healer practices at the Goodmedicine Clinic. Enter Dr. Healer's EIN in Block 25.
26	Enter the patient's account number as assigned by the provider. **NOTE:** When completing CMS-1500 claims for case studies, enter the case study number (e.g., 12-2). When the patient has both primary and secondary coverage, enter a P (for primary) (e.g., 12-2P) next to the number (on the primary claim) and an S (for secondary) (e.g., 12-2S) next to the number (on the secondary claim)
27	Enter an X in the YES box to indicate that the provider agrees to accept assignment. Otherwise, enter an X in the NO box.
28	Enter the total charges for services and/or procedures reported in Block 24. **NOTE:** If multiple claims are submitted for one patient because more than six procedures or services were reported, be sure the total charge reported on each claim accurately represents the total of the items on each submitted claim.
29	Enter the total amount the patient (or another payer) paid *toward covered services only.* If no payment was made, leave blank.
30	Enter the total amount due (by subtracting the amount entered in Block 29 from the amount entered in Block 28). *Do not report negative amounts or a credit due to the patient.*
31	Enter the provider's name and credential (e.g., MARY SMITH MD) and the date the claim was completed as MMDDYYYY (without spaces). *Do not enter any punctuation.*
32	Enter the name and address where procedures or services were provided *if at a location other than the provider's office or the patient's home, such as a hospital, outside laboratory facility, skilled nursing facility, or DMEPOS supplier.* Otherwise, leave blank. Enter the name on line 1, the address on line 2, and the city, state, and 5- or 9-digit zip code on line 3. *For a 9-digit zip code, enter the hyphen.* **NOTE:** If Block 18 contains dates of service for inpatient care and/or Block 20 contains an X in the YES box, enter the name and address of the facility that provided services.
32a	Enter the 10-digit NPI of the facility or supplier entered in Block 32.
32b	Leave blank.

(continues)

TABLE 12-1 (continued)

BLOCK	INSTRUCTIONS
33	Enter the provider's *billing* name, address, and telephone number. Enter the phone number in the area next to the Block title. *Do not enter parentheses for the area code.* Enter the name on line 1, enter the address on line 2, and enter the city, state, and 5- or 9-digit zip code on line 3. *For a 9-digit zip code, enter the hyphen.* **EXAMPLE:** • Dr. Brilliant is a solo practitioner. Enter Dr. Brilliant's name, credential, and address in Block 33. • Dr. Healer practices at the Goodmedicine Clinic. Enter Goodmedicine Clinic as the billing provider along with its address and telephone number in Block 33.
33a	Enter the 10-digit NPI of the *billing* provider (e.g., solo practitioner) or group practice (e.g., clinic). **EXAMPLE:** Dr. Healer (NPI: 6789012345) practices at Goodmedicine Clinic (NPI: 3345678901). Enter 3345678901 in Block 33a.
33b	Leave blank.

ERIN A. HELPER, M.D.
101 Medic Drive, Anywhere NY 12345
(101) 111-1234 (Office) • (101) 111-9292 (Fax)
EIN: 11-1234523
NPI: 1234567890

Case Study

PATIENT INFORMATION:

Name:	Public, John Q.
Address:	10A Senate Avenue
City:	Anywhere
State:	NY
Zip Code:	12345-1234
Telephone:	(101) 201-7891
Gender:	Male
Date of Birth:	03-09-1945
Occupation:	Supervisor
Employer:	Legal Research, Inc.

INSURANCE INFORMATION:

Patient Number:	12-1
Place of Service:	Office
Primary Insurance Plan:	Metropolitan
Primary Insurance Plan ID #:	225120661W
Group #:	23698
Primary Policyholder:	Public, John Q.
Policyholder Date of Birth:	03-09-1945
Relationship to Patient:	Self
Secondary Insurance Plan:	
Secondary Insurance Plan ID #:	
Secondary Policyholder:	

Patient Status   ☐ Married   ☐ Divorced   ☒ Single   ☐ Student

ICD-10-CM ALERT!

Bronchopneumonia	J18.0
Urinary frequency	R35.0

DIAGNOSIS INFORMATION

Diagnosis	Code	Diagnosis	Code
1. Bronchopneumonia	485	5.	
2. Urinary frequency	788.41	6.	
3.		7.	
4.		8.	

PROCEDURE INFORMATION

Description of Procedure or Service	Date	Code	Charge
1. Established patient office visit, level III	01-09-YYYY	99213	75.00
2. Urinalysis, dipstick, automatic microscopy	01-09-YYYY	81001	10.00
3. Chest x-ray, 2 views	01-09-YYYY	71020	50.00
4.			
5.			

SPECIAL NOTES: • Date symptoms started: 01-05-YYYY   • Referring physician: Ivan Goodoc, MD (NPI: 3456789012)
• Recheck: 01/19/YYYY   • Amount patient paid: $10 copayment

FIGURE 12-1 John Q. Public case study (Courtesy Delmar/Cengage Learning)

FIGURE 12-2 Completed John Q. Public primary claim (Courtesy Delmar/Cengage Learning)

ICD-10-CM ALERT!

21. DIAGNOSIS OR NATURE OF ILLNESS OR INJURY (Relate Items 1, 2, 3 or 4 to Item 24E by Line)

1. J18.0   3. _____

2. R35.0   4. _____

E. DIAGNOSIS POINTER

EXERCISE 12-1

Completing the Mary S. Patient CMS-1500 Claim

1. Review the Mary S. Patient case study (Figure 12-3).

2. Select the information needed for Blocks 1 through 33, and enter the required information on a blank CMS-1500 claim using optical scanning guidelines.

3. Review the completed claim to be sure that all required blocks are completed accurately.

4. Compare your claim with the completed Mary S. Patient claim (Figure 12-4).

ERIN A. HELPER, M.D.
101 Medic Drive, Anywhere NY 12345
(101) 111-1234 (Office) • (101) 111-9292 (Fax)
EIN: 11-1234523
NPI: 1234567890

Case Study

PATIENT INFORMATION:

Name:	Patient, Mary S.
Address:	91 Home Street
City:	Nowhere
State:	NY
Zip Code:	12367-1234
Telephone:	(101) 201-8989
Gender:	Female
Date of Birth:	10-10-1959
Occupation:	Homemaker
Employer:	

INSURANCE INFORMATION:

Patient Number:	12-2
Place of Service:	Hospital Inpatient
Primary Insurance Plan:	Conn General
Primary Insurance Plan ID #:	222017681
Group #:	6920
Primary Policyholder:	James W. Patient
Policyholder Date of Birth:	03-01-1948
Employer:	Alstom
Relationship to Patient:	Spouse
Secondary Insurance Plan:	
Secondary Insurance Plan ID #:	
Secondary Policyholder:	

Patient Status   ☒ Married   ☐ Divorced   ☐ Single   ☐ Student

---

ICD-10-CM ALERT!

Abnormal ECG	R94.30
Prinzmetal angina	I20.1
Familial combined hyperlipidemia	E78.4

DIAGNOSIS INFORMATION

Diagnosis	Code	Diagnosis	Code
1. Abnormal ECG	794.31	5.	
2. Prinzmetal angina	413.1	6.	
3. Familial combined hyperlipidemia	272.4	7.	

PROCEDURE INFORMATION

Description of Procedure or Service	Date	Code	Charge
1. Initial hospital visit, level III	01-07-YYYY	99223	150.00
2. Subsequent hospital visit, level I	01-08-YYYY	99231	75.00
3. Discharge visit, 30 minutes	01-09-YYYY	99238	75.00
4.			
5.			

SPECIAL NOTES:
• Date symptoms started: 01-07-YYYY   • Referred to: Dr. Cardiac for Thallium Stress test on 01-10-YYYY
• Recheck: 01/17/YYYY
• Hospital Information: Goodmedicine Hospital, Anywhere Street, Anywhere NY 12345-1234 (NPI: 2345678901)

FIGURE 12-3 Mary S. Patient case study (Courtesy Delmar/Cengage Learning)

1500

HEALTH INSURANCE CLAIM FORM

APPROVED BY NATIONAL UNIFORM CLAIM COMMITTE 08/05

☐☐ PICA   PICA ☐☐

1. MEDICARE (Medicare #)	MEDICAID (Medicaid #)	TRICARE CHAMPUS (Sponsor's SSN)	CHAMPVA (Member ID#)	GROUP HEALTH PLAN (SSN or ID)	FECA BLK LUNG (SSN)	OTHER [X] (ID)	1a. INSURED'S I.D. NUMBER (For Program in Item 1)

1a. INSURED'S I.D. NUMBER: 222017681

2. PATIENT'S NAME (Last Name, First Name, Middle Initial): PATIENT, MARY, S

3. PATIENT'S BIRTH DATE: 10 | 10 | 1959   SEX: M ☐ F [X]

4. INSURED'S NAME (Last Name, First Name, Middle Initial): PATIENT, JAMES, W

5. PATIENT'S ADDRESS (No., Street): 91 HOME STREET

6. PATIENT'S RELATIONSHIP TO INSURED: Self ☐ Spouse [X] Child ☐ Other ☐

7. INSURED'S ADDRESS (No., Street): 91 HOME STREET

CITY: NOWHERE   STATE: NY

8. PATIENT STATUS: Single ☐ Married [X] Other ☐

CITY: NOWHERE   STATE: NY

ZIP CODE: 12367-1234   TELEPHONE (Include Area Code): (101)2018989

Employed ☐   Full-Time Student ☐   Part-Time Student ☐

ZIP CODE: 12367-1234   TELEPHONE (Include Area Code): (101)2018989

9. OTHER INSURED'S NAME (Last Name, First Name, Middle Initial):

10. IS PATIENT'S CONDITION RELATED TO:

11. INSURED'S POLICY GROUP OR FECA NUMBER:

a. OTHER INSURED'S POLICY OR GROUP NUMBER:

a. EMPLOYMENT? (Current or Previous): YES ☐ NO [X]

a. INSURED'S DATE OF BIRTH: 03 | 01 | 1948   SEX: M [X] F ☐

b. OTHER INSURED'S DATE OF BIRTH: SEX: M ☐ F ☐

b. AUTO ACCIDENT? PLACE (State): YES ☐ NO [X]

b. EMPLOYER'S NAME OR SCHOOL NAME: ALSTOM

c. EMPLOYER'S NAME OR SCHOOL NAME:

c. OTHER ACCIDENT?: YES ☐ NO [X]

c. INSURANCE PLAN NAME OR PROGRAM NAME: CONN GENERAL

d. INSURANCE PLAN NAME OR PROGRAM NAME:

10d. RESERVED FOR LOCAL USE:

d. IS THERE ANOTHER HEALTH BENEFIT PLAN? YES ☐ NO [X]   *If yes*, return to and complete item 9 a-d.

READ BACK OF FORM BEFORE COMPLETING & SIGNING THIS FORM.

12. PATIENT'S OR AUTHORIZED PERSON'S SIGNATURE I authorize the release of any medical or other information necessary to process this claim. I also request payment of government benefits either to myself or to the party who accepts assignment below.

SIGNED SIGNATURE ON FILE   DATE

13. INSURED'S OR AUTHORIZED PERSON'S SIGNATURE I authorize payment of medical benefits to the undersigned physcian or supplier for services described below.

SIGNED SIGNATURE ON FILE

14. DATE OF CURRENT: 01 | 07 | YYYY   ILLNESS (First symptom) OR INJURY (Accident) OR PREGNANCY (LMP)

15. IF PATIENT HAS HAD SAME OR SIMILAR ILLNESS. GIVE FIRST DATE MM | DD | YY

16. DATES PATIENT UNABLE TO WORK IN CURRENT OCCUPATION: FROM   TO

17. NAME OF REFERRING PROVIDER OR OTHER SOURCE:

17a.   17b. NPI

18. HOSPITALIZATION DATES RELATED TO CURRENT SERVICES: FROM 01 | 07 | YYYY   TO 01 | 09 | YYYY

19. RESERVED FOR LOCAL USE:

20. OUTSIDE LAB? YES ☐ NO [X] $ CHARGES

21. DIAGNOSIS OR NATURE OF ILLNESS OR INJURY (Relate Items 1, 2, 3 or 4 to Item 24E by Line)

1. 794 31   3. 272 4

2. 413 1   4.

22. MEDICAID RESUBMISSION CODE   ORIGINAL REF. NO.

23. PRIOR AUTHORIZATION NUMBER

24. A. DATE(S) OF SERVICE From MM DD YY — To MM DD YY	B. PLACE OF SERVICE	C. EMG	D. PROCEDURES, SERVICES, OR SUPPLIES (Explain Unusual Circumstances) CPT/HCPCS	MODIFIER	E. DIAGNOSIS POINTER	F. $ CHARGES	G. DAYS OR UNITS	H. EPSDT Family Plan	I. ID. QUAL.	J. RENDERING PROVIDER ID. #
1	0107 YYYY	21		99223		1	150 00	1		NPI	
2	0108 YYYY	21		99231		1	75 00	1		NPI	
3	0109 YYYY	21		99238		1	75 00	1		NPI	
4										NPI	
5										NPI	
6										NPI	

25. FEDERAL TAX I.D. NUMBER: 111234523   SSN EIN [X]

26. PATIENT'S ACCOUNT NO.: 12-2

27. ACCEPT ASSIGNMENT? (For govt. claims, see back): [X] YES ☐ NO

28. TOTAL CHARGE: $ 300 00

29. AMOUNT PAID: $

30. BALANCE DUE: $ 300 00

31. SIGNATURE OF PHYSICIAN OR SUPPLIER INCLUDING DEGREES OR CREDENTIALS (I certify that the statements on the reverse apply to this bill and are made a part thereof.)

SIGNED ERIN A HELPER MD   DATE MMDDYYYY

32. SERVICE FACILITY LOCATION INFORMATION: GOODMEDICINE HOSPITAL ANYWHERE STREET ANYWHERE NY 12345-1234

a. 2345678901   b.

33. BILLING PROVIDER INFO & PH # (101)1111234

ERIN A HELPER MD 101 MEDIC DRIVE ANYWHERE NY 12345

a. 1234567890   b.

NUCC Instruction Manual available at: www.nucc.org

APPROVED OMB-0938-0999 FORM CMS-1500 (08/05)

FIGURE 12-4 Completed Mary S. Patient primary claim (Courtesy Delmar/Cengage Learning)

ICD-10-CM ALERT!

21. DIAGNOSIS OR NATURE OF ILLNESS OR INJURY (Relate Items 1, 2, 3 or 4 to Item 24E by Line)

1. R94 30   3. E78 4

2. I20 1   4.

E. DIAGNOSIS POINTER

Additional commercial claim case studies are found in Appendices I and II of this text.

COMMERCIAL SECONDARY COVERAGE

Modifications are made to the primary CMS-1500 claim instructions when patients are covered by primary (Table 12-2) and secondary or supplemental (Table 12-3) health insurance plans. Secondary health insurance plans provide coverage similar to that of primary plans; supplemental plans usually cover only deductible, copayment, and coinsurance expenses.

When the same payer issues the primary and secondary or supplemental policies, submit just one CMS-1500 claim. If the payers for the primary and secondary or supplemental policies are different, submit a CMS-1500 claim to the primary payer. When the primary payer has processed the claim (e.g., provider is reimbursed), generate a second CMS-1500 claim to send to the secondary payer, and include a copy of the primary payer's remittance advice.

TABLE 12-2   Modifications to commercial primary CMS-1500 claims completion instructions when the same commercial health insurance company provides secondary or supplemental policy

BLOCK	INSTRUCTIONS
1a	Enter the primary policyholder's commercial health plan identification number as it appears on the patient's insurance card. *Do not enter hyphens or spaces in the number.*
7	Enter the secondary or supplemental policyholder's last name, first name, and middle initial (separated by commas).
9	Enter the secondary or supplemental policyholder's last name, first name, and middle initial (if known) (separated by commas).
9a	Enter the secondary or supplemental policyholder's policy or group number.
9b	Enter the secondary or supplemental policyholder's birth date as MM DD YYYY (with spaces). Enter an X in the appropriate box to indicate the secondary or supplemental policyholder's gender.
9c	Enter the name of the secondary or supplemental policyholder's employer (if employed) or school (if unemployed and considered a full- or part-time student). Otherwise, leave blank.
9d	Enter the name of the secondary or supplemental policyholder's commercial health insurance plan.
11	Enter the secondary or supplemental policyholder's commercial group number if the patient is covered by a group health plan. *Do not enter hyphens or spaces in the group number.*
11a	Enter the secondary or supplemental policyholder's birth date as MM DD YYYY (with spaces). Enter an X in the appropriate box to indicate the policyholder's gender. If the policyholder's gender is unknown, leave blank.
11b	Enter the name of the secondary or supplemental policyholder's employer (if employed) or school (if unemployed and considered a full- or part-time student). Otherwise, leave blank.
11c	Enter the name of the secondary or supplemental policyholder's commercial health insurance plan.
11d	Enter an X in the YES box.

TABLE 12-3   Modifications to commercial primary CMS-1500 claims completion instructions when a different commercial health insurance company provides secondary or supplemental policy

BLOCK	INSTRUCTIONS
	NOTE: If the primary and secondary/supplemental payers are the same, do not generate a second CMS-1500 claim. Instead, modify the primary CMS-1500 claim using the instructions in Table 12-2.
1a	Enter the secondary or supplemental policyholder's health insurance identification number (HICN) as it appears on the insurance card. *Do not enter hyphens or spaces in the number.*
4	Enter the secondary or supplemental policyholder's last name, first name, and middle initial (separated by commas).
7	Enter the secondary or supplemental policyholder's mailing address and telephone number.
9	Enter the primary policyholder's last name, first name, and middle initial (if known) (separated by commas).
9a	Enter the primary policyholder's policy or group number.
9b	Enter the primary policyholder's birth date as MM DD YYYY (with spaces). Enter an X in the appropriate box to indicate the secondary or supplemental policyholder's gender.
9c	Enter the name of the primary policyholder's employer (if employed) or school (if unemployed and considered a full- or part-time student). Otherwise, leave blank.
9d	Enter the name of the primary policyholder's commercial health insurance plan.
11	Enter the primary policyholder's policy or group number. *Do not enter hyphens or spaces in the policy or group number.*
11a	Enter the primary policyholder's birth date as MM DD YYYY (with spaces). Enter an X in the appropriate box to indicate the policyholder's gender. If the policyholder's gender is unknown, leave blank.
11b	Enter the name of the primary policyholder's employer (if employed) or school (if unemployed and considered a full- or part-time student). Otherwise, leave blank.
11c	Enter the name of the primary policyholder's commercial health insurance plan.
11d	Enter an X in the YES box.
26	Add an S to the patient account number in to indicate the secondary policy.

EXERCISE 12-2

Filing Commercial Secondary Claims When the Same Commercial Payer Provides Primary and Secondary Coverage

1. Obtain a blank claim by making a copy of the claim in Appendix III.

2. Underline Blocks 7, 9 through 9d, and 11–11d on the claim.

3. Refer to the Mary S. Patient case study (Figure 12-3). Enter the following information in the appropriate blocks for the secondary policy (Table 12-2):
   Conn General ID # 22335544
   Policyholder: James W. Patient
   Birth date: 03/01/48
   Relationship: Spouse
   Add an "S" to the patient's account number in Block 26 (e.g., 12-2S)

4. Review the completed claim to be sure all required blocks are properly completed.

5. Compare your claim with the completed Mary S. Patient claim in Figure 12-5.

1500
HEALTH INSURANCE CLAIM FORM
APPROVED BY NATIONAL UNIFORM CLAIM COMMITTE 08/05

| | PICA | | | | | | | | PICA | | |

1. MEDICARE	MEDICAID	TRICARE CHAMPUS	CHAMPVA	GROUP HEALTH PLAN	FECA BLK LUNG	OTHER	1a. INSURED'S I.D. NUMBER (For Program in Item 1)
(Medicare #)	(Medicaid #)	(Sponsor's SSN)	(Member ID#)	(SSN or ID)	(SSN)	(ID)	222017681

2. PATIENT'S NAME (Last Name, First Name, Middle Initial)	3. PATIENT'S BIRTH DATE MM DD YY	SEX	4. INSURED'S NAME (Last Name, First Name, Middle Initial)
PATIENT, MARY, S	10 10 1959	M □ F X	PATIENT, JAMES, W

5. PATIENT'S ADDRESS (No., Street)	6. PATIENT'S RELATIONSHIP TO INSURED	7. INSURED'S ADDRESS (No., Street)
91 HOME STREET	Self □ Spouse X Child □ Other □	91 HOME STREET

CITY		STATE	8. PATIENT STATUS	CITY		STATE
NOWHERE		NY	Single □ Married X Other □	NOWHERE		NY

ZIP CODE	TELEPHONE (Include Area Code)		ZIP CODE	TELEPHONE (Include Area Code)
12367-1234	(101)2018989	Employed □ Full-Time Student □ Part-Time Student □	12367-1234	(101)2018989

9. OTHER INSURED'S NAME (Last Name, First Name, Middle Initial)	10. IS PATIENT'S CONDITION RELATED TO:	11. INSURED'S POLICY GROUP OR FECA NUMBER
PATIENT, JAMES, W		6920

a. OTHER INSURED'S POLICY OR GROUP NUMBER	a. EMPLOYMENT? (Current or Previous)	a. INSURED'S DATE OF BIRTH MM DD YY	SEX
22335544	YES □ X NO	03 01 1948	M X F □

b. OTHER INSURED'S DATE OF BIRTH MM DD YY	SEX	b. AUTO ACCIDENT? PLACE (State)	b. EMPLOYER'S NAME OR SCHOOL NAME
03 01 1948	M X F □	YES □ X NO	ALSTOM

c. EMPLOYER'S NAME OR SCHOOL NAME	c. OTHER ACCIDENT?	c. INSURANCE PLAN NAME OR PROGRAM NAME
ALSTOM	YES □ X NO	CONN GENERAL

d. INSURANCE PLAN NAME OR PROGRAM NAME	10d. RESERVED FOR LOCAL USE	d. IS THERE ANOTHER HEALTH BENEFIT PLAN?
CONN GENERAL		X YES □ NO If yes, return to and complete item 9 a-d.

READ BACK OF FORM BEFORE COMPLETING & SIGNING THIS FORM.

12. PATIENT'S OR AUTHORIZED PERSON'S SIGNATURE I authorize the release of any medical or other information necessary to process this claim. I also request payment of government benefits either to myself or to the party who accepts assignment below.

SIGNED SIGNATURE ON FILE   DATE

13. INSURED'S OR AUTHORIZED PERSON'S SIGNATURE I authorize payment of medical benefits to the undersigned physician or supplier for services described below.

SIGNED SIGNATURE ON FILE

14. DATE OF CURRENT: MM DD YY 01 07 YYYY	ILLNESS (First symptom) OR INJURY (Accident) OR PREGNANCY (LMP)	15. IF PATIENT HAS HAD SAME OR SIMILAR ILLNESS. GIVE FIRST DATE MM DD YY	16. DATES PATIENT UNABLE TO WORK IN CURRENT OCCUPATION MM DD YY FROM TO

17. NAME OF REFERRING PROVIDER OR OTHER SOURCE	17a.	18. HOSPITALIZATION DATES RELATED TO CURRENT SERVICES MM DD YY FROM 01 07 YYYY TO 01 09 YYYY
	17b. NPI	

19. RESERVED FOR LOCAL USE	20. OUTSIDE LAB? YES □ X NO	$ CHARGES

21. DIAGNOSIS OR NATURE OF ILLNESS OR INJURY (Relate Items 1, 2, 3 or 4 to Item 24E by Line)

1. 794 31   3. 272 4
2. 413 1   4.

22. MEDICAID RESUBMISSION CODE	ORIGINAL REF. NO.

23. PRIOR AUTHORIZATION NUMBER

24. A DATE(S) OF SERVICE From To MM DD YY MM DD YY	B. PLACE OF SERVICE	C. EMG	D. PROCEDURES, SERVICES, OR SUPPLIES (Explain Unusual Circumstances) CPT/HCPCS MODIFER	E. DIAGNOSIS POINTER	F. $ CHARGES	G. DAYS OR UNITS	H. EPSDT Family Plan	I. ID. QUAL.	J. RENDERING PROVIDER ID. #
1	0107 YYYY	21		99223	1	150 00	1		NPI	
2	0108 YYYY	21		99231	1	75 00	1		NPI	
3	0109 YYYY	21		99238	1	75 00	1		NPI	
4									NPI	
5									NPI	
6									NPI	

25. FEDERAL TAX I.D. NUMBER SSN EIN	26. PATIENT'S ACCOUNT NO.	27. ACCEPT ASSIGNMENT? (For govt. claims, see back)	28. TOTAL CHARGE	29. AMOUNT PAID	30. BALANCE DUE
111234523 X	12-2S	X YES □ NO	$ 300 00	$	$ 300 00

31. SIGNATURE OF PHYSICIAN OR SUPPLIER INCLUDING DEGREES OR CREDENTIALS (I certify that the statements on the reverse apply to this bill and are made a part thereof.) ERIN A HELPER MD SIGNED DATE MMDDYYYY	32. SERVICE FACILITY LOCATION INFORMATION GOODMEDICINE HOSPITAL ANYWHERE STREET ANYWHERE NY 12345-1234 a. 2345678901 b.	33. BILLING PROVIDER INFO & PH # (101)1111234 ERIN A HELPER MD 101 MEDIC DRIVE ANYWHERE NY 12345 a. 1234567890 b.

NUCC Instruction Manual available at: www.nucc.org

APPROVED OMB-0938-0999 FORM CMS-1500 (08/05)

FIGURE 12-5 Completed Mary S. Patient claim when primary and secondary payers are the same (Courtesy Delmar/Cengage Learning)

ICD-10-CM ALERT!

21. DIAGNOSIS OR NATURE OF ILLNESS OR INJURY (Relate Items 1, 2, 3 or 4 to Item 24E by Line)

1. R94 30   3. E78 4
2. I20 1   4.

E. DIAGNOSIS POINTER

EXERCISE 12-3

Filing Commercial Secondary Claims When Different Commercial Payers Provide Primary and Secondary Coverage

1. Obtain a blank claim by making a copy of the claim in Appendix III.

2. Underline Blocks 1a, 4, 7, 9, 9a–9d, 11, and 11a–11d on the claim.

3. Refer to the Mary S. Patient case study (Figure 12-3). Enter the following information in the appropriate blocks for the secondary policy:

   Aetna ID # 987654321

   Policyholder: James W. Patient

   Birth date: 03/01/48

   Relationship: Spouse

   Add an "S" to the patient's account number in Block 26 (e.g., 12-2S)

4. Review the completed claim to be sure all required blocks are properly completed.

5. Compare your claim with the completed Mary S. Patient claim in Figure 12-6.

1500
HEALTH INSURANCE CLAIM FORM
APPROVED BY NATIONAL UNIFORM CLAIM COMMITTEE 08/05

PICA			PICA

1. MEDICARE (Medicare #) **MEDICAID** (Medicaid #) **TRICARE CHAMPUS** (Sponsor's SSN) **CHAMPVA** (Member ID#) **GROUP HEALTH PLAN** (SSN or ID) **FECA BLK LUNG** (SSN) [X] **OTHER** (ID)

1a. INSURED'S I.D. NUMBER (For Program in Item 1)
987654321

2. PATIENT'S NAME (Last Name, First Name, Middle Initial)
PATIENT, MARY, S

3. PATIENT'S BIRTH DATE MM 10 DD 10 YY 1959 **SEX** M F [X]

4. INSURED'S NAME (Last Name, First Name, Middle Initial)
PATIENT, JAMES, W

5. PATIENT'S ADDRESS (No., Street)
91 HOME STREET

6. PATIENT'S RELATIONSHIP TO INSURED
Self Spouse [X] Child Other

7. INSURED'S ADDRESS (No., Street)
91 HOME STREET

CITY NOWHERE **STATE** NY

8. PATIENT STATUS
Single Married [X] Other
Employed Full-Time Student Part-Time Student

CITY NOWHERE **STATE** NY

ZIP CODE 12367-1234 **TELEPHONE (Include Area Code)** (101)2018989

ZIP CODE 12367-1234 **TELEPHONE (Include Area Code)** (101)2018989

9. OTHER INSURED'S NAME (Last Name, First Name, Middle Initial)
PATIENT, JAMES, W

10. IS PATIENT'S CONDITION RELATED TO:

11. INSURED'S POLICY GROUP OR FECA NUMBER

a. OTHER INSURED'S POLICY OR GROUP NUMBER
222017681

a. EMPLOYMENT? (Current or Previous)
YES [X] NO

a. INSURED'S DATE OF BIRTH MM 03 DD 01 YY 1948 **SEX** M [X] F

b. OTHER INSURED'S DATE OF BIRTH MM 03 DD 01 YY 1948 **SEX** M [X] F

b. AUTO ACCIDENT? **PLACE (State)**
YES [X] NO

b. EMPLOYER'S NAME OR SCHOOL NAME
ALSTOM

c. EMPLOYER'S NAME OR SCHOOL NAME
ALSTOM

c. OTHER ACCIDENT?
YES [X] NO

c. INSURANCE PLAN NAME OR PROGRAM NAME
AETNA

d. INSURANCE PLAN NAME OR PROGRAM NAME
CONN GENERAL

10d. RESERVED FOR LOCAL USE

d. IS THERE ANOTHER HEALTH BENEFIT PLAN?
[X] YES NO **If yes, return to and complete item 9 a-d.**

READ BACK OF FORM BEFORE COMPLETING & SIGNING THIS FORM.
12. PATIENT'S OR AUTHORIZED PERSON'S SIGNATURE I authorize the release of any medical or other information necessary to process this claim. I also request payment of government benefits either to myself or to the party who accepts assignment below.
SIGNED SIGNATURE ON FILE DATE

13. INSURED'S OR AUTHORIZED PERSON'S SIGNATURE I authorize payment of medical benefits to the undersigned physician or supplier for services described below.
SIGNED SIGNATURE ON FILE

14. DATE OF CURRENT: ILLNESS (First symptom) OR INJURY (Accident) OR PREGNANCY (LMP) MM 01 DD 07 YY YYYY

15. IF PATIENT HAS HAD SAME OR SIMILAR ILLNESS GIVE FIRST DATE MM DD YY

16. DATES PATIENT UNABLE TO WORK IN CURRENT OCCUPATION FROM MM DD YY TO MM DD YY

17. NAME OF REFERRING PROVIDER OR OTHER SOURCE
17a.
17b. NPI

18. HOSPITALIZATION DATES RELATED TO CURRENT SERVICES FROM MM 01 DD 07 YY YYYY TO MM 01 DD 09 YY YYYY

19. RESERVED FOR LOCAL USE

20. OUTSIDE LAB? YES [X] NO **$ CHARGES**

21. DIAGNOSIS OR NATURE OF ILLNESS OR INJURY (Relate Items 1, 2, 3 or 4 to Item 24E by Line)
1. 794.31
2. 413.1
3. 272.4
4.

22. MEDICAID RESUBMISSION CODE ORIGINAL REF. NO.

23. PRIOR AUTHORIZATION NUMBER

24. A DATE(S) OF SERVICE From MM DD YY To MM DD YY	B. PLACE OF SERVICE	C. EMG	D. PROCEDURES, SERVICES, OR SUPPLIES CPT/HCPCS	MODIFIER	E. DIAGNOSIS POINTER	F. $ CHARGES	G. DAYS OR UNITS	H. EPSDT Family Plan	I. ID. QUAL	J. RENDERING PROVIDER ID. #
1 01 07 YYYY	21		99223		1	150 00	1		NPI	
2 01 08 YYYY	21		99231		1	75 00	1		NPI	
3 01 09 YYYY	21		99238		1	75 00	1		NPI	
4									NPI	
5									NPI	
6									NPI	

25. FEDERAL TAX I.D. NUMBER 111234523 SSN EIN [X]

26. PATIENT'S ACCOUNT NO. 12-2S

27. ACCEPT ASSIGNMENT? (For govt. claims, see back) [X] YES NO

28. TOTAL CHARGE $ 300 00

29. AMOUNT PAID $

30. BALANCE DUE $ 300 00

31. SIGNATURE OF PHYSICIAN OR SUPPLIER INCLUDING DEGREES OR CREDENTIALS (I certify that the statements on the reverse apply to this bill and are made a part thereof.)
ERIN A HELPER MD
SIGNED DATE MMDDYYYY

32. SERVICE FACILITY LOCATION INFORMATION
GOODMEDICINE HOSPITAL
ANYWHERE STREET
ANYWHERE NY 12345-1234
a. 2345678901 b.

33. BILLING PROVIDER INFO & PH # (101)1111234
ERIN A HELPER MD
101 MEDIC DRIVE
ANYWHERE NY 12345
a. 1234567890 b.

NUCC Instruction Manual available at: www.nucc.org
APPROVED OMB-0938-0999 FORM CMS-1500 (08/05)

Figure 12-6 Completed Mary Sue Patient claim when primary and secondary payers are different (Courtesy Delmar/Cengage Learning)

COMMERCIAL GROUP HEALTH PLAN COVERAGE

NOTE: Individual and family health plans cover individuals and their families, and each person covered must qualify individually. Group health plans are required to accept employees and their family members, and may be more expensive than individual/family health plans.

Employers include group health plan coverage in fringe benefit programs to retain high-quality employees and ensure productivity by providing preventive medical care to create a healthy workforce. There are many group health plan options available to employers, including various payment options from paying 100% of annual premium costs for each employee to sharing a percentage (e.g., 80%) of the annual insurance costs with employees.

EXAMPLE: Linda Ryan is employed by a public school, which provides individual and family group health plan coverage. Her employer pays 80% of her annual premium. Linda selected family coverage for her group health plan, which means her employer pays $9,600 per year (of the $12,000 annual premium). Linda is responsible for 20% of the annual premium (or $2400), which means $92.31 is deducted from each of her 26 biweekly paychecks. (Copayments and deductibles also apply to her group health plan, such as a $20 copayment for office visits, a $50 copayment for hospital emergency department visits, and a $35 copayment for hospital outpatient ancillary tests.)

TABLE 12-4   Modifications to commercial primary CMS-1500 claims completion instructions when the policy is a group health plan

BLOCK	INSTRUCTIONS
1	Enter an X in the Group Health Plans box.
11	Enter the policyholder's group number. **NOTE:** Locate the group number on the policyholder's insurance identification card (or in case studies located in this textbook, workbook, and SimClaim software)

EXERCISE 12-4

Filing Group Health Plan Claims

1. Obtain a blank claim by making a copy of the claim in Appendix III.

2. Underline Blocks 1 and 11 on the claim.

3. Refer to the Mary S. Patient case study (see Figure 12-3). Enter the following information in the appropriate blocks for the group health plan policy:

   Group number: 123A

4. Review the completed claim to be sure all required blocks are properly completed.

5. Compare your claim with the completed Mary S. Patient claim in Figure 12-7.

1500

HEALTH INSURANCE CLAIM FORM

APPROVED BY NATIONAL UNIFORM CLAIM COMMITTE 08/05

PICA	PICA

1. MEDICARE (Medicare #)	MEDICAID (Medicaid #)	TRICARE CHAMPUS (Sponsor's SSN)	CHAMPVA (Member ID#)	GROUP HEALTH PLAN (SSN or ID) [X]	FECA BLK LUNG (SSN)	OTHER (ID)	1a. INSURED'S I.D. NUMBER (For Program in Item 1)
							987654321

2. PATIENT'S NAME (Last Name, First Name, Middle Initial)	3. PATIENT'S BIRTH DATE MM DD YY	SEX	4. INSURED'S NAME (Last Name, First Name, Middle Initial)
PATIENT, MARY, S	10 10 1959	M[ ] F[X]	PATIENT, JAMES, W

5. PATIENT'S ADDRESS (No., Street)	6. PATIENT'S RELATIONSHIP TO INSURED	7. INSURED'S ADDRESS (No., Street)
91 HOME STREET	Self [ ] Spouse [X] Child [ ] Other [ ]	91 HOME STREET

CITY	STATE	8. PATIENT STATUS	CITY	STATE
NOWHERE	NY	Single [ ] Married [X] Other [ ]	NOWHERE	NY

ZIP CODE	TELEPHONE (Include Area Code)		ZIP CODE	TELEPHONE (Include Area Code)
12367-1234	(101)2018989	Employed [ ] Full-Time Student [ ] Part-Time Student [ ]	12367-1234	(101)2018989

9. OTHER INSURED'S NAME (Last Name, First Name, Middle Initial)	10. IS PATIENT'S CONDITION RELATED TO:	11. INSURED'S POLICY GROUP OR FECA NUMBER
PATIENT, JAMES, W		123A

a. OTHER INSURED'S POLICY OR GROUP NUMBER	a. EMPLOYMENT? (Current or Previous)	a. INSURED'S DATE OF BIRTH MM DD YY	SEX
222017681	YES [ ] NO [X]	03 01 1948	M[X] F[ ]

b. OTHER INSURED'S DATE OF BIRTH MM DD YY	SEX	b. AUTO ACCIDENT?	PLACE (State)	b. EMPLOYER'S NAME OR SCHOOL NAME
03 01 1948	M[X] F[ ]	YES [ ] NO [X]		ALSTOM

c. EMPLOYER'S NAME OR SCHOOL NAME	c. OTHER ACCIDENT?	c. INSURANCE PLAN NAME OR PROGRAM NAME
ALSTOM	YES [ ] NO [X]	AETNA

d. INSURANCE PLAN NAME OR PROGRAM NAME	10d. RESERVED FOR LOCAL USE	d. IS THERE ANOTHER HEALTH BENEFIT PLAN?
CONN GENERAL		[X] YES [ ] NO *If yes,* return to and complete item 9 a-d.

READ BACK OF FORM BEFORE COMPLETING & SIGNING THIS FORM.

12. PATIENT'S OR AUTHORIZED PERSON'S SIGNATURE I authorize the release of any medical or other information necessary to process this claim. I also request payment of government benefits either to myself or to the party who accepts assignment below.	13. INSURED'S OR AUTHORIZED PERSON'S SIGNATURE I authorize payment of medical benefits to the undersigned physcian or supplier for services described below.
SIGNED SIGNATURE ON FILE DATE	SIGNED SIGNATURE ON FILE

14. DATE OF CURRENT: MM DD YY ILLNESS (First symptom) OR INJURY (Accident) OR PREGNANCY (LMP)	15. IF PATIENT HAS HAD SAME OR SIMILAR ILLNESS, GIVE FIRST DATE MM DD YY	16. DATES PATIENT UNABLE TO WORK IN CURRENT OCCUPATION MM DD YY MM DD YY
01 07 YYYY		FROM TO

17. NAME OF REFERRING PROVIDER OR OTHER SOURCE	17a.	18. HOSPITALIZATION DATES RELATED TO CURRENT SERVICES MM DD YY MM DD YY
	17b. NPI	FROM 01 07 YYYY TO 01 09 YYYY

19. RESERVED FOR LOCAL USE	20. OUTSIDE LAB?	$ CHARGES
	YES [ ] NO [X]	

21. DIAGNOSIS OR NATURE OF ILLNESS OR INJURY (Relate Items 1, 2, 3 or 4 to Item 24E by Line)	22. MEDICAID RESUBMISSION CODE	ORIGINAL REF. NO.
1. 794 31 3. 272 4		
2. 413 1 4.	23. PRIOR AUTHORIZATION NUMBER	

24. A. DATE(S) OF SERVICE From MM DD YY To MM DD YY	B. PLACE OF SERVICE	C. EMG	D. PROCEDURES, SERVICES, OR SUPPLIES (Explain Unusual Circumstances) CPT/HCPCS MODIFER	E. DIAGNOSIS POINTER	F. $ CHARGES	G. DAYS OR UNITS	H. EPSDT Family Plan	I. ID. QUAL.	J. RENDERING PROVIDER ID. #
1	01 07 YYYY	21		99223	1	150 00	1		NPI	
2	01 08 YYYY	21		99231	1	75 00	1		NPI	
3	01 09 YYYY	21		99238	1	75 00	1		NPI	
4									NPI	
5									NPI	
6									NPI	

25. FEDERAL TAX I.D. NUMBER SSN EIN	26. PATIENT'S ACCOUNT NO.	27. ACCEPT ASSIGNMENT? (For govt. claims, see back)	28. TOTAL CHARGE	29. AMOUNT PAID	30. BALANCE DUE
111234523 [X]	12-2	[X] YES [ ] NO	$ 300 00	$	$ 300 00

31. SIGNATURE OF PHYSICIAN OR SUPPLIER INCLUDING DEGREES OR CREDENTIALS (I certify that the statements on the reverse apply to this bill and are made a part thereof.)	32. SERVICE FACILITY LOCATION INFORMATION	33. BILLING PROVIDER INFO & PH # (101)1111234
ERIN A HELPER MD	GOODMEDICINE HOSPITAL ANYWHERE STREET ANYWHERE NY 12345-1234	ERIN A HELPER MD 101 MEDIC DRIVE ANYWHERE NY 12345
SIGNED DATE MMDDYYYY	a. 2345678901 b.	a. 1234567890 b.

NUCC Instruction Manual available at: www.nucc.org   APPROVED OMB-0938-0999 FORM CMS-1500 (08/05)

Figure 12-7 Completed Mary Sue Patient claim for commercial payer group health plan (Courtesy Delmar/Cengage Learning)

ICD-10-CM ALERT!

21. DIAGNOSIS OR NATURE OF ILLNESS OR INJURY (Relate Items 1, 2, 3 or 4 to Item 24E by Line)

1. R94 30   3. E78 4

2. I20 1   4.

E. DIAGNOSIS POINTER

SUMMARY

Automobile insurance coverage includes medical payments and PIP; disability insurance provides an individual with reimbursement for lost wages; liability insurance covers losses to a third party caused by the insured or on premises owned by the insured.

Although commercial claims completion instructions are generally recognized nationwide, it is important to check with each payer to determine if they require alternate information to be entered on the claim. Commercial payers also implement changes to claims completion requirements throughout the year, and most providers discover these changes when claims are denied. Commercial payers do not typically make available their billing manuals or updates, which is another reason it is important to routinely contact payers to request their specific CMS-1500 claims completion instructions.

When patients are covered by primary *and* secondary/supplemental health insurance plans, modifications are made to the CMS-1500 claim instructions:

- If the same payer provides both primary and secondary/supplemental coverage, just one claim is submitted, and information is entered in Blocks 9 through 11d.
- If the secondary/supplemental payer is different from the primary payer, a primary claim is submitted to the primary payer, and a new claim is generated and submitted to the secondary payer, with information entered in Blocks 1a, 4, 7, 9 through 9d, and 11 through 11d. A copy of the primary payer's remittance advice is attached to the secondary claim.

When completing commercial CMS-1500 claims for case studies in this text and the Workbook, the following special instructions apply:

- Block 12—Enter SIGNATURE ON FILE
- Block 13—Enter SIGNATURE ON FILE
- Block 20—Enter an X in the NO box
- Block 26—Enter the case study number (e.g., 12-2). If the patient has both primary and secondary coverage, enter a P (for primary) next to the number (on the primary claim) (e.g., 12-2P) and an S (for secondary) next to the number (on the secondary claim) (e.g., 12-2S)
- Block 27—Enter an X in the YES box
- Block 31—Enter the provider's complete name with credentials and the date as MMDDYYYY.

INTERNET LINKS

- Aetna
  www.aetna.com
- *Commercial Insurance*
  www.commercialinsurancefacts.org
- eHealthInsurance Services, Inc.
  www.ehealthinsurance.org
- Insurance Information Institute
  www.iii.org
- *International Insurance Fact Book*
  www.internationalinsurance.org
- State of Wisconsin Office of the Commissioner of Insurance
  www.oci.wi.gov
- Washington State Office of the Insurance Commissioner
  www.insurance.wa.gov
- Wolters Kluwer Financial Services, Insurance Compliance Solutions
  insurance.wolterskluwerfs.com

STUDY CHECKLIST

- ☐ Read this textbook chapter and highlight key terms.
- ☐ Access SimClaim software at the online companion, and become familiar with the software.
- ☐ Complete CMS-1500 claims for chapter case studies.
- ☐ Complete the chapter review, verifying answers with your instructor.
- ☐ Complete WebTutor assignments, and take online quizzes.
- ☐ Complete commercial claims for cases located in Appendices I and II.
- ☐ Complete the Workbook chapter, verifying answers with your instructor.
- ☐ Complete the StudyWare activities to receive immediate feedback.
- ☐ Form a study group with classmates to discuss chapter concepts in preparation for an exam.

REVIEW

MULTIPLE CHOICE Select the most appropriate response.

1. **When a patient is covered by a large employer group health plan (EGHP) and Medicare, which is primary?**
   a. EGHP
   b. Medicare
   c. no distinction is made between the plans
   d. the plan that has been in place longest

2. **When a child who is covered by two or more plans lives with his married parents, the primary policyholder is the parent**
   a. who is older.
   b. who is younger.
   c. whose birthday occurs first in the year.
   d. whose birthday occurs later in the year.

3. **When an insurance company uses the patient's social security number as the patient's insurance identification number, Block 1a of the CMS-1500 claim**
   a. contains the dashes associated with social security numbers.
   b. contains the identification number without hyphens or spaces.
   c. is left blank, because social security numbers are private.
   d. can contain spaces or dashes when the number is entered.

4. **When the CMS-1500 claim requires spaces in the data entry of a date, the entry looks like which of the following?**
   a. MM DD YYYY
   b. MM-DD-YYYY
   c. MM/DD/YYYY
   d. MMDDYYYY

5. **When completing a CMS-1500 claim using computer software, text should be entered in _____ case.**
   a. lower
   b. small caps
   c. title
   d. upper

6. **When the CMS-1500 claim requires a response to *Yes* or *No* entries, enter**

   a. a checkmark.

   b. an X.

   c. either an X or a checkmark.

   d. nothing.

7. **When SIGNATURE ON FILE is the appropriate entry for a CMS-1500 claim block, which is also acceptable as an entry?**

   a. FILED

   b. S/F

   c. SIGNED

   d. SOF

8. **Block 14 of the CMS-1500 claim requires entry of the date the patient first experienced signs or symptoms of an illness or injury (or the date of last menstrual period for obstetric visits). Upon completion of Jean Mandel's claim, you notice that there is no documentation of that date in the record. The provider does document that her pain began five days ago. Today is May 10, YYYY. What do you enter in block 14?**

   a. 05 05 YYYY

   b. 05 10 YYYY

   c. the word NONE

   d. nothing (leave the block blank)

9. **Blocks 24A–24J of the CMS-1500 contain shaded rows, which can contain**

   a. additional dates of service and code numbers.

   b. attachments to the CMS-1500 claim.

   c. modifiers that didn't fit in the unshaded block.

   d. supplemental information, per payer instructions.

10. **Block 24A of the CMS-1500 claim contains dates of service (*FROM* and *TO*). If a procedure was performed on May 10, YYYY in the office, what is entered in the *TO* block?**

    a. 05 10 YYYY

    b. 0510YYYY

    c. NONE

    d. nothing; leave the block blank

11. **Block 30 contains the balance due amount. What is entered in the block if the patient is owed a credit?**

    a. negative amount in that block

    b. credit amount due the patient

    c. zero balance in the block

    d. leave the block blank

12. **When Block 25 of the CMS-1500 contains the provider's EIN, enter _____ after the first two digits of the EIN.**

    a. a hyphen

    b. a space

    c. no punctuation or space

    d. the provider's SSN

13. **When a patient is covered by the same primary and secondary commercial health insurance plan,**

   a. complete and submit two CMS-1500 claims.

   b. mail the remittance advice to the payer.

   c. send the secondary CMS-1500, but not the primary claim.

   d. submit just one CMS-1500 to the payer.

14. **When entering the patient's name in Block 2 of the CMS-1500 claim, separate the last name, first name, and middle initial (if known) with**

   a. commas

   b. hyphens

   c. parentheses

   d. slashes

15. **Block 33a of the CMS-1500 claim contains the provider's**

   a. EIN.

   b. NPI.

   c. PIN.

   d. SSN.

Blue Cross Blue Shield

CHAPTER OUTLINE

History of Blue Cross Blue Shield

Blue Cross Blue Shield Plans

Billing Notes

Claims Instructions

Blue Cross Blue Shield Secondary Coverage

OBJECTIVES

Upon successful completion of this chapter, you should be able to:

1. Define key terms.
2. Explain the history of Blue Cross and Blue Shield.
3. Differentiate among Blue Cross Blue Shield plans.
4. Apply Blue Cross Blue Shield billing notes when completing CMS-1500 claims.
5. Complete Blue Cross Blue Shield primary and secondary claims.

KEY TERMS

American Hospital Association (AHA)
Away From Home Care® Program
BCBS basic coverage
BCBS major medical (MM) coverage
BlueCard® Program
Blue Cross (BC)
Blue Cross Blue Shield (BCBS)
Blue Shield (BS)
BlueWorldwide *Expat*
coordinated home health and
    hospice care

Federal Employee Health Benefits
    Program (FEHBP)
Federal Employee Program (FEP)
for-profit corporation
Government-Wide Service Benefit Plan
Healthcare Anywhere
indemnity coverage
medical emergency care rider
Medicare supplemental plans
member
member hospital
nonprofit corporation

outpatient pretreatment authorization
    plan (OPAP)
PPN provider
precertification
preferred provider network (PPN)
prepaid health plan
prospective authorization
rider
second surgical opinion (SSO)
service location
special accidental injury rider
usual, customary, and reasonable (UCR)

419

INTRODUCTION

> **NOTE:** Instructions for completing CMS-1500 claims in this chapter are for BCBS fee-for-service claims only.

Blue Cross (BC) and Blue Shield (BS) plans are perhaps the best known medical insurance programs in the United States. They began as two separate *prepaid health plans* selling contracts to individuals or groups for coverage of specified medical expenses as long as the premiums were paid.

Complete StudyWare practice quizzes and activities using the CD-ROM located inside the back cover of your textbook.

HISTORY OF BLUE CROSS BLUE SHIELD

Origin of Blue Cross

The forerunner of what is known today as the Blue Cross (BC) plan began in 1929 when Baylor University Hospital in Dallas, Texas, approached teachers in the Dallas school district with a plan that would guarantee up to 21 days of hospitalization per year for subscribers and each of their dependents, in exchange for a $6 annual premium. This prepaid health plan was accepted by the teachers and worked so well that the concept soon spread across the country. Early plans specified which hospital subscribers and their dependents could use for care. By 1932 some plans modified this concept and organized community-wide programs that allowed the subscriber to be hospitalized in one of several member hospitals, which had signed contracts to provide services for special rates.

The blue cross symbol was first used in 1933 by the St. Paul, Minnesota plan and was adopted in 1939 by the American Hospital Association (AHA) when it became the approving agency for accreditation of new prepaid hospitalization plans. In 1948 the need for additional national coordination among plans arose, and the Blue Cross Association was created. In 1973 the AHA deeded the right to both the name and the use of the blue cross symbol to the Blue Cross Association. At that time the symbol was updated to the trademark in use today.

Origin of Blue Shield

The Blue Shield (BS) plans began as a resolution passed by the House of Delegates at an American Medical Association meeting in 1938. This resolution supported the concept of voluntary health insurance that would encourage physicians to cooperate with prepaid healthcare plans. The first known plan was formed in Palo Alto, California, in 1939 and was called the California Physicians' Service. This plan stipulated that physicians' fees for covered medical services would be paid in full by the plan if the subscriber earned less than $3,000 a year. When the subscriber earned more than $3,000 a year, a small percentage of the physician's fee would be paid by the patient. This patient responsibility for a small percentage of the healthcare fee is the forerunner of today's industry-wide required patient coinsurance or copay.

The blue shield design was first used as a trademark by the Buffalo, New York plan in 1939. The name and symbol were formally adopted by the Associated Medical Care Plans, formed in 1948, as the approving agency for accreditation of new Blue Shield plans adopting programs created in the spirit of the California Physicians' Service program. In 1951 this accrediting organization changed its name to the National Association of Blue Shield Plans. Like the Blue Cross plans, each Blue Shield plan in the association was established as a separate, nonprofit corporate entity that issued its own contracts and plans within a specific geographic area.

Blue Cross Blue Shield Joint Ventures

Blue Cross plans originally covered only hospital bills, and Blue Shield plans covered fees for physician services. Over the years, both programs increased their coverage to include almost all healthcare services. In many areas of the country, there was close cooperation between Blue Cross and Blue Shield plans that resulted in the formation of joint ventures in some states where the two corporations were housed in one building. In these joint ventures, Blue Cross Blue Shield (BCBS) shared one building and computer services but maintained separate corporate identities.

BCBS Association

In 1977 the membership of the separate Blue Cross and Blue Shield national associations voted to combine personnel under the leadership of a single president, responsible to both boards of directors. Further consolidation occurred in 1986 when the boards of directors of the separate national Blue Cross and Blue Shield associations merged into a single corporation named the BlueCross BlueShield Association (BCBSA).

Today, BCBSA consists of more than 450 independent, locally operated Blue Cross and Blue Shield plans that collectively provide healthcare coverage to more than 80 million Americans and serve more than 1 million enrolled in the Medicare+Choice program (discussed in Chapter 14). The BCBSA is located in Chicago, Illinois, and performs the following functions:

- Establishes standards for new plans and programs
- Assists local plans with enrollment activities, national advertising, public education, professional relations, and statistical and research activities
- Serves as the primary contractor for processing Medicare hospital, hospice, and home healthcare claims
- Coordinates nationwide BCBS plans

The association is also the registered owner of the BC and BS trademarks (Figure 13-1).

FIGURE 13-1 Empire BlueCross BlueShield insurance card (Courtesy of Empire BlueCross BlueShield)

The Changing Business Structure

Strong competition among all health insurance companies in the United States emerged during the 1990s and resulted in the following:

- **Mergers occurred among BCBS regional corporations (within a state or with neighboring states) and names no longer had regional designations.**

> **EXAMPLE:** Care First BCBS is the name of the corporation that resulted from a merger between BCBS of Maryland and Washington, D.C. BCBS.

- **BlueCross BlueShield Association no longer required plans to be nonprofit (as of 1994).**

Regional corporations that needed additional capital, to compete with commercial for-profit insurance carriers, petitioned their respective state legislatures to allow conversion from their nonprofit status to for-profit corporations. **Nonprofit corporations** are charitable, educational, civic, or humanitarian organizations whose profits are returned to the program of the corporation rather than distributed to shareholders and officers of the corporation. Because no profits of the organization are distributed to shareholders, the government does not tax the organization's income. **For-profit corporations** pay taxes on profits generated by the corporation's enterprises and pay dividends to shareholders on after-tax profits.

Although some BCBS plans have converted to for-profit companies, state regulators and courts are scrutinizing these transactions, some on a retroactive basis, to ensure that charitable assets are preserved. For example, Empire BCBS in New York State publicly acknowledges its nonprofit obligations and agrees to preserve 100 percent of its assets for nonprofit charitable purposes as part of proposed conversions to for-profit corporations.

BCBS Distinctive Features

The "Blues" were pioneers in nonprofit, prepaid health care, and they possessed features that distinguished them from other commercial health insurance groups.

1. They maintain negotiated contracts with providers of care. In exchange for such contracts, BCBS agrees to perform the following services:

   - **Make prompt, direct payment of claims.**
   - **Maintain regional professional representatives to assist participating providers with claim problems.**
   - **Provide educational seminars, workshops, billing manuals, and newsletters to keep participating providers up-to-date on BCBS insurance procedures.**

NOTE: For-profit commercial plans have the right to cancel a policy at renewal time if the patient moves into a region of the country in which the company is not licensed to sell insurance *or* if the person is a high user of benefits and has purchased a plan that does not include a non-cancellation clause.

2. BCBS plans, in exchange for tax relief for their nonprofit status, are forbidden by state law from canceling coverage for an individual because he or she is in poor health or BCBS payments to providers have far exceeded the average. Policies issued by the nonprofit entity can be canceled, or an individual unenrolled, only:

   - **When premiums are not paid.**
   - **If the plan can prove that fraudulent statements were made on the application for coverage.**

3. BCBS plans must obtain approval from their respective state insurance commissioners for any rate increases and/or benefit changes that affect BCBS members within the state. For-profit commercial plans have more freedom to increase rates and modify general benefits without state approval when the premium is due for annual renewal (if there is no clause restricting such action in the policy).

4. BCBS plans must allow conversion from group to individual coverage and guarantee the transferability of membership from one local plan to another when a change in residency moves a policyholder into an area served by a different BCBS corporation.

> **NOTE:** The insurance claim is submitted to the BC/BS plan in the state where services were rendered. That *local plan* forwards the claim to the *home plan* for adjudication.

Participating Providers

As mentioned earlier, the "Blues" were pioneers in negotiating contracts with providers of care. A *participating provider (PAR)* is a healthcare provider who enters into a contract with a BCBS corporation and agrees to:

- Submit insurance claims for all BCBS subscribers.
- Provide access to the Provider Relations Department, which assists the PAR provider in resolving claims or payment problems.
- Write off (make a fee adjustment for) the difference or balance between the amount charged by the provider and the approved fee established by the insurer.
- Bill patients for only the deductible and copay/coinsurance amounts that are based on BCBS-allowed fees and the full charged fee for any uncovered service.

In return, BCBS corporations agree to:

- Make direct payments to PARs.
- Conduct regular training sessions for PAR billing staff.
- Provide free billing manuals and PAR newsletters.
- Maintain a provider representative department to assist with billing/payment problems.
- Publish the name, address, and specialty of all PARs in a directory distributed to BCBS subscribers and PARs.

Preferred Providers

PARs can also contract to participate in the plan's preferred provider network (PPN), a program that requires providers to adhere to managed care provisions. In this contractual agreement, the PPN provider (a provider who has signed a PPN contract) agrees to accept the PPN allowed rate, which is generally 10 percent lower than the PAR allowed rate. The provider further agrees to abide by all cost-containment, utilization, and quality assurance provisions of the PPN program. In return for a PPN agreement, the "Blues" agree to notify PPN providers in writing of new employer groups and hospitals that have entered into PPN contracts and to maintain a PPN directory.

Nonparticipating Providers

Nonparticipating providers (nonPARs) have not signed participating provider contracts, and they expect to be paid the full fee charged for services rendered. In these cases, the patient may be asked to pay the provider in full and then be reimbursed by BCBS the allowed fee for each service, minus the patient's deductible and copayment obligations. Even when the provider agrees to file the claim for the patient, the insurance company sends the payment for the claim directly to the patient and not to the provider.

BLUE CROSS BLUE SHIELD PLANS

Blue Cross Blue Shield coverage includes the following programs:

- Fee-for-service (traditional coverage).
- Indemnity.
- Managed care plans.
  - Coordinated home health and hospice care
  - Exclusive provider organization (EPO)
  - Health maintenance organization (HMO)
  - Outpatient pretreatment authorization plan (OPAP)
  - Point-of-service (POS) plan
  - Preferred provider organization (PPO)
  - Second surgical opinion (SSO)
- Federal Employee Program (FEP).
- Medicare supplemental plans.
- Healthcare Anywhere.

Fee-for-Service (Traditional Coverage)

BCBS *fee-for-service* or *traditional coverage* is selected by (1) individuals who do not have access to a group plan, and (2) many small business employers. These contracts are divided into two types of coverage within one policy:

- Basic coverage.
- Major medical (MM) benefits.

Minimum benefits under BCBS basic coverage routinely include the following services:

- Hospitalizations.
- Diagnostic laboratory services.
- X-rays.
- Surgical fees.
- Assistant surgeon fees.

- Obstetric care.
- Intensive care.
- Newborn care.
- Chemotherapy for cancer.

BCBS major medical (MM) coverage includes the following services in addition to basic coverage:

- Office visits.
- Outpatient nonsurgical treatment.
- Physical and occupational therapy.
- Purchase of durable medical equipment (DME).
- Mental health visits.
- Allergy testing and injections.

- Prescription drugs.
- Private duty nursing (when medically necessary).
- Dental care required as a result of a covered accidental injury.

Major medical services are usually subject to patient deductible and copayment requirements, and in a few cases the patient may be responsible for filing claims for these benefits.

Some of the contracts also include one or more **riders**, which are special clauses stipulating additional coverage over and above the standard contract. Common riders include special accidental injury and medical emergency care coverage.

The **special accidental injury rider** covers 100 percent of nonsurgical care sought and rendered within 24 to 72 hours (varies according to the policy) of the accidental injury. Surgical care is subject to any established contract basic plan deductible and patient copayment requirements. Outpatient follow-up care for these accidental injuries is not included in the accidental injury rider, but will be covered if the patient has supplemental coverage.

The **medical emergency care rider** covers *immediate treatment sought and received for sudden, severe, and unexpected conditions* that if not treated would place the patient's health in permanent jeopardy or cause permanent impairment or dysfunction of an organ or body part. Chronic or subacute conditions do not qualify for treatment under the medical emergency rider unless the symptoms suddenly become acute and require immediate medical attention. Special attention must be paid to the ICD-9-CM coding (Blocks 21 and 24D) on the CMS-1500 claim to ensure that services rendered under the medical emergency rider are linked to diagnoses or reported symptoms generally accepted as conditions that require immediate care. Nonspecific conditions such as "acute upper respiratory infection" or "bladder infection" would not be included on the medical emergency diagnosis list.

Indemnity Coverage

BCBS **indemnity coverage** offers choice and flexibility to subscribers who want to receive a full range of benefits along with the freedom to use any licensed healthcare provider. Coverage includes hospital-only or comprehensive hospital and medical coverage. Subscribers share the cost of benefits through coinsurance options, do not have to select a primary care provider, and do not need a referral to see a provider.

Managed Care Plans

Managed care is a healthcare delivery system that provides health care and controls costs through a network of physicians, hospitals, and other healthcare providers. BCBS managed care plans include the coordinated home health and hospice care program, exclusive provider organizations, health maintenance organizations, outpatient pretreatment authorization plans, point-of-service plans, preferred provider organizations, and second surgical opinions.

The **coordinated home health and hospice care** program allows patients with this option to elect an alternative to the acute care setting. The patient's physician must file a treatment plan with the case manager assigned to review and coordinate the case. All authorized services must be rendered by personnel from a licensed home health agency or approved hospice facility.

An *exclusive provider organization (EPO)* is similar to a health maintenance organization that provides healthcare services through a network of doctors, hospitals, and other healthcare providers, except that members are not required to select a primary care provider (PCP), and they do not need a referral to see a specialist. However, they must obtain services from EPO providers only or the patient is responsible for the charges. A *primary care provider (PCP)* is a physician or other medical professional who serves as a subscriber's first contact with a plan's healthcare system. The PCP is also known as a *personal care physician* or *personal care provider.*

All BCBS corporations now offer at least one *health maintenance organization (HMO)* plan that assumes or shares the financial and healthcare delivery risks associated with providing comprehensive medical services to subscribers in return for a fixed, prepaid fee. Some plans were for-profit acquisitions; others were developed as separate nonprofit plans. Examples of plan names are *Capital Care* and *Columbia Medical Plan.* Because familiar BCBS names are not always used in the plan name, some HMOs may not be easily recognized as BCBS plans. The BCBS trademarks, however, usually appear on the plan's ID cards and advertisements.

The **outpatient pretreatment authorization plan (OPAP)** requires preauthorization of outpatient physical, occupational, and speech therapy services. In addition, OPAP requires periodic treatment/progress plans to be filed. OPAP is a requirement for the delivery of certain healthcare services and is issued prior to the provision of services. OPAP is also known as **prospective authorization** or **precertification.**

A *point-of-service (POS) plan* allows subscribers to choose, at the time medical services are needed, whether they will go to a provider within the plan's network or outside the network. When subscribers go outside the network to seek care, out-of-pocket expenses and copayments generally increase. POS plans provide a full range of inpatient and outpatient services, and subscribers choose a primary care provider (PCP) from the payer's PCP list. The PCP assumes responsibility for coordinating subscriber and dependent medical care, and the PCP is often referred to as the *gatekeeper* of the patient's medical care. The name and telephone number of the PCP appears on POS plan ID cards, and written referral notices issued by the PCP are usually mailed to the appropriate local processing address following the transmission of an electronic claim. Because the PCP is responsible for authorizing all inpatient hospitalizations, a specialist's office should contact the PCP when hospitalization is necessary and follow up that call with one to the utilization control office at the local BCBS plan office.

> **NOTE:** When subscribers go outside the network for health care, the approval of the PCP is not required, and costs are usually higher.

A *preferred provider organization (PPO)* offers discounted healthcare services to subscribers who use designated healthcare providers (who contract with the PPO) but also provides coverage for services rendered by healthcare providers who are not part of the PPO network. The BCBS PPO plan is sometimes described as a subscriber-driven program, and BCBS substitutes the terms *subscriber* (or **member**) for *policyholder* (used by other commercial carriers). In this type of plan, the subscriber (member) is responsible for remaining within the network of PPO providers and must request referrals to PPO specialists whenever possible. The subscriber must also adhere to the managed care requirements of the PPO policy, such as obtaining required second surgical opinions and/or hospital admission review. Failure to adhere to these requirements will result in denial of the surgical claim or reduced payment to the provider. In such cases, the patient is responsible for the difference or balance between the reduced payment and the normal PPO allowed rate.

The mandatory **second surgical opinion (SSO)** requirement is necessary when a patient is considering elective, nonemergency surgical care. The initial surgical recommendation must be made by a physician qualified to perform the anticipated surgery. If a second surgical opinion is not obtained prior to surgery, the patient's out-of-pocket expenses may be greatly increased. The patient or surgeon should contact the subscriber's BCBS local plan for instructions. In some cases, the second opinion must be obtained from a member of a select surgical panel. In other cases, the concurrence of the need for surgery from the patient's PCP may suffice.

Federal Employee Program

The Federal Employee Health Benefits Program (FEHBP) (or Federal Employee Program, FEP) is an employer-sponsored health benefits program established by an Act of Congress in 1959. The FEP began covering federal employees on July 1, 1960, and now provides benefits to more than 9 million federal enrollees and dependents through contracts with about 300 insurance carriers. FEP is underwritten and administered by participating insurance plans (e.g., Blue Cross and Blue Shield plans) that are called *local plans.* Claims are submitted to local plans that serve the location where the patient was seen (called a service location), regardless of the member's FEP plan affiliation.

FEP cards contain the phrase Government-Wide Service Benefit Plan under the BCBS trademark. FEP enrollees have identification numbers that begin with the letter "R" followed by eight numeric digits (Figure 13-2). All ID cards contain the name of the government employee. Dependents' names do *not* appear on the card. A three-digit enrollment code is located on the front of the card to specify the option(s) elected when the government employee enrolled in the program. This code should be entered as the group ID number on BCBS claims.

The four enrollment options are:

- 101—Individual, High Option Plan.
- 102—Family, High Option Plan.
- 104—Individual Standard (Low) Option Plan.
- 105—Family Standard (Low) Option Plan.

The FEP is considered a managed fee-for-service program and has generally operated as a PPO plan. The patient is responsible for ensuring that precertification is obtained for all hospitalizations except routine maternity care, home health and hospice care, and emergency hospitalization within 48 hours of admission. In 1997, a POS product was introduced in specific geographic sections of the country, and gradual expansion to a nationwide POS program

NOTE: The federal government's Office of Personnel Management (OPM) oversees administration of the FEHBP, and BCBS is just one of several payers who reimburse healthcare services. Others include the Alliance Health Plan (AHP), American Postal Workers Union (APWU) Health Plan, Government Employee Hospital Association (GEHA), Mail Handlers Benefit Plan (MHBP), National Association of Letter Carriers (NALC), and People Before Profit (PBP) Health Plan sponsored by the National League of Postmasters.

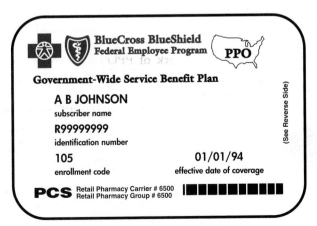

FIGURE 13-2 BCBS FEP PPO plan ID card (Courtesy of BlueCross BlueShield Association)

was implemented. The federal POS program requires that the subscriber select a PCP. This plan offers enhanced benefits and reduced out-of-pocket expenses when PCP referrals are obtained for specialty care.

Medicare Supplemental Plans

BCBS corporations offer several federally designed and regulated Medicare supplemental plans (described in Chapter 14), which augment the Medicare program by paying for Medicare deductibles and copayments. These plans are better known throughout the industry as *Medigap Plans* and are usually identified by the word *Medigap* on the patient's plan ID card.

Healthcare Anywhere

Suitcase logo for BlueCard® program

Healthcare Anywhere coverage allows "members of the independently owned and operated BCBS plans [to] have access to healthcare benefits throughout the United States and around the world, depending on their home plan benefits. Generally, the BlueCard® Program enables such members obtaining healthcare services while traveling or living in another BCBS Plan's service area to receive the benefits of their home Plan contract and to access local provider networks. As instructed by their home BCBS Plan, members call the phone number on their Plan ID card to arrange for pre-certification or prior authorization number, if necessary. Member identification cards (Figure 13-3) displaying a (suitcase) logo indicate that the BlueCard® Program is available to the member. The Away From Home Care® Program allows the participating BCBS Plan members who are temporarily residing outside of their home HMO service area for at least 90 days to temporarily enroll with a local HMO. Such members usually include dependent students attending school out-of-state, family members who reside in different HMO service areas, long-term travelers whose work assignment is in another state, and retirees with a dual residence." (BlueCard, Away From Home Care, and the PPO suitcase are registered marks of the BlueCross BlueShield Association and are used with permission.) BlueWorldwide *Expat* provides global medical coverage for active employees and their dependents who spend more than six months outside the United States. Any U.S. corporation, with new or existing Blue coverage, that sends members to work and reside outside the United States for six months or more is eligible for BlueWorldwide *Expat*.

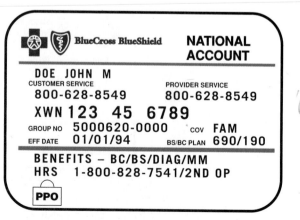

FIGURE 13-3 BCBS National Account PPO ID (Courtesy of BlueCross BlueShield Association)

BILLING NOTES

A summary follows of nationwide billing issues for traditional BCBS fee-for-service claims. PAR providers are required to submit claims for subscribers.

Claims Processing

BCBS plans process their own claims.

Deadline for Filing Claims

The deadline is customarily one year from the date of service, unless otherwise specified in the subscriber's or provider's contracts.

Forms Used

Most BCBS payers currently accept the CMS-1500 claim.

Inpatient and Outpatient Coverage

Inpatient and outpatient coverage may vary according to the plan. Many plans require second surgical opinions and prior authorization for elective hospitalizations. Information on the individual program requirements can be obtained from your BCBS payer(s).

Deductible

The deductible will vary according to the BCBS plan. Consult the BCBS billing manual or eligibility status computerized phone bank for specific patient requirements. Patients enrolled in PPO plans may have no applicable deductibles for certain preventive medicine services.

Copayment/Coinsurance

Patient copayment/coinsurance requirements vary according to the patient plan. The most common coinsurance amounts are 20 percent or 25 percent, although they may be as high as 50 percent for mental health services on some policies.

Allowable Fee Determination

The allowable fee varies according to the program. Many corporations have begun to use the physician fee schedule to determine the allowed fees for each procedure. Other plans use a usual, customary, and reasonable (UCR) basis, which is the amount commonly charged for a particular medical service by providers within a particular geographic region for establishing their allowable rates. Participating providers must accept the allowable rate on all covered services and write off or adjust the difference or balance between the plan determined allowed amount and the amount billed. Patients are responsible for any deductible and copay/coinsurance described in the policy, as well as full charges for uncovered services.

The remittance advice sent to PAR and PPN providers clearly states the patient's total deductible and copayment/coinsurance responsibility for each claim submission.

EXERCISE 13-1

Completing the Mary S. Patient BCBS CMS-1500 Claim

1. Review the Mary S. Patient case study (Figure 13-6).

2. Obtain a blank claim by making a copy of the claim in Appendix III.

3. Select the information needed from the case study (Figure 13-6) and enter the required information on the claim using optical scanning guidelines.

4. Review the completed claim to be sure all required blocks are completed accurately.

5. Compare your claim with the completed Mary S. Patient claim (Figure 13-7).

ERIN A. HELPER, M.D.
101 Medic Drive, Anywhere NY 12345
(101) 111-1234 (Office) • (101) 111-9292 (Fax)
EIN: 11-1234523
NPI: 1234567890

Case Study

PATIENT INFORMATION:

Name:	Patient, Mary S.
Address:	91 Home Street
City:	Nowhere
State:	NY
Zip Code:	12367-1234
Telephone:	(101) 201-8989
Gender:	Female
Date of Birth:	10-10-1959
Occupation:	Manager
Employer:	Happy Farm Day Care

INSURANCE INFORMATION:

Patient Number:	13-2
Place of Service:	Office
Primary Insurance Plan:	BCBS
Primary Insurance Plan ID #:	WWW1023456
Primary Policyholder:	Mary S. Patient
Policyholder Date of Birth:	10-10-1959
Relationship to Patient:	Self
Secondary Insurance Plan:	
Secondary Insurance Plan ID #:	
Secondary Policyholder:	

Patient Status   ☒ Married   ☐ Divorced   ☐ Single   ☐ Student

---

ICD-10-CM ALERT!

Strep throat	J03.00
Type I diabetes mellitus	E10.9

DIAGNOSIS INFORMATION

Diagnosis	Code	Diagnosis	Code
1. Strep throat	034.0	5.	
2. Type 1 diabetes mellitus	250.01	6.	
3.		7.	
4.		8.	

PROCEDURE INFORMATION

Description of Procedure or Service	Date	Code	Charge
1. Office visit, level II, established patient	01-12-YYYY	99212	65.00
2. Strep test	01-12-YYYY	87880	12.00
3.			
4.			
5.			

SPECIAL NOTES:

FIGURE 13-6 Mary Sue Patient case study (Courtesy Delmar/Cengage Learning)

TABLE 13-3   Modifications to BCBS secondary CMS-1500 claims completion instructions when patient is covered by BCBS secondary or supplemental plan (and primary payer is *not* BCBS)

BLOCK	INSTRUCTIONS
	NOTE: If the primary and secondary/supplemental payers are the same, do not generate a second CMS-1500 claim. Refer to Table 13-2 instructions.
1a	Enter the secondary or supplemental policyholder's BCBS identification number as it appears on the insurance card. *Do not enter hyphens or spaces in the number.*
4	Enter the secondary or supplemental policyholder's last name, first name, and middle initial (if known) (separated by commas).
7	Enter the secondary or supplemental policyholder's mailing address and telephone number. Enter the street address on line 1, enter the city and state on line 2, and enter the 5- or 9-digit zip code and phone number on line 3.
9	Enter the primary policyholder's last name, first name, and middle initial (if known) (separated by commas).
9a	Enter the primary policyholder's policy or group number. *Do not enter hyphens or spaces in the number.*
9b	Enter the primary policyholder's birth date as MM DD YYYY (with spaces). Enter an X in the appropriate box to indicate the primary policyholder's gender.
9c	Enter the name of the primary policyholder's employer (if employed) or school (if unemployed and considered a full- or part-time student). Otherwise, leave blank.
9d	Enter the name of the primary policyholder's health insurance plan (e.g., commercial health insurance plan name or government program).
11	Enter the secondary or supplemental policyholder's policy or group number. *Do not enter hyphens or spaces in the policy or group number.*
11a	Enter the secondary or supplemental policyholder's birth date as MM DD YYYY (with spaces). Enter an X in the appropriate box to indicate the policyholder's gender. If the policyholder's gender is unknown, leave blank.
11b	Enter the name of the secondary or supplemental policyholder's employer (if employed) or school (if unemployed and considered a full- or part-time student). Otherwise, leave blank.
11c	Enter the name of the secondary or supplemental policyholder's BCBS health insurance plan.
11d	Enter an X in the YES box.
26	Add an S to the patient account number in to indicate the secondary policy.
29	Enter reimbursement amount received from primary payer.
30	Enter the total amount due (by subtracting the amount entered in Block 29 from the amount entered in Block 28). *Do not report negative amounts or a credit due to the patient.*

Additional BCBS claim case studies are found in Appendix I and Appendix II.

ERIN A. HELPER, M.D.
101 Medic Drive, Anywhere NY 12345
(101) 111-1234 (Office) • (101) 111-9292 (Fax)
EIN: 11-1234523
NPI: 1234567890

Case Study

NOTE: Janet B. Cross is retired, and her primary health insurance plan is Medicare. Her secondary insurance plan is Blue Cross Blue Shield plan, which is provided by her former employer as a retirement benefit.

PATIENT INFORMATION:

Name:	Cross, Janet B.
Address:	1901 Beach Head Drive
City:	Anywhere
State:	NY
Zip Code:	12345-1234
Telephone:	(101) 201-1991
Gender:	Female
Date of Birth:	11-01-1934
Occupation:	Retired
Employer:	

INSURANCE INFORMATION:

Patient Number:	13-3
Place of Service:	Hospital Inpatient
Primary Insurance Plan:	Medicare
Primary Insurance Plan ID #:	191266844A
Policy #:	
Primary Policyholder:	Cross, Janet B.
Policyholder Date of Birth:	11-01-1934
Relationship to Patient:	Self
Secondary Insurance Plan:	BCBS
Secondary Insurance Plan ID #:	WWW191266844
Secondary Policyholder:	Cross, Janet B.
Relationship to Patient:	Self

Patient Status   ☒ Married   ☐ Divorced   ☐ Single   ☐ Student

DIAGNOSIS INFORMATION

	Diagnosis	Code		Diagnosis	Code
1.	Intracranial hemorrhage	432.9	5.		
2.	Dysphasia	784.59	6.		
3.			7.		
4.			8.		

ICD-10-CM ALERT!

Intracranial hemorrhage	I62.9
Dysphasia	R47.02

PROCEDURE INFORMATION

	Description of Procedure or Service	Date	Code	Charge
1.	Initial hospital visit, level III	01-13-YYYY	99223	150.00
2.	Discharge management, 60 minutes	01-14-YYYY	99239	100.00
3.				
4.				
5.				

SPECIAL NOTES: Patient transferred to University Medical Center via ambulance. Place of service: Goodmedicine Hospital, Anywhere Street, Anywhere NY 12345 (NPI: 2345678901)

FIGURE 13-9 Janet B. Cross case study (Courtesy Delmar/Cengage Learning)

1500

HEALTH INSURANCE CLAIM FORM REMITTANCE ADVICE ATTACHED

APPROVED BY NATIONAL UNIFORM CLAIM COMMITTE 08/05

| | PICA | | | | | | | | | | PICA | |

| 1. MEDICARE (Medicare #) | MEDICAID (Medicaid #) | TRICARE CHAMPUS (Sponsor's SSN) | CHAMPVA (Member ID#) | GROUP HEALTH PLAN (SSN or ID) | FECA BLK LUNG (SSN) | OTHER X (ID) | 1a. INSURED'S I.D. NUMBER (For Program in Item 1) WWW191266844 |

2. PATIENT'S NAME (Last Name, First Name, Middle Initial)
CROSS, JANET, B

3. PATIENT'S BIRTH DATE
MM 11 DD 01 YY 1934 M F X SEX

4. INSURED'S NAME (Last Name, First Name, Middle Initial)
CROSS, JANET, B

5. PATIENT'S ADDRESS (No., Street)
1901 BEACH HEAD DRIVE

6. PATIENT'S RELATIONSHIP TO INSURED
Self X Spouse Child Other

7. INSURED'S ADDRESS (No., Street)
1901 BEACH HEAD DRIVE

CITY ANYWHERE STATE NY

8. PATIENT STATUS
Single Married X Other
Employed Full-Time Student Part-Time Student

CITY ANYWHERE STATE NY

ZIP CODE 12345-1234 TELEPHONE (Include Area Code) (101)2011991

ZIP CODE 12345-1234 TELEPHONE (Include Area Code) (101)2011991

9. OTHER INSURED'S NAME (Last Name, First Name, Middle Initial)
CROSS, JANET, B

10. IS PATIENT'S CONDITION RELATED TO:

11. INSURED'S POLICY GROUP OR FECA NUMBER

a. OTHER INSURED'S POLICY OR GROUP NUMBER
191266844A

a. EMPLOYMENT? (Current or Previous)
YES X NO

a. INSURED'S DATE OF BIRTH
MM 11 DD 01 YY 1934 M F X SEX

b. OTHER INSURED'S DATE OF BIRTH
MM 11 DD 01 YY 1934 M F X SEX

b. AUTO ACCIDENT? PLACE (State)
YES X NO

b. EMPLOYER'S NAME OR SCHOOL NAME

c. EMPLOYER'S NAME OR SCHOOL NAME

c. OTHER ACCIDENT?
YES X NO

c. INSURANCE PLAN NAME OR PROGRAM NAME
BCBS

d. INSURANCE PLAN NAME OR PROGRAM NAME
MEDICARE

10d. RESERVED FOR LOCAL USE

d. IS THERE ANOTHER HEALTH BENEFIT PLAN?
X YES NO *If yes,* return to and complete item 9 a-d.

READ BACK OF FORM BEFORE COMPLETING & SIGNING THIS FORM.

12. PATIENT'S OR AUTHORIZED PERSON'S SIGNATURE I authorize the release of any medical or other information necessary to process this claim. I also request payment of government benefits either to myself or to the party who accepts assignment below.

SIGNED SIGNATURE ON FILE DATE

13. INSURED'S OR AUTHORIZED PERSON'S SIGNATURE I authorize payment of medical benefits to the undersigned physican or supplier for services described below.

SIGNED

14. DATE OF CURRENT: ILLNESS (First symptom) OR INJURY (Accident) OR PREGNANCY (LMP)
MM 01 DD 13 YY YYYY

15. IF PATIENT HAS HAD SAME OR SIMILAR ILLNESS, GIVE FIRST DATE MM DD YY

16. DATES PATIENT UNABLE TO WORK IN CURRENT OCCUPATION
MM DD YY FROM TO MM DD YY

17. NAME OF REFERRING PROVIDER OR OTHER SOURCE

17a.
17b. NPI

18. HOSPITALIZATION DATES RELATED TO CURRENT SERVICES
MM DD YY FROM 01 13 YYYY TO 01 14 YYYY

19. RESERVED FOR LOCAL USE

20. OUTSIDE LAB?
YES X NO $ CHARGES

21. DIAGNOSIS OR NATURE OF ILLNESS OR INJURY (Relate Items 1, 2, 3 or 4 to Item 24E by Line)
1. 432 . 9
2. 784 . 5
3.
4.

22. MEDICAID RESUBMISSION CODE ORIGINAL REF. NO.

23. PRIOR AUTHORIZATION NUMBER

24. A DATE(S) OF SERVICE From MM DD YY To MM DD YY	B. PLACE OF SERVICE	C. EMG	D. PROCEDURES, SERVICES, OR SUPPLIES (Explain Unusual Circumstances) CPT/HCPCS MODIFER	E. DIAGNOSIS POINTER	F. $ CHARGES	G. DAYS OR UNITS	H. EPSDT Family Plan	I. ID. QUAL.	J. RENDERING PROVIDER ID. #
1	01 13 YYYY	21		99223	2	150 00	1		NPI
2	01 14 YYYY	21		99239	1	100 00	1		NPI
3									NPI
4									NPI
5									NPI
6									NPI

25. FEDERAL TAX I.D. NUMBER SSN EIN
111234523 X

26. PATIENT'S ACCOUNT NO.
13-3S

27. ACCEPT ASSIGNMENT? (For govt. claims, see back)
X YES NO

28. TOTAL CHARGE
$ 250 00

29. AMOUNT PAID
$

30. BALANCE DUE
$

31. SIGNATURE OF PHYSICIAN OR SUPPLIER INCLUDING DEGREES OR CREDENTIALS (I certify that the statements on the reverse apply to this bill and are made a part thereof.)
ERIN A HELPER MD
SIGNED DATE MMDDYYYY

32. SERVICE FACILITY LOCATION INFORMATION
GOODMEDICINE HOSPITAL
ANYWHERE STREET
ANYWHERE NY 12345
a. 2345678901 b.

33. BILLING PROVIDER INFO & PH # (101)1111234
ERIN A HELPER MD
101 MEDIC DRIVE
ANYWHERE NY 12345
a. 1234567890 b.

NUCC Instruction Manual available at: www.nucc.org   APPROVED OMB-0938-0999 FORM CMS-1500 (08/05)

FIGURE 13-10 Completed Janet B. Cross secondary payer claim (Courtesy Delmar/Cengage Learning)

ICD-10-CM ALERT!

21. DIAGNOSIS OR NATURE OF ILLNESS OR INJURY (Relate Items 1, 2, 3 or 4 to Item 24E by Line)
1. I62 . 9
2. R47 . 02
3.
4.

E. DIAGNOSIS POINTER

SUMMARY

Blue Cross plans were initiated in 1929 and originally provided coverage for hospital bills, while Blue Shield was created in 1938 and originally covered fees for physician services. Blue Cross and Blue Shield (BCBS) plans entered into joint ventures that increased coverage of almost all healthcare services, and the BlueCross BlueShield Association (BCBSA) was created in 1986 when the separate Blue Cross association merged with the Blue Shield association. The BCBS plans were pioneers in nonprofit, prepaid health care; and competition among all health insurance payers in the United States resulted in further mergers. BCBS negotiates contracts with providers who are designated *participating providers (PARs)*. PARs are eligible to contract with preferred provider networks, and they qualify for assignment of benefits.

Nonparticipating providers do not sign such contracts, and they expect to be reimbursed the complete fee. They collect payment from the patient, and the patient receives reimbursement from BCBS. BCBS plans include fee-for-service, indemnity, managed care, Federal Employee Program, Medicare supplemental, and Healthcare Anywhere plans.

When completing BCBS CMS-1500 claims for case studies in this text and the Workbook, the following special instructions apply:

- Block 12—Enter SIGNATURE ON FILE, and leave date blank
- Block 19—Leave blank
- Block 20—Enter an X in the *NO* box
- Block 23—Leave blank
- Block 26—Enter the case study number (e.g., 13-4). If the patient has both primary and secondary coverage, enter a P (for primary) next to the case study number (on the primary claim) (e.g., 13-3P) and an S (for secondary) next to the number (on the secondary claim) (e.g., 13-3S); if the same BCBS plan provides both primary and secondary coverage, enter a BB next to the case study number (e.g., 13-2BB)
- Block 27—Enter an X in the *YES* box
- When completing secondary claims, enter REMITTANCE ADVICE ATTACHED in the top margin of the CMS-1500 claim (to simulate the attachment of a primary payer's remittance advice with a claim submitted to a secondary payer)

INTERNET LINKS

- BCBS Federal Employee Program
  www.fepblue.org
- BlueCross BlueShield Association
  www.bcbsa.com

STUDY CHECKLIST

- ☐ Read this textbook chapter and highlight key concepts.
- ☐ Access SimClaim software at the online companion, and become familiar with the software.
- ☐ Complete CMS-1500 claims for each chapter case study.
- ☐ Complete the chapter review, verifying answers with your instructor.
- ☐ Complete the chapter CD-ROM activities.
- ☐ Complete WebTutor assignments, and take online quizzes.
- ☐ Complete BCBS claims for case studies located in Appendices I and II.
- ☐ Complete the Workbook chapter, verifying answers with your instructor.
- ☐ Complete the StudyWare activities to receive immediate feedback.
- ☐ Form a study group with classmates to discuss chapter concepts in preparation for an exam.

MULTIPLE CHOICE Select the most appropriate response.

1. **One of the requirements that a participating provider must comply with is to**
   a. maintain a provider representative department to assist with billing and payment problems for submitted claims.
   b. make fee adjustments for the difference between amounts charged to patients for services provided and payer-approved fees.
   c. purchase billing manuals and newsletters published by the payer, and pay registration fees to attend payer training sessions.
   d. write off deductible and copay/coinsurance amounts, and accept as payment in full the BCBS-allowed fees.

2. **Which is a program that requires providers to adhere to managed care provisions?**
   a. fee-for-service
   b. indemnity
   c. preferred provider network
   d. traditional coverage

3. **One of the expectations that a nonparticipating provider has is to _____ for services rendered.**
   a. file the CMS-1500 claim on behalf of the patient
   b. obtain payment for the full fee charged
   c. receive reimbursement directly from the payer
   d. waive patient deductibles and copay/coinsurance

4. **Which is considered a minimum benefit under BCBS basic coverage?**
   a. hospitalizations
   b. office visits
   c. physical therapy
   d. prescription drugs

5. **Which is considered a service reimbursed by BCBS major medical coverage?**
   a. assistant surgeon fees
   b. chemotherapy for cancer
   c. diagnostic laboratory services
   d. mental health visits

6. **Which is a special clause in an insurance contract that stipulates additional coverage over and above the standard contract?**
   a. coinsurance
   b. copayment
   c. deductible
   d. rider

7. **BCBS indemnity coverage is characterized by certain limitations, including**
   a. hospital-only or comprehensive hospital and medical coverage.
   b. the requirement that patients identify and select a primary care provider.
   c. provision of care by participating licensed healthcare providers.
   d. the requirement that patients obtain a referral before seeing a provider.

8. **Prospective authorization or precertification is a requirement of the _____ BCBS managed care plan.**

    a. coordinated home health and hospice care

    b. outpatient pretreatment authorization

    c. second surgical opinion

    d. point-of-service

9. **Which phrase is located on a Federal Employee Program plan ID card?**

    a. enrollment option, such as *Family, High Option Plan*

    b. *Government-Wide Service Benefit Plan*

    c. *Office of Personnel Management*

    d. *Preferred Provider Organization*

10. **The plan ID card for a subscriber who opts for BCBS's Healthcare Anywhere PPO coverage uniquely contains the _____ logo.**

    a. dental

    b. eyeglass

    c. prescription drug

    d. suitcase

Medicare

CHAPTER OUTLINE

OBJECTIVES

Upon successful completion of this chapter, you should be able to:

1. Define key terms.
2. Explain Medicare eligibility guidelines.
3. Describe the Medicare enrollment process.
4. Differentiate among Medicare Part A, Part B, Part C, and Part D coverage.
5. Define other Medicare health plans, employer and union health plans, Medigap, and private contracting.
6. Calculate Medicare reimbursement amounts for participating and nonparticipating providers.

447

7. Determine when a Medicare surgical disclosure notice and an advance beneficiary notice are required.

8. Explain the Medicare mandatory claims submission process.

9. List and explain Medicare's experimental and investigational procedures.

10. Differentiate between Medicare as primary payer and Medicare as secondary payer.

11. Interpret a Medicare Summary Notice.

12. Apply Medicare billing notes when completing CMS-1500 claims.

13. Complete Medicare primary, Medigap, Medicare/Medicaid (Medi-Medi) crossover, secondary, and roster billing claims.

KEY TERMS

advance beneficiary notice (ABN)

benefit period

conditional primary payer status

coordinated care plan

demonstration/pilot program

general enrollment period (GEP)

hospice

initial enrollment period (IEP)

lifetime reserve days

medical necessity denial

Medicare Advantage (Medicare Part C)

Medicare Cost Plan

Medicare fee-for-service plan

Medicare Hospital Insurance (Medicare Part A)

Medicare Medical Insurance (Medicare Part B)

Medicare Part A

Medicare Part B

Medicare Part C

Medicare Part D

Medicare Prescription Drug Plans (Medicare Part D)

Medicare private contract

Medicare SELECT

Medicare special needs plans

Medicare Supplementary Insurance (MSI)

Medicare-Medicaid (Medi-Medi) crossover

original Medicare plan

private fee-for-service (PFFS)

Program of All-Inclusive Care for the Elderly (PACE)

qualified disabled working individual (QDWI)

qualified Medicare beneficiary program (QMBP)

qualifying individual (QI)

respite care

roster billing

special enrollment period (SEP)

specified low-income Medicare beneficiary (SLMB)

spell of illness

INTRODUCTION

Medicare, the largest single medical benefits program in the United States, is a federal program authorized by Congress and administered by the Centers for Medicare and Medicaid Services (CMS, formerly HCFA). CMS is responsible for the operation of the Medicare program and for selecting Medicare administrative contractors (MACs) to process Medicare fee-for-service Part A, Part B, and durable medicine equipment (DME) claims. Medicare is a two-part program:

- **Medicare Part A** reimburses institutional providers for inpatient, hospice, and some home health services.

- **Medicare Part B** reimburses institutional providers for outpatient services and physicians for inpatient and office services.

The Medicare program includes the following:

- **Medicare Hospital Insurance (Medicare Part A)** pays for inpatient hospital critical care access; skilled nursing facility stays; hospice care; and some home health care. (Submit UB-04 [CMS-1450] claim for services.)

- **Medicare Medical Insurance (Medicare Part B)** pays for doctors' services; outpatient hospital care; durable medical equipment; and some medical services that are not covered by Part A. (Submit CMS-1500 claim for services.)

- **Medicare Advantage (Medicare Part C)**, formerly called Medicare+Choice, includes managed care and private fee-for-service plans that provided contracted care to Medicare patients. Medicare Advantage is an alternative to the original Medicare plan reimbursed under Medicare Part A. (Submit CMS-1500 or UB-04, depending on type of services provided.)

- **Medicare Prescription Drug Plans (Medicare Part D)** add prescription drug coverage to the Original Medicare Plan, some Medicare Cost Plans, some Medicare Private Fee-for-Service Plans and Medicare Medical Savings Account Plans. (Medicare beneficiaries present a Medicare prescription drug discount card to pharmacies.)

Medicare beneficiaries can also obtain supplemental insurance, called *Medigap*, which helps cover costs not reimbursed by the original Medicare plan. Depending on the region of the country, more than one Medicare health plan may be available to enrollees.

The billing instructions in this chapter cover Medicare Part B services only. Medicare Part A claims are not filed by insurance specialists working in healthcare provider offices; the UB-04 is filed by hospitals, hospices, and home healthcare providers.

Complete StudyWare practice quizzes and activities using the CD-ROM located inside the back cover of your textbook.

MEDICARE ELIGIBILITY

General Medicare eligibility requires:

1. Individuals or their spouses to have worked at least 10 years in Medicare-covered employment.

2. Individuals to be the minimum of 65 years old.

3. Individuals to be citizens or permanent residents of the United States.

Individuals can also qualify for coverage if they are younger than 65 *and have* a disability or End-Stage Renal Disease. The *Social Security Administration (SSA)* (an agency of the federal government) bases its definition of *disability* on an individual's ability to work; an individual can be considered disabled if unable to do work as before and if it is determined that adjustments cannot be made to do other work because of a medical condition(s). In addition, the disability must last or be expected to last a year or to result in death. There is no premium for Part A if individuals meet one of these conditions; however, they do pay for Part B coverage. The Part B monthly premium changes annually and is deducted from Social Security, Railroad Retirement, or Civil Service Retirement checks.

Medicare Part A coverage is available to individuals *age 65 and over* who:

- Are already receiving retirement benefits from Social Security or the Railroad Retirement Board (RRB).
- Are eligible to receive Social Security or Railroad benefits but have not yet filed for them.
- Had Medicare-covered government employment.

Medicare Part A coverage is available to individuals *under age 65* who have:

- Received Social Security or RRB disability benefits for 24 months.
- End-Stage Renal Disease and meet certain requirements.

Provider Telephone Inquiries for Medicare Eligibility Information

The standard method for providers to obtain Medicare eligibility information is through electronic data interchange (EDI). EDI is the most efficient and cost-effective way to make eligibility information available because provider agreements ensure privacy safeguards. Instructions regarding provider EDI access to limited eligibility information can be found in Chapter 3 (Provider Inquiries) of the *Medicare Contractor Beneficiary and Provider Communications Manual*.

date of birth

Eligibility information is also available over the telephone, subject to conditions intended to ensure the protection of the beneficiary's privacy rights. The eligibility information that can be released by telephone is limited to *that information available via EDI.*

The provider's name and identification number must be verified and the following information obtained about each beneficiary:

> **NOTE:** The Privacy Act of 1974 prohibits release of information unless all the listed required information is accurately provided.

- **Last name and first initial**
- **Date of birth**
- **HICN (health insurance claim number)**
- **Gender**

MEDICARE ENROLLMENT

Medicare enrollment is handled in two ways: either individuals are enrolled automatically, or they apply for coverage. Individuals age 65 and over do not pay a monthly premium for Medicare Part A *if they or a spouse paid Medicare taxes while they were working.* Individuals age 65 and over and who do not pay Medicare taxes "buy in" to Medicare Part A by paying monthly premiums. The Medicare Part A buy-in premiums for 2010 are:

- **$461/month (less than 30 quarters of Medicare covered employment).**
- **$254/month (greater than 30 quarters of Medicare covered employment).**

Medicare Part B premiums are based on the modified adjusted gross income reported on an individual or joint tax return (Table 14-1).

Automatic Enrollment

Individuals not yet age 65 who already receive Social Security, Railroad Retirement Board, or disability benefits are automatically enrolled in Part A and Part B effective the month of their 65th birthday. About three months before the 65th birthday, or the 24th month of disability, individuals are sent an initial enrollment package that contains information about Medicare, a ques-

TABLE 14-1   Medicare Part B monthly premiums based on annual income (2010)

INDIVIDUAL TAX RETURN (SINGLE)	JOINT TAX RETURN (MARRIED)	INDIVIDUAL TAX RETURN (MARRIED)	MONTHLY PREMIUM
$85,000 or less	$170,000 or less	$85,000 or less	$110.50
$85,000-$107,000	$170,000 - $214,000	Not Applicable	$154.70
$107,000-$160,000	$214,000-$320,000	Not Applicable	$221.00
$160,000-$214,000	$320,000-$428,000	$85,000-$129,000	$287.30
Greater than $214,000	Greater than $428,000	Greater than $129,000	$353.60

tionnaire, and a Medicare card. If the individual wants both Medicare Part A (hospital insurance) and Part B (supplemental medical insurance), he or she just signs the Medicare card and keeps it in a safe place.

Individuals who do not want Part B coverage (because there is a monthly premium associated with it) must follow the instructions that accompany the Medicare card; these instructions direct the individual to mark an "X" in the refusal box on the back of the Medicare card form, sign the form, and return it *with* the Medicare card to the address indicated. The individual is then sent a new Medicare card showing coverage for Part A only.

Applying for Medicare

Individuals who do not receive Social Security, Railroad Retirement Board, or disability benefits must apply for Medicare Part A and Part B by contacting the Social Security Administration (or Railroad Retirement Board) approximately three months before the month in which they turn 65 or the 24th month of disability. Upon applying for Medicare Part A and Part B, a seven-month **initial enrollment period (IEP)** begins that provides an opportunity for the individual to enroll in Medicare Part A and/or Part B. Those who wait until they actually turn 65 to apply for Medicare will cause a delay in the start of Part B coverage, because they will have to wait until the next **general enrollment period (GEP)**, which is held January 1 through March 31 of each year; Part B coverage starts on July 1 of that year. The Part B premium is also increased by 10 percent for each 12-month period during which an individual was eligible for Part B coverage but did not participate.

Under certain circumstances, individuals can delay Part B enrollment without having to pay higher premiums.

- **Individuals age 65 or older who are working, or whose spouse is working, and who have group health insurance through the employer or union.**
- **Disabled individuals who are working and who have group health insurance or who have group health insurance coverage from a working family member.**

If Part B enrollment is delayed for one of these reasons, individuals can enroll anytime during the **special enrollment period (SEP)**, a set time when they can sign up for Medicare Part B, if they did not enroll in Part B during the initial enrollment period. For individuals who enroll in Medicare Part B while covered by a group health plan or during the first full month after group health plan coverage ends, coverage starts on the first day of the month of enrollment. Individuals can also delay the start date for Medicare Part B coverage until the first day of any of the subsequent three months. If the individual enrolls during any of the seven remaining months of the special enrollment period, coverage begins the month after enrollment. If an individual does not enroll during the special enrollment period, they must wait until the next general enrollment period (January 1 through March 31 of each year), and they may be required to pay a higher Medicare Part B premium.

Dual Eligible Medicare Beneficiary Groups

Medicare Savings Programs help people with low income and asset levels pay for healthcare coverage, and certain income and asset limits must be met to qualify for the following programs (Table 14-2):

- **Qualified Medicare beneficiary program (QMBP)** **(helps individuals whose assets are not low enough to qualify them for Medicaid by requiring states to pay their Medicare Part A and B premiums, deductibles, and coinsurance amounts)**

TABLE 14-2   Dual eligible Medicare beneficiary groups

MONTHLY INCOME LIMIT (2010)*		NAME OF PROGRAM	PROGRAM WILL PAY:
$923	Individual (or)	Qualified Medicare Beneficiary	Medicare Part A and Part B premiums, deductibles,
$1235	Couple	(QMB)	and coinsurance
$1103	Individual (or)	Specified Low-income Medicare	Medicare Part B premiums
$1477	Couple	Beneficiary (SLMB)	
$1239	Individual (or)	Qualifying Individual (QI)	Medicare Part B premiums
$1660	Couple		
$3695	Individual (or)	Qualified Disabled Working	Medicare Part A premiums
$4942	Couple	(QDWI)	

*Alaska and Hawaii income limits are slightly higher, and all income limits will increase slightly next year.

- Specified low-income Medicare beneficiary (SLMB) (helps low-income individuals by requiring states to pay their Medicare Part B premiums)
- Qualifying individual (QI) (helps low-income individuals by requiring states to pay their Medicare Part B premiums)
- Qualified disabled working individual (QDWI) (helps individuals who received Social Security and Medicare because of disability, but who lost their Social Security benefits and free Medicare Part A because they returned to work and their earnings exceed the limit allowed, by requiring states to pay their Medicare Part A premiums)

The asset limits are the same for all programs. Personal assets (e.g., cash, money in the bank, stocks, bonds, and so on) cannot exceed $4,000 for an individual or $6,000 for married couples. Exclusions include a home, household goods and personal belongings, one car, a life insurance policy up to a cash value of $1,500 per person, a prepaid burial plan (unlimited if irrevocable; up to $1,500 if revocable), a burial plot, and retroactive Social Security or SSI benefits (for six months after qualification in a Medicare savings program).

MEDICARE PART A

Medicare Part A (Medicare Hospital Insurance) helps cover inpatient care in acute care hospitals, critical access hospitals, and skilled nursing facilities. It also covers hospice care and some home healthcare services.

Hospitalizations

> **NOTE:** The original Medicare plan (or Medicare fee-for-service plan) includes Medicare Part A and Medicare Part B, and is available nationwide to anyone who is eligible for Medicare coverage. Original Medicare plan subscribers also subscribe to *Medigap* supplemental insurance coverage, which helps pay for healthcare costs not covered by the original Medicare plan (e.g., deductible and coinsurance amounts).

Medicare pays only a portion of a patient's acute care and critical access hospital (CAH) inpatient hospitalization expenses, and the patient's out-of-pocket expenses are calculated on a benefit-period basis. A **benefit period** begins with the first day of hospitalization and ends when the patient has been out of the hospital for 60 consecutive days. (Some Medicare literature uses the term **spell of illness**, formerly called "spell of sickness," in place of "benefit period.") After 90 continuous days of hospitalization, the patient may elect to use some or all of the allotted lifetime reserve days, or pay the full daily charges for hospitalization. **Lifetime reserve days** (60 days) may be used only once during a patient's lifetime and are usually reserved for use during the patient's final, terminal hospital stay. The 2010 Part A deductibles per benefit period are:

Days 1–60	$1,100 total
Days 61–90	$275/day
Days 91–150	Patient pays total charges, or elects to use lifetime reserve days at $550/day
150+ continuous days	Patient pays total charges

A person who has been out of the hospital for a period of 60 consecutive days will enter a new benefit period if rehospitalized, and the expenses for the first 90 days under this new benefit period are the same as stated earlier. Persons confined to a psychiatric hospital are allowed 190 lifetime reserve days instead of the 60 days allotted for a stay in an acute care hospital.

Skilled Nursing Facility Stays

Individuals who become inpatients at a skilled nursing facility after a three-day-minimum acute hospital stay, and who meet Medicare's qualified diagnosis and comprehensive treatment plan requirements, pay 2010 rates of:

Days 1–20	Nothing
Days 21–100	$137.50 per day
Days 101+	Full daily rate

Home Health Services

> **NOTE:** Medicare Part B also covers some home health services if the patient is *not* covered by Medicare Part A.

Individuals receiving physician-prescribed, Medicare-covered home health services have no deductible or coinsurance responsibilities for services provided. Patients must be confined to the home, but they do not have to be hospitalized in an acute care hospital before qualifying for home health benefits. The patient is responsible for a 20 percent deductible of the approved amount for durable medical equipment.

Hospice Care

All terminally ill patients qualify for hospice care. Hospice is an autonomous, centrally administered program of coordinated inpatient and outpatient palliative (relief of symptoms) services for terminally ill patients and their families. This program is for patients for whom the provider can do nothing further to stop the progression of disease; the patient is treated only to relieve pain or other discomfort. In addition to medical care, a physician-directed interdisciplinary team provides psychological, sociological, and spiritual care. Medicare limits hospice care to four benefit periods, which include:

- **Two periods of 90 days each**
- **One 30-day period**
- **A final "lifetime" extension of unlimited duration**

The hospice patient is responsible for:

- **5 percent of the cost of each prescription for symptom management or pain relief, but not more than $5 for any prescription.**
- **5 percent of the Medicare payment amount for inpatient respite care for up to five consecutive days at a time.**

Respite care is the temporary hospitalization of a terminally ill, dependent hospice patient for the purpose of providing relief for the nonpaid person who has the major day-to-day responsibility for care of that patient.

Patients who withdraw from the hospice program during the final benefit period are considered to have exhausted their hospice benefits. A patient who is receiving hospice benefits is not eligible for Medicare Part B services except for those services that are totally unrelated to the terminal illness. When a patient chooses Medicare hospice benefits, all other Medicare benefits stop, with the exception of physician services or treatment for conditions not related to the patient's terminal diagnosis.

MEDICARE PART B

Medicare Part B (Medicare Medical Insurance) helps cover physician services, outpatient hospital care, and other services not covered by Medicare Part A, including physical and occupational therapy and some home health care for patients who do not have Medicare Part A.

Deductible and Coinsurance Expenses

> **NOTE:** In hospital outpatient settings, the coinsurance amount is based on a national median amount per ambulatory payment classification (APC), which could be higher than 20 percent. Hospitals have the option of charging patients either the 20 percent or the higher national median coinsurance amount. Regardless, Medicare will reimburse hospitals the difference between the Medicare-approved amount and the national coinsurance of 20 percent. However, if the hospital collects the higher median coinsurance amount from the patient, Medicare will reduce its reimbursement accordingly.

Medicare Part B costs (2010) to the patient include:

- **$110.50 standard monthly premium for aged enrollees (and $270.40 for disabled enrollees) (some people pay a higher premium based on modified adjusted gross income.)**
- **$155 annual deductible**
- **20 percent coinsurance of Medicare-approved amount after deductible is met**
- **20 percent of all occupational, physical and speech-language therapy services**
- **20 percent of the Medicare-approved amount for durable medical equipment**
- **50 percent for most outpatient mental health care**
- **First three pints of blood plus 20 percent of the Medicare-approved amount for additional pints of blood (after the deductible has been met)**

Providers who do not routinely collect the patient's deductible and coinsurance are in violation of Medicare regulations and are subject to large fines and exclusion from the Medicare program.

Physician Fee Schedule

> **NOTE:** Medicare enrollees whose incomes are more than $85,000 (individual) or $170,000 (couple) pay higher Part B premiums than people with lower incomes.

Since 1992, Medicare has reimbursed provider services according to a *physician fee schedule* (also called the *Resource-Based Relative Value Scale, RBRVS*), which also limits amounts nonparticipating providers (nonPARs) can charge beneficiaries. Reimbursement under the fee schedule is based on relative value units (RVUs) that consider resources used in providing a service (physician work, practice expense, and malpractice expense). The schedule is revised annually and is organized in a table format that includes HCPCS/CPT code numbers and the Medicare-allowed fee for each.

> **EXAMPLE:** CPT E/M codes are listed in the physician fee schedule as indicated below. (This represents a sample listing, not based on any particular year.)
>
> | | | | | |
> |---|---|---|---|---|
> | 99201 | $ 35.68 | | 99211 | $ 21.47 |
> | 99202 | $ 64.48 | | 99212 | $ 38.02 |
> | 99203 | $ 96.32 | | 99213 | $ 52.76 |
> | 99204 | $ 136.57 | | 99214 | $ 82.57 |
> | 99205 | $ 173.30 | | 99215 | $ 120.93 |

MEDICARE PART C

Medicare Advantage Plans (Medicare Part C, formerly called *Medicare+Choice* as established by the Balanced Budget Act of 1997) are health plan options that are approved by Medicare but managed by private companies. These plans provide all Medicare Part A (hospital) and Medicare Part B (medical) coverage and must cover medically-necessary services. There is no need to purchase a Medigap policy. Medicare Advantage Plans may:

- Require referrals to see specialists.
- Offer lower premiums or copayments and deductibles than the Original Medicare Plan.
- Have networks, which means patients may have to see doctors who belong to the plan or go to certain hospitals to get covered services.
- Offer extra benefits, such as prescription drug coverage.
- Coordinate patient care, using networks and referrals, which can help with overall care management and result in cost savings.

Medicare enrollees have the option of enrolling in one of the following plans:

- Medicare health maintenance organization (HMO)
- Medicare medical savings account (MSA) plan
- Medicare special needs plan
- Preferred provider organization (PPO)
- Private fee-for-service (PFFS) plan

A Medicare Medical Savings Account (MSA) is used by an enrollee to pay healthcare bills, while Medicare pays the cost of a special healthcare policy that has a high deductible (not to exceed $6,000). Medicare also annually deposits into an account the difference between the policy costs and what Medicare pays for an average enrollee in the patient's region. The money deposited annually by Medicare into an MSA is managed by a Medicare-approved insurance company or other qualified company. It is not taxed if the enrollee uses it to pay qualified healthcare expenses. It may earn interest or dividends, and any funds left in the account at the end of a calendar year are carried over to the next year. The enrollee pays healthcare expenses using money from the MSA account until the high deductible has been met. (If the MSA is exhausted before the high deductible has been met, the enrollee pays out of pocket until the deductible has been met.) Once the deductible has been met, the insurance policy pays healthcare expenses.

> **EXAMPLE:** Jill selects the Medicare MSA plan option, establishes an account, and selects an MSA insurance policy with a $5,000 deductible. Medicare deposits $1,200 into Jill's MSA account on January 1. During the first year of the MSA plan, Jill receives healthcare services for which she pays $300, leaving $900 remaining in her MSA account. On January 1, Medicare deposits another $1,200 into her account; Jill now has $2,100 that she can use for healthcare expenses. During that next year, Jill undergoes surgery that costs $8,000. She uses the $2,100 in her account plus $2,900 of her own money to meet the policy's high deductible of $5,000; the remaining $3,000 is reimbursed by the MSA insurance policy.

Private fee-for-service (PFFS) plans are offered by private insurance companies and are available in some regions of the country. Medicare pays a pre-established amount of money each month to the insurance company, which decides how much it will pay for services. Such plans reimburse providers on a fee-for-service basis and are authorized to charge enrollees up to 115 percent of the plan's payment schedule.

Medicare special needs plans cover all Medicare Part A and Part B health care for individuals who can benefit the most from special care for chronic illnesses, care management of multiple diseases, and focused care management. Such plans may limit membership to individuals who:

- Are eligible for both Medicare and Medicaid (Medi-Medi coverage).
- Have certain chronic or disabling conditions.
- Reside in certain institutions (e.g., nursing facility).

MEDICARE PART D

Medicare Prescription Drug Plans (Medicare Part D) offer prescription drug coverage to all Medicare beneficiaries that may help lower prescription drug costs and help protect against higher costs in the future. Medicare Part D is optional, and individuals who join a Medicare drug plan pay a monthly premium. (Individuals who decide not to enroll in a Medicare prescription drug plan when first eligible may be required to pay a penalty if they choose to join later.)

Medicare prescription drug plans are administered by insurance companies and other private companies approved by Medicare. There are two ways to obtain Medicare prescription drug coverage:

1. Join a Medicare Prescription Drug Plan that adds coverage to the original Medicare plan, some Medicare private fee-for-service plans, some Medicare cost plans, and Medicare medical savings account plans. This plan requires subscribers to pay a monthly premium and an annual deductible.

2. Join a Medicare Advantage Plan (e.g., HMO) that includes prescription drug coverage as part of the plan. Monthly premiums and annual deductibles will vary, depending on the plan. In addition, all Medicare health care (including prescription drug coverage) is provided by such plans.

OTHER MEDICARE HEALTH PLANS

Other Medicare health plans generally provide all of an individual's Medicare-covered health care, and some cover prescription drugs. Other Medicare health plans include:

- Medicare Cost Plans.
- Demonstration/pilot program.
- Programs of All-inclusive Care for the Elderly (PACE).

A Medicare Cost Plan is a type of HMO that works in much the same way and has some of the same rules as a Medicare Advantage Plan. In a Medicare Cost Plan, if the individual receives health care from a non-network provider, the Original Medicare Plan covers the services. The individual pays Medicare Part A and Part B coinsurance and deductibles.

A **demonstration/pilot program** is a special project that tests improvements in Medicare coverage, payment, and quality of care. Some follow Medicare Advantage Plan rules, but others do not. Demonstrations usually apply to a specific group of people and/or are offered only in specific areas. They also include pilot programs for individuals with multiple chronic illnesses designed to reduce health risks, improve quality of life, and provide healthcare savings.

Programs of All-Inclusive Care for the Elderly (PACE) combine medical, social, and long-term care services for frail people who live and receive health care in the community. PACE is a joint Medicare and Medicaid option in some states. To be eligible, an individual must be:

- **55 years old, or older.**
- **A resident of the service area covered by the PACE program.**
- **Able to live safely in the community.**
- **Certified as eligible for nursing home care by the appropriate state agency.**

The goal of PACE is to help people stay independent and live in their community as long as possible, while receiving the high quality care they need.

High qualit

EMPLOYER AND UNION HEALTH PLANS

Some employer and union health insurance policies provide coverage for individuals who reach age 65 and who retire. Medicare has special rules that apply to beneficiaries who have group health plan coverage through their own or their spouse's current employment. Group health plans of employers with 20 or more employees must offer the same health insurance benefits under the same conditions that younger workers and spouses receive. When the individual or the individual's spouse stops working and the individual is already enrolled in Part B, the individual is responsible for:

- **Notifying Medicare that their or their spouse's employment situation has changed.**
- **Providing the name and address of the employer plan, policy number with the plan, the date the coverage stopped and why.**
- **Telling their provider that Medicare is their primary payer and should be billed first. The individual should also provide the date their group health coverage stopped.**

MEDIGAP

Medigap (or **Medicare Supplementary Insurance, MSI**) is offered by commercial health insurance companies and some BCBS companies. It is designed to supplement Medicare benefits by paying for services that Medicare does not cover. Although Medicare covers many healthcare costs, enrollees must still pay Medicare's deductibles and coinsurance amounts. In addition, there are many healthcare services that Medicare does not cover. A Medigap policy provides reimbursement for out-of-pocket costs not covered by Medicare, in addition to those that are the beneficiary's share of healthcare costs. There are 12 Medigap policies (Table 14-3), each offering a different combination of benefits. (Premium amounts are determined by payers.)

TABLE 14-3   Medigap plans

BASIC BENEFITS REQUIRED BY ALL MEDIGAP PLANS	A	B	C	D	E	F	G	H	I	J	K	L
Part A Hospital (Days 61–90)	√	√	√	√	√	√	√	√	√	√	√	√
Lifetime reserve days (91–150)	√	√	√	√	√	√	√	√	√	√	√	√
365 Life hospital days—100%	√	√	√	√	√	√	√	√	√	√	√	√
Parts A & B Blood	√	√	√	√	√	√	√	√	√	√	√	√
Part B Coinsurance—20%	√	√	√	√	√	√	√	√	√	√	√	√

ADDITIONAL BENEFITS	A	B	C	D	E	F	G	H	I	J	K	L
Skilled nursing facility coinsurance (Days 21–90)			√	√	√	√	√	√	√	√	50%	75%
Part A deductible		√	√	√	√	√	√	√	√	√	50%	75%
Part B deductible			√			√				√	√	
Part B excess charges						100%	80%		100%	100%	100%	
Foreign travel emergency			√	√	√	√	√	√	√	√	√	
At-home recovery			√				√		√	√	√	
Preventive medical care					√					√	√	

Medicare SELECT is a type of Medigap insurance that requires enrollees to use a network of providers (doctors and hospitals) in order to receive full benefits. Because of this requirement, Medicare SELECT policies may have lower premiums. However, if an out-of-network provider is used, Medicare SELECT generally will not pay benefits for nonemergency services. Medicare, however, will still pay its share of approved charges. Currently, Medicare SELECT is available only in limited geographic areas of the country.

PARTICIPATING PROVIDERS

Medicare has established a *participating provider (PAR)* agreement in which the provider contracts to *accept assignment* on all claims submitted to Medicare. By 2000, more than 85 percent of all physicians, practitioners, and suppliers in the United States were PARs. Congress mandated special incentives to increase the number of healthcare providers signing PAR agreements with Medicare, including:

- Direct payment of all claims.
- A 5 percent higher fee schedule than for nonparticipating providers.
- Bonuses provided to Medicare administrative contractors (MACs) for recruitment and enrollment of PARs.
- Publication of an annual, regional PAR directory (MedPARD) made available to all Medicare patients.
- A special message printed on all unassigned Medicare Summary Notice (MSN) forms mailed to patients, reminding them of the reduction in out-of-pocket expenses if they use PARs and stating how much they would save with PARs.
- Hospital referrals for outpatient care that provide the patient with the name and full address of at least one PAR provider each time the hospital provides a referral for care.
- Faster processing of assigned claims.

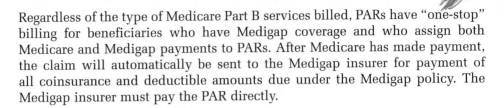

Regardless of the type of Medicare Part B services billed, PARs have "one-stop" billing for beneficiaries who have Medigap coverage and who assign both Medicare and Medigap payments to PARs. After Medicare has made payment, the claim will automatically be sent to the Medigap insurer for payment of all coinsurance and deductible amounts due under the Medigap policy. The Medigap insurer must pay the PAR directly.

NONPARTICIPATING PROVIDERS

Medicare *nonparticipating providers (nonPARs)* may elect to accept assignment on a claim-by-claim basis, but several restrictions must be adhered to:

- NonPARs must file all Medicare claims.
- Fees are restricted to not more than the "limiting charge" on nonassigned claims.
- Balance billing of the patient by a nonPAR is forbidden.
- Collections are restricted to only the deductible and coinsurance due at the time of service on an assigned claim.
- Patients must sign a Surgical Disclosure Notice for all nonassigned surgical fees over $500.
- NonPARs must accept assignment on clinical laboratory charges.

Limiting Charge

Nonparticipating physicians who do not accept assignment on Medicare claims are subject to a limit (established by federal law) on what can be charged to beneficiaries for covered services. The Medicare-allowed fee for nonPARs is 5 percent below the PAR fee schedule, but the nonPAR physician may charge a maximum of 15 percent above the nonPAR approved rate (or 10 percent above the PAR fee schedule). The *limiting charge* is the maximum fee a nonPAR may charge for a covered service. It applies regardless of who is responsible for payment and whether Medicare is primary or secondary.

EXAMPLE: Compare the PAR and nonPAR Medicare reimbursement rates.

Participating (PAR) Provider Medicare Reimbursement		Nonparticipating (nonPAR) Provider Medicare Reimbursement	
PAR usual charge for office visit	$110	nonPAR limiting charge[1]	$110
PAR Medicare-allowed fee schedule	$100	nonPAR Medicare-allowed fee schedule[2]	$95
Medicare pays 80% of fee schedule	$80	Medicare pays 80% of fee schedule	$76
PAR writes off amount[3]	$10	nonPAR bills patient[4]	$34
Patient coinsurance[5] (20% of PAR Medicare-allowed fee schedule)	$20	Patient coinsurance[6]	$19
Total payment to PAR	$100	Total payment to nonPAR	$110

Although it appears that the nonPAR is paid more than the PAR ($110 versus $100), the nonPAR has to collect $53 from the patient, whereas the PAR has to collect just $20 from the patient. (It is also more cost-effective for patients to seek treatment from PARs.)

[1] Even if nonPAR's usual charge for office visit is greater than $110, limiting charge in this example remains $110

[2] nonPAR Medicare-allowed fee schedule is 5% below PAR Medicare-allowed fee schedule (In the nonPAR example above, the $95 nonPAR Medicare-allowed fee schedule is calculated as: (1) $100 x 5% = $5 and (2) $100 - $5 = $95.)

[3] PAR writes off difference between usual charge and Medicare-allowed fee schedule

[4] nonPAR can bill patient difference between limiting charge and Medicare-allowed fee schedule

[5] 20% of PAR Medicare-allowed fee schedule

[6] 20% of nonPAR Medicare-allowed fee schedule

Accepting Assignment on a Claim

A nonparticipating provider who agrees to accept assignment on a claim will be reimbursed the Medicare-allowed fee. The nonPAR may also collect any unpaid deductible and the 20 percent coinsurance determined from the Medicare Physician Fee Schedule (MPFS). If the nonPAR collects the entire charge at the time of the patient's visit, the assigned status of the claim is voided and the nonPAR limiting fee is then in effect. The nonPAR may also be subject to a fine or may be in violation of MPFS requirements.

The nonPAR cannot revoke the agreement for an assigned claim *unless* it is by mutual written consent of the provider and the beneficiary. Even then, such an agreement must be communicated to the MAC *before* the MAC has determined the allowed amount. Providers who repeatedly violate the assignment agreement could be charged and found guilty of a misdemeanor, which is punishable by a fine, imprisonment, or both. In addition, a criminal violation may result in suspension from Medicare participation.

The following practitioners who submit claims for services must accept assignment:

- Anesthesiologist assistants
- Certified nurse midwives
- Certified registered nurse anesthetists
- Clinical nurse specialists
- Clinical psychologists
- Clinical social workers
- Mass immunization roster billers
- Nurse practitioners
- Physician assistants
- Registered dietitians

Providers who submit claims for the following services must accept assignment:

- ambulance services
- Ambulatory surgical center services
- Clinical diagnostic laboratory services
- Home dialysis supplies and equipment
- Medications
- Physician lab services
- Physician services to Medicare/Medicaid (Medi-Medi) crossover patients

> **EXAMPLE:** A patient undergoes laboratory procedures and sees the nonPAR physician during an office visit (evaluation and management service). If the nonPAR accepts assignment for just the laboratory procedures, two claims must be submitted: one for the laboratory services and another for the office visit.

Waiver of Medicare Billing Contracts

Medicare law specifically states that nonPARs are subject to sanctions, including fines and exclusions from the Medicare program, if they require patients to sign agreements stating that the patient waives the right to have the nonPAR provider file the patient's Medicare claims or that the patient agrees to pay charges for services that are in excess of the nonPAR charge limits.

Privacy Act

In addition to the other restrictions, the Privacy Act of 1974 forbids the Medicare administrative contractor (MAC) from disclosing the status of any unassigned claim beyond the following:

- **Date the claim was received by the MAC**
- **Date the claim was paid, denied, or suspended**
- **General reason the claim was suspended**

The nonPAR provider will *not* be told payment amounts or approved charge information.

SURGICAL DISCLOSURE NOTICE

Providers *must* notify beneficiaries in writing of projected out-of-pocket expenses for elective surgery and noncovered procedures when the charge for surgery is $500 or more. This notification is required of both surgeons and assistant surgeons. For Medicare purposes, *elective surgery* is defined as a surgery that:

- **Can be scheduled in advance;**
- **Is not an emergency; and**
- **If delayed, *would not* result in death or permanent impairment of health.**

The Omnibus Budget Reconciliation Act (OBRA) of 1986 requires the following information to be provided in writing to the patient:

- **Estimated actual charge for surgery**
- **Estimated Medicare payment**
- **Excess of the provider's actual charge as compared with the approved charge**
- **Applicable coinsurance amount**
- **Beneficiary's out-of-pocket expenses**

NonPARs must document the receipt and acknowledgment of this information by having the beneficiary or the beneficiary's representative sign and date a Surgical Disclosure Notice (Figure 14-1). A copy of the signed and dated notice must be maintained and provided upon request from the MAC. If the nonPAR fails to properly notify the beneficiary prior to performing surgery, any money collected from the beneficiary that exceeds the Medicare-approved amount must be refunded. Failure to make the appropriate refund could result in civil monetary penalties and/or exclusion from the Medicare program.

Goodmedicine Clinic ■ 1 Provider St ■ Anywhere US 12345 ■ (101) 111-2222

Name of Medicare Beneficiary   Date

As previously discussed, I am not accepting Medicare assignment for reimbursement of your surgery. Medicare regulations require that I provide the following information to patients who are considering surgery that will cost $500 or more.

Type of surgery: _____

Name of provider: _____

Estimated actual charge: $ _____

Estimated Medicare payment: $ _____

Patient's estimated payment (includes coinsurance): $ _____

ACKNOWLEDGED AND AGREED BY:

Signature of Medicare Beneficiary   Date   Signature of Provider   Date
or Legal Representative

FIGURE 14-1 Sample nonPAR Surgical Disclosure Notice (Courtesy Delmar/Cengage Learning)

MANDATORY CLAIMS SUBMISSION

Federal law requires that all providers and suppliers submit claims to Medicare if they provide a Medicare-covered service to a patient enrolled in Medicare Part B. This regulation does not apply if the:

- Patient is not enrolled in Part B.
- Patient disenrolled before the service was furnished.
- Patient or the patient's legal representative refuses to sign an authorization for release of medical information.
- Provider opts out of the Medicare program, and those patients enter into private contracts with the provider (see section on Private Contracting).

An exception may occur if a patient refuses to sign an authorization for the release of medical information to Medicare. However, if the patient later opts to sign a Medicare authorization and requests that claims for all prior services be filed with Medicare, the request must be honored.

PRIVATE CONTRACTING

Under the Balanced Budget Act of 1997, physicians were provided the option of withdrawing from Medicare and entering into private contracts with their Medicare patients. As of 2003, dentists, optometrists, and podiatrists were added to the list of providers who may opt out of Medicare. This **Medicare private contract** is an agreement between the Medicare beneficiary and a physician or other practitioner who has "opted out" of Medicare for two years for *all* covered items and services furnished to Medicare beneficiaries. This means that the physician/practitioner will not bill for any service or supplies provided to any Medicare beneficiary for at least two years.

Under a private contract:

- No Medicare payment will be made for services or procedures provided to a patient.
- The patient is required to pay whatever the physician/practitioner charges, and there is no limit on what the physician/practitioner can charge for Medicare approved services (the limiting charge will not apply).
- Medicare managed care plans will not pay for services rendered under a private contract.
- No claim is to be submitted to Medicare, and Medicare will not pay if a claim is submitted.
- Supplemental insurance (Medigap) will not pay for services or procedures rendered.
- Other insurance plans may not pay for services or procedures rendered.

The private contract applies only to services and procedures rendered by the physician or practitioner with whom the patient signed an agreement. Patients cannot be asked to sign a private contract when facing an emergency or urgent health situation. If patients want to pay for services that the original Medicare plan does not cover, the physician does not have to leave Medicare or ask the patient to sign a private contract. The patient is welcome to obtain noncovered services and to pay for those services.

A physician who enters into a Medicare private contract with one patient will be unable to bill Medicare for any patient for a period of two years with the exception of emergency or urgent care provided to a patient who has not signed an agreement with the provider to forgo Medicare benefits. In these cases, the claim for urgent or emergency care must be accompanied by an attachment explaining the following: (1) the nature of the emergency or urgent problem, and (2) a statement affirming that this patient has not signed an agreement with the provider to forgo Medicare. If a provider submits a nonemergency or urgent care claim for any patient before the opt-out agreement becomes effective, the provider must submit claims for all Medicare patients thereafter and abide by the limiting-fee rules. If, however, the patient files the claim, the provider will not be penalized.

ADVANCE BENEFICIARY NOTICE

An **advance beneficiary notice (ABN)** is a written document provided to a Medicare beneficiary by a supplier, physician, or provider prior to service being rendered (Figure 14-2). The ABN indicates that the service is unlikely to be reimbursed by Medicare, specifies why Medicare denial is anticipated, and requests the beneficiary to sign an agreement that guarantees personal payment for services. A beneficiary who signs an ABN agreement will be held responsible for payment of the bill if Medicare denies payment. ABNs should be generated whenever the supplier or provider believes that a claim for the services is likely to receive a Medicare **medical necessity denial** (a denial of otherwise covered services that were found to be not "reasonable and necessary").

> **BILLING TIP:**
> The purpose of obtaining the ABN is to ensure payment for a procedure or service that might not be reimbursed under Medicare.

(A) Notifier(s):

B) Patient Name: **(C) Identification Number:**

ADVANCE BENEFICIARY NOTICE OF NONCOVERAGE (ABN)

<u>NOTE:</u> If Medicare doesn't pay for **(D)**_____ below, you may have to pay.

Medicare does not pay for everything, even some care that you or your healthcare provider have good reason to think you need. We expect Medicare may not pay for the **(D)** _____ below.

(D)_____	**(E) Reason Medicare May Not Pay:**	**(F) Estimated Cost:**

WHAT YOU NEED TO DO NOW:

- Read this notice, so you can make an informed decision about your care.
- Ask us any questions that you may have after you finish reading.
- Choose an option below about whether to receive the **(D)**_____ listed above.
    Note: If you choose Option 1 or 2, we may help you to use any other insurance that you might have, but Medicare cannot require us to do this.

(G) OPTIONS: **Check only one box. We cannot choose a box for you.**

☐ **OPTION 1.** I want the **(D)**_____ listed above. You may ask to be paid now, but I also want Medicare billed for an official decision on payment, which is sent to me on a Medicare Summary Notice (MSN). I understand that if Medicare doesn't pay, I am responsible for payment, but **I can appeal to Medicare** by following the directions on the MSN. If Medicare does pay, you will refund any payments I made to you, less co-pays or deductibles.

☐ **OPTION 2.** I want the **(D)**_____ listed above, but do not bill Medicare. You may ask to be paid now as I am responsible for payment. **I cannot appeal if Medicare is not billed**.

☐ **OPTION 3.** I don't want the **(D)**_____ listed above. I understand with this choice I am **not** responsible for payment, and **I cannot appeal to see if Medicare would pay.**

(H) Additional Information:

This notice gives our opinion, not an official Medicare decision. If you have other questions on this notice or Medicare billing, call **1-800-MEDICARE** (1-800-633-4227/**TTY**: 1-877-486-2048).

Signing below means that you have received and understand this notice. You also receive a copy.

(I) Signature:	**(J) Date:**

According to the Paperwork Reduction Act of 1995, no persons are required to respond to a collection of information unless it displays a valid OMB control number. The valid OMB control number for this information collection is 0938-0566. The time required to complete this information collection is estimated to average 7 minutes per response, including the time to review instructions, search existing data resources, gather the data needed, and complete and review the information collection. If you have comments concerning the accuracy of the time estimate or suggestions for improving this form, please write to: CMS, 7500 Security Boulevard, Attn: PRA Reports Clearance Officer, Baltimore, Maryland 21244-1850.

Form CMS-R-131 (03/08)   Form Approved OMB No. 0938-0566

FIGURE 14-2 Advance beneficiary notice form approved for use by CMS (Reprinted according to **www.cms.hhs.gov** Web Site Content Reuse Policy)

Cost estimates are unnecessary when an ABN is generated, because the purpose of the ABN is to document that the beneficiary has received notice that a service is unlikely to be reimbursed by Medicare. Hospital ABNs are called Hospital-Issued Notices of Noncoverage (HINN) or Notices of Noncoverage (NONC).

Do not have a patient sign an ABN when a service is *never* covered by Medicare. Instead, have those patients sign a different form, called the Notice of Exclusion of Medicare Benefits (NEMB). The ABN is used when the service is sometimes covered by Medicare, but the provider does not think it will be covered for that patient. It communicates that the patient will be responsible for provider charges if Medicare

NOTE: CMS has announced that it will consider, for Medicare coverage, certain devices with an FDA-approved investigational device exemption (IDE) that are considered nonexperimental or investigational. The FDA categorizes all FDA-approved IDEs into either Category A (experimental) or Category B (nonexperimental/investigational) for Medicare reimbursement consideration. Only those IDEs placed in Category B by the FDA are eligible for Medicare coverage consideration.

denies the service. The NEMB clearly states that the service is never covered by Medicare, and that the patient is responsible for paying provider charges. Unlike the ABN, providers are not required to have patients sign an NEMB for a never-covered Medicare service in order to bill the patient; however, use of the form makes it clear to the patient *before* a service is provided that the patient will have to pay for it.

EXPERIMENTAL AND INVESTIGATIONAL PROCEDURES

Medicare law allows payment only for services or supplies that are considered reasonable and necessary for the stated diagnosis. Medicare will not cover procedures deemed to be experimental in nature. There are cases in which the provider determines that treatments or services are fully justified and such treatment options are then explained to the patient, who must pay the full cost of the non-covered procedure.

Medicare regulations specify that the provider must refund any payment received from a patient for a service denied by Medicare as investigational, unnecessary, unproved, or experimental, unless the patient agreed in writing prior to receiving the services to personally pay for such services. Figure 14-3 shows a CMS-approved medical necessity statement. An appeal of the denial of payment must be made in writing, and if the appeal is not granted, a refund must be paid to the patient within 30 days. A refund is not required if the provider "could not have known a specific treatment would be ruled unnecessary."

Goodmedicine Clinic ■ 1 Provider St ■ Anywhere US 12345 ■ (101) 111-2222

To My Medicare Patients:

My primary concern as your physician is to provide you with the best possible care. Medicare does not pay for all services and will only allow those which it determines, under the guidelines spelled out in the Omnibus Budget Reconciliation Act of 1986 Section 1862(a)(1), to be reasonable and necessary. Under this law, a procedure or service deemed to be medically unreasonable or unnecessary will be denied. Since I believe each scheduled visit or planned procedure is both reasonable and necessary, I am required to notify you in advance that the following procedures or services listed below, which we have mutually agreed on, may be denied by Medicare.

Date of Service _____

Description of Service   Charge

_____   _____
_____   _____
_____   _____

Denial may be for the following reasons:
1. Medicare does not usually pay for this many visits or treatments,
2. Medicare does not usually pay for this many services within this period of time, and/or
3. Medicare does not usually pay for this type of service for your condition.

I, however, believe these procedures/services to be both reasonable and necessary for your condition, and will assist you in collecting payment from Medicare. In order for me to assist you in this matter, the law requires that you read the following agreement and sign it.

I have been informed by (fill in the name and title of the provider) that he/she believes, in my case, Medicare is likely to deny payment for the services and reasons stated above. If Medicare denies payment, I agree to be personally and fully responsible for payment.

Beneficiary's Name: _____   Medicare ID# _____ or

Beneficiary's Signature: _____

or

Authorized Representative's Signature _____

FIGURE 14-3 Sample letter of medical necessity (Courtesy Delmar/Cengage Learning)

MEDICARE AS PRIMARY PAYER

Medicare is considered the primary payer under the following circumstances:

- The employee is eligible for a group health plan but has declined to enroll, or has recently dropped coverage.
- The individual is currently employed, but is not yet eligible for group plan coverage or has exhausted benefits under the plan.
- The health insurance plan is only for self-employed individuals.
- The health insurance plan was purchased as an individual plan and not obtained through a group.
- The patient is also covered by TRICARE, which provides health benefits to retired members of the uniformed services and spouses/children of active duty, retired, and deceased service members.
- The patient is under age 65, has Medicare because of a disability or ESRD, and is not covered by an employer-sponsored plan.
- The patient is under age 65, has ESRD, and has an employer-sponsored plan but has been eligible for Medicare for more than 30 months.
- The patient has left a company and has elected to continue coverage in the group health plan under federal COBRA rules.
- The patient has both Medicare and Medicaid (Medi-Medi crossover patient).

The Consolidated Omnibus Budget Reconciliation Act of 1985 (COBRA) requires employers with 20 or more employees to allow employees and their dependents to keep their employer-sponsored group health insurance coverage for up to 18 months for any of the following occurrences:

- Death of the employed spouse
- Loss of employment or reduction in work hours
- Divorce

The employee or dependents may have to pay their share as well as the employer's share of the premium.

Medicare Conditional Primary Payer Status

Medicare will award an assigned claim conditional primary payer status and process the claim under the following circumstances:

- A plan that is normally considered primary to Medicare issues a denial of payment that is under appeal.
- A patient who is physically or mentally impaired fails to file a claim with the primary payer.
- A workers' compensation claim has been denied, and the case is slowly moving through the appeal process.
- There is no response from a liability payer within 120 days of filing the claim.

Medicare is to be reimbursed immediately if payment is received from the primary payer at a later date.

MEDICARE AS SECONDARY PAYER

A clarification of the *Medicare Secondary Payer (MSP)* rules was published in 1996, stating that Medicare is secondary when the patient is eligible for Medicare and is also covered by one or more of the following plans:

- An employer-sponsored group health plan (EGHP) that has more than 20 covered employees.

- Disability coverage through an employer-sponsored group health plan that has more than 100 covered employees.

- An End-Stage Renal Disease case covered by an employer-sponsored group plan of any size during the first 18 months of the patient's eligibility for Medicare.

- A third-party liability policy, if the Medicare-eligible person is seeking treatment for an injury covered by such a policy (this category includes automobile insurance, no-fault insurance, and self-insured liability plans).

- A workers' compensation program; if the claim is contested, the provider should file a Medicare primary claim and include a copy of the workers' compensation notice declaring that the case is "pending a Compensation Board decision."

- Veterans Administration (VA) preauthorized services for a beneficiary who is eligible for both VA benefits and Medicare.

- Federal Black Lung Program that covers currently or formerly employed coal miners.

NOTE: Providers are required to collect or verify Medicare Secondary Payer (MSP) information during the initial beneficiary encounter instead of each time the patient is seen. Providers are also encouraged to retain MSP questionnaires for at least ten years, even though five years is the required retention period.

NOTE: Be sure to submit a claim to Medicare for services paid by a primary payer, even if the primary payer reimbursed the entire amount charged. Failure to submit claims to Medicare could result in patients being denied credit toward their Medicare deductible.

All primary plans, which are collectively described in the Medicare literature as *MSP plans,* must be billed first. Medicare is billed only after the remittance advice from the primary plan or plans has been received. (The remittance advice must be attached to the Medicare claim when the claim is submitted.)

Independent and hospital labs are to enter NONE in Block 11 of the CMS-1500 claim when they bill Medicare for reference lab services when there is no face-to-face encounter with a Medicare patient. This was changed because CMS no longer requires labs to collect Medicare secondary payer information to bill Medicare if they have had no face-to-face encounter with the patient. Entering NONE in Block 11 will prevent claims from being denied as unprocessable. When independent or hospital labs have face-to-face encounters with Medicare patients, they must collect MSP information.

To avoid fines and penalties for routinely billing Medicare as primary when it is the secondary payer, a more detailed Medicare secondary payer questionnaire (Figure 14-4) should be provided to all Medicare patients when they register/reregister (update demographic and/or insurance information) with the practice. This form is used to clarify primary and secondary insurance payers.

Goodmedicine Clinic ■ 1 Provider St ■ Anywhere US 12345 ■ (101) 111-2222

To: All Medicare Patients

In order for us to comply with the Medicare as Secondary Payer laws, you must complete this form before we can properly process your insurance claim.

Please complete this questionnaire and return it to the front desk. We will also need to make photocopies of all your insurance identification cards. Do not hesitate to ask for clarification of any item on this form.

CHECK ALL ITEMS THAT DESCRIBE YOUR HEALTH INSURANCE COVERAGE

1. I am working full time _____ part time _____ . I retired on ___/___/___.

2. _____ I am enrolled in a Medicare HMO plan.
   _____ I am entitled to Black Lung Benefits.
   _____ I had a job-related injury on ___/___/___.
   _____ I have a fee service card from the VA.
   _____ I had an organ transplant on ___/___/___.
   _____ I have been on kidney dialysis since ___/___/___.
   _____ I am being treated for an injury received in a car accident _____.
   _____ Other vehicle (please identify) _____
   _____ Other type of accident (please identify) _____
   _____.

3. _____ I am employed/My spouse is employed and I am covered by an employer-sponsored healthcare program covering more than 20 employees. Name of policy:
   _____

4. _____ I/My spouse has purchased a private insurance policy to supplement Medicare. Name of policy:
   _____

5. _____ I have health insurance through my/my spouse's previous employer or union. Name of previous employer or union:
   _____

6. _____ I am covered by Medicaid and my ID number is: _____

7. _____ I am retired and covered by an employer-sponsored retiree healthcare plan. Name of plan:
   _____

8. _____ I am retired, but have been called back temporarily and have employee health benefits while I am working. Name of plan:
   _____

Patient Signature _____ Date ____/____/____

FIGURE 14-4 Sample Medicare secondary payer questionnaire (Courtesy Delmar/Cengage Learning)

EXERCISE 14-1

Medicare as Secondary Payer

Review the following cases and determine the CMS-prescribed billing order for each.

> **EXAMPLE:** Patient is retired and covered by Medicare, an employer-sponsored retirement plan, and his spouse's employer-sponsored large group plan.
>
> *Billing order:* Employer-sponsored large group plan, Medicare, employer-sponsored retirement plan.

1. Patient is the policyholder in an employer-sponsored large group plan and has Medicare, a Medigap policy, and a $100-per-day extra coverage hospital plan.

   *Billing order:*_____

2. Patient has Medicare and an employer-sponsored retirement plan, and is a dependent on the spouse's employer-sponsored large group plan. The claim is for an injury received in a car accident.

   *Billing order:*_____

3. The patient has a retirement plan through his former employer, Medicare, and a cancer policy. The spouse is deceased.

   *Billing order:*_____

4. Patient is 67, working full time, and covered by Medicare, an employer-sponsored large group plan, and a Medigap plan. The spouse is retired, 62, and covered by an employer-sponsored plan for 18 employees.

   *Billing order:*_____

5. Patient is 50 and disabled, and has Medicare and an employer-sponsored group health plan that covers 50 employees.

   *Billing order:*_____

MEDICARE SUMMARY NOTICE

The *Medicare Summary Notice (MSN)* (Figure 14-5) is an easy-to-read, monthly statement that clearly lists health insurance claims information. It replaced the Explanation of Medicare Benefits (EOMB), the Medicare Benefits Notice (Part A), and benefit denial letters.

BILLING NOTES

Following is a summary of nationwide billing information for original Medicare plan claims submission.

Medicare Administrative Contractor (MAC)

The regional MAC for traditional Medicare claims is selected by CMS through a competitive bidding process. Obtain the name and mailing address of the MAC for your region.

CMS
MEDICARE · MEDICAID
Centers for Medicare & Medicaid Services

Medicare Summary Notice

July 10, YYYY

JOHN Q. PUBLIC
10A SENATE ST.
ANYWHERE NY 12345

CUSTOMER SERVICE INFORMATION
Your Medicare Number: 112-34-9801A

If you have questions, write or call:
Medicare Part A
101 Main St
Anywhere NY 12345

Local: 1-800-555-4606 (Maryland)
Toll-free: 1-800-555-1636 (Others)

HELP STOP FRAUD: Read your Medicare Summary
Notice carefully for accuracy of dates, services, and
amounts billed to Medicare.

This is a summary of claims processed on 06/26/YYYY.

PART B MEDICAL INSURANCE - OUTPATIENT FACILITY CLAIMS

Dates of Service	Services Provided	Amount Charged	Non-Covered Charges	Deductible and Coinsurance	You May Be Billed	See Notes Section
Claim number 12345678901245						
Goodmedicine Hospital						a, b
Anywhere St.						
Anywhere NY 12345						
Referred by: E Helper						
05/25/YY	CAT scan for therapy guide (76370)	$212.00	$0.00	$122.40	$0.00	c

Notes Section:

a. This information is being sent to your private insurer(s). Send any questions regarding your benefits to them.
b. $100.00 of the money approved by your primary insurer has been credited to your Medicare Part B deductible. You do not have to pay this amount.
c. $100.00 of this approved amount has been applied toward your deductible.

Your Medicare Number: 112-34-9801A

Deductible Information:

You have met the Part B deductible for YYYY.

General Information:

Who pays? You pay. Report Medicare fraud by calling 1-800-447-8477. An example of fraud would be claims for Medicare items or services you did not receive. If you have any other questions about your claim, please contact the Medicare contractor telephone number shown on this notice.

You can protect yourself from some pneumococcal infections by getting a pneumococcal vaccination. Medicare Part B will pay for your vaccination. One pneumococcal vaccination may be all you ever need.

Appeals Information - Part B (Outpatient)

If you disagree with any claims decision on this notice, you can request an appeal by **January 10, YYYY.**
Follow the instructions below:

1. Circle the item(s) you disagree with and explain why you disagree.
2. Send this notice, or a copy, to the address in the "Customer Service Information" box on Page 1.
3. Sign here _____ Phone number (_____) _____

THIS IS NOT A BILL - Keep this notice for your records.

FIGURE 14-5 Sample Medicare Summary Notice (Courtesy Delmar/Cengage Learning)

Medicare Split/Shared Visit Policy

The *Medicare split/shared visit payment policy* applies when the physician and a qualified nonphysician provider (NPP) (e.g., nurse practitioner, physician assistant) each personally perform a substantive portion of a medically necessary evaluation and management (E/M) service for the same patient on the same date of service. A *substantive portion of an E/M visit* involves performing all or some portion of the history, examination or medical decision making (the key components of an E/M service). The physician and qualified NPP must be in the same group practice or be employed by the same employer.

Durable Medical Equipment Claims

Durable medical equipment (DME) claims must be sent to one of four regional Medicare administrative contractors in the country. Check the Medicare manual for the one responsible for processing DME claims for your region.

Deadline for Filing Claims

The claim filing deadline for both regular Medicare and Railroad Retirement claims is within 12 months after the date of service.

> **EXAMPLE 1:** A claim for services performed on January 28 this year must be submitted on or before January 28 next year.

> **EXAMPLE 2:** A claim for services performed on November 5 this year can be submitted by November 5 next year.

Forms Used

All paper claims must be submitted on the CMS-1500 claim. A minimum of 45 days should pass before an unpaid paper claim is resubmitted. A Surgical Disclosure Notice is required for all nonassigned surgeries totaling $500 or more. A letter of medical necessity is required if the provider is to collect fees from the patient for procedures deemed by Medicare to be unreasonable, experimental, unproved, or investigational.

Medicare does not differentiate between basic and major medical benefits. Medicare is *not* the primary payer for accidental injuries covered by any third-party liability program.

Special Handling

All providers are required to file Medicare claims for their patients. Noncompliance with MSP rules and regulations may result in a substantial penalty or fine. For each filing, when Medicare is the secondary payer, a copy of the primary payer's remittance advice must be attached to the Medicare claim.

Two claims may be needed to describe one encounter in the following circumstances:

- When multiple referring, ordering, or supervising names and provider identifier numbers are required in Blocks 17 through 17a
- When multiple facility names and addresses are required in Block 32
- When DME is charged to the patient at the same time the patient had a reimbursable medical or surgical encounter
- When the patient has received covered lab services and other medical or surgical services during an encounter with a nonPAR provider

When more than one claim is needed to describe an encounter, be sure that the diagnoses on each claim prove the medical necessity for performing the service, and that the proper names and numbers required in Blocks 17, 17a, and 32 appear on the correct claims.

Before continuing with this chapter, complete the Review questions located at the end of this chapter.

CLAIMS INSTRUCTIONS

The law requires that all Medicare claims be filed using optical scanning guidelines. Practices must make certain that forms generated by computer software follow Medicare claims processing guidelines. Extraneous data on the claims or data appearing in blocks not consistent with Medicare guidelines will cause the claim to be rejected.

You should review Chapter 11, Essential CMS-1500 Claim Instructions, before working with Medicare claims instructions.

Read the following instructions carefully. Medicare requires many details that are not required for other payers discussed in this text.

These instructions (Table 14-4) are for filing primary original Medicare plan claims when the patient is not covered by additional insurance. (Instructions for filing Medicare-HMO fee-for-service claims are found in Chapter 12.)

During review of the instructions, refer to the John Q. Public case study in Figure 14-6 and the completed CMS-1500 claim (Figure 14-7).

TABLE 14-4   CMS-1500 claims completion instructions for Medicare primary claims

NOTE: Refer to Chapter 11 for clarification of claims completion (e.g., entering names, mailing addresses, ICD codes, diagnosis pointer numbers, NPI, and so on).

BLOCK	INSTRUCTIONS
1	Enter an X in the Medicare box.
1a	Enter the Medicare identification number as it appears on the patient's insurance card. *Do not enter hyphens or spaces in the number.*
2	Enter the patient's last name, first name, and middle initial (separated by commas) (e.g., DOE, JOHN, J).
3	Enter the patient's birth date as MM DD YYYY (with spaces). Enter an X in the appropriate box to indicate the patient's gender. If the patient's gender is unknown, leave blank.
4	Leave blank. *Block 4 is completed if the patient has other insurance primary to Medicare (e.g., employer group health plan) (discussed later in this chapter).*
5	Enter the patient's mailing address and telephone number. Enter the street address on line 1, enter the city and state on line 2, and enter the 5- or 9-digit zip code and phone number on line 3.
6	Leave blank.

(continues)

TABLE 14-4   (continued)

BLOCK	INSTRUCTIONS
7	Leave blank. *Block 7 is completed if the patient has other insurance primary to Medicare (e.g., employer group health plan) (discussed later in this chapter).*
8	Enter an X in the appropriate box to indicate the patient's marital status. If the patient is an unmarried domestic partner, enter an X in the *Other* box. Enter an X in the appropriate box to indicate the patient's employment or student status. If the patient is unemployed and/or not a full- or part-time student, leave blank.
9, 9a–9d	Leave blank. *Blocks 9 and 9a–9d are completed if the patient has secondary insurance coverage, such as Medigap (discussed later in this chapter).*
10a–c	Enter an X in the NO boxes. (If an X is entered in the YES box for auto accident, enter the 2-character state abbreviation of the patient's residence.)
10d	Leave blank.
11	Enter NONE, which indicates the provider has made a good-faith effort to determine whether Medicare is the primary or secondary payer.
11a	Leave blank.
11b	Leave blank. *If there is a change in the insured's insurance status (e.g., retired), enter the date of retirement as MM DD YYYY preceded by the word RETIRED (e.g., RETIRED 01 15 2008).*
11c–d	Leave blank.
12	Enter SIGNATURE ON FILE. Leave the date field blank. (The abbreviation SOF is also acceptable.)
13	Leave blank. *Block 13 is completed if the patient has Medigap coverage.*
14	Enter the date as MM DD YYYY (with spaces) to indicate when the patient first experienced signs or symptoms of the present illness or injury *or* the date of the last menstrual period (LMP) for obstetric visits. *If the date is not documented in the patient's record, but the history indicates an appropriate date (e.g., three weeks ago), simply count back to the approximate date and enter it on the claim.*
15	Leave blank.
16	Enter dates as MM DD YYYY (with spaces) to indicate the period of time the patient was unable to work in his current occupation, *if documented in the patient's record. An entry in this Block might indicate employment-related insurance coverage.* Otherwise, leave blank.
17	Enter the first name, middle initial (if known), last name, and credentials of the professional who referred or ordered healthcare service(s) or supply(s) reported on the claim. *Do not enter any punctuation.* Otherwise, leave blank.
17a	Leave blank.
17b	Enter the 10-digit national provider identifier (NPI) of the professional in Block 17. Otherwise, leave blank.
18	Enter the admission date and discharge date as MM DD YYYY (with spaces) if the patient received inpatient services (e.g., hospital, skilled nursing facility). *If the patient has not been discharged at the time the claim is completed, leave the discharge date blank.* Otherwise, leave blank.
19	Leave blank. This block can contain a variety of information, depending on services provided to the patient. Refer to the Medicare Claims Processing Manual, located at **www.cms.hhs.gov**, by scrolling down to the Top 10 Links heading, clicking on the Manual link, and clicking on the Internet-Only Manuals (IOMs) link.
20	Enter an X in the NO box if all laboratory procedures reported on the claim were performed in the provider's office. Otherwise, enter an X in the YES box, enter the total amount charged by the outside laboratory in $ CHARGES, and enter the outside laboratory's name, mailing address, and NPI in Block 32. (Charges are entered *without* punctuation. For example, $1,100.00 is entered as 110000 below $ CHARGES.)

(continues)

TABLE 14-4   (continued)

BLOCK	INSTRUCTIONS
21	Enter the ICD code for up to four diagnoses or conditions treated or medically managed during the encounter. Lines 1, 2, 3, and 4 in Block 21 will relate to CPT/HCPCS service/procedure codes reported in Block 24E.
22	Leave blank. Reserved for Medicaid claims.
23	Enter the applicable quality improvement organization (QIO) prior authorization number, investigational device exemption (IDE) number, NPI for a physician performing care plan oversight services of a home health agency or hospice, referral number, mammography pre-certification number, or 10-digit Clinical Laboratory Improvement Amendments (CLIA) certification number, or skilled nursing facility NPI. *Do not enter hyphens or spaces in the number.* Otherwise, leave blank.
24A	Enter the date the procedure or service was performed in the FROM column as MMDDYYYY (without spaces). Enter a date in the TO column *if the procedure or service was performed on consecutive days during a range of dates. Then, enter the number of consecutive days in Block 24G.* **NOTE:** The shaded area in each line is used to enter supplemental information to support reported services *if instructed by the payer to enter such information.* Data entry in Block 24 is limited to reporting six services. *Do not use the shaded lines to report additional services.* If additional services were provided, generate new CMS-1500 claim(s) to report the additional services.
24B	Enter the appropriate 2-digit Place of Service (POS) code to identify the location where the reported procedure or service was performed. (Refer to Appendix II for POS codes.)
24C	Leave blank.
24D	Enter the CPT or HCPCS level II code and applicable required modifier(s) for procedures or services performed. *Separate the CPT/HCPCS code and first modifier with one space. Separate additional modifiers with one space each. Up to four modifiers can be entered.*
24E	Enter the diagnosis pointer number from Block 21 that relates to the procedure/service performed on the date of service.
24F	Enter the fee charged for each reported procedure or service. When multiple procedures or services are reported on the same line, enter the total fee charged. *Do not enter commas, periods, or dollar signs. Do not enter negative amounts. Enter 00 in the cents area if the amount is a whole number.*
24G	Enter the number of days or units for procedures or services reported in Block 24D. *If just one procedure or service was reported in Block 24D, enter a 1 in Block 24G.*
24H	Leave blank. Reserved for Medicaid claims.
24I	Leave blank. The NPI abbreviation is preprinted on the CMS-1500 claim.
24J	Enter the 10-digit NPI for the: • provider who performed the service *if the provider is a member of a group practice.* (Leave blank if the provider is a solo practitioner.) • supervising provider *if the service was provided "incident to" the service of a physician or nonphysician practitioner* **and** *the physician or practitioner who ordered the service did not supervise the provider.* (Leave blank if the "incident to" service was performed under the supervision of the physician or nonphysician practitioner.) • DMEPOS supplier or outside laboratory *if the physician submits the claim for services provided by the DMEPOS supplier or outside laboratory.* (Leave blank if the DMEPOS supplier or outside laboratory submits the claim.) Otherwise, leave blank.
25	Enter the provider's social security number (SSN) or employer identification number (EIN*). Do not enter hyphens or spaces in the number.* Enter an X in the appropriate box to indicate which number is reported.

(continues)

TABLE 14-4 (continued)

BLOCK	INSTRUCTIONS
26	Enter the patient's account number as assigned by the provider. **NOTE:** When completing claims for case studies, enter the case study number (e.g., 14-7). If the patient has both primary and secondary coverage, enter a P (for primary) (e.g., 14-3P) next to the case study number (on the primary claim) and an S (for secondary) (e.g., 14-3S) next to the number (on the secondary claim); if the patient is eligible for the Medicare-Medicaid crossover plan, enter MM (e.g., 14-2MM) next to the case study number.
27	Enter an X in the YES box to indicate that the provider agrees to accept assignment. Otherwise, enter an X in the NO box.
28	Enter the total charges for services and/or procedures reported in Block 24. **NOTE:** If multiple claims are submitted for one patient because more than six procedures or services were reported, be sure the total charge reported on each claim accurately represents the total of the items on each submitted claim.
29	Enter the total amount the patient (or another payer) paid *toward covered services only*. If no payment was made, leave blank.
30	Leave blank.
31	Enter the provider's name and credential (e.g., MARY SMITH MD) and the date the claim was completed as MMDDYYYY (without spaces). *Do not enter any punctuation.*
32	Enter the name and address where procedures or services were provided *if at a location other than the patient's home, such as a hospital, outside laboratory facility, physician's office, skilled nursing facility, or DMEPOS supplier.* Otherwise, leave blank. Enter the name on line 1, the address on line 2, and the city, state and 5- or 9-digit zip code on line 3. *For a 9-digit zip code, enter the hyphen.* **EXAMPLE:** ● Dr. Brilliant is a solo practitioner. Enter Dr. Brilliant's name, credential, and address in Block 32. ● Dr. Healer practices at the Goodmedicine Clinic. Enter Goodmedicine Clinic and its address in Block 32. **NOTE:** ● If Block 18 contains dates of service for inpatient care and/or Block 20 contains an X in the YES box, enter the name and address of the facility that provided services. ● Effective April 1, 2004, when reporting services rendered in the physician's office, enter the physician's name, street address, city, state, and zip code. Failure to report the physician's office address in Block 32 will result in the claim being returned unprocessed, and the provider will not be allowed to appeal the claim. Although entering physician office address information in Blocks 32 and 33 may appear to be redundant, electronic data interchange (EDI) requires entry in both places.
32a	Enter the 10-digit NPI of the provider entered in Block 32.
32b	Leave blank.
33	Enter the provider's *billing* name, address, and telephone number. Enter the phone number in the area next to the Block title. *Do not enter parentheses for the area code.* Enter the name on line 1, enter the address on line 2, and enter the city, state, and 5- or 9-digit zip code on line 3. *For a 9-digit zip code, enter the hyphen.*
33a	Enter the 10-digit NPI of the *billing* provider (e.g., solo practitioner) or group practice (e.g., clinic).
33b	Leave blank.

ERIN A. HELPER, M.D.
101 Medic Drive, Anywhere NY 12345
(101) 111-1234 (Office) • (101) 111-9292 (Fax)
EIN: 11-1234523
NPI: 1234567890

Case Study

PATIENT INFORMATION:

Name:	Public, John Q.
Address:	10A Senate Avenue
City:	Anywhere
State:	NY
Zip Code:	12345-1234
Telephone:	(101) 201-7891
Gender:	Male
Date of Birth:	09-25-1930
Occupation:	
Employer:	
Spouse's Employer:	

INSURANCE INFORMATION:

Patient Number:	14-1
Place of Service:	Office
Primary Insurance Plan:	Medicare
Primary Insurance Plan ID #:	112349801A
Policy #:	
Primary Policyholder:	Public, John Q.
Policyholder Date of Birth:	09-25-1930
Relationship to Patient:	Self
Secondary Insurance Plan:	
Secondary Insurance Plan ID #:	
Secondary Policyholder:	

Patient Status ☐ Married   ☐ Divorced   ☒ Single   ☐ Student

ICD-10-CM ALERT!

Abdominal pain   R10.9

DIAGNOSIS INFORMATION

Diagnosis	Code	Diagnosis	Code
1. Abdominal pain	789.00	5.	
2.		6.	
3.		7.	
4.		8.	

PROCEDURE INFORMATION

Description of Procedure or Service	Date	Code	Charge
1. New patient office visit, level III	01-20-YYYY	99203	75.00
2.			
3.			
4.			
5.			

SPECIAL NOTES: Referring physician: Ivan Gooddoc, M.D. (NPI 3456789012).

FIGURE 14-6 John Q. Public case study (Courtesy Delmar/Cengage Learning)

FIGURE 14-7 Completed CMS-1500 claim for John Q. Public case study (Courtesy Delmar/Cengage Learning)

ICD-10-CM ALERT!

21. DIAGNOSIS OR NATURE OF ILLNESS OR INJURY (Relate Items 1, 2, 3 or 4 to Item 24E by Line)
1. R10 9
2.
3.
4.
E. DIAGNOSIS POINTER

EXERCISE 14-2

Completing the Mary S. Patient Medicare Primary CMS-1500 Claim

1. Review the Mary S. Patient case study (Figure 14-8). Obtain a blank claim by making a copy of the claim in Appendix III.

2. Refer to the claims completion instructions in Table 14-4.

3. Select the information needed from the case study (Figure 14-8) and enter the required information on the claim using optical scanning guidelines.

4. Review the claim to be sure all required blocks are properly completed.

5. Compare your claim with the completed Mary S. Patient claim in Figure 14-9.

ERIN A. HELPER, M.D.
101 Medic Drive, Anywhere NY 12345
(101) 111-1234 (Office) • (101) 111-9292 (Fax)
EIN: 11-1234523
NPI: 1234567890

Case Study

PATIENT INFORMATION:

Name:	Patient, Mary S.
Address:	91 Home Street
City:	Nowhere
State:	NY
Zip Code:	12367-1234
Telephone:	(101) 201-8989
Gender:	Female
Date of Birth:	03-08-1933
Occupation:	
Employer:	

INSURANCE INFORMATION:

Patient Number:	14-2
Place of Service:	Office
Primary Insurance Plan:	Medicare
Primary Insurance Plan ID #:	001287431D
Policy #:	
Primary Policyholder:	Mary S. Patient
Policyholder Date of Birth:	03-08-1933
Relationship to Patient:	Self
Secondary Insurance Plan:	
Secondary Insurance Plan ID #:	
Secondary Policyholder:	

Patient Status   ☐ Married   ☐ Divorced   ☒ Single   ☐ Student

---

ICD-10-CM ALERT!

Pleurisy	R09.1
Atrial tachycardia	I47.1
History of pulmonary embolism	Z86.71

DIAGNOSIS INFORMATION

	Diagnosis	Code		Diagnosis	Code
1.	Pleurisy	511.0	5.		
2.	Atrial tachycardia	427.89	6.		
3.	History of pulmonary embolism	V12.51	7.		
4.			8.		

PROCEDURE INFORMATION

	Description of Procedure or Service	Date	Code	Charge
1.	Office consultation, Level III	01-30-YYYY	99243	150.00
2.	Chest x-ray, two views (frontal and lateral)	01-30-YYYY	71020	50.00
3.	12-lead ECG with interpretation and report	01-30-YYYY	93000	50.00
4.				
5.				

SPECIAL NOTES: Date of onset 01-28-YYYY. Referred by Ivan M. Gooddoc M.D. (NPI 3456789012).

FIGURE 14-8 Mary S. Patient case study (Courtesy Delmar/Cengage Learning)

1500

HEALTH INSURANCE CLAIM FORM

APPROVED BY NATIONAL UNIFORM CLAIM COMMITTE 08/05

| | PICA | | | | | | | | | PICA | |

| 1. MEDICARE | MEDICAID | TRICARE CHAMPUS | CHAMPVA | GROUP HEALTH PLAN | FECA BLK LUNG | OTHER | 1a. INSURED'S I.D. NUMBER | (For Program in Item 1) |
| [X] (Medicare #) | (Medicaid #) | (Sponsor's SSN) | (Member ID#) | (SSN or ID) | (SSN) | (ID) | 001287431D | |

2. PATIENT'S NAME (Last Name, First Name, Middle Initial)
PATIENT, MARY, S

3. PATIENT'S BIRTH DATE MM DD YY
03 08 1933 **SEX** M F [X]

4. INSURED'S NAME (Last Name, First Name, Middle Initial)

5. PATIENT'S ADDRESS (No., Street)
91 HOME STREET

6. PATIENT'S RELATIONSHIP TO INSURED
Self Spouse Child Other

7. INSURED'S ADDRESS (No., Street)

CITY NOWHERE **STATE** NY

8. PATIENT STATUS
Single [X] Married Other

CITY **STATE**

ZIP CODE 12367-1234 **TELEPHONE (Include Area Code)** (101) 2018989

Employed Full-Time Student Part-Time Student

ZIP CODE **TELEPHONE (Include Area Code)** ( )

9. OTHER INSURED'S NAME (Last Name, First Name, Middle Initial)

10. IS PATIENT'S CONDITION RELATED TO:

11. INSURED'S POLICY GROUP OR FECA NUMBER
NONE

a. OTHER INSURED'S POLICY OR GROUP NUMBER

a. EMPLOYMENT? (Current or Previous)
YES [X] NO

a. INSURED'S DATE OF BIRTH MM DD YY SEX M F

b. OTHER INSURED'S DATE OF BIRTH MM DD YY SEX M F

b. AUTO ACCIDENT? PLACE (State)
YES [X] NO

b. EMPLOYER'S NAME OR SCHOOL NAME

c. EMPLOYER'S NAME OR SCHOOL NAME

c. OTHER ACCIDENT?
YES [X] NO

c. INSURANCE PLAN NAME OR PROGRAM NAME

d. INSURANCE PLAN NAME OR PROGRAM NAME

10d. RESERVED FOR LOCAL USE

d. IS THERE ANOTHER HEALTH BENEFIT PLAN?
YES NO **If yes,** return to and complete item 9 a-d.

READ BACK OF FORM BEFORE COMPLETING & SIGNING THIS FORM.
12. PATIENT'S OR AUTHORIZED PERSON'S SIGNATURE I authorize the release of any medical or other information necessary to process this claim. I also request payment of government benefits either to myself or to the party who accepts assignment below.

SIGNED SIGNATURE ON FILE DATE

13. INSURED'S OR AUTHORIZED PERSON'S SIGNATURE I authorize payment of medical benefits to the undersigned physican or supplier for services described below.

SIGNED

14. DATE OF CURRENT: MM DD YY
01 28 YYYY
ILLNESS (First symptom) OR INJURY (Accident) OR PREGNANCY (LMP)

15. IF PATIENT HAS HAD SAME OR SIMILAR ILLNESS. GIVE FIRST DATE MM DD YY

16. DATES PATIENT UNABLE TO WORK IN CURRENT OCCUPATION MM DD YY MM DD YY
FROM TO

17. NAME OF REFERRING PROVIDER OR OTHER SOURCE
IVAN M GOODDOC MD

17a.
17b. NPI 3456789012

18. HOSPITALIZATION DATES RELATED TO CURRENT SERVICES MM DD YY MM DD YY
FROM TO

19. RESERVED FOR LOCAL USE

20. OUTSIDE LAB? YES [X] NO $ CHARGES

21. DIAGNOSIS OR NATURE OF ILLNESS OR INJURY (Relate Items 1, 2, 3 or 4 to Item 24E by Line)
1. 511 0
2. 427 89
3. V12 51
4.

22. MEDICAID RESUBMISSION CODE ORIGINAL REF. NO.

23. PRIOR AUTHORIZATION NUMBER

24. A DATE(S) OF SERVICE From To MM DD YY MM DD YY	B. PLACE OF SERVICE	C. EMG	D. PROCEDURES, SERVICES, OR SUPPLIES (Explain Unusual Circumstances) CPT/HCPCS MODIFER	E. DIAGNOSIS POINTER	F. $ CHARGES	G. DAYS OR UNITS	H. EPSDT Family Plan	I. ID. QUAL.	J. RENDERING PROVIDER ID. #
1 01 30 YYYY	11		99243	1	150 00	1		NPI	
2 01 30 YYYY	11		71020	1	50 00	1		NPI	
3 01 30 YYYY	11		93000	2	50 00	1		NPI	
4								NPI	
5								NPI	
6								NPI	

25. FEDERAL TAX I.D. NUMBER SSN EIN
111234523 [X]

26. PATIENT'S ACCOUNT NO.
14-2

27. ACCEPT ASSIGNMENT? (For govt. claims, see back)
[X] YES NO

28. TOTAL CHARGE $ 250 00

29. AMOUNT PAID $

30. BALANCE DUE $

31. SIGNATURE OF PHYSICIAN OR SUPPLIER INCLUDING DEGREES OR CREDENTIALS (I certify that the statements on the reverse apply to this bill and are made a part thereof.)
ERIN A HELPER MD
SIGNED DATE MMDDYYYY

32. SERVICE FACILITY LOCATION INFORMATION
ERIN A HELPER MD
101 MEDIC DRIVE
ANYWHERE NY 12345
a. 1234567890 b.

33. BILLING PROVIDER INFO & PH # (101) 1111234
ERIN A HELPER MD
101 MEDIC DRIVE
ANYWHERE NY 12345
a. 1234567890 b.

NUCC Instruction Manual available at: www.nucc.org

APPROVED OMB-0938-0999 FORM CMS-1500 (08/05)

FIGURE 14-9 Completed Medicare primary CMS-1500 claim for Mary S. Patient case study (Courtesy Delmar/Cengage Learning)

ICD-10-CM ALERT!

21. DIAGNOSIS OR NATURE OF ILLNESS OR INJURY (Relate Items 1, 2, 3 or 4 to Item 24E by Line)
1. R09 1
2. I47 1
3. Z86 71
4.

E. DIAGNOSIS POINTER

MEDICARE AND MEDIGAP CLAIMS

Modifications must be made to the Medicare primary claim (Table 14-5) when the healthcare provider is a Medicare PAR, the patient has a Medigap policy in addition to Medicare, and the patient has signed an Authorization for Release of Medigap Benefits. If a separate Medigap release is on file, the words SIGNATURE ON FILE must appear in Block 13. No benefits will be paid to the PAR if Block 27, Accept Assignment, contains an X in the NO box.

TABLE 14-5   CMS-1500 claims completion instructions for Medicare and Medigap claims

BLOCK	INSTRUCTIONS
1	Enter an X in the *Medicare* and the *Other* boxes.
9	Enter SAME if the patient is the Medigap policyholder. If the patient is *not* the Medigap policyholder, enter policyholder's last name, first name, and middle initial (if known) (separated by commas).
9a	Enter MEDIGAP followed by the policy number and group number, separated by spaces (e.g., MEDIGAP 123456789 123). (The abbreviations MG or MGAP are also acceptable.)
9b	Enter the Medigap policyholder's birth date as MM DD YYYY (with spaces). Enter an X in the appropriate box to indicate the Medigap policyholder's gender.
9c	Leave blank if the Medigap plan identification number assigned by the payer is entered in Block 9d. Otherwise, enter the payer's mailing address.
9d	Enter the Medigap PlanID number. If there is no PlanID number, enter the plan's name (e.g., Aetna Medigap).
13	Enter SIGNATURE ON FILE. (The abbreviation SOF is also acceptable.) Leave the date field blank.

EXERCISE 14-3

Medicare and Medigap Claims Processing

Additional information needed for this case:
Dr. Helper is a Medicare PAR. The billing entity is Erin Helper, M.D.

1. Obtain a blank CMS-1500 claim by making a copy of the blank claim in Appendix III.

2. Underline the block identifiers on the new claim for the blocks discussed in the Medigap claim form instructions (Table 14-5).

3. Refer to the case study for John Q. Public (see Figure 14-6). Enter the following information in the blocks for the secondary policy:

   Aetna Medigap ID # 22233544

   PlanID: 11543299

   Policyholder: John Q. Public

   Employer: Retired

4. Complete the Medicare/Medigap claim using the data from the case study.

5. Compare the completed claim to the claim in Figure 14-10 to be sure all required blocks are properly completed.

FIGURE 14-10 Completed Medicare/Medigap CMS-1500 claim for John Q. Public case study (Courtesy Delmar/Cengage Learning)

ICD-10-CM ALERT!

21. DIAGNOSIS OR NATURE OF ILLNESS OR INJURY (Relate Items 1, 2, 3 or 4 to Item 24E by Line)

1. R09 . 1
2. I47 . 1
3. Z86 . 71
4.

E. DIAGNOSIS POINTER

MEDICARE-MEDICAID (MEDI-MEDI) CROSSOVER CLAIMS

A **Medicare–Medicaid (Medi-Medi) crossover** plan provides both Medicare and Medicaid coverage to certain eligible beneficiaries (Medicare beneficiaries with low incomes).

The following modifications must be added to the Medicare primary claim when the patient is covered by Medicare and also has Medicaid coverage for services rendered on a fee-for-service basis (Table 14-6).

TABLE 14-6   CMS-1500 claims completion instructions for Medicare-Medicaid (Medi-Medi) crossover claims

BLOCK	INSTRUCTIONS
1	Enter an X in both the Medicare *and* Medicaid boxes.
10d	Enter the abbreviation MCD followed by the patient's Medicaid ID number.
26	Add MM to the patient account number to indicate Medicare-Medicaid crossover coverage.
27	Enter an X in the YES box. (NonPAR providers must accept assignment on Medicare-Medicaid crossover claims.)

EXERCISE 14-4

Medicare-Medicaid Crossover Claims Processing

Additional information needed for this case:
Dr. Helper is a Medicare PAR. The billing entity is Erin Helper, M.D.

1. Obtain a blank CMS-1500 claim by making a copy of the claim in Appendix III.

2. Underline the blocks discussed in the Medicare-Medicaid crossover claims instructions (Table 14-6).

3. Refer to the Mary S. Patient case study in Figure 14-8, and enter additional Medicaid information in the secondary policy blocks:

   Insurance policy: Medicaid

   ID #: 101234591XT

   Relationship: Self

4. Complete the Medicare/Medicaid (Medi/Medi) claim.

5. Compare the completed claim with the claim in Figure 14-11.

MEDICARE AS SECONDARY PAYER CLAIMS

CMS-1500 claims instructions are modified when Medicare is secondary to another insurance plan (Table 14-7). The Medicare Secondary Payer (MSP) program coordinates benefits between Medicare and other payers to determine if another insurance plan is primary. CMS awards a coordination-of-benefits (COB) contract to consolidate activities that support the collection, management, and reporting of other insurance coverage primary to Medicare. The COB contractor uses the following to identify insurance primary to Medicare:

- *Initial Enrollment Questionnaire (IEQ)*—Medicare beneficiaries complete a questionnaire about other insurance coverage about three months before they are entitled to Medicare

1500

HEALTH INSURANCE CLAIM FORM

APPROVED BY NATIONAL UNIFORM CLAIM COMMITTE 08/05

☐ PICA PICA ☐☐

1. MEDICARE	MEDICAID	TRICARE CHAMPUS	CHAMPVA	GROUP HEALTH PLAN	FECA BLK LUNG	OTHER	1a. INSURED'S I.D. NUMBER (For Program in Item 1)
[X] (Medicare #)	[X] (Medicaid #)	☐ (Sponsor's SSN)	☐ (Member ID#)	☐ (SSN or ID)	☐ (SSN)	☐ (ID)	001287431D

2. PATIENT'S NAME (Last Name, First Name, Middle Initial)	3. PATIENT'S BIRTH DATE MM DD YY	SEX	4. INSURED'S NAME (Last Name, First Name, Middle Initial)
PATIENT, MARY, S	03 08 1933	M☐ F[X]	

5. PATIENT'S ADDRESS (No., Street)	6. PATIENT'S RELATIONSHIP TO INSURED	7. INSURED'S ADDRESS (No., Street)
91 HOME STREET	Self ☐ Spouse ☐ Child ☐ Other ☐	
CITY	STATE	8. PATIENT STATUS	CITY	STATE
NOWHERE	NY	Single [X] Married ☐ Other ☐	
ZIP CODE	TELEPHONE (Include Area Code)		ZIP CODE	TELEPHONE (Include Area Code)
12367-1234	(101)2018989	Employed ☐ Full-Time Student ☐ Part-Time Student ☐	( )

9. OTHER INSURED'S NAME (Last Name, First Name, Middle Initial)	10. IS PATIENT'S CONDITION RELATED TO:	11. INSURED'S POLICY GROUP OR FECA NUMBER
		NONE
a. OTHER INSURED'S POLICY OR GROUP NUMBER	a. EMPLOYMENT? (Current or Previous) ☐ YES [X] NO	a. INSURED'S DATE OF BIRTH MM DD YY SEX M☐ F☐
b. OTHER INSURED'S DATE OF BIRTH MM DD YY SEX M☐ F☐	b. AUTO ACCIDENT? PLACE (State) ☐ YES [X] NO	b. EMPLOYER'S NAME OR SCHOOL NAME
c. EMPLOYER'S NAME OR SCHOOL NAME	c. OTHER ACCIDENT? ☐ YES [X] NO	c. INSURANCE PLAN NAME OR PROGRAM NAME
d. INSURANCE PLAN NAME OR PROGRAM NAME	10d. RESERVED FOR LOCAL USE MCD 101234591XT	d. IS THERE ANOTHER HEALTH BENEFIT PLAN? ☐ YES ☐ NO If yes, return to and complete item 9 a-d.

READ BACK OF FORM BEFORE COMPLETING & SIGNING THIS FORM.
12. PATIENT'S OR AUTHORIZED PERSON'S SIGNATURE I authorize the release of any medical or other information necessary to process this claim. I also request payment of government benefits either to myself or to the party who accepts assignment below.

SIGNED SIGNATURE ON FILE DATE

13. INSURED'S OR AUTHORIZED PERSON'S SIGNATURE I authorize payment of medical benefits to the undersigned physician or supplier for services described below.

SIGNED

14. DATE OF CURRENT: ILLNESS (First symptom) OR INJURY (Accident) OR PREGNANCY (LMP) MM DD YY	15. IF PATIENT HAS HAD SAME OR SIMILAR ILLNESS. GIVE FIRST DATE MM DD YY	16. DATES PATIENT UNABLE TO WORK IN CURRENT OCCUPATION MM DD YY MM DD YY
01 28 YYYY		FROM TO

17. NAME OF REFERRING PROVIDER OR OTHER SOURCE	17a.	18. HOSPITALIZATION DATES RELATED TO CURRENT SERVICES MM DD YY MM DD YY
IVAN M GOODDOC MD	17b. NPI 3456789012	FROM TO

19. RESERVED FOR LOCAL USE	20. OUTSIDE LAB? ☐ YES [X] NO	$ CHARGES

21. DIAGNOSIS OR NATURE OF ILLNESS OR INJURY (Relate Items 1, 2, 3 or 4 to Item 24E by Line)

1. 511.0   3. V12.51
2. 427.89   4.

22. MEDICAID RESUBMISSION CODE	ORIGINAL REF. NO.

23. PRIOR AUTHORIZATION NUMBER

24. A DATE(S) OF SERVICE From MM DD YY To MM DD YY	B. PLACE OF SERVICE	C. EMG	D. PROCEDURES, SERVICES, OR SUPPLIES (Explain Unusual Circumstances) CPT/HCPCS MODIFER	E. DIAGNOSIS POINTER	F. $ CHARGES	G. DAYS OR UNITS	H. EPSDT Family Plan	I. ID. QUAL.	J. RENDERING PROVIDER ID. #
1	01 30 YYYY	11		99243	1	150 00	1		NPI	
2	01 30 YYYY	11		71020	1	50 00	1		NPI	
3	01 30 YYYY	11		93000	2	50 00	1		NPI	
4									NPI	
5									NPI	
6									NPI	

25. FEDERAL TAX I.D. NUMBER SSN EIN	26. PATIENT'S ACCOUNT NO.	27. ACCEPT ASSIGNMENT? (For govt. claims, see back)	28. TOTAL CHARGE	29. AMOUNT PAID	30. BALANCE DUE
111234523 [X]	14-2MM	[X] YES ☐ NO	$ 250 00	$	$

31. SIGNATURE OF PHYSICIAN OR SUPPLIER INCLUDING DEGREES OR CREDENTIALS (I certify that the statements on the reverse apply to this bill and are made a part thereof.)	32. SERVICE FACILITY LOCATION INFORMATION	33. BILLING PROVIDER INFO & PH # (101)1111234
ERIN A HELPER MD SIGNED DATE MMDDYYYY	ERIN A HELPER MD 101 MEDIC DRIVE ANYWHERE NY 12345 a. 1234587890 b.	ERIN A HELPER MD 101 MEDIC DRIVE ANYWHERE NY 12345 a. 1234587890 b.

NUCC Instruction Manual available at: www.nucc.org

APPROVED OMB-0938-0999 FORM CMS-1500 (08/05)

FIGURE 14-11 Completed Medicare/Medicaid (Medi/Medi) CMS-1500 claim for Mary S. Patient case study (Courtesy Delmar/Cengage Learning)

ICD-10-CM ALERT!

21. DIAGNOSIS OR NATURE OF ILLNESS OR INJURY (Relate Items 1, 2, 3 or 4 to Item 24E by Line)

1. K62.5   3.
2. Z85.03   4.

E. DIAGNOSIS POINTER

NOTE: Effective 2007, HCPCS level II modifier -M2 (Medicare secondary payer) was added to reported codes to communicate to private payers that Medicare is the secondary payer. Reporting modifier -M2 prevents claims denial based on the patient's age or another edit specific to a private payer.

- *IRS/SSA/CMS Data Match*—Employers complete a questionnaire that provides group health plan (GHP) information about identified workers who are either entitled to Medicare or married to a Medicare beneficiary
- *MSP Claims Investigation*—Collects data about other health insurance that may be primary to Medicare; is based on information submitted on a CMS-1500 claim or from other sources
- *Voluntary MSP Data Match Agreements*—Voluntary agreements with CMS and employers and payers that allow the electronic data exchange of group health plan eligibility and Medicare information

TABLE 14-7   CMS-1500 claims completion instructions for Medicare as secondary payer claims

BLOCK	INSTRUCTIONS
1	Enter an X in the *Medicare* and *Other* boxes.
4	If the policyholder is the patient, enter SAME. If the patient is not the policyholder, enter the primary insurance policyholder's name.
6	Enter an X in the appropriate box to indicate the patient's relationship to the primary insurance policyholder.
7	Enter SAME.
10, 10a–10c	Enter an X in the appropriate boxes to indicate whether the patient's condition is related to employment or an auto or other accident. **NOTE:** Entering an X in any of the YES boxes alerts the Medicare administrative contractor that another insurance plan might be liable for payment. Medicare will not process the claim until the provider submits a remittance advice from the liable party (e.g., auto insurance, workers' compensation).
11	Enter the primary policyholder's group number if the patient is covered by a group health plan. *Do not enter hyphens or spaces in the policy or group number.* Otherwise, leave blank.
11a	Enter the primary insurance policyholder's date of birth as MM DD YYYY (with spaces). Enter an X in the appropriate box to indicate the policyholder's gender.
11b	If the primary insurance is a large group health plan (LGHP), enter the name of the employer. If the primary insurance policyholder is retired, enter RETIRED and the date of retirement as MM DD YYYY (with spaces).
11c	Enter the name of the primary policyholder's insurance plan. **NOTE:** Be sure to attach a copy of the remittance advice to the claim, which must contain the payer's name and address.
16	If the patient is employed full time, enter the dates the patient is or was unable to work (if applicable).
26	Add an S to the patient account number to indicate the secondary policy.

EXERCISE 14-5

Medicare as Secondary Payer Claims Processing

Additional information needed for this case:

Dr. Helper is a Medicare PAR. The billing entity is Erin Helper, M.D. The ambulatory surgical center NPI is 5678901234.

1. Obtain a blank CMS-1500 claim by making a copy of the claim in Appendix III.
2. Underline the blocks discussed in the Medicare Secondary Payer claims instructions in Table 14-7.
3. Refer to the Jack L. Neely case study (Figure 14-12) and complete the Medicare Secondary Payer claim for this case.
4. Review the completed claim to be sure all required blocks are filled in.
5. Compare your claim with Figure 14-13.

ERIN A. HELPER, M.D.
101 Medic Drive, Anywhere NY 12345
(101) 111-1234 (Office) • (101) 111-9292 (Fax)
EIN: 11-1234523
NPI: 1234567890

Case Study

PATIENT INFORMATION:

Name:	Jack L. Neely
Address:	329 Water Street
City:	Nowhere
State:	NY
Zip Code:	12367-1234
Telephone:	(101) 201-1278
Gender:	Male
Date of Birth:	09-09-1929
Occupation:	Retired
Spouse's Employer:	Federal Investigative Services

INSURANCE INFORMATION:

Patient Number:	14-3
Place of Service:	Anywhere Surgical Center
Primary Insurance Plan:	BCBS Federal
Primary Insurance Plan ID #:	R1234567
Primary Policyholder:	Mary Neely
Primary Policyholder Birth Date:	03-19-1935
Relationship to Patient:	Spouse
Secondary Policy:	Medicare
Secondary Insurance Plan ID #:	111223344A
Secondary Policyholder:	Jack L. Neely

Patient Status ☒ Married   ☐ Divorced   ☐ Single   ☐ Student

ICD-10-CM ALERT!

Rectal bleeding (3 days) K62.5
History of polyps,
ascending colon Z85.03

DIAGNOSIS INFORMATION

Diagnosis	Code	Diagnosis	Code
1. Rectal bleeding (3 days)	569.3	5.	
2. History of polyps, ascending colon	V10.05	6.	
3.		7.	
4.		8.	

PROCEDURE INFORMATION

Description of Procedure or Service	Date	Code	Charge
1. Colonoscopy, flexible to ileum	01-08-YYYY	45378	700.00
2.			
3.			
4.			
5.			

SPECIAL NOTES: Referring physician: Arnold Younglove M.D. (NPI 4567890123)
Anywhere Surgical Center, 101 Park St, Anywhere NY 12345 (NPI 5678901234)

FIGURE 14-12 Jack L. Neely case study (Courtesy Delmar/Cengage Learning)

FIGURE 14-13 Completed Medicare Secondary Payer CMS-1500 claim for Jack L. Neely case study (Courtesy Delmar/Cengage Learning)

ICD-10-CM ALERT!

21. DIAGNOSIS OR NATURE OF ILLNESS OR INJURY (Relate Items 1, 2, 3 or 4 to Item 24E by Line)

1. K62 5

2. Z85 03

3.

4.

E. DIAGNOSIS POINTER

Additional Medicare case studies are found in Appendix I and Appendix II.

ROSTER BILLING FOR MASS VACCINATION PROGRAMS

The simplified roster billing process was developed to enable Medicare beneficiaries to participate in mass pneumococcal polysaccharide vaccine (PPV) and influenza virus vaccination programs offered by public health clinics (PHCs) and other entities that bill Medicare payers. (Medicare has not yet developed roster billing for hepatitis B vaccinations.) Properly licensed individuals and entities conducting mass immunization programs may submit claims using a simplified claims filing procedure to bill for the PPV and influenza virus vaccine benefit for multiple beneficiaries if they agree to accept assignment for these claims. Entities that submit claims on roster bills (and therefore must accept assignment) may not collect any donations or other cost-sharing of any kind from Medicare beneficiaries for PPV or influenza vaccinations. However, the entity may bill Medicare for the amount not subsidized from its own budget.

> **EXAMPLE:** A public health clinic (PHC) sponsors an influenza virus vaccination clinic for Medicare beneficiaries. The cost is $12.50 per vaccination, and the PHC pays $2.50 of the cost from its budget.
>
> The PHC is therefore eligible to roster-bill Medicare the $10 cost difference for each beneficiary. The PHC submits both the roster billing form (Figure 14-14) and CMS-1500 claim (Figure 14-15).

Provider Enrollment Criteria

All individuals and entities that submit PPV and influenza virus vaccination benefit claims to Medicare on roster bills must complete Form CMS-855, the Provider/Supplier Enrollment Application. Specialized instructions must be followed to simplify the enrollment process, and providers may not bill Medicare for any services other than PPV and influenza virus vaccinations.

Completing the CMS-1500 Claim for Roster Billing Purposes

Providers that qualify for roster billing may use a preprinted CMS-1500 claim that contains standardized information about the entity and the benefit (Table 14-8). Providers that submit roster bills to carriers must complete certain blocks on a single modified CMS-1500 claim, which serves as the cover sheet for the roster bill.

NOTE: There is no minimum requirement as to the number of beneficiaries to be reported on the same date (the rule used to be a minimum of five beneficiaries reported on the same date to qualify for roster billing). *However, the date of service for each vaccination administered must be entered.*

NOTE: Roster billing is not used to submit single patient bills.

NOTE: Providers should establish a computer edit to identify individuals and entities that plan to participate in the Medicare program only for the purpose of mass immunizing beneficiaries.

NOTE: During a mass immunization clinic, beneficiaries receive either the PPV *or* the influenza virus vaccination, not both. (This note applies to Blocks 21 and 24D.)

NOTE: If the provider is not charging for the vaccine or its administration, enter 0 00 or NC (for "no charge") on the appropriate line for that item. This information is required for both paper claims and electronic submissions.

Provider	Allegany Health Clinic
	100 Main St, Anywhere NY 12345
	(101) 555-1111
EIN	98-7654321
NPI	1123456789
Date of Service	November 15, YYYY
Diagnosis	Encounter for immunization (ICD code V04.81)
Type of Service	Flu vaccine (CPT code 90658; HCPCS level II code G0008)
	$10.00 ($50.00 to be billed to Medicare) (90658)
Cost	$1.00 ($5.00 to be billed to Medicare) (G0008)

ICD-10-CM ALERT!

Flu vaccine	Z23

Patient Information

HICN	Name	DOB	Sex	Address	Signature
215659849	Doe, John A	02/05/34	M	1 Hill, Anywhere NY 12345	John A. Doe
236595428	Doe, Jane M	12/24/30	F	5 Main, Anywhere NY 12345	Jane M. Doe
236595214	Smith, May J	02/18/32	F	8 Roe, Anywhere NY 12345	May J Smith
956325954	Brown, Lou	05/15/20	F	2 Sims, Anywhere NY 12345	Lou Brown
596524854	Green, Julie	09/30/25	F	6 Pine, Anywhere NY 12345	Julie Green

FIGURE 14-14 Sample roster billing form (attach to CMS-1500 claim) (Courtesy Delmar/Cengage Learning)

TABLE 14-8 CMS-1500 claims completion instructions for Medicare roster billing

BLOCK	INSTRUCTIONS
1	Enter an X in the Medicare box.
2	Enter SEE ATTACHED ROSTER.
11	Enter NONE.
20	Enter an X in the NO box.
21	On line 1, enter V03.82 for PPV *or* V04.81 for influenza virus.
24B	Enter 60 (place of service, POS, code for "mass immunization center")
24D	On line 1, enter 90732 for PPV *or* 90658 for influenza virus. On line 2, enter G0009 (administration code for PPV) *or* G0008 (administration code for influenza).
24E	On lines 1 and 2, enter the diagnosis pointer number from Block 21.
24F	On lines 1 and 2, enter the total charges for each service.
25	Enter the provider's EIN (without the hyphen). Enter an X in the EIN box.
27	Enter an X in the YES box.
29	Enter the total amount paid by Medicare beneficiaries (e.g., coinsurance amounts). If no amount was paid, enter 0 00.
31	Have the provider sign the claim or use a signature stamp. Enter the date as MMDDYYYY (without spaces).
32	Enter the provider's name and address.
32a	Enter the provider's NPI.
33	Enter the provider's name, address, and telephone number.
33a	Enter the provider's NPI.

1500

HEALTH INSURANCE CLAIM FORM

APPROVED BY NATIONAL UNIFORM CLAIM COMMITTEE 08/05

| PICA | | | | | | | | | | PICA |

1. MEDICARE	MEDICAID	TRICARE CHAMPUS	CHAMPVA	GROUP HEALTH PLAN	FECA BLK LUNG	OTHER	1a. INSURED'S I.D. NUMBER	(For Program in Item 1)
X (Medicare #)	(Medicaid #)	(Sponsor's SSN)	(Member ID#)	(SSN or ID)	(SSN)	(ID)		

2. PATIENT'S NAME (Last Name, First Name, Middle Initial)
SEE ATTACHED ROSTER

3. PATIENT'S BIRTH DATE MM DD YY SEX M F

4. INSURED'S NAME (Last Name, First Name, Middle Initial)

5. PATIENT'S ADDRESS (No., Street)

6. PATIENT'S RELATIONSHIP TO INSURED
Self Spouse Child Other

7. INSURED'S ADDRESS (No., Street)

CITY   STATE

8. PATIENT STATUS
Single Married Other
Employed Full-Time Student Part-Time Student

CITY   STATE

ZIP CODE   TELEPHONE (Include Area Code) ( )

ZIP CODE   TELEPHONE (Include Area Code) ( )

9. OTHER INSURED'S NAME (Last Name, First Name, Middle Initial)

10. IS PATIENT'S CONDITION RELATED TO:

11. INSURED'S POLICY GROUP OR FECA NUMBER
NONE

a. OTHER INSURED'S POLICY OR GROUP NUMBER

a. EMPLOYMENT? (Current or Previous)
YES NO

a. INSURED'S DATE OF BIRTH MM DD YY SEX M F

b. OTHER INSURED'S DATE OF BIRTH MM DD YY SEX M F

b. AUTO ACCIDENT? PLACE (State)
YES NO

b. EMPLOYER'S NAME OR SCHOOL NAME

c. EMPLOYER'S NAME OR SCHOOL NAME

c. OTHER ACCIDENT?
YES NO

c. INSURANCE PLAN NAME OR PROGRAM NAME

d. INSURANCE PLAN NAME OR PROGRAM NAME

10d. RESERVED FOR LOCAL USE

d. IS THERE ANOTHER HEALTH BENEFIT PLAN?
YES NO If yes, return to and complete item 9 a-d.

READ BACK OF FORM BEFORE COMPLETING & SIGNING THIS FORM.
12. PATIENT'S OR AUTHORIZED PERSON'S SIGNATURE I authorize the release of any medical or other information necessary to process this claim. I also request payment of government benefits either to myself or to the party who accepts assignment below.

SIGNED   DATE

13. INSURED'S OR AUTHORIZED PERSON'S SIGNATURE I authorize payment of medical benefits to the undersigned physician or supplier for services described below.

SIGNED

14. DATE OF CURRENT: ILLNESS (First symptom) OR INJURY (Accident) OR PREGNANCY (LMP) MM DD YY

15. IF PATIENT HAS HAD SAME OR SIMILAR ILLNESS, GIVE FIRST DATE MM DD YY

16. DATES PATIENT UNABLE TO WORK IN CURRENT OCCUPATION MM DD YY FROM TO MM DD YY

17. NAME OF REFERRING PROVIDER OR OTHER SOURCE
17a.
17b. NPI

18. HOSPITALIZATION DATES RELATED TO CURRENT SERVICES MM DD YY FROM TO MM DD YY

19. RESERVED FOR LOCAL USE

20. OUTSIDE LAB? YES X NO $ CHARGES

21. DIAGNOSIS OR NATURE OF ILLNESS OR INJURY (Relate Items 1, 2, 3 or 4 to Item 24E by Line)
1. V04.81
2.
3.
4.

22. MEDICAID RESUBMISSION CODE ORIGINAL REF. NO.

23. PRIOR AUTHORIZATION NUMBER

24. A DATE(S) OF SERVICE From MM DD YY	To MM DD YY	B. PLACE OF SERVICE	C. EMG	D. PROCEDURES, SERVICES, OR SUPPLIES (Explain Unusual Circumstances) CPT/HCPCS	MODIFIER	E. DIAGNOSIS POINTER	F. $ CHARGES	G. DAYS OR UNITS	H. EPSDT Family Plan	I. ID. QUAL.	J. RENDERING PROVIDER ID. #
1	1115YYYY		60	90658		1	50 00				NPI
2	1115YYYY		60	G0008		1	5 00				NPI
3											NPI
4											NPI
5											NPI
6											NPI

25. FEDERAL TAX I.D. NUMBER	SSN EIN	26. PATIENT'S ACCOUNT NO.	27. ACCEPT ASSIGNMENT? (For govt. claims, see back)	28. TOTAL CHARGE	29. AMOUNT PAID	30. BALANCE DUE
987654321	X		X YES NO	$	$ 0 00	$

31. SIGNATURE OF PHYSICIAN OR SUPPLIER INCLUDING DEGREES OR CREDENTIALS (I certify that the statements on the reverse apply to this bill and are made a part thereof.)
SIGNATURE STAMP
SIGNED   DATE MMDDYYYY

32. SERVICE FACILITY LOCATION INFORMATION
ALLEGANY HEALTH CLINIC
100 MAIN ST
ANYWHERE NY 12345
a. 1123456789 b.

33. BILLING PROVIDER INFO & PH # (101)5551111
ALLEGANY HEALTH CLINIC
100 MAIN ST
ANYWHERE NY 12345
a. 1123456789 b.

NUCC Instruction Manual available at: www.nucc.org

APPROVED OMB-0938-0999 FORM CMS-1500 (08/05)

FIGURE 14-15 Completed CMS-1500 claim as cover sheet for Medicare roster billing form (Courtesy Delmar/Cengage Learning)

ICD-10-CM ALERT!

21. DIAGNOSIS OR NATURE OF ILLNESS OR INJURY (Relate Items 1, 2, 3 or 4 to Item 24E by Line)
1. Z23
2.
3.
4.

E. DIAGNOSIS POINTER

SUMMARY

Medicare Part A reimburses institutional providers for inpatient hospital and skilled nursing facility stays; home health and hospice services; ESRD and kidney donor coverage; and heart/heart-lung, liver, and bone marrow transplants. Medicare Part B reimburses noninstitutional healthcare providers for all outpatient services, including physician services, diagnostic testing, ambulance services, DME, supplies used in the home and certified by a physician, and so on.

Medicare Advantage plans (Medicare Part C) include managed care plans and private fee-for-service plans that provide care under contract to Medicare and may include such benefits as coordination of care, reductions in out-of-pocket expenses, and prescription drugs. The Medicare outpatient prescription drug program consists of private prescription drug plans (PDPs) and Medicare Advantage prescription drug plans (MA–PDs), collectively referred to as Medicare Part D.

Participating providers (PARs) agree to accept assignment on all Medicare claims submitted, and PARs receive special incentives as part of the agreement. Nonparticipating providers (nonPARs) may elect to accept assignment on a claim-by-claim basis, and restrictions apply (e.g., limiting charge).

When completing Medicare CMS-1500 claims for case studies in this text and the Workbook, the following special instructions apply:

- Block 9a—Enter MEDIGAP followed by the policy and/or group number (this instruction applies to Medigap claims only); otherwise, leave blank
- Block 12—Enter SIGNATURE ON FILE (patients have signed a customized authorization that is filed in the patient's record), and leave date blank
- Block 19—Leave blank
- Block 20—Enter an X in the *NO* box
- Block 23—Leave blank
- Block 26—Enter the case study number (e.g., 14-7). If the patient has both primary and secondary coverage, enter a P (for primary) next to the case study number (on the primary claim) (e.g., 14-3P) and an S (for secondary) next to the number (on the secondary claim) (e.g., 14-3S); if the patient is eligible for the Medicare-Medicaid crossover plan, enter MM next to the case study number (14-2MM)
- Block 27—Enter an X in the *YES* box
- When completing secondary claims, enter REMITTANCE ADVICE ATTACHED in the top left margin of the CMS-1500 claim (to simulate the attachment of a primary payer's remittance advice with a claim submitted to a secondary payer)

INTERNET LINKS

- *Medicare Contractor Beneficiary and Provider Communications Manual*
  Go to **www.cms.hhs.gov,** scroll down to the Top 10 Links heading, click, on the Manuals link, click on the Internet-Only Manuals (IOM) link, click on the Publication 100-09 link, and click on the Chapter 3—Provider Customer Services link.

- Medicare coverage information
  Go to **www.cms.hhs.gov,** click on the Medicare link, locate the Coverage heading, and click on the Medicare Coverage—General Information link.

- Medicare physician fee schedules
  Go to **www.cms.hhs.gov,** click on the Medicare link, locate the Medicare Fee-for-Service Payment heading, and click on the Fee Schedules—General Information link.

- Medicare program manuals
  Go to **www.cms.hhs.gov,** scroll down and click on the Manuals link, click on the Internet-Only Manuals link, and click on Publication #100-04 (*Medicare Claims Processing Manual)* and 100-05 (*Medicare Secondary Payer Manual).*

- Medicare Summary Notice
  Go to **www.medicare.gov,** click on the Medicare Billing link, and click on the Medicare Summary Notice link.
- QualityNet healthcare quality data exchange
  www.qualitynet.org
- RBRVS EZ-Fees software
  www.rbrvs.net
- U.S. Government Site for people with Medicare
  www.medicare.gov

STUDY CHECKLIST

- ☐ Read this textbook chapter and highlight key concepts.
- ☐ Access SimClaim software at the online companion, and become familiar with the software.
- ☐ Complete CMS-1500 claims for each chapter case study.
- ☐ Complete the chapter review, verifying answer with your instructor.
- ☐ Complete the chapter CD-ROM activities.
- ☐ Complete WebTutor assignments, and take online quizzes.
- ☐ Complete the Workbook chapter, verifying answers with your instructor.
- ☐ Complete Medicare claims for cases located in Appendices I and II.
- ☐ Complete the StudyWare activities to receive immediate feedback.
- ☐ Form a study group with classmates to discuss chapter concepts in preparation for an exam.

REVIEW

MULTIPLE CHOICE Select the most appropriate response.

1. **CMS is responsible for administering the _____ program.**
   a. Medicaid
   b. Medicare
   c. TRICARE
   d. workers' compensation

2. **Medicare Part _____ reimburses institutional providers for inpatient, hospice, and some home health services.**
   a. A
   b. B
   c. C
   d. D

3. **Which is a characteristic of Medicare enrollment?**
   a. Eligible individuals are automatically enrolled, or they apply for coverage.
   b. Individuals who qualify for SSA benefits must "buy in" to Medicare Part A.
   c. The general enrollment period is between January 1 and December 31.
   d. Those who enroll in Medicare Part A must also enroll in Medicare Part B.

4. **A Medicare benefit period is defined as beginning the first day of hospitalization and ending when**

   a. the patient has been admitted to a skilled nursing facility.

   b. the patient has been officially discharged from the hospital.

   c. the patient has been out of the hospital for 60 consecutive days.

   d. the spell of illness has ended for the patient.

5. **Skilled nursing facility (SNF) inpatients who meet Medicare's qualified diagnosis and comprehensive treatment plan requirements when they are admitted after a three-day-minimum acute hospital stay are required to pay the Medicare rate for SNF inpatient care during which period?**

   a. days 1–20

   b. days 21–100

   c. days 101+

   d. days 1–101

6. **Which is the total number of Medicare *lifetime reserve days* (defined as the number of days that can be used just once during a patient's lifetime)?**

   a. 30

   b. 60

   c. 90

   d. 120

7. **The original Medicare plan is also called Medicare**

   a. Advantage.

   b. fee-for-service.

   c. SELECT.

   d. supplemental insurance.

8. **Medigap coverage is offered to Medicare beneficiaries by**

   a. commercial payers.

   b. Medicaid.

   c. employers.

   d. federal health plans.

9. **As the result of legislation passed by some states, a nonPAR is prohibited from participating in _____.**

   a. assignment of benefits

   b. balance billing

   c. limiting charges

   d. private contracting

10. **Which is a written document provided to a Medicare beneficiary by a provider prior to rendering a service that is unlikely to be reimbursed by Medicare?**

    a. advance beneficiary notice

    b. medical necessity denial

    c. MSP questionnaire

    d. waiver of Medicare billing contract

Medicaid

CHAPTER OUTLINE

Medicaid Eligibility

Medicaid-Covered Services

Payment for Medicaid Services

Billing Notes

Claims Instructions

Medicaid as Secondary Payer Claims

Mother/Baby Claims

SCHIP Claims

OBJECTIVES

Upon successful completion of this chapter, you should be able to:

1. Define key terms.
2. Explain Medicaid eligibility guidelines.
3. List Medicaid covered services required by the federal government.
5. Describe how payments for Medicaid services are processed.
6. Apply Medicaid billing notes when completing CMS-1500 claims.
   Complete Medicaid primary, secondary, and mother/baby claims.

KEY TERMS

adjusted claim

dual eligibles

Early and Periodic Screening, Diagnostic, and Treatment (EPSDT) services

Federal Medical Assistance Percentage (FMAP)

federal poverty level (FPL)

MassHealth

Medicaid

Medicaid eligibility verification system (MEVS)

Medicaid remittance advice

MediCal

medical assistance program

mother/baby claim

recipient eligibility verification system (REVS)

surveillance and utilization review subsystem (SURS)

Temporary Assistance for Needy Families (TANF)

TennCare

voided claim

...ssed Title 19 of the Social Security Act, establishing a federally ...medical assistance program for individuals with incomes below the f... ...federal name for this program is Medicaid; several states assign lc... ...ifornia uses MediCal; Massachusetts uses MassHealth; Tennessee uses... ...which is a nationwide entitlement program, the federal governme... ...quirements for Medicaid and gave states the flexibility to develop el... ...nal benefits if they assumed responsibility for the program's support.

...es medical and health-related services to certain individuals and fami... with low incomes and limited resources (the "medically indigent"). It is jointly funded b... federal and state governments to assist states in providing adequate medical care to qual... individuals. Within broad federal guidelines, each state:

- Establishes its own eligibility standards.
- Determines the type, amount, duration, and scope of services.
- Sets rates of payment for services.
- Administers its own program.

Thus, Medicaid varies considerably from state to state, and each state has modified its program over time.

StudyWARE™

Complete StudyWare practice quizzes and activities using the CD-ROM located inside the back cover of your textbook.

MEDICAID ELIGIBILITY

Medicaid policies for eligibility are complex and vary considerably, even among states of similar size and geographic proximity. Thus, a person who is eligible for Medicaid in one state may not be eligible in another state, and the services provided by one state may differ considerably in amount, duration, or scope as compared with services provided in a similar or neighboring state. In additio... state legislatures may change Medicaid eligibility requirements during the ye...

Medicaid Eligibility

Medicaid does not provide medical assistance for all poor persons, ...and it is important to realize that low income is only one test for Medicaid el...igibility; an individual's resources are also compared to limits established by ea...ch state in accordance with federal guidelines. To be eligible for federal funds..., states are required to provide Medicaid coverage for certain individuals who ...receive federally assisted income-maintenance payments and for related groups t...hat do not receive cash payments. In addition to their Medicaid programs, most ...states implement "state-only" programs to provide medical assistance for spe...cified poor persons who do not qualify for Medicaid. (Federal funds are *not* prov...ided for state-only programs.) The federal government provides matching f...unds to state Medicaid programs when certain healthcare services are provide...d to eligible individuals (e.g., children, disabled, seniors). Each state adminis...ters its own Medicaid program, and CMS monitors the programs and establis...hes requirements for the delivery, funding, and quality of services as well as eligi...bil- ity criteria.

Medicaid eligibility is limited to individuals who can be classified i...to three eligibility groups:

- Categorically needy
- Medically needy
- Special groups

Categorically Needy Groups

State Medicaid programs must be available to the following *mandatory Medicaid eligibility groups* (or *mandatory populations*) because the federal government provides matching funds:

NOTE: Go to www.coverageforall.org and click on the current "federal poverty level chart" link to locate federal poverty levels; calculations are based on family size (e.g., a pregnant woman counts as two in the chart) and state of residence (e.g., calculations for states of Alaska and Hawaii are higher than 48 contiguous states).

- **Families who meet states' Temporary Assistance for Needy Families (TANF) eligibility requirements in effect on July 16, 1996.**
- **Pregnant women and children under age 6 whose family income is at or below 133% of the federal poverty level (annual income guidelines established by the federal government).**
- **Caretakers (relatives or legal guardians who take care of children under age 18, or age 19 if still in high school)**
- **Supplemental Security Income (SSI) recipients (or, in certain states, aged, blind, and disabled people who meet more restrictive requirements than those of the SSI program).**
- **Individuals and couples living in medical institutions who have a monthly income up to 300% of the SSI income.**

Medically Needy Program

States that establish a *medically needy Medicaid program* expand eligibility to additional qualified persons who may have too much income to qualify under the categorically needy group. (Federal matching funds are available.) This option allows:

NOTE: Temporary Assistance for Needy Families (TANF) makes cash assistance available, for a limited time, for children deprived of support because of a parent's absence, death, incapacity, or unemployment. TANF was previously called the Aid to Families with Dependent Children (AFDC) program.

- **Individuals to "spend down" to Medicaid eligibility by incurring medical and/or remedial care expenses to offset their excess income. Thus, their income is reduced to a level below the maximum allowed by their state's Medicaid plan.**
- **Families to establish eligibility as medically needy by paying monthly premiums in an amount equal to the difference between family income (reduced by unpaid expenses, if any, incurred for medical care in previous months) and the income eligibility standard.**

NOTE: States are required to extend Medicaid eligibility to all children born after September 30, 1983, who reside in families with incomes at or below the federal poverty level, until they reach age 19. (States may choose to establish an earlier date.)

States that implement a medically needy Medicaid program are required to include pregnant women through a 60-day postpartum period, children under age 18, certain newborns for one year, and certain protected blind persons. States may also choose to provide coverage to other medically needy persons, including aged, blind, and/or disabled persons; caretaker relatives or legal guardians who live with and take care of children and other eligible children up to age 21 who are full-time students.

Special Groups

States are required to assist the following special groups:

- *Qualified Medicare beneficiaries (QMB)* (states pay Medicare premiums, deductibles and coinsurance amounts for individuals whose income is at or below 100 percent of the federal poverty level and whose resources are at or below twice the standard allowed under SSI)
- *Qualified working disabled individuals (QWDI)* (states pay Medicare Part A premiums for certain disabled individuals who lose Medicare coverage because of work; these individuals have incomes below 200 percent of the federal poverty level and resources that are no more than twice the standard allowed under SSI)
- *Qualifying individual (QI)* (states pay Medicare Part B premiums for individuals with incomes between 120 percent and 175 percent of the federal poverty level)

- *Specified low-income Medicare beneficiary (SLMB)* (states pay Medicare Part B premiums for individuals with incomes between 100 percent and 120 percent of the federal poverty level)

States may also improve access to employment, training, and placement of people with disabilities who want to work by providing expanded Medicaid eligibility to:

- Working disabled people between ages 16 and 65 who have income and resources greater than that allowed under the SSI program.
- Working individuals who become ineligible for the group described above because their medical conditions improve. (States may require these individuals to share in the cost of their medical care.)

Two additional eligibility groups are related to specific medical conditions, and states may provide coverage under their Medicaid plans:

- Time-limited eligibility for women who have breast or cervical cancer
- Individuals diagnosed with tuberculosis (TB) who are uninsured.

Women with breast or cervical cancer receive all Medicaid plan services. TB patients receive only services related to the treatment of TB.

State Children's Health Insurance Program

The *State Children's Health Insurance Program (SCHIP)* was implemented in accordance with the Balanced Budget Act (BBA), which allows states to create or expand existing insurance programs, providing more federal funds to states for the purpose of expanding Medicaid eligibility to include a greater number of currently uninsured children. With certain exceptions, these include low-income children who would not otherwise qualify for Medicaid. SCHIP may also be used to provide medical assistance to children during a presumptive eligibility period for Medicaid. Medicaid coverage can begin as early as the third month *prior to* application *if* the person would have been eligible for Medicaid had he or she applied during that time. Medicaid coverage is usually discontinued at the end of the month in which a person no longer meets the criteria for any Medicaid eligibility group. The BBA allows states to provide 12 months of continuous Medicaid coverage (without reevaluation) for eligible children under the age of 19.

Programs of All-Inclusive Care for the Elderly (PACE)

Programs of All-inclusive Care for the Elderly (PACE) use a capitated payment system to provide a comprehensive package of community-based services as an alternative to institutional care for persons age 55 or older who require a *nursing facility level of care.* PACE is part of the Medicare program, but is an optional service for state Medicaid plans. Thus, PACE programs operate only in states that have selected to include this option. PACE programs enter into contracts with various types of providers, physicians, and other entities to furnish care to participants. This PACE team offers and manages *all* health, medical, and social services and mobilizes other services as needed to provide preventive, rehabilitative, curative, and supportive care. The care is provided in day health centers, homes, hospitals, and nursing facilities, and its purpose is to help the person maintain independence, dignity, and quality of life. PACE providers receive payment only through the PACE agreement and must make available all items and services covered under both Medicaid and Medicare, without amount, duration, or scope limitations and without application of any deductibles, copayments, or other cost-sharing. The individuals enrolled in PACE receive benefits solely through the PACE program.

NOTE: When a PACE participant needs to use a noncontract provider, physician, or other entity, there is a limit on the amount that these noncontract entities can charge the PACE program.

Spousal Impoverishment Protection

The *Medicare Catastrophic Coverage Act of 1988 (MCCA)* implemented Spousal Impoverishment Protection Legislation in 1989 to prevent married couples from being required to *spend down* income and other *liquid assets* (cash and property) before one of the partners could be declared eligible for Medicaid coverage for nursing facility care. The spouse residing at home is called the *community spouse* (which has nothing to do with community property). Before monthly income is used to pay nursing facility costs, a minimum monthly maintenance needs allowance (MMMNA) is deducted.

To determine whether the spouse residing in a facility meets the state's resource standard for Medicaid, a *protected resource amount (PRA)* is subtracted from the couple's combined resources. The PRA is the greatest of the:

- Spousal share, up to a maximum of $109,560 in 2009.
- State spousal resource standard, which a state could set at any amount between $21,912 and 109,560 in 2009.
- Amount transferred to the community spouse for her or his support as directed by a court order.
- Amount designated by a state officer to raise the community spouse's protected resources up to the minimum monthly maintenance needs standard.

> **NOTE:** The couple's home, household goods, automobile, and burial funds are *not* included in the couple's combined resources.

> **NOTE:** The community spouse's income is *not* available to the spouse who resides in the facility, and the two individuals are not considered a couple for income eligibility purposes. The state uses the income eligibility standard for one person rather than two, and the standard income eligibility process for Medicaid is used.

After the PRA is subtracted from the couple's combined countable resources, the remainder is considered available as resources to the spouse residing in the facility. If the amount of resources is below the state's resource standard, the individual is eligible for Medicaid. Once resource eligibility is determined, any resources belonging to the community spouse are no longer considered available to the spouse in the facility.

> **EXAMPLE:** John Q. Public is required to reside in a nursing facility. His wife, Nancy Public, resides in the family home. At the time of Mr. Public's Medicaid application, they have $160,000 in resources (not including the family home, which is not included in resources as long as the spouse is in residence). John Q. Public's monthly Social Security income (SSI) is $1,000, and Nancy Public's monthly SSI is $600, totaling $1,600.
>
> - Under the *income-first approach*, the state attributes one-half of the resources (or $80,000) to Mrs. Public as her community spouse resource allowance (CSRA). This allows Mr. Public to retain $80,000, which must be reduced to $1,500 before he becomes eligible for Medicaid. This means the Publics are expected to convert the $78,500 in resources (e.g., stocks, bonds, summer home) to cash and spend it on nursing facility care for Mr. Public. Because the state's minimum monthly maintenance needs allowance (MMMNA) is $1,751 (in 2009), Mrs. Public keeps all her monthly SSI, in addition to all $1,000 of her husband's monthly SSI. None of the monthly income is expended on nursing facility care for Mr. Public.
>
> - Under the *resources-first approach*, Mr. Public is expected to expend his $1,000 monthly SSI on nursing facility care. This means that Mrs. Public has a monthly income of only $600, and because the state's MMMNA is $1,751, Mr. Public can transfer his $80,000 in resources to Mrs. Public. This increases her CSRA to an amount that generates an additional $1,000 per month. As a result, Mr. Public becomes immediately eligible for Medicaid, and Mrs. Public is allowed to retain all $160,000 in resources.

Confirming Medicaid Eligibility

Any time patients state that they receive Medicaid, they must present a valid Medicaid identification card.

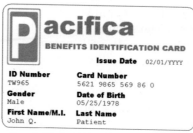

Sample Medicaid identification card

Eligibility, in many cases, will depend on the patient's monthly income. As eligibility may fluctuate from one month to the next, most states have a dedicated telephone line for verification of eligibility. Confirmation of eligibility should be obtained for each visit; failure to do so may result in a denial of payment. If residing in one of these states, be sure to access the Medicaid verification line. Some states have a point-of-service device similar to those used by credit card companies. Beneficiaries carry plastic cards containing encoded data strips. When the card is swiped, the printout indicates eligibility or noneligibility data.

Retroactive eligibility is sometimes granted to patients whose income has fallen below the state-set eligibility level and who had high medical expenses prior to filing for Medicaid. When patients notify the practice that they have become retroactively eligible for Medicaid benefits, confirm this information before proceeding. A refund of any payments made by the patient during the retroactive period must be made and Medicaid billed for these services.

MEDICAID-COVERED SERVICES

Medicaid allows considerable flexibility within state plans, but some federal requirements are mandatory if federal matching funds are to be received. A state's Medicaid program *must* offer medical assistance for certain *basic* services to eligible groups.

Mandatory Services

To receive federal matching funds, states must offer the following services:

Services for Categorically Needy Eligibility Groups

Medicaid eligibility groups classified as categorically needy are entitled to the following services unless waived under the Medicaid law. (These service entitlements do not apply to the SCHIP programs.)

- Inpatient hospital (excluding inpatient services in institutions for mental disease).
- Outpatient hospital including Federally Qualified Health Centers (FQHCs) and if permitted under state law, rural health clinic (RHC) and other ambulatory services provided by a rural health clinic that are otherwise included under states' plans.
- Other laboratory and x-ray.
- Certified pediatric and family nurse practitioners (when licensed to practice under state law).

> **NOTE:** Early and Periodic Screening, Diagnostic, and Treatment (EPSDT) services consist of routine pediatric checkups provided to all children enrolled in Medicaid, including dental, hearing, screening, and vision services. Other necessary health care, diagnostic services, treatment, and other measures must also be performed to correct or ameliorate defects and physical and mental illnesses and conditions discovered by the screening services, whether or not such services are covered by the state Medicaid plan.

- Nursing facility services for beneficiaries age 21 and older.
- Early and periodic screening, diagnosis, and treatment (EPSDT) for children under age 21.
- Family planning services and supplies.
- Physicians' services.
- Medical and surgical services of a dentist.
- Home health services for beneficiaries entitled to nursing facility services under the state's Medicaid plan.
- Intermittent or part-time nursing services provided by home health agency or by a registered nurse when there is no home health agency in the area.
- Home health aides.
- Medical supplies and appliances for use in the home.
- Nurse mid-wife services.
- Pregnancy-related services and service for other conditions that might complicate pregnancy.
- Sixty (60) days postpartum pregnancy-related services.

Services for Medically Needy Eligibility Groups

States must provide at least the following services when the medically needy are included under the Medicaid plans:

- Prenatal and delivery services
- Post-partum pregnancy-related services for beneficiaries who are under age 18 and are entitled to institutional and ambulatory services defined in a state's plan
- Home health services to beneficiaries entitled to receive nursing facility services under the state's Medicaid plan

States may provide different services to different groups of medically needy individuals, such as specified services for beneficiaries under age 21 and/or over age 65 in institutions for mental disease (IMDs); and/or intermediate care facilities for the mentally retarded (ICF/MRs), if included as medically needy. The services provided to a particular group must also be available to everyone within that group (unless the state has obtained a waiver).

PAYMENT FOR MEDICAID SERVICES

Medicaid operates as a vendor-payment program, which means that states pay healthcare providers on a fee-for-service basis *or* states pay for Medicaid services using prepayment arrangements (e.g., an HMO). When Medicaid makes payment directly to providers, those participating in Medicaid must accept the reimbursement as payment in full. States determine their own reimbursement methodology and payment rates for services, with three exceptions: (1) for institutional services, payment may not exceed amounts that would be paid under Medicare payment rates; (2) for *disproportionate share hospitals (DSHs)*, hospitals that treat a disproportionate number of Medicaid patients, different limits apply; and (3) for hospice care services, rates cannot be lower than Medicare rates.

States can require nominal deductibles, coinsurance, or copayments for certain services performed for some Medicaid recipients. Emergency services and family planning services are exempt from copayments. Certain Medicaid recipients are also excluded from this cost-sharing, including pregnant women, children under age 18, and hospital or nursing home patients who are expected to contribute most of their income to institutional care.

The portion of the Medicaid program paid by the federal government is known as the **Federal Medical Assistance Percentage (FMAP)** and is determined annually for each state using a formula that compares the state's average per capita income level with the national average. Wealthier states receive a smaller share of reimbursed costs, and the federal government shares in administration expenses (minimum 50 percent match).

The federal government also reimburses states for 100 percent of the cost of services provided through facilities of the Indian Health Service, provides financial help to the 12 states that furnish the highest number of emergency services to undocumented aliens, and shares in each state's expenditures for the administration of the Medicaid program. Most administrative costs are matched at 50 percent, although higher percentages are paid for certain activities and functions, such as development of mechanized claims processing systems.

Medicare-Medicaid Relationship

> **NOTE:** When an individual has both Medicare and Medicaid coverage, covered services are paid by Medicare first before any payments are made by the Medicaid program. The reason for this is because Medicaid is always the *payer of last resort.*

Medicare beneficiaries with low incomes and limited resources may also receive help from the Medicaid program. For those eligible for *full* Medicaid coverage, Medicare coverage is supplemented by services available under a state's Medicaid program. These additional services may include, for example, nursing facility care beyond the 100-day limit covered by Medicare, prescription drugs, eyeglasses, and hearing aids.

Dual Eligibles

Medicare beneficiaries with low incomes and limited resources may receive help with out-of-pocket medical expenses from state Medicaid programs. Various benefits are available to **dual eligibles**, individuals entitled to Medicare *and* eligible for some type of Medicaid benefit (abbreviated as Medi-Medi). Individuals eligible for full Medicaid coverage receive program supplements to their Medicare coverage via services and supplies available from the state's Medicaid program. Services covered by both programs are paid first by Medicare and the difference by Medicaid, up to the state's payment limit. Medicaid also covers the following additional services:

- **Nursing facility care beyond the 100-day limit covered by Medicare**
- **Prescription drugs**
- **Eyeglasses**
- **Hearing aids**

Medicaid as a Secondary Payer

Medicaid is always the *payer of last resort.* If the patient is covered by another medical or liability policy, including Medicare, TRICARE (formerly CHAMPUS), CHAMPVA, or Indian Health Services (IHS), this coverage must be billed first. Medicaid is billed only if the other coverage denies responsibility for payment, pays less than the Medicaid fee schedule, or if Medicaid covers procedures not covered by the other policy.

Participating Providers

Any provider who accepts a Medicaid patient must accept the Medicaid-determined payment as payment in full. Providers are forbidden by law to bill *(balance billing)* patients for Medicaid-covered benefits. A patient may be billed for any service that is not a covered benefit; however, some states have historically required providers to sign formal participating Medicaid contracts. Other states do not require contracts.

Medicaid and Managed Care

Medicaid managed care grew rapidly in the 1990s. In 1991, 2.7 million beneficiaries were enrolled in some form of managed care. By 2004 that number had grown to 27 million, an increase of 900 percent. That represents 60 percent of the Medicaid population who receive benefits through managed care. States can make managed care enrollment voluntary, or they can seek a waiver of the Social Security Act from CMS to require certain populations to enroll in an MCO.

Medicaid *managed care* does not always mean a comprehensive healthcare plan that requires a monthly premium and is at financial risk for the cost of care provided to all enrollees. Medicaid beneficiaries are also enrolled in *primary care case management (PCCM)* plans, which are similar to fee-for-service plans except that each PCCM enrollee has a primary care provider who authorizes access to specialty care but is not at risk for the cost of care provided.

Most states that have not placed all Medicaid beneficiaries into a prepaid HMO have some form of prior approval or preauthorization for recipients. Preauthorization is required for certain procedures and services (e.g., inpatient hospitalizations) as mandated by state and federal law. To be eligible for reimbursement, the provider must submit the appropriate preauthorization form, such as California's Department of Health Care Services (DHCS) treatment authorization request (TAR) and/or service authorization request (SAR), to the appropriate state Medicaid field office. Once approved, the procedure or service is provided to the patient and the provider is reimbursed by Medicaid. Preauthorization guidelines include:

> **NOTE:**
>
> • Go to www.medical.ca.gov, and click on the eTAR Tutorials link to learn how to use a Web-based Medicaid treatment preauthorization system.
>
> • Go to www.westernhighlands. org, click on Providers, click on Service Authorization Procedures, and click on the Service Authorization Request Form (SAR) (Word) link to view a SAR form.

- Elective inpatient admission (document medical necessity justification of inpatient treatment and admission diagnosis and treatment plan)

- Emergency inpatient admission (document medical necessity justification for inpatient treatment and admission diagnosis and treatment plan)

- More than one preoperative day (document reason[s] surgery cannot be performed within 24 hours of indication for surgery and specify number of additional preoperative day[s] requested)

- Outpatient procedure(s) to be performed in an inpatient setting (submit CPT code and description of surgical procedure along with medical necessity justification for performing surgery on an inpatient basis)

- Days exceeding state hospital stay limitation due to complication(s) (submit diagnosis stated on original preauthorization request, beginning and ending dates originally preauthorized, statement describing the complication[s], date complication[s] presented, principal diagnosis, and complication[s] diagnosis)

- Extension of inpatient days (document medical necessity justification for the extension and specify number of additional days requested)

NOTE: Go to www.eMedNY.org to view a web-based electronic Medicaid system.

NOTE: The provider should compare content on the remittance advice to claims submitted to determine whether proper payment was received. If improper payment was issued, the provider has the option to appeal the claim.

Medicaid Eligibility Verification System

The Medicaid eligibility verification system (MEVS) (sometimes called recipient eligibility verification system, or REVS) allows providers to electronically access the state's eligibility file using the methods listed below. Then, a "receipt ticket" (Figure 15-1) is generated upon eligibility verification by MEVS.

- *Point-of-service device:* The patient's medical identification card contains a magnetic strip, and when the provider "swipes" the card through a reader, accurate eligibility information is displayed. (The provider purchases magnetic card reader equipment.)
- *Computer software:* When the provider enters a Medicaid recipient's identification number into special computer software, accurate eligibility information is displayed.
- *Automated voice response:* Providers can call the state's Medicaid office to receive eligibility verification information through an automated voice response system.

US MEDICAID
Eligibility

05/15/YYYY	14:44:58
Date of Service:	05/15/YYYY
Provider NPI:	1234567890

Individual Status

Verification Number:	23659856236541
Name:	John Q. Public
RID #:	562365951
Card Generation #:	001
DOB/(age):	03/09/1945
Sex:	M
Restriction:	None
Co-Pay:	N

Managed Care

Managed Care:	N
PCP Name:	Dr. Erin Helper
PCP Telephone #:	101-111-1234

Third-Party Liability

Coverage Code:	LDO–4
Policy #:	DD1234
Carrier Name:	Any Insurance
Address:	111 Main St
City/State/Zip:	Anywhere, NY 12345
Phone #:	(101) 555-1234

Legend
LDO-4 = large dialysis organization #4

FIGURE 15-1 Sample Medicaid eligibility verification system (MEVS) receipt ticket (Courtesy Delmar/Cengage Learning)

Medicaid Remittance Advice

NOTE: Remittance advice documents should be maintained according to the statute of limits of the state in which the provider practices.

Providers receive reimbursement from Medicaid on a lump-sum basis, which means they will receive payment for several claims at once. A Medicaid remittance advice (Figure 15-2) is sent to the provider which contains the current status of all claims (including adjusted and voided claims). The provider should compare content on the remittance advice to claims submitted to determine whether proper payment was received. If improper payment was issued, the provider has the option to appeal the claim. An adjusted claim has a payment correction, resulting in additional payment(s) to the provider. A voided claim is one that Medicaid should not have originally paid, and results in a deduction from the lump-sum payment made to the provider. If a year-to-date negative balance appears on the Medicaid remittance advice as a result of voided claims, the provider receives no payment until the amount of paid claims exceeds the negative balance amount.

Utilization Review

The federal government requires states to verify the receipt of Medicaid services. Thus, a sample of Medicaid recipients is sent a monthly survey letter requesting verification of services paid the previous month on their behalf. (Such services are identified in nontechnical terms, and confidential services are omitted.) Federal regulations also required Medicaid to establish and maintain a surveillance and utilization review subsystem (SURS), which safeguards against unnecessary or inappropriate use of Medicaid services or excess payments and assesses the quality of those services. A postpayment review process monitors both the use of health services by recipients and the delivery of health services by providers. Overpayments to providers may be recovered by the SURS unit, regardless of whether the payment error was caused by the provider or by the Medicaid program.

The SURS unit is also responsible for identifying possible fraud or abuse, and most states organize the unit under the state's Office of Attorney General, which is certified by the federal government to detect, investigate, and prosecute fraudulent practices or abuse against the Medicaid program.

```
                        State of New York Medicaid
 Provider Number: 999   Remittance Advice as of 01-06-YY          RA#: 256295987

  RECIPIENT   MEDICAID   INTERNAL    SERVICE DATES  POS    CPT   QUANTITY  BILLED   ALLOWED   CUT/    PAYMENT   ADJUSTMENT
    NAME        ID     CONTROL NO.   FROM    TO            CODE            AMOUNT    AMOUNT    BACK    AMOUNT    REASON CODE

 DOE, JOHN    123654   4400367890   0105YY  0105YY   11   99213     1      45.00    24.00    21.00    24.00      A2
 REMARK CODES: N59                  *** CLAIMS TOTALS ***          1               24.00    21.00    24.00

 JONES, MARY  569562   5626594589   0106YY  0106YY   11   99213     1      54.00    24.00    30.00    24.00      A2
                                    0106YY  0106YY   11   82948     1      18.00     1.00    17.00     1.00      A2
 REMARK CODES: N59   MA66           0106YY  0106YY   11   36415     1       4.00     0.00     4.00     0.00      125
                                    *** CLAIMS TOTALS ***          3               25.00    51.00    25.00


 *** CATEGORY TOTALS:               NUMBER OF CLAIMS:        2     4       121.00   49.00    72.00    49.00

                        RA# 256295987 CHECK AMOUNT: $ 49.00

 ******************************************************************************************************************
 *** EARNINGS DATA ***              NO. OF CLAIMS PROCESSED YEAR TO DATE:     75
                                    DOLLAR AMOUNT PROCESSED YEAR TO DATE:     $1459.82
                                    CHECK AMOUNT YEAR TO DATE:                $1459.82

 *** CODE LEGEND ***                11 = Office
                                    125 = Submission/billing error(s)
                                    A2 = Contractual adjustment
                                    N59 = Refer to provider manual for program/provider information
```

FIGURE 15-2 Sample Medicaid remittance advice (RA) (Courtesy Delmar/Cengage Learning)

Medical Necessity

Medicaid-covered services are payable only when the service is determined by the provider to be medically necessary. Covered services must be:

- Consistent with the patient's symptoms, diagnosis, condition, or injury.
- Recognized as the prevailing standard and consistent with generally accepted professional medical standards of the provider's peer group.
- Provided in response to a life-threatening condition; to treat pain, injury, illness, or infection; to treat a condition that could result in physical or mental disability; or to achieve a level of physical or mental function consistent with prevailing community standards for diagnosis or condition.

In addition, medically necessary services are:

- Not furnished primarily for the convenience of the recipient or the provider.
- Furnished when there is no other equally effective course of treatment available or suitable for the recipient requesting the service that is more conservative or substantially less costly.

BILLING NOTES

Following is information on nationwide fee-for-service billing. Consult your state's Medicaid MCO billing manual to bill for noncapitated MCO services.

Fiscal Agent

The name of the state's Medicaid fiscal agent will vary from state to state. Contact the local county government for information about the Medicaid program in your area. (In some states, third-party payers contract with Medicaid to process claims.)

Underwriter

Underwriting responsibility is shared between state and federal governments. Federal responsibility rests with CMS. The name of the state agency will vary according to state preference.

Form Used

The CMS-1500 claim is required.

Timely Filing Deadline

Deadlines vary from state to state. Check with your State's Medicaid office. It is important to file a Medicaid fee-for-service claim as soon as possible. The only time a claim should be delayed is when the patient does not identify Medicaid eligibility or if the patient has applied for retroactive Medicaid coverage.

Medicare-Medicaid crossover claims follow the Medicare, not Medicaid, deadlines for claims. (Refer to Chapter 14 for details of the Medicare claim filing deadline.)

Allowable Determination

The state establishes the maximum reimbursement payable for each non-managed care service. It is expected that Medicaid programs will use the new Medicare physician fee schedule for these services, with each state establishing its own conversion factor. Medicaid recipients can be billed for any noncovered procedure performed. However, because most Medicaid patients have incomes below the poverty level, collection of fees for uncovered services is difficult.

Accept Assignment

> **NOTE:** Medicaid patients must assign benefits to providers.

Accept assignment must be selected on the CMS-1500 claim, or reimbursement (depending on state policy) may be denied. It is illegal to attempt collection of the difference between the Medicaid payment and the fee the provider charged, even if the patient did not reveal Medicaid status at the time services were rendered.

Deductibles

A deductible may be required. In such cases, eligibility cards usually are not issued until after the stated deductible has been met.

Copayments

Copayments are required for some Medicaid recipients.

Inpatient Benefits

All nonemergency hospitalizations must be preauthorized. If the patient's condition warrants an extension of the authorized inpatient days, the hospital must seek an authorization for additional inpatient days.

Major Medical/Accidental Injury Coverage

There is no special treatment for major medical or accidental injury categories. Medicaid will conditionally subrogate claims when there is liability insurance to cover a person's injuries. *Subrogation* is the assumption of an obligation for which another party is primarily liable.

Because Medicaid eligibility is determined by income, patients can be eligible one month and not the next. Check eligibility status on each visit. New work requirements may change this, as beneficiaries may continue coverage for a specific time even if their income exceeds the state eligibility levels. Prior authorization is required for many procedures and most nonemergency hospitalizations. Consult the current Medicaid handbook for a listing of the procedures that must have prior authorization. When in doubt, contact the state agency for clarification.

Cards may be issued for the "Unborn child of . . ." (the name of the pregnant woman is inserted in the blank space). These cards are good only for services that promote the life and good health of the unborn child.

Because other health and liability programs are primary to Medicaid, the remittance advice from the primary coverage must be attached to the Medicaid claim.

A combined Medicare-Medicaid (Medi-Medi) claim should be filed by the Medicaid deadline on the CMS-1500 claim.

Before working with Medicaid claims, complete the Review located at the end of this chapter.

CLAIMS INSTRUCTIONS

The instructions in Table 15-1 are for filing primary Medicaid fee-for-service claims when the patient is not covered by additional insurance. If the patient is covered by Medicare and Medicaid, follow the instructions for Medicare-Medicaid (Medi-Medi) crossover claims in Chapter 14.

Refer to the John Q. Public case study in Figure 15-3 and the completed claim in Figure 15-4 as you study Table 15-1.

TABLE 15-1　CMS-1500 claims completion instructions for Medicaid primary claims

NOTE: Refer to Chapter 11 for clarification of claims completion (e.g., entering names, mailing addresses, ICD codes, diagnosis pointer numbers, NPI, and so on).

BLOCK	INSTRUCTIONS
1	Enter an X in the *Medicaid* box.
1a	Enter the Medicaid identification number as it appears on the patient's Medicaid card. *Do not enter hyphens or spaces in the number.*
2	Enter the patient's last name, first name, and middle initial (separated by commas) (DOE, JANE, M).
3	Enter the patient's birth date as MM DD YYYY (with spaces). Enter an X in the appropriate box to indicate the patient's gender. If the patient's gender is unknown, leave blank.
4	Leave blank.
5	Enter the patient's mailing address and telephone number. Enter the street address on line 1, enter the city and state on line 2, and enter the 5- or 9-digit zip code and phone number on line 3.
6–8	Leave blank.
9–9d	Leave blank. *Blocks 9 and 9a–9d are completed if the patient has additional insurance coverage, such as commercial insurance.*
10a–c	Enter an X in the NO boxes. (If an X is entered in the YES box for auto accident, enter the 2-character state abbreviation of the patient's residence.)
10d	Leave blank. For Medicaid managed care programs, enter an E for emergency care or U for urgency care (if instructed to do so by the administrative contractor).
11–16	Leave blank.
17	Enter the first name, middle initial (if known), last name, and credentials of the professional who referred or ordered healthcare service(s) or supply(s) reported on the claim. *Do not enter any punctuation.* Otherwise, leave blank.
17a	Leave blank.
17b	Enter the 10-digit national provider identifier (NPI) of the professional in Block 17. Otherwise, leave blank.
18	Enter the admission date and discharge date as MM DD YYYY (with spaces) if the patient received inpatient services (e.g., hospital, skilled nursing facility). *If the patient has not been discharged at the time the claim is completed, leave the discharge date blank.* Otherwise, leave blank.
19	Reserved for local use. Some Medicaid programs require entry of the Medicaid provider's NPI, and others require entry of a description of unlisted procedure or service codes reported in Block 24E. (If the description does not fit, enter SEE ATTACHMENT, and attach documentation to the claim describing the unlisted procedures/services provided.)

(continues)

TABLE 15-1 (continued)

BLOCK	INSTRUCTIONS
20	Enter an X in the NO box if all laboratory procedures reported on the claim were performed in the provider's office. Otherwise, enter an X in the YES box, enter the total amount charged by the outside laboratory in $ CHARGES, and enter the outside laboratory's name, mailing address, and NPI in Block 32. (Charges are entered *without* punctuation. For example, $1,100.00 is entered as 110000 below $ CHARGES.)
21	Enter the ICD code for up to four diagnoses or conditions treated or medically managed during the encounter. Lines 1, 2, 3, and 4 in Block 21 will relate to CPT/HCPCS service/procedure codes reported in Block 24E.
22	Enter the original claim reference number plus Medicaid resubmission code, if applicable to the claim. Otherwise, leave blank.
23	Enter the Medicaid preauthorization number, which was assigned by the payer, if applicable. If written preauthorization was obtained, attach a copy to the claim. Otherwise, leave blank.
24A	Enter the date the procedure or service was performed in the FROM column as MMDDYYYY. Enter a date in the TO column *if the procedure or service was performed on consecutive days during a range of dates. Then, enter the number of consecutive days in Block 24G.* **NOTE:** The shaded area in each line is used to enter supplemental information to support reported services *if instructed by the payer to enter such information.* Data entry in Block 24 is limited to reporting six services. *Do not use the shaded lines to report additional services.* If additional services were provided, generate new CMS-1500 claim(s) to report the additional services.
24B	Enter the appropriate 2-digit Place of Service (POS) code to identify the location where the reported procedure or service was performed. (Refer to Appendix II for POS codes.)
24C	Enter an E *if the service was provided for a medical emergency,* regardless of where it was provided. Otherwise, leave blank.
24D	Enter the CPT or HCPCS level II code and applicable required modifier(s) for procedures or services performed. *Separate the CPT/HCPCS code and first modifier with one space. Separate additional modifiers with one space each. Up to four modifiers can be entered.*
24E	Enter the diagnosis pointer number from Block 21 that relates to the procedure/service performed on the date of service.
24F	Enter the fee charged for each reported procedure or service. When multiple procedures or services are reported on the same line, enter the total fee charged. *Do not enter commas, periods, or dollar signs. Do not enter negative amounts. Enter 00 in the cents area if the amount is a whole number.*
24G	Enter the number of days or units for procedures or services reported in Block 24D. *If just one procedure or service was reported in Block 24D, enter a 1 in Block 24G.*
24H	Enter an E if the service was provided under the EPSDT program, or enter an F if the service was provided for family planning. Enter a B if the service can be categorized as both EPSDT and family planning. Otherwise, leave blank.
24I	Leave blank. The NPI abbreviation is preprinted on the CMS-1500 claim.

(continues)

TABLE 15-1   (continued)

BLOCK	INSTRUCTIONS
24J	Enter the 10-digit NPI for the: • provider who performed the service *if the provider is a member of a group practice.* (Leave blank if the provider is a solo practitioner.) • supervising provider *if the service was provided "incident to" the service of a physician or nonphysician practitioner* **and** *the physician or practitioner who ordered the service did not supervise the provider.* (Leave blank if the "incident to" service was performed under the supervision of the physician or nonphysician practitioner.) • DMEPOS supplier or outside laboratory *if the physician submits the claim for services provided by the DMEPOS supplier or outside laboratory.* (Leave blank if the DMEPOS supplier or outside laboratory submits the claim.) Otherwise, leave blank.
25	Enter the provider's social security number (SSN) or employer identification number (EIN). *Do not enter hyphens or spaces in the number.* Enter an X in the appropriate box to indicate which number is reported.
26	Enter the patient's account number as assigned by the provider. **NOTE:** When completing CMS-1500 claims for case studies, if just one is generated enter the case study number (e.g., 15-5). When the patient has Medicaid as secondary coverage, enter an S (for secondary) (e.g., 15-2S) next to the number (on the secondary claim).
27	Enter an X in the YES box to indicate that the provider agrees to accept assignment. Otherwise, enter an X in the NO box.
28	Enter the total charges for services and/or procedures reported in Block 24. **NOTE:** If multiple claims are submitted for one patient because more than six procedures or services were reported, be sure the total charge reported on each claim accurately represents the total of the items on each submitted claim.
29–30	Leave blank.
31	Enter the provider's name and credential (e.g., MARY SMITH MD) and the date the claim was completed as MMDDYYYY (without spaces). *Do not enter any punctuation.*
32	Enter the name and address where procedures or services were provided *if at a location other than the patient's home, such as a hospital, outside laboratory facility, skilled nursing facility, or DMEPOS supplier.* Otherwise, leave blank. Enter the name on line 1, the address on line 2, and the city, state and 5- or 9-digit zip code on line 3. *For a 9-digit zip code, enter the hyphen.* **NOTE:** If Block 18 contains dates of service for inpatient care and/or Block 20 contains an X in the YES box, enter the name and address of the facility that provided services.
32a	Enter the 10-digit NPI of the provider entered in Block 32.
32b	Leave blank.
33	Enter the provider's *billing* name, address, and telephone number. Enter the phone number in the area next to the Block title. *Do not enter parentheses for the area code.* Enter the name on line 1, enter the address on line 2, and enter the city, state, and 5- or 9-digit zip code on line 3. *For a 9-digit zip code, enter the hyphen.*
33a	Enter the 10-digit NPI of the *billing* provider (e.g., solo practitioner) or group practice (e.g., clinic).
33b	Leave blank.

MEDICAID AS SECONDARY PAYER CLAIMS

The instructions in Table 15-2 are for cases in which the patient is covered by a commercial or liability insurance policy (Figures 15-7 and 15-8). These instructions modify the primary Medicaid instructions.

The instructions *do not* apply to Medicare-Medicaid (Medi-Medi) crossover cases, which are discussed in Chapter 14.

TABLE 15-2 CMS-1500 claims completion instructions for Medicaid as secondary payer

BLOCK	INSTRUCTIONS
4	Enter the primary policyholder's last name, first name, and middle initial (separated by commas).
6	Enter an X in the appropriate box to indicate the patient's relationship to the primary policyholder. If the patient is an unmarried domestic partner, enter an X in the *Other* box.
7	Enter the primary policyholder's mailing address and telephone number. Enter the street address on line 1, enter the city and state on line 2, and enter the 5- or 9-digit zip code and phone number on line 3.
9	Enter the primary policyholder's last name, first name, and middle initial (if known) (separated by commas). If the primary policyholder is the patient, enter SAME.
9a	Enter the primary policyholder's policy or group number. *Do not enter hyphens or spaces in the number.*
9b	Enter the primary policyholder's birth date as MM DD YYYY (with spaces). Enter an X in the appropriate box to indicate the secondary or supplemental policyholder's gender. *If the primary policyholder is the patient, leave blank.*
9d	Enter the name of the primary policyholder's health insurance plan (e.g., commercial health insurance plan name or government program).
10a–c	Enter an X in the appropriate box.
10d	Leave blank.
11	Enter the rejection code provided by the payer *if the patient has other third-party payer coverage and the submitted claim was rejected by that payer.* Otherwise, leave blank. **NOTE:** When a third-party payer has rejected the submitted claim, and a CMS-1500 claim is sent to Medicaid, enter the code that describes the reason for rejection by the payer (e.g., service not covered). The rejection code reported in Block 11 alerts Medicaid that another payer is not responsible for reimbursement of procedures/services provided. (The other payer's remittance advice or explanation of benefits may need to be submitted to Medicaid as proof.)
11d	Enter an X in the YES box.
26	Add an S to the patient account number in to indicate the secondary policy.
28	Enter the total charges for services and/or procedures reported in Block 24.
29	Enter the amount paid by the other payer. If the other payer denied the claim, enter 0 00.
30	Enter the total amount due (by subtracting the amount entered in Block 29 from the amount entered in Block 28). *Do not report negative amounts or a credit due to the patient.*

ERIN A. HELPER, M.D.
101 Medic Drive, Anywhere NY 12345
(101) 111-1234 (Office) • (101) 111-9292 (Fax)
EIN: 11-1234523
NPI: 1234567890

Case Study

PATIENT INFORMATION:

Name:	Connelly, Jennifer
Address:	45 Main Street
City:	Nowhere
State:	NY
Zip Code:	12367-1234
Telephone:	(101) 555-5624
Gender:	Female
Date of Birth:	05-05-1955
Occupation:	
Employer:	

INSURANCE INFORMATION:

Patient Number:	15-3
Place of Service:	Office
Primary Insurance Plan:	Aetna
Primary Insurance Plan ID #:	56265897
Policy #:	
Primary Policyholder:	Thomas Connelly
Policyholder Date of Birth:	05-25-1956
Employer:	Turbodyne
Relationship to Patient:	Spouse
Secondary Insurance Plan:	Medicaid
Secondary Insurance Plan ID #:	56215689
Secondary Policyholder:	Jennifer Connelly

Patient Status   [X] Married   [ ] Divorced   [ ] Single   [ ] Student

DIAGNOSIS INFORMATION

Diagnosis	Code	Diagnosis	Code
1. Hypertension	401.9	5.	
2.		6.	
3.		7.	
4.		8.	

ICD-10-CM ALERT!
Hypertension   I10

PROCEDURE INFORMATION

Description of Procedure or Service	Date	Code	Charge
1. New patient, office visit, level III	01-07-YYYY	99203	150.00
2.			
3.			
4.			
5.			

SPECIAL NOTES: Aetna paid $105.00 as primary payer.

FIGURE 15-7 Jennifer Connelly case study (Courtesy Cengage/Delmar Learning)

FIGURE 15-8 Completed Medicaid secondary payer CMS-1500 claim for Jennifer Connelly case study (Courtesy Cengage/Delmar Learning)

MOTHER/BABY CLAIMS

The instructions in Table 15-3 are for mother/baby claims. They modify the primary Medicaid instructions. Refer to Figures 15-9 and 15-10 for a completed claim based on a case study.

The infant of a Medicaid recipient is automatically eligible for Medicaid for the entire first year of life. Individual state Medicaid programs determine reimbursement procedures for services provided to newborns. When claims are submitted under the *mother's Medicaid identification number,* coverage is usually limited to the baby's first 10 days of life (during which time an application is made so the baby is assigned its own identification number). Medicaid usually covers babies through the end of the month of their first birthday (e.g., baby born January 5 this year, is covered until January 31 next year). The baby must continuously live with its mother to be eligible for the full year, and the baby remains eligible for Medicaid even if changes in family size or income occur and the mother is no longer eligible for Medicaid.

> **NOTE:** Medicaid *Baby Your Baby* programs cover the mother's prenatal care only.

A **mother/baby claim** is submitted for services provided to a baby under the mother's Medicaid identification number. (The mother's services are *not* reimbursed on the mother/baby claim; they are submitted on a separate CMS-1500 claim according to the instructions in Table 15-1.)

TABLE 15-3   CMS-1500 claims completion instructions for Medicaid mother/baby claims

BLOCK	INSTRUCTIONS
1a	Enter the mother's Medicaid ID number as it appears on the patient's Medicaid card. *Do not enter hyphens or spaces in the number.*
2	Enter the mother's last name followed by the word NEWBORN (separated by commas). **EXAMPLE:** VANDERMARK, NEWBORN
3	Enter the infant's birth date as MM DD YYYY (with spaces). Enter an X to indicate the infant's gender.
4	Enter the mother's name (separated by commas), followed by (MOM), as the responsible party. **EXAMPLE:** VANDERMARK, JOYCE (MOM)
21	Enter ICD secondary diagnosis codes in fields 2, 3, and/or 4, if applicable.

KIM A. CARRINGTON, M.D.
900 Medic Drive, Anywhere NY 12345
(101) 111-2365 (Office) • (101) 111-5625 (Fax)
EIN: 11-5623567
NPI: 7890123456

Case Study

PATIENT INFORMATION:

Name:	Muracek, Newborn
Address:	515 Hill Street
City:	Anywhere
State:	NY
Zip Code:	12367-1234
Telephone:	(101) 555-5598
Gender:	Female
Date of Birth:	01-10-2010
Occupation:	
Employer:	

INSURANCE INFORMATION:

Patient Number:	15-4
Place of Service:	Inpatient Hospital
Primary Insurance Plan:	Medicaid
Primary Insurance Plan ID #:	56265987
Policy #:	
Primary Policyholder:	Yvonne Muracek
Policyholder Date of Birth:	12-24-1980
Employer:	
Relationship to Patient:	Mother
Secondary Insurance Plan:	
Secondary Insurance Plan ID #:	
Secondary Policyholder:	

Patient Status   ☐ Married   ☐ Divorced   ☒ Single   ☐ Student

---

DIAGNOSIS INFORMATION

Diagnosis	Code	Diagnosis	Code
1. Healthy single liveborn infant, delivered vaginally	V30.00	5.	
2.		6.	
3.		7.	
4.		8.	

PROCEDURE INFORMATION

Description of Procedure or Service	Date	Code	Charge
1. History and examination of normal newborn	01-10-2010	99460	150.00
2. Attendance at delivery	01-10-2010	99464	400.00
3. Subsequent care for normal newborn	01-11-2010	99461	100.00
4.			
5.			

SPECIAL NOTES: Inpatient care provided at Goodmedicine Hospital, Anywhere St, Anywhere, NY 12345. (NPI: 2345678901) Application for infant's Medicaid ID number has been submitted.

> **ICD-10-CM ALERT!**
>
> Health single liveborn infant, delivered vaginally   Z38.00

FIGURE 15-9 Newborn Muracek case study (Courtesy Cengage/Delmar Learning)

FIGURE 15-10 Completed Medicaid mother/baby CMS-1500 claim for Newborn Muracek case study (Courtesy Cengage/Delmar Learning)

ICD-10-CM ALERT!

21. DIAGNOSIS OR NATURE OF ILLNESS OR INJURY (Relate Items 1, 2, 3 or 4 to Item 24E by Line)

1. Z38 00   3.

2.   4.

E. DIAGNOSIS POINTER

SCHIP CLAIMS

Each state selects a payer that administers its State Children's Health Insurance Program (SCHIP) program, and the payer develops its own CMS-1500 claims instructions. General instructions included in Table 15-4 are used to complete SCHIP CMS-1500 claims for case studies in this textbook and its workbook. (Refer to Figures 15-11 and 15-12 for a completed claim based on a case study.) It is important to obtain official CMS-1500 claims completion instructions from the SCHIP payer in your state.

> **EXAMPLE 1:** California's Healthy Kids program is administered by the Partnership HealthPlan of California (www.PartnershipHP.org), which requires entry of an X in the *Group Health Plan* box.

> **EXAMPLE 2:** New York State's Child Health Plus program is administered by Excellus BlueCross BlueShield (www.ExcellusBCBS.com), which requires entry of an X in the *Other* box.

TABLE 15-4   CMS-1500 claims completion instructions for SCHIP claims

BLOCK	INSTRUCTIONS
1	Enter an X in the *Other* box. **NOTE:** Some SCHIP payers, such as California's Healthy Kids program (administered by the Partnership HealthPlan of California), require an X to be entered in the *Group Health Plan box*.
1a	Enter the SCHIP identification number (assigned by the Health Plan) of the subscriber (person who holds the policy).
19	Leave blank.
22	Leave blank.
29	Enter the total amount the patient (or another payer) paid toward covered services only. If no payment was made, leave blank.
30	Enter the total amount due (by subtracting the amount entered in Block 29 from the amount entered in Block 28). *Do not report negative amounts or a credit due to the patient.*

ANGELA DILALIO, M.D.
99 Provider Street • Injury NY 12347 • (101) 201-4321
EIN: 11-1982342
NPI: 4567890123

Case Study

PATIENT INFORMATION:

Name:	Edgar Vasquez
Address:	1018 Bonita Ave
City:	Anywhere
State:	US
Zipcode:	12345
Telephone:	(101) 690-5244
Gender:	Male
Date of Birth:	10-18-2008
Occupation:	
Employer:	
Spouse's Employer	

INSURANCE INFORMATION:

Patient Number:	15-5
Place of Service:	Office
Primary Insurance Plan:	SCHIP
Primary Insurance Plan ID#:	CAM101919690
Group #:	987654Y
Primary Policyholder:	Edgar Vasquez
Policyholder Date of Birth:	10-18-2008
Relationship to Patient:	Self
Secondary Insurance Plan:	
Secondary Insurance Plan ID #:	
Secondary Policyholder:	

Patient status: ☐ Married   ☐ Divorced   ☒ Single   ☐ Employed   ☐ Student   ☐ Other

---

ICD-10-CM ALERT!

Asthma	J45.909

DIAGNOSIS INFORMATION

Diagnosis	Code	Diagnosis	Code
1. Asthma	493.90	5.	
2.		6.	
3.		7.	
4.		8.	

PROCEDURE INFORMATION

Description of Procedure or Service	Date	Code	Charge
1. Office visit, established visit, level II	12-18-YYYY	99212	$40.00
2.			
3.			
4.			
5.			

SPECIAL NOTES:

FIGURE 15-11 Edgar Vasquez case study (Courtesy Delmar/Cengage Learning)

1500

HEALTH INSURANCE CLAIM FORM

APPROVED BY NATIONAL UNIFORM CLAIM COMMITTEE 08/05

CARRIER →

PICA		PICA

1. MEDICARE MEDICAID TRICARE CHAMPUS (Sponsor's SSN) CHAMPVA (Member ID#) GROUP HEALTH PLAN (SSN or ID) FECA BLK LUNG (SSN) OTHER [X] (ID)
(Medicare #) (Medicaid #)

1a. INSURED'S I.D. NUMBER   (For Program in Item 1)
CAM101919690

2. PATIENT'S NAME (Last Name, First Name, Middle Initial)
VASQUEZ, EDGAR

3. PATIENT'S BIRTH DATE   MM 10 DD 18 YY 2008   SEX M [X] F

4. INSURED'S NAME (Last Name, First Name, Middle Initial)

5. PATIENT'S ADDRESS (No., Street)
1018 BONITA AVE

6. PATIENT'S RELATIONSHIP TO INSURED
Self Spouse Child Other

7. INSURED'S ADDRESS (No., Street)

CITY
ANYWHERE STATE US

8. PATIENT STATUS
Single Married Other
Employed Full-Time Student Part-Time Student

CITY STATE

ZIP CODE
12345

TELEPHONE (Include Area Code)
(101) 690-5244

ZIP CODE TELEPHONE (Include Area Code)
( )

9. OTHER INSURED'S NAME (Last Name, First Name, Middle Initial)

10. IS PATIENT'S CONDITION RELATED TO:

11. INSURED'S POLICY GROUP OR FECA NUMBER

a. OTHER INSURED'S POLICY OR GROUP NUMBER

a. EMPLOYMENT? (Current or Previous)
YES NO

a. INSURED'S DATE OF BIRTH MM DD YY   SEX M F

b. OTHER INSURED'S DATE OF BIRTH MM DD YY   SEX M F

b. AUTO ACCIDENT?   PLACE (State)
YES NO

b. EMPLOYER'S NAME OR SCHOOL NAME

c. EMPLOYER'S NAME OR SCHOOL NAME

c. OTHER ACCIDENT?
YES NO

c. INSURANCE PLAN NAME OR PROGRAM NAME

d. INSURANCE PLAN NAME OR PROGRAM NAME

10d. RESERVED FOR LOCAL USE

d. IS THERE ANOTHER HEALTH BENEFIT PLAN?
YES NO If yes, return to and complete item 9 a-d.

READ BACK OF FORM BEFORE COMPLETING & SIGNING THIS FORM.
12. PATIENT'S OR AUTHORIZED PERSON'S SIGNATURE I authorize the release of any medical or other information necessary to process this claim. I also request payment of government benefits either to myself or to the party who accepts assignment below.

SIGNED   DATE

13. INSURED'S OR AUTHORIZED PERSON'S SIGNATURE I authorize payment of medical benefits to the undersigned physician or supplier for services described below.

SIGNED

14. DATE OF CURRENT: MM DD YY ILLNESS (First symptom) OR INJURY (Accident) OR PREGNANCY (LMP)

15. IF PATIENT HAS HAD SAME OR SIMILAR ILLNESS, GIVE FIRST DATE MM DD YY

16. DATES PATIENT UNABLE TO WORK IN CURRENT OCCUPATION
FROM MM DD YY   TO MM DD YY

17. NAME OF REFERRING PROVIDER OR OTHER SOURCE
17a.
17b. NPI

18. HOSPITALIZATION DATES RELATED TO CURRENT SERVICES
FROM MM DD YY   TO MM DD YY

19. RESERVED FOR LOCAL USE

20. OUTSIDE LAB?
YES [X] NO $ CHARGES

21. DIAGNOSIS OR NATURE OF ILLNESS OR INJURY (Relate Items 1, 2, 3 or 4 to Item 24E by Line)
1. 493 . 90
2.
3.
4.

22. MEDICAID RESUBMISSION CODE   ORIGINAL REF. NO.

23. PRIOR AUTHORIZATION NUMBER

24. A. DATE(S) OF SERVICE From MM DD YY / To MM DD YY	B. PLACE OF SERVICE	C. EMG	D. PROCEDURES, SERVICES, OR SUPPLIES (Explain Unusual Circumstances) CPT/HCPCS / MODIFIER	E. DIAGNOSIS POINTER	F. $ CHARGES	G. DAYS OR UNITS	H. EPSDT Family Plan	I. ID. QUAL	J. RENDERING PROVIDER ID. #
1	12 18 YYYY	11		99212	1	40 00	1		NPI	
2									NPI	
3									NPI	
4									NPI	
5									NPI	
6									NPI	

25. FEDERAL TAX I.D. NUMBER   SSN EIN [X]
111982342

26. PATIENT'S ACCOUNT NO.
15-5

27. ACCEPT ASSIGNMENT? (For govt. claims, see back)
[X] YES NO

28. TOTAL CHARGE
$ 40 00

29. AMOUNT PAID
$

30. BALANCE DUE
$ 40 00

31. SIGNATURE OF PHYSICIAN OR SUPPLIER INCLUDING DEGREES OR CREDENTIALS (I certify that the statements on the reverse apply to this bill and are made a part thereof.)
ANGELA DILALIO MD
SIGNED   DATE MMDDYYYY

32. SERVICE FACILITY LOCATION INFORMATION
a. NPI   b.

33. BILLING PROVIDER INFO & PH # (101) 2014321
ANGELA DILALIO
99 PROVIDER STREET
INJURY NY 12347
a. 4567890123   b.

NUCC Instruction Manual available at: www.nucc.org

APPROVED OMB-0938-0999 FORM CMS-1500 (08/05)

FIGURE 15-12 Completed SCHIP CMS-1500 claim for Edgar Vasquez case study

---

ICD-10-CM ALERT!

21. DIAGNOSIS OR NATURE OF ILLNESS OR INJURY (Relate Items 1, 2, 3 or 4 to Item 24E by Line)
1. J45 . 909
2.
3.
4.

E. DIAGNOSIS POINTER

SUMMARY

Title 19 of the SSA created Medicaid, a medical assistance program for individuals with incomes below the FPL. The federal government establishes Medicaid eligibility requirements, and individual states have discretion in determining coverage policies as well as establishing financial criteria for eligibility. Medicaid eligibility criteria depend on which of the following a recipient is categorized as: mandatory eligibility groups, optional eligibility groups, SCHIP, and disabled Medicaid beneficiaries who work.

Preauthorization for services is often required by Medicaid programs that have not implemented managed care (e.g., HMOs). A *dual eligible* is an individual who is covered by both Medicare and Medicaid—Medicare is billed as the primary payer. Medicaid is always the *payer of last resort* when a recipient is covered by other insurance (e.g., Medicare, TRICARE, IHS, or commercial health insurance). Participating providers accept Medicaid payments as payment in full, and balance billing is illegal.

MEVS (or REVS) allow providers to electronically verify a recipient's eligibility for Medicaid coverage via a point-of-service device, computer software, or an automated voice response system. The Medicaid remittance advice sent to providers contains the status of claims submitted, including paid, adjusted, and voided claims. Medicaid's surveillance utilization review system assesses unnecessary or inappropriate use of Medicaid services or excess payments, as well as the quality of services rendered.

When completing Medicaid CMS-1500 claims for case studies in this text and the Workbook, the following special instructions apply:

- Block 20—Enter an X in the NO box
- Block 22—Leave blank
- Block 24C—Leave blank
- Block 24H—Leave blank
- Block 26—Enter the case study number (e.g., 15-5). If the patient has Medicaid as secondary coverage, enter an S (for secondary) (15-2S) next to the number (on the secondary claim)
- Block 27—Enter an X in the YES box
- Block 32—If Block 18 contains dates and/or Block 20 contains an X in the YES box, enter the name, address, and Medicaid NPI of the responsible provider (e.g., hospital, outside laboratory)
- When completing secondary claims, enter REMITTANCE ADVICE ATTACHED in the top margin of the CMS-1500 claim (to indicate that a primary payer's remittance advice would be attached to the claim submitted to the secondary payer)

INTERNET LINKS

- Medicaid
  Go to **www.cms.hhs.gov,** and click on the Medicaid link.
- BenefitsCheckUp®
  Go to **www.benefitscheckup.org** to locate information useful to seniors with limited income and resources.
- State Children's Health Insurance Program (SCHIP)
  Go to **www.cms.hhs.gov,** and click on the SCHIP link.
- Ticket to Work and Work Incentives Improvements Act (TWWIA)
  Go to **www.cms.hhs.gov,** click on the Medicaid link, locate the Medicaid Initiatives heading, and click on the Ticket to Work and Work Incentive Improvement Act (TWWIA) link.

- Your Benefits Connection®
  Go to **www.govbenefits.gov** (official benefits Web site of the U.S. government) for improved, personalized access to government assistance programs.
- Programs of All-Inclusive Care for the Elderly (PACE)
  Go to **www.cms.hhs.gov,** click on the Medicaid link, locate the Medicaid—General Information heading, and click on the Programs of All-Inclusive Care for the Elderly (PACE) link.

STUDY CHECKLIST

- ☐ Read this textbook chapter, and highlight key terms.
- ☐ Access SimClaim software at the online companion, and become familiar with the software.
- ☐ Complete CMS-1500 claims for each chapter case study.
- ☐ Complete the chapter review, verifying answers with your instructor.
- ☐ Complete the chapter CD-ROM activities.
- ☐ Complete WebTutor assignments, and take online quizzes.
- ☐ Complete Medicaid claims for cases located in Appendices I and II.
- ☐ Complete the Workbook chapter, verifying answers with your instructor.
- ☐ Complete the StudyWare activities to receive immediate feedback.
- ☐ Form a study group with classmates to discuss chapter concepts in preparation for an exam.

REVIEW

MULTIPLE CHOICE Select the most appropriate response.

1. **Medicaid is jointly funded by federal and state governments, and each state**
   a. administers its own Medicaid program.
   b. adopts the federal scope of services.
   c. establishes uniform eligibility standards.
   d. implements managed care for payment.

2. **State legislatures may change Medicaid eligibility requirements**
   a. as directed by the federal government.
   b. during the year, sometimes more than once.
   c. no more than once during each year.
   d. to clarify services and payments only.

3. **Which requirements are used to determine Medicaid eligibility for mandatory categorically needy eligibility groups?**
   a. AFDC
   b. EPSDT
   c. PACE
   d. TANF

4. **States that opt to include a medically needy eligibility group in their Medicaid program are required to include certain children and under the age of**
   a. 18.
   b. 19.
   c. 21.
   d. 25.

5. **Which allows states to create or expand existing insurance programs to include a greater number of children who are currently uninsured?**

    a. FMAP

    b. SCHIP

    c. SSDI

    d. TWIIA

6. **Which is considered a mandatory Medicaid service that states must offer to receive federal matching funds?**

    a. family planning services and supplies

    b. nursing facility services for those under age 21

    c. rehabilitation and physical therapy services

    d. transportation services

7. **Individuals who are eligible for both Medicare and Medicaid coverage are called**

    a. dual eligibles.

    b. Medicaid allowables.

    c. PACE participants.

    d. participating providers.

8. **When a patient has Medicaid coverage in addition to other, third-party payer coverage, Medicaid is always considered the**

    a. adjusted claim.

    b. medically necessary service.

    c. payer of last resort.

    d. remittance advice.

9. **Which is considered a voided claim?**

    a. a claim that has a negative balance for which the provider receives no payment until amounts exceed the negative balance amount

    b. a claim that has a payment correction submitted on it, which results in additional reimbursement being made to the provider

    c. a claim that Medicaid should not have originally paid and results in a deduction from the lump-sum payment made to the provider

    d. a claim that underwent review to safeguard against unnecessary or inappropriate use of Medicaid services or excess payments

10. **Medicaid-covered services are paid only when the service is determined by the provider to be medically necessary, which means the services are**

    a. consistent with the patient's symptoms, diagnosis, condition, or injury.

    b. furnished primarily for the convenience of the recipient or the provider.

    c. provided when other equally effective treatments are available or suitable.

    d. recognized as being inconsistent with generally accepted standards.

TRICARE

CHAPTER OUTLINE

TRICARE Background

TRICARE Administration

CHAMPVA

TRICARE Options

TRICARE Programs and Demonstration
Projects

TRICARE Supplemental Plans

Billing Notes

Claims Instructions

Primary TRICARE with a Supplemental
Policy

TRICARE as Secondary Payer

OBJECTIVES

Upon successful completion of this chapter, you should be able to:

1. Define key terms.
2. Explain the historical background of TRICARE.
3. Describe how TRICARE is administered.
4. Define CHAMPVA.
5. List and explain the TRICARE options, programs and demonstration projects, and supplemental plans.
6. Apply TRICARE billing notes when completing CMS-1500 claims.
7. Complete TRICARE claims properly.

KEY TERMS

beneficiary counseling and assistance
    coordinator (BCAC)
beneficiary services representative (BSR)
catastrophic cap benefit
catchment area
CHAMPUS Reform Initiative (CRI)
common access card (CAC)

critical pathway
debt collection assistance officer (DCAO)
Defense Enrollment Eligibility Reporting
    System (DEERS)
demonstration project
DSM (Diagnostic and Statistical
    Manual)
emergency care

fiscal year
Health Affairs (HA)
health care finder (HCF)
lead agent (LA)
Military Health Services System (MHSS)
military treatment facility (MTF)
nonavailability statement (NAS)

525

nurse advisor
other health insurance (OHI)
practice guidelines
primary care manager (PCM)
Program Integrity (PI) Office
TRICARE

TRICARE beneficiary
TRICARE Extra
TRICARE Management Activity (TMA)
TRICARE Prime
TRICARE Program Management
   Organization (PMO)

TRICARE Service Center (TSC)
TRICARE sponsor
TRICARE Standard
uniformed services

INTRODUCTION

TRICARE is a healthcare program for (1) active duty members of the military and their qualified family members, (2) CHAMPUS-eligible retirees and their qualified family members, and (3) eligible survivors of members of the uniformed services. CHAMPUS (now called TRICARE Standard) is an abbreviation for the Civilian Health and Medical Program of the Uniformed Services, a federal program created in 1966 (and implemented in 1967) as a benefit for dependents of personnel serving in the uniformed services (U.S. military branches that include the Army, Navy, Air Force, Marines, and Coast Guard), Public Health Service, and the National Oceanic and Atmospheric Administration (NOAA). TRICARE was created to expand healthcare access, ensure quality of care, control healthcare costs, and improve medical readiness.

Complete StudyWare practice quizzes and activities using the CD-ROM located inside the back cover of your textbook.

NOTE: The original 12 TRICARE regions were consolidated as part of restructuring initiatives in 2004.

TRICARE BACKGROUND

CHAMPUS (now called TRICARE) was implemented in 1967 as the result of an initiative to provide military medical care for families of active-duty members. The original budget was $106 million; the current budget is more than $24 billion (*2002 Tricare Stakeholders' Report,* volume IV). In the 1980s the Department of Defense (DoD) began researching ways to improve access to quality care while controlling costs, and demonstration projects were authorized. One demonstration project, the CHAMPUS Reform Initiative (CRI) carried out in California and Hawaii, offered military families a choice of how their healthcare benefits could be used. The DoD noted the successful operation and high levels of patient satisfaction associated with the CRI, and it was determined that its concepts should be expanded to a nationwide uniform program.

TRICARE

This new program became known as TRICARE, a regionally-managed healthcare program that joins the healthcare resources of the uniformed services (e.g., Army) and supplements them with networks of civilian healthcare professionals to provide access and high-quality service while maintaining the capability to support military operations. TRICARE is a healthcare program for active-duty members of the uniformed services and their families, retirees and their families, and survivors of all uniformed services who are not eligible for Medicare.

There are four TRICARE regions: three in the United States and TRICARE overseas (Figure 16-1). Each is managed by a Lead Agent staff that is responsible for the military health system in that region. Commanders of selected military treatment facilities (MTFs) are selected as lead agents (LA) for the TRICARE regions. The Lead Agent staff serves as a federal healthcare team created to work with regional military treatment facility commanders, uniformed service headquarters' staffs, and Health Affairs (HA) to support the mission of the Military Health Services System (MHSS). The Military Health Services System (MHSS) is the entire healthcare system of the U.S. uniformed services and includes MTFs as well as various programs in the civilian healthcare market, such as TRICARE. Health Affairs (HA) refers to the Office of the Assistant Secretary of

FIGURE 16-1 Map of TRICARE regions (Permission to reuse in accordance with **www.tricare.mil** Web Site policy)

Defense for Health Affairs, which is responsible for both military readiness and peacetime health care.

Eligibility for TRICARE is specified in Table 16-1.

TABLE 16-1 TRICARE eligibility

BENEFICIARY CATEGORY	DESCRIPTION
Active-duty and retired service members	Includes any of the seven uniformed services: ● Air Force ● Army ● Coast Guard ● Marine Corps ● National Oceanic and Atmospheric Administration ● Navy ● Public Health Service
Spouses and unmarried children (including stepchildren) of active-duty or retired service members	● Remain eligible even if parents divorce or remarry ● Eligibility ends at age 21 unless child is a full-time student (validation of student status is required), and eligibility ends at age 23 or when the full-time student status ends ● Eligibility may extend past age 21 if the child is incapable of self-support because of a mental or physical incapacity and the condition existed prior to age 21, or if the condition occurred between ages 21 and 23 while the child was a full-time student ● Illegitimate children of current or former service members or their spouses may be eligible under certain conditions ● Children placed in the custody of a service member or former service member, either by a court or by a recognized adoption agency, in anticipation of legal adoption by the member **NOTE:** Stepchildren lose eligibility after a divorce unless they are adopted by the sponsor.

(continues)

TABLE 16-1   (continued)

BENEFICIARY CATEGORY	DESCRIPTION
National Guard and Reserve Component members on active duty for more than 30 days—under Federal orders	Includes National Guard and any of the following Reserve Component services: • Air Force • Army • Coast Guard • Marine Corps • National Oceanic and Atmospheric Administration • Navy • Public Health Service
Spouses and unmarried children of National Guard and Reserve Component service members	• Covered while sponsor is on active duty for more than 30 consecutive days • Covered if sponsor was injured or died during, or on the way to or from, active-duty training for a period of 30 days or less
Retired National Guard and Reserve Component service members and their family members	• When retired service member is eligible for retirement pay (usually at age 60), member and his or her eligible family members become eligible for TRICARE
Widows or widowers and unmarried children of deceased active-duty or retired service members	• Are eligible as family members of deceased member *if* sponsor was serving or was ordered to active duty for more than 30 days at time of death • Claims will be cost-shared at the active-duty family member rate for three years after death of active-duty sponsor, and thereafter at the retiree rate • Widows or widowers remain eligible until they remarry (loss of benefits remains applicable even if remarriage ends in death or divorce) • Children remain eligible until age 21, unless they meet the exceptions listed earlier
Medal of Honor recipients and their family members	• Any service member who was awarded the Medal of Honor • Awardee's eligible family members and widow or widower are eligible for medical and dental benefits under TRICARE

Certain eligible former spouses of active-duty or retired service members	• Must not have remarried (if remarried, loss of benefits remains applicable even if remarriage ends in death or divorce)
	• Starting October 1, 2003, eligibility and medical records are listed under former spouse's own social security number, not that of the sponsor
	• Must not be covered by an employer-sponsored health plan
	• Must not be former spouse of a North Atlantic Treaty Organization (NATO) or Partners for Peace (PFP) nation member
	• Must meet the requirements of one of the following three situations:
	  • SITUATION 1: Must have been married to the *same* member or former member for at least 20 years, and at least 20 of those years must have been creditable in determining the member's eligibility for retirement pay. If the date of the final decree of divorce or annulment was on or after February 1, 1983, the former spouse is eligible for TRICARE coverage of health care that is received after that date. If the date of the final decree is before February 1, 1983, the former spouse is eligible for TRICARE coverage of health care received on or after January 1, 1985.
	  • SITUATION 2: Must have been married to the *same* military member or former member for at least 20 years, and at least 15—but less than 20—of those married years must have been creditable in determining the member's eligibility for retirement pay. If the date of the final decree of divorce or annulment is before April 1, 1985, the former spouse is eligible only for care received on or after January 1, 1985, or the date of the decree, whichever is later.
	  • SITUATION 3: Must have been married to the *same* military member or former member for at least 20 years, and at least 15—but less than 20—of those married years must have been creditable in determining the member's eligibility for retirement pay. If the date of the final decree of divorce or annulment is on or after September 29, 1988, the former spouse is eligible for care received for only one year from the date of the decree. Upon completion of the period of eligibility for TRICARE, explained in Situation 3, a former spouse is eligible for the Continued Health Care Benefit Program (CHCBP).

TRICARE ADMINISTRATION

The **TRICARE Management Activity (TMA)** (formerly called OCHAMPUS) is the office that coordinates and administers the TRICARE program and is accountable for quality health care provided to members of the uniformed services and their families. The TMA also serves as arbitrator for denied claims submitted for consideration by TRICARE sponsors and beneficiaries; its offices are located in Aurora, Colorado. **TRICARE sponsors** are uniformed service personnel who are either active duty, retired, or deceased. (Dependents of deceased sponsors are eligible for TRICARE benefits.) Sponsor information (e.g., SSN, DOB, and last name) can be verified in the **Defense Enrollment Eligibility Reporting System (DEERS)**, a computer system that contains up-to-date Defense Department workforce personnel information. **TRICARE beneficiaries** include sponsors and dependents of sponsors.

> **NOTE:** Do not submit TRICARE claims to the TMA; claims are processed by TRICARE contractors (similar to Medicare administrative contractors) for different regions of the country and overseas.

TRICARE Service Centers

TRICARE regions are served by one or more **TRICARE Service Centers (TSC)**, business offices staffed by one or more beneficiary services representatives and health-care finders who assist TRICARE sponsors with healthcare needs and answer questions about the program.

Beneficiary Services Representatives

A **beneficiary services representative (BSR)** is employed at a TRICARE Service Center, provides information about using TRICARE, and assists with other matters affecting access to health care (e.g., appointment scheduling).

Health Care Finders

A **health care finder (HCF)** is a registered nurse or physician assistant who assists primary care providers with preauthorizations and referrals to healthcare services in a military treatment facility or civilian provider network. A *preauthorization* is formal approval obtained from a health care finder before certain specialty procedures and inpatient care services are rendered. A *referral* is a request for a member to receive treatment from another provider.

Nurse Advisors

In most TRICARE regions, **nurse advisors** are also available 24/7 for advice and assistance with treatment alternatives and to discuss whether a sponsor should see a provider based on a discussion of symptoms. Nurse advisors will also discuss preventive care and ways to improve a family's health.

Military Treatment Facilities

A **military treatment facility (MTF)** is a healthcare facility operated by the military that provides inpatient and/or ambulatory (outpatient and emergency department) care to eligible TRICARE beneficiaries. The capabilities of MTFs vary from limited acute care clinics to teaching and tertiary care medical centers.

Beneficiary counseling and assistance coordinators (BCACs) are located at military treatment facilities (MTFs), and they are available to answer questions, help solve healthcare-related problems, and assist beneficiaries in obtaining medical care through TRICARE. BCACs were previously called *Health Benefits Advisors (HBAs)*. **Debt collection assistance officers (DCAOs)** are located at military treatment facilities to assist beneficiaries in resolving healthcare collection-related issues.

Case Management

TRICARE *case management* is organized under TRICARE utilization management and is a collaborative process that coordinates and monitors a beneficiary's healthcare options and services by assessing available resources to promote quality and cost-effective outcomes. The use of critical pathways, practice guidelines, and discharge planning can enhance the case management process. A critical pathway is the sequence of activities that can normally be expected to result in the most cost-effective clinical course of treatment. Practice guidelines are decision-making tools used by providers to determine appropriate health care for specific clinical circumstances. They offer the opportunity to improve healthcare delivery processes by reducing unwanted variation. The Institute of Medicine specifies that practice guidelines should be valid, reliable and reproducible, clinically applicable and flexible, a multidisciplinary process, reviewed on a scheduled basis, and well documented. *Discharge planning* assesses requirements so that arrangements can be made for the appropriate and timely discharge of patients from acute care or outpatient settings.

> **EXAMPLE:** Inpatient records undergo quarterly review (using predetermined screening criteria) to identify individuals whose frequency of services or cost of services makes them candidates for case management.

Program Integrity Office

The TMA Program Integrity (PI) Office is responsible for the surveillance of fraud and abuse activities worldwide involving purchased care for beneficiaries in the Military Health Care System. The PI Office develops policies and procedures for the prevention, detection, investigation, and control of TRICARE fraud, waste, and program abuse. It monitors contractor program integrity activities, coordinates with the Department of Defense and external investigative agencies, and initiates administrative remedies as required. TRICARE-authorized providers can be excluded from program participation if one of the following conditions applies:

- Any criminal conviction or civil judgment involving fraud
- Fraud or abuse under TRICARE
- Exclusion or suspension by another federal, state, or local government agency
- Participation in a conflict-of-interest situation
- When it is in the best interest of the TRICARE program or its beneficiaries

> **EXAMPLE:** A Colorado psychologist pled guilty to two felony counts of healthcare fraud, one felony count of conspiracy to defraud with respect to claims, and one felony count of criminal forfeiture. This judgment was the culmination of a six-year investigation of a counseling center where a billing-fraud scam involved filing claims for services not provided as well as using an authorized provider's identification number to submit claims for services that were provided by an unauthorized provider. TRICARE will recover almost $500,000 in damages. The psychologist received a sentence of 21 months of imprisonment and three years of released supervision.

CHAMPVA

The *Civilian Health and Medical Program of the Department of Veterans Affairs (CHAMPVA)* is a comprehensive healthcare program for which the Department of Veterans Affairs (VA) shares costs of covered healthcare services and supplies with eligible beneficiaries. The Health Administration Center, located in Denver, Colorado, administers the CHAMPVA program by:

- Processing applications.
- Determining eligibility.
- Authorizing benefits.
- Processing claims.

> **NOTE:** Due to the similarity between CHAMPVA and TRICARE (previously called CHAMPUS), the two are often confused. CHAMPVA is the Department of Veterans Affairs healthcare program. TRICARE is a regionally managed healthcare program for active duty and retired members of the uniformed services, their families, and survivors.

Eligibility for CHAMPVA

To be eligible for CHAMPVA, the beneficiary must be:

- The spouse or child of a veteran who has been rated permanently and totally disabled for a service-connected disability by a VA regional office.
- The surviving spouse or child of a veteran who died from a VA-rated service connected disability.
- The surviving spouse or child of a veteran who at the time of death was rated as permanently and totally disabled as the result of a service-connected disability.
- The surviving spouse or child of a military member who died in the line of duty (not due to misconduct) (however, these individuals may be eligible for TRICARE instead of CHAMPVA).

Eligible CHAMPVA sponsors may be entitled to receive medical care through the VA healthcare system based on their veteran status. If an eligible CHAMPVA sponsor is the spouse of another eligible CHAMPVA sponsor, both may be eligible for CHAMPVA benefits. In each instance where an eligible spouse requires medical attention, the spouse may choose to receive health care from the VA system or through CHAMPVA coverage.

> **NOTE:** For a CHAMPVA beneficiary who also has Medicare coverage, CHAMPVA is always the secondary payer to Medicare. Therefore, submit the beneficiary's claim to Medicare first. (CHAMPVA requires electronic submission of CMS-1500 claims.)

TRICARE OPTIONS

TRICARE offers three healthcare options:

1. *TRICARE Prime*: Military treatment facilities are the principal source of health care under this option.
2. *TRICARE Extra*: A preferred provider organization (PPO) option.
3. *TRICARE Standard* (formerly CHAMPUS): A fee-for-service option.

> **NOTE:** The TRICARE Extra option is not offered in all regions because of the limited availability of PPOs in some civilian markets; instead, TRICARE Standard is available.

TRICARE Prime

TRICARE Prime is a managed care option similar to a civilian health maintenance organization (HMO). Enrollment in TRICARE Prime guarantees priority access to care at military treatment facilities.

Features of TRICARE Prime

- Guaranteed access to timely medical care
- Priority for care at military treatment facilities
- Assignment of a primary care manager (PCM)
- Lowest cost option of the three TRICARE options
- Requires enrollment for one year
- Retired military pay an annual enrollment fee
- Care sought outside of TRICARE Prime network is costly
- May be unavailable in some TRICARE regions

TRICARE Prime provides comprehensive healthcare benefits at the lowest cost of the three options. *Eligible individuals are required to enroll in TRICARE Prime so that adequate professional staffing and resources are available in military treatment facilities and supporting civilian facilities.* Individuals eligible for TRICARE Prime include (1) active-duty military personnel, (2) family members of active-duty sponsors (no enrollment fee), and (3) retirees and their family members, all of whom are under 65. See Tables 16-2 and 16-3, which list out-of-pocket costs for TRICARE Prime.

A **primary care manager (PCM)** is a doctor assigned to a sponsor, and is part of the TRICARE provider network. The PCM guides TRICARE Prime members

TABLE 16-2   TRICARE deductible, copayment, and coinsurance amounts (2010)

	TRICARE PRIME	TRICARE EXTRA/STANDARD
Annual deductible	$0	$150 individual (E-5 and above)
		$300 family (E-5 and above)
		$50 individual (E-4 and below)
		$100 family (E-4 and below)
Civilian outpatient visit	$0	Extra: 15% of negotiated fee
		Standard: 20% of allowed charge
Civilian inpatient admission	$0	$15.65/day or $25 minimum, whichever is greater
Civilian inpatient behavioral health	$0	$20/day or $25 minimum, whichever is greater
Civilian inpatient SNF care	$0	$15.65/day or $25 minimum, whichever is greater

TABLE 16-3   TRICARE out-of-pocket expenses for retirees and their family members (2010)

	TRICARE PRIME	TRICARE EXTRA	TRICARE STANDARD
Annual deductible	$0	$150 individual	$150 individual
		$300 family	$300 family
Annual enrollment fees	$230 individual	$0	$0
	$460 family		
Civilian Provider Copays			
Outpatient visit	$12	20% of negotiated fees	25% of allowed charges
Emergency care	$30	20% of negotiated fees	25% of allowed charges
Mental health visit	$25	20% of negotiated fees	25% of allowed charges
	$17 (group visit)	20% of negotiated fees	25% of allowed charges
Civilian inpatient cost share	$11/day ($25 minimum)	Lesser of $250/day or 25% of billed charges; plus 20% of negotiated professional fees	Lesser of $535/day or 25% of billed charges; plus 25% of allowed professional charges
Civilian inpatient behavioral health	$40/day	20% of institutional charges; plus 25% of professional charges	Lesser of $193/day or 25% of institutional; plus 25% of professional charges

(Reprinted according to reuse policy at www.tricare.osd.mil/main/privacy.html)

through the healthcare system and coordinates all specialty medical needs. Prime members can choose a PCM from the MTF or the TRICARE provider directory. TRICARE Prime beneficiaries also receive care if they reside and work outside an MTF catchment area, the region defined by code boundaries within a 40-mile radius of an MTF. Note that certain TRICARE regions only allow a military doctor or medical clinic to serve as a PCM.

The PCM provides nonemergency care to eligible beneficiaries and arranges referrals for specialty care if needed, usually through a military hospital. If military specialty care is unavailable, the PCM authorizes care from a civilian specialist. For beneficiaries to receive coverage for specialty care, the PCM must make these arrangements. TRICARE Prime guarantees enrollees access to care; urgent care is rendered within one day, while less urgent care is provided within one week. In addition, travel is limited to no more than 30 minutes to the PCM. Preventive care is emphasized, and the following services are provided at no additional charge: eye exams, immunizations, hearing screenings, mammograms, Pap smears, prostate exams, and other cancer-prevention and early diagnosis exams.

TRICARE Prime covers nonemergency care if the beneficiary is away from home and receives prior approval from the PCM. Such authorization is required for all routine medical care provided out of the area or at another facility. If the beneficiary seeks medical care without prior approval, the *point-of-service option* is activated, requiring payment of an annual deductible plus 50 percent or more of visit or treatment fees.

Beneficiaries who require emergency care should seek that care at the nearest civilian or military treatment facility.

Catastrophic Cap Benefit

The catastrophic cap benefit protects TRICARE beneficiaries from devastating financial loss due to serious illness or long-term treatment by establishing limits over which payment is not required. Under TRICARE Prime, the maximum out-of-pocket cost per year for covered medical services is $1,000 for active-duty military sponsors' family members and $3,000 for retirees and their families per enrollment year.

TRICARE Extra

TRICARE Extra allows TRICARE Standard users to save 5 percent of their TRICARE Standard cost-shares by using healthcare providers in the TRICARE network. To receive care, enrollees simply go to any network doctor, hospital, or other provider and present their uniformed services common access card (CAC) (identification card issued by Department of Defense, DoD) (Figure 16-2), which is scanned. Care is also available at an MTF on a space-available basis.

(A)

(B)

FIGURE 16-2 (A) Sample TRICARE enrollment card (Reuse in accordance with www.tricare.mil.) (B) Sample uniformed services common access card (CAC) inserted in point-of-service device (Reuse in accordance with www.hanscom.af.mil.)

Features of TRICARE Extra

- Choice of any physician in the network
- Less costly than TRICARE Standard
- May be more expensive than TRICARE Prime
- Annual enrollment is not required
- Lower priority for care provided at MTFs

Unlike for TRICARE Prime, individuals eligible for TRICARE Extra do not have to enroll or pay an enrollment fee. They can use the option whenever they choose by selecting any healthcare provider from within the TRICARE Extra provider network. When a TRICARE Extra network provider renders care, it is just like using TRICARE Standard (formerly CHAMPUS), with the bonus of a 5 percent discount on most cost-shares (e.g., copayments).

TRICARE Extra offers enrollees the choice of receiving healthcare services from participating civilian hospitals, physicians, and other medical providers who have agreed to charge an approved fee for medical treatment and procedures. Two groups that usually prefer TRICARE Extra include (1) individuals and families whose regular physician is a participating member of the TRICARE Extra network, and (2) individuals who do not have convenient access to MTFs and want reduced healthcare costs as compared with TRICARE Standard.

Those eligible for TRICARE Extra coverage include (1) family members of active-duty sponsors (no enrollment fee), and (2) retirees (except most Medicare-eligible beneficiaries) and their family members under age 65.

TRICARE Extra Coverage

Individuals eligible to enroll in TRICARE Extra are not required to pay an annual fee, can seek care from a network provider, receive a discount on services, and usually pay reduced copayments (5 percent less than TRICARE Standard; participating providers are reimbursed the approved rate plus 5 percent). In addition, network providers file insurance claims for enrollees and are prohibited from balance billing. *Balance billing* refers to the practice of a provider billing a patient for all charges not reimbursed by a health plan.

TRICARE Extra enrollees can also seek healthcare services from an MTF on a space-available basis, and they can select between TRICARE Extra and TRICARE Standard options on a visit-by-visit basis. Tables 16-2 and 16-3 list out-of-pocket costs for TRICARE Extra.

Catastrophic Cap Benefit

Under TRICARE Extra, active-duty sponsors' family members are responsible for up to $1,000 and retirees for up to $3,000 per year in out-of-pocket costs for covered services.

TRICARE Standard

TRICARE Standard is the new name for traditional CHAMPUS. To use this option, enrollees either make an appointment at an MTF or seek care from any TRICARE-certified civilian healthcare provider (fee-for-service option). Enrollees are responsible for annual deductibles and copayments. It provides beneficiaries with the greatest freedom in selecting civilian providers; however, it has the highest out-of-pocket costs of the three plans. There is no enrollment requirement for TRICARE Standard.

UNIFORMED SERVICES MEDICAL TREATMENT FACILITY NONAVAILABILITY STATEMENT (NAS) | REPORT CONTROL SYMBOL

Privacy Act Statement

AUTHORITY: 44 USC 3101, 41 CFR 101 et seq., 10 USC 1066 and 1079, and EO 9397, November 1943 (SSN).

PRINCIPAL PURPOSE: To evaluate eligibility for civilian health benefits authorized by 10 USC, Chapter 55, and to issue payment upon establishment of eligibility and determination that the medical care received is authorized by law. The information is subject to verification with the appropriate Uniformed Service.

ROUTINE USE: CHAMPUS and its contractors use the information to control and process medical claims for payment; for control and approval of medical treatments and interface with providers of medical care; to control and accomplish reviews of utilization; for review of claims related to possible third party liability cases and initiation of recovery actions; and for referral to Peer Review Committees or similar professional review organizations to control and review providers' medical care.

DISCLOSURE: Voluntary; however, failure to provide information will result in denial of, or delay in payment of, the claim.

1. NAS NUMBER *(Facility) (Yr-Julian) (Seq. No.)*

2. PRIMARY REASON FOR ISSUANCE *(X one)*
- a. PROPER FACILITIES ARE TEMPORARILY NOT AVAILABLE IN A SAFE OR TIMELY MANNER
- b. PROFESSIONAL CAPABILITY IS TEMPORARILY NOT AVAILABLE IN A SAFE OR TIMELY MANNER
- c. PROPER FACILITIES OR PROFESSIONAL CAPABILITY ARE PERMANENTLY NOT AVAILABLE AT THIS FACILITY
- d. IT WOULD BE MEDICALLY INAPPROPRIATE TO REQUIRE THE BENEFICIARY TO USE THE MTF *(Explain in Remarks)*

3. MAJOR DIAGNOSIC CATEGORY FOR WHICH NAS IS ISSUED *(Use code from reverse)*

4. PATIENT DATA
- a. NAME *(Last, First, Middle Initial)*
- b. DATE OF BIRTH *(YYMMDD)*
- c. SEX
- d. ADDRESS *(Street, City, State, and ZIP Code)*
- e. PATIENT CATEGORY *(X one)*
  - (1) Dependent of Active Duty
  - (2) Dependent of Retiree
  - (3) Retiree
  - (4) Survivor
  - (5) Former Spouse
- f. OTHER NON CHAMPUS HEALTH INSURANCE *(X one)*
  - (1) Yes, but only CHAMPUS Supplemental
  - (2) Yes *(List in Remarks)*
  - (3) No

5. SPONSOR DATA *(If you marked 4e(3) Retiree above, print "Same" in 5a.)*
- a. NAME *(Last, First, Middle Initial)*
- b. SPONSOR'S OR RETIREE'S SOCIAL SECURITY NO.

6. ISSUING OFFICIAL DATA
- a. NAME *(Last, First, Middle Initial)*
- b. TITLE
- c. SIGNATURE
- d. PAY GRADE
- e. DATE ISSUED *(YYMMDD)*

7. REMARKS *(Indicate block number to which the answer applies.)*

DD Form 1251 — Outside the United States and Puerto Rico, previous editions may be used until exhausted. Inside the United States and Puerto Rico, previous editions are obsolete

FIGURE 16-3 Sample nonavailability statement (NAS) (Courtesy Delmar/Cengage Learning)

Features of TRICARE Standard

- **Greatest flexibility in selecting healthcare providers**
- **Most convenient when traveling or away from home**
- **Potentially most expensive of all options**
- **Enrollment not required**
- **TRICARE Extra can be used**
- **Space-available care in MTFs is a provision (low priority is assigned to TRICARE Standard enrollees)**

NOTE: TRICARE Standard does not enroll participating providers; they participate voluntarily and may do so on a case-by-case basis. When using TRICARE Standard, enrollees should ask the selected providers whether they participate in TRICARE Standard.

TRICARE Standard Coverage

Annual deductibles, cost-shares, and benefits are the same as they were for CHAMPUS. Under TRICARE Standard, enrollees can select their healthcare provider; however, out-of-pocket costs are higher when compared with other TRICARE options.

Also, enrollees who seek care from nonparticipating providers may have to file their own claim forms and, perhaps, pay more for care (up to 15 percent more than the allowable charge). Participating providers accept the TRICARE Standard allowable charge as payment in full for care rendered and they will file insurance claims for enrollees.

Catastrophic Cap Benefit

Under TRICARE Standard, active-duty sponsors' family members are responsible for up to $1,000 and retirees for up to $3,000 per year in out-of-pocket costs for covered services.

Dual Medicare and TRICARE Eligibility

Sponsors and dependents who are eligible for Medicare qualify for *dual Medicare/TRICARE eligibility* in the following situations:

- Beneficiaries who become eligible for Medicare Part A on the basis of age and who also purchase Medicare Part B coverage continue to be eligible for TRICARE, which is secondary to Medicare.

- Family members of active-duty service members who are eligible for Medicare for any reason are also eligible for TRICARE Prime, Extra, or Standard, whether or not they purchase Medicare Part B.

- Beneficiaries under age 65 who are entitled to Medicare Part A because of disability or end-stage renal disease (ESRD) and who have purchased Medicare Part B are also eligible for TRICARE Prime, Extra, or Standard until they turn 65 (when they become eligible only for TRICARE for Life, discussed later in this chapter).

TRICARE PROGRAMS AND DEMONSTRATION PROJECTS

The TRICARE Program Management Organization (PMO) manages TRICARE programs (e.g., pharmacy program) and demonstration projects (e.g., Healthy Eating and Active Living in TRICARE Households, abbreviated as HEALTH). A demonstration project tests and establishes the feasibility of implementing a new program during a trial period, after which the program is evaluated, modified, and/or abandoned. If, upon evaluation, it is determined that program implementation criteria are met (e.g., cost-effectiveness and meets intended needs of a population), the demonstration project is approved as a program, and enrollment is expanded to include all eligible individuals. (TRICARE was originally a demonstration project.)

TRICARE SUPPLEMENTAL PLANS

TRICARE supplemental insurance policies are offered by most military associations and by some private firms. They are designed to reimburse patients for the civilian medical care expenses that must be paid after TRICARE reimburses the government's share of healthcare costs. Each TRICARE supplemental policy has its own rules concerning preexisting conditions, eligibility requirements for family members, deductibles, mental health limitations, long-term care illnesses, well-baby care, disability care, claims processed under the diagnosis related group (DRG) payment system for inpatient hospital charges, and rules concerning allowable charges.

BILLING NOTES

The following is a summary of the nationwide billing information for TRICARE Standard and TRICARE Extra out-of-network services. Providers of services are required to file these claims.

TRICARE Contractors

In recent years, TRICARE contractors were grouped in large regional districts covering many states. Each regional contractor assigned post office box numbers and an associated nine-digit zip code for each state served. Be sure to use and proofread carefully both the post office box number and its associated zip code when submitting claims or correspondence to the contractor. Contact the nearest military facility to obtain the current address of the contractor assigned to your area, or access the TRICARE Web site of the U.S. Department of Defense Military Health System at **www.tricare.osd.mil.**

Underwriter

TRICARE is based in Colorado. Changes in general benefits are enacted by the United States Congress.

Forms Used

NOTE: Inpatient and outpatient hospital (and other institution) claims are submitted on the UB-04 (CMS-1450). If inpatient or outpatient health care was provided at a civilian hospital, a *nonavailability statement (NAS)* must be submitted electronically. (Do not submit an NAS for emergency care provided at a civilian hospital.)

Providers submit the CMS-1500 claim to TRICARE. If the patient has other health insurance (OHI), attach the remittance advice to the TRICARE claim. This includes coverage such as automobile insurance and workers' compensation. If the other health insurance plan does not pay the claim, submit the exclusion section of its policy or a copy of the denial. (A denial from an HMO or PPO stating that the patient did not use available services is not considered an exclusion.) If hospital care was provided (or physician's charges are $500 or higher) for an accidental injury, submit a *DD Form 2527* (Personal Injury Questionnaire) that was completed by the patient.

- Providers receive a remittance advice from TRICARE third-party payers, which illustrates how claims were processed and the amount for which the enrollee is responsible. If a claim is denied, an explanation of the denial is also provided.
- Enrollees receive a TRICARE explanation of benefits (EOB), which is an itemized statement that includes the action taken by TRICARE submitted CMS-1500 claims.

Filing Deadline

Claims will be denied if they are filed more than one year after the date of service for outpatient care or more than one year from the date of discharge for inpatient care.

NOTE: Patients who file claims directly with TRICARE submit a *DD Form 2642* (Patient's Request for Medical Payment) and attach a copy of the provider's itemized bill to the claim. (Go to **www.tricare.osd.mil/ claims/DD_2642.pdf** to view the four-page DD Form 2642.)

Allowable Fee Determination

TRICARE follows the principles of the RBRVS system, but has made some adjustments to the geographic regions and assigned a slightly higher conversion factor. Fee schedules are available from regional carriers. The TRICARE fee schedule must still be followed when TRICARE is a secondary payer.

Deductibles

All deductibles are applied to the government's fiscal year, which runs from October 1 of one year to September 30 of the next. This is different from other insurance programs, for which deductibles are usually calculated on a calendar-year basis.

Confirmation of Eligibility

Confirmation of TRICARE eligibility is obtained by entering the sponsor's social security number in the nationwide computerized Defense Enrollment Eligibility Reporting System (DEERS). The SSN is located on the reverse of the sponsor's uniformed services common access card (CAC). (The CAC is a smart card that replaced the military identification card. Photocopying the CAC is permitted to facilitate eligibility verification and to provide healthcare services.)

Accepting Assignment

Accepting assignment for nonPARs is determined on a claim-by-claim basis. Be sure to indicate the provider's choice in Block 27 of the claim. All deductibles and cost-shares may be collected at the time service is rendered. When assignment is elected, the local beneficiary services representative can assist if there are problems collecting the deductible and cost-share (copayment) from the patient. The TRICARE contractor's provider representative can assist with claims review or intervene when a claim payment is overdue.

TRICARE has established a "good faith policy" for assigned claims when the copy of the front and back of the patient's uniformed services common access card (CAC) on file turns out to be invalid. If copies of the CAC are on file and TRICARE provides notification that the patient is ineligible for payment, the local BSR can help in investigation of the claim. If the investigation reveals that the CAC is invalid, refile the claim with a note stating: "We treated this patient in good faith. Please note the enclosed copy of the CAC that was presented at the time the treatment was rendered." *Do not send* your file copy of the CAC card. The provider should receive payment of the TRICARE-approved fee for these services.

TRICARE Limiting Charges

All TRICARE nonPAR providers are subject to a limiting charge of 15 percent above the TRICARE fee schedule for PAR providers. Patients can no longer be billed for the difference between the provider's normal fee and the TRICARE limiting charge (called *balance billing*). Exceptions to the 15 percent limiting charge are claims from independent laboratory and diagnostic laboratory companies, for durable medical equipment, and from medical supply companies.

EXERCISE 16-1

Completion of TRICARE as Primary CMS-1500 Claim

1. Obtain a blank copy of the CMS-1500 claim by making a copy of the claim in Appendix III.
2. Review claims instructions on your comparison chart.
3. Review Figure 16-6, Mary S. Patient case study.
4. Select the information needed from Figure 16-6, and enter the required information on the claim using optical scanning guidelines.
5. Review the claim to be sure all required blocks are properly completed.
6. Compare your claim with the completed claim in Figure 16-7.

PRIMARY TRICARE WITH A SUPPLEMENTAL POLICY

The modifications in Table 16-5 must be made to the TRICARE primary claim when the healthcare provider is a TRICARE participating provider and the patient has a supplemental policy in addition to TRICARE.

TABLE 16-5   Modifications to TRICARE primary CMS-1500 claims completion instructions when patient has supplemental health insurance coverage

BLOCK	INSTRUCTIONS
NOTE: Blocks 11 and 11a–11c remain blank on a TRICARE Supplemental CMS-1500 claim.	
9	Enter the supplemental policyholder's last name, first name, and middle initial (if known) (separated by commas).
9a	Enter the supplemental policyholder's policy or group number.
9b	Enter the supplemental policyholder's birth date as MM DD YYYY (with spaces). Enter an X in the appropriate box to indicate the supplemental policyholder's gender.
9c	Enter the name of the supplemental policyholder's employer (if employed) or school (if unemployed and considered a full- or part-time student). Otherwise, leave blank.
9d	Enter the name of the supplemental policyholder's health insurance plan.
10d	Enter the word ATTACHMENT. (Attach the remittance advice received from the supplemental health insurance payer to the CMS-1500 claim.)
11d	Enter an X in the YES box.

ERIN A. HELPER, M.D.
101 Medic Drive, Anywhere NY 12345
(101) 111-1234 (Office) • (101) 111-9292 (Fax)
EIN: 11-1234523
NPI: 1234567890

Case Study

PATIENT INFORMATION:

Name:	Patient, Mary S.
Address:	91 Home Street
City:	Nowhere
State:	NY
Zip Code:	12367-1234
Telephone:	(101) 201-8989
Gender:	Female
Occupation:	Homemaker
Date of Birth:	10-10-1959
Employer:	

INSURANCE INFORMATION:

Patient Number:	16-2
Place of Service:	Office
Primary Insurance Plan:	TRICARE Standard
Primary Insurance Plan ID #:	101 23 9945
Policy #:	
Primary Policyholder:	Patient, James L.
Policyholder Date of Birth:	08-22-1944
Employer:	US Navy
Relationship to Patient:	Spouse
Address:	Dept 07 Naval Station
City/State/Zip Code:	Nowhere NY 12367-1234

Patient Status [X] Married [ ] Divorced [ ] Single [ ] Student

---

ICD-10-CM ALERT!

Fracture, distal radius, left	S52.509A
Fell at home	Y92.099
Fell down stairs	W10.8xxA

DIAGNOSIS INFORMATION

Diagnosis	Code	Diagnosis	Code
1. Fracture, distal radius, left	813.42	5.	
2. Fell at home	E849.0	6.	
3. Fell down stairs	E880.9	7.	
4.		8.	

PROCEDURE INFORMATION

Description of Procedure or Service	Date	Code	Charge
1. Closed manipulation, left distal radius	01-10-YYYY	25600-LT	300.00
2. X-ray, left wrist, 3 views	01-10-YYYY	73110-LT	50.00
3. X-ray, left forearm, 1 view	01-10-YYYY	73090-LT	25.00
4.			
5.			

SPECIAL NOTES: Fell down stairs at home today.

FIGURE 16-6 Mary S. Patient case study (Courtesy Delmar/Cengage Learning)

1500

HEALTH INSURANCE CLAIM FORM

APPROVED BY NATIONAL UNIFORM CLAIM COMMITTEE 08/05

PICA	PICA

1. MEDICARE (Medicare #)	MEDICAID (Medicaid #)	TRICARE CHAMPUS (Sponsor's SSN) [X]	CHAMPVA (Member ID#)	GROUP HEALTH PLAN (SSN or ID)	FECA BLK LUNG (SSN)	OTHER (ID)	1a. INSURED'S I.D. NUMBER (For Program in Item 1) 101239945

2. PATIENT'S NAME (Last Name, First Name, Middle Initial) PATIENT, MARY, S	3. PATIENT'S BIRTH DATE MM 10 DD 10 YY 1959 SEX M F [X]	4. INSURED'S NAME (Last Name, First Name, Middle Initial) PATIENT, JAMES, L

5. PATIENT'S ADDRESS (No., Street) 91 HOME STREET	6. PATIENT'S RELATIONSHIP TO INSURED Self Spouse [X] Child Other	7. INSURED'S ADDRESS (No., Street) DEPT 07 NAVAL STATION
CITY NOWHERE	STATE NY	8. PATIENT STATUS Single Married [X] Other	CITY NOWHERE	STATE NY
ZIP CODE 12367-1234	TELEPHONE (Include Area Code) (101)2018989	Employed Full-Time Student Part-Time Student	ZIP CODE 12367-1234	TELEPHONE (Include Area Code) ( )

9. OTHER INSURED'S NAME (Last Name, First Name, Middle Initial)	10. IS PATIENT'S CONDITION RELATED TO:	11. INSURED'S POLICY GROUP OR FECA NUMBER
a. OTHER INSURED'S POLICY OR GROUP NUMBER	a. EMPLOYMENT? (Current or Previous) YES NO [X]	a. INSURED'S DATE OF BIRTH MM DD YY SEX M F
b. OTHER INSURED'S DATE OF BIRTH MM DD YY SEX M F	b. AUTO ACCIDENT? PLACE (State) YES NO [X]	b. EMPLOYER'S NAME OR SCHOOL NAME
c. EMPLOYER'S NAME OR SCHOOL NAME	c. OTHER ACCIDENT? YES NO [X]	c. INSURANCE PLAN NAME OR PROGRAM NAME
d. INSURANCE PLAN NAME OR PROGRAM NAME	10d. RESERVED FOR LOCAL USE	d. IS THERE ANOTHER HEALTH BENEFIT PLAN? YES NO [X] If yes, return to and complete item 9 a-d.

READ BACK OF FORM BEFORE COMPLETING & SIGNING THIS FORM.

12. PATIENT'S OR AUTHORIZED PERSON'S SIGNATURE I authorize the release of any medical or other information necessary to process this claim. I also request payment of government benefits either to myself or to the party who accepts assignment below.

SIGNED SIGNATURE ON FILE   DATE

13. INSURED'S OR AUTHORIZED PERSON'S SIGNATURE I authorize payment of medical benefits to the undersigned physician or supplier for services described below.

SIGNED SIGNATURE ON FILE

14. DATE OF CURRENT: MM 01 DD 10 YY YYYY ILLNESS (First symptom) OR INJURY (Accident) OR PREGNANCY (LMP)	15. IF PATIENT HAS HAD SAME OR SIMILAR ILLNESS. GIVE FIRST DATE MM DD YY	16. DATES PATIENT UNABLE TO WORK IN CURRENT OCCUPATION FROM MM DD YY TO MM DD YY
17. NAME OF REFERRING PROVIDER OR OTHER SOURCE	17a. 17b. NPI	18. HOSPITALIZATION DATES RELATED TO CURRENT SERVICES FROM MM DD YY TO MM DD YY
19. RESERVED FOR LOCAL USE		20. OUTSIDE LAB? YES NO [X] $ CHARGES

21. DIAGNOSIS OR NATURE OF ILLNESS OR INJURY (Relate Items 1, 2, 3 or 4 to Item 24E by Line)	22. MEDICAID RESUBMISSION CODE ORIGINAL REF. NO.
1. 813.42 3. E8809	23. PRIOR AUTHORIZATION NUMBER
2. E8490 4.	

24. A. DATE(S) OF SERVICE From MM DD YY To MM DD YY	B. PLACE OF SERVICE	C. EMG	D. PROCEDURES, SERVICES, OR SUPPLIES (Explain Unusual Circumstances) CPT/HCPCS MODIFER	E. DIAGNOSIS POINTER	F. $ CHARGES	G. DAYS OR UNITS	H. EPSDT Family Plan	I. ID. QUAL.	J. RENDERING PROVIDER ID. #
1	01 10 YYYY	11		25600 LT	1	300 00	1		NPI	
2	01 10 YYYY	11		73110 LT	1	50 00	1		NPI	
3	01 10 YYYY	11		73090 LT	1	25 00	1		NPI	
4									NPI	
5									NPI	
6									NPI	

25. FEDERAL TAX I.D. NUMBER SSN EIN 111234523 [X]	26. PATIENT'S ACCOUNT NO. 16-2	27. ACCEPT ASSIGNMENT? (For govt. claims, see back) YES [X] NO	28. TOTAL CHARGE $ 375 00	29. AMOUNT PAID $	30. BALANCE DUE $ 375 00
31. SIGNATURE OF PHYSICIAN OR SUPPLIER INCLUDING DEGREES OR CREDENTIALS (I certify that the statements on the reverse apply to this bill and are made a part thereof.) ERIN A HELPER MD SIGNED DATE MMDDYYYY	32. SERVICE FACILITY LOCATION INFORMATION a. NPI b.	33. BILLING PROVIDER INFO & PH # (101)1111234 ERIN A HELPER MD 101 MEDIC DRIVE ANYWHERE NY 12345 a. 1234567890 b.

NUCC Instruction Manual available at: www.nucc.org

APPROVED OMB-0938-0999 FORM CMS-1500 (08/05)

FIGURE 16-7 Completed TRICARE as primary CMS-1500 claim for Mary S. Patient case study (Courtesy Delmar/Cengage Learning)

ICD-10-CM ALERT!

21. DIAGNOSIS OR NATURE OF ILLNESS OR INJURY (Relate Items 1, 2, 3 or 4 to Item 24E by Line)	
1. S52.509A	3. W10.8xxA
2. Y92.099	4.
	E. DIAGNOSIS POINTER

TRICARE AS SECONDARY PAYER

Table 16-6 contains modifications to the CMS-1500 claims instructions when a claim is generated with TRICARE as the secondary payer. In this situation the patient's primary health insurance coverage is another payer, such as Medicare or an employer group health plan (e.g., BCBS).

TABLE 16-6   Modifications to CMS-1500 claims completion instructions when TRICARE is secondary payer

BLOCK	INSTRUCTIONS
NOTE: Blocks 11 and 11a–11c remain blank on a TRICARE as Secondary CMS-1500 claim.	
9	Enter the primary policyholder's last name, first name, and middle initial (if known) (separated by commas).
9a	Enter the primary policyholder's policy or group number.
9b	Enter the primary policyholder's birth date as MM DD YYYY (with spaces). Enter an X in the appropriate box to indicate the secondary policyholder's gender.
9c	Enter the name of the primary policyholder's employer (if employed) or school (if unemployed and considered a full- or part-time student). Otherwise, leave blank.
9d	Enter the name of the primary policyholder's health insurance plan.
11d	Enter an X in the YES box.
26	Add an S to the patient account number in to indicate the secondary policy.
29	Enter the reimbursement amount received from the primary payer. Attach the remittance advice received from the primary payer to the CMS-1500 claim.

EXERCISE 16-2

Completion of TRICARE as Secondary CMS-1500 Claim

1. Obtain a blank claim.
2. Refer to Figure 16-8, the John R. Neely case study.
3. Complete the TRICARE secondary claim for this case.
4. Review the completed claim to be sure all required blocks are properly completed. Refer to Figure 16-9.

Additional TRICARE case studies are found in Appendices I and II of this text and in the Workbook.

ERIN A. HELPER, M.D.
101 Medic Drive, Anywhere NY 12345
(101) 111-1234 (Office) • (101) 111-9292 (Fax)
EIN: 11-1234523
NPI: 1234567890

Case Study

PATIENT INFORMATION:

Name:	John R. Neely
Address:	1 Military Drive
City:	Nowhere
State:	NY
Zip Code:	12345-1234
Telephone:	(101) 111-9941
Gender:	Male
Date of Birth:	10-25-1945
Occupation:	Retired Navy Captain
Employer:	
Spouse's Employer:	

INSURANCE INFORMATION:

Patient Number:	16-3
Place of Service:	Office
Primary Insurance Plan:	Blue Cross Blue Shield
Primary Insurance Plan ID #:	WXY7031
Policy #:	AS101
Primary Policyholder:	Janet B. Neely
Policyholder Date of Birth:	09-09-1945
Employer:	State College
Relationship to Patient:	Spouse
Secondary Insurance Plan:	TRICARE Standard
Secondary Insurance Plan ID #:	001 06 7019
Secondary Policyholder:	John R. Neely

Patient Status ☒ Married   ☐ Divorced   ☐ Single   ☐ Student

DIAGNOSIS INFORMATION

Diagnosis	Code	Diagnosis	Code
1. Abnormal ECG	794.31	5.	
2. Coronary artery disease, native vessel	414.00	6.	
3. Family history of heart disease	V17.49	7.	
4.		8.	

PROCEDURE INFORMATION

Description of Procedure or Service	Date	Code	Charge
1. Established patient office visit, level III	03-10-YYYY	99213	75.00
2. ECG, 12-lead with interpretation and report	03-10-YYYY	93000	60.00
3.			
4.			

SPECIAL NOTES: Schedule stress test for tomorrow.   BCBS paid $80 on claim.

FIGURE 16-8 John R. Neely case study (Courtesy Delmar/Cengage Learning)

ICD-10-CM ALERT!

Abnormal ECG	R94.30
Coronary artery disease, native vessel	I25.10
Family history of heart disease	Z82.49

FIGURE 16-9 Completed TRICARE as secondary CMS-1500 claim for John R. Neely case study (Courtesy Delmar/Cengage Learning)

ICD-10-CM ALERT!

21. DIAGNOSIS OR NATURE OF ILLNESS OR INJURY (Relate Items 1, 2, 3 or 4 to Item 24E by Line)

1. R94 30   3. Z82 49

2. I25 10   4.

E. DIAGNOSIS POINTER

SUMMARY

TRICARE is a regionally-managed healthcare program for active-duty and retired military members and their qualified family members, as well as eligible survivors of deceased uniformed services members. CHAMPUS (previous name of TRICARE) was created in 1966 as a benefit for dependents of personnel serving in the uniformed services. TRICARE regions are managed by Lead Agent staff, responsible for the military health system in their region. Lead Agents serve as a federal healthcare team to support the mission of the Military Health Services System (MHSS), which is the entire healthcare system of the U.S. uniformed services. TRICARE Management Activity (TMA) (formerly OCHAMPUS) coordinates and administers the TRICARE program. TRICARE options include TRICARE Prime, TRICARE Extra, and TRICARE Standard. All active-duty military personnel are enrolled in TRICARE Prime. TRICARE beneficiaries who have other health insurance (OHI) that is primary to TRICARE must submit documentation (e.g., remittance advice) when submitting TRICARE claims. TRICARE is the secondary payer to civilian insurance plans, workers' compensation, liability insurance plans, and employer-sponsored HMO plans. TRICARE is the primary payer to Medicaid and TRICARE supplemental plans. CHAMPVA is a healthcare benefits program for dependents of veterans who are rated by Veterans Affairs (VA) as having a total and permanent disability, survivors of veterans who died from VA-rated service-connected conditions, and survivors of veterans who died in the line of duty and not from misconduct.

When completing TRICARE CMS-1500 claims for case studies in this text and the Workbook, the following special instructions apply:

- Blocks 9 through 9d—Complete if TRICARE beneficiary has a secondary or supplemental plan; otherwise, leave blank
- Blocks 11 through 11c—Complete if TRICARE beneficiary has a health plan that is primary to TRICARE; otherwise, leave blank
- Block 14—Leave blank
- Block 15—Leave blank
- Block 16—Leave blank
- Block 20—Enter an X in the NO box
- Block 23—Leave blank
- Blocks 24H through block 24I—Leave blank
- Block 26—Enter the case study number (e.g., 16-5). If the patient has TRICARE as secondary coverage, enter an S (for secondary) next to the number (on the secondary claim) (16-3S)
- Block 27—Enter an X in the YES box
- Block 32—Enter the name and address of the MTF
- When completing secondary claims, enter REMITTANCE ADVICE ATTACHED in the top margin of the CMS-1500 (to simulate the attachment of a primary payer's remittance advice with a claim submitted to a secondary payer)

INTERNET LINKS

- CHAMPVA
  Go to **www.va.gov,** scroll over the Health Care heading, and click on the CHAMPVA link.
- TRICARE Dental Program
  www.tricaredentalprogram.com
- TRICARE manuals
  manuals.tricare.osd.mil
- TRICARE Retiree Dental Program
  www.trdp.org

- TRICARE Supplemental Insurance
  Go to **www.tricare.mil,** and select Supplemental Insurance from the Beneficiary Jump To: dropdown menu.
- US Family Health Plan
  www.usfamilyhealthplan.org

STUDY CHECKLIST

☐ Read this textbook chapter and highlight key terms.

☐ Access SimClaim software at the online companion, and become familiar with the software.

☐ Complete CMS-1500 claims for each chapter case study.

☐ Complete the chapter reviews, verifying answers with your instructor.

☐ Complete the chapter CD-ROM activities.

☐ Complete WebTutor assignments, and take online quizzes.

☐ Complete TRICARE claims for cases located in Appendices I and II.

☐ Complete the Workbook chapter, verifying answers with your instructor.

☐ Complete the StudyWare activities to receive immediate feedback.

☐ Form a study group with classmates to discuss chapter concepts in preparation for an exam.

REVIEW

MULTIPLE CHOICE Select the most appropriate response.

1. **The healthcare program for active-duty members of the military and their qualified dependents is called**
   a. CHAMPUS.
   b. CHAMPVA.
   c. MHSS.
   d. TRICARE.

2. **Commanders of selected military treatment facilities for TRICARE regions are called**
   a. health care finders.
   b. lead agents.
   c. service centers.
   d. sponsors.

3. **Which office coordinates and administers the TRICARE program and is accountable for the quality of health care provided to members of the uniformed services and their eligible dependents?**
   a. Defense Enrollment Reporting System (DEERS)
   b. Military Health Services System (MHSS)
   c. Military Treatment Facility (MTF)
   d. TRICARE Management Activity (TMA)

4. **Who assists TRICARE sponsors with information about the health program, along with other matters affecting access to health care (e.g., appointment scheduling)?**
   a. beneficiary services representative
   b. health care finder
   c. nurse advisor
   d. primary care manager

5. **A critical pathway is the**

   a. approval process obtained from a health care finder before certain specialty procedures are provided.

   b. decision-making tool used by providers to determine appropriate health care for specific clinical circumstances.

   c. mechanism for surveillance of fraud and abuse activities worldwide involving purchased care.

   d. sequence of activities that can normally be expected to result in the most cost-effective clinical course of treatment.

6. **The managed care option that is similar to a civilian HMO is called TRICARE**

   a. Extra.

   b. Prime.

   c. Standard.

   d. Worldwide.

7. **The new name for CHAMPUS is TRICARE**

   a. Extra.

   b. Prime.

   c. Standard.

   d. Worldwide.

8. **TRICARE nonparticipating providers are subject to a limiting charge of _____ above the TRICARE fee schedule for participating providers.**

   a. 5 percent

   b. 10 percent

   c. 15 percent

   d. 20 percent

9. **What is the abbreviation for the computer system that contains up-to-date Defense Department workforce personnel information and is used to verify TRICARE eligibility?**

   a. DEERS

   b. HCF

   c. MHSS

   d. TMA

10. **The number of TRICARE regions has _____ since 1999.**

    a. decreased

    b. diminished in scope

    c. increased

    d. remained the same

Workers' Compensation

CHAPTER OUTLINE

OBJECTIVES

Upon successful completion of this chapter, you should be able to:

1. Define key terms.
2. Describe federal and state workers' compensation programs.
3. List eligibility requirements for workers' compensation coverage.
4. Classify workers' compensation cases.
5. Describe special handling practices for workers' compensation cases.
6. Explain how managed care applies to workers' compensation coverage.
7. Submit first report of injury and progress reports.
8. Describe workers' compensation appeals and adjudication processes.
9. State examples of workers' compensation fraud and abuse.
10. Apply workers' compensation billing notes when completing CMS-1500 claims.
11. Complete workers' compensation claims properly.

KEY TERMS

adjudication

arbitration

Energy Employees Occupational Illness
  Compensation Program

Federal Black Lung Program

Federal Employment Liability Act (FELA)

First Report of Injury

Longshore and Harbor Workers'
  Compensation Program

Material Safety Data Sheet (MSDS)

Merchant Marine Act (Jones Act)

Mine Safety and Health Administration
  (MSHA)

Occupational Safety and Health
  Administration (OSHA)

Office of Workers' Compensation
  Programs (OWCP)

on-the-job injury

permanent disability

State Insurance Fund (or State
  Compensation Fund)

survivor benefits

temporary disability

vocational rehabilitation

Workers' Compensation Board (or
  Workers' Compensation Commission)

INTRODUCTION

Federal and state laws require employers to maintain workers' compensation coverage to meet minimum standards, covering a majority of employees for work-related illnesses and injuries (as long as the employee was not negligent in performing the assigned duties). Employees receive health care and monetary awards (if applicable), and dependents of workers killed on the job receive benefits. Workers' compensation laws also protect employers and fellow workers by limiting the award an injured employee can recover from an employer and by eliminating the liability of coworkers in most accidents. Federal workers' compensation statutes (laws) apply to federal employees or workers employed in a significant aspect of interstate commerce. Individual state workers' compensation laws establish comprehensive programs and are applicable to most employers. For example, California laws (1) limit the liability of employer and fellow employees for work-related illness and injuries, (2) require employers to obtain workers' compensation coverage for potential claims, and (3) establish a state fund to pay claims when employers have illegally failed to obtain coverage.

> **NOTE:** *Workers' compensation* is sometimes mistakenly referred to by its previous name, *workman's compensation.* The name change occurred years ago to reflect an increase in the number of women in the workforce.

Complete StudyWare practice quizzes and activities using the CD-ROM located inside the back cover of your textbook.

FEDERAL WORKERS' COMPENSATION PROGRAMS

The U.S. Department of Labor's (DOL) Office of Workers' Compensation Programs (OWCP) administers programs that provide wage-replacement benefits, medical treatment, vocational rehabilitation, and other benefits to federal workers (or eligible dependents) who are injured at work or acquire an occupational disease. The four programs include:

- **Energy Employees Occupational Illness Compensation Program**
- **Federal Black Lung Program**
- **Federal Employees' Compensation Act (FECA) Program**
- **Longshore and Harbor Workers' Compensation Program**

The Department of Labor also manages the following programs designed to prevent work-related injuries and illnesses:

- **Mine Safety and Health Administration (MSHA)**
- **Occupational Safety and Health Administration (OSHA)**

Other federal programs include:

- **Federal Employment Liability Act (FELA)**
- **Merchant Marine Act (Jones Act)**

Energy Employees Occupational Illness Compensation Program

Effective July 31, 2001, the Energy Employees Occupational Illness Compensation Program started providing benefits to eligible employees and former employees of the Department of Energy, its contractors and subcontractors or to certain survivors of such individuals, and to certain beneficiaries of the Radiation Exposure Compensation Act. The OWCP is responsible for adjudicating and administering claims filed by employees or former employees or certain qualified survivors.

Federal Black Lung Program

The Federal Black Lung Program, enacted in 1969 as part of the *Black Lung Benefits Act,* provides medical treatment and other benefits for respiratory conditions related to former employment in the nation's coal mines. The *Division of Coal Mine Workers' Compensation* administers and processes claims filed by coal miners (and their surviving dependents) who are or were employed in or around U.S. coal mines. Monthly benefit checks are sent to coal miners (or their eligible surviving dependents) who are totally disabled by *pneumoconiosis* (black lung disease) arising from their employment in or around the nation's coal mines.

Federal Employees' Compensation Act Program

> **NOTE:** Federal agencies reimburse FECA for workers' compensation expenses through an annual *budget chargeback process,* which transfers funds from a responsible federal agency's budget (e.g., U.S. Postal Service) to the DFEC.

Enacted in 1908, the *Federal Employees' Compensation Act (FECA)* is administered by the OWCP and provides workers' compensation coverage to all federal and postal workers throughout the world for employment-related injuries and occupational diseases. Benefits include wage replacement, payment for medical care, and where necessary, medical and vocational rehabilitation assistance in returning to work. The OWCP's *Division of Federal Employees' Compensation (DFEC)* processes new claims for benefits and manages ongoing cases, pays medical expenses and compensation benefits to injured workers and survivors, and helps injured employees return to work when they are medically able to do so.

Longshore and Harbor Workers' Compensation Program

> **NOTE:** The program is also responsible for more than $2 billion in negotiable securities, cash, and bonds maintained for the payment of benefits in the event an employer or insurance payer goes out of business.

The Longshore and Harbor Workers' Compensation Program, administered by the U.S. Department of Labor, provides medical benefits, compensation for lost wages, and rehabilitation services to longshoremen, harbor workers, and other maritime workers who are injured during the course of employment or suffer from diseases caused or worsened by conditions of employment. The program also covers private-industry workers who are engaged in the extraction of natural resources from the outer continental shelf, employees on American defense bases, and those working under contract with the U.S. government for defense or public-works projects outside the continental United States.

Mine Safety and Health Administration

The U.S. Labor Department's **Mine Safety and Health Administration (MSHA)** helps to reduce deaths, injuries, and illnesses in U.S. mines through a variety of activities and programs. MSHA develops and enforces safety and health rules that apply to all U.S. mines, helps mine operators who have special compliance problems, and makes available technical, educational, and other types of assistance. MSHA works cooperatively with industry, labor, and other federal and state agencies toward improving safety and health conditions for all miners. MSHA's responsibilities are delineated in the *Federal Mine Safety and Health Act of 1977.*

> **NOTE:** U.S. federal mine safety laws were first enacted in 1911 and have since become increasingly stronger, culminating in the 1977 law.

Occupational Safety and Health Administration

The *Occupational Safety and Health Act of 1970* created the **Occupational Safety and Health Administration (OSHA)** to protect employees against injuries from occupational hazards in the workplace. OSHA and its state partners (of approximately 2,100 inspectors) establish protective standards, enforce those standards, and reach out to employers and employees by providing technical assistance and consultation programs. OSHA has special significance for those employed in health care because employers are required to obtain and retain manufacturers' **Material Safety Data Sheets (MSDS)**, which contain information about chemical and hazardous substances used on site. Training employees in the safe handling of these substances is also required.

Healthcare workers who might come into contact with human blood and infectious materials must be provided specific training in their handling (including use of Standard Precautions) to avoid contamination. Healthcare workers who might be exposed to infectious materials must be offered hepatitis B vaccinations.

> **NOTE:** Comprehensive records of all vaccinations administered and any accidental exposure incidences (e.g., needle sticks) must be retained for 20 years.

Federal Employment Liability Act

The **Federal Employment Liability Act (FELA)** is not a workers' compensation statute, but it provides railroad employees with protection from employer negligence, and makes railroads engaged in interstate commerce liable for injuries to employees if the railroad was negligent.

Merchant Marine Act (Jones Act)

The **Merchant Marine Act** (or **Jones Act)** is also not a workers' compensation statute, but it provides seamen with the same protection from employer negligence as FELA provides railroad workers.

STATE WORKERS' COMPENSATION PROGRAMS

> **NOTE:** In New York State (NYS), the maximum weekly benefit was $500 in 2007 (ranking fifth lowest in the country). (www.wcb.state.ny.us)

Workers' compensation insurance provides weekly cash payments and reimburses healthcare costs for covered employees who develop a work-related illness or sustain an injury while on the job. It also provides payments to qualified dependents of a worker who dies from a compensable illness or injury. Each state establishes a **Workers' Compensation Board** or **Commission**, a state agency responsible for administering workers' compensation laws and handling appeals for denied claims or cases in which a worker feels compensation was too low.

State workers' compensation legislation resulted in the following types of coverage:

- **State Insurance (or Compensation) Fund**: a quasi-public agency that provides workers' compensation insurance coverage to private and public employers and acts as an agent in state workers' compensation cases involving state employees.
- *Self-insurance plans:* employers with sufficient capital to qualify can self-insure, which means they are required to set aside a state-mandated percentage of capital funds to cover medical expenses, wage compensation, and other benefits (e.g., death benefit to an employee's dependents) payable to employees who develop on-the-job illnesses and/or incur injuries.
- *Commercial workers' compensation insurance:* employers are permitted to purchase policies from commercial insurance companies that meet state mandates for workers' compensation coverage.
- *Combination programs:* employers in some states are allowed to choose a combination of any of the above to comply with workers' compensation coverage requirements (e.g., companies with a majority of employees who are at high risk for injury participate in the State Insurance Fund, but may purchase commercial insurance coverage for office workers).

NOTE: The *State Insurance Fund* must offer workers' compensation insurance to any employer requesting it, thereby making the fund an insurer of last resort for employers otherwise unable to obtain coverage.

ELIGIBILITY FOR WORKERS' COMPENSATION COVERAGE

To qualify for workers' compensation benefits, the employee must be either injured while working within the scope of the job description, injured while performing a service required by the employer, or develops a disorder that can be directly linked to employment, such as asbestosis or mercury poisoning. In some states, coverage has been awarded for stress-related disorders to workers in certain high-stress occupations, including emergency services personnel, air traffic controllers, and persons involved in hostage situations at work.

The worker does not have to be physically on company property to qualify for workers' compensation. An **on-the-job injury** would include, for example, a medical assistant who is injured while picking up reports for the office at the local hospital or a worker who is making a trip to the bank to deposit checks. These both qualify as job-related assignments. An employee sent to a workshop in another state who falls during the workshop would also be eligible for compensation, but not if she was injured while sightseeing.

NOTE: In a workers' compensation case, no one party is determined to be at fault, and the amount a claimant receives is not decreased by proof of carelessness (nor increased by proof of employer's fault). A worker will lose the right to workers' compensation coverage if the injury resulted solely from intoxication from drugs or alcohol or from the intent to injure himself or someone else.

CLASSIFICATION OF WORKERS' COMPENSATION CASES

The injured employee's healthcare provider determines the extent of disability; cash benefits are directly related to established disability classifications. Federal law mandates the following classification of workers' compensation cases:

- **Medical treatment**
- **Temporary disability**
- **Permanent disability**
- **Vocational rehabilitation**
- **Survivor benefits**

NOTE: The term *disability* associated with the following classifications does not refer to *disability insurance (or benefits)*, which are temporary cash benefits paid to an eligible wage earner when he or she is disabled by an off-the-job injury or illness. This concept was discussed in Chapter 2.

Medical Treatment

Medical treatment claims are the easiest to process because they are filed for minor illness or injuries that are treated by a healthcare provider. In these cases, the employee continues to work or returns to work within a few days.

Temporary Disability

Temporary disability claims cover healthcare treatment for illness and injuries, as well as payment for lost wages. *Temporary disability* is subclassified as:

- *Temporary total disability,* in which the employee's wage-earning capacity is totally lost, but only on a temporary basis.
- *Temporary partial disability,* in which the employee's wage-earning capacity is partially lost, but only on a temporary basis.

Permanent Disability

Permanent disability refers to an ill or injured employee's diminished capacity to return to work. In this case, a provider has determined that although the employee's illness or injury has stabilized, he or she has been permanently impaired. The employee is therefore unable to return to the position held prior to the illness or injury. Subclassifications include:

- *Permanent total disability,* in which the employee's wage-earning capacity is permanently and totally lost. (There is no limit on the number of weeks payable, and an employee may continue to engage in business or employment if his or her wages, combined with the weekly benefit, do not exceed the maximums established by law.)
- *Permanent partial disability,* in which part of the employee's wage-earning capacity has been permanently lost. Benefits are payable as long as the partial disability exists, except in the following circumstances:
  - *Schedule loss of use,* in which the employee has a loss of eyesight, hearing, or a part of the body or its use. Compensation is limited to a certain number of weeks, according to a schedule set by law.
  - *Disfigurement,* in which serious and permanent disfigurement to the face, head, or neck may entitle the employee to compensation (up to a maximum benefit, depending on the date of the accident).

NOTE: Providers who treat established patients for work-related disorders should create a compensation file (separate from the established medical record). Caution must be used to ensure that treatment data, progress notes, diagnostic test reports, and other pertinent chart entries pertaining to non-work-related disorders or injuries are not combined with notes and reports covering work-related disorders.

Vocational Rehabilitation

Vocational rehabilitation claims cover expenses for vocational retraining for both temporary and permanent disability cases. Vocational rehabilitation retrains an ill or injured employee so he or she can return to the workforce, although the employee may be incapable of resuming the position held prior to the illness or injury.

Survivor Benefits

Survivor benefits claims provide death benefits to eligible dependents. These benefit amounts are calculated according to the employee's earning capacity at the time of illness or injury.

SPECIAL HANDLING OF WORKERS' COMPENSATION CASES

Providers are required to accept the workers' compensation-allowable fee as payment in full for covered services rendered on cases involving on-the-job illnesses and injuries. An adjustment to the patient's account must be made if the amount charged for the treatment is greater than the approved reimbursement for the treatment.

State Compensation Boards/Commissions and insurance payers are entitled by law to review only history and treatment data pertaining to a patient's on-the-job injury.

> **EXAMPLE:** Patient A has been treated for diabetes by his doctor for the past two years. The patient was then treated by the same doctor for a broken ankle after falling at his place of employment. The patient was told to return in five days for a recheck. Three days after the original treatment for the broken ankle, the patient was seen in the office for "strep throat." The doctor also checks on the ankle. The treatment for the throat condition should be reported in the patient's medical record; the progress report on the broken ankle will be recorded in the workers' compensation record.

Out-of-State Treatment

Billing regulations vary from state to state. Contact the workers' compensation board/commission in the state where the injury occurred for billing instructions if an injured worker presents for treatment of a work-related injury that occurred in another state.

WORKERS' COMPENSATION AND MANAGED CARE

Both employees and employers have benefited from incorporating managed care into workers' compensation programs, thereby improving the quality of medical benefits and services provided. For employers, managed care protects human resources and reduces workers' compensation costs. For employees, the benefits include:

- More comprehensive coverage, because states continue to eliminate exemptions under current law (e.g., small businesses and temporary workers)
- Expanded healthcare coverage if the injury or illness is work-related and the treatment/service is reasonable and necessary
- Provision of appropriate medical treatment to facilitate healing and promote prompt return to work (lack of treatment can result in increased permanent disability, greater wage replacement benefits, and higher total claim costs)
- Internal grievance and dispute resolution procedures involving the care and treatment provided by the workers' compensation program, along with an appeals process to the state workers' compensation agency
- Coordination of medical treatment and services with other services designed to get workers back to work (research by the Florida Division of Workers' Compensation suggests that managed care may reduce the time it takes an injured worker to return to work)
- No out-of-pocket costs for coverage or provision of medical services and treatment; cost/time limits do not apply when an injury or illness occurs

FIRST REPORT OF INJURY FORM

NOTE: There is no patient signature line on this form. The law says that when a patient requests treatment for a work-related injury or disorder, the patient has given consent for the filing of compensation claims and reports. The required state forms may be obtained from the state board/commission. Necessary forms for filing federal forms may be obtained from the personnel office where the employee works or from the workers' compensation Federal District Office listed under the United States Government listings in the phone book.

First Report of Injury forms are completed by the provider (e.g., physician) when the patient first seeks treatment for a work-related illness or injury (Figure 17-1). This report must be completed in quadruplicate with one copy distributed to each of the following parties:

- **State Workers' Compensation Board/Commission**
- **Employer-designated compensation payer**
- **Ill or injured party's employer**
- **Patient's work-related injury chart**

The time limit for filing this form varies from 24 hours to 14 calendar days, depending on state requirements. It is best to make a habit of completing the form immediately, thus ensuring that the form is filed on time and not overlooked.

The First Report of Injury form requires some information that is not automatically furnished by a patient. When the patient tells you this was a work-related injury, it will be necessary to obtain the following information:

- **Name and address of present employer**
- **Name of immediate supervisor**
- **Date and time of the accident or onset of the disease**
- **Site where injury occurred**
- **Patient's description of the onset of the disorder; if the patient is claiming injury due to exposure to hazardous chemicals or compounds, these should be included in the patient's description of the problem**

In addition, the patient's employer must be contacted to obtain the name and mailing address of the compensation payer. Ask for a faxed confirmation from the employer of the worker with the on-the-job injury. If the employer disputes the legitimacy of the claim, you should still file the First Report of Injury. The employer must also file an injury report with the compensation commission/board.

Completing the First Report of Injury Form

Item 1

NOTE: The *physician* is responsible for completing this form.

Enter the employee's full name as shown on personnel files (last, first, middle). Enter the employee's social security number and date of birth (MMDDYYYY). Indicate the employee's gender by entering an X in the appropriate box.

Item 2

Enter the employee's complete home address. This is very important, as workers' compensation disability payments, when due, will be mailed to this address. An incorrect address will delay receipt.

Item 3

NOTE: The date of the claimed accident must be specific. For example, if an employee was lifting heavy boxes on Tuesday (11/6) and called in sick on Thursday (11/8) because of a sore back, the date that is entered in Item 4 is 11/6.

Enter the complete name and address of the employer.

Item 4

Enter the date (MMDDYYYY) on which the accident or onset of disease occurred. Enter the time of the day at which the accident or onset of disease occurred, and check the appropriate box to indicate a.m. or p.m.

INSTRUCTIONS

1. Type answers to ALL questions and file original with the Workers' Compensation Commission within 72 hours after first treatment.
2. DO NOT FAIL to forward to the Workers' Compensation Commission PROGRESS REPORTS and FINAL REPORT upon discharge of patient.

WORKERS' COMPENSATION COMMISSION
6 NORTH LIBERTY STREET, BALTIMORE, MD 21201-3785
SURGEON'S REPORT

This is   First Report ☐   Progress Report ☐   Final Report ☐

DO NOT WRITE IN THIS SPACE

WCC CLAIM #

EMPLOYER'S REPORT Yes ☐   No ☐

1. Name of Injured Person:	Soc. Sec. No. — D.O.B. — Sex M ☐ F ☐
2. Address: (No. and Street) — (City or Town) — (State) — (Zip Code)	
3. Name and Address of Employer:	
4. Date of Accident or Onset of Disease: — Hour: — A.M. ☐ P.M. ☐	5. Date Disability Began:
6. Patient's Description of Accident or Cause of Disease:	
7. Medical Description of Injury or Disease:	
8. Will Injury result in: (a) Permanent defect? Yes ☐ No ☐ If so, what? — (b) Disfigurement? Yes ☐ No ☐	
9. Causes, other than injury, contributing to patient's condition:	
10. Is patient suffering from any disease of the heart, lungs, brain, kidneys, blood, vascular system or any other disabling condition not due to this accident? Give particulars.	
11. Is there any history or evidence present of previous accident or disease? Give particulars.	
12. Has normal recovery been delayed for any reason? Give particulars.	
13. Date of first treatment: — Who engaged your services?	
14. Describe treatment given by you:	
15. Were X-rays taken? Yes ☐ No ☐ — By whom? — (Name and Address) — Date:	
16. X-ray Diagnosis:	
17. Was patient treated by anyone else? Yes ☐ No ☐ — By whom? — (Name and Address) — Date:	
18. Was patient hospitalized? Yes ☐ No ☐ — Name and Address of Hospital — Date of Admission: Date of Discharge:	
19. Is further treatment needed? Yes ☐ No ☐ — For how long? — 20. Patient was ☐ will be ☐ able resume regular work on: Patient was ☐ will be ☐ able resume light work on:	
21. If death ensued give date: — 22. Remarks: (Give any information of value not included above.)	
23. I am a qualified specialist in: — I am a duly licensed Physician in the State of: — I graduated from Medical School: (Name) — Year:	
Date of this report: — (Signed)	
(This report must be signed PERSONALLY by Physician.)	
Address: — Phone:	

(left margin, vertical) EVERY QUESTION MUST BE ANSWERED AND FORM SIGNED

FIGURE 17-1 First Report of Injury Form completed by provider (e.g., physician) (Courtesy of Maryland Workers' Compensation Commission)

Item 5

Enter the last date the employee worked after having the accident. If no time was lost from work, enter STILL WORKING.

Item 6

Enter the employee's word-for-word description of the accident. A complete description of the accident is required. Attach an additional page if space provided on the First Report of Injury is insufficient.

Item 7

Enter the description of the injury or disease. Explain the physical injuries or disease (e.g., laceration, fracture, or contusion). Enter the anatomic part(s) of the body that required medical attention. Be specific, and indicate the location of the injured part when necessary (e.g., left middle finger, right thumb, left shoulder). Enter the location and address where the accident occurred.

Items 8 through 12

Enter as appropriate.

Item 13

Enter the date (MMDDYYYY) the patient initially received services and/or treatment.

Items 14 through 19

Enter as appropriate.

Item 20

Enter an X in the appropriate box.

Item 21

If the employee died as a result of the injury sustained, enter the date of death (MMDDYYYY). Notify the appropriate state agency immediately upon the work-related death of an employee.

Item 22

Enter additional information of value that was not previously documented on the form.

Item 23

Enter the physician's specialty (e.g., internal medicine), the state in which the physician is licensed, and the name of the medical school from which the physician graduated, along with the year of graduation (YYYY).

Be sure the physician dates (MMDDYYYY) and signs the report. Enter the physician's office address and telephone number.

PROGRESS REPORTS

A detailed narrative progress/supplemental report (Figure 17-2) should be filed to document any significant change in the worker's medical or disability status. This report should document:

- Patient's name and compensation file/case number
- Treatment and progress report
- Work status at the present time
- Statement of further treatment needed
- Estimate of the future status with regard to work or permanent loss or disability
- Copies of substantiating x-ray, laboratory, or consultation reports

Employee Name (First, Middle, Last)

Name of Employer:

Type of Report   ☐ Initial   ☐ Supplement   ☐ Final   ☐ Reopened

Workers' Compensation # _____

Social Security Number: _____

Date of Injury: _____

Disability Date: _____

Treatment Now Being Administered:

Diagnosis:

Patient is under my care.	☐ Yes ☐ No	**If no, care was transferred to:** _____
Patient is totally disabled.	☐ Yes ☐ No	**Patient is partially disabled.** ☐ Yes ☐ No
Patient is working.	☐ Yes ☐ No	**Date patient returned to work:** _____
Patient may be able to return to work.	☐ Yes ☐ No	**Date patient may be able to return to work:** _____

Work Limitations:

☐ None: _____

☐ Cannot Work: _____

☐ Light Work: _____

☐ Weightlifting limit: _____

Present Condition:

☐ Improved: _____

☐ Unchanged: _____

☐ Worsening: _____

Anticipated Date of Maximum Medical Improvement or Discharge:

☐ Weeks: _____

☐ Months: _____

☐ Specific Date: _____

☐ Undetermined: _____

Signature of Provider: _____   **EIN:** _____

FIGURE 17-2 Sample workers' compensation narrative progress (supplemental) report (Courtesy Delmar/Cengage Learning)

The physician should personally sign the original and all photocopies of these reports. No patient signature is required for the release of any report to the compensation payer or commission/board. These reports should be generated in duplicate because:

- **One copy is sent to the compensation payer.**
- **One copy is retained in the patient's file.**

The physician is required to answer all requests for further information sent from the compensation payer or the commission/board. Acknowledgment of receipt of a claim will be made by the payer or the commission/board. This acknowledgment will contain the file or case number assigned to the claim. This file/claim number should be written on all further correspondence forwarded to the employer, the payer, the commission/board, and, of course, on all billings sent to the payer.

APPEALS AND ADJUDICATION

> **NOTE:** Adjudication is different from **arbitration**, a dispute resolution process in which a final determination is made by an impartial person who may not have judicial powers.

When a workers' compensation claim is denied, the employee (or eligible dependents) can appeal the denial to the state Workers' Compensation Board (or Commission) and undergo a process called adjudication, a judicial dispute resolution process in which an appeals board makes a final determination. All applications for appeal should include supporting medical documentation of the claim when there is a dispute about medical issues. During the appeal process, involved parties will undergo a *deposition,* a legal proceeding during which a party answers questions under oath (but not in open court). If the appeal is successful, the board (commission) will notify the healthcare provider to submit a claim to the employer's compensation payer and refund payments made by the patient to cover medical expenses for the on-the-job illness or injury.

FRAUD AND ABUSE

Workers' compensation fraud occurs when individuals knowingly obtain benefits for which they are not eligible (e.g., provider who submits a false claim for workers' compensation coverage of patient treatment). *Workers' compensation abuse* occurs when the workers' compensation system is used in a way contrary to its intended purpose or to the law; fraud is a form of abuse. Penalties include fines and imprisonment, and most states offer a toll-free hotline to report fraud and abuse. Categories of fraud include:

- *Employer fraud:* committed by an employer who misrepresents payroll amounts or employee classification or who attempts to avoid higher insurance risk by transferring employees to a new business entity that is rated in a lower-risk category.
- *Employee fraud:* committed when an employee lies or provides a false statement, intentionally fails to report income from work, or willfully misrepresents a physical condition to obtain benefits from the state compensation fund.
- *Provider fraud:* committed by healthcare providers and attorneys who inflate their bills for services or bill for treatment of non-work-related illnesses and/or injuries.

BILLING NOTES

The following is a summary of the general nationwide billing information for workers' compensation claims. Local requirements will vary by state. Be sure to follow all the regulations established by your state commission.

Eligibility

For-profit and not-for-profit (non-profit) company/corporation or state employees with work-related injuries are eligible for workers' compensation benefits. Coal miners, longshoremen, harbor workers, and all federal employees except those in the uniformed services with a work-related injury are eligible for federal compensation plans.

Fiscal Agent

State Plans

Any one of the following can be designated the fiscal agent by state law and the corporation involved.

1. State insurance or compensation fund (do not confuse this with the state's Workers' Compensation Board or Commission)
2. A third-party payer (e.g., commercial insurance company)
3. The employer's special company capital funds set aside for compensation cases

Federal Plans

Information may be obtained from the human resources officer at the agency where the patient is employed.

Underwriter

The federal or state government is the plan's underwriter, depending on the case.

Forms Used

The forms used include:

- First Report of Injury form
- Narrative progress/supplemental reports
- CMS-1500 claim

Filing Deadline

The filing deadline for the first injury report is determined by state law. The deadline for filing of the claim for services performed will vary from payer to payer.

Deductible

There is no deductible for workers' compensation claims.

Copayment

There is no copayment for workers' compensation cases.

Premium

The employer pays all premiums.

Approved Fee Basis

The state compensation board or commission establishes a schedule of approved fees. Many states use a relative value study (RVS) unit-value scale; others have implemented managed care. Contact the state commission/board for information.

Accept Assignment

All providers must accept the compensation payment as payment in full.

Special Handling

Contact the employer immediately when an injured worker presents for the first visit without a written or personal referral from the employer. Contact the workers' compensation board/commission of the state where the work-related injury occurred if treatment is sought in another state.

No patient signature is needed on the First Report of Injury form, Progress Report, or billing forms. If an established patient seeks treatment of a work-related injury, a separate compensation chart and ledger/account must be established for the patient.

The First Report of Injury form requires a statement from the patient describing the circumstances and events surrounding the injury. Progress reports should be filed when there is any significant change in the patient's condition and when the patient is discharged. Prior authorization may be necessary for nonemergency treatment.

Private Payer Mistakenly Billed

When a patient fails to inform a provider that an illness or injury is work-related, the patient's primary payer is billed for services or procedures rendered. If the patient subsequently requests that the workers' compensation payer be billed instead, the claim will probably be denied. The patient must then initiate the appeal process (and the provider will be responsible for submitting appropriate documentation to support the workers' compensation claim). Any reimbursement paid by the primary payer must be returned.

Before working with workers' compensation claims, complete the Review located at the end of this chapter.

CLAIMS INSTRUCTIONS

Refer to Figures 17-3 and 17-4 as you study the claims instructions in Table 17-1.

Additional workers' compensation cases are found in Appendices I and II.

TABLE 17-1 CMS-1500 claims completion instructions for workers' compensation claims

> **NOTE:** Refer to Chapter 11 for clarification of claims completion (e.g., entering names, mailing addresses, ICD codes, diagnosis pointer numbers, NPI, and so on).

BLOCK	INSTRUCTIONS
1	Enter an X in the *FECA* box. **NOTE:** FECA is the abbreviation for the Federal Employee Compensation Act.
1a	Enter the patient's social security number. *Do not enter hyphens or spaces in the number.*
2	Enter the patient's last name, first name, and middle initial (separated by commas) (e.g., DOE, JANE, M).
3	Enter the patient's birth date as MM DD YYYY (with spaces). Enter an X in the appropriate box to indicate the patient's gender. If the patient's gender is unknown, leave blank.
4	Enter the name of the patient's employer.
5	Enter the patient's mailing address and telephone number. Enter the street address on line 1, enter the city and state on line 2, and enter the 5- or 9-digit zip code and phone number on line 3.
6	Enter an X in the *Other* box.
7	Enter the employer's mailing address and telephone number. Enter the street address on line 1, enter the city and state on line 2, and enter the 5- or 9-digit zip code and phone number on line 3.
8	Enter an X in the EMPLOYED box.
9, 9a–9d	Leave blank.
10a	Enter an X in the YES box.
10b–c	Enter an X in the appropriate boxes to indicate whether the patient's condition is related to an automobile accident and/or another accident. If an X is entered in the YES box for auto accident, enter the 2-character state abbreviation of the patient's residence.
10d	Leave blank.
11	Enter the workers' compensation claim number, if known. *Do not enter hyphens or spaces in the policy or group number.* Otherwise, leave blank. **NOTE:** For workers' compensation (WC) claims, the identifier (claim number) assigned by the state WC payer is entered. If a patient claims work-related condition(s) under the Federal Employees Compensation Act (FECA), the 9-digit FECA identifier assigned to the claim is entered.
11a	Leave blank.
11b	Enter the name of the patient's employer.
11c	Enter the name of the workers' compensation payer.
11d	Leave blank.
12–13	Leave blank.
14	Enter the date as MM DD YYYY (with spaces) to indicate when the patient first experienced signs or symptoms of the illness or injury. *If the date is not documented in the patient's record, but the history indicates an appropriate date (e.g., three weeks ago), simply count back to the approximate date and enter it on the claim.* **EXAMPLE:** For encounter date 06/08/YYYY, when the record documents that the patient was "injured on the job three months ago," enter 03 08 YYYY in Block 14.
15	Enter the date as MM DD YYYY (with spaces) to indicate that a prior episode of the same or similar illness began, *if documented in the patient's record.* Otherwise, leave blank.

(continues)

TABLE 17-1 (continued)

BLOCK	INSTRUCTIONS
16	Enter dates as MM DD YYYY (with spaces) to indicate the period of time the patient was unable to work in his current occupation, *if documented in the patient's record*. Otherwise, leave blank.
17	Enter the first name, middle initial (if known), last name, and credentials of the professional who referred or ordered healthcare service(s) or supply(s) reported on the claim. *Do not enter any punctuation*. Otherwise, leave blank.
17a	Leave blank.
17b	Enter the 10-digit national provider identifier (NPI) of the professional in Block 17. Otherwise, leave blank.
18	Enter the admission date and discharge date as MM DD YYYY (with spaces) if the patient received inpatient services (e.g., hospital, skilled nursing facility). *If the patient has not been discharged at the time the claim is completed, leave the discharge date blank*. Otherwise, leave blank.
19	Leave blank.
20	Enter an X in the NO box if all laboratory procedures reported on the claim were performed in the provider's office. Enter an X in the YES box if laboratory procedures reported on the claim were performed by an outside laboratory and billed to the provider. Enter the total amount charged by the outside laboratory in $ CHARGES, and enter the outside laboratory's name, mailing address, and NPI in Block 32. (Charges are entered *without* punctuation. For example, $1,100.00 is entered as 110000 below $ CHARGES.)
21	Enter the ICD code for up to four diagnoses or conditions treated or medically managed during the encounter. Lines 1, 2, 3, and 4 in Block 21 will relate to CPT/HCPCS service/procedure codes reported in Block 24E.
22	Leave blank. Reserved for Medicaid claims.
23	Enter any preauthorization number assigned by the workers' compensation payer. *Do not enter hyphens or spaces in the number*. Otherwise, leave blank.
24A	Enter the date the procedure or service was performed in the FROM column as MMDDYYYY (without spaces). Enter a date in the TO column *if the procedure or service was performed on consecutive days during a range of dates. Then, enter the number of consecutive days in Block 24G.* **NOTE:** The shaded area in each line is used to enter supplemental information to support reported services *if instructed by the payer to enter such information.* Data entry in Block 24 is limited to reporting six services. *Do not use the shaded lines to report additional services.* If additional services were provided, generate new CMS-1500 claim(s) to report the additional services.
24B	Enter the appropriate 2-digit Place of Service (POS) code to identify the location where the reported procedure or service was performed. (Refer to Appendix II for POS codes.)
24C	Leave blank.
24D	Enter the CPT or HCPCS level II code and applicable required modifier(s) for procedures or services performed. *Separate the CPT/HCPCS code and first modifier with one space. Separate additional modifiers with one space each. Up to four modifiers can be entered.*
24E	Enter the diagnosis pointer number from Block 21 that relates to the procedure/service performed on the date of service.
24F	Enter the fee charged for each reported procedure or service. When multiple procedures or services are reported on the same line, enter the total fee charged. *Do not enter commas, periods, or dollar signs. Do not enter negative amounts. Enter 00 in the cents area if the amount is a whole number.*

(continues)

TABLE 17-1   (continued)

BLOCK	INSTRUCTIONS
24G	Enter the number of days or units for procedures or services reported in Block 24D. *If just one procedure or service was reported in Block 24D, enter a 1 in Block 24G.*
24H–I	Leave blank.
24J	Enter the 10-digit NPI for: • The provider who performed the service *if the provider is a member of a group practice.* (Leave blank if the provider is a solo practitioner.) • The supervising provider *if the service was provided "incident to" the service of a physician or nonphysician practitioner* **and** *the physician or practitioner who ordered the service did not supervise the provider.* (Leave blank if the "incident to" service was performed under the supervision of the physician or nonphysician practitioner.) • The DMEPOS supplier or outside laboratory *if the physician submits the claim for services provided by the DMEPOS supplier or outside laboratory.* (Leave blank if the DMEPOS supplier or outside laboratory submits the claim.) Otherwise, leave blank.
25	Enter the provider's social security number (SSN) or employer identification number (EIN). *Do not enter hyphens or spaces in the number.* Enter an X in the appropriate box to indicate which number is reported.
26	Enter the patient's account number as assigned by the provider.
27	Enter an X in the YES box to indicate that the provider agrees to accept assignment. Otherwise, enter an X in the NO box.
28	Enter the total charges for services and/or procedures reported in Block 24. NOTE: If multiple claims are submitted for one patient because more than six procedures or services were reported, be sure the total charge reported on each claim accurately represents the total of the items on each submitted claim.
29–30	Leave blank.
31	Enter the provider's name and credential (e.g., MARY SMITH MD) and the date the claim was completed as MMDDYYYY (without spaces). *Do not enter any punctuation.*
32	Enter the name and address where procedures or services were provided *if at a location other than the provider's office or the patient's home, such as a hospital, outside laboratory facility, skilled nursing facility, or DMEPOS supplier.* Otherwise, leave blank. Enter the name on line 1, the address on line 2, and the city, state and 5- or 9-digit zip code on line 3. *For a 9-digit zip code, enter the hyphen.* NOTE: If Block 18 contains dates of service for inpatient care and/or Block 20 contains an X in the YES box, enter the name and address of the facility that provided services.
32a	Enter the 10-digit NPI of the facility entered in Block 32.
32b	Leave blank.
33	Enter the provider's *billing* name, address, and telephone number. Enter the phone number in the area next to the Block title. *Do not enter parentheses for the area code.* Enter the name on line 1, enter the address on line 2, and enter the city, state, and 5- or 9-digit zip code on line 3. *For a 9-digit zip code, enter the hyphen.*
33a	Enter the 10-digit NPI of the *billing* provider (e.g., solo practitioner) or group practice (e.g., clinic).
33b	Leave blank.

ERIN A. HELPER, M.D.
101 Medic Drive, Anywhere NY 12345
(101) 111-1234 (Office) • (101) 111-9292 (Fax)
EIN: 11-1234523
NPI: 1234567890

Case Study

PATIENT INFORMATION:

Name:	Public, John Q.
Address:	10A Senate Avenue
City:	Anywhere
State:	NY
Zip Code:	12345-1234
Telephone:	(101) 201-7891
Gender:	Male
Date of Birth:	10-10-1959
Occupation:	Technician
Employer:	BIO Laboratory
Spouse's Employer:	

INSURANCE INFORMATION:

Patient Number:	17-1
Place of Service:	Office
WC Insurance Plan:	High Risk, Inc.
WC Claim #:	BL3638B
Group #:	
WC Policyholder:	BIO Laboratory
Address:	Bio Drive, Anywhere NY 12345
Relationship to Patient:	Employer

Patient Status   ☒ Married   ☐ Divorced   ☐ Single   ☐ Student

DIAGNOSIS INFORMATION

Diagnosis	Code	Diagnosis	Code
1. Whiplash	847.0	5.	
2. Motor vehicle accident (street)	E849.5	6.	
3.		7.	
4.		8.	

PROCEDURE INFORMATION

Description of Procedure or Service	Date	Code	Charge
1. Established patient office visit, level III	01-03-YYYY	99213	40.00
2.			
3.			
4.			
5.			

SPECIAL NOTES: Originally injured driving delivery car while working 12/29/YYYY. Return to work 01/05/YYYY. NOTE: Submit claim to workers' compensation payer.

FIGURE 17-3 John Q. Public case study (Courtesy Delmar/Cengage Learning)

ICD-10-CM ALERT!

Whiplash	S13.8xxD
Motor vehicle accident (street)	V49.9xxA
	Y92.410

ICD-10-CM tabular list notes state that each code requires assignment of a seventh character. The "x" placeholder characters are included in the code so that the seventh character can be entered.

1500

HEALTH INSURANCE CLAIM FORM

APPROVED BY NATIONAL UNIFORM CLAIM COMMITTE 08/05

| | PICA | | | | | | | PICA | | |

1. MEDICARE ☐ (Medicare #) MEDICAID ☐ (Medicaid #) TRICARE CHAMPUS ☐ (Sponsor's SSN) CHAMPVA ☐ (Member ID#) GROUP HEALTH PLAN ☐ (SSN or ID) FECA BLK LUNG ☒ (SSN) OTHER ☐ (ID)

1a. INSURED'S I.D. NUMBER (For Program in Item 1)
252459568

2. PATIENT'S NAME (Last Name, First Name, Middle Initial)
PUBLIC, JOHN, Q

3. PATIENT'S BIRTH DATE MM **10** DD **10** YY **1959** SEX M ☒ F ☐

4. INSURED'S NAME (Last Name, First Name, Middle Initial)
BIO LABORATORY

5. PATIENT'S ADDRESS (No., Street)
10A SENATE AVENUE

6. PATIENT'S RELATIONSHIP TO INSURED
Self ☐ Spouse ☐ Child ☐ Other ☒

7. INSURED'S ADDRESS (No., Street)
BIO DRIVE

CITY **ANYWHERE**   STATE **NY**

8. PATIENT STATUS
Single ☐ Married ☐ Other ☐

CITY **ANYWHERE**   STATE **NY**

ZIP CODE **12345-1234**   TELEPHONE (Include Area Code) **(101) 2017891**

Employed ☒ Full-Time Student ☐ Part-Time Student ☐

ZIP CODE **12345**   TELEPHONE (Include Area Code) **(101) 5559876**

9. OTHER INSURED'S NAME (Last Name, First Name, Middle Initial)

10. IS PATIENT'S CONDITION RELATED TO:

11. INSURED'S POLICY GROUP OR FECA NUMBER
BL3638B

a. OTHER INSURED'S POLICY OR GROUP NUMBER

a. EMPLOYMENT? (Current or Previous)
YES ☒ NO ☐

a. INSURED'S DATE OF BIRTH MM DD YY   SEX M ☐ F ☐

b. OTHER INSURED'S DATE OF BIRTH MM DD YY SEX M ☐ F ☐

b. AUTO ACCIDENT?   PLACE (State)
YES ☒ NO ☐ **NY**

b. EMPLOYER'S NAME OR SCHOOL NAME
BIO LABORATORY

c. EMPLOYER'S NAME OR SCHOOL NAME

c. OTHER ACCIDENT?
YES ☐ NO ☒

c. INSURANCE PLAN NAME OR PROGRAM NAME
HIGH RISK INC

d. INSURANCE PLAN NAME OR PROGRAM NAME

10d. RESERVED FOR LOCAL USE

d. IS THERE ANOTHER HEALTH BENEFIT PLAN?
YES ☐ NO ☐ If yes, return to and complete item 9 a-d.

READ BACK OF FORM BEFORE COMPLETING & SIGNING THIS FORM.

12. PATIENT'S OR AUTHORIZED PERSON'S SIGNATURE I authorize the release of any medical or other information necessary to process this claim. I also request payment of government benefits either to myself or to the party who accepts assignment below.

SIGNED _____ DATE _____

13. INSURED'S OR AUTHORIZED PERSON'S SIGNATURE I authorize payment of medical benefits to the undersigned physican or supplier for services described below.

SIGNED _____

14. DATE OF CURRENT: MM **12** DD **29** YY **YYYY** ILLNESS (First symptom) OR INJURY (Accident) OR PREGNANCY (LMP)

15. IF PATIENT HAS HAD SAME OR SIMILAR ILLNESS, GIVE FIRST DATE MM DD YY

16. DATES PATIENT UNABLE TO WORK IN CURRENT OCCUPATION
FROM MM **12** DD **29** YY **YYYY** TO MM **01** DD **03** YY **YYYY**

17. NAME OF REFERRING PROVIDER OR OTHER SOURCE
17a.
17b. NPI

18. HOSPITALIZATION DATES RELATED TO CURRENT SERVICES
FROM MM DD YY TO MM DD YY

19. RESERVED FOR LOCAL USE

20. OUTSIDE LAB? YES ☐ NO ☒ $ CHARGES

21. DIAGNOSIS OR NATURE OF ILLNESS OR INJURY (Relate Items 1, 2, 3 or 4 to Item 24E by Line)
1. **847 0**
2. **E8190**
3. **E8495**
4.

22. MEDICAID RESUBMISSION CODE   ORIGINAL REF. NO.

23. PRIOR AUTHORIZATION NUMBER

24. A. DATE(S) OF SERVICE From MM DD YY To MM DD YY	B. PLACE OF SERVICE	C. EMG	D. PROCEDURES, SERVICES, OR SUPPLIES (Explain Unusual Circumstances) CPT/HCPCS | MODIFER	E. DIAGNOSIS POINTER	F. $ CHARGES	G. DAYS OR UNITS	H. EPSDT Family Plan	I. ID. QUAL.	J. RENDERING PROVIDER ID. #
1	**01 03 YYYY**	**11**		**99213**	**1**	**40 00**	**1**		NPI
2									NPI
3									NPI
4									NPI
5									NPI
6									NPI

25. FEDERAL TAX I.D. NUMBER **111234523** SSN ☐ EIN ☒

26. PATIENT'S ACCOUNT NO. **17-1**

27. ACCEPT ASSIGNMENT? (For govt. claims, see back) YES ☒ NO ☐

28. TOTAL CHARGE $ **40 00**

29. AMOUNT PAID $

30. BALANCE DUE $

31. SIGNATURE OF PHYSICIAN OR SUPPLIER INCLUDING DEGREES OR CREDENTIALS (I certify that the statements on the reverse apply to this bill and are made a part thereof.)
ERIN A HELPER MD
SIGNED _____ DATE **MMDDYYYY**

32. SERVICE FACILITY LOCATION INFORMATION
a. NPI   b.

33. BILLING PROVIDER INFO & PH # **(101) 1111234**
ERIN A HELPER MD
101 MEDIC DRIVE
ANYWHERE NY 12345
a. **1234567890**   b.

APPROVED OMB-0938-0999 FORM CMS-1500 (08/05)

FIGURE 17-4 Completed Workers' Compensation as primary CMS-1500 claim for John Q. Public case study (Courtesy Delmar/Cengage Learning)

ICD-10-CM ALERT!

21. DIAGNOSIS OR NATURE OF ILLNESS OR INJURY (Relate Items 1, 2, 3 or 4 to Item 24E by Line)
1. **S13 8xxD**
2. **V49 9xxA**
3.
4.

E. DIAGNOSIS POINTER

Completion of Workers' Compensation as Primary CMS-1500 Claim

1. Obtain a blank CMS-1500 claim by making a copy of the claim in Appendix III.
2. Review the instructions on your comparison chart.
3. Review the Mary S. Patient case study (Figure 17-5).
4. Select the information needed from the case study, and enter the required information on the claim using optical scanning guidelines.
5. Review the claim to be sure all required blocks are properly completed. Compare it to the completed claim in Figure 17-6.

ERIN A. HELPER, M.D.
101 Medic Drive, Anywhere NY 12345
(101) 111-1234 (Office) • (101) 111-9292 (Fax)
EIN: 11-1234523
NPI: 1234567890

Case Study

PATIENT INFORMATION:

Name:	Patient, Mary S.
Address:	91 Home Street
City:	Nowhere
State:	NY
Zip Code:	12367-1234
Telephone:	(101) 201-8989
Gender:	Female
Date of Birth:	10-10-1959
Occupation:	Clerk
Employer:	A1 Grocery
Address:	1 Main St, Nowhere NY 12367
Telephone:	(101) 555-4561

INSURANCE INFORMATION:

Patient Number:	17-2
Place of Service:	Office
Primary Insurance Plan:	
Primary Insurance Plan ID #:	
Policy #:	
Primary Policyholder:	
Policyholder Date of Birth:	
Relationship to Patient:	
Workers' Compensation Plan:	State Insurance Fund
Workers' Compensation Claim #:	MSP9761
Patient's SSN:	467980123

Patient Status   ☒ Married   ☐ Divorced   ☐ Single   ☐ Student

DIAGNOSIS INFORMATION

	Diagnosis	Code		Diagnosis	Code
1.	Muscle spasms, trapezius	728.85	5.		
2.	Weakness, both arms	728.9	6.		
3.	Cervical osteoarthritis	721.90	7.		
4.	Accident at work	E849.3	8.		

ICD-10-CM ALERT!

Muscle spasms, trapezius	M62.40
Weakness, both arms	M68.9
Cervical osteoarthritis	M47.819
Accident at work	Y92.69

PROCEDURE INFORMATION

	Description of Procedure or Service	Date	Code	Charge
1.	Office visit, established patient, level II	01-27-YYYY	99212	45.00
2.	Trigger point injections (upper and medial trapezius muscles)	01-27-YYYY	20552	75.00
3.				
4.				
5.				

SPECIAL NOTES: Injured at work 01-20-YYYY. Return to work 01-22-YYYY.

FIGURE 17-5 Mary S. Patient case study (Courtesy Delmar/Cengage Learning)

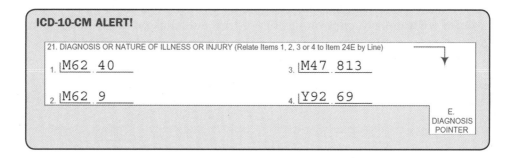

FIGURE 17-6 Completed Mary S. Patient claim (Courtesy Delmar/Cengage Learning)

ICD-10-CM ALERT!

21. DIAGNOSIS OR NATURE OF ILLNESS OR INJURY (Relate Items 1, 2, 3 or 4 to Item 24E by Line)

1. M62.40   3. M47.813

2. M62.9   4. Y92.69

E. DIAGNOSIS POINTER

SUMMARY

The U.S. DOL Office of Workers' Compensation Programs administers programs that provide wage-replacement benefits, medical treatment, vocational rehabilitation, and other benefits to federal workers (or eligible dependents) who are injured at work or who acquire an occupational disease. Federal programs include Energy Employees Occupational Illness Compensation Program, Federal Black Lung Program, Federal Employees' Compensation Program, Longshore and Harbor Workers' Compensation Program, Mine Safety and Health Administration, and Occupational Safety and Health Administration. State programs include the following types of coverage: State Insurance (or Compensation) Fund; employer self-insured programs; private, commercial workers' compensation programs; and combination programs.

To qualify for workers' compensation, employees must either be injured while working within the scope of their job description, injured while performing a service required by the employer, or contracts an illness that can be directly linked to employment. Workers' compensation cases are classified as (1) medical claims with no disability, (2) temporary disability, (3) permanent disability, (4) vocational rehabilitation, and (5) death of the worker.

Providers are required to accept workers' compensation reimbursement as payment in full. Balance billing of patients is prohibited. Many workers' compensation programs incorporate managed care to improve quality of medical benefits and services provided, as well as to control costs.

The First Report of Injury form is completed when the patient first seeks treatment for a work-related illness or injury. The report is filed in quadruplicate with a copy distributed to the State Workers' Compensation Board/Commission, employer-designated compensation payer, ill or injured party's employer, and patient's work-related injury chart. When employers initially deny workers' compensation claims, the employee has the right to appeal the denial. Detailed narrative progress/supplemental reports document significant changes in the employee's medical or disability status.

When completing workers' compensation CMS-1500 claims for case studies in this text and the Workbook, the following special instructions apply:

- Block 14—Review the case study to locate the date of the on-the-job illness or injury
- Block 15—Review the case study to locate the date of any prior episode of the same or similar illness or injury
- Block 16—Review the case study to locate the dates the patient was unable to work
- Block 20—Enter an X in the NO box
- Block 23—Leave blank
- Block 26—Enter the case study number (e.g., 17-4)
- Blocks 29–30—Leave blank
- Block 32—If Block 18 contains dates, enter the name and address of the responsible provider (e.g., hospital)

INTERNET LINKS

- California Workers' Compensation Institute
  www.cwci.org
- Federal workers' compensation resources
  Go to **www.dol.gov,** click on the Topics link, and click on the Workers' Compensation link.
- Mine Safety and Health Administration
  www.msha.gov
- National Workers' Compensation Web site
  www.workerscompensation.com

- Occupational Safety and Health Administration
  www.osha.gov

- State Compensation Fund of Arizona
  www.scfaz.com

STUDY CHECKLIST

☐ Read this textbook chapter and highlight key terms.

☐ Access SimClaim software at the online companion, and become familiar with the software.

☐ Complete CMS-1500 claims for each chapter case study.

☐ Complete the chapter review, verifying answers with your instructor.

☐ Complete the chapter CD-ROM activities.

☐ Complete WebTutor assignments, and take online quizzes.

☐ Complete workers' compensation claims for cases located in Appendices I and II.

☐ Complete the Workbook chapter, verifying answers with your instructor.

☐ Complete the StudyWare activities to receive immediate feedback.

☐ Form a study group with classmates to discuss chapter concepts in preparation for an exam.

REVIEW

MULTIPLE CHOICE Select the most appropriate response.

1. **The Office of Workers' Compensation Programs (OWCP) administers programs that provide**

   a. medical treatment.

   b. vocational rehabilitation.

   c. wage replacement benefits.

   d. all of the above.

2. **The Energy Employees Occupational Illness Compensation Program began providing benefits to eligible employees and former employees of the Department of Energy in**

   a. 1999.

   b. 2000.

   c. 2001.

   d. 2002.

3. **The Federal Black Lung Program was enacted in 1969 to provide _____ and other benefits for respiratory conditions related to persons formerly employed in the nation's coal mines.**

   a. medical treatment

   b. vocational rehabilitation

   c. wage replacement benefits

   d. all of the above

4. **The Federal Employees' Compensation Act (FECA) program provides workers' compensation to all federal and postal workers throughout the world for employment-related injuries and occupational diseases, and includes**

   a. medical and vocational rehabilitation.

   b. payment for medical care.

   c. wage replacement.

   d. all of the above.

5. **The Longshore and Harbor Workers' Compensation Program covers private-industry workers who are**
   a. employees that work for American companies in foreign countries.
   b. engaged in extracting natural resources from the outer continental shelf.
   c. those associated with industry, labor, and other federal and state agencies.
   d. working under contract for foreign countries outside the continental United States.

6. **Material Safety Data Sheets contain information about**
   a. activities and programs associated with mining.
   b. chemical and hazardous substances used on site.
   c. interstate commerce injuries from railroads.
   d. occupational hazards in the workplace.

7. **Which is responsible for administering workers' compensation laws?**
   a. Office of Workers' Compensation Programs
   b. State Compensation Commission
   c. State Insurance Fund
   d. Workers' Compensation Board

8. **Which situation qualifies a worker for workers' compensation coverage?**
   a. Cindy Frasier administered an injection to a patient and stuck her finger with the needle; this required immediate treatment at the hospital and follow-up treatment by her primary care provider.
   b. Jenny Baker traveled to the local hospital from her place of employment to have lunch with friends; after eating lunch, she suffered food poisoning and underwent emergency care.
   c. Peter Mills attended an out-of-state conference for which his employer had preapproved reimbursement of his expenses; while attending a concert one evening during the trip, he fell and broke his arm.
   d. Sally Jones left the doctor's office where she is employed and stopped at the bank to deposit the day's accounts receivable; thereafter, while on the way to her residence, she was injured in a car accident.

9. **The judicial dispute resolution process in which an appeals board makes a final determination is called**
   a. adjudication.
   b. intercession.
   c. mediation.
   d. negotiation.

10. **Which is completed when the patient initially seeks treatment for a work-related illness or injury?**
    a. billing information notes
    b. First Report of Injury
    c. Material Safety Data Sheet
    d. progress report

Case Studies Set One

HOW TO ACCESS SIMCLAIM

To access the SimClaim student practice software program online, please refer to the information on the printed access card found in the front of this textbook. The SimClaim case studies are also available for reference in Appendix I and II of this textbook. Additional information on how to use the SimClaim software program is provided at the online site.

GENERAL INSTRUCTIONS FOR SIMCLAIM

- **Turn on Caps Lock**—all data entered into SimClaim must be in ALL CAPS
- **Do not abbreviate**—spell out words like street, drive, avenue, Signature on File, Blue Cross Blue Shield, etc.—no abbreviations (other than state abbreviations) will be accepted by the program
- **Do not use 'Same As' or 'None' in any block**—even if patient information is the same as insured information, enter that information again on the claim
- **More than one Diagnosis Pointer in Block 24E**—for the SimClaim case studies, there may be more than one diagnosis pointer required in Block 24E
- **No Amount Paid indicated**—if there is no amount paid indicated on the case study, **enter '0 00' in Block 29**
- **Secondary Insurance Claims**—If a Case Study indicates that a patient's **primary payer has paid an amount,** complete a second claim form for the secondary insurance that reflects the amount reimbursed by the primary payer
- **More than one CMS form**—Remember, if the place of service or the provider changes, another CMS-1500 claim is completed
- **Block 32**—always enter service facility location information in SimClaim Block 32
- **Enter all dates as given in case study.** For dates that aren't given (ex: signature dates), use **'MM DD YY'**. **'YY'** or **'YYYY'** is always used in place of an actual year except for birthdates.
- **For additional help using SimClaim, refer to the Block Help within SimClaim.**

GENERAL INSTRUCTIONS AND HINTS FOR SET ONE CASE STUDIES (1-1 THROUGH 1-20)

The case studies in Appendix I (see Table I-1) provide additional practice completing CMS-1500 claims for different payers. These case studies are available in the SimClaim software, and are reprinted here for your convenience. Be sure to read through the following instructions prior to beginning work.

TABLE I-1

CASE	PAYER	CASE	PAYER
1-1	Commercial	1-11	Commercial/Medicaid
1-2	Commercial	1-12	Medicare
1-3	Commercial	1-13	Medicaid
1-4	Blue Cross Blue Shield	1-14	TRICARE
1-5	Blue Cross Blue Shield	1-15	TRICARE
1-6	Blue Cross Blue Shield	1-16	TRICARE
1-7	Medicare	1-17	Commercial TRICARE
1-8	Medicare	1-18	Commercial
1-9	Medicare/Medigap	1-19	Commercial
1-10	Blue Cross Blue Shield	1-20	Commercial

- The provider name for all cases in Case Studies: Set One is also the practice name. Please note that this differs from the cases in Case Studies: Set Two

- Primary and secondary insurance information should be entered on the claim even if the secondary insurance is not being filed at this time

- Pay careful attention to the Special Notes section of each case study for those cases requiring two claims, a primary claim and a secondary claim may be required when the primary payer has already processed or adjudicated the claim.

- Make certain that diagnosis pointers are appropriately matched to the diagnosis that corresponds to the specific service for each line item

- Only one (1) payer should be designated in Block 1. This should reflect the insurance that is being filed on the current claim form only. In those instances where both primary and secondary claims are being completed, the "X" should reflect the payer for that specific claim only.

- When commercial insurance is provided and the policy is through an employer, enter an X in the "group" box in Block 1 as well as the appropriate group number in Block 11.

- For these case studies, claims completion should be based on the most *generically correct* claims completion guidelines. Specific payer, state, or insurance company guidelines should **not** be utilized for completing the claims in Case Studies for Set One or Set Two. For more information, the NUCC Claim Form Instruction Manual may be downloaded by going to www.nucc.org.

CASE STUDY 1-1

Mary S. Hightower

IRMINA M BRILLIANT MD
25 MEDICAL DRIVE
INJURY NY 12347
101   2013145

Patient Number: 1-1

EIN: 117654312   **NPI:** 2345678901

PATIENT INFORMATION:
Name: HIGHTOWER, MARY, S
Address: 61 WATER TOWER STREET
City: ANYWHERE
State: NY
Zip/4: 12345-1234
Telephone: 101 2016987

Gender: **M**   F X
Status: Single   Married X   Other
Date of Birth: 08   07   1951
Employer:
Student: FT   PT   School:

Work Related?   Y   N X
Employment Related?   Y   N X
Other Accident: Y   N X
Date of Accident:

Referring Physician: IM GOODDOC MD
Address:
Telephone:
NPI #: 5678901234

INSURANCE INFORMATION:
Primary Insurance
   Primary Insurance Name: AETNA
   Address: PO BOX 45
   City: STILLWATER
   State: PA
   Zip/4: 12345-0045

   Plan ID#: 272034109
   Group #: NPW
   Policyholder: HIGHTOWER, WALTER, W
   Address: 61 WATER TOWER STREET
   City: ANYWHERE
   State: NY
   Zip/4: 12345-1234
   Policyholder Date of Birth: 04   09   1951
   Pt Relationship to Insured: Self   Spouse X Child   Other
   Employer/School Name: ANYWHERE WATER CO

Secondary Insurance
   Secondary Insurance Name:
   Address:
   City:
   State:
   Zip/4:

   Plan ID#:
   Group #:
   Policyholder:
   Address:
   City:
   State:
   Zip/4:
   Policyholder Date of Birth:
   Pt Relationship to Insured: Self   Spouse   Child   Other
   Employer/School Name:

ENCOUNTER INFORMATION:
Place of Service: 22

DIAGNOSIS INFORMATION

	Code	Diagnosis		Code	Diagnosis
1.	414 . 05	CAD of grafted artery	5.	.	
2.	.		6.	.	
3.	.		7.	.	
4.	.		8.	.	

PROCEDURE INFORMATION

Description of Procedure/Service	Dates	Code	Mod	Dx Order	Unit Charge	Days/ Units
1. Left heart catheterization	01 10 YY⁻	93510		1	2000 00	1
2. Injection for catheterization	01 10 YY⁻	93540		1	250 00	1
3. Angiography, venous bypass graft	01 10 YY⁻	93556		1	750 00	1
4.						
5.						
6.						

Special Notes: Patient diagnosed with CAD 5 years ago (6/15/YYYY).
   Referring provider: I.M. Gooddoc, M.D., NPI: 5678901234. Care rendered at Goodmedicine Hospital,
   1 Provider Street, Anywhere, NY 12345. NPI: 1123456789. Revisit 5 days. Admit/discharge date: 1/10/YYYY.

CASE STUDY 1-2
Ima Gayle

SEJAL RAJA MD
1 MEDICAL DRIVE
INJURY NY 12347
101   2022923

Patient Number: 1-2

EIN: 111397992   **NPI:** 7890123456

PATIENT INFORMATION:
Name: GAYLE, IMA
Address: 101 HAPPY DRIVE
City: ANYWHERE
State: NY
Zip/4: 12345-1234
Telephone: 101 1119876

Gender: **M**   F X
Status: **Single** X   **Married**   **Other**
Date of Birth: 09   30   1945
Employer: MAIL BOXES INCORPORATED
Student: FT   PT   School:

Work Related?   Y   **N** X
Employment Related?   Y   **N** X
Other Accident: Y   **N** X
Date of Accident:

Referring Physician:
Address:
Telephone:
NPI #:

INSURANCE INFORMATION:
Primary Insurance
    Primary Insurance Name: CONNECTICUT GENERAL
    Address: PO BOX 1234
    City: HEALTH
    State: CT
    Zip/4: 01234-1234

    Plan ID#: 210010121
    Group #: 101
    Policyholder: GAYLE, IMA
    Address: 101 HAPPY DRIVE
    City: ANYWHERE
    State: NY
    Zip/4: 12345-1234
    Policyholder Date of Birth: 09   30   1945
    Pt Relationship to Insured: Self X **Spouse   Child   Other**
    Employer/School Name:

Secondary Insurance
    Secondary Insurance Name:
    Address:
    City:
    State:
    Zip/4:

    Plan ID#:
    Group #:
    Policyholder:
    Address:
    City:
    State:
    Zip/4:
    Policyholder Date of Birth:
    Pt Relationship to Insured: Self   Spouse   Child   Other
    Employer/School Name:

ENCOUNTER INFORMATION:
Place of Service: 11

DIAGNOSIS INFORMATION

	Code	Diagnosis		Code	Diagnosis
1.	782.0	Numbness, left arm	5.	.	
2.	715.96	Osteoarthritis, left leg	6.	.	
3.	.		7.	.	
4.	.		8.	.	

PROCEDURE INFORMATION

Description of Procedure/Service	Dates	Code	Mod	Dx Order	Unit Charge	Days/ Units
1. Office visit, est patient, level II	03 01 YY¯	99213	25	12	60 00	1
2. Trigger point injection, trapezius, left	03 01 YY¯	20552		1	75 00	1
3.	¯					
4.	¯					
5.	¯					
6.	¯					

Special Notes: Patient paid $50 of today's total.

CASE STUDY 1-3

Sandy Spencer

IRMINA M BRILLIANT MD
25 MEDICAL DRIVE
INJURY NY 12347
101   2013145

Patient Number: 1-3

EIN: 117654312   **NPI:**   2345678901

PATIENT INFORMATION:
Name: SPENCER, SANDY
Address: 101 HIGH STREET
City: ANYWHERE
State: NY
Zip/4: 12345-1234
Telephone: 101 5555698

Gender: **M**   F X
Status: Single X   Married   Other
Date of Birth: 08   05   1985
Employer: GOODMEDICINE MEDICAL CLINIC
Student: FT   PT   School:

Work Related?   Y   N X
Employment Related?   Y   N X
Other Accident: Y   N X
Date of Accident:

Referring Physician:
Address:
Telephone:
NPI #:

INSURANCE INFORMATION:
Primary Insurance
    Primary Insurance Name: AFLAC
    Address: PO BOX 33
    City: ASHBURY
    State: TN
    Zip/4: 23456-0033

    Plan ID#: 5623569
    Group #:
    Policyholder: SPENCER, SANDY
    Address: 101 HIGH STREET
    City: ANYWHERE
    State: NY
    Zip/4: 12345-1234
    Policyholder Date of Birth: 08   05   1985
    Pt Relationship to Insured: Self X Spouse   Child   Other
    Employer/School Name: GOODMEDICINE MEDICAL CLINIC

Secondary Insurance
    Secondary Insurance Name:
    Address:
    City:
    State:
    Zip/4:

    Plan ID#:
    Group #:
    Policyholder:
    Address:
    City:
    State:
    Zip/4:
    Policyholder Date of Birth:
    Pt Relationship to Insured: Self   Spouse   Child   Other
    Employer/School Name:

ENCOUNTER INFORMATION:
Place of Service: 11

DIAGNOSIS INFORMATION

	Code	Diagnosis		Code	Diagnosis
1.	401 .9	Hypertension	5.	.	
2.	.		6.	.	
3.	.		7.	.	
4.	.		8.	.	

PROCEDURE INFORMATION

Description of Procedure/Service	Dates	Code	Mod	Dx Order	Unit Charge	Days/ Units
1. Office visit, est patient, level IV	10 15 YY⁻	99214		1	100 00	1
2.	⁻					
3.	⁻					
4.	⁻					
5.	⁻					
6.	⁻					

Special Notes:

CASE STUDY 1-4

Katlyn Tiger

ARNOLD J YOUNGLOVE MD
21 PROVIDER STREET
INJURY NY 12347
101   2027754

Patient Number: 1-4

EIN: 111234632   **NPI:**   0123456789

PATIENT INFORMATION:
Name: TIGER, KATLYN
Address: 2 JUNGLE ROAD
City: NOWHERE
State: NY
Zip/4: 12346-1234
Telephone: 101 1112222

Gender: M   F X
Status: Single X   **Married   Other**
Date of Birth: 01   03   1954
Employer: JOHN LION CPA
Student: FT   PT   School:

Work Related?   **Y   N** X
Employment Related?   **Y   N** X
Other Accident: **Y   N** X
Date of Accident:

Referring Physician:
Address:
Telephone:
NPI #:

INSURANCE INFORMATION:
Primary Insurance
   Primary Insurance Name: BLUE CROSS BLUE SHIELD
   Address: PO BOX 1121
   City: MEDICAL
   State: PA
   Zip/4: 12357-1121

   Plan ID#: ZJW334444
   Group #: W310
   Policyholder: TIGER, KATLYN
   Address: 2 JUNGLE ROAD
   City: NOWHERE
   State: NY
   Zip/4: 12346-1234
   Policyholder Date of Birth: 01   03   1954
   Pt Relationship to Insured: Self X **Spouse   Child   Other**
   Employer/School Name: JOHN LION CPA

Secondary Insurance
   Secondary Insurance Name:
   Address:
   City:
   State:
   Zip/4:

   Plan ID#:
   Group #:
   Policyholder:
   Address:
   City:
   State:
   Zip/4:
   Policyholder Date of Birth:
   Pt Relationship to Insured: Self   Spouse   Child   Other
   Employer/School Name:

ENCOUNTER INFORMATION:
Place of Service: 21

DIAGNOSIS INFORMATION

	Code	Diagnosis		Code	Diagnosis
1.	485 .	Bronchopneumonia	5.	.	
2.	.		6.	.	
3.	.		7.	.	
4.	.		8.	.	

PROCEDURE INFORMATION

Description of Procedure/Service	Dates	Code	Mod	Dx Order	Unit Charge	Days/ Units
1. Initial observation, comprehensive	02 28 YY⁻	99220		1	175 00	1
2. Discharge home	03 01 YY⁻	99217		1	65 00	1
3.	⁻					
4.	⁻					
5.	⁻					
6.	⁻					

Special Notes:
   Care rendered at Goodmedicine Hospital, 1 Provider Street, Anywhere, NY 12345, NPI: 1123456789.

CASE STUDY 1-5

Jeffrey A. Green

SEJAL RAJA MD
1 MEDICAL DRIVE
INJURY NY 12347
101   2022923

Patient Number: 1-5

EIN: 111397992   **NPI:** 7890123456

PATIENT INFORMATION:
Name: GREEN, JEFFREY, A
Address: 103 MOUNTAIN VIEW ROAD
City: NOWHERE
State: NY
Zip/4: 12346-1234
Telephone: 101 1178765

Gender: M X   F
Status: Single X   Married   Other
Date of Birth: 02   03   1997
Employer: AFLAC
Student: FT   PT   School:

Work Related?   Y   N X
Employment Related?   Y   N X
Other Accident: Y   N X
Date of Accident:

Referring Physician:
Address:
Telephone:
NPI #:

INSURANCE INFORMATION:
Primary Insurance
   Primary Insurance Name: BLUE CROSS BLUE SHIELD
   Address: PO BOX 1121
   City: MEDICAL
   State: PA
   Zip/4: 12357-1121

   Plan ID#: XWV7794483
   Group #: 876
   Policyholder: GREEN, JEFFREY, G
   Address: 103 MOUNTAIN VIEW DRIVE
   City: NOWHERE
   State: NY
   Zip/4: 12346-1234
   Policyholder Date of Birth: 07   01   1955
   Pt Relationship to Insured: Self   Spouse   Child X Other
   Employer/School Name: AFLAC

Secondary Insurance
   Secondary Insurance Name:
   Address:
   City:
   State:
   Zip/4:

   Plan ID#:
   Group #:
   Policyholder:
   Address:
   City:
   State:
   Zip/4:
   Policyholder Date of Birth:
   Pt Relationship to Insured: Self   Spouse   Child   Other
   Employer/School Name:

ENCOUNTER INFORMATION:
Place of Service: 11

DIAGNOSIS INFORMATION

	Code	Diagnosis		Code	Diagnosis
1.	466 .0	Acute bronchitis	5.	.	
2.	472 .0	Purulent rhinitis	6.	.	
3.	.		7.	.	
4.	.		8.	.	

PROCEDURE INFORMATION

Description of Procedure/Service	Dates	Code	Mod	Dx Order	Unit Charge	Days/ Units
1. Office visit, est patient, level II	03 10 YY⁻	99212		12	26 00	1
2.	⁻					
3.	⁻					
4.	⁻					
5.	⁻					
6.	⁻					

Special Notes:
   Patient's mother paid $15 of today's total. Return visit as needed.

CASE STUDY 1-6

Christine Noel

ARNOLD J YOUNGLOVE MD
21 PROVIDER STREET
INJURY NY 12347
101   2027754

Patient Number: 1-6

EIN: 111234632   **NPI:**   0123456789

PATIENT INFORMATION:
Name: NOEL, CHRISTINE
Address: 100 CHRISTMAS TREE LANE
City: ANYWHERE
State: NY
Zip/4: 12345-1234
Telephone: 101 1158123

Gender: **M**   F X
Status: Single   **Married** X   Other
Date of Birth: 09   03   1977
Employer: WORLD UNIVERSITY
Student: **FT**   **PT**   **School:**

Work Related?   **Y**   **N** X
Employment Related?   **Y**   **N** X
Other Accident: **Y**   **N** X
Date of Accident:

Referring Physician:
Address:
Telephone:
NPI #:

INSURANCE INFORMATION:
Primary Insurance
    Primary Insurance Name: BLUE CROSS BLUE SHIELD
    Address: PO BOX 1121
    City: MEDICAL
    State: PA
    Zip/4: 12357-1121

    Plan ID#: 123W476
    Group #:
    Policyholder: NOEL, CHRISTINE
    Address: 100 CHRISTMAS TREE LANE
    City: ANYWHERE
    State: NY
    Zip/4: 12345-1234
    Policyholder Date of Birth: 09   03   1977
    Pt Relationship to Insured: Self X **Spouse   Child   Other**
    Employer/School Name: WORLD UNIVERSITY

Secondary Insurance
    Secondary Insurance Name:
    Address:
    City:
    State:
    Zip/4:

    Plan ID#:
    Group #:
    Policyholder:
    Address:
    City:
    State:
    Zip/4:
    Policyholder Date of Birth:
    Pt Relationship to Insured: Self   Spouse   Child   Other
    Employer/School Name:

ENCOUNTER INFORMATION:
Place of Service: 11

DIAGNOSIS INFORMATION

	Code	Diagnosis		Code	Diagnosis
1.	462 .	Acute pharyngitis	**5.**	.	
2.	788 .41	Urinary frequency	**6.**	.	
3.	.		**7.**	.	
4.	.		**8.**	.	

PROCEDURE INFORMATION

Description of Procedure/Service	Dates	Code	Mod	Dx Order	Unit Charge	Days/ Units
1. Office visit, est patient, level II	03 01 YY¬	99212		12	45 00	1
2. Urinalysis, dipstick and microscopy	03 01 YY¬	81000		2	8 00	1
3. Strep test (CLIA-approved office lab)	03 01 YY¬	87880		1	12 00	1
4.	¬					
5.	¬					
6.	¬					

Special Notes: Patient paid $20 toward today's bill.

CASE STUDY 1-7

Gladys Phish

ANGELA DILALIO MD
99 PROVIDER DRIVE
INJURY NY 12347
101   2014321

Patient Number: 1-7

EIN: 111982342   **NPI:** 4567890123

PATIENT INFORMATION:
Name: PHISH, GLADYS
Address: 21 WINDWHISPER DRIVE
City: INJURY
State: NY
Zip/4: 12347-1234
Telephone: 101 1112397

Gender: M   F X
Status: Single   Married X   **Other**
Date of Birth: 11   21   1930
Employer:
Student: FT   PT   School:

Work Related?   Y   N X
Employment Related?   Y   N X
Other Accident: Y   N X
Date of Accident:

Referring Physician: IM GOODDOC MD
Address:
Telephone:
NPI #: 5678901234

INSURANCE INFORMATION:
Primary Insurance
   Primary Insurance Name: MEDICARE
   Address: PO BOX 9929
   City: BOXBURY
   State: MD
   Zip/4: 45678-9929

   Plan ID#: 101891701A
   Group #:
   Policyholder: PHISH, GLADYS
   Address: 21 WINDWHISPER DRIVE
   City: INJURY
   State: NY
   Zip/4: 12347-1234
   Policyholder Date of Birth: 11   21   1930
   Pt Relationship to Insured: Self X **Spouse   Child   Other**
   Employer/School Name:

Secondary Insurance
   Secondary Insurance Name:
   Address:
   City:
   State:
   Zip/4:

   Plan ID#:
   Group #:
   Policyholder:
   Address:
   City:
   State:
   Zip/4:
   Policyholder Date of Birth:
   Pt Relationship to Insured: Self   Spouse   Child   Other
   Employer/School Name:

ENCOUNTER INFORMATION:
Place of Service: 22

DIAGNOSIS INFORMATION

	Code	Diagnosis		Code	Diagnosis
1.	682 .4	Abscess, right hand	5.	.	
2.	.		6.	.	
3.	.		7.	.	
4.	.		8.	.	

PROCEDURE INFORMATION

Description of Procedure/Service	Dates	Code	Mod	Dx Order	Unit Charge	Days/ Units
1. Incision & drainage, abscess, subcut.	03 10 YY⁻	10060		1	450 00	1
2.	⁻					
3.	⁻					
4.	⁻					
5.	⁻					
6.	⁻					

Special Notes: Hospital info: Goodmedicine Hospital, 1 Provider St, Anywhere, NY 12345, NPI: 1123456789.
Admission/Discharge date: 3/10/YYYY.

CASE STUDY 1-8

Elaine Blueberry

IRMINA M BRILLIANT MD
25 MEDICAL DRIVE
INJURY NY 12347
101   2013145

Patient Number: 1-8

EIN: 117654312   **NPI:**   2345678901

PATIENT INFORMATION:
Name: BLUEBERRY, ELAINE
Address: 101 BUST STREET
City: ANYWHERE
State: NY
Zip/4: 12345-1234
Telephone: 101 5555689

Gender: M   F X
Status: Single X   **Married   Other**
Date of Birth: 10   02   1925
Employer:
Student: FT   PT   School:

Work Related?   Y   N X
Employment Related? Y   N X
Other Accident: Y   N X
Date of Accident:

Referring Physician: IM GOODDOC MD
Address:
Telephone:
NPI #:   5678901234

INSURANCE INFORMATION:
Primary Insurance
    Primary Insurance Name: MEDICARE
    Address: PO BOX 9929
    City: BOXBURY
    State: MD
    Zip/4: 45678-9929

    Plan ID#:   102623434B
    Group #:
    Policyholder: BLUEBERRY, ELAINE
    Address: 101 BUST STREET
    City: ANYWHERE
    State: NY
    Zip/4: 12345-1234
    Policyholder Date of Birth: 10   02   1925
    Pt Relationship to Insured: Self X **Spouse   Child   Other**
    Employer/School Name:

Secondary Insurance
    Secondary Insurance Name:
    Address:
    City:
    State:
    Zip/4:

    Plan ID#:
    Group #:
    Policyholder:
    Address:
    City:
    State:
    Zip/4:
    Policyholder Date of Birth:
    Pt Relationship to Insured: Self   Spouse   Child   Other
    Employer/School Name:

ENCOUNTER INFORMATION:
Place of Service: 21

DIAGNOSIS INFORMATION

	Code	Diagnosis		Code	Diagnosis
1.	578 .9	Gastrointestinal bleeding	5.	.	
2.	691 .0	Perianal rash due to adult diaper	6.	.	
3.	.		7.	.	
4.	.		8.	.	

PROCEDURE INFORMATION

Description of Procedure/Service	Dates	Code	Mod	Dx Order	Unit Charge	Days/ Units
1. Inpatient consultation, level III	03 01 YY⁻	99253		12	125 00	1
2.	⁻					
3.	⁻					
4.	⁻					
5.	⁻					
6.	⁻					

Special Notes: Care rendered at Goodmedicine Hospital, 1 Provider Street, Anywhere, NY 12345, NPI: 1123456789.
Admission Date: 03/01/YYYY. Discharge Date: 03/05/YYYY.

CASE STUDY 1-9

Emma Berry

ARNOLD J YOUNGLOVE MD
21 PROVIDER STREET
INJURY NY 12347
101 2027754

Patient Number: 1-9

EIN: 111234632 **NPI:** 0123456789

PATIENT INFORMATION:
Name: BERRY, EMMA
Address: 15 GOLDEN AGE ROAD
City: ANYWHERE
State: NY
Zip/4: 12345-1234
Telephone: 101 1117700

Gender: M F X
Status: Single X Married Other
Date of Birth: 03 08 1935
Employer:
Student: FT PT School:

Work Related? Y N X
Employment Related? Y N X
Other Accident: Y N X
Date of Accident:

Referring Physician:
Address:
Telephone:
NPI #:

INSURANCE INFORMATION:
Primary Insurance
  Primary Insurance Name: MEDICARE
  Address: PO BOX 9929
  City: BOXBURY
  State: MD
  Zip/4: 45678-9929

  Plan ID#: 888441234A
  Group #:
  Policyholder: BERRY, EMMA
  Address: 15 GOLDEN AGE ROAD
  City: ANYWHERE
  State: NY
  Zip/4: 12345-1234
  Policyholder Date of Birth: 03 08 1935
  Pt Relationship to Insured: Self X Spouse Child Other
  Employer/School Name:

Secondary Insurance
  Secondary Insurance Name: MEDIGAP
  Address: PO BOX 212
  City: BALTIMORE
  State: MD
  Zip/4: 45678-0212

  Plan ID#: 995432992
  Group #:
  Policyholder: BERRY, EMMA
  Address: 15 GOLDEN AGE ROAD
  City: ANYWHERE
  State: NY
  Zip/4: 12345-1234
  Policyholder Date of Birth: 03 08 1935
  Pt Relationship to Insured: Self X Spouse Child Other
  Employer/School Name:

ENCOUNTER INFORMATION:
Place of Service: 31

DIAGNOSIS INFORMATION

	Code	Diagnosis		Code	Diagnosis
1.	290.0	Stable senile dementia	5.	.	
2.	782.3	Peripheral edema	6.	.	
3.	.		7.	.	
4.	.		8.	.	

PROCEDURE INFORMATION

Description of Procedure/Service	Dates	Code	Mod	Dx Order	Unit Charge	Days/Units
1. SNF care, subsequent, level II	03 01 YY	99308		12	45 00	1
2.						
3.						
4.						
5.						
6.						

Special Notes: Care rendered at Good Life SNF, 200 Golden Age Road, Anywhere, NY 12345, NPI: 2234567890.
Admission date: 03/01/YYYY. Discharge date: 03/03/YYYY.
Daughter is Anne Peach, 1234 Beneficiary St, Faraway WA 99999.

CASE STUDY 1-10

Peter Cartright

ANGELA DILALIO MD
99 PROVIDER DRIVE
INJURY NY 12347
101   2014321

Patient Number: 1-10

EIN: 111982342   **NPI:** 4567890123

PATIENT INFORMATION:
Name: CARTRIGHT, PETER
Address: 250 HILL STREET
City: ANYWHERE
State: NY
Zip/4: 12345-1234
Telephone: 101 5557843

Gender: **M** X   **F**
Status: **Single** X   **Married**   **Other**
Date of Birth: 12   24   1975
Employer:
Student: **FT**   **PT**   School:

Work Related?   **Y**   **N** X
Employment Related?   **Y**   **N** X
Other Accident: **Y**   **N** X
Date of Accident:

Referring Physician:
Address:
Telephone:
NPI #:

INSURANCE INFORMATION:
Primary Insurance
   Primary Insurance Name: BLUE CROSS BLUE SHIELD
   Address: PO BOX 1121
   City: MEDICAL
   State: PA
   Zip/4: 12357-1121

   Plan ID#: 5626598
   Group #:
   Policyholder: CARTRIGHT, PETER
   Address: 250 HILL STREET
   City: ANYWHERE
   State: NY
   Zip/4: 12345-1234
   Policyholder Date of Birth: 12   24   1975
   Pt Relationship to Insured: Self X Spouse   Child   Other
   Employer/School Name:

Secondary Insurance
   Secondary Insurance Name:
   Address:
   City:
   State:
   Zip/4:

   Plan ID#:
   Group #:
   Policyholder:
   Address:
   City:
   State:
   Zip/4:
   Policyholder Date of Birth:
   Pt Relationship to Insured: Self   Spouse   Child   Other
   Employer/School Name:

ENCOUNTER INFORMATION:
Place of Service: 11

DIAGNOSIS INFORMATION

	Code	Diagnosis		Code	Diagnosis
1.	250 .00	Diabetes mellitus, type II	5.	.	
2.	.		6.	.	
3.	.		7.	.	
4.	.		8.	.	

PROCEDURE INFORMATION

	Description of Procedure/Service	Dates	Code	Mod	Dx Order	Unit Charge	Days/ Units
1.	Office visit, est patient, level II	04 15 YY⁻	99212		1	50 00	1
2.		-					
3.		-					
4.		-					
5.		-					
6.		-					

Special Notes:

CASE STUDY 1-11

Fred Cartwheel

ANGELA DILALIO MD
99 PROVIDER DRIVE
INJURY NY 12347
101 2014321

Patient Number: 1-11

EIN: 111982342 **NPI:** 4567890123

PATIENT INFORMATION:
Name: CARTWHEEL, FRED
Address: RED WAGON ROAD
City: NOWHERE
State: NY
Zip/4: 12346-1234
Telephone: 101 1135567

Gender: M X   F
Status: Single   Married X   Other
Date of Birth: 01 03 1965
Employer: WORLD UNIVERSITY
Student: FT   PT   School:

Work Related?   Y   N X
Employment Related?   Y   N X
Other Accident: Y   N X
Date of Accident:

Referring Physician:
Address:
Telephone:
NPI #:

INSURANCE INFORMATION:
Primary Insurance
  Primary Insurance Name: METLIFE
  Address: PO BOX 67
  City: HIGHLAND
  State: TX
  Zip/4: 76543-0067

  Plan ID#: XYZ332999009
  Group #:
  Policyholder: CARTWHEEL, FRED
  Address: RED WAGON ROAD
  City: NOWHERE
  State: NY
  Zip/4: 12346-1234
  Policyholder Date of Birth: 01 03 1965
  Pt Relationship to Insured: Self X **Spouse   Child   Other**
  Employer/School Name: WORLD UNIVERSITY

Secondary Insurance
  Secondary Insurance Name: MEDICARE
  Address: PO BOX 9929
  City: BOXBURY
  State: MD
  Zip/4: 45678-9929

  Plan ID#: 332999999D
  Group #:
  Policyholder: CARTWHEEL, FRED
  Address: RED WAGON ROAD
  City: NOWHERE
  State: NY
  Zip/4: 12346-1234
  Policyholder Date of Birth: 01 03 1965
  Pt Relationship to Insured: Self X **Spouse   Child   Other**
  Employer/School Name: WORLD UNIVERSITY

ENCOUNTER INFORMATION:
Place of Service: 21

DIAGNOSIS INFORMATION

	Code	Diagnosis		Code	Diagnosis
1.	401 .0	Essential hypertensive crisis, malig.	5.	.	
2.	.		6.	.	
3.	.		7.	.	
4.	.		8.	.	

PROCEDURE INFORMATION

Description of Procedure/Service	Dates	Code	Mod	Dx Order	Unit Charge	Days/ Units
1. Initial hospital visit, level III	03 14 YY⁻	99223		1	165 00	1
2. Subsequent hospital visit, level II (x2)	03 15 YY⁻ 03 16 YY	99232		1	190 00	2
3. Discharge management, 30 minutes	03 17 YY⁻	99238		1	55 00	1
4.	⁻					
5.	⁻					
6.	⁻					

Special Notes: Onset of illness 3/12/YYYY. Discharge home. Care provided at Goodmedicine Hospital,
1 Provider Street, Anywhere, NY 12345, NPI: 1122345789.
Update: MetLife paid $100.00. Patient on Medicare disability.

CASE STUDY 1-14

Gregory Willowtree

ANGELA DILALIO MD
99 PROVIDER DRIVE
INJURY NY 12347
101   2014321

Patient Number: 1-14

EIN: 111982342   **NPI:** 4567890123

PATIENT INFORMATION:
Name: WILLOWTREE, GREGORY
Address: 150 TREE LANE
City: NOWHERE
State: NY
Zip/4: 12346-1234
Telephone: 101 5552356

Gender: M X   F
Status: Single X   Married   Other
Date of Birth: 12   12   1942
Employer: RETIRED ARMY CAPTAIN
Student: FT   PT   School:

Work Related?   Y   N X
Employment Related?   Y   N X
Other Accident: Y   N X
Date of Accident:

Referring Physician:
Address:
Telephone:
NPI #:

INSURANCE INFORMATION:
Primary Insurance
   Primary Insurance Name: TRICARE
   Address: PO BOX 555
   City: TRICITY
   State: SC
   Zip/4: 76654-0555

   Plan ID#: 071269845
   Group #:
   Policyholder: WILLOWTREE, GREGORY
   Address: 150 TREE LANE
   City: NOWHERE
   State: NY
   Zip/4: 12346-1234
   Policyholder Date of Birth: 12   12   1942
   Pt Relationship to Insured: Self X **Spouse   Child   Other**
   Employer/School Name: RETIRED ARMY CAPTAIN

Secondary Insurance
   Secondary Insurance Name:
   Address:
   City:
   State:
   Zip/4:

   Plan ID#:
   Group #:
   Policyholder:
   Address:
   City:
   State:
   Zip/4:
   Policyholder Date of Birth:
   Pt Relationship to Insured: Self   Spouse   Child   Other
   Employer/School Name:

ENCOUNTER INFORMATION:
Place of Service: 22

DIAGNOSIS INFORMATION

	Code	Diagnosis		Code	Diagnosis
1.	836 .0	Medial meniscus tear, rt knee	5.	.	
2.	727 .83	Plica, right knee	6.	.	
3.	.		7.	.	
4.	.		8.	.	

PROCEDURE INFORMATION

Description of Procedure/Service	Dates	Code	Mod	Dx Order	Unit Charge	Days/ Units
1. Arthroscopy w/ medial meniscectomy, right knee	03 19 YY⁻	29881	RT	1	2000 00	1
2.	-					
3.	-					
4.	-					
5.	-					
6.	-					

Special Notes: Hospital info: Goodmedicine Hospital, 1 Provider St, Anywhere, NY 12345, NPI: 1123456789.
   Date of injury: 03/19/YYYY. Return visit in 3 days.
   Admission/discharge date: 03/19/YYYY.

CASE STUDY 1-15

Agnes Patty

IRMINA M BRILLIANT MD
25 MEDICAL DRIVE
INJURY NY 12347
101   2013145

Patient Number: 1-15

EIN: 117654312   **NPI:** 2345678901

PATIENT INFORMATION:
Name: PATTY, AGNES
Address: 1 PATTY CAKE DRIVE
City: NOWHERE
State: NY
Zip/4: 12346-1234
Telephone: 101 1122701

Gender: M   F X
Status: Single   Married X   Other
Date of Birth: 09   03   1947
Employer: Retired Army Captain
Student: FT   PT   School:

Work Related?   Y   N X
Employment Related?   Y   N X
Other Accident: Y   N X
Date of Accident:

Referring Physician:
Address:
Telephone:
NPI #:

INSURANCE INFORMATION:
Primary Insurance
   Primary Insurance Name: TRICARE
   Address: PO BOX 555
   City: TRICITY
   State: SC
   Zip/4: 76654-0555

   Plan ID#: 103236666
   Group #:
   Policyholder: PATTY, GERRY
   Address: 1 PATTY CAKE DRIVE
   City: NOWHERE
   State: NY
   Zip/4: 12346-1234
   Policyholder Date of Birth: 03   09   1940
   Pt Relationship to Insured: Self   Spouse X Child   Other
   Employer/School Name: RETIRED ARMY CAPTAIN

Secondary Insurance
   Secondary Insurance Name:
   Address:
   City:
   State:
   Zip/4:

   Plan ID#:
   Group #:
   Policyholder:
   Address:
   City:
   State:
   Zip/4:
   Policyholder Date of Birth:
   Pt Relationship to Insured: Self   Spouse   Child   Other
   Employer/School Name:

ENCOUNTER INFORMATION:
Place of Service: 11

DIAGNOSIS INFORMATION

	Code	Diagnosis		Code	Diagnosis
1.	427.9	Cardiac arrhythmia	5.	.	
2.	784.7	Epistaxis	6.	.	
3.	.		7.	.	
4.	.		8.	.	

PROCEDURE INFORMATION

Description of Procedure/Service	Dates	Code	Mod	Dx Order	Unit Charge	Days/ Units
1. Office visit, new patient, level III	03 01 YY¯	99203		12	100 00	1
2. Nasal cautery	03 01 YY¯	30901		2	65 00	1
3. ECG with interpretation	03 01 YY¯	93000		1	50 00	1
4.	¯					
5.	¯					
6.	¯					

Special Notes: First symptoms 2/10/YYYY. Patient paid $35.00 toward today's charges.

CASE STUDY 1-16

Terry Lewis

ANGELA DILALIO MD
99 PROVIDER DRIVE
INJURY NY 12347
101   2014321

Patient Number: 1-16

EIN: 111982342   **NPI:**   4567890123

PATIENT INFORMATION:
Name: LEWIS, TERRY
Address: 9 RANDOLPH ROAD
City: ANYWHERE
State: NY
Zip/4: 12345-1234
Telephone: 101 5555169

Gender: M X   F
Status: Single X   Married   Other
Date of Birth: 05   05   1986
Employer: US NAVY
Student: FT   PT   School:

Work Related?   Y   N X
Employment Related?   Y   N X
Other Accident: Y   N X
Date of Accident:

Referring Physician:
Address:
Telephone:
NPI #:

INSURANCE INFORMATION:
Primary Insurance
   Primary Insurance Name: TRICARE
   Address: PO BOX 555
   City: TRICITY
   State: SC
   Zip/4: 76654-0555

   Plan ID#: 562356989
   Group #:
   Policyholder: LEWIS, TERRY
   Address: 9 RANDOLPH ROAD
   City: ANYWHERE
   State: NY
   Zip/4: 12345-1234
   Policyholder Date of Birth: 05   05   1986
   Pt Relationship to Insured: Self X Spouse   Child   Other
   Employer/School Name: US NAVY

Secondary Insurance
   Secondary Insurance Name:
   Address:
   City:
   State:
   Zip/4:

   Plan ID#:
   Group #:
   Policyholder:
   Address:
   City:
   State:
   Zip/4:
   Policyholder Date of Birth:
   Pt Relationship to Insured: Self   Spouse   Child   Other
   Employer/School Name:

ENCOUNTER INFORMATION:
Place of Service: 11

DIAGNOSIS INFORMATION

	Code	Diagnosis		Code	Diagnosis
1.	300 . 00	Anxiety	5.	.	
2.	.		6.	.	
3.	.		7.	.	
4.	.		8.	.	

PROCEDURE INFORMATION

Description of Procedure/Service	Dates	Code	Mod	Dx Order	Unit Charge	Days/ Units
1. Office visit, est visit, level II	06 19 YY⁻	99212		1	35 00	1
2.	⁻					
3.	⁻					
4.	⁻					
5.	⁻					
6.	⁻					

Special Notes:

CASE STUDY 1-17

Mary Parker

ANGELA DILALIO MD
99 PROVIDER DRIVE
INJURY NY 12347
101   2014321

Patient Number: 1-17

EIN: 111982342   **NPI:**   4567890123

PATIENT INFORMATION:
Name: PARKER, MARY
Address: 15 MAIN STREET
City: ANYWHERE
State: NY
Zip/4: 12345-1234
Telephone: 101 5555658

Gender: M   F X
Status: Single   Married X   Other
Date of Birth: 06   06   1975
Employer: WORLD UNIVERSITY
Student: FT   PT   School:

Work Related?   Y   N X
Employment Related?   Y   N X
Other Accident: Y   N X
Date of Accident:

Referring Physician:
Address:
Telephone:
NPI #:

INSURANCE INFORMATION:
Primary Insurance
   Primary Insurance Name: AETNA
   Address: PO BOX 45
   City: STILLWATER
   State: PA
   Zip/4: 12345-0045

   Plan ID#: 562156
   Group #:
   Policyholder: PARKER, MARY
   Address: 15 MAIN STREET
   City: ANYWHERE
   State: NY
   Zip/4: 12345-1234
   Policyholder Date of Birth: 06   06   1975
   Pt Relationship to Insured: Self X Spouse   Child   Other
   Employer/School Name: WORLD UNIVERSITY

Secondary Insurance
   Secondary Insurance Name: TRICARE
   Address: PO BOX 555
   City: TRICITY
   State: SC
   Zip/4: 76654-0555

   Plan ID#: 23562598
   Group #:
   Policyholder: PARKER, MARK
   Address: USS EISENHOWER
   City: FPO
   State: AE
   Zip/4: 11600-3982
   Policyholder Date of Birth: 04   30   1970
   Pt Relationship to Insured: Self   Spouse X Child   Other
   Employer/School Name: US NAVY

ENCOUNTER INFORMATION:
Place of Service: 11

DIAGNOSIS INFORMATION

	Code	Diagnosis		Code	Diagnosis
1.	493 .90	Asthma	5.	.	
2.	.		6.	.	
3.	.		7.	.	
4.	.		8.	.	

PROCEDURE INFORMATION

Description of Procedure/Service	Dates	Code	Mod	Dx Order	Unit Charge	Days/ Units
1. Office visit, est visit, level II	06 19 YY⁻	99212		1	35 00	1
2.	⁻					
3.	⁻					
4.	⁻					
5.	⁻					
6.	⁻					

Special Notes: Mark Parker is stationed on the USS Eisenhower. FPO AE 11600-3982.
   Update: Aetna paid $10.00.

CASE STUDY 1-18

Iona J. Million

ANGELA DILALIO MD
99 PROVIDER DRIVE
INJURY NY 12347
101   2014321

Patient Number: 1-18

EIN: 111982342   **NPI:**   4567890123

PATIENT INFORMATION:
Name: MILLION, IONA, J
Address: 100A PASTURES COURT
City: ANYWHERE
State: NY
Zip/4: 12345-1234
Telephone: 101 7590839

Gender: M   F X
Status: Single   Married X   **Other**
Date of Birth: 01   01   1970
Employer: ANYWHERE GOLF COURSE
Student: FT   PT   School:

Work Related?   Y X **N**
Employment Related?   Y   **N** X
Other Accident: Y   **N** X
Date of Accident:

Referring Physician:
Address:
Telephone:
NPI #:

INSURANCE INFORMATION:
Primary Insurance
   Primary Insurance Name: HIGH RISK INSURANCE
   Address: 22 RISKY PROVIDER STREET
   City: RISKERTON
   State: IN
   Zip/4: 90909

   Plan ID#: 235568956
   Group #: 10173
   Policyholder: ANYWHERE GOLF COURSE
   Address: ROUTE 20
   City: GOLF
   State: NY
   Zip/4: 12348-1234
   Policyholder Date of Birth:
   Pt Relationship to Insured: Self   Spouse   Child   Other X
   Employer/School Name: ANYWHERE GOLF COURSE

Secondary Insurance
   Secondary Insurance Name:
   Address:
   City:
   State:
   Zip/4:

   Plan ID#:
   Group #:
   Policyholder:
   Address:
   City:
   State:
   Zip/4:
   Policyholder Date of Birth:
   Pt Relationship to Insured: Self   Spouse   Child   Other
   Employer/School Name:

ENCOUNTER INFORMATION:
Place of Service: 22

DIAGNOSIS INFORMATION

	Code	Diagnosis		Code	Diagnosis
1.	V54 .01	Retained hardware	5.	.	
2.	V45 .89	Status post fracture surgery	6.	.	
3.	719 .47	Pain, healed fracture site, lt ankle	7.	.	
4.	905 .4	Late eff of path fracture, lt ankle	8.	.	

PROCEDURE INFORMATION

Description of Procedure/Service	Dates	Code	Mod	Dx Order	Unit Charge	Days/ Units
1. Rem. intrnl fix device, lt ankle, deep	03 10 YY⁻	20680	LT	1234	650 00	1
2.	⁻					
3.	⁻					
4.	⁻					
5.	⁻					
6.	⁻					

Special Notes: Hospital info: Goodmedicine Hospital, 1 Provider St, Anywhere, NY 12345, NPI: 1123456789.
   DOI: 09/08/YYYY. Pt may return to work 04/01/YYYY. Admission/Discharge date: 03/10/YYYY.
   Patient's SSN is 235-56-8956.

CASE STUDY 1-19

Mike R. Scope

ANGELA DILALIO MD
99 PROVIDER DRIVE
INJURY NY 12347
101   2014321

Patient Number: 1-19

EIN: 111982342   **NPI:** 4567890123

PATIENT INFORMATION:
Name: SCOPE, MIKE, R
Address: 5 SPRUCE STREET
City: NOWHERE
State: NY
Zip/4: 12346-1234
Telephone: 101 1135567

Gender: M X   F
Status: Single X   Married   Other
Date of Birth: 06   20   1972
Employer: BIO LABS
Student: FT   PT   School:

Work Related?   Y X N
Employment Related?   Y   N X
Other Accident: Y   N X
Date of Accident: 03   12   YYYY

Referring Physician:
Address:
Telephone:
NPI #:

INSURANCE INFORMATION:
Primary Insurance
    Primary Insurance Name: HIGH RISK INSURANCE
    Address: 22 RISKY PROVIDER STREET
    City: RISKERTON
    State: IN
    Zip/4: 90909

    Plan ID#: 356898459
    Group #:
    Policyholder: BIO LABS
    Address: 10 LABORATORY COURT
    City: NOWHERE
    State: NY
    Zip/4: 12346-1234
    Policyholder Date of Birth:
    Pt Relationship to Insured: Self   Spouse   Child   Other X
    Employer/School Name: BIO LABS

Secondary Insurance
    Secondary Insurance Name:
    Address:
    City:
    State:
    Zip/4:

    Plan ID#:
    Group #:
    Policyholder:
    Address:
    City:
    State:
    Zip/4:
    Policyholder Date of Birth:
    Pt Relationship to Insured: Self   Spouse   Child   Other
    Employer/School Name:

ENCOUNTER INFORMATION:
Place of Service: 11

DIAGNOSIS INFORMATION

	Code	Diagnosis		Code	Diagnosis
1.	847.0	Cervical strain	5.	.	
2.	847.2	Low back strain	6.	.	
3.	E888.9	Accident at work	7.	.	
4.	E849.3		8.	.	

PROCEDURE INFORMATION

Description of Procedure/Service	Dates	Code	Mod	Dx Order	Unit Charge	Days/ Units
1. Office visit, est pt, level II	03 20 YY⁻	99212		1	26 00	1
2.	⁻					
3.	⁻					
4.	⁻					
5.	⁻					
6.	⁻					

Special Notes: Onset of illness 03/12/YYYY. Discharge home. Patient's SSN: 356-89-8459.

CASE STUDY 1-20

Jim Gallo

ANGELA DILALIO MD
99 PROVIDER DRIVE
INJURY NY 12347
101   2014321

Patient Number: 1-20

EIN: 111982342   **NPI:**   4567890123

PATIENT INFORMATION:
Name: GALLO, JIM
Address: 115 GLENN STREET
City: ANYWHERE
State: NY
Zip/4: 12345-1234
Telephone: 101 5558457

Gender: M X   F
Status: Single X   Married   Other
Date of Birth: 05   02   1975
Employer: WORLD UNIVERSITY
Student: FT   PT   School:

Work Related?   Y X N
Employment Related?   Y   N X
Other Accident: Y   N X
Date of Accident: 02   15   YYYY

Referring Physician:
Address:
Telephone:
NPI #:

INSURANCE INFORMATION:
Primary Insurance
    Primary Insurance Name: HIGH RISK INSURANCE
    Address: 22 RISKY PROVIDER STREET
    City: RISKERTON
    State: IN
    Zip/4: 90909

    Plan ID#: 467909560
    Group #: 10225
    Policyholder: WORLD UNIVERSITY
    Address: COLLEGE DRIVE
    City: ANYWHERE
    State: NY
    Zip/4: 12345
    Policyholder Date of Birth:
    Pt Relationship to Insured: Self   Spouse   Child   Other X
    Employer/School Name: WORLD UNIVERSITY

Secondary Insurance
    Secondary Insurance Name:
    Address:
    City:
    State:
    Zip/4:

    Plan ID#:
    Group #:
    Policyholder:
    Address:
    City:
    State:
    Zip/4:
    Policyholder Date of Birth:
    Pt Relationship to Insured: Self   Spouse   Child   Other
    Employer/School Name:

ENCOUNTER INFORMATION:
Place of Service: 11

DIAGNOSIS INFORMATION

	Code	Diagnosis		Code	Diagnosis
1.	724 .8	Muscle spasms, back	5.	.	
2.	E888 .9	Accidental fall at work	6.	.	
3.	E849 .3	Place of occurrence, industrial	7.	.	
4.	.		8.	.	

PROCEDURE INFORMATION

	Description of Procedure/Service	Dates	Code	Mod	Dx Order	Unit Charge	Days/ Units
1.	Office visit, est pt, level II	02 15 YY⁻	99212		1	35 00	1
2.		-					
3.		-					
4.		-					
5.		-					
6.		-					

Special Notes: Onset of illnes 02/15/YYYY. Return to work 02/21/YYYY. Patient's SSN: 467-90-9560

Case Studies: Set Two

NOTE: With the tenth edition of UHI, Case Studies: Set Two contain codes, which serves to facilitate claims entry in *SimClaim*. Students are provided with additional coding practice in the *Workbook to Accompany Understanding Health Insurance* where codes are <u>not</u> included in the case studies.

GENERAL INSTRUCTIONS AND HINTS FOR SET TWO CASE STUDIES (2-1 THROUGH 2-20)

The case studies in Appendix II provide practice completing CMS-1500 claims for physicians who practice at the Goodmedicine Clinic, which is a medical group practice. (A *medical group practice* consists of three or more physicians who enter into a formal agreement to provide single-specialty or multi-specialty health care services. They jointly share the use of equipment and personnel, and income generated from the practice is distributed according to a predetermined formula.)

Be sure to make special note of the following information prior to completing Case Studies 2-1 through 2-20:

- Unlike the claims in Set One, the provider and practice information is NOT always the same for the cases in Set Two. All the providers in this set are members of the practice, "Goodmedicine Clinic." As such, the information in Block 33, should reflect the practice name, while the information in Block 31 should reflect the actual service provider.
- All EIN and NPI information needed to complete each CMS-1500 claim is provided on each case study.
- When Goodmedicine Hospital is the place of service, the address and NPI are listed in the Special Notes on the case study and should be entered in Block 32.
- All providers participate in all payer plans; therefore, enter an X in the Yes box of Block 27.
- Table II-1 contains place of service (POS) codes reported in Block 24B of the CMS-1500 claim.
- Table II-2 contains the list of Case Studies Set Two according to payer.
- Please remember that services for only one place of service or one provider may be completed on a CMS-1500 claim. In those instances where services are provided by more than one physician or at more than one location, two separate CMS-1500 claims will need to be completed.
- Note that the physician who performed the service should be recorded in the following blocks:

Block 24J:	NPI for providing physician
Block 25:	EIN for providing physician
Block 31:	Providing physician name

- Note that the billing provider should be entered in Blocks 33 and 33A.

TABLE II-1   Place of service codes for CMS-1500 claim, Block 24B

CODE	DESCRIPTION	CODE	DESCRIPTION
01	Pharmacy	34	Hospice
02	Unassigned	35-40	Unassigned
03	School	41	Ambulance—Land
04	Homeless Shelter	42	Ambulance—Air or Water
05	Indian Health Service Free-standing Facility	43-48	Unassigned
06	Indian Health Service Provider-based Facility	49	Independent Clinic
07	Tribal 638 Free-standing Facility	50	Federally Qualified Health Center
08	Tribal 638 Provider-based Facility	51	Inpatient Psychiatric Facility
09	Prison Correctional Facility	52	Psychiatric Facility—Partial Hospitalization
10	Unassigned	53	Community Mental Health Center
11	Office	54	Intermediate Care Facility/Mentally Retarded
12	Home	55	Residential Substance Abuse Treatment Facility
13	Assisted Living Facility	56	Psychiatric Residential Treatment Facility
14	Group Home	57	Nonresidential Substance Abuse Treatment Facility
15	Mobile Unit	58-59	Unassigned
16-19	Unassigned	60	Mass Immunization Center
20	Urgent Care Facility	61	Comprehensive Inpatient Rehabilitation Facility
21	Inpatient Hospital	62	Comprehensive Outpatient Rehabilitation Facility
22	Outpatient Hospital	63-64	Unassigned
23	Emergency Room—Hospital	65	End-Stage Renal Disease Treatment Facility
24	Ambulatory Surgical Center	66-70	Unassigned
25	Birthing Center	71	Public Health Clinic
26	Military Treatment Facility	72	Rural Health Clinic
27-30	Unassigned	73-80	Unassigned
31	Skilled Nursing Facility	81	Independent Laboratory
32	Nursing Facility	82-98	Unassigned
33	Custodial Care Facility	99	Other Place of Service

TABLE II-2   List of cases according to payer for Case Studies: Set Two

CASE	PAYER	CASE	PAYER
2-1	Commercial	2-11	Medicaid
2-2	Commercial	2-12	Medicaid
2-3	Commercial	2-13	TRICARE
2-4	Blue Cross Blue Shield	2-14	Commercial/TRICARE
2-5	Blue Cross Blue Shield	2-15	Workers' Compensation
2-6	Medicare	2-16	Commercial
2-7	Medicare	2-17	TRICARE
2-8	Medicare/Medigap	2-18	TRICARE
2-9	Medicare	2-19	Medicare/Medicaid
2-10	Medicare/Medigap	2-20	Blue Cross Blue Shield

CASE STUDY 2-1

GOODMEDICINE CLINIC
1 PROVIDER STREET
ANYWHERE NY 12345
101 1112222

Patient Number: 2-1

EIN: 221234567   **NPI:** 3345678901

PATIENT INFORMATION:
Name: RAUL, JOSE, X
Address: 10 MAIN STREET
City: ANYWHERE
State: NY
Zip/4: 12345-1234
Telephone: 101 1115454

Gender: M X   F
Status: Single X   Married   Other
Date of Birth: 01 01 1968
Employer: ANYWHERE TELEPHONE COMPANY
Student: FT   PT   **School:**

Work Related?   Y   N X
Employment Related?   Y   N X
Other Accident: Y   N X
Date of Accident:

Referring Physician: IM GOODDOC MD
Address:
Telephone:
NPI #: 5678901234

INSURANCE INFORMATION:
Primary Insurance
   Primary Insurance Name: BELL ATLANTIC
   Address: 100 PROVIDER ROW
   City: ANYWHERE
   State: NY
   Zip/4: 12345-9597

   Plan ID#: 222304040
   Group #: MD1
   Policyholder: RAUL, JOSE, X
   Address: 10 MAIN STREET
   City: ANYWHERE
   State: NY
   Zip/4: 12345-1234
   Policyholder Date of Birth: 01 01 1968
   Pt Relationship to Insured: Self X **Spouse   Child   Other**
   Employer/School Name: ANYWHERE TELEPHONE COMPANY

Secondary Insurance
   Secondary Insurance Name:
   Address:
   City:
   State:
   Zip/4:

   Plan ID#:
   Group #:
   Policyholder:
   Address:
   City:
   State:
   Zip/4:
   Policyholder Date of Birth:
   Pt Relationship to Insured: Self   Spouse   Child   Other
   Employer/School Name:

ENCOUNTER INFORMATION:
Place of Service: 11

DIAGNOSIS INFORMATION

	Code	Diagnosis		Code	Diagnosis
1.	789.35	Periumbilic Mass	5.	.	
2.	569.3	Rectal bleeding/hemorrhage	6.	.	
3.	.		7.	.	
4.	.		8.	.	

PROCEDURE INFORMATION

Description of Procedure/Service	Dates	Code	Mod	Dx Order	Unit Charge	Days/ Units
1. Consultation, office, level 3	06 20 YY¯	99243		12	100 00	1
2.	¯					
3.	¯					
4.	¯					
5.	¯					
6.	¯					

Special Notes: Referring Physician IM Gooddoc, MD, NPI: 5678901234
   Provider: Henry C. Cardiac, MD, NPI: 3456789012

CASE STUDY 2-2

GOODMEDICINE CLINIC
1 PROVIDER STREET
ANYWHERE NY 12345
101 1112222

Patient Number: 2-2

EIN: 221234567   **NPI:** 3345678901

PATIENT INFORMATION:
Name: MOUTAINE, KAY
Address: 634 GOODVIEW AVENUE
City: ANYWHERE
State: NY
Zip/4: 12345-1234
Telephone: 101 1151234

Gender: M   F X
Status: Single   Married X   Other
Date of Birth: 03 04 1952
Employer:
Student: FT   PT   School:

Work Related?   Y   N X
Employment Related?   Y   N X
Other Accident: Y   N X
Date of Accident:

Referring Physician:
Address:
Telephone:
NPI #:

INSURANCE INFORMATION:
Primary Insurance
  Primary Insurance Name: CONNECTICUT GENERAL
  Address: PO BOX 1234
  City: HEALTH
  State: CT
  Zip/4: 01234-1234

  Plan ID#: 877345567
  Group #: V143
  Policyholder: MOUTAINE, CHARLES, W
  Address: 634 GOODVIEW AVENUE
  City: ANYWHERE
  State: NY
  Zip/4: 12345-1234
  Policyholder Date of Birth: 03 04 1952
  Pt Relationship to Insured: Self   Spouse X Child   Other
  Employer/School Name: GENERAL ELECTRIC

Secondary Insurance
  Secondary Insurance Name:
  Address:
  City:
  State:
  Zip/4:

  Plan ID#:
  Group #:
  Policyholder:
  Address:
  City:
  State:
  Zip/4:
  Policyholder Date of Birth:
  Pt Relationship to Insured: Self   Spouse   Child   Other
  Employer/School Name:

ENCOUNTER INFORMATION:
Place of Service: 11

DIAGNOSIS INFORMATION

	Code	Diagnosis		Code	Diagnosis
1.	345.40	Epilepsy, temporal lobe	5.	.	
2.	346.90	Migraine, NOS	6.	.	
3.	493.90	Asthma NOS	7.	.	
4.	477.9	Allergic sinusitis	8.	.	

PROCEDURE INFORMATION

Description of Procedure/Service	Dates	Code	Mod	Dx Order	Unit Charge	Days/ Units
1. Office Visit, new patient, level 3	06 20 YY⁻	99203		1234	75 00	1
2.	⁻					
3.	⁻					
4.	⁻					
5.	⁻					
6.	⁻					

Special Notes: Insurance through spouse's employer. Return visit as needed. Pt paid $30 on total.
  Physician: Henry C. Cardiac MD, NPI: 3456789012

CASE STUDY 2-3

GOODMEDICINE CLINIC
1 PROVIDER STREET
ANYWHERE NY 12345
101 1112222

Patient Number: 2-3

EIN: 331234567   **NPI:**   3345678901

PATIENT INFORMATION:
Name: PING, CHANG, L
Address: 100 CHRISTA STREET
City: INJURY
State: NY
Zip/4: 12347-1234
Telephone: 101 1114545

Gender: M X   F
Status: Single   Married X   Other
Date of Birth: 01   06   1945
Employer:
Student: FT   PT   School:

Work Related?   Y   N X
Employment Related?   Y   N X
Other Accident: Y   N X
Date of Accident:

Referring Physician:
Address:
Telephone:
NPI #:

INSURANCE INFORMATION:
Primary Insurance
   Primary Insurance Name: CONNECTICUT GENERAL
   Address: PO BOX 1234
   City: HEALTH
   State: CT
   Zip/4: 01234-1234

   Plan ID#: 333669999
   Group #: 93939
   Policyholder: PING, SONG
   Address: 100 CHRISTA STREET
   City: INJURY
   State: NY
   Zip/4: 12347-1234
   Policyholder Date of Birth: 06   01   1942
   Pt Relationship to Insured: Self   Spouse X Child   Other
   Employer/School Name: HUNAN INCORPORATED

Secondary Insurance
   Secondary Insurance Name:
   Address:
   City:
   State:
   Zip/4:

   Plan ID#:
   Group #:
   Policyholder:
   Address:
   City:
   State:
   Zip/4:
   Policyholder Date of Birth:
   Pt Relationship to Insured: Self   Spouse   Child   Other
   Employer/School Name:

ENCOUNTER INFORMATION:
Place of Service: 11

DIAGNOSIS INFORMATION

	Code	Diagnosis		Code	Diagnosis
1.	235 .2	Neoplasm,uncertain beh, sigmoid colon	5.	.	
2.	.		6.	.	
3.	.		7.	.	
4.	.		8.	.	

PROCEDURE INFORMATION

Description of Procedure/Service	Dates	Code	Mod	Dx Order	Unit Charge	Days/ Units
1. Office visit, new patient, Level 3	06 14 YY⁻	99203	57	1	75 00	1
2. Prostatectomy, w/ 1-stage colostomy	06 14 YY⁻	45110		1	800 00	1
3.	⁻					
4.	⁻					
5.	⁻					
6.	⁻					

Special Notes: Insurance is through spouse's employer.
   Admitted to Goodmedicine Hospital, 1 Provider Street, Anywhere, NY 12345, NPI: 1123456789.
   Provider: Janet B. Surgeon MD, NPI: 9012345678. Discharged 6-20-YYYY.

CASE STUDY 2-4

GOODMEDICINE CLINIC
1 PROVIDER STREET
ANYWHERE NY 12345
101 1112222

Patient Number: 2-4

EIN: 331234567   **NPI:** 3345678901

PATIENT INFORMATION:
Name: RECALL, JOHN, J
Address: 10 MEMORY LANE
City: ANYWHERE
State: NY
Zip/4: 12345-1234
Telephone: 101 1114444

Gender: M X   F
Status: Single X   Married   Other
Date of Birth: 06   03   1942
Employer: WILL SOLVE IT, INC.
Student: FT   PT   School:

Work Related?   Y   N X
Employment Related?   Y   N X
Other Accident: Y   N X
Date of Accident:

Referring Physician: ARNOLD YOUNGLOVE MD
Address:
Telephone:
NPI #: 0123456789

INSURANCE INFORMATION:
Primary Insurance
   Primary Insurance Name: BLUE CROSS BLUE SHIELD
   Address: PO BOX 1121
   City: MEDICAL
   State: PA
   Zip/4: 12357-1121

   Plan ID#: ZJW55544
   Group #: 650
   Policyholder: RECALL, JOHN, J
   Address: 10 MEMORY LANE
   City: ANYWHERE
   State: NY
   Zip/4: 12345-1234
   Policyholder Date of Birth: 06   03   1942
   Pt Relationship to Insured: Self X Spouse   Child   Other
   Employer/School Name: WILL SOLVE IT, INC.

Secondary Insurance
   Secondary Insurance Name:
   Address:
   City:
   State:
   Zip/4:

   Plan ID#:
   Group #:
   Policyholder:
   Address:
   City:
   State:
   Zip/4:
   Policyholder Date of Birth:
   Pt Relationship to Insured: Self   Spouse   Child   Other
   Employer/School Name:

ENCOUNTER INFORMATION:
Place of Service: 11

DIAGNOSIS INFORMATION

	Code	Diagnosis		Code	Diagnosis
1.	574.10	Cholelith w/chronic cholecystitis	5.	.	
2.	250.00	Diabetes mellitus NOS	6.	.	
3.	414.00	Atherosclerotic Hrt Dz	7.	.	
4.	V45.81	S/P CABG	8.	.	

PROCEDURE INFORMATION

Description of Procedure/Service	Dates	Code	Mod	Dx Order	Unit Charge	Days/ Units
1. Office visit, new patient, Level 3	06 18 YY⁻	99203	57	1234	75 00	1
2. Open cholecystectomy	06 19 YY⁻	47600				
3.	⁻					
4.	⁻					
5.	⁻					
6.	⁻					

Special Notes: Provider: Janet B. Surgeon, MD, NPI: 9012345678
   Admitted to Goodmedicine Hospital, 1 Provider Street, Anywhere, NY 12345, NPI: 1123456789.

CASE STUDY 2-5

GOODMEDICINE CLINIC
1 PROVIDER STREET
ANYWHERE NY 12345
101   1112222

Patient Number: 2-5

EIN: 221234567   **NPI:**   3345678901

PATIENT INFORMATION:
Name: ISLANDER, PHILAMENA
Address: 129 HENRY COURT
City: ANYWHERE
State: NY
Zip/4: 12345-1234
Telephone: 101 1117218

Gender: M   F X
Status: Single   Married X   Other
Date of Birth: 11   21   1953
Employer:
Student: FT   PT   School:

Work Related?   Y   N X
Employment Related?   Y   N X
Other Accident: Y   N X
Date of Accident:

Referring Physician:
Address:
Telephone:
NPI #:

INSURANCE INFORMATION:
Primary Insurance
  Primary Insurance Name: BLUE CROSS BLUE SHIELD
  Address: PO BOX 1121
  City: MEDICAL
  State: PA
  Zip/4: 12357-1121

  Plan ID#: XWJ473655
  Group #: 101
  Policyholder: ISLANDER, RICHARD, T
  Address: 129 HENRY COURT
  City: ANYWHERE
  State: NY
  Zip/4: 12345-1234
  Policyholder Date of Birth: 02   11   1952
  Pt Relationship to Insured: Self   Spouse X **Child   Other**
  Employer/School Name: WONDERFUL PHOTOS

Secondary Insurance
  Secondary Insurance Name:
  Address:
  City:
  State:
  Zip/4:

  Plan ID#:
  Group #:
  Policyholder:
  Address:
  City:
  State:
  Zip/4:
  Policyholder Date of Birth:
  Pt Relationship to Insured: Self   Spouse   Child   Other
  Employer/School Name:

ENCOUNTER INFORMATION:
Place of Service: 11

DIAGNOSIS INFORMATION

	Code	Diagnosis		Code	Diagnosis
1.	565 . 0	Anal fissure	5.	.	
2.	.		6.	.	
3.	.		7.	.	
4.	.		8.	.	

PROCEDURE INFORMATION

Description of Procedure/Service	Dates	Code	Mod	Dx Order	Unit Charge	Days/ Units
1. Office visit, est patient, level 2	06 20 YY¯	99212	25	1	50 00	1
2. Anoscopy w/ bx	06 20 YY¯	46606		1	100 00	1
3.	¯					
4.	¯					
5.	¯					
6.	¯					

Special Notes: Insurance through employer. Provider: Henry C. Cardiac MD, NPI: 3456789012

CASE STUDY 2-6

GOODMEDICINE CLINIC
1 PROVIDER STREET
ANYWHERE NY 12345
101 1112222

Patient Number: 2-6

EIN: 441234567   **NPI:** 3345678901

PATIENT INFORMATION:
Name: SUGAR, IMOGENE
Address: 120 YOUNG STREET
City: INJURY
State: NY
Zip/4: 12347-1234
Telephone: 101 1118675

Gender: **M**   F X
Status: Single X   **Married**   **Other**
Date of Birth: 03   09   1924
Employer:
Student: FT   **PT**   **School:**

Work Related?   **Y**   **N** X
Employment Related?   **Y**   **N** X
Other Accident: **Y**   **N** X
Date of Accident:

Referring Physician:
Address:
Telephone:
NPI #:

INSURANCE INFORMATION:
Primary Insurance
    Primary Insurance Name: MEDICARE
    Address: PO BOX 9929
    City: BOXBURY
    State: MD
    Zip/4: 45678-9929

    Plan ID#: 77722888W
    Group #:
    Policyholder: SUGAR, IMOGENE
    Address: 120 YOUNG STREET
    City: INJURY
    State: NY
    Zip/4: 12347-1234
    Policyholder Date of Birth: 03   09   1924
    Pt Relationship to Insured: Self X **Spouse**   **Child**   **Other**
    Employer/School Name:

Secondary Insurance
    Secondary Insurance Name:
    Address:
    City:
    State:
    Zip/4:

    Plan ID#:
    Group #:
    Policyholder:
    Address:
    City:
    State:
    Zip/4:
    Policyholder Date of Birth:
    Pt Relationship to Insured: Self   Spouse   Child   Other
    Employer/School Name:

ENCOUNTER INFORMATION:
Place of Service: 12

DIAGNOSIS INFORMATION

	Code	Diagnosis		Code	Diagnosis
1.	250 . 73	DMI w/peripheral neuropathy	**5.**	.	
2.	443 . 9	Peripheral vascular disease	**6.**	.	
3.	V49 . 73	S/P amputation, metatarsal/foot	**7.**	.	
4.	.		**8.**	.	

PROCEDURE INFORMATION

	Description of Procedure/Service	Dates	Code	Mod	Dx Order	Unit Charge	Days/ Units
1.	Home visit, est patient, level 2	06 20 YY¯	99348		123	45 00	1
2.		¯					
3.		¯					
4.		¯					
5.		¯					
6.		¯					

Special Notes: Home visit was performed at patient's home address.
   Provider: Nancy J. Healer MD, NPI: 6789012345.

CASE STUDY 2-7

GOODMEDICINE CLINIC
1 PROVIDER STREET
ANYWHERE NY 12345
101 1112222

Patient Number: 2-7

EIN: 221234567   **NPI:** 3345678901

PATIENT INFORMATION:
Name: GONZALES, ESAU
Address: 14 RIDLEY STREET
City: NOWHERE
State: NY
Zip/4: 12346-1234
Telephone: 101 1117689

Gender: M X   F
Status: Single X   Married   Other
Date of Birth: 09 10 1933
Employer:
Student: FT   PT   School:

Work Related? Y   N X
Employment Related? Y   N X
Other Accident: Y   N X
Date of Accident:

Referring Physician:
Address:
Telephone:
NPI #:

INSURANCE INFORMATION:
Primary Insurance
   Primary Insurance Name: MEDICARE
   Address: PO BOX 9929
   City: BOXBURY
   State: MD
   Zip/4: 45678-9929

   Plan ID#: 101234591A
   Group #:
   Policyholder: GONZALES, ESAU
   Address: 14 RIDLEY STREET
   City: NOWHERE
   State: NY
   Zip/4: 12346-1234
   Policyholder Date of Birth: 09 10 1933
   Pt Relationship to Insured: Self X Spouse   Child   Other
   Employer/School Name:

Secondary Insurance
   Secondary Insurance Name:
   Address:
   City:
   State:
   Zip/4:

   Plan ID#:
   Group #:
   Policyholder:
   Address:
   City:
   State:
   Zip/4:
   Policyholder Date of Birth:
   Pt Relationship to Insured: Self   Spouse   Child   Other
   Employer/School Name:

ENCOUNTER INFORMATION:
Place of Service: 11

DIAGNOSIS INFORMATION

	Code	Diagnosis		Code	Diagnosis
1.	786.09	Dyspnea	5.	.	
2.	401.9	Hypertension	6.	.	
3.	272.4	Hypercholesterolemia	7.	.	
4.	V45.81	S/P bypass graft	8.	.	

PROCEDURE INFORMATION

Description of Procedure/Service	Dates	Code	Mod	Dx Order	Unit Charge	Days/ Units
1. Office visit, est patient, level 4	06 20 YY⁻	99214		1234	100 00	1
2. EKG w/ interpretation	06 20 YY⁻	93000		14	65 00	1
3.	⁻					
4.	⁻					
5.	⁻					
6.	⁻					

Special Notes: Provider: Henry C. Cardiac MD, NPI: 3456789012

CASE STUDY 2-8

GOODMEDICINE CLINIC
1 PROVIDER STREET
ANYWHERE NY 12345
101   1112222

Patient Number: 2-8

EIN: 441234567   **NPI:**   3345678901

PATIENT INFORMATION:
Name: BUSH, MARY, B
Address: 9910 WILLIAMS ROAD
City: NOWHERE
State: NY
Zip/4: 12346-1234
Telephone: 101 1119922

Gender: M   F X
Status: Single X   Married   Other
Date of Birth: 04   01   1930
Employer:
Student: FT   PT   School:

Work Related?   Y   N X
Employment Related? Y   N X
Other Accident: Y   N X
Date of Accident:

Referring Physician:
Address:
Telephone:
NPI #:

INSURANCE INFORMATION:
Primary Insurance
   Primary Insurance Name: MEDICARE
   Address: PO BOX 9929
   City: BOXBURY
   State: MD
   Zip/4: 45678-9929

   Plan ID#: 071269645B
   Group #:
   Policyholder: BUSH, MARY, B
   Address: 9910 WILLIAMS ROAD
   City: NOWHERE
   State: NY
   Zip/4: 12346-1234
   Policyholder Date of Birth: 04   01   1930
   Pt Relationship to Insured: Self X **Spouse   Child   Other**
   Employer/School Name:

Secondary Insurance
   Secondary Insurance Name: CIGNA MEDIGAP
   Address: PO BOX 212
   City: BALTIMORE
   State: MD
   Zip/4: 45678-0212

   Plan ID#: 9912345678
   Group #:
   Policyholder: BUSH, MARY, B
   Address: 9910 WILLIAMS ROAD
   City: NOWHERE
   State: NY
   Zip/4: 12346-1234
   Policyholder Date of Birth: 04   01   1930
   Pt Relationship to Insured: Self X **Spouse   Child   Other**
   Employer/School Name:

ENCOUNTER INFORMATION:
Place of Service: 11

DIAGNOSIS INFORMATION

	Code	Diagnosis		Code	Diagnosis
1.	345 .90	Seizure disorder	5.	.	
2.	.		6.	.	
3.	.		7.	.	
4.	.		8.	.	

PROCEDURE INFORMATION

Description of Procedure/Service	Dates	Code	Mod	Dx Order	Unit Charge	Days/ Units
1. Office visit, est patient, level 4	06 20 YY-	99214		1	100 00	1
2.	-					
3.	-					
4.	-					
5.	-					
6.	-					

Special Notes: Provider Nancy J. Healer MD, NPI: 6789012345
   Note: deductible not met--no payment.

CASE STUDY 2-9

GOODMEDICINE CLINIC
1 PROVIDER STREET
ANYWHERE NY 12345
101   1112222

Patient Number: 2-9

EIN: 551234567   **NPI:**   3345678901

PATIENT INFORMATION:
Name: CADILLAC, MARY, A
Address: 500 CARR STREET
City: ANYWHERE
State: NY
Zip/4: 12345-1234
Telephone: 101 2223333

Gender: **M**   F X
Status: Single X   **Married**   **Other**
Date of Birth: 04   30   1929
Employer:
Student: FT   PT   **School:**

Work Related?   Y   N X
Employment Related?   Y   N X
Other Accident: Y   N X
Date of Accident:

Referring Physician:
Address:
Telephone:
NPI #:

INSURANCE INFORMATION:
Primary Insurance
    Primary Insurance Name: MEDICARE
    Address: PO BOX 9929
    City: BOXBURY
    State: MD
    Zip/4: 45678-9929

    Plan ID#:   001266811B
    Group #:
    Policyholder: CADILLAC, MARY, A
    Address: 500 CARR STREET
    City: ANYWHERE
    State: NY
    Zip/4: 12345-1234
    Policyholder Date of Birth: 04   30   1929
    Pt Relationship to Insured: Self X **Spouse**   **Child**   **Other**
    Employer/School Name:

Secondary Insurance
    Secondary Insurance Name:
    Address:
    City:
    State:
    Zip/4:

    Plan ID#:
    Group #:
    Policyholder:
    Address:
    City:
    State:
    Zip/4:
    Policyholder Date of Birth:
    Pt Relationship to Insured: Self   **Spouse**   **Child**   **Other**
    Employer/School Name:

ENCOUNTER INFORMATION:
Place of Service: 22

DIAGNOSIS INFORMATION

	Code	Diagnosis		Code	Diagnosis
1.	574 . 10	Cholelith w/chronic cholecystititis	5.	.	
2.	573 . 8	Liver nodules	6.	.	
3.	.		7.	.	
4.	.		8.	.	

PROCEDURE INFORMATION

Description of Procedure/Service	Dates	Code	Mod	Dx Order	Unit Charge	Days/ Units
1. Lap cholecystectomy w/intraop cholangio	06 20 YY⁻	47563		1	1350 00	1
2. Percut needle liver bx	06 20 YY⁻	47001	51	2	100 00	1
3.	⁻					
4.	⁻					
5.	⁻					
6.	⁻					

Special Notes: Outpatient surgery at Goodmedicine Hospital, 1 Provider St, Anywhere NY 12345, NPI: 1123456789.
   Provider: TJ Stitcher, MD, NPI: 8901234567

CASE STUDY 2-10

GOODMEDICINE CLINIC
1 PROVIDER STREET
ANYWHERE NY 12345
101   1112222

Patient Number: 2-10

EIN: 551234567   **NPI:**   3345678901

PATIENT INFORMATION:
Name: HAMMERCLAW, JOHN, W
Address: 111 LUMBER STREET
City: ANYWHERE
State: NY
Zip/4: 12345-1234
Telephone: 101 1119191

Gender: M X   F
Status: Single X   Married   Other
Date of Birth: 05   30   1930
Employer:
Student: FT   PT   School:

Work Related?   Y   N X
Employment Related? Y   N X
Other Accident: Y   N X
Date of Accident:

Referring Physician: NANCY J HEALER MD
Address:
Telephone:
NPI #:   6789012345

INSURANCE INFORMATION:
Primary Insurance
    Primary Insurance Name: MEDICARE
    Address: PO BOX 9929
    City: BOXBURY
    State: MD
    Zip/4: 45678-9929

    Plan ID#:   101101010A
    Group #:
    Policyholder: HAMMERCLAW, JOHN, W
    Address: 111 LUMBER STREET
    City: ANYWHERE
    State: NY
    Zip/4: 12345-1234
    Policyholder Date of Birth: 05   30   1930
    Pt Relationship to Insured: Self X Spouse   Child   Other
    Employer/School Name:

Secondary Insurance
    Secondary Insurance Name: MEDIGAP
    Address: PO BOX 212
    City: BALTIMORE
    State: MD
    Zip/4: 45678-0212

    Plan ID#: 8812345678
    Group #: YXW10110
    Policyholder: HAMMERCLAW, JOHN, W
    Address: 111 LUMBER STREET
    City: ANYWHERE
    State: NY
    Zip/4: 12345-1234
    Policyholder Date of Birth: 05   30   1930
    Pt Relationship to Insured: Self X Spouse   Child   Other
    Employer/School Name:

ENCOUNTER INFORMATION:
Place of Service: 11

DIAGNOSIS INFORMATION

	Code	Diagnosis		Code	Diagnosis
1.	706 .2	Sebaceous cyst	5.	.	
2.	.		6.	.	
3.	.		7.	.	
4.	.		8.	.	

PROCEDURE INFORMATION

Description of Procedure/Service	Dates	Code	Mod	Dx Order	Unit Charge	Days/ Units
1. Exc ben lesion, back, >4.0 cm	06 20 YY⁻	11406		1	360 00	1
2. Exc ben lesion, neck, 2.5 cm	06 20 YY⁻	11423	51	1	300 00	1
3.	—					
4.	—					
5.	—					
6.	—					

Special Notes: Referring physician: Nancy J Healer MD, NPI: 6789012345.
Provider: TJ Stitcher, MD, NPI: 8901234567.
Note: Deductible not met.

CASE STUDY 2-11

GOODMEDICINE CLINIC
1 PROVIDER STREET
ANYWHERE NY 12345
101   1112222

Patient Number: 2-11

EIN: 221234567   **NPI:** 3345678901

PATIENT INFORMATION:
Name: FONTAINE, GERMANE
Address: 132 CANAL STREET
City: INJURY
State: NY
Zip/4: 12347-1234
Telephone: 101 1119685

Gender: M   F X
Status: Single X   **Married   Other**
Date of Birth: 05   07   1965
Employer:
Student: FT   PT   School:

Work Related?   **Y   N** X
Employment Related?   **Y   N** X
Other Accident: **Y   N** X
Date of Accident:

Referring Physician:
Address:
Telephone:
NPI #:

INSURANCE INFORMATION:
Primary Insurance
    Primary Insurance Name: MEDICAID
    Address: PO BOX 9900
    City: NEW YORK
    State: NY
    Zip/4: 12300-9900

    Plan ID#: 11347765
    Group #:
    Policyholder: FONTAINE, GERMANE
    Address: 132 CANAL STREET
    City: INJURY
    State: NY
    Zip/4: 12347-1234
    Policyholder Date of Birth: 05   07   1965
    Pt Relationship to Insured: Self X **Spouse   Child   Other**
    Employer/School Name:

Secondary Insurance
    Secondary Insurance Name:
    Address:
    City:
    State:
    Zip/4:

    Plan ID#:
    Group #:
    Policyholder:
    Address:
    City:
    State:
    Zip/4:
    Policyholder Date of Birth:
    Pt Relationship to Insured: Self   Spouse   Child   Other
    Employer/School Name:

ENCOUNTER INFORMATION:
Place of Service: 11

DIAGNOSIS INFORMATION

	Code	Diagnosis		Code	Diagnosis
1.	473 .9	Chronic sinusitis	5.	.	
2.	462 .	Pharyngitis	6.	.	
3.	.		7.	.	
4.	.		8.	.	

PROCEDURE INFORMATION

Description of Procedure/Service	Dates	Code	Mod	Dx Order	Unit Charge	Days/ Units
1. Office visit, level 2	06 20 YY¯	99212		12	26 00	1
2. Strep screen	06 20 YY¯	87430		2	12 00	1
3.	¯					
4.	¯					
5.	¯					
6.	¯					

Special Notes: Provider: Henry C. Cardiac MD, NPI: 3456789012.

CASE STUDY 2-12

GOODMEDICINE CLINIC
1 PROVIDER STREET
ANYWHERE NY 12345
101   1112222

Patient Number: 2-12

EIN: 221234567   **NPI:** 3345678901

PATIENT INFORMATION:
Name: APPLE, JAMES
Address: 1 APPLEBLOSSOM COURT
City: HOMETOWN
State: NY
Zip/4: 15123-1234
Telephone: 201 1112011

Gender: M X   F
Status: Single X   Married   Other
Date of Birth: 11   12   1984
Employer:
Student: FT   PT   School:

Work Related?   Y   N X
Employment Related?   Y   N X
Other Accident: Y   N X
Date of Accident:

Referring Physician:
Address:
Telephone:
NPI #:

INSURANCE INFORMATION:
Primary Insurance
    Primary Insurance Name: MEDICAID
    Address: PO BOX 9900
    City: NEW YORK
    State: NY
    Zip/4: 12300-9900

    Plan ID#: 1234567
    Group #:
    Policyholder: APPLE, JAMES
    Address: 1 APPLEBLOSSOM COURT
    City: HOMETOWN
    State: NY
    Zip/4: 15123-1234
    Policyholder Date of Birth: 11   12   1984
    Pt Relationship to Insured: Self X Spouse   Child   Other
    Employer/School Name:

Secondary Insurance
    Secondary Insurance Name:
    Address:
    City:
    State:
    Zip/4:

    Plan ID#:
    Group #:
    Policyholder:
    Address:
    City:
    State:
    Zip/4:
    Policyholder Date of Birth:
    Pt Relationship to Insured: Self   Spouse   Child   Other
    Employer/School Name:

ENCOUNTER INFORMATION:
Place of Service: 21

DIAGNOSIS INFORMATION

	Code	Diagnosis		Code	Diagnosis
1.	540 .9	Acute appendicitis	5.	.	
2.	.		6.	.	
3.	.		7.	.	
4.	.		8.	.	

PROCEDURE INFORMATION

Description of Procedure/Service	Dates	Code	Mod	Dx Order	Unit Charge	Days/ Units
1. Hospital admit, Level 1	06 19 YY⁻	99221		1	165 00	1
2. Laparoscopic appendectomy	06 19 YY⁻	44970		1	1400 00	1
3.	⁻					
4.	⁻					
5.	⁻					
6.	⁻					

Special Notes: Dr. Henry C. Cardiac, attending physician, NPI: 3456789012.
TJ Stitcher, surgeon, NPI: 8901234567.
Hospital: Goodmedicine Hospital, 1 Provider Street, Anywhere NY 12345, NPI: 1123456789, patient discharged 06/20/YY.

CASE STUDY 2-13

GOODMEDICINE CLINIC
1 PROVIDER STREET
ANYWHERE NY 12345
101 1112222

Patient Number: 2-13

EIN: 331234567 **NPI:** 3345678901

PATIENT INFORMATION:
Name: BANANA, STANLEY, N
Address: 1 BARRACK STREET
City: ANYWHERE
State: NY
Zip/4: 12345-1234
Telephone: 101 1117676

Gender: M X F
Status: Single X Married Other
Date of Birth: 11 11 1956
Employer: US ARMY
Student: FT PT School:

Work Related? Y N X
Employment Related? Y N X
Other Accident: Y N X
Date of Accident:

Referring Physician: NANCY HEALER MD
Address:
Telephone:
NPI #: 6789012345

INSURANCE INFORMATION:
Primary Insurance
  Primary Insurance Name: TRICARE
  Address: PO BOX 555
  City: TRICITY
  State: SC
  Zip/4: 76654-0555

  Plan ID#: 123445555
  Group #:
  Policyholder: BANANA, STANLEY, N
  Address: 1 BARRACK STREET
  City: ANYWHERE
  State: NY
  Zip/4: 12345-1234
  Policyholder Date of Birth: 11 11 1956
  Pt Relationship to Insured: Self X Spouse Child Other
  Employer/School Name: US ARMY

Secondary Insurance
  Secondary Insurance Name:
  Address:
  City:
  State:
  Zip/4:

  Plan ID#:
  Group #:
  Policyholder:
  Address:
  City:
  State:
  Zip/4:
  Policyholder Date of Birth:
  Pt Relationship to Insured: Self Spouse Child Other
  Employer/School Name:

ENCOUNTER INFORMATION:
Place of Service: 22

DIAGNOSIS INFORMATION

	Code	Diagnosis		Code	Diagnosis
1.	565 .0	Anal fissure	5.	.	
2.	.		6.	.	
3.	.		7.	.	
4.	.		8.	.	

PROCEDURE INFORMATION

Description of Procedure/Service	Dates	Code	Mod	Dx Order	Unit Charge	Days/ Units
1. Flexible sigmoidoscopy	06 20 YY⁻	45330		1	600 00	1
2.	⁻					
3.	⁻					
4.	⁻					
5.	⁻					
6.	⁻					

Special Notes: Nancy J Healer MD referred patient (NPI: 6789012345).
Care provided at Goodmedicine Hospital, 1 Provider Street, Anywhere, NY 12345, NPI: 112456789.
Provider: Janet B Surgeon MD, NPI: 9012345678.

CASE STUDY 2-14

GOODMEDICINE CLINIC
1 PROVIDER STREET
ANYWHERE NY 12345
101   1112222

Patient Number: 2-14

EIN: 331234567   **NPI:**   3345678901

PATIENT INFORMATION:
Name: KAROT, REGINALD, T
Address: 15 CARING STREET
City: ANYWHERE
State: NY
Zip/4: 12345-1234
Telephone: 101 2220022

Gender: M X   F
Status: Single   Married X   Other
Date of Birth: 10   01   1936
Employer: A CONSTRUCTION CO.
Student: FT   PT   School:

Work Related?   Y   N X
Employment Related? Y   N X
Other Accident: Y   N X
Date of Accident:

Referring Physician: NANCY J HEALER MD
Address:
Telephone:
NPI #: 6789012345

INSURANCE INFORMATION:
Primary Insurance
    Primary Insurance Name: METROPOLITAN
    Address: PO BOX 5678
    City: NEW YORK
    State: NY
    Zip/4: 32214-5678

    Plan ID#: 22222222A
    Group #:
    Policyholder: KAROT, LOUISE
    Address: 15 CARING STREET
    City: ANYWHERE
    State: NY
    Zip/4: 12345-1234
    Policyholder Date of Birth: 10   11   1936
    Pt Relationship to Insured: Self   Spouse X Child   Other
    Employer/School Name: ANYWHERE SCHOOL DISTRICT

Secondary Insurance
    Secondary Insurance Name: TRICARE STANDARD
    Address: PO BOX 555
    City: TRICITY
    State: SC
    Zip/4: 76654-0555

    Plan ID#: 0123456543
    Group #:
    Policyholder: KAROT, REGINALD, T
    Address: 15 CARING STREET
    City: ANYWHERE
    State: NY
    Zip/4: 12345-1234
    Policyholder Date of Birth: 10   01   1936
    Pt Relationship to Insured: Self X Spouse   Child   Other
    Employer/School Name: A CONSTRUCTION CO.

ENCOUNTER INFORMATION:
Place of Service: 11

DIAGNOSIS INFORMATION

	Code	Diagnosis		Code	Diagnosis
1.	550 .92	Bilateral inguinal hernia	5.	.	
2.	.		6.	.	
3.	.		7.	.	
4.	.		8.	.	

PROCEDURE INFORMATION

Description of Procedure/Service	Dates	Code	Mod	Dx Order	Unit Charge	Days/ Units
1. Office visit, new patient, level 3	06 20 YY-	99203	57	1	75 00	1
2.	-					
3.	-					
4.	-					
5.	-					
6.	-					

Special Notes: Referring MD: Nancy J Healer, MD, NPI: 6789012345.
   Provider: Janet B Surgeon MD, NPI: 9012345678.
   Update: Metropolitan paid $10.00 towards total.

CASE STUDY 2-15

GOODMEDICINE CLINIC
1 PROVIDER STREET
ANYWHERE, NY 12345
101   1112222

Patient Number: 2-15

EIN: 551234567   **NPI:**   3345678901

PATIENT INFORMATION:
Name: BUTCHER, JAMES, L
Address: 14 PIGFEET ROAD
City: ANYWHERE
State: NY
Zip/4: 12345-1234
Telephone: 101 3334567

Gender: M X   **F**
Status: Single X   **Married   Other**
Date of Birth: 02   29   1977
Employer: PIGLET MEAT PACKERS
Student: FT   PT   School:

Work Related?   **Y** X **N**
Employment Related?   Y   N X
Other Accident: Y   N X
Date of Accident: 06   19

Referring Physician:
Address:
Telephone:
NPI #:

INSURANCE INFORMATION:
Primary Insurance
   Primary Insurance Name: WORKERS COMP FUND
   Address: 113 INSURANCE AVENUE
   City: ANYWHERE
   State: NY
   Zip/4: 12345

   Plan ID#: 321458765
   Group #: 987123
   Policyholder: PIGLET MEAT PACKERS
   Address: 100 REYNOLDS WAY
   City: ANYWHERE
   State: NY
   Zip/4: 12345
   Policyholder Date of Birth:
   Pt Relationship to Insured: Self   Spouse   Child   Other X
   Employer/School Name: PIGLET MEAT PACKERS

Secondary Insurance
   Secondary Insurance Name:
   Address:
   City:
   State:
   Zip/4:

   Plan ID#:
   Group #:
   Policyholder:
   Address:
   City:
   State:
   Zip/4:
   Policyholder Date of Birth:
   Pt Relationship to Insured: Self   Spouse   Child   Other
   Employer/School Name:

ENCOUNTER INFORMATION:
Place of Service: 23

DIAGNOSIS INFORMATION

	Code	Diagnosis		Code	Diagnosis
1.	883 .2	Open wound, finger w/tendon involved	5.	.	
2.	E920 .3	Cut with knife	6.	.	
3.	E849 .3	Place of occurrence industrial prem	7.	.	
4.	.		8.	.	

PROCEDURE INFORMATION

Description of Procedure/Service	Dates	Code	Mod	Dx Order	Unit Charge	Days/ Units
1. Repair left extensor tendon	06 19 YY¯	26410	LT	123	1400 00	1
2.	¯					
3.	¯					
4.	¯					
5.	¯					
6.						

Special Notes: Admit date: 06/19/YYYY. DC: 06/19 Return to light duty work: 08/19/YYYY. DOI: 06/19/YYYY.
   Surgeon: TJ Stitcher, MD, NPI: 8901234567.
   Care provided at: Goodmedicine Hospital, 1 Provider Street, Anywhere, NY 12345, NPI: 1123456789.

CASE STUDY 2-16

GOODMEDICINE CLINIC
1 PROVIDER STREET
ANYWHERE NY 12345
101   1112222

Patient Number: 2-16

EIN: 661234567   **NPI:**   3345678901

PATIENT INFORMATION:
Name: HURTS, DAVID, J
Address: 4321 NOWHERE STREET
City: ANYWHERE
State: NY
Zip/4: 12345-1234
Telephone: 101 3141414

Gender: M X   F
Status: Single X   Married   Other
Date of Birth: 02 28 1955
Employer: UC PAINTERS
Student: FT   PT   School:

Work Related? Y X N
Employment Related? Y   N X
Other Accident: Y   N X
Date of Accident: 06 20 YYYY

Referring Physician:
Address:
Telephone:
NPI #:

INSURANCE INFORMATION:
Primary Insurance
   Primary Insurance Name: INDUSTRIAL INDEMNITY
   Address: 10 POLICY STREET
   City: ANYWHERE
   State: NY
   Zip/4: 12345

   Plan ID#: 112102121
   Group #: 123987
   Policyholder: UC PAINTERS
   Address: 1 CIRCLE DRIVE
   City: ANYWHERE
   State: NY
   Zip/4: 12345-1234
   Policyholder Date of Birth:
   Pt Relationship to Insured: Self   Spouse   Child   Other X
   Employer/School Name: UC PAINTERS

Secondary Insurance
   Secondary Insurance Name:
   Address:
   City:
   State:
   Zip/4:

   Plan ID#:
   Group #:
   Policyholder:
   Address:
   City:
   State:
   Zip/4:
   Policyholder Date of Birth:
   Pt Relationship to Insured: Self   Spouse   Child   Other
   Employer/School Name: UC PAINTERS

ENCOUNTER INFORMATION:
Place of Service: 11

DIAGNOSIS INFORMATION

	Code	Diagnosis		Code	Diagnosis
1.	813 .41	Colles fracture	5.	.	
2.	873 .44	Open wound jaw	6.	.	
3.	E881 .0	Fall from ladder	7.	.	
4.	E849 .3	At work	8.	.	

PROCEDURE INFORMATION

Description of Procedure/Service	Dates	Code	Mod	Dx Order	Unit Charge	Days/ Units
1. Repair closed Colles fracture	06 20 YY~	25605	LT	134	300 00	1
2. Wrist x-ray	06 20 YY~	73090	LT	134	80 00	1
3. Repair open wound, jaw	06 20 YY~	12011		234	80 00	1
4.	~					
5.	~					
6.	~					

Special Notes: Provider: Gail R Bones, MD, NPI: 1234567890

CASE STUDY 2-17

GOODMEDICINE CLINIC
1 PROVIDER STREET
ANYWHERE NY 12345
101 1112222

Patient Number: 2-17

EIN: 331234567 **NPI:** 3345678901

PATIENT INFORMATION:
Name: SMITH, PETER, M
Address: 1000 MAIN STREET APARTMENT B
City: ANYWHERE
State: NY
Zip/4: 12345-1234
Telephone: 101 5629654

Gender: M X F
Status: Single Married X Other
Date of Birth: 02 20 1965
Employer: PEPPLES & CLARK
Student: FT PT School:

Work Related? Y N X
Employment Related? Y N X
Other Accident: Y N X
Date of Accident:

Referring Physician:
Address:
Telephone:
NPI #:

INSURANCE INFORMATION:
Primary Insurance
 Primary Insurance Name: TRICARE
 Address: PO BOX 555
 City: TRICITY
 State: SC
 Zip/4: 76654-0555

 Plan ID#: 235236594
 Group #:
 Policyholder: SMITH, PETER, M
 Address: 1000 MAIN STREET APARTMENT B
 City: ANYWHERE
 State: NY
 Zip/4: 12345-1234
 Policyholder Date of Birth: 02 20 1965
 Pt Relationship to Insured: Self X Spouse Child Other
 Employer/School Name: PEPPLES & CLARK

Secondary Insurance
 Secondary Insurance Name:
 Address:
 City:
 State:
 Zip/4:

 Plan ID#:
 Group #:
 Policyholder:
 Address:
 City:
 State:
 Zip/4:
 Policyholder Date of Birth:
 Pt Relationship to Insured: Self Spouse Child Other
 Employer/School Name:

ENCOUNTER INFORMATION:
Place of Service: 11

DIAGNOSIS INFORMATION

	Code	Diagnosis		Code	Diagnosis
1.	998 .59	Postoperative infection	5.	.	
2.	E879 .8	Complication of procedure, other	6.	.	
3.	.		7.	.	
4.	.		8.	.	

PROCEDURE INFORMATION

Description of Procedure/Service	Dates	Code	Mod	Dx Order	Unit Charge	Days/Units
1. Office visit, est patient, level 4	06 20 YY⁻	99214		12	100 00	1
2.	⁻					
3.	⁻					
4.	⁻					
5.	⁻					
6.	⁻					

Special Notes: Provider: Janet B Surgeon, MD, NPI: 9012345678.

CASE STUDY 2-18

GOODMEDICINE CLINIC
1 PROVIDER STREET
ANYWHERE NY 12345
101 1112222

Patient Number: 2-18

EIN: 331234567   **NPI:**   3345678901

PATIENT INFORMATION:
Name: MARTIN, MARY, A
Address: 5005 SOUTH AVENUE
City: ANYWHERE
State: NY
Zip/4: 12345-1234
Telephone: 101 1117676

Gender: M   F X
Status: Single X   **Married   Other**
Date of Birth: 10   05   1955
Employer: US NAVY
Student: FT   PT   School:

Work Related?   **Y   N** X
Employment Related?   **Y   N** X
Other Accident: **Y   N** X
Date of Accident:

Referring Physician:
Address:
Telephone:
NPI #:

INSURANCE INFORMATION:
Primary Insurance
   Primary Insurance Name: TRICARE
   Address: PO BOX 555
   City: TRICITY
   State: SC
   Zip/4: 76654-0555

   Plan ID#: 232589571
   Group #:
   Policyholder: MARTIN, MARY, A
   Address: 5005 SOUTH AVENUE
   City: ANYWHERE
   State: NY
   Zip/4: 12345-1234
   Policyholder Date of Birth: 10   05   1955
   Pt Relationship to Insured: Self X **Spouse   Child   Other**
   Employer/School Name: US NAVY

Secondary Insurance
   Secondary Insurance Name:
   Address:
   City:
   State:
   Zip/4:

   Plan ID#:
   Group #:
   Policyholder:
   Address:
   City:
   State:
   Zip/4:
   Policyholder Date of Birth:
   Pt Relationship to Insured: Self   Spouse   Child   Other
   Employer/School Name:

ENCOUNTER INFORMATION:
Place of Service: 22

DIAGNOSIS INFORMATION

	Code	Diagnosis		Code	Diagnosis
1.	626 .2	Menorrhagia	5.	.	
2.	.		6.	.	
3.	.		7.	.	
4.	.		8.	.	

PROCEDURE INFORMATION

Description of Procedure/Service	Dates	Code	Mod	Dx Order	Unit Charge	Days/ Units
1. Hysteroscopic endometrial ablation	06 20 YY⁻	58563		1	950 00	1
2.	⁻					
3.	⁻					
4.	⁻					
5.	⁻					
6.	⁻					

Special Notes: Surgery at: Goodmedicine Hospital, 1 Provider Street, Anywhere, NY 12345, NPI: 1123456789.
   Surgeon: Janet B Surgeon, MD, NPI: 9012345678.

CASE STUDY 2-19

GOODMEDICINE CLINIC
1 PROVIDER STREET
ANYWHERE NY 12345
101 1112222

Patient Number: 2-19

EIN: 441234567   **NPI:** 3345678901

PATIENT INFORMATION:
Name: SANTOS, CINDY
Address: 3902 MAIN STREET
City: ANYWHERE
State: NY
Zip/4: 12345-1234
Telephone: 101 1115128

Gender: **M**   **F** X
Status: **Single** X   **Married**   **Other**
Date of Birth: 04   29   1935
Employer:
Student: FT   **PT**   **School:**

Work Related?   **Y**   **N** X
Employment Related? **Y**   **N** X
Other Accident: **Y**   **N** X
Date of Accident:

Referring Physician:
Address:
Telephone:
NPI #:

INSURANCE INFORMATION:
Primary Insurance
   Primary Insurance Name: MEDICARE
   Address: PO BOX 9929
   City: BOXBURY
   State: MD
   Zip/4: 45678-9929

   Plan ID#: 53231589A
   Group #:
   Policyholder: SANTOS, CINDY
   Address: 3902 MAIN STREET
   City: ANYWHERE
   State: NY
   Zip/4: 12345-1234
   Policyholder Date of Birth: 04   29   1935
   Pt Relationship to Insured: Self X **Spouse   Child   Other**
   Employer/School Name:

Secondary Insurance
   Secondary Insurance Name: MEDICAID
   Address: PO BOX 9900
   City: NEW YORK
   State: NY
   Zip/4: 12300-9900

   Plan ID#: 231562584
   Group #:
   Policyholder: SANTOS, CINDY
   Address: 3902 MAIN STREET
   City: ANYWHERE
   State: NY
   Zip/4: 12345-1234
   Policyholder Date of Birth: 04   29   1935
   Pt Relationship to Insured: Self X **Spouse   Child   Other**
   Employer/School Name:

ENCOUNTER INFORMATION:
Place of Service: 11

DIAGNOSIS INFORMATION

	Code	Diagnosis		Code	Diagnosis
1.	401 .9	Hypertension	5.	.	
2.	.		6.	.	
3.	.		7.	.	
4.	.		8.	.	

PROCEDURE INFORMATION

Description of Procedure/Service	Dates	Code	Mod	Dx Order	Unit Charge	Days/ Units
1. Office visit, est patient, level 2	06 20 YY⁻	99212		1	50 00	1
2.	⁻					
3.	⁻					
4.	⁻					
5.	⁻					
6.	⁻					

Special Notes: Provider: Nancy J Healer MD, NPI: 6789012345.

CASE STUDY 2-20

GOODMEDICINE CLINIC
1 PROVIDER STREET
ANYWHERE NY 12345
101 1112222

Patient Number: 2-20

EIN: 551234567   **NPI:** 3345678901

PATIENT INFORMATION:
Name: TOBIAS, LANA
Address: 3920 HILL STREET
City: ANYWHERE
State: NY
Zip/4: 12345-1234
Telephone: 101 5551235

Gender: **M**   F X
Status: **Single**   **Married** X   **Other**
Date of Birth: 12   15   1967
Employer:
Student: FT   **PT**   **School:**

Work Related?   **Y**   **N** X
Employment Related?   **Y**   **N** X
Other Accident: **Y**   **N** X
Date of Accident:

Referring Physician:
Address:
Telephone:
NPI #:

INSURANCE INFORMATION:
Primary Insurance
  Primary Insurance Name: BLUE CROSS BLUE SHIELD
  Address: PO BOX 1121
  City: MEDICAL
  State: PA
  Zip/4: 12357-1121

  Plan ID#: ABC123456
  Group #: AB103
  Policyholder: TOBIAS, CASEY
  Address: 3920 HILL STREET
  City: ANYWHERE
  State: NY
  Zip/4: 12345-1234
  Policyholder Date of Birth: 12   15   1967
  Pt Relationship to Insured: Self   Spouse X **Child   Other**
  Employer/School Name: STATE UNIVERSITY

Secondary Insurance
  Secondary Insurance Name:
  Address:
  City:
  State:
  Zip/4:

  Plan ID#:
  Group #:
  Policyholder:
  Address:
  City:
  State:
  Zip/4:
  Policyholder Date of Birth:
  Pt Relationship to Insured: Self   Spouse   Child   Other
  Employer/School Name:

ENCOUNTER INFORMATION:
Place of Service: 11

DIAGNOSIS INFORMATION

	Code	Diagnosis		Code	Diagnosis
1.	719 .45	Hip pain	5.	.	
2.	E880 .9	Fall on stairs	6.	.	
3.	E849 .0	Place of occurence, home	7.	.	
4.	.		8.	.	

PROCEDURE INFORMATION

Description of Procedure/Service	Dates	Code	Mod	Dx Order	Unit Charge	Days/ Units
1. Office visit, est patient, level 2	06 20 YY⁻	99212		123	50 00	1
2.	⁻					
3.	⁻					
4.	⁻					
5.	⁻					
6.	⁻					

Special Notes: Provider: TJ Stitcher, MD, NPI: 8901234567.
Goodmedicine Clinic, 1 Provider Street, Anywhere, NY 12345, NPI: 3345678901

Forms

You are welcome to copy the following forms for use when completing exercises in the textbook and Workbook:

NOTE: The CMS-1500 claim can also be printed from the CD-ROM that accompanies this textbook. You'll need to make approximately 65 copies of the claim if you plan to complete all case studies in the textbook.

- **CMS-1500 claim (as black and white form suitable for photocopying)**
- **Coding Case Study Form (for Chapter 10 exercises)**
- **E/M CodeBuilder**

1500

HEALTH INSURANCE CLAIM FORM

APPROVED BY NATIONAL UNIFORM CLAIM COMMITTEE 08/05

PICA								PICA

1. MEDICARE	MEDICAID	TRICARE CHAMPUS	CHAMPVA	GROUP HEALTH PLAN	FECA BLK LUNG	OTHER	1a. INSURED'S I.D. NUMBER	(For Program in Item 1)
(Medicare #)	(Medicaid #)	(Sponsor's SSN)	(Member ID#)	(SSN or ID)	(SSN)	(ID)		

2. PATIENT'S NAME (Last Name, First Name, Middle Initial)

3. PATIENT'S BIRTH DATE MM | DD | YY   SEX   M   F

4. INSURED'S NAME (Last Name, First Name, Middle Initial)

5. PATIENT'S ADDRESS (No., Street)

6. PATIENT RELATIONSHIP TO INSURED Self Spouse Child Other

7. INSURED'S ADDRESS (No., Street)

CITY   STATE

8. PATIENT STATUS Single Married Other

CITY   STATE

ZIP CODE   TELEPHONE (Include Area Code) ( )

Employed Full-Time Student Part-Time Student

ZIP CODE   TELEPHONE (Include Area Code) ( )

9. OTHER INSURED'S NAME (Last Name, First Name, Middle Initial)

10. IS PATIENT'S CONDITION RELATED TO:

11. INSURED'S POLICY GROUP OR FECA NUMBER

a. OTHER INSURED'S POLICY OR GROUP NUMBER

a. EMPLOYMENT? (Current or Previous) YES NO

a. INSURED'S DATE OF BIRTH MM | DD | YY   SEX   M   F

b. OTHER INSURED'S DATE OF BIRTH MM | DD | YY   SEX   M   F

b. AUTO ACCIDENT? PLACE (State) YES NO

b. EMPLOYER'S NAME OR SCHOOL NAME

c. EMPLOYER'S NAME OR SCHOOL NAME

c. OTHER ACCIDENT? YES NO

c. INSURANCE PLAN NAME OR PROGRAM NAME

d. INSURANCE PLAN NAME OR PROGRAM NAME

10d. RESERVED FOR LOCAL USE

d. IS THERE ANOTHER HEALTH BENEFIT PLAN? YES NO *If yes*, return to and complete item 9 a-d.

READ BACK OF FORM BEFORE COMPLETING & SIGNING THIS FORM.

12. PATIENT'S OR AUTHORIZED PERSON'S SIGNATURE I authorize the release of any medical or other information necessary to process this claim. I also request payment of government benefits either to myself or to the party who accepts assignment below.

SIGNED _____ DATE _____

13. INSURED'S OR AUTHORIZED PERSON'S SIGNATURE I authorize payment of medical benefits to the undersigned physician or supplier for services described below.

SIGNED _____

14. DATE OF CURRENT: MM | DD | YY   ILLNESS (First symptom) OR INJURY (Accident) OR PREGNANCY(LMP)

15. IF PATIENT HAS HAD SAME OR SIMILAR ILLNESS. GIVE FIRST DATE MM | DD | YY

16. DATES PATIENT UNABLE TO WORK IN CURRENT OCCUPATION MM | DD | YY   FROM   TO   MM | DD | YY

17. NAME OF REFERRING PROVIDER OR OTHER SOURCE

17a.

17b. NPI

18. HOSPITALIZATION DATES RELATED TO CURRENT SERVICES MM | DD | YY   FROM   TO   MM | DD | YY

19. RESERVED FOR LOCAL USE

20. OUTSIDE LAB? YES NO $ CHARGES

21. DIAGNOSIS OR NATURE OF ILLNESS OR INJURY (Relate Items 1, 2, 3 or 4 to Item 24E by Line)

1. |___.___   3. |___.___

2. |___.___   4. |___.___

22. MEDICAID RESUBMISSION CODE   ORIGINAL REF. NO.

23. PRIOR AUTHORIZATION NUMBER

24. A. DATE(S) OF SERVICE From MM DD YY To MM DD YY	B. PLACE OF SERVICE	C. EMG	D. PROCEDURES, SERVICES, OR SUPPLIES (Explain Unusual Circumstances) CPT/HCPCS | MODIFIER	E. DIAGNOSIS POINTER	F. $ CHARGES	G. DAYS OR UNITS	H. EPSDT Family Plan	I. ID. QUAL.	J. RENDERING PROVIDER ID. #
1								NPI	
2								NPI	
3								NPI	
4								NPI	
5								NPI	
6								NPI	

25. FEDERAL TAX I.D. NUMBER   SSN EIN

26. PATIENT'S ACCOUNT NO.

27. ACCEPT ASSIGNMENT? (For govt. claims, see back) YES NO

28. TOTAL CHARGE $

29. AMOUNT PAID $

30. BALANCE DUE $

31. SIGNATURE OF PHYSICIAN OR SUPPLIER INCLUDING DEGREES OR CREDENTIALS (I certify that the statements on the reverse apply to this bill and are made a part thereof.)

SIGNED _____ DATE _____

32. SERVICE FACILITY LOCATION INFORMATION

a. NPI   b.

33. BILLING PROVIDER INFO & PH # ( )

a. NPI   b.

NUCC Instruction Manual available at: www.nucc.org

APPROVED OMB-0938-0999 FORM CMS-1500 (08-05)

CASE STUDY NO.	DIAGNOSIS CODE #s	PROCEDURE CODE #s
Sample: 2-1	789.35, 569.3	99242

E/M CODEBUILDER

For use with 1995 and 1997 *CMS Documentation Guidelines for Evaluation & Management Coding.*
Go to **www.cms.hhs.gov** and click on Outreach & Education, MLN Educational Web Guides, and Documentation Guidelines for E&M Services to print the guidelines and use with the E/M CodeBuilder.

Introduction

The evaluation and management (E/M) code reported to a third-party payer must be supported by documentation in the patient's record (e.g., SOAP or clinic note, diagnostic test results, operative findings). Although providers are responsible for selecting the E/M code from the encounter form, superbill, or chargemaster at the time patient care is rendered, insurance specialists audit records to make sure that the appropriate level of E/M code was reported to the third-party payer.

This *E/M CodeBuilder* form can be used for that purpose, and it can also be used as a tool to teach appropriate assignment of E/M level codes. To assign a code, just review the documentation in the patient's record, record your findings (based on the directions provided), and refer to the CPT coding manual to select the E/M code to be reported.

E/M code selection is based on three key components: *history, examination,* and *medical decision making.* This *E/M CodeBuilder* form emphasizes those components. It is important to be aware that contributory components (*counseling* and *coordination of care*) also play an important role in selecting the E/M code when documentation in the patient record indicates that counseling or coordination of care dominated the visit. In this situation, the contributory component of *time* can be considered a key or controlling factor in selecting a level of E/M service (code).

> **NOTE:** *Time* and *nature of presenting problem* are listed in some E/M code descriptions to assist in determining which code number to report.

Selecting the Level of History

To select the level of history, review the following elements in the patient record. If an element is not documented, it cannot be considered when selecting the level of E/M service code.

- **History of present illness (HPI)**
- **Review of systems (ROS)**
- **Past, family, and/or social history (PFSH)**

History of Present Illness (HPI)

Review the clinic or SOAP note in the patient's record, and for each documented HPI element (below), enter an X in the box in front of the element on this form. Then, total the Xs and enter that number on the line in front of the Total Score (below). Finally, select the level of HPI based on the total number of elements documented, and enter an X in the appropriate box.

- ☐ **Duration:** of pain/discomfort; length of time condition has persisted (e.g., pain began three days ago).
- ☐ **Location:** of pain/discomfort (e.g., is pain diffused/localized or unilateral/bilateral; does it radiate or refer?).
- ☐ **Quality:** a description of the quality of the symptom (e.g., is pain described as sharp, dull, throbbing, stabbing, constant, intermittent, acute or chronic, stable, improving, or worsening?).
- ☐ **Severity:** use of self-assessment scale to measure subjective levels (e.g., on a scale of 1–10, how severe is the pain?), or comparison of pain quantitatively with previously experienced pain.
- ☐ **Timing:** establishing onset of pain and chronology of pain development (e.g., migraine in the morning).
- ☐ **Context:** where was the patient and what was he doing when pain began (e.g., was patient at rest or involved in an activity; was pain aggravated or relieved, or does it recur, with a specific activity; did situational stress or some other factor precede or accompany the pain?).
- ☐ **Modifying factors:** what has patient attempted to do to relieve pain (e.g., heat vs. cold; does it relieve or exacerbate pain; what makes the pain worse; have over-the-counter drugs been attempted—with what results?).
- ☐ **Associated signs/symptoms:** clinician's impressions formulated during the interview may lead to questioning about additional sensations or feelings (e.g., diaphoresis associated with indigestion or chest pain, blurred vision accompanying a headache, etc.).

____ **Total Score:** Enter the score for number of Xs entered above (representing number of HPI elements), and enter an X in front of the type of HPI below:

☐ Brief HPI (1–3 elements)

☐ Extended HPI (4 or more elements)

Review of Systems (ROS)

Review the clinic or SOAP note in the patient's record, and for each documented ROS element (below), enter an X in the box in front of the element on this form. Then, total the Xs and enter that number on the line in front of the Total Score (below). Finally, select the level of ROS based on the total number of elements documented, and enter an X in the appropriate box.

> **NOTE:** To properly assess review of systems documentation, have *CMS Documentation Guidelines for Evaluation & Management Coding* available as you review the patient's record.

☐ Constitutional symptoms   ☐ Respiratory   ☐ Allergic/Immunologic

☐ Eyes   ☐ Gastrointestinal   ☐ Hematologic/Lymphatic

☐ Musculoskeletal   ☐ Integumentary (including   ☐ Neurologic

☐ Ears, nose, mouth, throat   skin & breast)   ☐ Endocrine

☐ Cardiovascular   ☐ Genitourinary   ☐ Psychiatric

____ **Total Score:** Enter the score for number of Xs entered above (representing number of ROS elements), and enter an X in front of the type of ROS below:

☐ None

☐ Problem pertinent (1 body system documented)

☐ Extended (2–9 body systems documented)

☐ Complete (all body systems documented)

Past, Family, and/or Social History (PFSH)

Review the clinic or SOAP note in the patient's record, and for each documented PFSH element (below), enter an X in the box in front of the element on this form. Then, total the Xs and enter that number on the line in front of the Total Score (below). Finally, select the level of PFSH based on the total number of elements documented, and enter an X in the appropriate box.

☐ Past history (patient's past experience with illnesses, operations, injuries, and treatments)

☐ Family history (review of medical events in the patient's family, including diseases that may be hereditary or place the patient at risk)

☐ Social history (an age-appropriate review of past and current activities)

____ **Total Score:** Enter the score for number of Xs entered above (representing number of PFSH elements), and enter an X in front of the type of PFSH below:

☐ None

☐ Pertinent (1 history area documented)

☐ Complete (2 or 3 history areas documented)

Level of History

Circle the type of HPI, ROS, and PFSH determined above; then circle the appropriate level of history below.

HPI	Brief	Brief	Extended	Extended
ROS	None	Problem Pertinent	Extended	Complete
PFSH	None	None	Pertinent	Complete
Level of History	Problem Focused	Expanded Problem Focused	Detailed	Comprehensive

Selecting the Level of Examination

To select the level of examination, first determine whether a *single organ examination* (specialist exam; e.g., ophthalmologist) or *a general multisystem examination* (e.g., family practitioner) was completed.

Single Organ System Examination

Refer to the single organ system examination requirements in the *CMS Documentation Guidelines for Evaluation & Management Services,* and enter an X in front of the appropriate level of exam below.

☐ PROBLEM FOCUSED EXAMINATION (1–5 elements identified by a bullet)

☐ EXPANDED PROBLEM FOCUSED EXAMINATION (at least 6 elements identified by a bullet)

☐ DETAILED EXAMINATION (at least 12 elements identified by a bullet)

☐ COMPREHENSIVE EXAMINATION (all elements identified by a bullet; document every element in each box with a shaded border and at least one element in each box with an unshaded box)

> **NOTE:** For eye and psychiatric examinations, at least nine elements in each box with a shaded border and at least one element in each box with a shaded or unshaded border is documented.

General Multisystem Exam

Refer to the general multisystem examination requirements in the *CMS Documentation Guidelines for Evaluation & Management Services.* Enter an X in front of the organ system or body area for up to the total number of allowed elements (e.g., up to two elements can be documented for the Neck exam).

☐ Constitutional (2)   ☐ Gastrointestinal (5)   ☐ Musculoskeletal (6)

☐ Eyes (3)   ☐ Chest (breasts) (2)   ☐ Neurologic (3)

☐ Ears, nose, mouth, throat (6)   ☐ Skin (2)   ☐ Psychiatric (4)

☐ Neck (2)   ☐ Genitourinary (male–3;

☐ Cardiovascular (7)   female–6)

☐ Respiratory (4)

____ **Total Score:** Enter the score for number of Xs entered above (representing number of exam elements), and enter an X in front of the level of exam below:

☐ PROBLEM FOCUSED EXAMINATION (1–5 elements identified by a bullet on *CMS Documentation Guidelines for Evaluation & Management Services*)

☐ EXPANDED PROBLEM FOCUSED EXAMINATION (at least 6 elements identified by a bullet on *CMS Documentation Guidelines for Evaluation & Management Services*)

☐ DETAILED EXAMINATION (at least 2 elements identified by a bullet from each of 6 organ systems or body areas, or at least 12 elements identified by a bullet in two or more systems or areas, on *CMS Documentation Guidelines for Evaluation & Management Services*)

☐ COMPREHENSIVE EXAMINATION (documentation of all elements identified by a bullet in at least 9 organ systems or body areas, and documentation of at least 2 elements identified by a bullet from each of 9 organ systems or body areas, on *CMS Documentation Guidelines for Evaluation & Management Services*)

Medical Decision Making

Select the appropriate level of medical decision making based upon the following criteria:

NUMBER OF DIAGNOSIS OR MANAGEMENT OPTIONS	AMOUNT/COMPLEXITY OF DATA TO BE REVIEWED	RISK OF COMPLICATIONS AND/OR MORBIDITY/ MORTALITY	MEDICAL DECISION MAKING
Minimal	Minimal or none	Minimal	Straightforward
Limited	Limited	Low	Low complexity
Multiple	Moderate	Moderate	Moderate complexity
Extensive	Extensive	High	High complexity

E/M Code Selection

Select the E/M code based on selection of level of history, examination, and medical decision making:

History	Problem focused	Expanded problem focused	Expanded problem focused	Detailed	Comprehensive
Examination	Problem focused	Expanded problem focused	Expanded problem focused	Detailed	Comprehensive
Medical Decision Making	Straightforward	Low complexity	Moderate complexity	Moderate complexity	High complexity
Go to the appropriate E/M category/subcategory, and select the code based upon the information selected above.					

Dental Claims Processing

INTRODUCTION

Dental benefits programs offer a variety of options in the form of either fee-for-service or managed care plans that reimburse a portion of a patient's dental expenses and may exclude certain treatments (e.g., dental sealants). It is, therefore, important for the insurance specialist to become familiar with the specifics of dental plans in which the dental professional participates. It is equally important to become familiar with dental terminology (Table IV-1).

DENTAL CLAIMS PROCESSING

Dental claims (Figures IV-1 and IV-2) are submitted on the American Dental Association (ADA)–approved claim, and instructions (Table IV-2) should be carefully followed. Dental offices also have the option of submitting electronic claims according to HIPAA's electronic transaction standard, *ASC X12N 837 v.4010–Health Care Claim: Dental.*

Dental treatment is reported using codes assigned from the *Current Dental Terminology (CDT)*. CDT is published by the American Dental Association (ADA), which ensures that codes are:

- Created according to a standard format.
- At an appropriate level of specificity.
- Uniformly applied to dental treatment.
- Used to report dental procedures.

The American Dental Association periodically reviews and revises CDT to update codes according to recognized changes in dental procedures. Published revisions are implemented biannually, at the beginning of odd-numbered years. CDT contains the following features:

- Codes and descriptions
- A section on implant-supported prosthetics
- Glossaries of dental and dental benefit terminology
- The new ADA claim
- An introduction to the Systematized Nomenclature of Dentistry (SNODENT). SNODENT contains standard terms to describe dental disease, captures clinical detail and patient characteristics, and allows for the analysis of patient care services and outcomes

CURRENT DENTAL TERMINOLOGY (CDT)

The **Current Dental Terminology (CDT)** is published by the American Dental Association (ADA) as an annual revision. It classifies dental procedures and services.

> **NOTE:** CDT codes are also included in HCPCS level II, beginning with the first digit of D.

Dental providers and ambulatory care settings use the CDT to report procedures and services. CDT also includes the Code on Dental Procedures and Nomenclature (Code), which contains instructions for use of the Code, questions and answers, ADA dental claim form completion instructions, and tooth numbering systems.

> **EXAMPLE:** Patient underwent incision and drainage of intraoral soft tissue abscess. Report CDT code D7510.

CDT CODING PRACTICE

Instructions: Use the CDT coding manual to assign a code to each item below. If you do not have access to a CDT coding manual, use your HCPCS level II coding manual. Its Dental Procedures (D0000-D9999) chapter is identical to the codes located in the CDT coding manual.

_____   1. Frenulectomy

_____   2. Sialolithotomy

_____   3. Administration of general anesthesia for deep sedation, during dental procedure 45 minutes

_____   4. Fixed appliance therapy

_____   5. Administration of local anesthesia, during dental procedure

_____   6. Enamel microabrasion

_____   7. External bleaching, teeth #8 and #9

_____   8. Core buildup with pins

_____   9. Bone replacement graft, first site in quadrant

_____   10. Interim partial denture, mandible

_____   11. Repair, cast framework

_____   12. Adjust partial denture, maxilla

_____   13. Modification of palatal lift prosthesis

_____   14. Surgical stent

_____   15. Connector bar

_____   16. Stress breaker

_____   17. Removal of impacted tooth, soft tissue

_____   18. Brush biopsy, transepithelial sample collection

_____   19. Closure of fistula, salivary

_____   20. Surgical removal, residual tooth roots

_____	21.	Removal of torus mandibularis
_____	22.	Incision and drainage of abscess, extraoral soft tissue, complicated by drainage of multiple fascial spaces
_____	23.	Closed reduction of mandible with immobilization of teeth
_____	24.	Replacement of broken retainer
_____	25.	Comprehensive orthodontic treatment, adult dentition

ANSWER KEY TO CDT CODING PRACTICE

1.	D7960		14.	D5982
2.	D7980		15.	D6920
3.	D2220, D2221		16.	D6940
4.	D8220		17.	D7220
5.	D9215		18.	D7288
6.	D9970		19.	D7983
7.	D9973, D9973		20.	D7250
8.	D2950		21.	D7473
9.	D4263		22.	D7521
10.	D5821		23.	D7640
11.	D5620		24.	D8692
12.	D5421		25.	D8090
13.	D5959			

TABLE IV-1   Glossary of common dental terms

DENTAL TERM	DEFINITION
abscess	acute or chronic, localized inflammation associated with tissue destruction
Academy of General Dentistry (AGD)	serves needs and represents interests of general dentists
Alliance for the Best Clinical Practices in Dentistry (ABCPD)	organization that encourages development of evidence-based prevention and treatment protocols through the process of organizing focused seminars
American Academy of Pediatric Dentistry (AAPD)	dedicated to improving and maintaining the oral health of infants, children, adolescents, and persons with special healthcare needs
American Academy of Periodontology (AAP)	dedicated to advancing the art and science of periodontics and improving the periodontal health of the public
American Dental Association (ADA)	promotes public health through commitment of member dentists to provide high-quality oral health care and promotes accessible oral health care
amalgam	alloy used in direct dental restorations; also called a *silver filling*
attrition	normal wearing away of the surface of a tooth from chewing
baby bottle tooth decay	severe decay in baby teeth due to sleeping with a bottle of milk or juice; natural sugars from drinks combine with bacteria in the mouth to produce acid that decays teeth
bitewing radiograph	x-rays of top and bottom molars and premolars
bruxism	involuntary clenching or grinding of teeth
calculus	hard deposit of mineralized material that adheres to teeth; also called *tartar* or *calcified plaque*
caries	tooth decay
crown	artificial covering of a tooth with metal, porcelain, or porcelain fused to metal
deciduous teeth	baby teeth or primary teeth
endentulous	having no teeth
endodontics	dental specialty concerned with treatment of the root and nerve of a tooth
fluoride	chemical compound that prevents cavities and makes tooth surface stronger
gingivitis	inflammation of gums surrounding teeth, caused by buildup of plaque or food
gum disease	*see* periodontitis
halitosis	bad breath
malocclusion	improper alignment of biting or chewing surfaces of upper and lower teeth
orthodontics	dental specialty concerned with straightening or moving misaligned teeth and/or jaws with braces and/or surgery
panoramic radiograph	single, large x-ray of jaws taken by a machine that rotates around the head
pedodontics	dental specialty concerned with treatment of children; also called *pediatric dentistry*
periodontics	dental specialty concerned with treatment of gums, tissue, and bone that supports the teeth
periodontitis	inflammation and loss of connective tissue of the supporting or surrounding structure of the teeth; also called *gum disease*
plaque	bacteria-containing substance that collects on the surface of teeth, which can cause decay and gum irritation when not removed by daily brushing and flossing
Prevent Abuse and Neglect through Dental Awareness (PANDA)	educational program that educates oral health professionals about child abuse and helps them learn how to diagnose and report potential abuse situations to appropriate authorities
prophylaxis	professional cleaning to remove plaque, calculus, and stains
prosthodontics	dental specialty concerned with restoration and/or replacement of missing teeth with artificial materials
radiograph	x-ray
scaling	removal of plaque, calculus, and stains from teeth
sealant	thin plastic material used to cover biting surface of a child's tooth
supernumerary tooth	extra tooth
tartar	*see* calculus

ADA Dental Claim Form

HEADER INFORMATION

1. Type of Transaction (Mark all applicable boxes)

- [ ] Statement of Actual Services
- [ ] Request for Predetermination / Preauthorization
- [ ] EPSDT / Title XIX

2. Predetermination / Preauthorization Number

INSURANCE COMPANY/DENTAL BENEFIT PLAN INFORMATION

3. Company/Plan Name, Address, City, State, Zip Code

OTHER COVERAGE

4. Other Dental or Medical Coverage? [ ] No (Skip 5-11) [ ] Yes (Complete 5-11)

5. Name of Policyholder/Subscriber in #4 (Last, First, Middle Initial, Suffix)

6. Date of Birth (MM/DD/CCYY)

7. Gender [ ] M [ ] F

8. Policyholder/Subscriber ID (SSN or ID#)

9. Plan/Group Number

10. Patient's Relationship to Person Named in #5 [ ] Self [ ] Spouse [ ] Dependent [ ] Other

11. Other Insurance Company/Dental Benefit Plan Name, Address, City, State, Zip Code

POLICYHOLDER/SUBSCRIBER INFORMATION (For Insurance Company Named in #3)

12. Policyholder/Subscriber Name (Last, First, Middle Initial, Suffix), Address, City, State, Zip Code

13. Date of Birth (MM/DD/CCYY)

14. Gender [ ] M [ ] F

15. Policyholder/Subscriber ID (SSN or ID#)

16. Plan/Group Number

17. Employer Name

PATIENT INFORMATION

18. Relationship to Policyholder/Subscriber in #12 Above [ ] Self [ ] Spouse [ ] Dependent Child [ ] Other

19. Student Status [ ] FTS [ ] PTS

20. Name (Last, First, Middle Initial, Suffix), Address, City, State, Zip Code

21. Date of Birth (MM/DD/CCYY)

22. Gender [ ] M [ ] F

23. Patient ID/Account # (Assigned by Dentist)

RECORD OF SERVICES PROVIDED

	24. Procedure Date (MM/DD/CCYY)	25. Area of Oral Cavity	26. Tooth System	27. Tooth Number(s) or Letter(s)	28. Tooth Surface	29. Procedure Code	30. Description	31. Fee
1								
2								
3								
4								
5								
6								
7								
8								
9								
10								

MISSING TEETH INFORMATION

34. (Place an 'X' on each missing tooth)

Permanent

| 1 | 2 | 3 | 4 | 5 | 6 | 7 | 8 | 9 | 10 | 11 | 12 | 13 | 14 | 15 | 16 |
| 32 | 31 | 30 | 29 | 28 | 27 | 26 | 25 | 24 | 23 | 22 | 21 | 20 | 19 | 18 | 17 |

Primary

| A | B | C | D | E | F | G | H | I | J |
| T | S | R | Q | P | O | N | M | L | K |

32. Other Fee(s)

33. Total Fee

35. Remarks

AUTHORIZATIONS

36. I have been informed of the treatment plan and associated fees. I agree to be responsible for all charges for dental services and materials not paid by my dental benefit plan, unless prohibited by law, or the treating dentist or dental practice has a contractual agreement with my plan prohibiting all or a portion of such charges. To the extent permitted by law, I consent to your use and disclosure of my protected health information to carry out payment activities in connection with this claim.

X _____

Patient/Guardian signature   Date

37. I hereby authorize and direct payment of the dental benefits otherwise payable to me, directly to the below named dentist or dental entity.

X _____

Subscriber signature   Date

BILLING DENTIST OR DENTAL ENTITY (Leave blank if dentist or dental entity is not submitting claim on behalf of the patient or insured/subscriber)

48. Name, Address, City, State, Zip Code

49. NPI

50. License Number

51. SSN or TIN

52. Phone Number ( ) –

52A. Additional Provider ID

ANCILLARY CLAIM/TREATMENT INFORMATION

38. Place of Treatment [ ] Provider's Office [ ] Hospital [ ] ECF [ ] Other

39. Number of Enclosures (00 to 99) Radiograph(s) Oral Image(s) Model(s)

40. Is Treatment for Orthodontics? [ ] No (Skip 41-42) [ ] Yes (Complete 41-42)

41. Date Appliance Placed (MM/DD/CCYY)

42. Months of Treatment Remaining

43. Replacement of Prosthesis? [ ] No [ ] Yes (Complete 44)

44. Date Prior Placement (MM/DD/CCYY)

45. Treatment Resulting from [ ] Occupational illness/injury [ ] Auto accident [ ] Other accident

46. Date of Accident (MM/DD/CCYY)

47. Auto Accident State

TREATING DENTIST AND TREATMENT LOCATION INFORMATION

53. I hereby certify that the procedures as indicated by date are in progress (for procedures that require multiple visits) or have been completed.

X _____

Signed (Treating Dentist)   Date

54. NPI

55. License Number

56. Address, City, State, Zip Code

56A. Provider Specialty Code

57. Phone Number ( ) –

58. Additional Provider ID

© 2006 American Dental Association

J400 (Same as ADA Dental Claim Form – J401, J402, J403, J404)

To Reorder call 1-800-947-4746
or go online at www.adacatalog.org

FIGURE IV-1 ADA Dental Claim Form © 2006 American Dental Association. Reprinted with permission.

American Dental Association
www.ada.org

Comprehensive completion instructions for the ADA Dental Claim Form are found in Section 4 of the ADA Publication titled *CDT-2009/2010.* Five relevant extracts from that section follow:

GENERAL INSTRUCTIONS

A. The form is designed so that the name and address (Item 3) of the third-party payer receiving the claim (insurance company/dental benefit plan) is visible in a #10 window envelope. Please fold the form using the 'tick-marks' printed in the margin.

B. In the upper-right of the form, a blank space is provided for the convenience of the payer or insurance company, to allow the assignment of a claim or control number.

C. All Items in the form must be completed unless it is noted on the form or in the following instructions that completion is not required.

D. When a name and address field is required, the full name of an individual or a full business name, address and zip code must be entered.

E. All dates must include the four-digit year.

F. If the number of procedures reported exceeds the number of lines available on one claim form, the remaining procedures must be listed on a separate, fully completed claim form.

COORDINATION OF BENEFITS (COB)

When a claim is being submitted to the secondary payer, complete the form in its entirety and attach the primary payer's Explanation of Benefits (EOB) showing the amount paid by the primary payer. You may indicate the amount the primary payer paid in the "Remarks" field (Item # 35).

NATIONAL PROVIDER IDENTIFIER (NPI)

49 and 54   NPI (National Provider Identifier): This is an identifier assigned by the Federal government to all providers considered to be HIPAA covered entities. Dentists who are not covered entities may elect to obtain an NPI at their discretion, or may be enumerated if required by a participating provider agreement with a third-party payer or applicable state law/regulation. An NPI is unique to an individual dentist (Type 1 NPI) or dental entity (Type 2 NPI), and has no intrinsic meaning. Additional information on NPI and enumeration can be obtained from the ADA's Web Site: **www.ada.org/goto/npi**

ADDITIONAL PROVIDER IDENTIFIER

52A and 58   Additional Provider ID: This is an identifier assigned to the billing dentist or dental entity other than a Social Security Number (SSN) or Tax Identification Number (TIN). It is not the provider's NPI. The additional identifier is sometimes referred to as a Legacy Identifier (LID). LIDs may not be unique as they are assigned by different entities (e.g., third-party payer; Federal government). Some Legacy IDs have an intrinsic meaning.

PROVIDER SPECIALTY CODES

56A   Provider Specialty Code: Enter the code that indicates the type of dental professional who delivered the treatment. Available codes describing treating dentists are listed below. The general code listed as 'Dentist' may be used instead of any other dental practitioner code.

Category / Description Code	Code
Dentist A dentist is a person qualified by a doctorate in dental surgery (D.D.S) or dental medicine (D.M.D.) licensed by the state to practice dentistry, and practicing within the scope of that license.	122300000X
General Practice	1223G0001X
Dental Specialty (see following list)	Various
Dental Public Health	1223D0001X
Endodontics	1223E0200X
Orthodontics	1223X0400X
Pediatric Dentistry	1223P0221X
Periodontics	1223P0300X
Prosthodontics	1223P0700X
Oral & Maxillofacial Pathology	1223P0106X
Oral & Maxillofacial Radiology	1223D0008X
Oral & Maxillofacial Surgery	1223S0112X

Dental provider taxonomy codes listed above are a subset of the full code set that is posted at:
www.wpc-edi.com/codes/taxonomy

Should there be any updates to ADA Dental Claim Form completion instructions, the updates will be posted on the ADA's web site at:
www.ada.org/goto/dentalcode

FIGURE IV-2 Reverse of ADA Dental Claim Form © 2006 American Dental Association. Reprinted with permission.

TABLE IV-2   Instructions for completing the ADA claim

BLOCK	INSTRUCTIONS
	HEADER INFORMATION
1	Enter an X in the appropriate box. Select the *Statement of Actual Services* to obtain reimbursement for services provided. Select the *Request for Predetermination/Preauthorization* to obtain preapproval of dental services. Select the *EPSDT/Title XIX* if the patient is covered by Medicaid's Early and Periodic Screening, Diagnosis, and Treatment program for persons under age 21.
2	Enter the predetermination or preauthorization number assigned by the payer, if applicable. Otherwise, leave blank.
	PRIMARY PAYER INFORMATION (INSURANCE COMPANY/DENTAL BENEFIT PLAN INFORMATION)
3	Enter the primary payer's name, address, city, state, and zip code.
	OTHER COVERAGE
	NOTE: Always complete Block 4. Complete Blocks 5–11 *only* if the patient has a secondary dental plan.
4	Enter an X in the NO box if the patient is not covered by another dental insurance plan, and go to Block 12. Enter an X in the YES box if the patient is covered by another dental insurance plan, and complete Blocks 5–11. **REMEMBER!** Complete Blocks 5–11 *only* if the patient has a secondary dental plan. Otherwise, leave Blocks 5–11 blank.
5	*If the patient has secondary dental plan coverage,* enter the complete name (last, first, middle initial, suffix) of the individual named as policyholder on the secondary plan.
6	*If the patient has secondary dental plan coverage,* enter the secondary policyholder's date of birth as MMDDYYYY (without spaces).
7	*If the patient has secondary dental plan coverage,* enter an X in the appropriate box to indicate the secondary policyholder's gender.
8	*If the patient has secondary dental plan coverage,* enter the secondary policyholder's social security number (SSN) or dental plan identification number, as it appears on the dental plan card.
9	*If the patient has secondary dental plan coverage,* enter the secondary policyholder's dental plan number and group number (e.g., 123456 001).
10	*If the patient has secondary dental plan coverage,* enter an X in the appropriate box to indicate the relationship of the patient to the policyholder.
11	*If the patient has secondary dental plan coverage,* enter the dental plan's name, address, city, state, and zip code.
	PRIMARY SUBSCRIBER INFORMATION (POLICYHOLDER/SUBSCRIBER INFORMATION)
12	Enter the primary policyholder's complete name, address, city, state, and zip code.
13	Enter the primary policyholder's date of birth as MMDDYYYY (without spaces).
14	Enter an X in the appropriate box to indicate the primary policyholder's gender.
15	Enter the primary policyholder's social security number (SSN) or dental plan identification number and group number, as it appears on the dental plan card.
16	Enter the dental plan number and/or group number. **NOTE:** Plan number is also called *certificate number.*
17	Enter the name of the primary policyholder's employer.

(continues)

TABLE IV-2   (continued)

BLOCK	INSTRUCTIONS
	PATIENT INFORMATION
	NOTE: Always complete Block 18. Complete Blocks 19–23 only if the patient is *not* the primary policyholder (e.g., if "Self" does not contain an X in Block 18).
18	Enter an X in the appropriate box to indicate the relationship of the patient to the primary subscriber.
19	*If the patient is not the primary policyholder* and if the patient is a full-time student, enter an X in the FTS box. If the patient is a part-time student, enter an X in the PTS box. If the patient is *not* a student, leave blank.
20	*If the patient is not the primary policyholder*, enter the patient's complete name, address, city, state, and zip code.
21	*If the patient is not the primary policyholder*, enter the patient's date of birth as MMDDYYYY (without spaces).
22	*If the patient is not the primary policyholder*, enter an X in the appropriate box to indicate the patient's gender.
23	*If the patient is not the primary policyholder*, enter the account number assigned to the patient by the dental practice.
	RECORD OF SERVICES PROVIDED
24	For each procedure performed, enter the date of service on a different line. **NOTE:** There is no units/days column on the ADA claim.
25	Enter the area of oral cavity treated using the *ANSI/ADA/ISO Specification No. 3950 for Dentistry-Designation System for Teeth and Areas of the Oral Cavity*, which provides a system for designating teeth or areas of the oral cavity using two digits. It also provides a system for designating surfaces of the teeth using letters of the alphabet. The system was created by the International Dental Federation (IDF) and approved by the World Health Organization (WHO). **EXAMPLE:** UL = Upper Left Quadrant UR = Upper Right Quadrant LR = Lower Right Quadrant LL = Lower Left Quadrant
26	Enter the applicable ANSI ASC X12N code list qualifier JP or JO: • JP = ADA's Universal/National Tooth Designation System (numbers teeth 1–32) • JO = ANSI/ADA/ISO Specification No. 3950 (numbers teeth 11–18, 21–28, 31–38, 41–48)
27	Identify tooth/teeth number(s) when procedure directly involves a tooth (e.g., restoration, tooth extraction, root canal, crown, or dentition-related surgical excision): • Report a range of teeth by entering a hyphen between first and last tooth (e.g., 1–5) • Report separate individual teeth by entering a comma between teeth numbers (e.g., 1, 3, 5) **NOTE:** Use numerical identification (1–32) for permanent teeth and capital letter identification (A–T) for primary teeth. Leave blank if treatment of a specific tooth (e.g., oral examination) is not performed. For supernumerary tooth numbering, contact the dental plan.
28	When procedure(s) directly involve one or more tooth surface(s), enter up to five of the following codes (without spaces): B = Buccal F = Facial M = Mesial D = Distal L = Lingual O = Occlusal
29	Enter the CDT procedure code for dental treatment provided.

(continues)

TABLE IV-2 (continued)

BLOCK	INSTRUCTIONS
	RECORD OF SERVICES PROVIDED (continued)
30	Enter terminology to describe the service provided. **NOTE:** If service is for a supernumerary tooth, enter the word "supernumerary" and include information to identify the closest numbered tooth.
31	Enter the fee charged for the procedure.
32	Enter other fees (e.g., state taxes where applicable, fees imposed by regulatory agencies).
33	Enter the total of all fees reported on the claim.
	MISSING TEETH INFORMATION
34	Enter an X on each number that corresponds to a missing tooth.
35	Enter additional applicable information (e.g., multiple supernumerary teeth).
	AUTHORIZATIONS
36	Obtain patient/guardian signature and date, which authorizes payment and release of information to dental plan.
37	Obtain policyholder's signature and date, which authorizes the dental plan to make payment directly to the provider (e.g., dentist).
	ANCILLARY CLAIM/TREATMENT INFORMATION
38	Enter an X in the appropriate box to indicate place of treatment. **NOTE:** ECF refers to extended care facility (e.g., nursing facility).
39	Enter an X in the appropriate box if the claim has attached radiograph(s), oral image(s), and/or model(s). If nothing is attached to the claim, leave blank.
40	Enter an X in the NO box if treatment is not for orthodontics, and go to Block 43. Enter an X in the YES box if treatment is for orthodontics, and complete Blocks 41 and 42.
41	Enter the date appliances (e.g., braces) were placed as MMDDYYYY (without spaces). Leave blank if an X was entered in the NO box in Block 40.
42	Enter a number that represents the remaining months of treatment (e.g., 26). Leave blank if an X was entered in the NO box in Block 40.
43	Enter an X in the NO box if treatment is not for replacement of prosthesis, and go to Block 45. Enter an X in the YES box if treatment is for replacement of prosthesis, and complete Block 44.
44	Enter the date the prior prosthesis was placed as MMDDYYYY (without spaces). Leave blank if an X was entered in the NO box in Block 43.
45	Enter an X in the appropriate box, if applicable, and complete Blocks 46 and 47. Otherwise, leave blank.
46	If an X was entered in a box in Block 47, enter the date of accident as MMDDYYYY (without spaces). Otherwise, leave blank.
47	If an X was entered in the AUTO ACCIDENT box in Block 47, enter the state in which the accident occurred. Otherwise, leave blank.
	BILLING DENTIST OR DENTAL ENTITY
	REMEMBER! Complete Blocks 48–52 *only* if the provider is submitting a claim on behalf of the patient or policyholder.
48	*If the provider is submitting a claim on behalf of the patient or policyholder,* enter the provider's name, address, city, state, and zip code.

(continues)

TABLE IV-2 (continued)

BLOCK	INSTRUCTIONS
BILLING DENTIST OR DENTAL ENTITY (continued)	
49	*If the provider is submitting a claim on behalf of the patient or policyholder,* enter the provider's NPI. **NOTE:** This is *not* the provider's social security number or employer identification number.
50	*If the provider is submitting a claim on behalf of the patient or policyholder,* enter the provider's license number.
51	*If the provider is submitting a claim on behalf of the patient or policyholder,* enter the provider's social security number or employer identification number.
52	*If the provider is submitting a claim on behalf of the patient or policyholder,* enter the provider's telephone number.
52A	Leave blank.
TREATING DENTIST AND TREATMENT LOCATION INFORMATION	
53	Have the treating dentist provider sign and date the completed claim. **NOTE:** Check with the dental plan to determine if the signature can be typed or stamped, instead of signed by the provider.
54	Enter the treating dentist's NPI.
55	Enter the treating dentist's license number.
56	Enter the treating dentist's address, city, state, and zip code.
56A	Leave blank.
57	Enter the treating dentist's telephone number.
58	Leave blank.

APPENDIX V

Abbreviations

A

837	claims validation tables (as in ANSI ASC X12 837)
AAMA	American Association of Medical Assistants
ABN	Advance Beneficiary Notice
ADA	Americans with Disabilities Act
AHA	American Hospital Association
AHFS	American Hospital Formulary Service
AHIMA	American Health Information Management Association
AMA	American Medical Association
ANSI	American National Standards Institute
APC	ambulatory payment classification
AP-DRG	All Patient diagnosis-related group
APR-DRG	All Patient refined diagnosis-related group
ASC	Accredited Standards Committee
ASC	ambulatory surgical center

B

BC	Blue Cross
BCAC	Beneficiary Counseling and Assistance Coordinator
BCBS	Blue Cross Blue Shield
BCBSA	Blue Cross and Blue Shield Association
BRAC	base realignment and closure
BS	Blue Shield
BSR	Beneficiary Services Representative

C

Ca	cancer or carcinoma
CAC	common access card
CAC	computer-assisted coding
CAT	computerized axial tomography
CCS	Certified Coding Specialist
CDAC	Clinical Data Abstracting Center

CDHP	consumer-directed health plan
CDHS	California Department of Health Services
CDT	*Current Dental Terminology*
CERT	Comprehensive Error Rate Testing
CF	conversion factor
CHAMPUS	Civilian Health and Medical Program of the Uniformed Services
CHAMPVA	Civilian Health and Medical Program of Veterans Affairs
CLIA	Clinical Laboratory Improvement Act
CMP	competitive medical plan
CMS	Centers for Medicare and Medicaid Services
CMS-1450	UB-04 claim used by institutional and other selected providers to bill payers
CMS-1500	Insurance claim used by noninstitutional providers and suppliers to bill payers
CNS	clinical nurse specialist
COB	coordination of benefits
COBRA	Consolidated Omnibus Budget Reconciliation Act of 1985
CPC	Certified professional coder
CPT	Current Procedural Terminology
CRI	CHAMPUS Reform Initiative
CSCP	customized sub-capitation plan
CT	computed tomography

D

DCAO	debt collection assistance officer
DEERS	Defense Enrollment Eligibility Reporting System
DME	durable medical equipment
DMEPOS	durable medical equipment, prosthetic and orthotic supplies
DMERC	durable medical equipment regional carriers

641

DoD	Department of Defense
DRG	diagnosis-related groups
DSH	disproportionate share hospital (adjustment)
DSM	*Diagnostic and Statistical Manual*

E

EDD	(California) Employment Development Department
EDI	electronic data interchange
EFT	electronic funds transfer
EGHP	employer group health plan
EHNAC	Electronic Healthcare Network Accreditation Commission
EHR	electronic health record
E/M	evaluation and management
EMC	electronic media claim
EMR	electronic medical record
EOB	explanation of benefits
EPO	exclusive provider organization
EPSDT	early and periodic screening, diagnostic, and treatment
EQRO	external quality review organization
ERA	electronic remittance advice
ERISA	Employee Retirement Income Security Act of 1974

F

FATHOM	First-look Analysis for Hospital Outlier Monitoring
FCA	False Claims Act
FDCPA	Fair Debt Collection Practices Act
FECA	Federal Employment Compensation Act
FEHBP	Federal Employee Health Benefits Program
FELA	Federal Employment Liability Act
FEP	Federal Employee Program
FMAP	federal medical assistance percentage
FPL	federal poverty level
FR	*Federal Register*
FSA	flexible spending account

G

GEM	general equivalency mapping
GEP	general enrollment period
GCPI	geographic cost practice index
GPWW	group practice without walls

H

HA	Health Affairs
HAVEN	Home Assessment Validation and Entry
HCF	Health Care Finder
HCPCS	Healthcare Common Procedure Coding System
HCRA	healthcare reimbursement account
HEDIS	Health Plan Employer Data and Information Set
HHRG	home health resource group
HICN	health insurance claim number
HIPAA	Health Insurance Portability and Accountability Act of 1996
HIPPS	health insurance prospective payment system (code set)
HMO	health maintenance organization
HPMP	Hospital Payment Monitoring Program
HPSA	health personnel shortage area
HRA	health reimbursement arrangement
HSA	health savings account
HSSA	health savings security account

I

ICD	International Classification of Diseases
ICD-9-CM	*International Classification of Diseases, 9th revision, Clinical Modification*
ICD-10-CM	*International Classification of Diseases, 10th revision, Clinical Modification*
ICD-10-PCS	*International Classification of Diseases, 10th revision, Procedural Coding System*
IDS	integrated delivery system
IEP	initial enrollment period
IME	indirect medical education (adjustment)
IPA	independent practice association
IPIA	Improper Payments Information Act of 2002
IPO	integrated provider organization
IPPS	inpatient prospective payment system
IRVEN	Inpatient Rehabilitation Validation and Entry

L

LA	lead agent
LC	limiting charge
LCD	local coverage determination
LGHP	large group health plan

LHWCA	Longshore and Harbor Workers' Compensation Act
LLP	limited license practitioners
LTCPPS	long-term (acute) care hospital prospective payment system

M

MAC	Medicare administrative contractor
MAC	monitored anesthesia care
MDC	major diagnostic category
MCO	managed care organization
Medi-Medi	Medicare-Medicaid (crossover)
MEVS	Medicaid eligibility verification system
MFN	most favored nation
MHSS	Military Health Services System
MIP	Medicaid Integrity Program
MM	major medical
MN	medically needy
MPFS	Medicare physician fee schedule
MRI	magnetic resonance imaging
MSA	medical savings account
MS-DRG	Medicare severity diagnosis-related groups
MSDS	Material Safety Data Sheet
MSHA	Mine Safety and Health Administration
MSI	Medicare Supplementary Insurance
MSN	Medicare Summary Notice
MSO	management service organization
MSP	Medicare Secondary Payer
MSN	Medicare Summary Notice
MTF	military treatment facility

N

NAS	nonavailability statement
NCCI	National Correct Coding Initiative
NCD	national coverage determination
NCHS	National Center for Health Statistics
NCQA	National Committee for Quality Assurance
NDC	National Drug Code
NEC	not elsewhere classifiable
NMOP	National Mail Order Pharmacy
nonPAR	nonparticipating provider
NOS	not otherwise specified
NP	nurse practitioner
NPI	national provider identifier
NPPES	National Plan and Provider Enumeration System

NSF	national standard format
NUCC	National Uniform Claims Committee

O

OBRA	Omnibus Budget Reconciliation Act of 1981
OCE	outpatient code editor
OCR	optical character reader
OHI	other health insurance
OIG	Office of Inspector General
OPM	Office of Personnel Management
OPAP	outpatient pretreatment authorization plan
OSHA	Occupational Safety and Health Administration
OWCP	Office of Workers' Compensation Programs

P

PA	physician assistant
PACE	Program of All-Inclusive Care for the Elderly
PAR	participating provider
PAT	preadmission testing
PATH	Physicians at Teaching Hospitals
PCM	primary care manager
PCP	primary care provider
PDAC	Pricing, Data Analysis and Coding
PEPP	Payment Error Prevention Program
PEPPER	Program for Evaluating Payment Patterns Electronic Report
PERM	Payment Error Rate Measurement
PFFS	private fee-for-service plan
PFPWD	program for persons with disabilities
PHI	protected health information
PI	program integrity (office)
PIN	provider identification number
PlanID	national health plan identification number
PMO	program management organization (TRICARE)
POS	place of service
PPA	preferred provider arrangement
PPN	preferred provider network
PPO	preferred provider organization
PRN	Provider Remittance Notice
PSO	provider-sponsored organization

Q

QAPI	quality assessment and performance improvement
QDWI	qualified disabled and working individual

QI	qualifying individual
QISMC	Quality Improvement System for Managed Care
QMB	qualified Medicare beneficiary
QMBP	qualified Medicare beneficiary program
QPU	Quarterly Provider Update (published by CMS)

R

RAVEN	Resident Assessment Validation and Entry
RBRVS	resource-based relative value scale
REVS	recipient eligibility verification system
ROM	risk of mortality
RVU	relative value unit

S

SCHIP	State Children's Health Insurance Program
SEP	special enrollment period
SLMB	specified low-income Medicare beneficiary
SOAP	subjective, objective, assessment, plan
SOI	severity of illness
SSA	Social Security Administration
SSI	Supplemental Security Income
SSN	social security number
SSO	second surgical opinion
SURS	surveillance and utilization review subsystem

T

TANF	Temporary Assistance for Needy Families
TEFRA	Tax Equity and Fiscal Responsibility Act of 1982

TMA	TRICARE Management Activity
TOS	type of service
TPA	third-party administrator
TPMS	total practice management system
TRHCA	Tax Relief and Health Care Act of 2006
TSC	TRICARE Service Center

U

UB-04	uniform bill (claim) created in 2004; also called CMS-1450
UCR	usual, customary, and reasonable
UPIN	unique provider identification number
URO	utilization review organization

V

VA	Veterans Administration
VAN	value-added network

W

WHO	World Health Organization

X

X12N	Insurance Subcommittee (as in ANSI ASC X12N 837)

Common Medical Terminology

Prefixes, Suffixes, and Combining Forms

a-, an-	no; not	-emia	blood condition
ab-	away from	en-	in; within
abdomin-	abdomen	end-, endo-	in; within
acr-	extremities; top	epi-	above; upon
ad-	toward	erythr-	red
-ad	toward	-esis	condition
adip-	fat	-esthesia	nervous sensation
-al	pertaining to	eti-	cause
angi-	vessel	ex-	out; away from
ankyl-	crooked; bent	extra-	outside
anti-	against	fibr-	fiber
arthr-	joint	fore-	before
-asis, -esis, -iasis, -isis, -sis	condition	galact-, lact-	milk
		gaster-, gastr-	stomach
bi-	two	genit-	genitals
blephar-	eyelid	gloss-	tongue
brachy-	short	gluc-, glyc-	sugar; glucose
brady-	slow	-gram	record
bronch-	bronchial tube	-graph	instrument for reading
cardi-	heart	-graphy	process of recording
cephal-	head	gyn-, gyne-, gynec-	women; female
cervic-	neck; cervix	hem-, hema-, hemat-	blood
colp-, kolp-	vagina	hemi-	half
contra-	against; opposite	hepat-	liver
crani-	skull	hyp-, hyph-	below; under
cry-	cold	hyper-	above; excessive
cyan-	blue	hyster-	uterus; womb
dacry-	tear	-ia, -iasis	condition
dactyl-	fingers; toes	-ic	pertaining to
de-	lack of; down	ileo-	ileum (small intestine)
demi-	half	ilio-	ilium (hip bone)
derm-, dermat-	skin	in-	in; into; not
dextr-	right	infra-	within; into
di-	two	inter-	between
dis-	separation	intra-, intro-	within; into
-dynia	pain	ipsi-	same
dys-	bad; painful	-isis	condition
-ectomy	excision; removal	-itis	inflammation
-emesis	vomiting	juxta-	near

645

laryng-	larynx (voice box)	-poiesis, -poietic	formation
later-	side	poly-	many; much
leuk-	white	post-	after; behind
lingu-	tongue	poster-	back; behind
lip-	fat; lipid	pro-	before; forward
-lith	stone	pseud-	false
-lysis	breakdown	psych-	mind
mal-	bad	pyelo-	renal pelvis
-mania	obsessive preoccupation	re-	back; again
med-, medi-	middle	ren-	kidney
mega-, megal-	large	retr-	behind; back
melan-	black	rhe-, -rrhea	flow
meta-	change; beyond	rhin-	nose
metr-, metra-	uterus; measure	-rrhage, -rhagia	bursting forth (as of blood)
mon-	one; single		
musculo-, my-	muscle	-rrhaphy	suture
myel-	spinal cord; bone marrow	salping-	fallopian tube; auditory tube
nas-	nose		
necr-	death	scirrh-	hard
neo-	new	-sclerosis	hardening
nephr-, nephra-	kidney	-scope	instrument for visual examination
non-	not; no		
norm-	rule; order	-scopy	visual examination
ob-	obstetrics	semi-	half
oculo-, optico-, opto-	eye	soma-, somat-	body
-oma	tumor; mass	sphygm-	pulse
omphal-	umbilicus (navel)	splen-	spleen
onych-	nail	spondyl-	vertebra
oo-, ovi-, ovo-	egg	sten-	narrowness
oophor-, oophoron-	ovary	steth-	chest
-osis	condition—usually abnormal	sub-	below
oste-	bone	super-	above, superior
-ostomosis, -ostomy, -stomosis, -stomy	new opening	supra-	above, upper
		tachy-	fast
ot-	ear	tel-, tele-	complete
-otomy	incision	tend-, ten-	tendon
-ous	pertaining to	thorac-, thoraci-	chest; pleural cavity
pach-, pachy-	heavy; thick	thromb-	clot
pan-	all	-tomy	process of cutting
para-, -para	near; besides	trans-	across
path-, -pathic, -pathy	disease	trich-, trichi-	hair
per-	through	tympan-	tympanic membrane
peri-	surrounding	ultra-	beyond; excess
-pexy	fixation	uni-	one
pharyng-	throat (pharynx)	ureter-	ureter
phleb-	vein	urethr-	urethra
-phobia	fear	-uria	urination
-plegia	paralysis	vas-	vessel; duct
pleur-	pleura	ven-	vein
pneum-, pneumat-	lung; air	vesic-	urinary bladder

Bibliography

BOOKS AND MANUALS

Accounts Receivable Management for the Medical Practice. (2009). Los Angeles, CA: Practice Management Information Corporation.

American Medical Association. (2009). *CPT 2010.* Chicago, IL.

Blue Cross Association. (1972). *The Blue Cross story.* Chicago, IL.

Blue Cross and Blue Shield Association. (1987). *The history of Blue Cross and Blue Shield plans.* Chicago, IL.

Butler, A. & Dobbins, L. (2010). *Outcomes in coding practice: A roadmap from provider to payer.* Clifton Park, NY: Delmar Cengage Learning.

Davis, J. B. (2010). *Medical fees in the United States.* CA: Practice Management Information Corporation.

Davison, J., & Lewis, M. (2007). *Working with insurance and managed care plans: A guide for getting paid.* Los Angeles, CA: Practice Management Information Corporation.

Diamond, M. (2007). *Understanding hospital billing and coding: A worktext.* Clifton Park, NY: Delmar Learning.

Dictionary of coding and billing terminology. (2009). Los Angeles, CA: Practice Management Information Corporation.

E/M coding made easy! (2010). Los Angeles, CA: Practice Management Information Corporation.

Fordney, M. T., French, L. L., & Follis, J. F. (2008). *Administrative medical assisting.* Clifton Park, NY: Delmar Learning.

Frisch, B. (2007). *Correct coding for Medicare, compliance, and reimbursement.* Clifton Park, NY: Delmar Cengage Learning.

Garrett, T. M., Baillie, H. W., & Garrett, R. M. (2001). *Health care ethics: Principles and problems.* Upper Saddle River, NJ: Prentice Hall.

Green, M. (2009). *3-2-1 Code It!* Clifton Park, NY: Delmar Cengage Learning.

Ingenix Publishing. (2010). 2010 *HCPCS level II professional.* Salt Lake City, UT.

Ingenix Publishing. (2010). 2010 *ICD-9-CM professional for hospitals, volumes 1, 2 & 3.* Salt Lake City, UT.

Ingenix Publishing. (2008). *ICD-10-CM: the complete official draft code set.* Salt Lake City, UT: Ingenix Publishing.

___ (2009). *ICD-10-CM mapping file (2009 draft).* Salt Lake City, UT: Ingenix Publishing.

___ (2009). *ICD-10-PCS: The complete official draft code set.* Salt Lake City, UT: Ingenix Publishing.

___ (2009). *ICD-10-PCS mapping files (2009 draft).* Salt Lake City, UT: Ingenix Publishing.

___ (2010). *Medicare desk reference for physicians.* Salt Lake City, UT: Ingenix Publishing.

___ (2010). *Medicare correct coding guide.* Salt Lake City, UT: Ingenix Publishing.

___ (2010). *Uniform billing editor.* Salt Lake City, UT: Ingenix Publishing.

Keir, L., Wise, B., Krebs, C., & Kelley-Arney, C. (2008). *Medical assisting: Administrative and clinical competencies.* Clifton Park, NY: Delmar Learning.

Kelly-Farwell, D., & Favreau, C. (2008). *Coding for medical necessity in the physician's office.* Clifton Park, NY: Delmar Cengage Learning.

Krager, D., & Krager, C. (2008). *HIPAA for health care professionals.* Clifton Park, NY: Delmar Cengage Learning.

Lind, W. Q., Pooler, M. S., Tamparo, C. D., & Dahl, B. M. *Delmar's Comprehensive Medical Assisting: Administrative and Clinical Competencies.* (2010). Clifton Park, NY: Delmar Cengage Learning.

Maki, S. E., & Petterson, B. *Using the electronic health record in the healthcare provider practice.* Clifton Park, NY: Delmar Cengage Learning.

Moore, C. D. (2009). *Understanding workers' compensation insurance.* Clifton Park, NY: Delmar Cengage Learning.

National Association of Blue Shield Plans. *The Blue Shield story: All of us helping each of us.* Chicago, IL: Blue Cross and Blue Shield Association.

Richards, C. (2010). *Coding basics: medical billing and reimbursement fundamentals.* Clifton Park, NY: Delmar Cengage Learning.

Rimmer, M. (2009). *Coding basics, understanding medical collections.* Clifton Park, NY: Delmar Cengage Learning.

Rimmer, M. (2008). Medical Billing 101. Clifton Park, NY: Delmar Cengage Learning.

BROCHURES AND BULLETINS

CMS-1500 claim filing instructions. Albuquerque, NM: BlueCross BlueShield of New Mexico.

Coverage policy bulletins. Hartford, CT: Aetna US Healthcare, Aetna Life Insurance Company.

Electronic data revolution in the health care industry. Marlborough, MA: 3Com.

FEP service benefit plan brochure. Chicago, IL: Blue Cross and Blue Shield Federal Employees Program.

Follow that claim: Claims submission, adjudication and payment. Chicago, IL: American Medical Association.

Health Insurance Portability and Accountability Act of 1996—Administrative simplification care fact sheet. Washington, D.C.: Centers for Medicare and Medicaid Services.

Health insurance, the history. Seattle, WA: Health Insurance Association of America.

HIPAA: Health care transformation to electronic communications. Bellevue, WA: Captaris, Inc.

Medicare & you 2010. Washington, D.C.: Centers for Medicare and Medicaid Services.

Medicare and other health benefits: Your guide to who pays first. Washington, D.C.: Centers for Medicare and Medicaid Services.

Medigap policies: The basics. Washington, D.C.: Centers for Medicare and Medicaid Services.

Protecting Medicare and you from fraud. Washington, D.C.: Centers for Medicare and Medicaid Services.

Quick facts about Medicare's new coverage for prescription drugs for people with Medicare and Medicaid. Washington, D.C.: Centers for Medicare and Medicaid Services.

The facts about Medicare advantage. Washington, D.C.: Centers for Medicare and Medicaid Services.

The facts about Medicare prescription drug plans. Washington, D.C.: Centers for Medicare and Medicaid Services.

TRICARE grand rounds. Falls Church, VA: TRICARE Management Activity.

Understanding the choice you have in how you get your Medicare health care coverage. Washington, D.C.: Centers for Medicare and Medicaid Services.

Your Medicare benefits. Washington, D.C.: Centers for Medicare and Medicaid Services.

INSURANCE MANUALS

Blue Cross and Blue Shield of Maryland guide to programs & benefits. Owings Mills, MD: Carefirst Blue Cross and Blue Shield.

CHAMPVA handbook. Denver, CO: VA Health Administration Center.

Medicare claims processing manual. Washington, D.C.: Centers for Medicare and Medicaid Services.

Medicare contractor beneficiary and provider communications manual. Washington, D.C.: Centers for Medicare and Medicaid Services.

Medicare financial management manual. Washington, D.C.: Centers for Medicare and Medicaid Services.

Medicare general information, eligibility and entitlement manual. Washington, D.C.: Centers for Medicare and Medicaid Services.

Medicare managed care manual. Washington, D.C.: Centers for Medicare and Medicaid Services.

Medicare prescription drug benefit manual. Washington, D.C.: Centers for Medicare and Medicaid Services.

Medicare program integrity manual. Washington, D.C.: Centers for Medicare and Medicaid Services.

Medicare secondary payer manual. Washington, D.C.: Centers for Medicare and Medicaid Services.

Quality improvement organization manual. Washington, D.C.: Centers for Medicare and Medicaid Services.

State Medicaid manual. Washington, D.C.: Centers for Medicare and Medicaid Services.

TRICARE reimbursement manual. Aurora, CO: TRICARE Management Activity.

JOURNALS, NEWSMAGAZINES, AND NEWSLETTERS

Advance for health information professionals. King of Prussia, PA: Merion Publications.

BlueReview for contracting institutional & professional providers. Chicago, IL: Blue Cross and Blue Shield of Illinois.

Coding edge. Salt Lake City, UT: American Association of Professional Coders.

Compliance (free e-zine). Gaithersburg, MD: DecisionHealth.

Corporate compliance (free e-newsletter). Marblehead, MA: HCPro, Inc.

CPT assistant. Chicago, IL: American Medical Association.

Dental care news. Detroit, MI: Blue Cross and Blue Shield of Michigan.

Family practice management. Leawood, KS: American Academy of Family Physicians.

For the record. Spring City, PA: Great Valley Publishing.

Healthcare Auditing Weekly (free e-newsletter). Marblehead, MA: HCPro, Inc.

ICD-9/CPT CodingPro. Rockville, MD: Decision Health.

InFocus. Owings Mills, MD: CareFirst Blue Cross and Blue Shield.

Journal of Medical Practice Management®. Phoenix, MD: Greenbranch Publishing.

Journal of the American Health Information Management Association. Chicago, IL: American Health Information Management Association.

Managed Care Magazine. Yardley, PA: MultiMedia USA.

Medicare Update for Physician Services (free e-newsletter). Marblehead, MA: HCPro, Inc.

Medicare Weekly Update (free e-newsletter). Marblehead, MA: HCPro, Inc.

Physician billing & reimbursement (free e-zine). Gaithersburg, MD: DecisionHealth.

Physician coding (free e-zine). Gaithersburg, MD: DecisionHealth.

TrailBlazer eBulletin. Denison, TX: TrailBlazer Health Enterprises, LLC.

INTERNET-BASED REFERENCES

www.carefirst.com—BCBS affiliate in Maryland.

cms.meridianski.com—self-paced Medicare training by downloading free interactive courses and attending free satellite programs designed to teach Medicare billing guidelines.

www.codecorrect.com—subscription service that provides CPT, ICD-9, CCI, Coding Crosswalk and APC data, and searchable Medicare newsletters and *Federal Register* issues.

www.usa.gov—resource for locating government information on the Internet.

www.trailblazerhealth.com—Medicare Part A and Part B Newsletter and Special Bulletins.

www.worldofquotes.com—archive of historic quotes and proverbs.

SOFTWARE

Encoder Pro. Salt Lake City, UT: Ingenix Publishing.

SIMClaim. Clifton Park, NY: Delmar Cengage Learning.

Glossary

 # (7) - the number (#) symbol precedes CPT codes that appear out of numerical order.

abuse (5) - actions inconsistent with accepted, sound medical, business, or fiscal practices.

accept assignment (4) - provider accepts as payment in full whatever is paid on the claim by the payer (except for any copayment and/or coinsurance amounts).

accounts receivable (4) - the amount owed to a business for services or goods provided.

accounts receivable aging report (4) - shows the status (by date) of outstanding claims from each payer, as well as payments due from patients.

accounts receivable management (4) - assists providers in the collection of appropriate reimbursement for services rendered; include functions such as insurance verification/eligibility and preauthorization of services.

accreditation (3) - voluntary process that a healthcare facility or organization (e.g., hospital or managed care plan) undergoes to demonstrate that it has met standards beyond those required by law.

adjudication (17) - judicial dispute resolution process in which an appeals board makes a final determination.

adjusted claim (15) - payment correction resulting in additional payment(s) to the provider.

advance beneficiary notice (ABN) (14) - document that acknowledges patient responsibility for payment if Medicare denies the claim.

adverse effect (6) - also called *adverse reaction;* the appearance of a pathologic condition due to ingestion or exposure to a chemical substance properly administered or taken.

adverse reaction (6) - *see* adverse effect.

adverse selection (3) - covering members who are sicker than the general population.

allowable charge (9) - *see* limiting charge.

allowed charge (4) - the maximum amount the payer will reimburse for each procedure or service, according to the patient's policy.

All Patient DRG (AP–DRG) (9) - DRG system adapted for use by third-party payers to reimburse hospitals for inpatient care provided to *non*-Medicare beneficiaries (e.g., Blue Cross Blue Shield, commercial health plans, TRICARE); DRG assignment is based on intensity of resources.

All Patient Refined DRG (APR–DRG) (9) - adopted by Medicare in 2008 to reimburse hospitals for inpatient care provided to Medicare beneficiaries; expanded original DRG system (based on intensity of resources) to add two subclasses to each DRG that adjusts Medicare inpatient hospital reimbursement rates for severity of illness (SOI) (extent of physiological decompensation or organ system loss of function) and risk of mortality (ROM) (likelihood of dying); each subclass, in turn, is subdivided into four areas: (1) minor, (2) moderate, (3) major, and (4) extreme.

ambulance fee schedule (9) - payment system for ambulance services provided to Medicare beneficiaries.

Ambulatory Payment Classification (APC) (2) - prospective payment system used to calculate reimbursement for outpatient care according to similar clinical characteristics and in terms of resources required.

ambulatory surgical center (ASC) (9) - state-licensed, Medicare-certified supplier (not provider) of surgical healthcare services that must *accept assignment* on Medicare claims.

ambulatory surgical center payment rate (9) - predetermined amount for which ASC services are reimbursed, at 80 percent after adjustment for regional wage variations.

Amendment to the HMO Act of 1973 (3) - legislation that allowed federally qualified HMOs to permit members to occasionally use non-HMO physicians and be partially reimbursed.

American Academy of Professional Coders (AAPC) (1) - professional association established to provide a national certification and credentialing process, to support the national and local membership by providing educational products and opportunities to network, and to increase and promote national recognition and awareness of professional coding.

American Association of Medical Assistants (AAMA) (1) - enables medical assisting professionals to enhance and demonstrate the knowledge, skills, and professionalism required by employers and patients; and protect medical assistants' right to practice.

American Health Information Management Association (AHIMA) (1) - founded in 1928 to improve the quality of medical records, and currently advances the health information management (HIM) profession toward an electronic and global environment, including implementation of ICD-10-CM and ICD-10-PCS in 2013.

American Hospital Association (AHA) (13) - national organization that represents and serves all types of hospitals, healthcare networks, and their patients and communities; the AHA began as the accreditation agency for new prepaid hospitalization plans in 1939.

American Medical Billing Association (AMBA) (1) - offers the Certified Medical Reimbursement Specialist (CMRS) exam, which recognizes competency of members who have met high standards of proficiency.

American Recovery and Reinvestment Act of 2009 (5) - authorized an expenditure of $1.5 billion for grants for construction, renovation and equipment, and for the acquisition of health information technology systems.

ANSI ASC X12 standards (4) - use a variable-length file format to process transactions for institutional, professional, dental, and drug claims.

ANSI ASC X12N 837 (5) - variable-length file format used to bill institutional, professional, dental, and drug claims.

appeal (4) - documented as a letter, signed by the provider, explaining why a claim should be reconsidered for payment.

arbitration (17) - dispute-resolution process in which a final determination is made by an impartial person who may not have judicial powers.

assessment (10) - contains the diagnostic statement and may include the physician's rationale for the diagnosis.

assignment of benefits (4) - the provider receives reimbursement directly from the payer.

auditing process (10) - review of patient records and CMS-1500 (or UB-04) claims to assess coding accuracy and whether documentation is complete.

authorization (5) - document that provides official instruction, such as the customized document that gives covered entities permission to use specified protected health information (PHI) for specified purposes or to disclose PHI to a third party specified by the individual.

automobile insurance policy (12) - contract between an individual and an insurance company whereby the individual pays a premium and in exchange, the insurance company agrees to pay for specific car-related financial losses during the term of the policy; typically includes medical-payments coverage and personal injury protection (PIP) to reimburse healthcare expenses sustained as the result of injury from an automobile accident.

Away From Home Care® Program (13) - provides continuous BCBS healthcare coverage for subscribers who will be out of their service area for more than 90 consecutive days.

axis of classification (6) - organizes entities, diseases, and other conditions according to etiology, anatomy, or severity (as in ICD-10-CM).

bad debt (4) - accounts receivable that cannot be collected by the provider or a collection agency.

balance billing (9) - billing beneficiaries for amounts not reimbursed by payers (not including copayments and coinsurance amounts); this practice is prohibited by Medicare regulations.

Balanced Budget Act of 1997 (BBA) (2) - addresses healthcare fraud and abuse issues, and provides for Department of Health and Human Services (DHHS) Office of the Inspector General (OIG) investigative and audit services in healthcare fraud cases.

base period (12) - period of time that usually covers 12 months and is divided into four consecutive quarters.

BCBS basic coverage (13) - Blue Cross and Blue Shield (BCBS) coverage for the following services: hospitalization, diagnostic laboratory services, x-rays, surgical fees, assistant surgeon fees, obstetric care, intensive care, newborn care, and chemotherapy for cancer.

BCBS major medical (MM) coverage (13) - BCBS coverage for the following services, in addition to basic coverage: office visits, outpatient nonsurgical treatment, physical and occupational therapy, purchase of durable medical equipment (DME), mental health visits, allergy testing and injections, prescription drugs, private duty nursing (when medically necessary), and dental care required as a result of a covered accidental injury.

beneficiary (4) - the person eligible to receive healthcare benefits.

beneficiary counseling and assistance coordinator (BCAC) (16) - individuals available at a military treatment facility (MTF) to answer questions, help solve healthcare-related problems, and assist beneficiaries in obtaining medical care through TRICARE; were previously called *health benefits advisors (HBA).*

beneficiary services representative (BSR) (16) - employed at a TRICARE Service Center; provides information about using TRICARE and assists with other matters affecting access to health care (e.g., appointment scheduling).

benefit period (Medicare) (14) - begins with the first day of hospitalization and ends when the patient has been out of the hospital for 60 consecutive days.

benign (6) - not cancerous.

billing entity (11) - the legal business name of the provider's practice.

birthday rule (4) - determines coverage by primary and secondary policies when each parent subscribes to a different health insurance plan.

black box edits (5) - nonpublished code edits, which were discontinued in 2000.

BlueCard® Program (13) - program that allows BCBS subscribers to receive local Blue Plan healthcare benefits while traveling or living outside of their plan's area.

Blue Cross (BC) (13) - insurance plan created in 1929 when Baylor University Hospital, in Dallas, TX, approached teachers in the Dallas school district with a plan that guaranteed up to 21 days of hospitalization per year for subscribers and each dependent for a $6 annual premium.

Blue Cross/Blue Shield (BCBS) (13) - joint venture between Blue Cross and Blue Shield where the corporations shared one building and computer services but maintained separate corporate identities.

BlueCross BlueShield Association (BCBSA) (2) - an association of independent Blue Cross and Blue Shield plans.

Blue Shield (BS) (13) - began as a resolution passed by the House of Delegates at an American Medical Association meeting in 1938; incorporates a concept of voluntary health insurance that encourages physicians to cooperate with prepaid health plans.

BlueWorldwide *Expat* (13) - provides global medical coverage for active employees and their dependents who spend more than six months outside the United States; any U.S. corporation with new or existing Blue coverage that sends members to work and reside outside the United States for six months or more is eligible for BlueWorldwide *Expat*.

bonding insurance (1) - an insurance agreement that guarantees repayment for financial losses resulting from the act or failure to act of an employee. It protects the financial operations of the employer.

breach of confidentiality (5) - unauthorized release of patient information to a third party.

business liability insurance (1) - protects business assets and covers the cost of lawsuits resulting from bodily injury, personal injury, and false advertising.

cafeteria plan (3) - also called *triple option plan;* provides different health benefit plans and extra coverage options through an insurer or third-party administrator.

capitation (3) - provider accepts preestablished payments for providing healthcare services to enrollees over a period of time (usually one year).

carcinoma (Ca) *in situ* (6) - a malignant tumor that is localized, circumscribed, encapsulated, and noninvasive (has not spread to deeper or adjacent tissues or organs).

care plan oversight services (7) - cover the physician's time supervising a complex and multidisciplinary care treatment program for a specific patient who is under the care of a home health agency, hospice, or nursing facility.

case law (5) - also called *common law;* based on a court decision that establishes a precedent.

case management (3) - development of patient care plans to coordinate and provide care for complicated cases in a cost-effective manner.

case management services (7) - process by which an attending physician coordinates and supervises care provided to a patient by other providers.

case manager (3) - submits written confirmation, authorizing treatment, to the provider.

case mix (9) - the types and categories of patients treated by a healthcare facility or provider.

catastrophic cap benefit (16) - protects TRICARE beneficiaries from devastating financial loss due to serious illness or long-term treatment by establishing limits over which payment is not required.

catchment area (16) - the region defined by code boundaries within a 40-mile radius of a military treatment facility.

Category I codes (7) - procedures/services identified by a five-digit CPT code and descriptor nomenclature; these codes are traditionally associated with CPT and organized within six sections.

Category II codes (7) - optional performance measurement tracking codes that are assigned an alphanumeric identifier with a letter in the last field (e.g., 1234A); these codes will be located after the Medicine section; *their use is optional.*

Category III codes (7) - temporary codes for data collection purposes that are assigned an alphanumeric identifier with a letter in the last field (e.g., 0001T); these codes are located after the Medicine section, and will be archived after five years unless accepted for placement within Category I sections of CPT.

Centers for Medicare and Medicaid Services (CMS) (1) - formerly known as the Health Care Financing Administration (HCFA); an administrative agency within the federal Department of Health and Human Services (DHHS).

CHAMPUS Reform Initiative (CRI) (2, 16) - conducted in 1988; resulted in a new health program called TRICARE, which includes three options: TRICARE Prime, TRICARE Extra, and TRICARE Standard.

charge description master (CDM) (9) - *see* chargemaster.

chargemaster (4) - term hospitals use to describe a patient encounter form.

check digit (5) - one-digit character, alphabetic or numeric, used to verify the validity of a unique identifier.

civil law (5) - area of law not classified as criminal.

Civilian Health and Medical Program of the Department of Veterans Affairs (CHAMPVA) (2) - program that provides health benefits for dependents of veterans rated as 100 percent permanently and totally disabled as a result of service-connected conditions, veterans who died as a result of service-connected conditions, and veterans who died on duty with less than 30 days of active service.

Civilian Health and Medical Program—Uniformed Services (CHAMPUS) (2) - originally designed as a benefit for dependents of personnel serving in the armed forces and uniformed branches of the Public Health Service and the National Oceanic and Atmospheric Administration; now called TRICARE.

claims adjudication (4) - comparing a claim to payer edits and the patient's health plan benefits to verify that the required information is available to process the claim; the claim is not a duplicate; payer rules and procedures have been followed; and procedures performed or services provided are covered benefits.

claims attachment (4) - medical report substantiating a medical condition.

claims examiner (1) - employed by third-party payers to review health-related claims to determine whether the charges are reasonable and medically necessary based on the patient's diagnosis.

claims processing (4) - sorting claims upon submission to collect and verify information about the patient and provider.

claims submission (4) - the transmission of claims data (electronically or manually) to payers or clearinghouses for processing.

Classification of Drugs by AHFS List (6) - Appendix C of ICD-9-CM that contains the American Hospital Formulary Services list number and its ICD-9-CM equivalent code number; organized in numerical order according to AHFS list number.

Classification of Industrial Accidents According to Agency (6) - Appendix D of ICD-9-CM; based on employment injury statistics adopted by the Tenth International Conference of Labor Statisticians.

clean claim (4) - a correctly completed standardized claim (e.g., CMS-1500 claim).

clearinghouse (4) - performs centralized claims processing for providers and health plans.

Clinical Data Abstracting Center (CDAC) (5) - requests and screens medical records for the Payment Error Prevention Program (PEPP) to survey samples for medical review, DRG validation, and medical necessity.

clinical laboratory fee schedule (9) - data set based on local fee schedules (for outpatient clinical diagnostic laboratory services).

Clinical Laboratory Improvement Act (CLIA) (2) - established quality standards for all laboratory testing to ensure the accuracy, reliability, and timeliness of patient test results regardless of where the test was performed.

clinical nurse specialist (CNS) (9) - a registered nurse licensed by the state in which services are provided, has a master's degree in a defined clinical area of nursing from an accredited educational institution, and is certified as a CNS by the American Nurses Credentialing Center.

closed claim (4) - claims for which all processing, including appeals, has been completed.

closed-panel HMO (3) - health care is provided in an HMO-owned center or satellite clinic or by physicians who belong to a specially formed medical group that serves the HMO.

CMS-1500 (2) - form used to submit Medicare claims; previously called the HCFA-1500.

CMS Quarterly Provider Update (QPU) (9) - an online CMS publication that contains information about regulations and major policies currently under development, regulations and major policies completed or cancelled, and new or revised manual instructions.

code pairs (5) - edit pairs included in the Correct Coding Initiative (CCI) cannot be reported on the same claim if each has the same date of service.

coding (1) - process of reporting diagnoses, procedures, and services as numeric and alphanumeric characters on the insurance claim.

coding conventions (6) - rules that apply to the assignment of ICD-9-CM codes.

coinsurance (2, 4) - also called *coinsurance payment;* the percentage the patient pays for covered services after the deductible has been met and the copayment has been paid.

commercial insurance (12) - covers the medical expenses of individuals and groups; and premiums and benefits vary according to the type of plan offered.

common access card (CAC) (16) - identification card issued by the Department of Defense (DoD), which TRICARE enrollees show to receive healthcare services.

common data file (4) - abstract of all recent claims filed on each patient.

common law (5) - also called *case law;* is based on a court decision that establishes a precedent.

comorbidity (6) - secondary diagnosis or concurrent condition that coexists with the primary condition, has the potential to affect treatment of the primary condition, and is an active condition for which the patient is treated or monitored.

competitive medical plan (CMP) (3) - an HMO that meets federal eligibility requirements for a Medicare risk contract, but is not licensed as a federally qualified plan.

complication (6) - condition that develops subsequent to inpatient admission.

comprehensive assessment (7) - must include an assessment of the patient's functional capacity, identification of potential problems, and a nursing plan to enhance, or at least maintain, the patient's physical and psychosocial functions.

computer-assisted coding (CAC) (6) - uses a natural language processing engine to "read" patient records and generate ICD-9-CM and HCPCS/CPT codes.

concurrent care (7) - provision of similar services, such as hospital inpatient visits, to the same patient by more than one provider on the same day.

concurrent review (3) - review for medical necessity of tests and procedures ordered during an inpatient hospitalization.

conditional primary payer status (14) - Medicare claim process that includes the following circumstances: a plan that is normally considered to be primary to Medicare issues a denial of payment that is under appeal;

a patient who is physically or mentally impaired failed to file a claim to the primary payer; a workers' compensation claim has been denied and the case is slowly moving through the appeal process; or there is no response from a liability payer within 120 days of filing the claim.

confidentiality (5) - restricting patient information access to those with proper authorization and maintaining the security of patient information.

congenital anomaly (6) - disorder diagnosed in infants at birth.

Consolidated Omnibus Budget Reconciliation Act of 1985 (COBRA) (2) - allows employees to continue healthcare coverage beyond the benefit termination date.

consultation (7) - examination of a patient by a healthcare provider, usually a specialist, for the purpose of advising the referring or attending physician in the evaluation and/or management of a specific problem with a known diagnosis.

Consumer Credit Protection Act of 1968 (4) - was considered landmark legislation because it launched truth-in-lending disclosures that required creditors to communicate the cost of borrowing money in a common language so that consumers could figure out the charges, compare costs, and shop for the best credit deal.

consumer–directed health plan (CDHP) (3) - *see* consumer-driven health plan.

consumer–driven health plan (2) - healthcare plan that encourages individuals to locate the best health care at the lowest possible price, with the goal of holding down costs; also called *consumer-directed health plan.*

contiguous site (6) - also called *overlapping site;* occurs when the origin of the tumor (primary site) involves two adjacent sites.

continuity of care (2) - documenting patient care services so that others who treat the patient have a source of information on which to base additional care and treatment

contributory components (7) - include counseling, coordination of care, nature of presenting problem, and time.

conversion factor (9) - dollar multiplier that converts relative value units (RVUs) into payments.

coordinated care plan (14) - also called *managed care plan;* includes health maintenance organizations (HMOs), preferred provider organizations (PPOs), and provider-sponsored organizations (PSOs), through which a Medicare beneficiary may choose to receive healthcare coverage and services. CCPs often provide a greater array of services and smaller copayment than conventional Medicare.

coordinated home health and hospice care (13) - allows patients with this option to elect an alternative to the acute care setting.

coordination of benefits (COB) (4) - provision in group health insurance policies that prevents multiple insurers from paying benefits covered by other policies; also specifies that coverage will be provided in a specific sequence when more than one policy covers the claim.

coordination of care (7) - physician makes arrangements with other providers or agencies for services to be provided to a patient.

copayment (copay) (2) - provision in an insurance policy that requires the policyholder or patient to pay a specified dollar amount to a healthcare provider for each visit or medical service received.

counseling (7) - discussion with a patient and/or family concerning one or more of the following areas: diagnostic results, impressions, and/or recommended diagnostic studies; prognosis; risks and benefits of management (treatment) options; instructions for management (treatment) and/or follow-up; importance of compliance with chosen management (treatment) options; risk factor reduction; and patient and family education.

covered entity (4) - private sector health plans (excluding certain small self-administered health plans), managed care organizations, ERISA-covered health benefit plans (Employee Retirement Income Security Act of 1974), and government health plans (including Medicare, Medicaid, Military Health System for active duty and civilian personnel; Veterans Health Administration, and Indian Health Service programs); all healthcare clearinghouses; and all healthcare providers that choose to submit or receive transactions electronically.

CPT-5 (7) - fifth edition of CPT, developed by the American Medical Association in response to the electronic data interchange requirements of the Health Insurance Portability and Accountability Act of 1996 (HIPAA).

CPT-5 Project (7) - improvements to CPT that address the needs of hospitals, managed care organizations, and long-term care facilities.

CPT Coding Conventions (7)

boldface type - highlights main terms in the CPT index and categories, subcategories, headings, and code numbers in the CPT manual.

cross-reference term (See) - directs coders to a different CPT index entry because no codes are found under the original entry.

descriptive qualifiers - terms that clarify assignment of a CPT code.

guidelines - define terms and explain the assignment of codes for procedures and services located in a particular section.

inferred words - used to save space in the CPT index when referencing subterms.

instructional notes - appear throughout CPT sections to clarify the assignment of codes.

italicized type - used for the cross-reference term, *See*, in the CPT index.

separate procedure - follows a code description that identifies procedures that are an integral part of another procedure or service.

CPT Symbols (7)

● bullet located to the left of a code number identifies new CPT procedures and services.

▲ triangle located to the left of a code number identifies a revised code description.

►◄ horizontal triangles surround revised guidelines and notes. *This symbol is not used for revised code descriptions.*

; semicolon saves space in CPT so that some code descriptions are not printed in their entirety next to a code number; the entry is indented and the coder refers back to the common portion of the code description located before the semicolon.

+ plus symbol identifies add-on codes for procedures that are commonly, but not always, performed at the same time and by the same surgeon as the primary procedure.

∅ symbol identifies codes that are not to be appended with modifier -51.

⊙ bull's eye symbol identifies a procedure that includes conscious sedation. (CPT Appendix G includes a list of codes that include conscious sedation.)

⫫ flash symbol indicates that a code is pending FDA approval but that it has been assigned a CPT code.

criminal law (5) - public law governed by statute or ordinance that deals with crimes and their prosecution.

critical care services (7) - reported when a physician directly delivers medical care for a critically ill or critically injured patient.

critical pathway (16) - sequence of activities that can normally be expected to result in the most cost-effective clinical course of treatment.

Current Dental Terminology (CDT) **(5)** - medical code set maintained and copyrighted by the American Dental Association.

Current Procedural Terminology (CPT) **(1)** - published by the American Medical Association; includes five-digit numeric codes and descriptors for procedures and services performed by providers (e.g., 99203 identifies a detailed office visit for a new patient).

customized sub-capitation plan (CSCP) (3) - managed care plan in which healthcare expenses are funded by insurance coverage; the individual selects one of each type of provider to create a customized network and pays the resulting customized insurance premium; each provider is paid a fixed amount per month to provide only the care that an individual needs from that provider (called a *sub-capitation payment*).

day sheet (4) - also called *manual daily accounts receivable journal;* chronological summary of all transactions posted to individual patient ledgers/accounts on a specific day.

debt collection assistance officer (DCAO) (16) - individuals located at military treatment facilities to assist beneficiaries in resolving healthcare collection-related issues.

decrypt (5) - to decode an encoded computer file so that it can be viewed.

deductible (2, 4) - amount for which the patient is financially responsible before an insurance policy provides coverage.

Defense Enrollment Eligibility Reporting System (DEERS) (16) - computer system that contains up-to-date Defense Department Workforce personnel information.

delinquent account (4) - *see* past due account.

delinquent claim (4) - claim usually more than 120 days past due; some practices establish time frames that are less than or more than 120 days past due.

delinquent claim cycle (4) - advances through various aging periods (30 days, 60 days, 90 days, and so on), with practices typically focusing internal recovery efforts on older delinquent accounts (e.g., 120 days or more).

demonstration/pilot program (14) - special project that tests improvements in Medicare coverage, payment, and quality of care.

demonstration project (16) - tests and establishes the feasibility of implementing a new program during a trial period, after which the program is evaluated, modified, and/or abandoned.

deposition (5) - legal proceeding during which a party answers questions under oath (but not in open court).

diagnosis pointer numbers (11) - item numbers 1 through 4 preprinted in Block 21 of the CMS-1500 claim.

diagnosis-related group (DRG) (2) - prospective payment system that reimburses hospitals for inpatient stays.

Diagnostic and Statistical Manual (DSM) **(9, 16)** - classifies mental health disorders and is based on ICD; published by the American Psychiatric Association.

Diagnostic Coding and Reporting Guidelines for Outpatient Services: Hospital-Based and Physician Office (6) - developed by the federal government for use in reporting diagnoses for claims submission.

digital (5) - application of a mathematical function to an electronic document to create a computer code that can be encrypted (encoded).

direct contract model HMO (3) - contracted healthcare services delivered to subscribers by individual physicians in the community.

direct patient contact (7) - refers to face-to-face patient contact (outpatient or inpatient).

disability insurance (12) - reimbursement for income lost as a result of a temporary or permanent illness or injury.

discharge planning (3) - involves arranging appropriate healthcare services for the discharged patient (e.g., home health care).

disproportionate share hospital (DSH) adjustment (9) - hospitals that treat a high-percentage of low-income patients receive increased Medicare payments.

downcoding (4) - assigning lower-level codes than documented in the record.

DSM (16) - *see Diagnostic and Statistical Manual.*

dual eligibles (15) - individuals entitled to Medicare and eligible for some type of Medicaid benefit.

durable medical equipment (DME) (8) - canes, crutches, walkers, commode chairs, blood glucose monitors, and so on.

durable medical equipment, prosthetics and orthotic supplies (DMEPOS) (8) - defined by Medicare as equipment that can withstand repeated use, is primarily used to serve a medical purpose, is used in the patient's home, and would not be used in the absence of illness or injury.

durable medical equipment, prosthetics, orthotics, and supplies (DMEPOS) dealers (8) - supply patients with durable medical equipment (DME) (e.g., canes, crutches); DMEPOS claims are submitted to DME Medicare administrative contractors (MACs) awarded contracts by CMS; each DME MAC covers a specific geographic region of the country and is responsible for processing DMEPOS claims for its specific region.

durable medical equipment, prosthetics/orthotics, and supplies (DMEPOS) fee schedule (9) - Medicare reimburses DMEPOS dealers according to either the actual charge or the amount calculated according to formulas that use average reasonable charges for items during a base period from 1986 to 1987, whichever is lower.

E code (6) - located in the ICD-9-CM Tabular List, describes external causes of injury, poisoning, or other adverse reactions affecting a patient's health.

Early and Periodic Screening, Diagnostic, and Treatment (EPSDT) services (15) – legislation that mandates states to provide routine pediatric checkups to all children enrolled in Medicaid.

edit pairs (5) - *see code pairs.*

electronic claims processing (4) - sending data in a standardized machine-readable format to an insurance company via disk, telephone, or cable.

electronic data interchange (EDI) (4) - computer-to-computer exchange of data between provider and payer.

electronic flat file format (4) - series of fixed-length records (e.g., 25 spaces for patient's name) submitted to payers to bill for healthcare services.

electronic funds transfer (EFT) (4) - system by which payers deposit funds to the provider's account electronically.

Electronic Funds Transfer Act (4) - established the rights, liabilities, and responsibilities of participants in electronic funds transfer systems.

electronic health record (2) - global concept that includes the collection of patient information documented by a number of providers at different facilities regarding one patient.

Electronic Healthcare Network Accreditation Commission (EHNAC) (4) - organization that accredits clearinghouses.

electronic media claim (4) - *see* electronic flat file format.

electronic medical record (EMR) (2) - considered part of the electronic health record (EHR), the EMR is created on a computer using a keyboard, a mouse, an optical pen device, a voice recognition system, a scanner, or a touch screen; records are created using vendor software, which assists in provider decision making; numerous vendors offer EMR software, mostly to physician office practices that require practice management solutions.

electronic remittance advice (ERA) (4) - remittance advice that is submitted to the provider electronically and contains the same information as a paper-based remittance advice; providers receive the ERA more quickly.

electronic transaction standards (5) - also called *transactions rule;* a uniform language for electronic data interchange.

E/M codes (2) - *see* Evaluation and Management (E/M).

embezzle (1) - the illegal transfer of money or property as a fraudulent action.

emergency care (16) - care for the sudden and unexpected onset of a medical or mental health condition that is threatening to life, limb, or sight.

emergency department services (7) - services provided in an organized, hospital-based facility, which is open on a 24-hour basis, for the purpose of "providing unscheduled episodic services to patients requiring immediate medical attention."

Employee Retirement Income Security Act of 1974 (ERISA) (2) - mandated reporting and disclosure requirements for group life and health plans (including managed care plans), permitted large employers to self-insure employee healthcare benefits, and exempted large employers from taxes on health insurance premiums.

employer group health plan (EGHP) (9) - contributed to by an employer or employee pay-all plan; provides coverage to employees and dependents without regard to the enrollee's employment status (i.e., full-time, part-time, or retired).

encoder (6) - automates the coding process using computerized or Web-based software; instead of manually looking up conditions (or procedures) in the coding manual's index, the coder uses the software's search feature to locate and verify diagnosis and procedure codes.

encounter form (4) - financial record source document used by providers and other personnel to record treated diagnoses and services rendered to the patient during the current encounter.

encrypt (5) - to convert information to a secure language format for transmission.

end-stage renal disease (ESRD) (14) - chronic kidney disorder that requires long-term hemodialysis or kidney transplantation because the patient's filtration system in the kidneys has been destroyed.

Energy Employees Occupational Illness Compensation Program (17) - provides benefits to eligible employees and former employees of the Department of Energy, its contractors and subcontractors, certain survivors of such individuals, and certain beneficiaries of the Radiation Exposure Compensation Act.

enrollees (3) - also called *covered lives;* employees and dependents who join a managed care plan; known as *beneficiaries* in private insurance plans.

Equal Credit Opportunity Act (4) - prohibits discrimination on the basis of race, color, religion, national origin, sex, marital status, age, receipt of public assistance, or good faith exercise of any rights under the Consumer Credit Protection Act.

errors and omissions insurance (1) - *see* professional liability insurance.

ESRD composite payment rate system (9) - bundles end-state renal disease (ESRD) drugs and related laboratory tests with the composite rate payments, resulting in one reimbursement amount paid for ESRD services provided to patients; the rate is case-mix adjusted to provide a mechanism to account for differences in patients' utilization of healthcare resources (e.g., patient's age).

established patient (7) - one who has received professional services from the physician or from another physician of the same specialty who belongs to the same group practice, within the past three years.

ethics (1) - principle of right or good conduct; rules that govern the conduct of members of a profession.

Evaluation and Management (E/M) (2) - services that describe patient encounters with providers for evaluation and management of general health status.

Evaluation and Management Documentation Guidelines (7) - federal (CMS) guidelines that explain how E/M codes are assigned according to elements associated with comprehensive multisystem and single-system examinations.

Evaluation and Management (E/M) section (7) - located at the beginning of CPT because these codes describe services (e.g., office visits) that are most frequently provided by physicians.

exclusive provider organization (EPO) (3) - managed care plan that provides benefits to subscribers if they receive services from network providers.

explanation of benefits (EOB) (1) - report that details the results of processing a claim (e.g., payer reimburses provider $80 on a submitted charge of $100).

extent of examination (CPT) (7)

> *comprehensive* - general multisystem examination or a complete examination of a single organ system.

> *detailed* - extended examination of the affected body area(s) and other symptomatic or related organ system(s).

> *expanded problem focused* - limited examination of the affected body area or organ system and other symptomatic or related organ system(s).

> *problem focused* - limited examination of the affected body area or organ system.

extent of history (CPT) (7)

> *comprehensive* - chief complaint, extended history of present illness, review of systems directly related to the problem(s) identified in the history of the present illness, plus a review of all additional body systems and complete past/family/social history.

> *detailed* - chief complaint, extended history of present illness, problem-pertinent system review extended to include a limited number of additional systems, pertinent past/family/social history directly related to patient's problem.

> *expanded problem focused* - chief complaint, brief history of present illness, problem-pertinent system review.

> *problem focused* - chief complaint, brief history of present illness or problem.

external quality review organization (EQRO) (3) - responsible for reviewing health care provided by managed care organizations.

face-to-face time (7) - amount of time the office or outpatient care provider spends with the patient and/or family.

Fair Credit and Charge Card Disclosure Act (4) - amended the Truth in Lending Act, requiring credit and charge card issuers to provide certain disclosures in direct mail, telephone, and other applications and solicitations for open-end credit and charge accounts and under other circumstances; this law applies to providers that accept credit cards.

Fair Credit Billing Act (4) - federal law passed in 1975 that helps consumers resolve billing issues with card issuers; protects important credit rights, including rights to dispute billing errors, unauthorized use of an account, and charges for unsatisfactory goods and services; cardholders cannot be held liable for more than $50 of fraudulent charges made to a credit card.

Fair Credit Reporting Act (4) - protects information collected by consumer reporting agencies such as credit bureaus, medical information companies and tenant screening services; organizations that provide information to consumer reporting agencies also have specific legal obligations, including the duty to investigate disputed information.

Fair Debt Collection Practices Act (FDCPA) (4) - specifies what a collection source may and may not do when pursuing payment of past due accounts.

False Claims Act (FCA) (5) - passed by the federal government during the Civil War to regulate fraud associated with military contractors selling supplies and equipment to the Union Army.

Federal Black Lung Program (17) - enacted in 1969 as part of the *Black Lung Benefits Act;* provides medical treatment and other benefits for respiratory conditions related to former employment in the nation's coal mines.

Federal Claims Collection Act (5) - requires Medicare administrative contractors (previously called carriers and fiscal intermediaries), as agents of the federal government, to attempt the collection of overpayments.

Federal Employee Health Benefits Program (FEHBP) (13) - also called the *Federal Employee Program (FEP);* an employer-sponsored health benefits program established by an Act of Congress in 1959, which now provides benefits to more than 9 million federal enrollees and dependents through contracts with about 300 third-party payers.

Federal Employee Program (FEP) (13) - *see* Federal Employee Health Benefits Program (FEHBP).

Federal Employees' Compensation Act (FECA) (2) - replaced the 1908 workers' compensation legislation; civilian employees of the federal government are provided medical care, survivors' benefits, and compensation for lost wages.

Federal Employment Liability Act (FELA) (17) - not a workers' compensation statute, but provides railroad employees with protection from employer negligence, making railroads engaged in interstate commerce liable for injuries to employees if the railroad was negligent.

Federal Medical Assistance Percentage (FMAP) (15) - portion of the Medicaid program paid by the federal government.

federal poverty level (FPL) (15) - income guidelines established annually by the federal government.

Federal Register (5) - legal newspaper published every business day by the National Archives and Records Administration (NARA).

federally qualified HMO (3) - certified to provide healthcare services to Medicare and Medicaid enrollees.

fee-for-service (3) - reimbursement methodology that increases payment if the healthcare service fees increase, if multiple units of service are provided, or if more expensive services are provided instead of less expensive services (e.g., brand-name vs. generic prescription medication).

fee schedule (2) - list of predetermined payments for healthcare services provided to patients (e.g., a fee is assigned to each CPT code).

Financial Services Modernization Act (2) - prohibits sharing of medical information among health insurers and other financial institutions for use in making credit decisions; also allows banks to merge with investment and insurance houses, which allows them to make a profit no matter what the status of the economy, because people usually house their money in one of the options; also called *Gramm-Leach-Bliley Act.*

First Report of Injury (17) - workers' compensation form completed when the patient first seeks treatment for a work-related illness or injury.

first-listed diagnosis (6) - reported on outpatient claims (instead of inpatient *principal diagnosis);* it is determined in accordance with ICD-9-CM's coding conventions (or rules) as well as general and disease-specific coding guidelines.

First-look Analysis for Hospital Outlier Monitoring (FATHOM) (5) - data analysis tool, which provides administrative hospital and state-specific data for specific CMS target areas.

fiscal year (16) - for the federal government, October 1 of one year to September 30 of the next.

flexible benefit plan (3) - *see* cafeteria plan and triple option plan.

flexible spending account (FSA) (3) - tax-exempt account offered by employers with any number of employees, which individuals use to pay healthcare bills; participants enroll in a relatively inexpensive, high-deductible insurance plan, and a tax-deductible savings account is opened to cover current and future medical expenses; money deposited (and earnings) is tax-deferred, and money is withdrawn to cover qualified medical expenses tax-free; money can be withdrawn for purposes other than healthcare expenses after payment of income tax plus a 15 percent penalty; also called *health savings account (HSA)* or *health savings security account (HSSA).*

for-profit corporation (13) - pays taxes on profits generated by the corporation's for-profit enterprises and pays dividends to shareholders on after-tax profits.

fraud (5) - intentional deception or misrepresentation that could result in an unauthorized payment.

gag clause (3) - prevents providers from discussing all treatment options with patients, whether or not the plan would provide reimbursement for services.

gatekeeper (3) - primary care provider for essential healthcare services at the lowest possible cost, avoiding nonessential care, and referring patients to specialists.

general enrollment period (GEP) (14) - enrollment period for Medicare Part B held January 1 through March 31 of each year.

general equivalency mapping (GEM) (6) - translation dictionaries or crosswalks of codes that can be used to roughly identify ICD-10-CM/PCS codes for their ICD-9-CM equivalent codes (and vice versa).

global period (7) - includes all services related to a procedure during a period of time (e.g., 10 days, 30 days, 90 days, depending on payer guidelines).

global surgery (7) - also called *package concept* or *surgical package;* includes the procedure, local infiltration, metacarpal/digital block or topical anesthesia when used, and normal, uncomplicated follow-up care.

Government-Wide Service Benefit Plan (13) - phrase printed below the BCBS trademark on federal employee plan (FEP) insurance cards, which indicates that the enrollee has federal employer-sponsored health benefits.

Gramm–Leach–Bliley Act (2) - *see* Financial Services Modernization Act.

group health insurance (2) - traditional healthcare coverage subsidized by employers and other organizations (e.g., labor unions, rural and consumer health cooperatives) whereby part or all of premium costs are paid for and/or discounted group rates are offered to eligible individuals.

group model HMO (3) - contracted healthcare services delivered to subscribers by participating physicians who are members of an independent multispecialty group practice.

group practice without walls (GPWW) (3) - contract that allows physicians to maintain their own offices and share services (e.g., appointment scheduling and billing).

grouper software (9) - determines appropriate group (e.g., diagnosis-related group, home health resource group, and so on) to classify a patient after data about the patient is input.

guarantor (4) - person responsible for paying healthcare fees.

HCPCS level II (1) - national codes published by CMS, which include five-digit alphanumeric codes for procedures, services, and supplies not classified in CPT.

HCPCS level II code types (8)

dental codes - contained in *Current Dental Terminology (CDT)*.

miscellaneous codes - reported when a DMEPOS dealer submits a claim for a product or service for which there is no existing permanent national code.

modifiers - provide additional information about a procedure or service (e.g., left-sided procedure).

permanent national codes - maintained by the HCPCS National Panel, composed of representatives from the BlueCross BlueShield Association (BCBSA), the Health Insurance Association of America (HIAA), and CMS.

temporary codes - maintained by the CMS and other members of the HCPCS National Panel; independent of permanent national codes.

Health Affairs (HA) (16) - refers to the Office of the Assistant Secretary of Defense for Health Affairs, which is responsible for both military readiness and peacetime health care.

health care (2) - expands the definition of medical care to include preventive services.

Healthcare Anywhere (13) - BCBS program that allows members of independently owned and operated plans to have access to healthcare benefits throughout the U.S. and around the world.

Healthcare Common Procedure Coding System (HCPCS) (1) - coding system that consists of CPT, national codes (level II), and local codes (level III); local codes were discontinued in 2003; previously known as HCFA Common Procedure Coding System.

health care finder (HCF) (16) - registered nurse or physician assistant who assists primary care providers with preauthorizations and referrals to healthcare services in a military treatment facility or civilian provider network.

healthcare provider (1) - physician or other healthcare practitioner (e.g., physician's assistant).

health care reimbursement account (HCRA) (3) - tax-exempt account used to pay for healthcare expenses; individual decides, in advance, how much money to deposit in an HCRA (and unused funds are lost).

health information technician (1) - professionals who manage patient health information and medical records, administer computer information systems, and code diagnoses and procedures for healthcare services provided to patients.

health insurance (2) - contract between a policyholder and a third-party payer or government program to reimburse the policyholder for all or a portion of the cost of medically necessary treatment or preventive care by healthcare professionals.

health insurance claim (1) - documentation submitted to an insurance plan requesting reimbursement for healthcare services provided (e.g., CMS-1500 and UB-04 claims).

Health Insurance Portability and Accountability Act of 1996 (HIPAA) (2) - mandates regulations that govern privacy, security, and electronic transactions standards for healthcare information.

health insurance prospective payment system (HIPPS) code set (9) - Five-digit alphanumeric codes that represent case-mix groups about which payment determinations are made for the HH PPS.

health insurance specialist (1) - person who reviews health-related claims to determine the medical necessity for procedures or services performed before payment (reimbursement) is made to the provider; *see also* reimbursement specialists.

health maintenance organization (HMO) (3) - responsible for providing healthcare services to subscribers in a given geographical area for a fixed fee.

Health Maintenance Organization Assistance Act of 1973 (3) - authorized grants and loans to develop HMOs under private sponsorship; defined a federally qualified HMO as one that has applied for, and met, federal standards established in the HMO Act of 1973; required most employers with more than 25 employees to offer HMO coverage if local plans were available.

Healthcare Effectiveness Data and Information Set (HEDIS) (3) - created standards to assess managed-care systems using data elements that are collected, evaluated, and published to compare the performance of managed healthcare plans.

health reimbursement arrangement (HRA) (3) - tax-exempt accounts offered by employers with more than 50 employees.

health savings account (HSA) (3) - *see* flexible spending account.

health savings security account (HSSA) (3) - *see* flexible spending account.

Hill-Burton Act (2) - provided federal grants for modernizing hospitals after the Great Depression and WWII (1929–1945); facilities were required to provide services free, or at reduced rates, to patients unable to pay for care.

history (7) - interview of patient that includes history of the present illness (HPI) (including the patient's chief complaint), a review of systems (ROS), and a past/family/social history (PFSH).

hold harmless clause (1) - patient is not responsible for paying what the insurance plan denies.

Home Assessment Validation and Entry (HAVEN) (9) - data entry software used to collect OASIS assessment data for transmission to state databases.

Home Health Prospective Payment System (HH PPS) (2) - reimbursement methodology that uses a classification system called home health resource groups (HHRGs), which establishes a predetermined rate for healthcare services provided to patients for each 60-day episode of home health care.

home health resource group (HHRG) (9) - classifies patients into one of 80 groups, which range in severity level according to three domains: clinical, functional, and service utilization.

home services (7) - healthcare services provided in a private residence.

hospice (14) - autonomous, centrally administered program of coordinated inpatient and outpatient palliative (relief of symptoms) services for terminally ill patients and their families.

hospital discharge service (7) - includes final examination of the patient, discussion of hospital stay with the patient and/or caregiver; instructions for continuing care provided to the patient and/or caregiver; and preparation of discharge records, prescriptions, and referral forms.

Hospital Payment Monitoring Program (HPMP) (5) - measures, monitors, and reduces incidence of Medicare fee-for-service payment errors for short-term, acute care, inpatient PPS hospitals.

iatrogenic illness (6) - illness that results from medical intervention (e.g., adverse reaction to contrast material injected prior to a scan).

ICD-9-CM Coordination and Maintenance Committee (6) - NCHS and CMS federal agencies responsible for overseeing changes and modifications to ICD-9-CM diagnosis (NCHS) and procedure (CMS) codes.

ICD-10 Coordination and Maintenance Committee (6) - NCHS and CMS agencies responsible for overseeing all changes and modifications to ICD-10-CM (NCHS) and ICD-10-PCS (CMS).

ICD-9-CM Index to Diseases coding conventions (6)

code in slanted brackets - always reported as secondary codes because they are manifestations (results) of other conditions.

eponym - disease (or procedure) named for an individual (e.g., physician who originally discovered the disease, first patient diagnosed with the disease).

essential modifier - subterms that are indented below the main term in alphabetical order (except for "with" and "without"); clarifies the main term and must be contained in the diagnostic statement for the code to be assigned.

main term - condition printed in boldface type and followed by the code number.

NEC (not elsewhere classifiable) - identifies codes to be assigned when information needed to assign a more specific code cannot be located in the ICD-9-CM coding book.

nonessential modifier - subterm enclosed in parentheses following the main term that clarify code selection, but do not have to be present in the provider's diagnostic statement.

note - contained in boxes to define terms, clarify index entries, and list choices for additional digits (e.g., fourth and fifth digits).

qualifier - supplementary term that further modifies subterms and other qualifiers.

See - directs the coder to a more specific term under which the code can be found.

See also - refers the coder to an index entry that may provide additional information to assign the code.

See also condition - directs the coder to the condition in the index (because the coder referenced an anatomic site, etc.).

See category - directs the coder to a specific three-digit category code in the Tabular List of Diseases for code assignment.

subterm - essential modifiers that qualify the main term by listing alternate sites, etiology, or clinical status.

ICD-9-CM Index to Procedures and Tabular List of Procedures coding conventions (6)

code also any synchronous procedures - refers to operative procedures that are to be coded to completely classify a procedure.

omit code - term that identifies procedures or services that may be components of other procedures; this instruction means that the procedure or service is not coded.

ICD-9-CM Tabular List of Diseases coding conventions (6)

and - when two disorders are separated by the word "and," it is interpreted as "and/or" and indicates that either of the two disorders is associated with the code number.

bold type - all category and subcategory codes and descriptions are printed in bold type.

braces - enclose a series of terms, each of which modifies the statement located to the right of the brace.

brackets - enclose synonyms, alternate wording, or explanatory phrases.

category - printed in bold upper- and lowercase type and are preceded by a three-digit code.

code first underlying disease - appears when the code referenced is to be sequenced as a secondary code; the code, title, and instructions are italicized.

colon - used after an incomplete term and is followed by one or more modifiers (additional terms).

excludes - directs the coder to another location in the codebook for proper assignment of the code.

format - all subterms are indented below the term to which they are linked; if a definition or disease requires more than one line, that text is printed on the next line and further indented.

fourth and fifth digits - create ICD-9-CM subcategory and subclassification codes, respectively. (In the ICD-9-CM Tabular List of Procedures, third and fourth digits create ICD-9-CM subcategory and subclassification codes, respectively.)

includes - includes notes appear below a three-digit category code description to further define, clarify, or provide an example.

major topic heading - printed in bold uppercase letters and followed by a range of codes enclosed in parentheses.

not otherwise specified (NOS) - indicates that the code is unspecified; coders should ask the provider for a more specific diagnosis before assigning the code.

parentheses - enclose supplementary words that may be present or absent in the diagnostic statement, without affecting assignment of the code number.

subcategory - indented and printed in the same fashion as the major category headings.

subclassification - requires the assignment of a fifth digit.

use additional code - indicates that a second code is to be reported to provide more information about the diagnosis.

with - when codes combine one disorder with another (e.g., code that combines primary condition with a complication), the provider's diagnostic statement must clearly indicate that both conditions are present and that a relationship exists between the conditions.

Improper Payments Information Act of 2002 (IPIA) (5) – established the *Payment Error Rate Measurement (PERM) program* to measure improper payments in the Medicaid program and the State Children's Health Insurance Program (SCHIP); *Comprehensive Error Rate Testing (CERT) program* to calculate the paid claims error rate for submitted Medicare claims by randomly selecting a statistical sample of claims to determine whether claims were paid properly (based on reviewing selected claims and associated medical record documentation); and the *Hospital Payment Monitoring Program (HPMP)* to measure, monitor, and reduce the incidence of Medicare fee-for-service payment errors for short-term, acute care, inpatient PPS hospitals.

incident to (9) - Medicare regulation which permitted billing Medicare under the physician's billing number for ancillary personnel services when those services were "incident to" a service performed by a physician.

indemnity coverage (13) - offers choice and flexibility to subscribers who want to receive a full range of benefits along with the freedom to use any licensed healthcare provider.

independent contractor (1) - defined by the *'Lectric Law Library's Lexicon* as "a person who performs services for another under an express or implied agreement and who is not subject to the other's control, or right to control, of the manner and means of performing the services. The organization that hires an independent contractor is not liable for the acts or omissions of the independent contractor."

independent practice association (IPA) HMO (3) - also called *individual practice association (IPA)*; type of HMO where contracted health services are delivered to subscribers by physicians who remain in their independent office settings.

Index to Diseases (Volume 2) (6) - contains Alphabetical Index of Diseases and Injuries, Table of Drugs and Chemicals, and Index to External Causes of Injury and Poisoning.

Index to Procedures and Tabular List of Procedures (Volume 3) (ICD-9-CM) (6) - included only in the hospital version of the commercial ICD-9-CM; is a combined alphabetical index and numerical listing of inpatient procedures.

indexing (6) - cataloging diseases and procedures by code number.

indirect medical education (IME) adjustment (9) - approved teaching hospitals receive increased Medicare payments, which are adjusted depending on the ratio of residents-to-beds (to calculate operating costs) and residents-to-average daily census (to calculate capital costs).

individual health insurance (2) - private health insurance policy purchased by individuals or families who do not have access to group health insurance coverage; applicants can be denied coverage, and they can also be required to pay higher premiums due to age, gender, and/or preexisting medical conditions.

individual practice association (IPA) HMO (3) - *see* independent practice association (IPA).

initial enrollment period (IEP) (14) - seven-month period that provides an opportunity for the individual to enroll in Medicare Part A and/or Part B.

initial hospital care (7) - covers the first inpatient encounter the *admitting/attending physician* has with the patient for each admission.

injury (6) - traumatic wound or damage to an organ.

inpatient prospective payment system (IPPS) (9) - system in which Medicare reimburses hospitals for inpatient hospital services according to a predetermined rate for each discharge.

Inpatient Psychiatric Facility Prospective Payment System (IPF PPS) (2) - system in which Medicare reimburses inpatient psychiatric facilities according to a patient classification system that reflects differences in patient resource use and costs; it replaces the cost-based payment system with a *per diem* IPF PPS.

Inpatient Rehabilitation Facilities Prospective Payment System (IRF PPS) (2) - implemented as a result of the BBA of 1997; utilizes information from a patient assessment instrument to classify patients into distinct groups based on clinical characteristics and expected resource needs.

Inpatient Rehabilitation Validation and Entry (IRVEN) (9) - software used as the computerized data entry system by inpatient rehabilitation facilities to create a file in a standard format that can be electronically transmitted to a national database; data collected is used to assess the clinical characteristics of patients in rehabilitation hospitals and rehabilitation units in acute care hospitals, and provide agencies and facilities with a means to objectively measure and compare facility performance and quality; data also provides researchers with information to support the development of improved standards.

insurance (2) - contract that protects the insured from loss.

integrated delivery system (IDS) (3) - organization of affiliated provider sites (e.g., hospitals, ambulatory surgical centers, or physician groups) that offer joint healthcare services to subscribers.

integrated provider organization (IPO) (3) - manages the delivery of healthcare services offered by hospitals, physicians employed by the IPO, and other healthcare organizations (e.g., an ambulatory surgery clinic and a nursing facility).

intensity of resources (9) - relative volume and types of diagnostic, therapeutic, and inpatient bed services used to manage an inpatient disease.

International Classification of Diseases (ICD) (2) - classification system used to collect data for statistical purposes.

International Classification of Diseases, 9th Revision, Clinical Modification (ICD-9-CM) (1) - coding system used to report diagnoses and reasons for encounters on physician office claims.

International Classification of Diseases, 10th Revision, Clinical Modification (ICD-10-CM) (1) - coding system to be implemented on October 1, 2013, and used to report diagnoses and reasons for encounters on outpatient and physician office claims.

International Classification of Diseases, 10th Revision, Procedural Coding System (ICD-10-PCS) (1) - coding system to be implemented on October 1, 2013, and used to report procedures in all inpatient claims.

internship (1) - nonpaid professional practice experience that benefits students and facilities that accept students for placement; students receive on-the-job experience prior to graduation, and the internship assists them in obtaining permanent employment.

interrogatory (5) - document containing a list of questions that must be answered in writing.

IPPS 3-day payment window (9) - requires that outpatient preadmission services provided by a hospital for a period of up to three days prior to a patient's inpatient admission be covered by the IPPS DRG payment for diagnostic services (e.g., lab testing) and therapeutic (or nondiagnostic) services when the inpatient principal diagnosis code (ICD-9-CM) exactly matches that for pre-admission services.

IPPS 72-hour rule (9) - *see* IPPS 3-day payment window.

IPPS transfer rule (9) - any patient with a diagnosis from one of ten CMS-determined DRGs, who is discharged to a post acute provider, is treated as a transfer case; this means hospitals are paid a graduated *per diem* rate for each day of the patient's stay, not to exceed the prospective payment DRG rate.

key components (7) - extent of history, extent of examination, and complexity of medical decision making.

large group health plan (LGHP) (9) - provided by an employer that has 100 or more employees *or* a multiemployer plan in which at least one employer has 100 or more full- or part-time employees.

late effect (6) - residual effect or sequela of a previous acute illness, injury, or surgery.

lead agent (LA) (16) - serves as a federal healthcare team created to work with regional military treatment facility commanders, uniformed service headquarters' staffs, and Health Affairs (HA) to support the mission of the Military Health Services System (MHSS).

legislation (3) - laws.

lesion (6) - any discontinuity of tissue (e.g., skin or organ) that may or may not be malignant.

level of service (7) - reflects the amount of work involved in providing health care to patients.

liability insurance (12) - policy that covers losses to a third party caused by the insured, by an object owned by the insured, or on the premises owned by the insured.

lien (12) - pledges or secures a debtor's property as security or payment for a debt; may be used in a potential liability case, but use varies on a federal and state basis.

lifetime maximum amount (2) - maximum benefit payable to a health plan participant.

lifetime reserve days (14) - may be used only once during a patient's lifetime and are usually reserved for use during the patient's final, terminal hospital stay.

limiting charge (9) - maximum fee a physician may charge.

List of Three-Digit Categories (6) - found in Appendix E of ICD-9-CM; contains a breakdown of three-digit category codes organized beneath section headings.

listserv (5) - subscriber-based question-and-answer forum that is available through e-mail.

litigation (4) - legal action to recover a debt; usually a last resort for a medical practice.

local coverage determination (LCD) (10) - formerly called *local medical review policy (LMRP);* Medicare administrative contractors create edits for national coverage determination rules that are called LCDs.

Longshore and Harbor Workers' Compensation Program (17) - administered by the U.S. Department of Labor; provides medical benefits, compensation for lost wages, and rehabilitation services to longshoremen, harbor workers, and other maritime workers who are injured during the course of employment or suffer from diseases caused or worsened by conditions of employment.

long–term (acute) care hospital prospective payment system (LTCPPS) (9) - classifies patients according to long-term (acute) care DRGs, which are based on patients' clinical characteristics and expected resource needs; replaced the reasonable cost-based payment system.

major diagnostic category (MDC) (9) - organizes diagnosis-related groups (DRGs) into mutually exclusive categories, which are loosely based on body systems (e.g., nervous system).

major medical insurance (2) - coverage for catastrophic or prolonged illnesses and injuries.

malignant (6) - cancerous.

managed care (3) - *see* managed health care.

managed care organization (MCO) (3) - responsible for the health of a group of enrollees; can be a health plan, hospital, physician group, or health system.

managed health care (managed care) (3) - combines health-care delivery with the financing of services provided.

management service organization (MSO) (3) - usually owned by physicians or a hospital and provides practice management (administrative and support) services to individual physician practices.

mandate (3) - laws.

manual daily accounts receivable journal (4) - also called the *day sheet;* a chronological summary of all transactions posted to individual patient ledgers/accounts on a specific day.

MassHealth (15) - name of Massachusetts' Medicaid program.

Material Safety Data Sheet (MSDS) (17) - contains information about chemical and hazardous substances used on-site.

Medicaid (2, 15) - cost-sharing program between the federal and state governments to provide healthcare services to low-income Americans; originally administered by the Social and Rehabilitation Service (SRS).

Medicaid eligibility verification system (MEVS) (15) - sometimes called *recipient eligibility verification system* or *REVS;* allows providers to electronically access the state's eligibility file through point-of-sale device, computer software, and automated voice response.

Medicaid Integrity Program (MIP) (5) - increased resources available to CMS to combat fraud, waste, and abuse in the Medicaid program; Congress requires annual reporting by CMS about the use and effectiveness of funds appropriated for the MIP.

Medicaid remittance advice (15) - sent to the provider; serves as an explanation of benefits from Medicaid and contains the current status of all claims (including adjusted and voided claims).

MediCal (15) - name of California's Medicaid program.

medical assistance program (15) - program for individuals with incomes below the federal poverty level.

medical assistant (1) - employed by a provider to perform administrative and clinical tasks that keep the office or clinic running smoothly.

Medical Association of Billers (MAB) (1) - created in 1995 to provide medical billing and coding specialists with a reliable source for diagnosis and procedure coding education and training.

medical care (2) - includes the identification of disease and the provision of care and treatment as provided by members of the healthcare team to persons who are sick, injured, or concerned about their health status.

medical decision making (7) - refers to the complexity of establishing a diagnosis and/or selecting a management option as measured by the number of diagnoses or management options, amount and/or complexity of data to be reviewed, and risk of complications and/or morbidity or mortality.

medical emergency care rider (13) - covers immediate treatment sought and received for sudden, severe, and unexpected conditions that, if not treated, would place the patient's health in permanent jeopardy or cause permanent impairment or dysfunction of an organ or body part.

medical foundation (3) - nonprofit organization that contracts with and acquires the clinical and business assets of physician practices; the foundation is assigned a provider number and manages the practice's business.

Medical Integrity Program (MIP) (5) - fraud and abuse detection program created by the Deficit Reduction Act of 2005.

medical malpractice insurance (1) - a type of liability insurance that covers physicians and other healthcare professionals for liability claims arising from patient treatment.

medical necessity (1) - involves linking every procedure or service reported to the insurance company to a condition that justifies the necessity for performing that procedure or service.

medical necessity denial (14) - denial of otherwise covered services that were found to be not "reasonable and necessary."

medical record (2) - *see* patient record.

medical savings account (MSA) (3) - tax-exempt trust or custodial account established for the purpose of paying medical expenses in conjunction with a high-deductible health plan; allows individuals to withdraw tax-free funds for healthcare expenses, which are not covered by a qualifying high-deductible health plan.

Medicare severity diagnosis–related groups (MS–DRGs) (9) - adopted by Medicare in 2008 to improve recognition of severity of illness and resource consumption and reduce cost variation among DRGs; bases DRG relative weights on hospital costs and greatly expanded the number of DRGs; re-evaluated complications/comorbidities (CC) list to assign *all* ICD-9-CM codes as non-CC status (conditions that should not be treated as CCs for specific clinical conditions), CC status, or major CC status; handles diagnoses closely associated with patient mortality differently depending on whether the patient lived or expired.

medically managed (10) - a particular diagnosis (e.g., hypertension) may not receive direct treatment during an office visit, but the provider had to consider that diagnosis when considering treatment for other conditions.

medically unlikely edits (MUE) project (11) - implemented to improve accuracy of Medicare payments by detecting and denying unlikely Medicare claims on prepayment basis. MUEs are used to compare units of service with code numbers as reported on submitted claims. On the CMS-1500, Block 24G (units of service) is compared with Block 24D (code number) on the same line. On the UB-04, Form Locator 46 (service units) is compared with Form Locator 44.

Medicare (2) - reimburses healthcare services to Americans over the age of 65.

Medicare administrative contractor (MAC) (5) - an organization (e.g., third-party payer) that contracts with CMS to process claims and perform program integrity tasks for Medicare Part A and Part B and DMEPOS; each contractor makes program coverage decisions and publishes a newsletter, which is sent to providers who receive Medicare reimbursement. Medicare is transitioning fiscal intermediaries and carriers to create Medicare Administrative Contractors (MACs).

Medicare Advantage (Medicare Part C) (14) - includes managed care plans and *private* fee-for-service plans, which provide care under contract to Medicare and may include such benefits as coordination of care, reductions in out-of-pocket expenses, and prescription drugs. Medicare enrollees have the option of enrolling in one of several plans; formerly called Medicare+Choice.

Medicare Benefit Policy Manual **(9)** - replaced current Medicare general coverage instructions that were found in Chapter II of the *Medicare Carriers Manual, Intermediary Manual,* various provider manuals, and *Program Memorandum* documents.

Medicare Cost Plan (14) - type of HMO similar to a medicare Advantage Plan; if an individual receives care from a non-network provider, the original medicare plan covers the services.

Medicare coverage database (MCD) (10) - used by Medicare administrative contractors, providers, and other health-care industry professionals to determine whether a procedure or service is reasonable and necessary for the diagnosis or treatment of an illness or injury; contains national coverage determinations (NCDs), including draft policies and proposed decisions; local coverage determinations (LCDs), including policy articles; and national coverage analyses (NCAs), coding analyses for labs (CALs), Medicare Evidence Development & Coverage Advisory Committee (MedCAC) proceedings, and Medicare coverage guidance documents.

Medicare+Choice (3) - *see* Medicare Advantage.

Medicare fee-for-service plan (14) - *see* original Medicare plan.

Medicare Hospital Insurance (14) - *see* Medicare Part A.

Medicare, Medicaid, and SCHIP Benefits Improvement and Protection Act of 2003 (BIPA) (2) - requires implementation of a $400 billion prescription drug benefit, improved Medicare Advantage (formerly called Medicare+Choice) benefits, faster Medicare appeals decisions, and more.

Medicare Medical Insurance (14) - *see* Medicare Part B.

Medicare National Coverage Determinations Manual **(9)** - replaced the *Medicare Coverage Issues Manual;* contains two chapters: Chapter 1 includes a description of national coverage determinations made by CMS, and Chapter 2 contains a listing of HCPCS codes that are related to each determination.

Medicare Part A (14) - reimburses institutional providers for inpatient, hospice, and some home health services.

Medicare Part B (14) - reimburses noninstitutional healthcare providers for outpatient services.

Medicare Part C (14) - *see* Medicare Advantage.

Medicare Part D (14) - The *MMA private prescription drug plans (PDPs)* and the *Medicare Advantage prescription drug plans (MA–PDs)* are collectively referred to as *Medicare Part D;* MMA requires coordination of Medicare Part D with State Pharmaceutical Assistance Programs (SPAPs), Medicaid plans, group health plans, Federal Employee Health Benefit Plans (FEHBPs), and military plans such as TRICARE); Medicare Part D enrollment is voluntary, and beneficiaries must apply for the benefit.

Medicare physician fee schedule (MPFS) (9) - payment system that reimburses providers for services and procedure by classifying services according to relative value units (RVUs); also called resource-based relative value scale (RBRVS) system.

Medicare Prescription Drug, Improvement, and Modernization Act (2) - adds new prescription drug and preventive benefits and provides extra assistance to people with low incomes.

Medicare Prescription Drug Plans (14) - *see* Medicare Part D.

Medicare private contract (14) - agreement between Medicare beneficiary and physician or other practitioner who has "opted out" of Medicare for two years for *all* covered items and services furnished to Medicare beneficiaries; physician/practitioner will not bill for any service or supplies provided to any Medicare beneficiary for at least two years.

Medicare risk program (3) - federally qualified HMOs and competitive medical plans (CMPs) that meet specified Medicare requirements provide Medicare covered services under a risk contract.

Medicare Savings Account (MSA) (14) - used by an enrollee to pay healthcare bills; Medicare pays for a special healthcare policy that has a high deductible and annually deposits into an account the difference between the policy cost and what it pays for an average Medicare enrollee in the patient's region.

Medicare Secondary Payer (MSP) (9) - situations in which the Medicare program does not have primary responsibility for paying a beneficiary's medical expenses.

Medicare SELECT (14) - type of Medigap policy available in some states where beneficiaries choose from a standardized Medigap plan.

Medicare special needs plan (14) - covers all Medicare Part A and Part B health care for individuals who can benefit the most from special care for chronic illnesses, care management of multiple diseases, and focused care management; such plans may limit membership to individuals who are eligible for both Medicare and Medicaid, have certain chronic or disabling conditions, and reside in certain institutions (e.g., nursing facility).

Medicare Summary Notice (MSN) (9) - previously called an *Explanation of Medicare Benefits* or *EOMB;* notifies Medicare beneficiaries of actions taken on claims.

Medicare supplemental plans (13) - augment the Medicare program by paying for Medicare deductibles and copayments.

Medicare Supplementary Insurance (MSI) (14) - *see* Medigap.

Medicare–Medicaid crossover (14) - combination of Medicare and Medicaid programs; available to Medicare-eligible persons with incomes below the federal poverty level.

Medigap (11) - supplemental plans designed by the federal government but sold by private commercial insurance companies to cover the costs of Medicare deductibles, copayments, and coinsurance, which are considered "gaps" in Medicare coverage.

member (13) - subscriber.

member hospital (13) - hospital that has signed a contract to provide services for special rates.

Merchant Marine Act (Jones Act) (17) - not a workers' compensation statute, but provides seamen with the same protection from employer negligence as FELA provides railroad workers.

message digest (5) - representation of text as a single string of digits, which was created using a formula, and for the purpose of electronic signatures the message digest is encrypted (encoded) and appended (attached) to an electronic document.

metastasize (6) - the spread of cancer from primary to secondary sites.

metastatic (6) - descriptive term that indicates a primary cancer has spread to another part of the body.

Military Health Services System (MHSS) (16) - entire healthcare system of the U.S. uniformed services and includes military treatment facilities (MTFs) as well as various programs in the civilian healthcare market, such as TRICARE.

military treatment facility (MTF) (16) - healthcare facility operated by the military that provides inpatient and/or ambulatory (outpatient and emergency department) care to eligible TRICARE beneficiaries; capabilities of MTFs vary from limited acute care clinics to teaching and tertiary care medical centers.

Mine Safety and Health Administration (MSHA) (17) - helps reduce deaths, injuries, and illnesses in U.S. mines through a variety of activities and programs.

Minimum Data Set (MDS) (2) - data elements collected by long-term care facilities.

moderate (conscious) sedation (7) - administration of moderate sedation or analgesia, which results in a drug-induced depression of consciousness; CPT established a package concept for moderate (conscious) sedation, and the bull's-eye (⊙) symbol located next to the code number identifies moderate (conscious) sedation as an inherent part of providing specific procedures.

modifier (5) - two-digit code attached to the main code; indicates that a procedure/service has been altered in some manner (e.g., bilateral procedure).

monitored anesthesia care (MAC) (7) - provision of local or regional anesthetic services with certain conscious altering drugs when provided by a physician, anesthesiologist, or medically-directed CRNA; monitored anesthesia care involves sufficiently monitoring the patient to anticipate the potential need for administration of general anesthesia, and it requires continuous evaluation of vital physiologic functions as well as recognition and treatment of adverse changes.

morbidity (6) - pertaining to illness or disease.

morphology (6) - indicates the tissue type of a neoplasm; though M codes are not reported on provider office claims, they are reported to state cancer registries.

Morphology of Neoplasms (M codes) (6) - Appendix A of ICD-9-CM; contains a reference to the World Health Organization publication entitled *International Classification of Diseases for Oncology (ICD-O).*

mortality (6) - pertaining to death.

mother/baby claim (15) - submitted for services provided to a baby under the mother's Medicaid identification number.

multiple surgical procedures (7) - two or more surgeries performed during the same operative session.

narrative clinic note (10) - using paragraph format to document health care.

National Center for Health Statistics (NCHS) (6) - one of the U.S. Department of Health and Human Services agencies responsible for overseeing all changes and modifications to the ICD-9-CM.

national codes (level II codes) (1) - commonly referred to as HCPCS codes; include five-digit alphanumeric codes for procedures, services, and supplies that are not classified in CPT (e.g., J-codes are used to assign drugs administered).

National Committee for Quality Assurance (NCQA) (3) - a private, not-for-profit organization that assesses the quality of managed care plans in the United States and releases the data to the public for its consideration when selecting a managed care plan.

National Correct Coding Initiative (NCCI) (2) - developed by CMS to promote national correct coding methodologies and to eliminate improper coding practices.

national coverage determination (NCD) (10) - rules developed by CMS that specify under what clinical circumstances a service or procedure is covered (including clinical circumstances considered reasonable and necessary) and correctly coded; Medicare administrative contractors create edits for NCD rules, called local coverage determinations (LCDs).

National Drug Code (NDC) **(5)** - maintained by the Food and Drug Administration (FDA); identifies prescription drugs and some over-the-counter products.

National Electronic Billers Alliance (NEBA) (1) - created in 1996 to assist professionals entering the medical billing industry and those already working in the field; offers Certified Healthcare Reimbursement Specialist (CHRS) and Certified HIPAA Information Specialist (CHIS) credentials.

National Health PlanID (PlanID) (5) - unique identifier, previously called PAYERID, that will be assigned to third-party payers and is expected to have 10 numeric positions, including a check digit in the tenth position.

National Individual Identifier (5) - unique identifier to be assigned to patients.

National Plan and Provider Enumeration System (NPPES) (5, 11) - developed by CMS to assign unique identifiers to healthcare providers (NPI) and health plans (PlanID).

National Provider Identifier (NPI) (5) - unique identifier to be assigned to healthcare providers as an 8- or possibly 10-character alphanumeric identifier, including a check digit in the last position.

National Standard Employer Identification Number (EIN) (5) - unique identifier assigned to employers who, as sponsors of health insurance for their employees, need to be identified in healthcare transactions.

National Standard Format (NSF) (5) - flat-file format used to bill physician and noninstitutional services, such as services reported by a general practitioner on a CMS-1500 claim.

nature of the presenting problem (7) - defined by CPT as a disease, condition, illness, injury, symptom, sign, finding, complaint, or other reason for the encounter, with or without a diagnosis being established at the time of the encounter.

neoplasm (6) - new growth, or tumor, in which cell reproduction is out of control.

network model HMO (3) - contracted healthcare services provided to subscribers by two or more physician multispecialty group practices.

network provider (3) - physician or healthcare facility under contract to the managed care plan.

new patient (7) - one who has *not* received any professional services from the physician or from another physician of the same specialty who belongs to the same group practice, within the past three years.

newborn care (7) - covers examinations of normal or high-risk neonates in the hospital or other locations, subsequent newborn care in a hospital, and resuscitation of high-risk babies.

nonavailability statement (NAS) (16) - certificate issued by a military treatment facility that cannot provide needed care to TRICARE Standard beneficiaries.

noncovered benefit (4) - any procedure or service reported on a claim that is not included on the payer's master benefit list, resulting in denial of the claim; also called *noncovered procedure* or *uncovered benefit.*

nonparticipating provider (nonPAR) (4) - does not contract with the insurance plan; patients who elect to receive care from nonPARs will incur higher out-of-pocket expenses.

nonprofit corporation (13) - charitable, educational, civic, or humanitarian organization whose profits are returned to the program of the corporation rather than distributed to shareholders and officers of the corporation.

nurse advisor (16) - available 24/7 for advice and assistance with treatment alternatives and to discuss whether a TRICARE sponsor should see a provider based on a discussion of symptoms.

nurse practitioner (NP) (9) - has two or more years of advanced training, has passed a special exam, and often works as a primary care provider along with a physician.

nursing facility services (7) - performed at the following sites: skilled nursing facilities (SNFs), intermediate care facilities (ICFs), and long-term care facilities (LTCFs).

objective (10) - documentation of measurable or objective observations made during physical examination and diagnostic testing.

observation or inpatient care services (7) - CPT codes used to report observation or inpatient hospital care services provided to patients admitted and discharged on the same date of service.

observation services (7) - furnished in a hospital outpatient setting to determine whether further treatment or inpatient admission is needed; when a patient is placed under observation, the patient is categorized as an outpatient; if the duration of observation care is expected to be 24 hours or more, the physician must order an inpatient admission (and the date the physician orders the inpatient stay is the date of inpatient admission).

Occupational Safety and Health Administration (OSHA) (17) - agency created to protect employees against injuries from occupational hazards in the workplace.

Occupational Safety and Health Administration Act of 1970 (OSHA) (2) - legislation designed to protect all employees against injuries from occupational hazards in the workplace.

Office of Managed Care (3) - CMS agency that facilitates innovation and competition among Medicare HMOs.

Office of Workers' Compensation Programs (OWCP) (17) - administers programs that provide wage replacement benefits, medical treatment, vocational rehabilitation, and other benefits to federal workers (or eligible dependents) who are injured at work or acquire an occupational disease.

Omnibus Budget Reconciliation Act of 1981 (OBRA) (2) - federal law that requires physicians to keep copies of any government insurance claims and copies of all attachments filed by the provider for a period of five years; also expanded Medicare and Medicaid programs.

on-the-job-injury (17) - occurrence when the employee is either injured while working within the scope of the job description, injured while performing a service required by the employer, or succumbs to a disorder that can be directly linked to employment, such as asbestosis or mercury poisoning.

open claim (4) - submitted to the payer, but processing is not complete.

open-panel HMO (3) - health care provided by individuals who are not employees of the HMO or who do not belong to a specially-formed medical group that serves the HMO.

operative report (10) - varies from a short narrative description of a minor procedure that is performed in the physician's office to a more formal report dictated by the surgeon in a format required by the hospitals and ambulatory surgical centers (ASCs).

optical character reader (OCR) (11) - device used for optical character recognition.

optical scanning (11) - uses a device (e.g., scanner) to convert printed or handwritten characters into text that can be viewed by an optical character reader.

organ- or disease-oriented panel (7) - series of blood chemistry studies routinely ordered by providers at the same time to investigate a specific organ (e.g., liver panel) or disease (e.g., thyroid panel).

original Medicare plan (14) - fee-for-service or traditional pay-per-visit plans for which beneficiaries are usually charged a fee for each healthcare service or supply received.

other health insurance (OHI) (16) - insurance policy considered primary to TRICARE (e.g., civilian insurance plan, workers' compensation, liability insurance plan).

out-of-pocket payment (4) - established by health insurance companies for a health insurance plan; usually has limits of $1,000 or $2,000; when the patient has reached the limit of an out-of-pocket payment (e.g., annual deductible) for the year, appropriate patient reimbursement to the provider is determined; not all health insurance plans include an out-of-pocket payment provision.

Outcomes and Assessment Information Set (OASIS) (2, 9) - group of data elements that represent core items of a comprehensive assessment for an adult home care patient and form the basis for measuring patient outcomes for purposes of outcome-based quality improvement.

outlier (9) - hospitals that treat unusually costly cases receive increased Medicare payments; the additional payment is designed to protect hospitals from large financial losses due to unusually expensive cases.

outpatient (6) - person treated in one of three settings: healthcare provider's office; hospital clinic, emergency department, hospital same-day surgery unit, or ambulatory surgical center (ASC) where the patient is released within 23 hours; or hospital admission solely for observation where the patient is released after a short stay.

outpatient code editor (OCE) (10) - software that edits outpatient claims submitted by hospitals, community mental health centers, comprehensive outpatient rehabilitation facilities, and home health agencies; the software reviews submissions for coding validity (e.g., missing fifth digits) and coverage (e.g., medical necessity); OCE edits result in one of the following dispositions: rejection, denial, return to provider (RTP), or suspension.

outpatient encounter (9) - includes all outpatient procedures and services (e.g., same day surgery, x-rays, laboratory tests, and so on) provided during one day to the same patient.

outpatient pretreatment authorization plan (OPAP) (13) - also called *prospective authorization* or *precertification;* requires preauthorization of outpatient physical, occupational, and speech therapy services.

Outpatient Prospective Payment System (OPPS) (2) - uses ambulatory payment classifications (APCs) to calculate reimbursement; was implemented for billing of hospital-based Medicare outpatient claims.

outpatient visit (9) - *see* outpatient encounter.

outsource (4) - contract out.

overlapping site (6) - *see* contiguous site.

overpayment (5) - funds a provider or beneficiary has received in excess of amounts due and payable under Medicare and Medicaid statutes and regulations.

partial hospitalization (7) - short term, intensive treatment program where individuals who are experiencing an acute episode of an illness (e.g., geriatric, psychiatric, or rehabilitative) can receive medically supervised treatment during a significant number of daytime or nighttime hours; this type of program is an alternative to 24-hour inpatient hospitalization and allows the patients to maintain their everyday life without the disruption associated with an inpatient hospital stay.

participating provider (PAR) (4) - contracts with a health insurance plan and accepts whatever the plan pays for procedures or services performed.

past-due account (4) - one that has not been paid within a certain time frame (e.g., 120 days); also called *delinquent account.*

patient account record (4) - also called *patient ledger;* a computerized permanent record of all financial transactions between the patient and the practice.

patient ledger (4) - *see* patient account record.

patient record (2) - documents healthcare services provided to a patient.

Patient Safety and Quality Improvement Act (5) - amends Title IX of the Public Health Service Act to provide for improved patient safety by encouraging voluntary and confidential reporting of events that adversely affect patients; creates patient safety organizations (PSOs) to collect, aggregate, and analyze confidential information reported by healthcare providers; and designates information reported to PSOs as privileged and not subject to disclosure (except when a court determines that the information contains evidence of a criminal act or each provider identified in the information authorizes disclosure).

Payment Error Prevention Program (PEPP) (5) - required facilities to identify and reduce improper Medicare payments and, specifically, the Medicare payment error rate. The hospital payment monitoring program (HPMP) replaced PEPP in 2002.

payment error rate (5) - number of dollars paid in error out of total dollars paid for inpatient prospective payment system services.

payment system (9) - reimbursement method the federal government uses to compensate providers for patient care.

***per diem* (2)** - Latin term meaning "for each day," which is how retrospective cost-based rates were determined; payments were issued based on daily rates.

perinatal condition (6) – occurs before birth, during birth, or within the perinatal period.

perinatal period (6) - first 28 days of life.

permanent disability (17) - refers to an ill or injured employee's diminished capacity to return to work.

personal health record (2) - web-based application that allows individuals to maintain and manage their health information (and that of others for whom they are authorized, such as family members) in a private, secure, and confidential environment.

physical examination (7) - assessment of the patient's organ (e.g., extremities) and body systems (e.g., cardiovascular).

physical status modifier (7) - indicates the patient's condition at the time anesthesia was administered.

physician assistant (PA) (9) - has two or more years of advanced training, has passed a special exam, works with a physician, and can do some of the same tasks as the doctor.

physician incentive plan (3) - requires managed care plans that contract with Medicare or Medicaid to disclose information about physician incentive plans to CMS or state Medicaid agencies before a new or renewed contract receives final approval.

physician incentives (3) - include payments made directly or indirectly to healthcare providers to serve as encouragement to reduce or limit services (e.g., discharge an inpatient from the hospital more quickly) to save money for the managed care plan.

physician-hospital organization (PHO) (3) - owned by hospital(s) and physician groups that obtain managed care plan contracts; physicians maintain their own practices and provide healthcare services to plan members.

physician self-referral law (5) - *see* Stark I.

physician standby services (7) - involve a physician spending a prolonged period of time without patient contact, waiting for an event to occur that will require the physician's services.

Physicians at Teaching Hospitals (PATH) (5) - HHS implemented audits in 1995 to examine the billing practices of physicians at teaching hospitals; focus was on two issues: (1) compliance with the Medicare rule affecting payment for physician services provided by residents (e.g., whether a teaching physician was present for Part B services billed to Medicare between 1990 and 1996), and (2) whether the level of the physician service was coded and billed properly.

place of service (POS) (7) - the physical location where health care is provided to patients (e.g., office or other outpatient settings, hospitals, nursing facilities, home health care, or emergency departments); the two-digit location code is required by Medicare.

plan (10) - statement of the physician's future plans for the work-up and medical management of the case.

point-of-service plan (3) - delivers healthcare services using both managed care network and traditional indemnity coverage so patients can seek care outside the managed care network.

poisoning (6) - occurs as the result of an overdose, wrong substance administered or taken, or intoxication (e.g., combining prescribed drugs with nonprescribed drugs or alcohol).

PPN provider (13) - provider who has signed a PPN contract and agrees to accept the PPN allowed rate, which is generally 10 percent lower than the PAR allowed rate.

practice guidelines (16) - decision-making tools used by providers to determine appropriate health care for specific clinical circumstances.

preadmission certification (PAC) (3) - review for medical necessity of inpatient care prior to the patient's admission.

preadmission review (3) - review for medical necessity of inpatient care prior to the patient's admission.

preadmission testing (PAT) (6) - completed prior to an inpatient admission or outpatient surgery to facilitate the patient's treatment and reduce the length of stay.

preauthorization (1) - prior approval.

precedent (5) - standard.

precertification (13) - *see* outpatient pretreatment authorization plan (OPAP).

preexisting condition (4) - any medical condition that was diagnosed and/or treated within a specified period of time immediately preceding the enrollee's effective date of coverage.

Preferred Provider Health Care Act of 1985 (3) - eased restrictions on preferred provider organizations (PPOs) and allowed subscribers to seek health care from providers outside of the PPO.

preferred provider network (PPN) (13) - program that requires providers to adhere to managed care provision.

preferred provider organization (PPO) (3) - network of physicians and hospitals that have joined together to contract with insurance companies, employers, or other organizations to provide health care to subscribers for a discounted fee.

preoperative clearance (7) - occurs when a surgeon requests that a specialist or other physician (e.g., general practice) examine a patient and give an opinion as to whether that patient can withstand the expected risks of a specific surgery.

prepaid health plan (13) - contract between employer and healthcare facility (or physician) where specified medical services were performed for a predetermined fee that was paid on either a monthly or yearly basis.

preventive medicine services (7) - routine examinations or risk management counseling for children and adults exhibiting no overt signs or symptoms of a disorder while presenting to the medical office for a preventive medical physical; also called "wellness visits."

preventive services (2) - designed to help individuals avoid health and injury problems.

primary care manager (PCM) (16) - provider (e.g., physician) who is assigned to a sponsor and part of the TRICARE provider network.

primary care provider (PCP) (3) - responsible for supervising and coordinating healthcare services for enrollees and preauthorizing referrals to specialists and inpatient hospital admissions (except in emergencies).

primary insurance (4) - associated with how an insurance plan is billed—the insurance plan responsible for paying healthcare insurance claims first is considered primary.

primary malignancy (6) - original cancer site.

principal diagnosis (6) - condition determined, after study, that resulted in the patient's admission to the hospital.

principal procedure (6) - procedure performed for definitive treatment rather than diagnostic purposes; one performed to treat a complication; or that which is most closely related to the principal diagnosis.

privacy (5) - right of individuals to keep their information from being disclosed to others.

Privacy Act of 1974 (5) - forbids the Medicare regional payer from disclosing the status of any unassigned claim beyond the following: date the claim was received by the payer; date the claim was paid, denied, or suspended; or general reason the claim was suspended.

privacy rule (5) - HIPAA provision that creates national standards to protect individuals' medical records and other personal health information.

private fee-for-service (PFFS) (14) - healthcare plan offered by private insurance companies; not available in all areas of the country.

privileged communication (5) - private information shared between a patient and healthcare provider; disclosure must be in accordance with HIPAA and/or individual state provisions regarding the privacy and security of protected health information (PHI).

problem-oriented record (POR) (2) - a systematic method of documentation that consists of four components: database, problem list, initial plan, and progress notes.

professional component (7) - supervision of procedure, interpretation, and writing of the report.

professional liability insurance (1) - provides protection from claims resulting from errors and omissions associated with professional services provided to clients as expected of a person in their profession; also called *errors and omissions insurance.*

professionalism (1) - conduct or qualities that characterize a professional person.

Program for Evaluating Payment Patterns Electronic Report (PEPPER) (5) - contains hospital-specific administrative claims data for a number of CMS-identified problem areas (e.g., specific DRGs, types of discharges); a hospital uses PEPPER data to compare its performance with that of other hospitals.

Program Integrity (PI) Office (16) - responsible for the worldwide surveillance of fraud and abuse activities involving purchased care for beneficiaries in the Military Health Services System.

Program of All-Inclusive Care for the Elderly (PACE) (14) - optional Medicaid benefit for eligible enrollees (e.g., adult day health center, home health care, and/or inpatient facilities).

Program Safeguard Contract (PSC) (5) - fraud and abuse detection program established by CMS in 1999; replaced detection activities previously performed by CMS's fiscal intermediaries (FIs) and carriers; Zone Program Integrity Contractor (ZPIC) program replaced PSC program in 2009.

program transmittal (5) - document published by Medicare containing new and changed policies and/or procedures that are to be incorporated into a specific CMS program manual (e.g., *Medicare Claims Processing Manual*); cover page (or transmittal page) summarizes new and changed material, and subsequent pages provide details; transmittals are sent to each Medicare administrative contractor.

prolonged services (7) - assigned in addition to other E/M services when treatment exceeds by 30 minutes or more the time included in the CPT description of the service.

property insurance (1) - protects business contents (e.g., buildings and equipment) against fire, theft, and other risks.

prospective authorization (13) - *see* outpatient pretreatment authorization plan (OPAP).

prospective cost-based rates (9) - rates established in advance, but based on reported healthcare costs (charges) from which a prospective *per diem* rate is determined.

prospective payment system (PPS) (2) - issues predetermined payment for services.

prospective price-based rates (9) - rates associated with a particular category of patient (e.g., inpatients) and established by the payer (e.g., Medicare) prior to the provision of healthcare services.

prospective review (3) - reviewing appropriateness and necessity of care provided to patients prior to administration of care.

protected health information (PHI) (5) - information that is identifiable to an individual (or individual identifiers) such as name, address, telephone numbers, date of birth, Medicaid ID number, medical record number, social security number (SSN), and name of employer.

Provider Remittance Notice (PRN) (4) - remittance advice submitted by Medicare to providers that includes payment information about a claim.

public health insurance (2) - Federal and state government health programs (e.g., Medicare, Medicaid, SCHIP, TRICARE) available to eligible individuals.

qualified diagnosis (6) - working diagnosis that is not yet proven or established.

qualified disabled working individual (QDWI) (14) - program that helps individuals who receive Social Security and Medicare because of disability, but who lost their Social Security benefits and free Medicare Part A because they returned to work and their earning exceed the limit allowed; states are required to pay their Medicare Part A premiums.

qualified Medicare beneficiary program (QMBP) (14) - program in which the federal government requires state Medicaid programs to pay Medicare premiums, patient deductibles, and coinsurance for individuals who have Medicare Part A, a low monthly income, and limited resources, and who are not otherwise eligible for Medicaid.

qualifiers (6) - supplementary terms in the ICD-9-CM Index to Diseases that further modify subterms and other qualifiers.

qualifying circumstances (7) - CPT Medicine Section codes reported in addition to Anesthesia Section codes when situations or circumstances make anesthesia administration more difficult (e.g., patient of extreme age, such as under one year or over 70).

qualifying individual (QI) (14) - program that helps low-income individuals by requiring states to pay their Medicare Part B premiums.

quality assessment and performance improvement (QAPI) (3) - program implemented so that quality assurance activities are performed to improve the functioning of Medicare Advantage organizations.

quality assurance program (3) - activities that assess the quality of care provided in a healthcare setting.

quality improvement organization (QIO) (2) - performs utilization and quality control review of health care furnished, or to be furnished, to Medicare beneficiaries.

Quality Improvement System for Managed Care (QISMC) (3) - established by Medicare to ensure the accountability of managed care plans in terms of objective, measurable standards.

***qui tam* (5)** - abbreviation for the Latin phrase *qui tam pro domino rege quam pro sic ipso in hoc parte sequitur*, which means "who as well for the king as for himself sues I this matter." It is a provision of the False Claims Act that allows a private citizen to file a lawsuit in the name of the U.S. government, charging fraud by government contractors and other entities.

radiologic views (7) - studies taken from different angles.

recipient eligibility verification system (REVS) (15) - also called *Medicaid eligibility verification system (MEVS)*; allows providers to electronically access the state's eligibility file through point-of-sale device, computer software, and automated voice response.

record linkage (2) - allows patient information to be created at different locations according to a unique patient identifier or identification number.

record retention (5) - storage of documentation for an established period of time, usually mandated by federal and/or state law; its purpose is to ensure the availability of records for use by government agencies and other third parties.

Recovery Audit Contractor (RAC) program (5) - mandated by the Medicare Prescription Drug, Improvement, and Modernization Act of 2003 (MMA) to find and correct improper Medicare payments paid to healthcare providers participating in fee-for-service Medicare.

re-excision (6) - occurs when the pathology report recommends that the surgeon perform a second excision to widen the margins of the original tumor site.

referral (7) - a patient who reports that another provider referred him or her.

regulation (5) - guidelines written by administrative agencies (e.g., CMS).

reimbursement specialist (1) - *see* health insurance specialist.

relative value units (RVUs) (9) - payment components consisting of physician work, practice expense, and malpractice expense.

remittance advice (remit) (1) - electronic or paper-based report of payment sent by the payer to the provider; includes patient name, patient health insurance claim (HIC) number, facility provider number/name, dates of service (from date/thru date), type of bill (TOB), charges, payment information, and reason and/or remark codes.

report card (3) - contains data regarding a managed care plan's quality, utilization, customer satisfaction, administrative effectiveness, financial stability, and cost control.

Resident Assessment Validation and Entry (RAVEN) (9) - data entry system used to enter MDS data about SNF patients and transmit those assessments in CMS-standard format to individual state databases.

Resource Utilization Groups (RUGs) (2) - based on data collected from resident assessments (using data elements called the Minimum Data Set, or MDS) and relative weights developed from staff time data.

Resource–Based Relative Value Scale (RBRVS) system (2) - payment system that reimburses physicians' practice expenses based on relative values for three components of each physician's services: physician work, practice expense, and malpractice insurance expense.

respite care (14) - the temporary hospitalization of a hospice patient for the purpose of providing relief from duty for the nonpaid person who has the major day-to-day responsibility for the care of the terminally ill, dependent patient.

***respondeat superior* (1)** - Latin for "let the master answer"; legal doctrine holding that the employer is liable for the actions and omissions of employees performed and committed within the scope of their employment.

retrospective reasonable cost system (9) - reimbursement system in which hospitals report actual charges for inpatient care to payers after discharge of the patient from the hospital.

retrospective review (3) - reviewing appropriateness and necessity of care provided to patients after the administration of care.

revenue code (9) - four-digit codes that indicate location or type of service provided to an institutional patient; reported in FL 42 of UB-04.

revenue cycle management (9) - process facilities and providers use to ensure financial viability.

rider (13) - special contract clause stipulating additional coverage above the standard contract.

risk contract (3) - an arrangement among providers to provide capitated (fixed, prepaid basis) healthcare services to Medicare beneficiaries.

risk of mortality (9) - likelihood of dying.

risk pool (3) - created when a number of people are grouped for insurance purposes (e.g., employees of an organization); the cost of healthcare coverage is determined by employees' health status, age, sex, and occupation.

roster billing (14) - enables Medicare beneficiaries to participate in mass PPV (pneumococcal pneumonia virus) and influenza virus vaccination programs offered by Public Health Clinics (PHCs) and other entities that bill Medicare payers.

scope of practice (1) - healthcare services, determined by the state, that an NP and PA can perform.

second surgical opinion (SSO) (3, 13) - second physician is asked to evaluate the necessity of surgery and recommend the most economical, appropriate facility in which to perform the surgery (e.g., outpatient clinic or doctor's office versus inpatient hospitalization).

secondary diagnosis (6) - also called *concurrent condition* or *comorbidity;* coexists with the primary condition, has the potential to affect treatment of the primary condition, and is an active condition for which the patient is treated or monitored.

secondary malignancy (6) - tumor has metastasized to a secondary site, either adjacent to the primary site or to a remote region of the body.

secondary procedure (6) - additional procedure performed during the same encounter as the principal procedure.

security (5) - involves the safekeeping of patient information by controlling access to hard copy and computerized records; protecting patient information from alteration, destruction, tampering, or loss; providing employee training in confidentiality of patient information; and requiring employees to sign a confidentiality statement that details the consequences of not maintaining patient confidentiality.

security rule (5) - HIPAA standards and safeguards that protect health information collected, maintained, used, or transmitted electronically; covered entities affected by this rule include health plans, healthcare clearinghouses, and certain healthcare providers.

Self–insured (or self–funded) employer–sponsored group health plan (2) - allows a large employer to assume the financial risk for providing healthcare benefits to employees; employer does not pay a fixed premium to a health insurance payer, but establishes a trust fund (of employer and employee contributions) out of which claims are paid.

self–referral (3) - enrollee who sees a non-HMO panel specialist without a referral from the primary care physician.

sequelae (6) - late effects of injury or illness.

service location (13) - location where the patient was seen.

severity of illness (SOI) (9) - extent of physiological decompensation or organ system loss of function.

single–payer system (2) - centralized healthcare system adopted by some Western nations (e.g., Canada, Great Britain) and funded by taxes. The government pays for each resident's health care, which is considered a basic social service.

site of service differential (9) - reduction of payment when office-based services are performed in a facility, such as a hospital or outpatient setting, because the doctor did not provide supplies, utilities, or the costs of running the facility.

Skilled Nursing Facility Prospective Payment System (SNF PPS) (2) - implemented (as a result of the BBA of 1997) to cover all costs (routine, ancillary, and capital) related to services furnished to Medicare Part A beneficiaries.

SOAP notes (10) - outline format for documenting health care; "SOAP" is an acronym derived from the first letter of the headings used in the note: Subjective, Objective, Assessment, and Plan.

socialized medicine (2) - type of single-payer system in which the government owns and operates healthcare facilities and providers (e.g., physicians) receive salaries; the VA healthcare program is a form of socialized medicine.

source document (4) - the routing slip, charge slip, encounter form, or superbill from which the insurance claim was generated.

special accidental injury rider (13) - covers 100 percent of nonsurgical care sought and rendered within 24 to 72 hours (varies according to policy) of the accidental injury.

special enrollment period (SEP) (14) - a set time when individuals can sign up for Medicare Part B if they did not enroll in Part B during the initial enrollment period.

special report (7) - must accompany the claim when an unlisted procedure or service code is reported to describe the nature, extent, and need for the procedure or service.

specified low-income Medicare beneficiary (SLMB) (14) - federally mandated program that required states to cover just the Medicare Part B premium for persons whose income is slightly above the poverty level.

spell of illness (14) - formerly called *spell of sickness;* is sometimes used in place of *benefit period.*

staff model HMO (3) - healthcare services are provided to subscribers by physicians employed by the HMO.

standards (3) - requirements.

Stark I (5) - responded to concerns about physicians' conflicts of interest when referring Medicare patients for a variety of services; prohibits physicians from referring Medicare patients to clinical laboratory services in which the physician or a member of the physician's family has a financial ownership/investment interest and/or compensation arrangement; also called *physician self-referral law.*

State Children's Health Insurance Program (SCHIP) (2) - also abbreviated as CHIP; provides health insurance coverage to uninsured children whose family income is up to 200 percent of the federal poverty level (monthly income limits for a family of four also apply).

State Insurance Fund (or State Compensation Fund) (17) - a quasi-public agency that provides workers' compensation insurance coverage to private and public employers and acts as an agent in workers' compensation cases involving state employees.

statistical analysis Medicare administrative contractor (SAMAC) (8) - responsible for providing suppliers and manufacturers with assistance in determining HCPCS codes to be used.

statutes (5) - also called *statutory law;* laws passed by legislative bodies (e.g., federal Congress and state legislatures).

statutory law (5) - *see* statutes.

sub-capitation payment (3) - each provider is paid a fixed amount per month to provide only the care that an individual needs from that provider.

subjective (10) - part of the note that contains the chief complaint and the patient's description of the presenting problem.

subpoena (5) - an order of the court that requires a witness to appear at a particular time and place to testify.

subpoena duces tecum (5) - requires documents (e.g., patient record) to be produced.

subrogation (12) - process of the third-party payer recovering healthcare expenses from the liable party.

subscribers (policyholders) (3) - person in whose name the insurance policy is issued.

subsequent hospital care (7) - includes review of patient's chart for changes in the patient's condition, the results of diagnostic studies, and/or reassessment of the patient's condition since the last assessment performed by the physician.

superbill (4) - term used for an encounter form in the physician's office.

supplemental plan (11) - covers the deductible and copay or coinsurance of a primary health insurance policy.

surgical package (7) - *see* global surgery.

surveillance and utilization review subsystem (SURS) (15) - safeguards against unnecessary or inappropriate use of Medicaid services or excess payments and assesses the quality of those services.

survey (3) - conducted by accreditation organizations (e.g., the Joint Commission) and/or regulatory agencies (e.g., CMS) to evaluate a facility's compliance with standards and/or regulations.

survivor benefits (17) - claim that provides death benefits to eligible dependents, which are calculated according to the employee's earning capacity at the time of illness or injury.

suspense (4) - pending.

Tabular List of Diseases (Volume 1) (ICD-9-CM) (6) - contains 17 chapters that classify diseases and injuries, two supplemental classifications, and five appendices.

Tax Equity and Fiscal Responsibility Act of 1982 (TEFRA) (2) - created Medicare risk programs, which allowed federally qualified HMOs and competitive medical plans that met specified Medicare requirements to provide Medicare-covered services under a risk contract.

Tax Relief and Health Care Act of 2006 (TRHCA) (5) - created physician quality reporting initiative (PQRI) system that establishes a financial incentive for eligible professionals who participate in a voluntary quality reporting program.

technical component (7) - use of equipment and supplies for services performed.

Temporary Assistance for Needy Families (TANF) (15) - makes cash assistance available on a time-limited basis for children deprived of support because of a parent's death, incapacity, absence, or unemployment.

temporary disability (17) - claim that covers healthcare treatment for illness and injuries, as well as payment for lost wages.

TennCare (15) - name of Tennessee's Medicaid program.

third-party administrator (TPA) (2, 13) - company that provides health benefits claims administration and other outsourcing services for self-insured companies; provides administrative services to healthcare plans; specializes in mental health case management; and processes claims, serving as a system of "checks and balances" for labor-management.

total practice management software (TPMS) (2) - used to generate the EMR, automating medical practice functions of registering patients, scheduling appointments, generating insurance claims and patient statements, processing payments from patient and third-party payers, and producing administrative and clinical reports.

transfer of care (7) - occurs when a physician who is managing some or all of a patient's problems releases the patient to the care of another physician who is not providing consultative services.

transitional pass-through payment (8) - temporary additional payment(s) (above the OPPS reimbursement rate) made for certain innovative medical devices, drugs, and biologicals provided to Medicare beneficiaries.

TRICARE (16) - healthcare program for active duty members of the military and their qualified family members, CHAMPUS-eligible retirees and their qualified family members, and eligible survivors of members of the uniformed services.

TRICARE beneficiary (16) - includes sponsors and dependents of sponsors.

TRICARE Extra (16) - allows TRICARE Standard users to save 5 percent of their TRICARE Standard cost-shares by using healthcare providers in the TRICARE network.

TRICARE Management Activity (TMA) (16) - formerly OCHAMPUS; the office that coordinates and administers the TRICARE program and is accountable for quality healthcare provided to members of the uniformed services and their families.

TRICARE Prime (16) - managed care option similar to a civilian health maintenance organization (HMO).

TRICARE Program Management Organization (PMO) (16) - manages TRICARE programs and demonstration projects.

TRICARE Service Center (TSC) (16) - business offices staffed by one or more beneficiary services representatives and healthcare finders who assist TRICARE sponsors with healthcare needs and answer questions about the program.

TRICARE sponsor (16) - uniformed service personnel who are either active duty, retired, or deceased.

TRICARE Standard (16) - new name for traditional CHAMPUS.

triple option plan (3) - usually offered by either a single insurance plan or as a joint venture among two or more third-party payers, and provides subscribers or employees with a choice of HMO, PPO, or traditional health insurance plans; also called *cafeteria plan* or *flexible benefit plan.*

Truth in Lending Act (4) - *see* Consumer Credit Protection Act of 1968.

two-party check (4) - check made out to both patient and provider.

type of service (TOS) (7) - refers to the kind of healthcare services provided to patients; a code required by Medicare to denote anesthesia services.

UB-04 (5) - insurance claim or flat file used to bill institutional services, such as services performed in hospitals.

unassigned claim (4) - generated for providers who do not accept assignment; organized by year.

unauthorized service (4) - services that are provided to a patient without proper authorization or that are not covered by a current authorization.

unbundling (4) - submitting multiple CPT codes when one code should be submitted.

uncertain behavior (6) - it is not possible to predict subsequent morphology or behavior from the submitted specimen.

uniformed services (16) - U.S. military branches that include the Army, Navy, Air Force, Marines, Coast Guard, Public Health Service, and the North Atlantic Treaty Organization (NATO).

unique bit string (5) - computer code that creates an electronic signature message digest that is encrypted (encoded) and appended (attached) to an electronic document (e.g., CMS-1500 claim).

unit/floor time (7) - amount of time the provider spends at the patient's bedside and managing the patient's care on the unit or floor (e.g., writing orders for diagnostic tests or reviewing test results).

universal health insurance (2) - goal of providing every individual with access to health coverage, regardless of the system implemented to achieve that goal.

unlisted procedure (7) - also called *unlisted service;* assigned when the provider performs a procedure of service for which there is no CPT code.

unlisted service (7) - *see* unlisted procedure.

unspecified nature (6) - neoplasm is identified, but no further indication of the histology or nature of the tumor is reflected in the documented diagnosis.

upcoding (5) - assignment of an ICD-9-CM diagnosis code that does not match patient record documentation for the purpose of illegally increasing reimbursement (e.g., assigning the ICD-9-CM code for heart attack when angina was actually documented in the record).

usual and reasonable payments (2) - based on fees typically charged by providers in a particular region of the country.

usual, customary, and reasonable (UCR) (13) - description of amount commonly charged for a particular medical service by providers within a particular geographic region; used for establishing allowable rates.

utilization management (utilization review) (3) - method of controlling healthcare costs and quality of care by reviewing the appropriateness and necessity of care provided to patients prior to the administration of care.

utilization review organization (URO) (3) - entity that establishes a utilization management program and performs external utilization review services.

V code (6) - located in the Tabular List of Diseases and assigned for patient encounters when a circumstance other than a disease or injury is present.

value–added network (VAN) (4) - clearinghouse that involves value-added vendors, such as banks, in the processing of claims; using a VAN is more efficient and less expensive for providers than managing their own systems to send and receive transactions directly from numerous entities.

vocational rehabilitation (17) - claim that covers expenses for vocational retraining for both temporary and permanent disability cases.

voided claim (15) - claim Medicaid should not have originally paid, resulting in a deduction from the lump-sum payment made to the provider.

wage index (9) - adjusts payments to account for geographic variations in hospitals' labor costs.

without direct patient contact (7) - includes non-face-to-face time spent by the physician on an outpatient or inpatient basis and occurring before and/or after direct patient care.

Workers' Compensation Board (Commission) (17) - state agency responsible for administering workers' compensation laws and handling appeals for denied claims or cases in which a worker feels compensation was too low.

workers' compensation insurance (1) - insurance program, mandated by federal and state governments, that requires employers to cover medical expenses and loss of wages for workers who are injured on the job or who have developed job-related disorders.

World Health Organization (WHO) (2) - developed the International Classification of Diseases (ICD).

Zone Program Integrity Contractor (ZPIC) (5) - reviews billing trends and patterns, focusing on providers whose billings for Medicare services are higher than the majority of providers in the community; assigned to each Medicare administrative contractor jurisdiction; replaced CMS's Program Safeguard Contract (PSC) program in 2009.

Index

Page numbers followed by b refer to boxes; page numbers followed by f refer to figures; page numbers followed by t refer to tables

A

ABN. *See* Advance beneficiary notice (ABN)
Abuse, in health care, 106–107, 566
Accept assignment
    for ASCs, 291
    defined, 54
    in Medicaid, 505
    for nonPARs, 459–460
    and overpayments, 111
    for PARs, 490
    refusal of, 57b, 80
    in roster billing, 487
    vs. assignment of benefits, 380–381
    for workers' compensation, 568
Accidental injury rider, 425
Accounts receivable management, 54, 56, 84–88
Accreditation, 48
Acts
    Balanced Budget Refinement Act (1999), 24t, 97b
    Clinical Laboratory Improvement Act (CLIA), 23t, 121b, 257b, 279b
    Consolidated Omnibus Budget Reconciliation Act of 1985 (COBRA), 23t, 101t
    Consumer Credit Protection Act (1968), 84
    Deficit Reduction Act (2005), 104t, 119–120
    Department of Education Organization Act, 101t
    Drug Abuse and Treatment Act, 100t
    Electronic Funds Transfer Act, 84
    Employee Retirement Income Security Act of 1974 (ERISA), 23t, 39t, 101t
    Equal Credit Opportunity Act, 84
    Fair Credit and Charge Card Disclosure Act, 84
    Fair Credit Billing Act, 84
    Fair Credit Reporting Act, 84
    Fair Debt Collection Practices Act (FDCPA), 84
    False Claims Act (FCA), 99t, 107
    Federal Claims Collection Act, 100t, 109
    Federal Employees Compensation Act (FECA), 21t, 557
    Federal Employment Liability Act (FELA), 558
    Federal Privacy Act, 392
    Financial Services Modernization Act (Gramm-Leach-Bliley Act), 24t
    Food and Drug Act, 99t
    Health Maintenance Organization Assistance Act (1973), 22t, 39t
    Hill-Burton Act, 21t, 99t
    HIPAA. See Health Insurance Portability and Accountability Act of 1996 (HIPAA)
    Improper Payments Information Act of 2002 (IPIA), 88, 103t
    McKinney Act, 102t
    Medicare, Medicaid, and SCHIP Benefits Improvement and Protection Act of 2008 (BIPA), 25t
    Medicare Catastrophic Coverage Act (1988), 133, 497
    Medicare Prescription Drug, Improvement, and Modernization Act (MMA), 25t, 103t, 109, 134
    Merchant Marine Act (Jones Act), 558
    Migrant Health Act, 99t
    National Cancer Act, 100t
    National Correct Coding Initiative (NCCI), 103t
    Nursing Home Reform Act, 102t
    Occupational Safety and Health Administration Act of 1970 (OSHA), 22t, 100t
    Omnibus Budget Reconciliation Act of 1981 (OBRA), 23t, 39t, 101t, 102t, 461
    Patient Safety and Quality Improvement Act, 104t, 126b
    Peer Review Improvement Act, 101t
    Privacy Act of 1974, 101t, 461
    Social Security Act, 99t, 100t
    Stark II, 102t
    Taft-Hartley Act (1947), 21t
    Tax Equity and Fiscal Responsibility Act of 1982 (TEFRA), 23t, 39t, 101t
    Tax Relief and Health Care Act of 2006 (TRHCA), 104t
    Ticket to Work and Work Incentives Improvement Act, 103t
    Truth in Lending Act, 84, 85t
    Utilization Review Act, 101t
Acupuncture, 262t
Addresses, on CMS-1500 claims, 379
Adjudication, 73, 75–76, 566
Adjustments, of PPS, 304
Administrative simplifications, 118
Advance beneficiary notice (ABN), 133, 342–343, 463–465
Adverse effect (reaction), 177
Adverse selection, 47
Aging report, for claims, 87
Allergy, immunology studies, 261t
Allowed charges, 75
All-Patient diagnosis-related groups (AP-DRGs), 298
All-Patient Refined diagnosis-related groups (APR-DRGs), 298
Ambulance fee schedules, 290
Ambulatory (outpatient) surgery, 145
Ambulatory patient classifications (APCs), 345

677

StudyWare™ to Accompany Understanding Health Insurance:
A Guide to Billing and Reimbursement, 10th Edition

Minimum System Requirements

- Operating systems: Microsoft Windows XP w/SP 2, Windows Vista w/ SP 1, Windows 7
- Processor: Minimum required by Operating System
- Memory: Minimum required by Operating System
- Hard Drive Space: 120MB
- Screen resolution: 1024 x 768 pixels
- CD-ROM drive
- Sound card & listening device required for audio features
- Flash Player 10. The Adobe Flash Player is free, and can be downloaded from http://www.adobe.com/products/flashplayer/

Setup Instructions

1. Insert disc into CD-ROM drive. The StudyWare™ installation program should start automatically. If it does not, go to step 2.
2. From My Computer, double-click the icon for the CD drive.
3. Double-click the setup.exe file to start the program.

Technical Support

Telephone: 1-800-648-7450
8:30 A.M.-6:30 P.M. Eastern Time
E-mail: delmar.help@cengage.com

StudyWare™ is a trademark used herein under license.

Microsoft® and Windows® are registered trademarks of the Microsoft Corporation.

Pentium® is a registered trademark of the Intel Corporation.

IMPORTANT! READ CAREFULLY: This End User License Agreement ("Agreement") sets forth the conditions by which Cengage Learning will make electronic access to the Cengage Learning-owned licensed content and associated media, software, documentation, printed materials, and electronic documentation contained in this package and/or made available to you via this product (the "Licensed Content"), available to you (the "End User"). BY CLICKING THE "I ACCEPT" BUTTON AND/OR OPENING THIS PACKAGE, YOU ACKNOWLEDGE THAT YOU HAVE READ ALL OF THE TERMS AND CONDITIONS, AND THAT YOU AGREE TO BE BOUND BY ITS TERMS, CONDITIONS, AND ALL APPLICABLE LAWS AND REGULATIONS GOVERNING THE USE OF THE LICENSED CONTENT.

1.0 SCOPE OF LICENSE

1.1 Licensed Content. The Licensed Content may contain portions of modifiable content ("Modifiable Content") and content which may not be modified or otherwise altered by the End User ("Non-Modifiable Content"). For purposes of this Agreement, Modifiable Content and Non-Modifiable Content may be collectively referred to herein as the "Licensed Content." All Licensed Content shall be considered Non-Modifiable Content, unless such Licensed Content is presented to the End User in a modifiable format and it is clearly indicated that modification of the Licensed Content is permitted.

1.2 Subject to the End User's compliance with the terms and conditions of this Agreement, Cengage Learning hereby grants the End User, a nontransferable, nonexclusive, limited right to access and view a single copy of the Licensed Content on a single personal computer system for noncommercial, internal, personal use only. The End User shall not (i) reproduce, copy, modify (except in the case of Modifiable Content), distribute, display, transfer, sublicense, prepare derivative work(s) based on, sell, exchange, barter or transfer, rent, lease, loan, resell, or in any other manner exploit the Licensed Content; (ii) remove, obscure, or alter any notice of Cengage Learning's intellectual property rights present on or in the Licensed Content, including, but not limited to, copyright, trademark, and/or patent notices; or (iii) disassemble, decompile, translate, reverse engineer, or otherwise reduce the Licensed Content.

2.0 TERMINATION

2.1 Cengage Learning may at any time (without prejudice to its other rights or remedies) immediately terminate this Agreement and/or suspend access to some or all of the Licensed Content, in the event that the End User does not comply with any of the terms and conditions of this Agreement. In the event of such termination by Cengage Learning, the End User shall immediately return any and all copies of the Licensed Content to Cengage Learning.

3.0 PROPRIETARY RIGHTS

3.1 The End User acknowledges that Cengage Learning owns all rights, title and interest, including, but not limited to all copyright rights therein, in and to the Licensed Content, and that the End User shall not take any action inconsistent with such ownership. The Licensed Content is protected by U.S., Canadian and other applicable copyright laws and by international treaties, including the Berne Convention and the Universal Copyright Convention. Nothing contained in this Agreement shall be construed as granting the End User any ownership rights in or to the Licensed Content.

3.2 Cengage Learning reserves the right at any time to withdraw from the Licensed Content any item or part of an item for which it no longer retains the right to publish, or which it has reasonable grounds to believe infringes copyright or is defamatory, unlawful, or otherwise objectionable.

4.0 PROTECTION AND SECURITY

4.1 The End User shall use its best efforts and take all reasonable steps to safeguard its copy of the Licensed Content to ensure that no unauthorized reproduction, publication, disclosure, modification, or distribution of the Licensed Content, in whole or in part, is made. To the extent that the End User becomes aware of any such unauthorized use of the Licensed Content, the End User shall immediately notify Cengage Learning. Notification of such violations may be made by sending an e-mail to infringement@cengage.com.

5.0 MISUSE OF THE LICENSED PRODUCT

5.1 In the event that the End User uses the Licensed Content in violation of this Agreement, Cengage Learning shall have the option of electing liquidated damages, which shall include all profits generated by the End User's use of the Licensed Content plus interest computed at the maximum rate permitted by law and all legal fees and other expenses incurred by Cengage Learning in enforcing its rights, plus penalties.

6.0 FEDERAL GOVERNMENT CLIENTS

6.1 Except as expressly authorized by Cengage Learning, Federal Government clients obtain only the rights specified in this Agreement and no other rights. The Government acknowledges that (i) all software and related documentation incorporated in the Licensed Content is existing commercial computer software within the meaning of FAR 27.405(b)(2); and (2) all other data delivered in whatever form, is limited rights data within the meaning of FAR 27.401. The restrictions in this section are acceptable as consistent with the Government's need for software and other data under this Agreement.

7.0 DISCLAIMER OF WARRANTIES AND LIABILITIES

7.1 Although Cengage Learning believes the Licensed Content to be reliable, Cengage Learning does not guarantee or warrant (i) any information or materials contained in or produced by the Licensed Content, (ii) the accuracy, completeness or reliability of the Licensed Content, or (iii) that the Licensed Content is free from errors or other material defects. THE LICENSED PRODUCT IS PROVIDED "AS IS," WITHOUT ANY WARRANTY OF ANY KIND AND CENGAGE LEARNING DISCLAIMS ANY AND ALL WARRANTIES, EXPRESSED OR IMPLIED, INCLUDING, WITHOUT LIMITATION, WARRANTIES OF MERCHANTABILITY OR FITNESS FOR A PARTICULAR PURPOSE. IN NO EVENT SHALL CENGAGE LEARNING BE LIABLE FOR: INDIRECT, SPECIAL, PUNITIVE OR CONSEQUENTIAL DAMAGES INCLUDING FOR LOST PROFITS, LOST DATA, OR OTHERWISE. IN NO EVENT SHALL CENGAGE LEARNING'S AGGREGATE LIABILITY HEREUNDER, WHETHER ARISING IN CONTRACT, TORT, STRICT LIABILITY OR OTHERWISE, EXCEED THE AMOUNT OF FEES PAID BY THE END USER HEREUNDER FOR THE LICENSE OF THE LICENSED CONTENT.

8.0 GENERAL

8.1 Entire Agreement. This Agreement shall constitute the entire Agreement between the Parties and supercedes all prior Agreements and understandings oral or written relating to the subject matter hereof.

8.2 Enhancements/Modifications of Licensed Content. From time to time, and in Cengage Learning's sole discretion, Cengage Learning may advise the End User of updates, upgrades, enhancements and/or improvements to the Licensed Content, and may permit the End User to access and use, subject to the terms and conditions of this Agreement, such modifications, upon payment of prices as may be established by Cengage Learning.

8.3 No Export. The End User shall use the Licensed Content solely in the United States and shall not transfer or export, directly or indirectly, the Licensed Content outside the United States.

8.4 Severability. If any provision of this Agreement is invalid, illegal, or unenforceable under any applicable statute or rule of law, the provision shall be deemed omitted to the extent that it is invalid, illegal, or unenforceable. In such a case, the remainder of the Agreement shall be construed in a manner as to give greatest effect to the original intention of the parties hereto.

8.5 Waiver. The waiver of any right or failure of either party to exercise in any respect any right provided in this Agreement in any instance shall not be deemed to be a waiver of such right in the future or a waiver of any other right under this Agreement.

8.6 Choice of Law/Venue. This Agreement shall be interpreted, construed, and governed by and in accordance with the laws of the State of New York, applicable to contracts executed and to be wholly preformed therein, without regard to its principles governing conflicts of law. Each party agrees that any proceeding arising out of or relating to this Agreement or the breach or threatened breach of this Agreement may be commenced and prosecuted in a court in the State and County of New York. Each party consents and submits to the nonexclusive personal jurisdiction of any court in the State and County of New York in respect of any such proceeding.

8.7 Acknowledgment. By opening this package and/or by accessing the Licensed Content on this Web site, THE END USER ACKNOWLEDGES THAT IT HAS READ THIS AGREEMENT, UNDERSTANDS IT, AND AGREES TO BE BOUND BY ITS TERMS AND CONDITIONS. IF YOU DO NOT ACCEPT THESE TERMS AND CONDITIONS, YOU MUST NOT ACCESS THE LICENSED CONTENT AND RETURN THE LICENSED PRODUCT TO CENGAGE LEARNING (WITHIN 30 CALENDAR DAYS OF THE END USER'S PURCHASE) WITH PROOF OF PAYMENT ACCEPTABLE TO CENGAGE LEARNING, FOR A CREDIT OR A REFUND. Should the End User have any questions/comments regarding this Agreement, please contact Cengage Learning at Delmar.help@cengage.com.